Transforming Mathematics Instruction

Advances in Mathematics Education

For further volumes:
http://www.springer.com/series/8392

Yeping Li • Edward A. Silver • Shiqi Li
Editors

Transforming Mathematics Instruction

Multiple Approaches and Practices

 Springer

Editors
Yeping Li
Department of Teaching, Learning
    and Culture
Texas A&M University
College Station, TX, USA

Edward A. Silver
School of Education
University of Michigan
Ann Arbor, MI, USA

Shiqi Li
Department of Mathematics
East China Normal University
Putuo, China

ISSN 1869-4918   ISSN 1869-4926 (electronic)
ISBN 978-3-319-04992-2   ISBN 978-3-319-04993-9 (eBook)
DOI 10.1007/978-3-319-04993-9
Springer Cham Heidelberg New York Dordrecht London

Library of Congress Control Number: 2014938206

Springer is part of Springer Science+Business Media (www.springer.com)

Series Preface

This volume of the series Advances in Mathematics Education edited by Yeping Li, Edward Silver, and Shiqi Li on "Transforming Mathematics Instruction" provides the reader with an overview on different approaches for transforming mathematics instruction. Departing from the evidence from large-scale assessments pointing out to strong weaknesses of many educational systems from all over the world, especially the strong learning gap between East Asian and Western learners, the current book seeks to survey and synthesize current research developments on innovative approaches for the change of mathematics classroom culture. There is a wealth of studies on the quality of education in general and the quality of mathematics education in particular, partly summarized by current meta-studies. However, most of these studies focus on Western countries. The current book overcomes this weakness by including not only studies and approaches from Western countries but also approaches from East Asian countries as well, reflecting their own way of innovative mathematics teaching. With this impressive overview on transforming mathematics instruction from Eastern and Western countries, this book will provide an insightful summary on possible ways to improve mathematics education while considering various cultural influences which the reader will hopefully find interesting.

University of Hamburg, Hamburg, Germany   Gabriele Kaiser
University of Montana, Missoula, MT, USA   Bharath Sriraman
                                                       Series editors

Preface and Acknowledgements

Classroom instruction is commonly seen as one of the key factors contributing to students' learning of mathematics, but much remains to be understood about teachers' instructional practices that lead to the development and enactment of effective classroom instruction, and approaches and practices developed and used to transform classroom instruction in different education systems.

This book surveys and examines several different approaches and practices that contribute to the changes in mathematics instruction, including: (1) innovative approaches that bring direct changes in classroom instructional practices, (2) curriculum reforms that introduce changes in content and requirements in classroom instruction, and (3) approaches in mathematics teacher education that aim to improve teachers' expertise and practices. It also surveys relevant theory and methodology development in studying and assessing mathematics instruction.

Transforming Mathematics Instruction is organized to help readers learn not only from reading individual chapters, but also from reading across chapters and sections to explore broader themes, including:

- Identifying what is important in mathematics for teaching and learning emphasized in different approaches
- Exploring how students' learning are considered and facilitated through different approaches and practices
- Learning and understanding the nature of various approaches that are valued in different systems and cultural contexts
- Probing culturally valued approaches in identifying and evaluating effective instructional practices

The book brings new research and insights into multiple approaches and practices for transforming mathematics instruction to the international community of mathematics education, with 25 chapters and four section prefaces contributed by 56 scholars from 10 different education systems. This rich collection is indispensable reading for mathematics educators, researchers, teacher educators, curriculum developers, and graduate students interested in learning about different instructional practices, approaches for instructional transformation, and research in different education systems.

It will help readers to reflect on approaches and practices that are useful for instructional changes in their own education systems, and also inspire them to identify and further explore new areas of research and program development in improving mathematics teaching and learning.

We want to take this opportunity to thank and acknowledge all of those who have been involved in the process of preparing this book. This has been a wonderful collaboration. The work on this book has not only brought together long time friends and colleagues, but also created new professional connections and new friends. We want to thank all those who were so ready and willing to contribute to the topic that is proven to be very important to the international mathematics education community.

Texas A&M University, USA   Yeping Li
University of Michigan, USA   Edward A. Silver
East China Normal University, China   Shiqi Li

Contents

Contributors

Fran Arbaugh Department of Curriculum and Instruction, Pennsylvania State University, University Park, PA, USA

Deborah Loewenberg Ball School of Education, University of Michigan, Ann Arbor, MI, USA

Hilda Borko Graduate School of Education, Stanford University, Stanford, CA, USA

Rita Borromeo Ferri Department of Mathematics, University of Kassel, Kassel, Germany

Melissa D. Boston School of Education, Duquesne University, Pittsburgh, PA, USA

Justin Boyle College of Education, University of New Mexico, Albuquerque, NM, USA

Neusa Branco Escola Superior de Educação de Santarém and Instituto de Educação, Universidade de Lisboa, Alameda da Universidade, Lisboa, Portugal

David Clarke Melbourne Graduate School of Education, University of Melbourne, Carlton, VIC, Australia

João Pedro da Ponte Instituto de Educação, Universidade de Lisboa, Alameda da Universidade, Lisboa, Portugal

Shelley Dole School of Education, The University of Queensland, St Lucia, QLD, Australia

Ruhama Even Department of Science Teaching, Weizmann Institute of Science, Rehovot, Israel

Evan Fuller Department of Mathematics, Montclair State University, Laurel, MD, USA

Vince Geiger School of Education, Australian Catholic University, Virginia, QLD, Australia

Merrilyn Goos School of Education, The University of Queensland, St Lucia, QLD, Australia

Koeno P.E. Gravemeijer Eindhoven School of Education, Eindhoven University of Technology, Leiden, The Netherlands

Guershon Harel Department of Mathematics, University of California, San Diego, La Jolla, CA, USA

Mark Hoover School of Education, University of Michigan, Ann Arbor, MI, USA

Rongjin Huang Department of Mathematical Sciences, Middle Tennessee State University, Murfreesboro, TN, USA

Jennifer Jacobs Institute of Cognitive Science, University of Colorado Boulder, Boulder, CO, USA

Barbara Jaworski Mathematics Education Centre, Loughborough University, Loughborough, UK

Tyrone John Urban Education, Graduate Center, City University of New York, Albans, NY, USA

Gabriele Kaiser Faculty of Education, University of Hamburg, Hamburg, Germany

Carolyn D. King Queensborough Community College, City University of New York, Brooklyn, NY, USA

Karen Koellner Department of Curriculum and Teaching, Hunter College, The City University of New York, New York, NY, USA

Elaine Lande Mathematics Education, School of Education, University of Michigan, Ann Arbor, MI, USA

Roza Leikin Faculty of Education, University of Haifa, Haifa, Israel

Jun Li Faculty of Arts and Education, School of Education, Deakin University, Australia

Qiong Li Teacher Education Research Center, School of Education, Beijing Normal University, Beijing, People's Republic of China

Shiqi Li Department of Mathematics, East China Normal University, Shanghai, China

Xiaoqing Li Rm B432, Department of Psychology, Normal College, Shenzhen University, Nanshan, Shenzhen, Guangdong, China

Yeping Li Department of Teaching, Learning and Culture, Texas A&M University, College Station, TX, USA

Peter Liljedahl Faculty of Education, Simon Fraser University, Burnaby, BC, Canada

Charmaine Mangram Graduate School of Education, Stanford University, Stanford, CA, USA

Vilma Mesa School of Education, University of Michigan, Ann Arbor, MI, USA

Célia Mestre Research Unity of the Institute of Education, University of Lisbon, Alameda da Universidade, Lisboa, Portugal

Yu-Jing Ni Ho Tim Building, Faculty of Education, The Chinese University of Hong Kong, Shatin, NT, Hong Kong, China

Hélia Oliveira Institute of Education, University of Lisbon, Alameda da Universidade, Lisboa, Portugal

Norma Presmeg Illinois State University, Normal, IL, USA

Marisa Quaresma Instituto de Educação, Universidade de Lisboa, Alameda da Universidade, Lisboa, Portugal

Nanette Seago WestEd, Redwood City, CA, USA

Edward A. Silver School of Education, University of Michigan, Ann Arbor, MI, USA

Margaret S. Smith Department of Instruction and Learning, School of Education, University of Pittsburgh, Pittsburgh, PA, USA

Osvaldo D. Soto Department of Mathematics, Patrick Henry High School, University of California, San Diego, La Jolla, CA, USA

Michael D. Steele Department of Curriculum and Instruction, School of Education, University of Wisconsin-Milwaukee, Milwaukee, WI, USA

Michelle Stephan College of Education, Middle/Secondary, Suite 312E, University of North Carolina Charlotte, Charlotte, NC, USA

Gabriel Stylianides Department of Education, University of Oxford, Oxford, UK

Heejoo Suh College of Education, Michigan State University, East Lansing, MI, USA

Peter Sullivan Faculty of Education, Monash University, Clayton, Australia

Diana Underwood-Gregg Department of Mathematics, Computer Science, and Statistics, Purdue University Calumet, Hammond, IN, USA

Katrin Vorhölter Faculty of Education, University of Hamburg, Hamburg, Germany

Tad Watanabe Department of Mathematics and Statistics, Kennesaw State University, Kennesaw, GA, USA

Erna Yackel Department of Mathematics, Computer Science, and Statistics, Purdue University Calumet, Dyer, IN, USA

Yudong Yang Shanghai Academy of Educational Sciences, Shanghai, People's Republic of China

Orit Zaslavsky New York University, New York, NY, USA

Technion – Israel Institute of Technology, Technion City, Haifa, Israel

Dehui Zhou Department of Counseling and Psychology, Hong Kong Shue Yan University, Hong Kong, China

Iris Zodik Technion – Israel Institute of Technology, Nesher, Israel

Transforming Mathematics Instruction: What Do We Know and What Can We Learn from Multiple Approaches and Practices?

Yeping Li, Edward A. Silver, and Shiqi Li

Abstract Mathematics classroom instruction, often seen as a key contributing factor to students' learning, has remained virtually unchanged for the past several decades. Efforts to improve the quality of mathematics education have led to multiple approaches and research that target different contributing factors but lack a systematic account of diverse approaches and practices for improving mathematics instruction. This book is thus designed to survey, synthesize, and extend current research on specific approaches and practices that are developed and used in different education systems for transforming mathematics instruction. In this introduction chapter, we highlight the background of this book project, its purposes, and what can be learned from reading this book.

Keywords Cultural context • Curriculum changes • Education system • Instructional transformation • International perspective • Mathematics instruction • Mathematics teacher education

Y. Li (✉)
Department of Teaching, Learning and Culture, Texas A&M University,
MS 4232, College Station, TX 77843-4232, USA
e-mail: yepingli@tamu.edu

E.A. Silver
School of Education, University of Michigan,
610 E. University Ave., Ann Arbor, MI 48109, USA
e-mail: easilver@umich.edu

S. Li
Department of Mathematics, East China Normal University,
500 Dongchuan Rd., Shanghai 200241, China
e-mail: sqli@math.ecnu.edu.cn; sqli1761@gmail.com

Y. Li et al. (eds.), *Transforming Mathematics Instruction: Multiple Approaches and Practices*, Advances in Mathematics Education, DOI 10.1007/978-3-319-04993-9_1,
© Springer International Publishing Switzerland 2014

Introduction

Mathematics instruction is ubiquitous in compulsory schooling across the globe. In virtually every country, at every grade level, on every day during the academic year, a student attending school is likely to receive mathematics instruction. Moreover, among all the school subjects that a student may study, the learning of mathematics is generally viewed as the one most contingent on classroom instruction. Whereas students may have many opportunities to sharpen literacy skills or to learn history or science independent of classroom instruction, it is generally acknowledged that the learning of mathematics depends to a great extent on the quantity and quality of classroom instruction and the completion of associated assignments. Thus, parents, educators, and education policy professionals across the world share a common interest in improving the quality of mathematics instruction. Despite this strong, shared interest, we currently lack clarity about the nature of effective mathematics instruction, and we know too little about how to improve the quality of classroom instruction.

One pathway toward better understanding that has been pursued in recent years and that has borne some fruits is cross-national examination of mathematics classroom instruction. In a pioneering effort in 1995, the Third International Mathematics and Science Study (TIMSS) – a large-scale international survey of mathematics and science achievement conducted by the International Association for the Evaluation of Educational Achievement (IEA) – included for the first time a component that involved an analysis of videotaped classroom instruction from three participating countries (Germany, Japan, and the United States) (Stigler and Hiebert 1999). The examination of classroom instruction was also included in the following TIMSS survey and was expanded to include more education systems. The TIMSS classroom video studies revealed that while mathematics classroom instruction was generally quite similar within a country, it varied considerably across countries, though there were few observable characteristics of classroom instruction that differentiated teaching in countries where students performed relatively well on the TIMSS mathematics assessment from that found in countries where students performed relatively poorly.

The TIMSS classroom video studies have prompted others to examine mathematics classroom instruction across different education systems, such as the Learner's Perspective Study (e.g., Clarke et al. 2006) and studies on classroom instruction in East Asia (e.g., Li and Huang 2013; Li and Shimizu 2009). These studies, and others, have collectively suggested the value of examining classroom instruction in diverse settings as a way to draw explicit attention to features of instruction that might otherwise remain implicit and to suggest alternative possibilities for mathematics teaching that might enrich efforts to improve classroom instruction. Nevertheless, our understanding of mathematics classroom instruction and its improvement remains fragmented. In particular, much remains to be understood about how to facilitate and support the development and enactment of effective classroom instruction. A systematic examination of different approaches and practices for classroom instruction improvement is critically important, especially in the current context in which the improvement of students' mathematics learning is a focus of emphasis around the world.

Our currently limited knowledge is due in no small measure to the inherent difficulty of capturing and analyzing the complexity of classroom instruction. Considered independently, student learning and teaching practices are each complex domains of inquiry, and inquiry becomes further complicated when these domains are seen as interacting with each other, and also with curriculum materials and mathematical ideas, within classroom settings. Nonetheless, some successes have begun to emerge in recent years in the quest to improve the quality of mathematics instruction, deriving from three different approaches that target different potential levers for change and improvement:

1. Approaches that directly target innovative classroom instruction practices (see, e.g., Bergmann and Sams 2012; Carpenter et al. 1999; Smith and Stein 2011; Stillman et al. 2013)
2. Approaches that seek to change instructional practice indirectly through the introduction of curriculum reforms that alter content or performance requirements (see, e.g., Huang and Li 2009; Leung and Li 2010; Li and Lappan 2014; Stein et al. 2007)
3. Approaches that seek to change instructional practice through professional development aimed at augmenting teachers' mathematics pedagogical knowledge and proficiency (see, e.g., Fernandez and Yoshida 2004; Li and Even 2011a; Li and Kaiser 2011; Stein et al. 2009; Yang and Ricks 2013)

Given the recent emergence of promising work related to each of these three approaches, the time appears to be ripe to survey and synthesize current research development on transforming mathematics instruction.

In this book, we have assembled a sample of contemporary research efforts aimed at understanding and transforming mathematics instruction. In addition to work exemplifying the three approaches described above, this book also extends to recent international studies focusing on mathematics classroom instruction and its improvement in different education systems.

In summary, then, our production of this volume was undergirded by two major motivations. First, we wished to build upon our previous work on mathematics classroom instruction in different education systems (e.g., Li 2006; Li and Huang 2013; Li and Shimizu 2009; Silver et al. 1990; Stein et al. 2009). Examining and learning about classroom instruction in different systems and cultural contexts can enrich our understanding of effective mathematics classroom instruction. This book contains 25 chapters and four section prefaces contributed by a total of 56 mathematics educators and researchers from ten different education systems (Australia, Canada, China, Germany, Hong Kong, Israel, the Netherlands, Portugal, the United Kingdom, and the United States). This variety of perspectives ensures that readers will be able to gain insights into the approaches and practices that are found and valued in different education systems. Second, we wished to consider a variety of perspectives, other than those that derive from cross-national contrasts, about mathematics instruction that would inform transformative efforts. A recent publication on different approaches and practices for improving mathematics teachers' expertise

(Li and Even 2011a) contained 18 articles that provided an array of perspectives and approaches on the nature of expert mathematics teaching and its improvement. Similarly, some others of our recent work on mathematics curriculum and teacher education (e.g., Leung and Li 2010; Li and Kaiser 2011; Li and Lappan 2014) suggest that those perspectives also offer important insights that can contribute to our conceptualization, analysis, and transformative efforts regarding mathematics classroom instruction. This book contains a rich collection of chapters that spans a variety of issues and factors relevant to classroom mathematics instruction.

In the following section, we provide general information about the book, its structure, and chapters.

What Do We Know and What Can We Learn from Multiple Approaches and Practices?

This book contains 25 chapters, with Ch 1 as an introduction to the book and the remaining chapters distributed into five parts. Part I contains seven chapters that examine different approaches and practices for improving mathematics instruction with a focus on classroom instruction itself. Parts II and III contain 13 chapters (six in Part II and seven in Part III) that expand the perspectives on transforming classroom instruction by attending to issues of mathematics curriculum and teacher education. Part IV contains seven chapters on recent development in theory and methods for studying and assessing mathematics classroom instruction. Part V is a section for commentary and conclusion; one commentary chapter is included to reflect on the research reported in Parts I to IV. Each chapter stands as an independent contribution. Moreover, the chapters comprising each section offer readers an opportunity to synthesize within the perspective represented by a section. And readers will likely find other productive ways to synthesize across chapters.

Knowing and Learning About Multiple Approaches and Practices as Presented in Individual Chapters

The simplest way of knowing and learning about multiple approaches and practices is to follow the book's structure. In the first part describing approaches and changes to classroom instruction practices, readers should discover several different perspectives and approaches that are highlighted in these seven chapters. They include the modeling approach (Vorhölter et al. 2014), guided reinvention (Stephan et al. 2014), the use of multiple solution tasks and mathematical investigations (Leikin 2014), the use of numeracy teaching model (Goos et al. 2014), exploratory work (da Ponte et al. 2014), and random grouping in classroom instruction (Liljedahl 2014). These diverse approaches and practices vary in terms of not only the nature of these approaches but also the rationale behind these approaches and practices. Such information is very important for readers to understand not only what these different approaches and practices are, but also why developing and using these approaches and practices is important. With no specific system or cultural constraints being specified, readers can certainly consider the feasibility of adapting and modifying a certain approach or practice for implementation in their system contexts. At the same time, however, David Clarke (2014) also pointed out in his preface that the effectiveness of these approaches and practices could be better supported with further empirical evidence and studies.

Parts II and III focus on other approaches and practices that can possibly lead to mathematics instruction transformation, with Part II concentrating on school curriculum changes and Part III concentrating on teacher changes through education and practices. Each part has its own preface that summarizes the various approaches and practices presented in that part (see Silver 2014; Sullivan 2014). A total of 13 chapters are included in these two parts, with some providing general perspectives on factors contributing to mathematics instruction transformation (e.g., Gravemeijer 2014; Watanabe 2014) and others providing specific approaches and practices (e.g., Borko et al. 2014; Oliveira and Mestre 2014; Smith et al. 2014; Yang 2014). As these approaches and practices are often presented within specific system and cultural contexts, readers also have the opportunity to appreciate the possible cultural value and significance of these approaches. At the same time, since these approaches and practices focus on curriculum and teacher changes, questions remain about the effectiveness of these approaches and practices on transforming mathematics instruction. Readers are encouraged to take further steps to explore and discuss how these approaches and practices can help lead to a successful transformation of classroom instruction in specific systems and cultural contexts.

The last two parts (Parts IV and V) view mathematics instruction as professional practices that call for further research and ongoing improvement. Part IV has six chapters and its own preface contributed by Norma Presmeg (2014). These chapters present readers with several new perspectives and approaches for studying and assessing mathematics instruction. Although the last part contains only one chapter, Ball and Hoover (2014) provide an inspiring commentary that calls for research transformation to support instructional transformation in classrooms.

Learning Through Reflecting on Multiple Approaches and Practices Across Chapters and Parts

Readers should learn much from reading the book, as outlined above, and can learn even more through reflecting on these approaches and practices across chapters and parts. In the following subsections, we will share with readers four aspects that are built upon our research and perspectives. The first two aspects refer to those that are not designed as the foci of this book, but we call for readers' special attention to these inseparable components when considering mathematics instruction and its changes. The last two culture-related aspects are pertinent to this book as multiple approaches and practices are situated in different systems and cultural contexts, and we share with readers what may be learned from these approaches and practices.

Identifying What Is Important in Mathematics for Teaching and Learning Emphasized in Different Approaches

It is clear that transforming mathematics instruction is not the purpose by itself, but a way of helping students learn *mathematics better*. However, what *mathematics* is important for teaching and learning and how to assess the quality of teaching and learning (i.e., *better*) are not the focus of this book. This does not mean that curriculum is an optional part of mathematics instruction, but rather requires readers to go beyond knowing multiple approaches and practices for transforming mathematics instruction to reflect on and identify what is important in mathematics for teaching and learning as is highlighted in different approaches. Some approaches have such information clearly presented, but others do not. For example, several approaches and practices presented in the first three parts contain more specific curriculum information that include numeracy as the use of mathematics in real-world contexts and different school subjects (Goos et al. 2014), algebraic thinking (Oliveira and Mestre 2014), algorithms as a core concept in secondary school mathematics (Huang and Li 2014), mathematical exploration (da Ponte et al. 2014), and reasoning and proving (Smith et al. 2014). Others contain less explicit curriculum information but with such information demonstrated through their research focus. As an example, several chapters in this book focus on the cognitive and mathematical challenges of specific tasks (e.g., Leikin 2014; Ni et al. 2014; Yang 2014). Such a focus reflects the importance placed on students' cognitive ability development (as opposed to procedural skills) through mathematics instruction.

At the same time, identifying and reflecting on what is important in mathematics for teaching and learning are also critical for readers who think about adapting and using specific approaches and practices. For example, the emphasis on cognitive challenges of mathematical tasks should help readers to think about the use of specific approaches and practices for developing students' ability in problem solving and doing mathematics. The approaches of modeling (Vorhölter et al. 2014) and numeracy (Goos et al. 2014) can likely help students connect mathematics with real-world contexts and improve their mathematical application ability. Certainly, different approaches and practices may also be constrained by their content focuses. Recognizing the diversity in curricular foci across different approaches and practices can help readers understand these approaches and practices better.

Exploring How Students' Learning Is Considered and Facilitated Through Different Approaches and Practices

With a focus on mathematics instruction transformation, readers may notice that the attention to students and their learning can be clear in some approaches and practices but not in others. For example, students and their learning are clearly considered in many chapters in Part I and some chapters in other parts, such as Even (2014), Ni et al. (2014), and Silver and Suh (2014). The less explicit attention to students and their learning in other chapters does not mean that students and their learning should not be focused on when considering mathematics instruction changes. Instead, as we pointed out at the beginning, classroom instruction is a very complex process that involves many different factors. Various simplifications are often needed to focus on certain aspects and factors related to classroom instruction at a specific time, instead of all areas of mathematics classroom instruction simultaneously. Thus, readers should go beyond knowing and learning specific approaches and practices to consider how students and their learning may be affected. Such considerations can possibly be carried out (at least) in the following two ways:

1. Readers can cross-examine various approaches and practices highlighted in different chapters and parts to explore how students and their learning may be considered and improved. Adding the explicit dimension of students and their learning should help readers to learn and better understand different approaches and practices.
2. Readers can view students and their learning as the focus of possible follow-up research efforts, especially when considering how to adapt and use a specific approach or practice. As the book's editors, we encourage readers to discuss, document, and assess specific approaches and practices supported with empirical evidence of students' learning improvement.

Learning and Understanding the Nature of Various Approaches That Are Valued in Different Systems and Cultural Contexts

With these approaches and practices contributed by authors from different education systems, it is natural to consider possible differences (and thus constraints) imposed by the system and cultural contexts. It is not difficult to notice that some approaches and practices are system and culture specific. For example, the textbook transformation in Japan over years (Watanabe 2014), the development and use of exemplary lessons in China (Huang and Li 2014), the Teaching Research Group (Yang 2014), and teaching contests (Li and Li 2014) are quite unique and suited to specific system and cultural contexts. Knowing and learning about these approaches and practices require readers to take further steps in learning and understanding their cultural niches. However, this system and cultural specificity does not mean that these approaches and practices are totally infeasible for implementation in another system and cultural context. One good example is lesson study, a cultural-pedagogical practice in Japan (Fernandez and Yoshida 2004), which has been disseminated and adapted in many other countries, including the United States.

At the same time, what can be learned from culture-specific approaches and practices is another important question to consider. If we take lesson study as an example, Schoenfeld (2013) argued that it is important to have a reasoned understanding of lesson study in its culture-specific elements, including its goals and the cultural support needed for its implementation. Without such a reasoned understanding, it is naïve to simply adopt and implement lesson study in the United States. However, Schoenfeld recognized and acknowledged the significance of learning important lessons from such culturally valued approaches, including teacher practice and collaboration. It is in the same idea that readers, from all over the world, can also identify culture-specific elements of these approaches and practices presented in this book and take important lessons that can be used in another system and cultural context.

There are quite a few approaches and practices presented in this book that don't give readers a sense of cultural uniqueness. Partially, this is due to the fact that many approaches and practices focus on the cognitive dimension of changes. It should be noted that being "culturally neutral" does not automatically grant such approaches and practices the capacity for direct adoption into another system and cultural context. Indeed, the development and use of any specific approach and practice contain its specific goal and supporting mechanism. As an example, Sullivan (2014) pointed out that chapters included in Part III present approaches from two different countries, China and the United States, and there are important differences among these approaches. The two approaches from China stem from the work of practitioners as teacher driven. In contrast, all of the approaches from the United States share an important similarity with substantial input from researchers. Sullivan's point coincides with the observation made by Li and Even (2011b) when examining various approaches and practices used in developing mathematics teachers' expertise in the West and East. Such differences suggest that, even for such "culturally neutral" approaches, they incorporate unique and culturally embedded support (from researchers) that may not be readily available in another system and cultural context. Nevertheless, there are also some important lessons (e.g., the quality of mathematical tasks designed and the generalizability of specific approaches) for others to recognize and use in their own system and cultural contexts.

Probing Culturally Valued Approaches in Identifying and Evaluating Effective Instructional Practices

The action of transforming mathematics instruction in different systems and cultural contexts itself contains special cultural elements. Such cultural elements can be thought of as special values and considerations *placed on* developing and using a specific approach or practice. In this regard, we already shared with readers in the above subsection what may or may not be taken away from specific approaches and practices situated in different systems and cultural contexts.

Such cultural elements can also be thought of as special values and consideration *placed behind* developing and using specific approach and practice. In this regard, special values and consideration can include the specification of what can be counted as effective instructional practice, how such effective instructional practice can be identified, what changes need to be made in order to develop such effective instructional practice, and how to evaluate the effectiveness of instructional practices. The learning and understanding of such cultural elements can help ensure that the intended transformation will help lead to the expected effectiveness of mathematics instruction that is valued in specific system and cultural context. However, attempting to answer these questions goes beyond the scope of this book. We shall encourage readers to uncover possible hints for identifying and evaluating effective instructional approaches valued in different systems and cultural contexts, within this book.

Significance and Limitations

With a focus on ways of transforming mathematics instruction, we hope this book will help to organize and synthesize several different strands of mathematics education research that are often viewed as unrelated. As the chapters in this volume attest, many different factors can be the focus of efforts to understand or improve mathematics instruction and ultimately students' learning of mathematics. Though they differ in approach and focus, they share similar goals, and each offers an important independent contribution to our collective understanding and the development of a comprehensive approach to improvement. This book thus provides a broadened perspective to survey, synthesize, and extend current research on specific approaches and practices that are developed and used in different education systems. Several parts of the book (esp. Parts I, II, and III), as structured, help provide a systematic account of multiple approaches and practices that can lead to mathematics instruction improvement. Such a broadened perspective allows readers to see possible connections among these seemingly disconnected approaches and practices and also see the complexity and challenge of making mathematics instruction improvement a success.

At the same time, we affirm the view promoted by Stigler and Hiebert (1999) that classroom instruction is a culturally constituted activity. As such, this book is not designed to promote simple and direct adoption of a specific approach or practice from one education system to another, but rather to provide a platform for mathematics educators all over the world to share and learn important lessons from others. It is in the process of sharing, learning, and reflecting on different approaches and practices, rather than taking away specific approaches and practices as final products, that readers can benefit the most from reading the book.

We close with a few cautionary words to the reader. Our decision to include particular approaches and practices in this volume should not be taken to imply that we endorse them or attest to their efficacy. Our goal was to display richness and diversity. Furthermore, the specific approaches and practices presented and discussed in different chapters are sometimes presented with reference to the cultural and education system within which they are embedded, but we are not attesting that these specific approaches and practices are representative of typical practice in the designated education systems. Nevertheless, keeping these cautions in mind, we invite readers to avail themselves of the rich collection of examples contained herein. We affirm the value of sharing and exchanging information regarding different approaches and practices for transforming mathematics instruction within and across education systems. Sharing and examining multiple approaches and practices developed and used in different education systems can allow us to learn important lessons that are otherwise not available when we look only at ourselves.

References

Ball, D. L., & Hoover, M. (2014). Transforming research to transform mathematics instruction. In Y. Li, E. A. Silver, & S. Li (Eds.), *Transforming mathematics instruction: Multiple approaches and practices*. Cham, Switzerland: Springer.

Bergmann, J., & Sams, A. (2012). *Flip your classroom: Reach every student in every class every day*. Eugene: International Society for Technology in Education.

Borko, H., Jacobs, J., Seago, N., & Mangram, C. (2014). Facilitating video-based professional development: Planning and orchestrating productive discussions. In Y. Li, E. A. Silver, & S. Li (Eds.), *Transforming mathematics instruction: Multiple approaches and practices*. Cham, Switzerland: Springer.

Carpenter, T. P., Fennema, E., Franke, M. L., Levi, L., & Empson, S. B. (1999). *Children's mathematics: Cognitively guided instruction*. Portsmouth: Heinemann.

Clarke, D. (2014). Preface to part I. In Y. Li, E. A. Silver, & S. Li (Eds.), *Transforming mathematics instruction: Multiple approaches and practices*. Cham, Switzerland: Springer.

Clarke, D., Keitel, C., & Shimizu, Y. (Eds.). (2006). *Mathematics classrooms in twelve countries: The insider's perspective*. Rotterdam: Sense Publishers.

da Ponte, J. P., Branco, N., & Quaresma, M. (2014). Exploratory activity in the mathematics classroom. In Y. Li, E. A. Silver, & S. Li (Eds.), *Transforming mathematics instruction: Multiple approaches and practices*. Cham, Switzerland: Springer.

Even, R. (2014). The interplay of factors involved in shaping students' opportunities to learn mathematics. In Y. Li, E. A. Silver, & S. Li (Eds.), *Transforming mathematics instruction: Multiple approaches and practices*. Cham, Switzerland: Springer.

Fernandez, C., & Yoshida, M. (2004). *Lesson study: A Japanese approach to improving mathematics teaching and learning*. Mahwah: Lawrence Erlbaum Associates.

Goos, M., Geiger, V., & Dole, S. (2014). Transforming professional practice in numeracy teaching. In Y. Li, E. A. Silver, & S. Li (Eds.), *Transforming mathematics instruction: Multiple approaches and practices*. Cham, Switzerland: Springer.

Gravemeijer, K. (2014). Transforming mathematics education: The role of textbooks and teachers. In Y. Li, E. A. Silver, & S. Li (Eds.), *Transforming mathematics instruction: Multiple approaches and practices*. Cham, Switzerland: Springer.

Huang, R., & Li, Y. (2009). Pursuing excellence in mathematics classroom instruction through exemplary lesson development in China: A case study. *ZDM – The International Journal on Mathematics Education, 41*, 297–309.

Huang, R., & Li, Y. (2014). Improving mathematics classroom instruction through exemplary lesson development: A Chinese approach. In Y. Li, E. A. Silver, & S. Li (Eds.), *Transforming mathematics instruction: Multiple approaches and practices*. Cham, Switzerland: Springer.

Leikin, R. (2014). Challenging mathematics with multiple solution tasks and mathematical investigations in geometry. In Y. Li, E. A. Silver, & S. Li (Eds.), *Transforming mathematics instruction: Multiple approaches and practices*. Cham, Switzerland: Springer.

Leung, F. K. S., & Li, Y. (Eds.). (2010). *Reforms and issues in school mathematics in East Asia – Sharing and understanding mathematics education policies and practices*. Rotterdam: Sense Publishers.

Li, S. (2006). Practice makes perfect: A key belief in China. In F. K. Leung, K. D. Graf, & F. J. Lopez-Real (Eds.), *Mathematics education in different cultural traditions-A comparative study of East Asia and the West: The 13th ICMI study* (Vol. 9, pp. 129–138). New York: Springer.

Li, Y., & Even, R. (Eds.). (2011a). Approaches and practices in developing teachers' expertise in mathematics instruction. *ZDM – The International Journal on Mathematics Education, 43*(6–7), 759–1024.

Li, Y., & Even, R. (2011b). Approaches and practices in developing teachers' expertise in mathematics instruction: An introduction. *ZDM – The International Journal on Mathematics Education, 43*, 759–762.

Li, Y., & Huang, R. (Eds.). (2013). *How Chinese teach mathematics and improve teaching*. New York: Routledge.

Li, Y., & Kaiser, G. (Eds.). (2011). *Expertise in mathematics instruction: An international perspective*. New York: Springer.

Li, Y., & Lappan, G. (Eds.). (2014). *Mathematics curriculum in school education*. Cham, Switzerland: Springer.

Li, Y., & Li, J. (2014). Pursuing mathematics classroom instruction excellence through teaching contests. In Y. Li, E. A. Silver, & S. Li (Eds.), *Transforming mathematics instruction: Multiple approaches and practices*. Cham, Switzerland: Springer.

Li, Y., & Shimizu, Y. (Eds.). (2009). Exemplary mathematics instruction and its development in East Asia. *ZDM – The International Journal on Mathematics Education, 41*, 257–395.

Liljedahl, P. (2014). The affordances of using visibly random groups in a mathematics classroom. In Y. Li, E. A. Silver, & S. Li (Eds.), *Transforming mathematics instruction: Multiple approaches and practices*. Cham, Switzerland: Springer.

Ni, Y., Li, X., Zhou, D., & Li, Q. (2014). Changes in instructional tasks and their influence on classroom discourse in reformed mathematics classrooms of Chinese primary schools. In Y. Li, E. A. Silver, & S. Li (Eds.), *Transforming mathematics instruction: Multiple approaches and practices*. Cham, Switzerland: Springer.

Oliveira, H., & Mestre, C. (2014). Opportunities to develop algebraic thinking in elementary grades throughout the school year in the context of mathematics curriculum changes. In Y. Li, E. A. Silver, & S. Li (Eds.), *Transforming mathematics instruction: Multiple approaches and practices*. Cham, Switzerland: Springer.

Presmeg, N. (2014). Preface to part IV. In Y. Li, E. A. Silver, & S. Li (Eds.), *Transforming mathematics instruction: Multiple approaches and practices*. Cham, Switzerland: Springer.

Schoenfeld, A. H. (2013). Foreword. In Y. Li & R. Huang (Eds.), *How Chinese teach mathematics and improve teaching* (pp. xii–xv). New York: Routledge.

Silver, E. A. (2014). Preface to part II. In Y. Li, E. A. Silver, & S. Li (Eds.), *Transforming mathematics instruction: Multiple approaches and practices*. Cham, Switzerland: Springer.

Silver, E. A., & Suh, H. (2014). Professional development for secondary school mathematics teachers using student work: Some challenges and promising possibilities. In Y. Li, E. A. Silver, & S. Li (Eds.), *Transforming mathematics instruction: Multiple approaches and practices*. Cham, Switzerland: Springer.

Silver, E. A., Kilpatrick, J., & Schlesinger, B. (1990). *Thinking through mathematics: Fostering inquiry and communication in mathematics classrooms*. New York: College Board.

Smith, M. S., & Stein, M. K. (2011). *Five practices for orchestrating productive mathematics discussions*. Reston: National Council of Teachers of Mathematics.

Smith, M. S., Boyle, J., Arbaugh, F., Steele, M. D., & Stylianides, G. (2014). Cases as a vehicle for developing knowledge needed for teaching. In Y. Li, E. A. Silver, & S. Li (Eds.), *Transforming mathematics instruction: Multiple approaches and practices*. Cham, Switzerland: Springer.

Stein, M. K., Remillard, J., & Smith, M. S. (2007). How curriculum influences student learning. In F. K. Lester Jr. (Ed.), *Second handbook of research on mathematics teaching and learning* (pp. 319–369). Charlotte: Information Age.

Stein, M. K., Smith, M. S., Henningsen, M. A., & Silver, E. A. (2009). *Implementing standards-based mathematics instruction: A casebook for professional development* (2nd ed.). New York: Teachers College Press.

Stephan, M., Underwood-Gregg, D., & Yackel, E. (2014). Guided reinvention: What is it and how do teachers learn this teaching approach? In Y. Li, E. A. Silver, & S. Li (Eds.), *Transforming mathematics instruction: Multiple approaches and practices*. Cham, Switzerland: Springer.

Stigler, J. W., & Hiebert, J. (1999). *The teaching gap: Best ideas from the world's teachers for improving education in the classroom*. New York: Free Press.

Stillman, G. A., Kaiser, G., Blum, W., & Brown, J. P. (Eds.). (2013). *Teaching mathematical modeling: Connecting to research and practice*. Cham, Switzerland: Springer.

Sullivan, P. (2014). Preface to part III. In Y. Li, E. A. Silver, & S. Li (Eds.), *Transforming mathematics instruction: Multiple approaches and practices*. Cham, Switzerland: Springer.

Vorhölter, K., Kaiser, G., & Ferri, R. B. (2014). Modelling in mathematics classroom instruction: An innovative approach for transforming mathematics education. In Y. Li, E. A. Silver, & S. Li (Eds.), *Transforming mathematics instruction: Multiple approaches and practices*. Cham, Switzerland: Springer.

Watanabe, T. (2014). Transformation of Japanese elementary mathematics textbooks: 1958–2012. In Y. Li, E. A. Silver, & S. Li (Eds.), *Transforming mathematics instruction: Multiple approaches and practices*. Cham, Switzerland: Springer.

Yang, Y. (2014). How classroom instruction was improved in a Teaching Research Group: A case study from Shanghai. In Y. Li, E. A. Silver, & S. Li (Eds.), *Transforming mathematics instruction: Multiple approaches and practices*. Cham, Switzerland: Springer.

Yang, Y., & Ricks, T. E. (2013). Chinese lesson study: Developing classroom instruction through collaborations in school-based teaching research group activities. In Y. Li & R. Huang (Eds.), *How Chinese teach mathematics and improve teaching* (pp. 51–65). New York: Routledge.

Part I
Transforming Mathematics Instruction with a Focus on Changes in Instructional Practice

Preface to Part I

David Clarke

Some approaches to the transformation of mathematics instruction might involve indirect approaches such as: change teacher education, change the curriculum or change assessment. It can be safely assumed that changes to teacher education, changes to the curriculum or changes to assessment will have their consequences for instruction. Part I of this book takes the direct route and addresses the possibility of changing mathematics instruction directly. But the other parts of this book remind us that any such change in instructional practice must occur within the constraints imposed by the curriculum, by existing assessment practices and by the teacher education programmes that equip teachers to engage in transformative practice. Acknowledging the significance of these different contexts within which we might attempt the transformation of instruction, the question remains: "In what direction, for what purpose and in what form might mathematics instruction be transformed?" The chapters in Part I offer some possible answers to this question.

Vorhölter, Kaiser and Ferri extol "the innovative power of the teaching and learning of mathematical modelling" and support their advocacy with examples from innovative projects designed to integrate modelling into the practices of mathematics classrooms. In part, their advocacy is based on a perceived need to make school mathematics more relevant to students and the community. This argument has been with us since Mogens Niss labelled it the "Relevance Paradox".

> The discrepancy between the objective social significance of mathematics and its subjective invisibility constitutes one form of what the author often calls the *relevance paradox*

D. Clarke (✉)
Melbourne Graduate School of Education, University of Melbourne,
109 Barry Street, Carlton, VIC, Australia
e-mail: d.clarke@unimelb.edu.au

Y. Li et al. (eds.), *Transforming Mathematics Instruction: Multiple Approaches and Practices*, Advances in Mathematics Education, DOI 10.1007/978-3-319-04993-9_2,
© Springer International Publishing Switzerland 2014

formed by the simultaneous objective relevance and subjective irrelevance of mathematics in society. (Niss 1994)

Vorhölter, Kaiser and Ferri restate this as, "a gap exists between the high relevance of mathematics in daily life, sciences, and this feeling of the uselessness of school mathematics". It should be humbling to the mathematics education community that we find ourselves still addressing this same "paradox" 20 years after Niss' original formulation. Yet the argument that mathematical modelling provides at least part of the key to establishing the relevance of classroom mathematics to situations of everyday life seems a convincing one. Having established the need and identified the strategy, we now address the question of tactics. How might mathematical modelling be used to transform mathematics instruction?

The chapter by Vorhölter, Kaiser and Ferri succeeds in addressing this question in at least three respects. Most importantly, it provides a well-referenced rationale for the inclusion of "applications and modelling" in the enacted curriculum and distinguishes usefully between the alternative attractions of holistic and atomistic approaches to the teaching of modelling, echoing past debates over the relative merits of teaching problem solving as a discrete or pervasive component of the mathematics curriculum. A variety of research projects are usefully cited to demonstrate the "innovative potential of modelling to change mathematics education". Any suggestion of single, simple approach is problematised by statements such as "there exist not only 'the modelling cycle', but modelling cycles for different purposes" and the demonstrated difference between research projects (and related approaches to instructional change) focusing on student behaviours and those focusing on teacher education.

The discussion of "scaffolding and adaptive interventions" is particularly interesting and leads naturally to the assertion that "modelling activities need to be carried out in a permanent balance between minimal teacher guidance and maximal students' independence, following well-known pedagogical principles such as the principal of minimal help". In this case, it is clear that it is the need for balance that is "permanent" and not the composition of that balance, which is based on "individual, adaptive, independence-preserving teacher interventions within modelling activities".

The chapter by Stephan, Underwood-Gregg and Yackel proposes a teaching approach they call "guided reinvention" that "moves beyond" inquiry approaches to mathematics teaching to an integration of aspects of "Realistic Mathematics Education" (Freudenthal 1973) with more recent conceptions of hypothetical learning trajectories (Simon and Tzur 2004). As with all the chapters in this book, it is legitimate to ask, "What's new?" and the answer is encouraging. In this case, the transformation of mathematics instruction is advanced by the advocacy of an approach to teaching that demonstrably and usefully builds on established and relevant research. This is sufficiently novel within the discipline as to be highly encouraging. Education as a discipline and mathematics education as a specific case do not have a happy history when it comes to the integration, consolidation and extension of knowledge. Guided reinvention is presented as a powerful approach that draws its warrant from firm foundations in existing theory and research. In a book titled "Transforming Mathematics Instruction", this is both reassuring and inspiring.

Leikin examines the interplay between multiple solution tasks (MSTs) and mathematical investigations (MIs). Analysis of the several examples of each takes as its utility function[1] "a student's mathematical potential" and posits a four-variable model of mathematical potential that encompasses mathematical ability, affective characteristics, personality traits and learning opportunities. The inclusion of "learning opportunities" immediately establishes the author's relativist position, further elaborated in relation to mathematical creativity. Recruiting Vygotsky's characterisation of imagination as further endorsement of the role of creativity in learning, Leikin then proposes MSTs and MIs as the vehicles by which student mathematical potential might be optimally realised.

Optimisation of the instructional use of MSTs and MIs is linked to "mathematical challenge" and thence back to Vygotsky again through connection to the Zone of Proximal Development. The author's relativist position is further consolidated by the assertion that "mathematical challenge is subjective". The transformation of mathematics instruction advocated in this chapter comes from tasks that "facilitate students with different levels of mathematical potential in overcoming mathematical challenges". As promised, the geometry tasks presented take conventional task forms and morph them into MST and MI versions with much greater capacity to stimulate, promote and realise student mathematical potential.

Goos, Geiger and Dole focus specifically on numeracy teaching. The project described in this chapter is shaped by a particularly rich conception of numeracy that encompasses "real-life contexts, application of mathematical knowledge, use of representational, physical, and digital tools, and positive dispositions towards mathematics" within the framework of a coherent, structured "model for numeracy in the 21st century". Central to this model is "a critical orientation towards numeracy" that connects the authors' conception of numeracy to some of the more emancipatory aspects of mathematical literacy (Jablonka 2003). The vehicle of change was a yearlong action research programme involving workshops and school visits. The structure, sequencing and rationale for this programme are provided in useful detail. The numeracy model is used to provide a particularly revealing representation of one teacher's trajectory towards transformed numeracy teaching. A case study outlines the teacher's professional development in compelling detail.

In evaluating the effectiveness of the professional development approach, teacher responses to a questionnaire administered before and after the action research programme are analysed. Emphasis is given to the increase in teachers' confidence in the various aspects of numeracy teaching. With respect to the classroom realisation of numeracy, "teachers seemed most comfortable with incorporating the *knowledge, dispositions,* and *contexts* components of the model into their thinking about numeracy", but the overarching "critical orientation" to numeracy was not widely achieved. The challenge of integrating this critical orientation

---

[1] A useful construct from economics, meaning "that which is maximised".

into their numeracy teaching proved too much for most participating teachers. The authors highlight the need for further research into how teachers might be better supported in implementing a critical orientation to numeracy. Notwithstanding the unevenness with which this critical orientation was achieved, the programme outlined provides a wonderful foundation on which further efforts to transform numeracy teaching might be undertaken.

From numeracy the focus shifts to exploratory work in the mathematics classroom (da Ponte, Branco and Quaresma). Examples are provided of the integration of exploratory work into the daily activities of the mathematics classroom. This is contrasted with the "exposition of concepts and procedures" and the "presentation of examples and practice of exercises" associated with "conventional education". The distinctive features of the problems used to initiate student mathematical exploration were "elements of uncertainty or openness, requiring students to undertake a significant work of interpreting the situation". The purpose of the chapter is to show how exploration tasks can be used to create a productive classroom environment and a teaching experiment is described with this focus.

Results of the research indicate student improvement in their understanding of fractions, percent and decimals. Representations (particularly student-generated representations) appear to play a critical role in the instructional approach, and the description of student activity as rebuilding their representations of the problem situation is particularly evocative. The emphasis on student presentation of their findings clearly contributes to the development of student learning while providing important information on that learning. In common with other instructional innovations discussed in Part I, student achievement of the more sophisticated learning goals was uneven; nonetheless, the examples provided constitute a form of proof of concept or validation of the viability of the use of exploration tasks in successfully promoting both conventional mathematics learning and more ambitious learning goals such as mathematical reasoning and communication.

The final chapter in Part I (Liljedahl) takes group work as its focus and explores the consequences of random assignment of students to groups. These consequences include student affect, classroom social flexibility and affordances and the devolution of the responsibility for generating mathematical knowledge from the teacher to the students. The recurrent argument of the chapter is that random assignment of students to groups has definite advantages in comparison with the strategic structuring of group membership advocated elsewhere.

Interestingly, the emphasis of this chapter is on social organisation, collegial activity and the emergence of a sense of community within the classroom, rather than on conventional cognitive outcomes. Randomised groupings served to destabilise existing classroom norms, particularly those related to the teacher's role as "expert" and compelled a reconceptualisation of classroom mathematical activity. It is also suggested that the role of mathematical tasks changed from fragmented assemblages of loosely connected examples and opportunities for skill practice to a more central role as the vehicle for group work and mathematical discussion. One of the most appealing aspects of this chapter is the relative simplicity of the change strategy and the extensive and sophisticated nature of its consequences in terms of social function, student engagement and classroom mathematical activity.

If our goal is "Transforming Mathematics Instruction", then we need not only the mechanisms of transformation but a compelling rationale for the direction of change and the reassurance that evidence exists that each advocated transformation is likely to lead to productive learning. The chapters of Part I provide the examples and the rationale, the strategies and the consequences. The claims made are tempered by the recognition that more could still be achieved, but each chapter provides plausible evidence of fruitful development. In combination, we have a picture of the sophistication and complexity of mathematics instruction, amenable to constructive transformation from several different perspectives.

Additional References

Freudenthal, H. (1973). *Mathematics as an educational task*. Dordrecht: Reidel.

Jablonka, E. (2003). Mathematical literacy. In A. Bishop, M. A. Clements, C. Keitel, J. Kilpatrick, & F. Leung (Eds.), *Second international handbook of mathematics education* (pp. 75–102). Dordrecht: Kluwer.

Niss, M. (1994). Mathematics in society. In R. Biehler, R. W. Scholz, R. Straesser, & B. Winkelmann (Eds.), *The didactics of mathematics as a scientific discipline* (s. 367–378). Dordrecht: Kluwer Academic Publishers.

Simon, M., & Tzur, R. (2004). Explicating the role of mathematical tasks in conceptual learning: An elaboration of the hypothetical learning trajectory. *Mathematical Thinking and Learning, 6*(2), 91–104.

Modelling in Mathematics Classroom Instruction: An Innovative Approach for Transforming Mathematics Education

Katrin Vorhölter, Gabriele Kaiser, and Rita Borromeo Ferri

Abstract The attitude of many students all over the world is shaped by the experience of learning impractical algorithms without any relevance for their actual or future life. Many students only learn algorithms and concepts in order to pass examinations and forget them afterwards. The inclusion of mathematical modelling in schools is one current innovative approach, which has the potential to offer students insight into the usefulness of mathematics in their life. In this chapter, the development of the current discussion on teaching and learning mathematical modelling is described by detailing the goals of implementing mathematical modelling in schools and ways of integrating modelling into classrooms. Innovative projects for the integration of modelling into classrooms are described, displaying the innovative power of the teaching and learning of mathematical modelling in school. Based on the results of empirical studies, scaffolding as an approach to support students' independent modelling processes is discussed in detail distinguishing approaches at a macro- and a micro-level.

Keywords Mathematical modelling • Scaffolding • Modelling cycle • Theoretical perspectives • Modelling competencies • Beliefs • Intervention

K. Vorhölter (✉) • G. Kaiser
Faculty of Education, University of Hamburg, Von-Melle-Park 8, 20146 Hamburg, Germany
e-mail: Katrin.Vorhoelter@uni-hamburg.de; gabriele.kaiser@uni-hamburg.de

R. Borromeo Ferri
Department of Mathematics, University of Kassel,
Heinrich-Plett-Strasse 40, 34132 Kassel, Germany
e-mail: borromeo@mathematik.uni-kassel.de

Y. Li et al. (eds.), *Transforming Mathematics Instruction: Multiple Approaches and Practices*, Advances in Mathematics Education, DOI 10.1007/978-3-319-04993-9_3,
© Springer International Publishing Switzerland 2014

Introduction

The relevance of promoting applications and mathematical modelling in schools is currently accepted in most parts of the world. Departing from literacy studies claiming that mathematics education aims to promote responsible citizenship, the promotion of modelling competencies, i.e. the competencies to solve real-world problems using mathematics, is accepted as a central goal for mathematics education worldwide. The reasons for this change in mathematics education are multifaceted. Amongst other motives, the negative attitudes towards mathematics of many students are responsible for this change, which became apparent in various large-scale assessments such as TIMSS and PISA and in the daily work at school (cf. Mullis et al. 2012; OECD 2010). This is not a new phenomenon, but has been well known for decades. Especially in Western countries, many students are complaining about the uselessness of the mathematics learned in school for their actual and future life. They express that they do not see any sense in learning mathematics. A gap exists between the high relevance of mathematics in daily life and the sciences and this feeling of the uselessness of school mathematics. Furthermore, large-scale studies like PISA, which are focused on assessing mathematical literacy in a broad sense or, more concrete, on evaluating the competencies of the students to use mathematics in order to solve problems based on real-world contexts, show the unsatisfactory results of many students in this domain. Especially complex, multistep solution processes of contextual-rich problems, which require translation processes between mathematics and the real world, are of high difficulty for students in school (see OECD 2010).

The inclusion of real-world and modelling examples in many national curricula worldwide emphasising modelling competencies on a broad level reflects the concerns of politicians and mathematics educators, who are afraid that the young generation acquires neither the competencies for being mathematically literate nor the positive attitudes towards mathematics necessary for an open-minded acquaintance with mathematics. It is nowadays mostly agreed in the broad international debate on mathematical education, especially at the official curricular discussion, that applications and modelling have to play a decisive role at school, covering all age levels and ability strands (although there are still contesters against a strong role of applications and modelling in school). However, beyond this consensus on the relevance of modelling, it is still discussed how to integrate mathematical modelling in mathematical teaching and learning processes. There is still a lack of strong empirical evidence on the effects of the integration of modelling examples into school practice, although there exist many smaller and several large-scale projects aiming to include mathematical modelling into school practice. We will describe in the next section the development of the discussion on the integration of mathematical modelling into school practice, and then we exhibit projects and practical approaches for the promotion of mathematical modelling into school in section "Ways of Implementing Modelling into Day-to-Day Teaching" and conclude with results of empirical studies on the inclusion of mathematical modelling in school practice in section "Scaffolding and Adaptive Interventions in Modelling Processes".

Theoretical Framework and Strands
of the Modelling Discussion

Although applications and modelling have already played an important role in mathematics education in the nineteenth century, the request to teach mathematics in an application-oriented way has become more prominent at the turn from the nineteenth to the twentieth century, when innovative new syllabi, which included applications in mathematics teaching, were developed. This development was forced by the fast technological progress at the turn from the nineteenth to the twentieth century, which necessitated a better understanding of real-world examples, especially of problems in technology and engineering. Despite this technological necessity, mathematics education was, in many parts of the world, dominated by pure algorithms with no relations to the real world. This unsatisfactory situation has changed dramatically in the last decades with the famous symposium 'Why to teach mathematics so as to be useful' (Freudenthal 1968; Pollak 1968), which was carried out in 1968. Since then, the question of how to change mathematics education in order to include applications and modelling in daily teaching has been the focus of many research studies. However, this high amount of studies has not led to a consistent argumentation of how to teach mathematics so as to be useful. There have been several attempts to analyse the various theoretical approaches to teach mathematical modelling and applications and to clarify possible commonalities and differences. For example, Kaiser-Messmer (1986) distinguished in her analysis, from the beginning of the recent debate on modelling until the mid-1980s of the last century, two main streams within the international debate on applications and modelling, a so-called pragmatic perspective, focusing on utilitarian or pragmatic goals with Henry Pollak (1968) as protagonist, and a scientific-humanistic perspective oriented more towards mathematics as a science and humanistic ideals of education with Hans Freudenthal (1968) as main protagonist. The different goals emphasised had consequences concerning how to include mathematical modelling, namely, either based on cyclic modelling processes as requested by Pollak (1968) or as complex mathematising interplay between mathematics and the real world as described by Freudenthal (1973).

A few years later, Blum and Niss (1991, p. 43f) focused on the arguments and goals for the inclusion of applications and modelling and discriminated five layers of arguments in their extensive survey on the state of the art, namely:

- The formative argument is related to the promotion of general competencies and attitudes, in 'particular orientated towards fostering overall explorative, creative and problem solving capacities (such as attitudes, strategies, heuristics, techniques etc.), as well as open-mindedness, self-reliance and confidence in their own powers'.
- The critical competence argument aims 'to enable students to "see and judge" independently, to recognize, understand, analyse and assess representative examples of actual uses of mathematics, including (suggested) solutions to socially significant problems'.

- The utility argument requires that 'mathematics instruction should enable students to practice applications and modelling in a variety of contexts where mathematics has instrumental services to offer without occupying in itself the focal point of interest'.
- The 'picture of mathematics' argument 'insists that it is an important task of mathematics education to establish with students a rich and comprehensive picture of mathematics in all its facets, as a science, as a field of activity in society and culture'.
- The promotion of mathematics learning argument emphasises that the 'incorporation of problem solving, applications and modelling aspects and activities in mathematics instruction is well suited to assist students in acquiring, learning and keeping mathematical concepts, notions, methods and results, by providing motivation for and relevance of mathematical studies'.

Blum and Niss (1991) emphasised especially the promotion of three goals: that a student should be able to perform the modelling processes, to acquire knowledge of existing models, and to critically analyse given examples of modelling processes.

Various other classifications exist amongst others by Kaiser-Meßmer (1986) and Blum (1996), however, the core and intention of these multilayered systems of goals remain the same.

Various approaches on how to consider applications and modelling in mathematics instruction have been proposed since the beginning of the debate ranging from a simple inclusion of applications and modelling into a mainly mathematically structured curriculum to the organising of the curriculum along real-world examples. Blum and Niss (1991, p. 60f) distinguished several ways to include applications and modelling in mathematics instruction:

1. *The separation approach and two-compartment approach.* The mathematical programme is divided into distinct parts, a usual course in 'pure' mathematics, whereas the second one deals with one or more 'applied' items, utilising mathematics established in the first part or earlier.
2. *The islands approach.* The mathematical programme is divided into several parts each organised according to the two-compartment approach.
3. *The mixing approach.* Applications and modelling examples are included frequently into the mathematical programme in order 'to assist the introduction of mathematical concepts etc. Conversely, newly developed mathematical concepts, methods and results are activated towards applicational and modelling situations whenever possible'.
4. *The mathematics curriculum integrated approach and the interdisciplinary integrated approach.* 'Here problems, whether mathematical or applicational, come first and mathematics to deal with them is sought and developed subsequently' or 'one operates with a full integration between mathematical and extramathematical activities within an interdisciplinary framework where "mathematics" is not organized as a separate subject'.

Which approaches or which combination of approaches is favourable and should be chosen depends, according to Blum and Niss (1991), on 'a multitude of factors: the arguments for and the purposes and goals of problem solving, modelling and applications in mathematics instruction, or the characteristics and peculiarities (legal restrictions and other boundary conditions, specific task traditions, resources etc.) of the educational (sub)system under consideration' (p. 61). However, Blum and Niss (1991) emphasised the relation to the school level. According to their standpoint, the islands and mixing approaches are especially favourable for elementary school level, because the fundamental mathematics needs to be acquired. At the secondary level, a more integrated approach seems to be favourable, for experimental curricula even the interdisciplinary integrated approach might be appropriate. At the tertiary level, for example, in a mathematics service subject programme, all approaches are possible; however, the two-compartment, the islands, and the mixing approaches might be the most favoured.

Apart from the goals for the inclusion of applications and modelling in mathematics education and the approaches to including modelling into mathematics teaching, there is another key characteristic of the discussion on mathematical modelling, specifically, how the mathematical modelling process is understood, i.e. how the relation between mathematics and the 'rest of the world' (Pollak 1968) is described. Analyses show that the modelling processes are differently described by various perspectives and streams within the modelling debate. The perspectives mentioned above developed different notions of the modelling process: emphasising either the solution of the original problem, as it is done by an applied modelling perspective, or the development of mathematical theory as it is done by more theoretically oriented approaches (for a description of these different perspectives, see Kaiser and Sriraman 2006). So, corresponding to different perspectives on mathematical modelling, there exist various modelling cycles with specific emphasis (for an overview, see Borromeo Ferri 2006). That means that there exists not only 'the modelling cycle' but modelling cycles for different purposes.

A kind of a modelling cycle nowadays used in many empirical studies was developed by Blum (1996) and Kaiser-Messmer (1986) and is based, amongst others, on work by Pollak (1968). This description contains the characteristics, which can be found in various modelling cycles used in various strands of the debate on modelling: the given real problem is simplified in order to build a real model of the situation, many assumptions have to be made, and central influencing factors have to be identified. To create a mathematical model, the real model has to be translated into mathematics. However, the distinction between a real and a mathematical model is not always well defined, because the process of developing a real model and a mathematical model is interwoven, partly because the developed real problem is related to the mathematical knowledge of the modeller. Inside the mathematical model, mathematical results are worked out by using mathematics. After interpreting the mathematical results, the real results have to be validated as well as the whole modelling process itself. Individual parts or the whole process may have to be repeated.

The modelling cycle by Kaiser and Stender (2013) in Fig. 1 contains these core elements and is a slight variation of a description proposed by Maaß (2005).

Fig. 1 Modelling process by
Kaiser and Stender
(2013, p. 279)

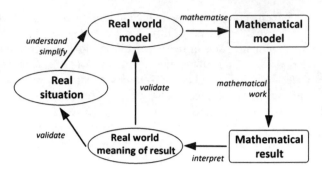

The cycle idealises the modelling process. In reality, several mini-modelling cycles occur that are worked out either in linear sequential steps like the cycle or in a less ordered way. Most modelling processes include frequent switching between different steps of the modelling cycles (Borromeo Ferri 2011). All of these steps are potential cognitive barriers for students, as well as essential stages in real modelling processes (Matos and Carreira 1997; Stillman 2011). These individual modelling processes – so-called modelling routes (Borromeo Ferri 2011) – are strongly influenced by the mathematical thinking style of the students as described by Borromeo Ferri (2011) in her extensive study. Students with a preference to an analytic thinking style usually switch to the mathematical model immediately and return to the real model only afterwards, when the need arises to understand the task in a better way. They work mainly in a formalistic manner and are better at 'perceiving' the mathematical aspects of a given real situation. Students with a preference towards a visual thinking style mostly imagine the situation in pictures and use pictographic drawings. Their argumentation during the modelling process is strongly related to the real world, even when they work within the mathematical model.

Especially important for modelling activities are modelling competencies, i.e. the ability and the volition to work out problems with mathematical means taken from the real-world problem through mathematical modelling. Based on the concept of the modelling cycle, the modelling debate distinguishes between sub-competencies and global competencies; sub-competencies relate to the single steps of the modelling cycle, and global modelling competencies, in contrast, relate to necessary abilities to perform the whole modelling process and to reflect on it (see Kaiser 2007). Based on the extensive studies by Maaß (2006) and work by Kaiser and Schwarz (2010), extensive work by Haines et al. (2000), Houston and Neill (2003), and Galbraith et al. (2007), and further studies which are summarised by Blomhøj (2011), different sub-competencies can be distinguished, whereby this list is far from being complete:

- 'Competency to solve at least partly a real world problem through mathematical description (that is, model) developed by oneself;
- Competency to reflect about the modelling process by activating meta-knowledge about modelling processes;

- Insight into the connections between mathematics and reality;
- Insight into the perception of mathematics as process and not merely as product;
- Insight into the subjectivity of mathematical modelling, that is, the dependence of modelling processes on the aims and the available mathematical tools and students competencies;
- Social competencies such as the ability to work in a group and to communicate about and via mathematics.' (Kaiser 2007, p. 111)

It is an open question whether special sub-competencies or modelling competencies in general should be fostered in the teaching and learning of mathematical modelling. Blomhøj and Jensen (2003) distinguish the two fundamentally different ways of teaching modelling, namely, in a holistic or an atomistic way. It is still an unanswered question if modelling can be better learned when focusing on one phase of the modelling cycle (atomistic way) and so using non-complex modelling problems or to start with complex tasks and carry out a whole modelling cycle (holistic way). The ongoing empirical study by Grünewald (2013) is measuring the efficiency of both approaches based on the increase of modelling competencies by students taught each way. The first results already point out that both approaches have advantages and disadvantages and seem to be able to support different sub-competencies of modelling.

Another influencing factor is the personal meaning students create when engaging in mathematics or working on mathematical tasks in class. As already mentioned, one reason for the implementation of mathematical modelling at a broader level is the negative attitudes of many students towards mathematics. Based on the concept of personal meaning as a special relation between mathematics and its relevance for the single student, the study by Vorhölter (2009) shows the high importance of the personal relation to the context taught and the necessity to include meaningful examples offering insight into a better understanding of the world around us. In detail the study emphasised that the personal meanings of mathematics as a service tool (i.e. students want to use mathematics in their present or future private life or at work as a tool and want to be prepared in school to this use) and self-fulfilment (i.e. students want to experience joy in mathematical activities and feel challenged by these) are decisive factors for students' learning and need to be considered in innovative teaching and learning approaches.

In the following, we want to show the innovative potential of modelling to change mathematics education by various projects, which attempt to implement mathematical modelling into the day-to-day teaching of mathematical classrooms.

Ways of Implementing Modelling into Day-to-Day Teaching

Due to the high number of both large and small projects, we concentrate on two different kinds of projects. The first focuses on students and, in this special case, on future teachers within the framework of teacher education. The second is embedded into the activities of in-service teacher education and focuses on practising teachers (for an overview on projects, cf. Blum et al. 2007; Kaiser et al. 2011; Stillman et al. 2013).

An influential way of implementing modelling into mathematics education is project-oriented work, amongst other so-called modelling weeks or modelling days, which are focused on students and future teachers. Originally developed at the University of Kaiserslautern and carried out for more than a decade at the University of Hamburg, they are now implemented at several other German universities. During modelling weeks, students from the upper secondary level (aged 16–18) work on a single modelling problem for a whole week at the university, whereas modelling days with students from the lower secondary level (aged 14–16) are organised at the participating school and last only 3 days. Students choose at the beginning of the activity one problem, which they tackle for the duration of the programme. The most important purpose of these projects is that the participating students will acquire competencies that enable them to carry out modelling examples independently, i.e. the ability to extract mathematical questions from the given problem contexts and to develop the solutions autonomously. Furthermore, it is hoped that students will be enabled to work purposefully on their own in open problem situations and will experience the feelings of uncertainty and insecurity, which are characteristics of real applications of mathematics in everyday life and the sciences. An overarching goal is that students' experiences with mathematics and their mathematical world views or mathematical beliefs are broadened (for details, see Kaiser et al. 2013). This can be described as a holistic approach, using the terminology of Blomhøj and Jensen (2003), i.e. the whole mathematical modelling process is carried out, covering all phases of the modelling cycle described above. The central feature of these projects is the use of authentic examples coming from industry, which are only simplified slightly. For example, the following themes have been tackled so far:

- Pricing for Internet booking of flights
- Optimal automated irrigation of a garden
- Development of ladybugs
- Chlorination of a swimming pool
- Optimal design of a bus stop

Quite often only a problematic situation is described, and the students have to develop a question that can be solved – the development and description of the problem to be tackled are the most important and most ambitious part of a modelling process, mostly neglected in ordinary mathematics lessons. Another feature of the problems is their openness, which means that various problem definitions and solutions are possible, depending on the views of the modellers.

One special feature of the activities carried out at the University of Hamburg is the integration of future teachers, i.e. that future teachers support the students during modelling activities as part of their university study.

The teaching and learning process is characterised as autonomous, self-organised learning, i.e. the students decide their ways of tackling the problem and no fast intervention by the tutors or teacher shall take place. That implies that various scaffolding and supporting measures need to be known by teachers, or in this case the student tutors, who therefore need to be trained beforehand. However, empirical research on the possibilities of supporting students with scaffolding measures and the efficiency of various measures has just started departing from the discussion on scaffolding in modelling at a micro-level described in the next section (see amongst others Kaiser and Stender 2013).

The other kind of projects we wish to describe focuses on practising teachers and takes place in the context of in-service teacher education. The international project LEMA (Learning and Education in and through Modelling and Applications) has developed different ways of implementing modelling into the mathematics classrooms of primary and secondary schools. The main aim is to implement mathematical modelling into day-to-day teaching by changing the teacher's practice and beliefs towards modelling and application. In order to achieve this goal, a teacher training course was designed, piloted, and evaluated in the classrooms of six participating countries from Europe. The core of the teacher training consists of five modules covering modelling tasks, lessons, assessment, and reflection. Sub-modules offered training in guidelines, resources, and teaching diaries. The modular design of the training course allows for flexible use in the different participating countries, considering national specifics as well as cultural aspects. The work of this international group reflects the difficulties of implementing a joint approach into classrooms of different cultures. Amongst others, the different theoretical backgrounds of the participating countries resulted in a multi-perspective approach and led to a critical consideration of the developed materials from different perspectives, which needed to be improved in further research (for details, see García et al. 2010). The main findings of the evaluation of the teacher training course point out that the course had no effect on the teachers' beliefs but had a positive effect on their pedagogical content knowledge and self-efficacy in terms of modelling. Furthermore, a high degree of satisfaction regarding the teachers' professional development and the intention to implement modelling tasks in day-to-day teaching could be determined (for details, see García and Ruiz-Higueras 2011; Maaß and Gurlitt 2011). This project shows clearly the difficulties that arise when modelling is implemented in ordinary classrooms, which are apparently quite similar in different countries despite the cultural differences.

In spite of the strong claims for the inclusion of mathematical modelling in schools and the variety of projects, applications and modelling still do not play a central role in the day-to-day teaching of mathematics around the world, as one would expect in the light of the curricular and didactical debate. As already mentioned, there exist worldwide many proposals for modelling examples, so the reason for this still unsatisfactory situation apparently does not lay in the scarcity of examples. However, in contrast to the wealth of examples, there still does not exist secure knowledge of how to teach mathematical modelling. In the beginning of the more recent modelling tradition, starting with the famous Freudenthal symposium, the rare empirical studies focused mainly on the aim of implementing mathematical modelling in classroom and how to implement it (cf. the study by Kaiser-Messmer 1986).

More recently, the focus has changed towards the question of how modelling can be taught and learned more effectively. Based on evidence from empirical studies and large-scale projects dealing with the teaching and learning of modelling, it was pointed out that mathematical modelling is not only a challenge for students but for teachers as well. The central question arises, how can teachers support their students within their modelling activities without destroying the independency of these modelling activities? The theoretical approach of scaffolding as a comprehensive, long-term approach combined with interventions as direct and immediate adaptive actions by the teachers – stemming from the tradition of self-directed independent learning approaches – seems to be highly adequate for these kinds of co-operative, self-directed activities, which are decisive for the modelling debate. In the following chapter, we will present research on various forms of scaffolding and adaptive interventions in modelling processes.

Scaffolding and Adaptive Interventions in Modelling Processes

Teaching and learning modelling is a complex interactional process influenced by many factors, ranging from the learning environment to teachers' knowledge. In order to support students effectively, teachers not only have to have a high content knowledge about modelling and the underlying mathematical and real-world knowledge but also sound knowledge of the different kinds of teaching methods. In the last decade, within the framework of constructivist teaching and learning approaches emphasising the construction of the own knowledge by the students and their independency within learning processes, the pedagogical approach of scaffolding and adaptive teaching interventions has been developed, which aims for tailored and temporary support that teachers can offer students during autonomous teaching and learning processes. Within the current debate on scaffolding, there exist different approaches and conceptualisations, as has been pointed out by van de Pol et al. (2010) in their survey on state of the art on scaffolding. Despite various differences, the central goal of scaffolding approaches is to enable students to solve a problem on their own. Therefore, adequate measures are provided in order to support the students in case they are not able to solve the given problem or when they are stuck. The support focuses on cognitive level means (such as required strategies and concepts) and metacognitive level measures (such as instructing self-regulated learning). The main principle is a consequent orientation on the individual learning process. Van de Pol et al. (2010) call this 'contingency' as one of the three central attributes of scaffolding. A condition, therefore, is the willingness and the competency of teachers to be responsible for the demands of thinking and understanding processes of students. When students work on complex modelling tasks and can choose mathematical algorithms on their own, the teacher must be able to decide, in a short time, if the student's path is goal-oriented or not. Depending on how self-regulated students are in this process, the teacher may try to reduce the support given to them, which is called 'fading' by van de Pol et al. (2010), because the teachers are 'transferring the responsibility' to their students.

The pedagogical approach of scaffolding is used in many studies concerning classroom instruction, and the approach by Hammond and Gibbons (2005) seems to be especially interesting. Hammond and Gibbons distinguish between macro-scaffolding, which covers all aspects of planning, and micro-scaffolding, which refers to interactional aspects, e.g. all kinds of teacher interventions. Both kinds of scaffolding are important for students' success and learning effects.

There exists extensive research on aspects, which refer to macro-scaffolding, especially effective lesson settings for modelling lessons. The large-scale project DISUM (didactical intervention modes for mathematics teaching oriented towards self-regulation) describes in its findings the motivational and challenging aspects of modelling tasks, the important role of motivational feedback by the teachers, the potential of individual work within group work, and the practicability of modelling activities with low-achieving students (Blum and Leiss 2007). In addition, two ways of teaching modelling problems were contrasted: a directive (teacher-centred) versus an operative-strategic (more student centred, emphasising group work and strategic scaffolding) instruction. Findings of this comparison point out that learning in operative-strategic groups promotes significantly higher performances in modelling than learning in directive groups. Furthermore, in the operative-strategic group, students' self-regulation was strongly improved. Students' self-reported enjoyment, effort, and use of learning strategies (Schukajlow et al. 2012) were positively related to performance. The modelling cycle introduced explicitly to students and used by them within the modelling process had positive impacts on student performance, settings, and strategies. However, teachers need to be trained for an adequate usage (Schukajlow et al. 2010). The effects of feedback given by the teachers were studied by the project Co²CA (Conditions and Consequences of Classroom Assessment), whose results point out that a differentiated feedback such as process-related, social comparative, or criteria-based feedback results in higher student motivation, but does not lead to higher achievement results.

The impact of heuristic worked-out examples on the promotion of modelling competencies was analysed by the project KOMMA (Kompendium Mathematik). The study showed that working with worked-out examples within the learning environment seems to be more appropriate for students with lower modelling competencies at the beginning (Zöttl et al. 2011). The influence of the promotion of multiple solution methods in modelling processes was evaluated in the project MultiMa (multiple solutions for mathematics teaching oriented towards students' self-regulation), which identified the better modelling performance of students who had been encouraged to develop multiple solutions of modelling problems. In addition, their self-regulation increased and their cognitive activation was much higher (Schukajlow and Krug 2013). To summarise, there is a wealth of studies that show the high potential of modelling in classrooms; however, it becomes clear that the way modelling is treated in daily teaching is decisive whether modelling competencies are promoted or not.

In the didactical research on scaffolding and interventions, several theoretical approaches for the support of learners by teachers are discussed. A distinction between different kinds of interventions – well known in the German debate – is offered by the taxonomy of assistance developed by Zech (1998), which refers to the principle of minimal help developed by Aebli (1983). This taxonomy was developed by Zech (1998) for problem-solving activities and departs from the norm in stating that the intensity and strength of the intervention shall increase step by step in relation to the lack of success of the students and that these interventions shall support the students to develop a solution on their own, if possible. This taxonomy differentiates motivational, feedback, general-strategic, content-oriented strategic, and content-oriented assistance. The intensity of the intervention increases gradually from motivational assistance to the content-oriented assistance. This classification has already been used in modelling activities for a long time but only at a practical level and without empirical evaluation of its efficiency. Based on this categorisation, Leiß (2007) evaluated the usage of various kinds of support given by teachers in modelling processes in a laboratory study within the project DISUM (cf. Blum 2011). The main results of Leiß's study were, amongst others, that strategic interventions are included in the intervention repertoire of the observed teachers only very marginally and that the teachers often choose indirect advice where students have to find only one step by themselves in order to overcome the difficulty. Further studies from Link (2011) and Beutel and Krosanke (2012) did not confirm these results. Link's study departed from the taxonomy developed by Zech and identified in laboratory studies a high amount of general-strategic interventions. Both studies found that particular strategic interventions lead to metacognitive activities in learners. The ongoing study by Stender on effective adaptive interventions has already identified one powerful and effective general-strategic intervention, namely, the request by the teacher to the students to present their state of work to him/her when approaching the group in a co-operative learning environment (Kaiser and Stender 2013). This intervention is a prerequisite of an adequate scaffold by the teacher, because scaffolding has to be based on a careful diagnosis of students' work, if it is to be efficient and successful. This kind of intervention is also, as the synthesis of meta-studies by Hattie (2009) has pointed out, a central part of an effective feedback and is closely related to the kind of feedback questions Hattie (2009) identifies as being effective.

Besides studies on this principle of minimal help, the role of metacognition within mathematical modelling for a basis of possible interventions was studied by Stillman et al. (2007) and Stillman et al. (2010). These studies identify mental or cognitive blockages, which prevent students from successful modelling. They emphasise the necessity of the metacognitive activities of the students, i.e. students should observe their own modelling process as 'looking over one's own shoulder'. Stillman (2011) claims the necessity for teachers' reflections about students' metacognitive activity within the specific situation and with respect to the teacher's role in the modelling process and calls for a meta-metacognitive process to be included in modelling activities. It is accepted within these studies that teacher interventions are necessary in order to facilitate reflective learning, e.g. as teachers' actions 'on the fly'.

Summary and Prospects

As discussed in this paper, the potential of mathematical modelling as an innovative teaching and learning approach has been shown in many studies. However, so far, the role of the teacher within modelling activities has not been researched sufficiently: not enough secure empirical evidence exists on how teachers can support students in independent modelling activities, how they can support them in overcoming cognitive blockages, or how can they foster metacognitive competencies. It is agreed that modelling activities need to be carried out in a permanent balance between minimal teacher guidance and maximal students' independence, following well-known pedagogical principles such as the principle of minimal help. Research calls for individual, adaptive, independence-preserving teacher interventions within modelling activities, which relates modelling activities to the approach of scaffolding. Scaffolding can be described, according to well-known definitions, as a metaphor for the tailored and temporary support that teachers offer students to help them solve a task that they would otherwise not be able to perform. So, it can be assumed that scaffolding is useful for the facilitation of student learning. Although scaffolding has been studied extensively in the last few decades, it was found to be rare in classroom practice. Scaffolding seems to be especially necessary and appropriate for modelling processes, which comprise complex cognitive activities. However, scaffolding has to be based on a diagnosis of students' understanding of the learning content, which most teachers did not usually ascertain; in contrast, most teachers provided immediate support or even favoured their own solution.

In the future, learning environments for modelling which support independent modelling activities need to be established, for example, by sense-making or using meaningful tasks (Freudenthal 1973; Vorhölter 2009), by model-eliciting activities based on challenging tasks (Lesh and Doerr 2003), or by the usage of authentic tasks (Kaiser and Schwarz 2010).

References

Aebli, H. (1983). *Zwölf Grundformen des Lehrens*. Stuttgart: Klett-Cotta.

Beutel, M., & Krosanke, N. (2012). *Rekonstruktion von Handlungsabläufen in komplexen Modellierungsprozessen – Schülerprobleme und Lehrerverhalten*, Unpublished master thesis. University of Hamburg, Hamburg.

Blomhøj, M. (2011). Modelling competency: Teaching, learning and assessing competencies – Overview. In G. Kaiser, W. Blum, R. Borromeo Ferri, & G. Stillman (Eds.), *Trends in teaching and learning of mathematical modelling* (pp. 343–349). New York: Springer.

Blomhøj, M., & Højgaard Jensen, T. (2003). Developing mathematical modelling competence: Conceptual clarification and educational planning. *Teaching Mathematics and Its Applications, 22*(3), 123–139.

Blum, W. (1996). Anwendungsbezüge im Mathematikunterricht – Trends und Perspektiven. In G. Kadunz, H. Kautschitsch, G. Ossimitz, & E. Schneider (Eds.), *Trends und Perspektiven* (pp. 15–38). Wien: Hölder-Pichler-Tempsky.

Blum, W. (2011). Can modelling be taught and learnt? Some answers from empirical research. In G. Kaiser, W. Blum, R. Borromeo Ferri, & G. Stillman (Eds.), *Trends in teaching and learning of mathematical modelling* (pp. 15–30). New York: Springer.

Blum, W., & Leiss, D. (2007). How do students and teachers deal with modeling problems? In C. P. Haines, P. Galbraith, W. Blum, & S. Khan (Eds.), *Mathematical modeling (ICTMA 12): Education, engineering and economics* (pp. 222–231). Chichester: Horwood.

Blum, W., & Niss, M. (1991). Applied mathematical problem solving, modelling, applications, and links to other subjects – State, trends and issues in mathematics instruction. *Educational Studies in Mathematics, 22,* 37–68.

Blum, W., Galbraith, P. L., Henn, H.-W., & Niss, M. (Eds.). (2007). *Modeling and applications in mathematics education. The 14th ICMI study.* New York: Springer.

Borromeo Ferri, R. (2006). Theoretical and empirical differentiations of phases in the modelling process. *ZDM – The International Journal on Mathematics Education, 38*(2), 86–95.

Borromeo Ferri, R. (2011). *Wege zur Innenwelt des mathematischen Modellierens.* Wiesbaden: Vieweg-Teubner.

Freudenthal, H. (1968). Why to teach mathematics so as to be useful. *Educational Studies in Mathematics, 1*(1/2), 3–8.

Freudenthal, H. (1973). *Mathematics as an educational task.* Dordrecht: Riedel.

Galbraith, P., Stillman, G., Brown, J., & Edwards, I. (2007). Facilitating middle secondary modeling competencies. In C. P. Haines, P. Galbraith, W. Blum, & S. Khan (Eds.), *Mathematical modelling (ICTMA 12): Education, engineering and economics* (pp. 130–141). Chichester: Horwood.

García, F. J., Maaß, K., & Wake, G. (2010). Theory meets practice: Working pragmatically within different cultures and traditions. In R. Lesh, P. L. Galbraith, C. R. Haines, & A. Hurford (Eds.), *Modeling students' mathematical modeling competencies. ICTMA 13* (pp. 445–457). New York: Springer.

García, F. J., & Ruiz-Higueras, L. (2011). Modifying teachers' practices: The case of a European training course on modelling and applications. In G. Kaiser, W. Blum, R. Borromeo Ferri, & G. Stillman (Eds.), *Trends in teaching and learning of mathematical modelling. ICTMA14* (pp. 569–578). Cham, Switzerland: Springer.

Grünewald, S. (2013). The development of modelling competencies by year 9 students: Effects of a modelling project. In G. Stillman, G. Kaiser, W. Blum, & J. Brown (Eds.), *Teaching mathematical modelling: Connecting to teaching and research practices* (pp. 185–194). Cham, Switzerland: Springer.

Haines, C. R., Crouch, R. M., & Davis, J. (2000). Understanding students' modelling skills. In J. F. Matos, W. Blum, K. Houston, & S. Carreira (Eds.), *Modelling and mathematics education: ICTMA9 applications in science and technology* (pp. 366–381). Chichester: Horwood.

Hammond, J., & Gibbons, P. (2005). Putting scaffolding to work: The contribution of scaffolding in articulating ESL education. *Prospect, 20*(1), 6–30.

Hattie, J. (2009). *Visible learning. A synthesis of over 800 meta-analyses relating to achievement.* London: Routledge.

Houston, K., & Neill, N. (2003). Investigating students' modelling skills. In Q. Ye, W. Blum, S. K. Houston, & Q. Jiang (Eds.), *Mathematical modelling in education and culture: ICTMA 10* (pp. 54–66). Chichester: Horwood.

Kaiser, G. (2007). Modelling and modelling competencies in school. In C. Haines, P. Galbraith, W. Blum, & S. Khan (Eds.), *Mathematical modelling (ICTMA 12): Education, engineering and economics* (pp. 110–119). Chichester: Horwood.

Kaiser, G., & Schwarz, B. (2010). Authentic modelling problems in mathematics education – Examples and experiences. *Journal für Mathematik-Didaktik, 31*(1), 51–76.

Kaiser, G., & Sriraman, B. (2006). A global survey of international perspectives on modeling in mathematics education. *ZDM – The International Journal on Mathematics Education, 38*(3), 302–310.

Kaiser, G., & Stender, P. (2013). Complex modelling problems in co-operative, self-directed learning environments. In G. Stillman, G. Kaiser, W. Blum, & J. Brown (Eds.), *Teaching mathematical modelling: Connecting to teaching and research practices* (pp. 277–293). Cham, Switzerland: Springer.

Kaiser, G., Blum, W., Borromeo Ferri, R., & Stillman, G. (Eds.). (2011). *Trends in teaching and learning of mathematical modelling*. Cham, Switzerland: Springer.

Kaiser, G., Bracke, M., Göttlich, S., & Kaland, C. (2013). Realistic complex modelling problems in mathematics education. In R. Strässer & A. Damlamian (Eds.), *Educational interfaces between mathematics and industry (ICMI-ICIAM-Study)* (pp. 299–307). New York: Springer.

Kaiser-Messmer, G. (1986). Anwendungen im Mathematikunterricht. *Vol. 1: Theoretische Konzeptionen. Vol. 2: Empirische Untersuchungen.* Bad Salzdetfurth: Franzbecker.

Leiß, D. (2007). *Hilf mir es selbst zu tun*. Hildesheim: Franzbecker.

Lesh, R., & Doerr, H. (Eds.). (2003). *Beyond constructivism: Models and modeling perspectives on mathematics problem solving, learning, and teaching*. Mahwah: Lawrence Erlbaum Associates.

Link, F. (2011). *Problemlöseprozesse selbstständigkeitsorientiert begleiten: Kontexte und Bedeutungen strategischer Lehrerinterventionen in der Sekundarstufe I*. Hildesheim: Franzbecker.

Maaß, K. (2005). Modellieren im Mathematikunterricht der Sekundarstufe I. *Journal für Mathematik-Didaktik, 26*(2), 114–142.

Maaß, K. (2006). What are modelling competencies? *Zentralblatt für Didaktik der Mathematik, 38*(2), 113–142.

Maaß, K., & Gurlitt, J. (2011). LEMA – Professional development of teachers in relation to mathematical modelling. In G. Kaiser, W. Blum, R. Borromeo Ferri, & G. Stillman (Eds.), *Trends in teaching and learning of mathematical modelling. ICTMA14* (pp. 629–639). Cham, Switzerland: Springer.

Matos, J., & Carreira, S. (1997). The quest for meaning in students' mathematical modelling. In K. Houston, W. Blum, I. Huntley, & N. Neill (Eds.), *Teaching and learning mathematical modelling (ICTMA 7)* (pp. 63–75). Chichester: Horwood Publishing.

Mullis, I. V. S., Martin, M. O., Foy, P., & Arora, A. (2012). *TIMSS 2011 international results in mathematics*. Chestnut Hill: Chestnut Hill TIMSS & PIRLS International Study Center, Boston College.

OECD. (2010). *PISA 2009 results: What students know and can do – Student performance in reading, mathematics and science* (Vol. 1). Paris: OECD.

Pollak, H. O. (1968). On some of the problems of teaching applications of mathematics. *Educational Studies in Mathematics, 1*(1/2), 24–30.

Schukajlow, S., & Krug, A. (2013). Considering multiple solutions for modelling problems – Design and first results from the MultiMa-project. In G. Stillman, G. Kaiser, W. Blum, & J. Brown (Eds.), *Teaching mathematical modelling: Connecting to teaching and research practices*. Cham, Switzerland: Springer.

Schukajlow, S., Krämer, J., Blum, W., Besser, M., Brode, R., Leiß, D., et al. (2010). Lösungsplan in Schülerhand: zusätzliche Hürde oder Schlüssel zum Erfolg? In *Beiträge zum Mathematikunterricht 2010* (pp. 771–774). Münster: WTM.

Schukajlow, S., Leiss, D., Pekrun, R., Blum, W., Müller, M., & Messner, R. (2012). Teaching methods for modelling problems and students' task-specific enjoyment, value, interest and self-efficacy expectations. *Educational Studies in Mathematics, 79*(2), 215–237.

Stillman, G. (2011). Applying metacognitive knowledge and strategies in applications and modelling tasks at secondary school. In G. Kaiser, W. Blum, R. Borromeo Ferri, & G. Stillman (Eds.), *Trends in teaching and learning of mathematical modelling. ICTMA14* (pp. 165–180). Cham, Switzerland: Springer.

Stillman, G., Galbraith, P., Brown, J., & Edwards, I. (2007). A framework for success in implementing mathematical modelling in the secondary classroom. In J. Watson & K. Beswick (Eds.), *Mathematics: Essential research, essential practice* (Vol. 2, pp. 688–697). Adelaide: MERGA.

Stillman, G., Brown, J., & Galbraith, P. (2010). Identifying challenges within transition phases of mathematical modeling activities at year 9. In R. Lesh, P. Galbraith, C. R. Haines, & A. Hurford (Eds.), *Modelling students' mathematical modeling competencies ICTMA13* (pp. 385–398). New York: Springer.

Stillman, G., Kaiser, G., Blum, W., & Brown, J. (Eds.). (2013). *Teaching mathematical modelling: Connecting to teaching and research practices*. Cham, Switzerland: Springer.
Van de Pol, J., Volman, M., & Beishuizen, J. (2010). Scaffolding in teacher-student interaction: A decade of research. *Educational Psychology Review, 22*, 271–293.
Vorhölter, K. (2009). *Sinn im Mathematikunterricht*. Opladen: Budrich.
Zech, F. (1998). *Grundkurs Mathematikdidaktik*. Weinheim: Beltz Verlag.
Zöttl, L., Ufer, S., & Reiss, K. (2011). Assessing modelling competencies. Using a multidimensional IRT approach. In G. Kaiser, W. Blum, R. Borromeo Ferri, & G. Stillman (Eds.), *Trends in teaching and learning of mathematical modelling* (pp. 427–437). Cham, Switzerland: Springer.

Guided Reinvention: What Is It and How Do Teachers Learn This Teaching Approach?

Michelle Stephan, Diana Underwood-Gregg, and Erna Yackel

Abstract In this chapter, the theoretical construct of guided reinvention is extended to include desirable pedagogical practices for teachers implementing RME sequences. First, we explain what a guided reinvention teaching approach looks like and how it evolved out of over 25 years of research. We then articulate the planning and teaching practices of guided reinvention teachers and describe how those practices move beyond what many call "inquiry approaches" to mathematics teaching. We end the chapter by offering a set of learning goals that professional developers might use when mentoring aspiring guided reinvention teachers.

Keywords Inquiry mathematics • Cognitive coaching • Planning and classroom practices • Guided reinvention • Realistic Mathematics Education

In this chapter, we discuss a form of mathematics instructional practice that is informed by several decades of classroom-based design research, challenges to implementing such instruction including major shifts in teachers' planning practices, and approaches to mentoring that we have found to be effective in supporting

M. Stephan (✉)
College of Education, Middle/Secondary, Suite 312E,
University of North Carolina Charlotte, 9201 University City Blvd.,
Charlotte, NC 28223-0001, USA
e-mail: Michelle.Stephan@uncc.edu

D. Underwood-Gregg
Department of Mathematics, Computer Science, and Statistics,
Purdue University Calumet, 2200 169th ST, Hammond, IN 46323, USA
e-mail: diana@purduecal.edu

E. Yackel
Department of Mathematics, Computer Science, and Statistics,
Purdue University Calumet, 730 Roy Street, Dyer, IN 46311, USA
e-mail: Erna.Yackel@purduecal.edu

Y. Li et al. (eds.), *Transforming Mathematics Instruction: Multiple Approaches and Practices*, Advances in Mathematics Education, DOI 10.1007/978-3-319-04993-9_4,
© Springer International Publishing Switzerland 2014

teachers as they develop this form of teaching practice. All three authors have been directly involved in a number of classroom-based design research projects that have resulted in both further elaborating and extending an approach to instruction that Cobb et al. (1992), following Richards (1991), called the "inquiry mathematics tradition" and in the development of instructional resources for various content areas (Stephan and Akyuz 2012; Underwood-Gregg 2002; Underwood-Gregg and Yackel 2002). The instructional approach that Cobb and colleagues called the inquiry mathematics tradition differs sharply from recent use of the term *inquiry* that is associated with student-centered, discovery, and standards-based approaches to teaching. Further, since the 1990s, Cobb and colleagues, including the authors of this chapter, have substantially extended their approach to mathematics instruction to incorporate specific aspects of instructional design theory. In this chapter, we describe this extension, which we call the "guided reinvention" approach to teaching, to avoid confusion with current uses of the term *inquiry instruction*. In the first section of this chapter, we explain in detail what we mean by the guided reinvention approach to teaching.

In addition, the authors have all worked with practicing teachers to support them as they restructure their instructional practice to the guided reinvention approach and, in some cases, make use of the developed resources. We contend that in order for teachers to become experts in the guided reinvention approach to teaching, a mentor teacher or mathematics education research practitioner should engage them in activities that focus the novice on the planning and classroom practices that characterize this teaching approach. Thus, the second section of our chapter focuses on defining the planning and classroom teaching practices that are specific to guided reinvention.

We end the chapter with a discussion of the learning goals that can be effective when mentoring teachers who strive to implement a guided reinvention approach to teaching. We use the authors' work with teachers to illustrate a possible set of learning goals inherent in inducting a new teacher into the guided reinvention approach. The chapter can be viewed as a demonstration of how a body of mathematics education research and mentoring is being used to dramatically restructure the learning experiences of students and the instructional practices of ordinary, albeit highly motivated, teachers.

Guided Reinvention

The guided reinvention teaching approach grew out of our work with not only students and teachers over the last 25 years but also our interactions with teams of researchers and teachers who conducted design experiments in a variety of classrooms. One of the goals of these experiments was to use an instructional design theory from the Netherlands called Realistic Mathematics Education (RME) to create mathematics instruction that would result in students reinventing important mathematical concepts, with careful guidance from their teacher. In the sections below, we elaborate some of the most important aspects of this design approach as a way to ground later discussions regarding the complexity that teachers face when learning to guide students' reinventions.

Origin and Characteristics of Instructional Resources for Guided Reinvention Teachers

The initial instructional activities we used in the beginning years of our research were constructed by teams of researchers who had been involved in constructivist teaching experiments (Steffe and Thompson 2000). With no clear articulation of any design principles, we searched for a heuristic-based design theory for mathematics instruction which led us to the theory of Realistic Mathematics Education (RME). All of our more recent instructional resources were created using the RME design theory and incorporate the following heuristics that often differ from most reform textbooks.

Heuristic One: Guided Reinvention

One of the most important heuristics of RME is that the instructional resources should be designed to encourage students' reinvention of key mathematical concepts (Freudenthal 1973). To start developing an instructional sequence, the designer first engages in a thought experiment to envision a learning route the class might invent itself (Gravemeijer 2004). Whereas some of what we consider to be basic mathematical concepts today took mathematicians decades or even centuries to fully develop, students are expected to develop comprehensive conceptual understandings of mathematical concepts within the span of several weeks or months of a single school year. RME instructional resources help students reinvent these ideas in shortened time periods using carefully sequenced problems and tools and guidance from the teacher. In this reinvention approach, mathematical concepts are not presented to students in a top-down manner, as in traditional instruction. Rather, the learning route is designed so that the concepts emerge as students engage in the instructional sequence. It is in this sense that we say that students "reinvent" mathematics.

As an example, in 2009 a hypothetical learning trajectory and associated instructional sequence was created by a group of 7th grade teachers with the first author. The intention of this sequence was to help students reinvent the meaning underlying positive and negative integers and to develop a basis for computation with integers, including integer addition, subtraction, and simple multiplication. To this end, the teachers began instruction within the context of finance, helping students understand the meaning of net worth, assets, and debts. The instructional sequence was then designed to support students making sense of "transactions" on a net worth such as what happens when a person adds a debt of $50, symbolized as +(−50), to a net worth of $10. By the end of the instructional sequence, together with the teacher's guidance through tools, discourse, and gestures, students reinvent their own meaning and rules for integer operations.

Heuristic Two: Sequences Should Be Experientially Real for Students

One of the central heuristics of RME is that the starting points of instructional sequences should be experientially real in that the students are able to engage in personally meaningful activity (Gravemeijer 1994). Often, this means grounding students' initial mathematical activity in experientially real scenarios (which can include mathematical situations). The 7th grade integer instruction serves as a typical example of this heuristic since students' work was grounded in the context of finance, net worths, and transactions on them. Finance turned out to be a realistic context for students since many of them could imagine incurring debts and obtaining assets, especially during a period of economic hardships. While many textbook authors see the value of using real-world problems in instruction, RME goes beyond simply situating mathematics in the real world. Rather, instructional tasks draw on realistic situations as a semantic grounding for students' mathematizations, and activities are sequenced so that students will organize their activity within the realistic context to reinvent important mathematics. Students begin to reason with abstract symbols as their reinventions become more and more sophisticated.

Heuristic Three: Emergent Models

The third heuristic involves designing instructional activities that encourage students to transition from reasoning with models of their informal mathematical activity to modeling their formal mathematical activity, also called *emergent modeling* (Gravemeijer and Stephan 2002). During the transition from informal to formal, the designer/teacher supports students' modeling by introducing new tools or using student-created tools, such as physical devices, inscriptions, and symbols that can be shared by students to explain their mathematical reasoning. The integer instructional sequence was designed such that a vertical number line might first emerge as a model of students' ordering of integers on the number line. Then, it might evolve to become a model for formal addition/subtraction strategies for integers (see Stephan and Akyuz 2012).

Hypothetical Learning Trajectory

Guided by the three heuristics described above, the designer creates an instructional sequence while at the same time envisioning a path that the class may follow as they engage in the tasks (Gravemeijer 2004). The anticipated path has been labeled a *hypothetical learning trajectory* (Simon 1995) because the designer makes conjectures about the mathematical route the class, as a community, will travel, including the mathematical goals and tool use, as they engage with the instructional tasks and anticipate the means by which the teacher can support that route.[1] After implementation, the designer analyzes the collective learning of the class (and individual student development) and revises the instructional sequence accordingly. Another classroom experiment occurs with a newly revised, hypothesized learning trajectory (HLT) and the results feedback to inform future implementations. At the completion of testing and revising, a well-researched, stable instructional theory is ready for future adaptation by other teachers.

The HLT that served as the instructional backbone for integers can be seen in Appendix A. It is organized in a table that is separated into five categories: the tools, imagery, activity/interest, possible topics of mathematical discourse, and gestures that would support students' reinventions. The tools, imagery, interests, and discourse, in addition to the tasks themselves, can all be seen as a variety of supports that can be used by the teacher to guide students in their reinvention processes.

A teacher who attempts to adapt this HLT to her own classroom might use this table as a way to preplan an integer unit in order to form a big picture of the overarching sequence of instruction with goals, tools, and mathematical ideas that can be used throughout the unit. A more detailed description of the purposes of the activities can be used for day-to-day planning, with the table illustrating the global picture.

The importance of RME instructional design and guided reinvention cannot be understated. Very few reform textbooks actually use a formal, operational instructional design theory *specific to mathematics* to guide the design of their instruction. The teacher's responsibility in guided reinvention is to provide the opportunities necessary to guide students progressively in their reinvention of sophisticated mathematics.

The Teacher's Guidance

As the former section suggests, the first major tool for guiding students' mathematical development is grounded in the careful design of the sequenced tasks themselves. We also maintain that the teacher serves an essential role in guiding students' reinvention. In this section, we elaborate on the theory of learning and the associated constructs that have emerged from our work in mathematics classrooms over the last three decades. This learning theory and interpretive framework guides our work with teachers as we collaborate with them in learning how to guide students' reinventions.

In our work with classroom teachers who are transitioning to guided reinvention teaching (GR teaching), we find the framework developed by Cobb and Yackel

---

[1] It is important to emphasize that the hypothetical learning trajectory describes the learning of the class as a collective. That is, it refers to the taken-as-shared learning of the group of students as a whole. It does not refer to the learning of individual students.

(1996) extremely helpful for orienting our initial conversations. The interpretive framework grew out of their attempts to develop a way to understand the mathematical interactions among classroom members. The *emergent perspective* argues that individuals make shifts in their cognition as they participate in and contribute to the social and mathematical practices of the classroom community (Cobb and Yackel 1996). Cobb and Yackel developed three constructs that describe the social dynamics of the mathematics classroom: social norms, sociomathematical norms, and classroom mathematical practices.

Norms refer to regularities in interaction patterns and, as such, are interactively constituted by the classroom participants, including the teacher and the students. Social norms can be described by indicating the expectations and obligations that the teacher and students have for one another during mathematical discussions. Cobb and colleagues (Cobb et al. 1988) have documented at least four social norms that sustain classroom microcultures characterized by explanation, justification, and argumentation: Students are expected to (1) explain and justify their solutions and methods, (2) attempt to make sense of others' explanations, (3) indicate agreement or disagreement, and (4) ask clarifying questions when the need arises. Sociomathematical norms, on the other hand, are normative aspects of mathematical discussions that are specific to mathematical activity. They involve the *criteria* for what counts as an acceptable mathematical explanation, a different solution, an efficient solution, and a sophisticated solution. For example, the understanding that students are expected to explain their thinking is a social norm, whereas the understanding of what counts as an acceptable mathematical explanation is a sociomathematical norm. In guided reinvention classrooms, acceptable explanations and justifications have to involve descriptions of actions on mathematical objects that are experientially real for the students rather than procedural instructions (Yackel and Cobb 1996).

Classroom mathematical practices can be described as the taken-as-shared ways of reasoning and arguing mathematically that are content specific (Cobb et al. 2001). Like social and sociomathematical norms, classroom mathematical practices are interactively constituted. In this sense, classroom mathematical practices evolve as the teacher and students discuss situations, problems, and solution methods and often include aspects of symbolizing and notating (Cobb et al. 1997). Classroom mathematical practices differ from social and sociomathematical norms in that they are content specific. While social and sociomathematical norms describe the normative ways of communicating with one another, both in general and mathematically, classroom mathematical practices can best be thought of as specific mathematical interpretations that become normative through these interactions (e.g., normative *integer* interpretations and methods).

When working with teachers, we have found ourselves discussing the meaning of each of these three constructs as well as techniques the teachers can use in their classroom to initiate the constitution of these norms and practices. Additionally, Akyuz (2010) documented the classroom teaching practices of an expert GR teacher and found that attention to social and sociomathematical norms that characterize guided reinvention teaching constituted a major portion of her decision making regarding classroom interactions. Moreover, it was the learning trajectory that served as a tool to help her orchestrate whole-class discussions in which certain classroom mathematical practices were established. In the section below, we elaborate the five classroom teaching practices of a GR teacher found by Akyuz (2010) that ground our work with teachers in the field today.

Classroom Teaching Practices of the GR Teacher

Practice One: Initiating and Sustaining Social Norms

Practice one involves the role that the teacher plays in establishing and sustaining classroom social norms that are conducive to children's reinvention. Elsewhere we have written about the role of the teacher in establishing these social norms (Cobb et al. 1989). In our experience, this practice is one that most GR teachers are able to establish (cf. Inoue and Buczynski 2011). Furthermore, they are typically successful in doing so within the first several months of the school year.

Practice Two: Supporting the Development of Sociomathematical Norms

Another important part of establishing the learning environment involves initiating and maintaining sociomathematical norms. While the teacher's role in this process has been detailed elsewhere at various grade levels (Stephan and Whitenack 2003; Yackel and Cobb 1996; Yackel et al. 1999, 2000), in guided reinvention classrooms, students' explanations are acceptable if they meet the criterion that they describe the students' actions on mathematical objects that are experientially real to them. Descriptions of only procedural steps are not counted as acceptable. Descriptions of procedures for finding an answer must be accompanied by the reasons for the calculations as well as what these calculations and their results mean in terms of the problem (Stephan et al. 2003). That is, the discourse is conceptual rather than calculational in nature (Cobb et al. 2001; Thompson et al. 1994). Furthermore, we emphasize that when the social norms described above are in place, students are obliged to ask questions when they disagree or do not understand. As a consequence, the decision about whether or not an explanation is acceptable is not the province of the teacher but of the entire class. Since we take an explanation to be a clarification of one's thinking for others (Cobb et al. 1992), an explanation is inadequate if others in the class have questions.

Practice Three: Capitalizing on Students' Imagery to Create Inscriptions and Notations

Practice three revolves around the teacher's encouragement of students' imagery through notations and tools use. She does this by capitalizing on the tool development that is part of the RME instructional design and the rich imagery that the design can foster. For example, in the integer instruction, the teacher capitalized on some students' imagery of marking numbers on a horizontal number line to introduce an empty vertical number line. Students used the vertical number line to record two net worths (e.g., $2,000 and $3,000) and find their difference ($5,000).

Practice Four: Developing Small Groups as Communities of Learners

This practice focuses on establishing the criteria for engaging in productive small groups. One of the roles of the teacher is to help students learn the value of working with peers as well as ways to do so. It is the teacher's responsibility to initiate the constitution of small group social norms that are conducive to reinvention. These include that students (1) develop personally meaningful solutions, (2) explain their reasoning to their partner(s), (3) listen to and attempt to understand the explanations of their partner(s), (4) persist on challenging problems, and (5) collaborate to complete the activities including indicating agreement or disagreement with their partner(s) (Wood and Yackel 1990; Yackel et al. 1991). Another small group norm is that if a student needs help, he is obligated to ask his partner(s) first before asking the teacher.

Practice Five: Facilitating Genuine Mathematical Discourse

The last practice involves the methods by which a GR teacher facilitates genuine and meaningful discourse about mathematics. She does this by (1) introducing mathematical vocabulary and tools to record students' inventions, (2) asking questions that promote students' strategies, (3) restating students' solutions in clearer or more advanced ways, and (4) using students' strategies during exploration time to orchestrate an effective whole-class discussion. This practice, in our experience, has been the most difficult to develop among novice guided reinvention teachers (cf. Inoue and Buczynski 2011) and requires the teacher to develop a thorough knowledge of both the HLT and the mathematics content.

The classroom teaching practices of a GR teacher are complex and thus may take many years to develop to sophistication. It is important to note that establishing productive social and sociomathematical norms, productive group norms, and genuine mathematical discourse alone is insufficient. Reinventions occur not only as students work together and explain their thinking but also as the teacher incorporates modeling and certain questioning and debate in her classroom. For this reason, it is essential that establishing specific classroom mathematical practices that are part of a well-designed learning trajectory becomes an integral part of the guided reinvention teacher's approach. Choosing appropriate instructional materials and *mindfully planning* for class discussion are therefore essential for maintaining the GR teaching approach. In the next section, we elaborate on the planning practices that are crucial for guided reinvention teaching.

Planning Practices of the GR Teacher

Practice One: Preparation

When planning the implementation of an RME instructional sequence, the teacher must plan lessons not only on a *daily* basis but, equally important, *long range* (Akyuz et al. 2013). Preparing long range means familiarizing herself with the goals of the entire unit of study. This includes becoming intimately familiar with the outlined hypothetical learning trajectory. Just like the designer, the teacher should understand the mathematics to be learned and students' preconceptions. The teacher then works through the instructional activities herself to unpack the intent of the tasks and to create a hypothetical image of the variety of pathways that can emerge as a result of the diversity of her students' reasoning. She also envisions the possible topics of conversation that might transpire as students work through and discuss the tasks and the potential classroom mathematical practices (and associated tools) that can be established through discourse. At times, it can become useful for the teacher to read relevant research to help her fill out her picture of the HLT more completely. The HLT as illustrated in Appendix A can be a helpful artifact for teachers to discuss together as they imagine ways of guiding their students' reinvention with the instructional tasks. While practice one focuses on creating a general long-range vision of the unit, practices 2, 3, and 4 involve the planning that occurs daily.

Practice Two: Anticipation (Looking Forward)

Before each class period, the teacher(s) hypothesizes the best ways to introduce the tasks, works out problems to anticipate possible student thinking and how it fits with current mathematical practices, and uses conjectured student thinking to imagine potential discussion topics that may or may not be aligned with current learning goals. She uses this analysis to lesson image (Schoenfeld 2000), that is, to create an image of how the next lesson will flow (i.e., what strategies students will develop, which are important for progress toward reinventing the mathematical ideas, which student should be called on first, second, and third, to help realize the learning goals).

From a theoretical point of view, the teacher is using both a collective and an individual lens in this practice. As she anticipates the diverse ways that students will engage in the tasks, she takes an individual lens while putting the collective learning in the background. When she lesson images to create a vision of how to use individual reasoning to structure the whole-class discussion and the practices that might become taken as shared in the collective, she has switched to a social lens.

Practice Three: Reflection (Looking Back)

After each class period, the teacher reflects on (1) the student reinventions and discourse to determine the status of classroom mathematical practices, including students' tool use, (2) the mathematical learning that emerged, and (3) the status of the social and sociomathematical norms. She then uses her reflective analysis to make revisions to the instruction for subsequent class periods.

Practice Four: Assessment

The GR teacher creates and implements formative assessments to ascertain the daily evolution of the classroom mathematical practices and individual students' growth. Short problems given at the beginning or end of class can assess their current understanding. Also, during students' exploration time, the teacher gathers data on student thinking as they attempt to solve the problems posed in class. Summative assessments can be used to document students' cumulative learning.

Practice Five: Revision

Revising occurs at two levels, one involving daily revisions based upon ongoing formative assessments. The other revision occurs at the end of the instructional sequence in the form of noting changes that should be made to the materials, tools, or questions that should be asked for the next year.

The planning practices, in a sense, mirror the practices of an RME instructional designer except that the GR teacher is not attempting to create an HLT and instructional activities from scratch. However, like the designer, a GR teacher must think and plan long range, which requires familiarizing herself with an already-constructed HLT. Furthermore, she must anticipate student strategies and possible whole-class discussions, together with the tools she can introduce. She must develop a reflective disposition in which she uses students' strategies and classroom mathematical practices to make informed decisions about future instruction. Finally, she must conduct formative and summative assessments for the purposes of revising in action as well as upon completion of the unit. These complex planning practices require unique forms of mentoring to help teachers develop them. In the next section, we highlight the learning goals that are associated with supporting aspiring GR teachers.

Mentoring Aspiring Guided Reinvention Teachers

It is well accepted that a variety of mentoring approaches including coaching, co-teaching, co-planning, model teaching, lesson study, and a diversity of professional development programs can have a positive effect on teacher change and, hence, student achievement. While coaching is becoming a popular mentoring approach, only a few studies have shown a statistically significant effectiveness of mathematics coaching on student achievement (e.g., Campbell and Malkus 2010; McCombs 1995). Of the many types of coaching, cognitive coaching (Costa and

Garmston 1994) is touted as the approach that engages teachers in the deepest reflection on their practice. Others including content-focused coaching (West and Staub 2003), instructional coaching (Kowal and Steiner 2007), and collaborative coaching and learning (Neufeld 2002) show additional promise, with peer coaching showing the least (Murray et al. 2009). However, it is less clear what approach works best with which teachers or if there are aspects of each that can be blended together to optimize the experience. In addition to a variety of coaching approaches, other notable programs involve teachers attending weeklong summer institutes with follow-up mentoring during the school year (cf. Yackel 2008).

We have argued that a guided reinvention approach to teaching requires highly specialized knowledge in the form of a different type of planning and of classroom teaching practices. It is not clear which of the mentoring approaches above can be used to best induct teachers into this approach. However, we have identified some possible learning goals for supporting teachers' shifts toward GR teaching and will specify these, along with associated mentoring activities, in the remainder of the chapter.

Catalysts for Change

We contend that some event typically occurs that serves as an impetus for a teacher to rethink their teaching practice, such as the adoption of a reform-based textbook, mandate from a principal, inspiration from a graduate education class, attendance at a conference, observation of a peer teacher, or some self-provocation. Without proper and meaningful guidance, however, the journey can be short-lived or even tumultuous. It is therefore important to develop and retain strong GR mentors within a school so that when teachers express a desire to change, adequate staff and resources are available. For example, the first author, Stephan, worked as a full-time middle school teacher in a suburb of Orlando, Florida. At the suggestion of the assistant principal, a first-year teacher, Sean, visited her classroom in order to observe a master GR teacher in action. Having quickly noticed how different her approach was with the students, Sean began discussing teaching with Stephan during their shared lunch periods as often as possible and subsequently shared his desire to shift from traditional teaching to an approach that valued students' thinking and explanation. At this time, they made an intentional decision to work together in an unofficial mentoring capacity the following school year. The catalyst for change in Sean's case was an opportunity provided by an administrator to provide a peer observation for a novice teacher. We will draw on Stephan and Sean's five-year collaboration throughout this paper to ground many of the suggestions we make regarding mentoring goals.

Once the recognition for change occurs to a teacher and a GR mentor is found, there are five learning goals we have identified that serve as the foundation for future mentoring activities: *develop an ear for listening hermeneutically, effectively interpret and implement the results of cognitive formative assessments, understand*

and implement GR planning practices, implementing GR classroom practices, and *coach self and others in the GR teaching approach.* These learning goals are not to be considered as isolated objectives or as occurring in a linear fashion. Rather, we contend that a mentor works toward all five goals simultaneously, with one or more goals enjoying heightened attention at times within certain activities.

Learning Goal 1: Develop an Ear for Listening Hermeneutically

A chief learning goal for aspiring GR teachers is to develop an ear for listening to students hermeneutically (Davis 1997). Basically, listening hermeneutically goes beyond listening to evaluate students' answers. Rather, teachers listen to students' strategies and explanations in order to *alter* instruction both on the fly and in planning later lessons. This is a complex form of listening because student thinking drives instruction and often results in changing the tasks and questions in the moment. For example, during discussions in his first mentoring year, Sean repeatedly asked Stephan's advice about his teaching techniques, like "What should I have done instead to address this problem?" Stephan always answered, "Well, how were your students thinking?" Sean often replied that he did not know how his students were reasoning and learned fairly quickly that, in his words, "I had better start listening to my students so I will have an answer to her questions next time." Sean also commented that the fact that Stephan repeatedly turned the conversation back to his students often took the pressure off him and led to a risk-free collaboration in which his teaching practice was not under evaluation.

This initial focus on listening skills is not typically the starting point for professional development experiences. Often, coaches offer to model teach in order to illustrate good classroom teaching practices. Or the coach observes the mentee teach a lesson and provides evaluative feedback on his practice. In contrast, a GR mentor might start from the viewpoint that good GR teaching practice is only possible when a teacher listens to the reasoning of his students and uses that as the basis for his teaching practice (cf. Ball 1991).

Learning Goal 2: Effectively Interpret and Implement the Results of Cognitive Formative Assessments

Another learning goal we have found powerful for helping GR teachers shift their practice is to become skilled at interviewing and interpreting the results of students' cognitive assessments. Cognitive interviews do not assess students' facility with basic skills but rather prompt students to reveal their understanding of a topic (for a sample problem, see Appendix B). The purpose of the interview is to listen hermeneutically to the student to understand their thinking and use that knowledge to organize instruction. Formative assessment has gained prominence in mathematics teaching, but the message that is typically sent to teachers (as was the case at Stephan and Sean's school) is that they should assess students on a *more consistent basis* than at the end of a unit. However, most techniques presented to teachers are basic skills-driven assessments that reveal only which skills and facts students have mastered, but not the meaning students hold for a concept. A cognitive-based assessment would give them both the reasons that a child may not be performing a skill well and the means for making better-informed decisions about problem choices in the classroom.

While Stephan has used cognitive assessments to guide individual teachers in their learning, we have also used cognitive interviewing to help teams of both in-service and preservice teachers learn to listen hermeneutically (Stephan et al. 2012; Yackel 2003). Results from our work with preservice teachers show that interviewing and listening hermeneutically was an extremely important part of shifting their envisioned teaching practice.

Learning Goal 3: Understand and Implement GR Planning Practices

A third learning goal involves supporting new GR teachers in their attempts to adopt the planning practices of GR teaching. While learning to listen, analyzing student thinking, and using student ideas to inform instruction are an important part of GR teaching, equally crucial is mindfully anticipating beforehand how students might think, so that the teacher can be more prepared to draw on those student contributions which align with the learning goals in the HLT. The five planning practices of a GR teacher outlined in a previous section constitute the basis with which we work with teachers to learn new planning techniques. Understanding how to plan like a GR teacher cannot be accomplished through reading or lecturing alone, but rather requires working with a more experienced teacher. For example, we have worked as co-teachers and co-planners with a variety of teachers. One way to co-plan is for the university or teacher mentor to coach other teachers during their planning period.

A second way that we have found successful is for an expert GR teacher to teach the same class as the aspiring teacher and plan their lessons collaboratively on a daily basis. The expert GR teacher, then, models the five planning practices in a very genuine way as they are both planning for and teaching the same lessons in their classrooms simultaneously. This relationship is different from coaching or other professional development experiences where the expert is not teaching the lesson and thus is an outsider to the experience. The expert and aspiring GR teacher, in the second case, share similar goals, purposes, and experiences, and thus, the entirety of the teacher's energy can be focused on supporting both her own students and those of the aspiring GR teacher. In the section below, we share an example from Stephan's work with Sean to show how GR planning practices can be supported by a mentor who is working alongside an aspiring teacher.

Collaborative Lesson Planning

Sean and Stephan lesson-planned collaboratively before each mathematics unit to prepare long range for the unit they would teach (planning practice 1 [PP1]). These conversations often involved a discussion of the HLT (if one existed) or of the long-range goals of a textbook unit. Stephan engaged Sean in conversations in which they attempted to highlight the mathematical concepts that formed the basis for the unit (or instructional sequence) as well as the tools and inscriptions that would be used to support students' reasoning. Once they were comfortable with the overarching mathematical goals, tool use, and student thinking that was intended throughout the unit, they then focused on implementing the sequence. Each day, they worked through the problems and anticipated how students might reinvent the relevant mathematical ideas. Then, they used their anticipations to imagine who they would call on during the summary whole-class discussion and in what order so that the relevant mathematical idea would emerge from the students during the discussion (PP2). They also planned certain questions based upon how they expected the discussion to unfold. These questions were intended to help students present their strategies in ways that other students could make sense of them, contrast them with theirs and others' strategies, and make decisions about the accuracy, sophistication, and efficiency of the ideas. The teachers also looked for ways that they could notate anticipated student strategies to move their thinking toward more efficiency and sophistication.

When the lesson was completed that day, Stephan and Sean met again briefly at the end of the day to discuss the ways in which their hypothesized image of the classes compared with what actually happened (PP3). In these discussions, student strategies were shared as well as the techniques each teacher used to structure the whole-class discussion. At this point, the teachers would decide if any changes needed to be made to their plan for the subsequent lesson. The next day, the cycle of anticipation and reflection began again. These cycles occurred on an almost daily basis throughout each unit. When appropriate, the teachers planned more formal formative assessments in the form of short quizzes or student presentations (PP4) and wrote a final unit assessment to determine the learning of individual students over the course of the instructional sequence. They then used their daily reflections as well as results from the unit assessment to record changes that needed to be made for the instructional sequence the following year (PP5).

For a coach who may not be teaching the same subject or may not be teaching at all, the strategies above can still be utilized with the intent to recreate, as closely as possible, some of the same activities. For instance, if the coach is not teaching full time, she can still co-plan with the teacher and develop formative assessments. However, since she doesn't teach, she has the added benefit of being able to be present during the implementation of their plan in her mentee's classroom that day. Then, they have a shared classroom experience through which to reflect on the current status of the HLT as well as fodder for follow-up co-planning sessions. Furthermore, they have a shared classroom experience that can be referred to as they discuss the teacher's GR classroom practices.

Learning Goal 4: Implementing GR Classroom Practices

The GR classroom practices are just as important as planning. Generally, our discussions with teachers begin with classroom practice 1 (CP1) that deals with establishing a teaching and learning environment conducive to the reinvention of mathematics. Focusing on social norms is a rich place to begin mentoring because a guided reinvention approach to teaching necessarily presumes a classroom participation structure in which students explain their thinking, make sense of other's thinking, and ask each other questions. We use teachers' classroom experiences (i.e., taught lessons) as an opportunity for discussing ways to initiate and establish strong GR social norms. However, what counts as acceptable mathematical explanations (CP2) are integral to discussions about social norms. Not only does a teacher want to establish a safe-discursive environment (CP1), but she must also think about the mathematical and discursive quality of those explanations (CP2). During these conversations with an experienced GR teacher, the other practices necessarily come into play because the teacher needs to anticipate what kinds of questions will help students develop acceptable explanations. She must also attend to students' symbolizations and what types of tools and inscriptions can support students' explanations and mathematical development. So, while discussions about social norms are a helpful starting point for learning about the GR classroom practices, they are conducted in the context of teacher's actual teaching and are not discussed in isolation of the other practices.

In attempting to support this learning goal, coaching can be an integral part of the mentoring experience. We have used a variety of coaching approaches with teachers, namely, the cognitive coaching approach (Costa and Garmston 1994) and less formal approaches such as observing a lesson and discussing the teacher's practice afterward. Additionally, model teaching can be effective in some instances if the expert GR teacher is intentional about illuminating the rationale for certain pedagogical moves (related to GR classroom practices) she made during the lesson. Co-teaching can also be effective as well as videotaping an aspiring or model teacher's lesson and analyzing their GR classroom practices.

The list of GR practices themselves can be useful during discussion. A more detailed version of the GR classroom practices (see Appendix C) was developed by a team of GR teachers at Stephan's school and can be used to frame discussions about a teacher's practice, both before and after the class session.

Learning Goal 5: Coach Self and Others in the GR Teaching Approach

The final learning goal involves learning to be a self-directed and reflective teacher and teaching those skills and GR practices to other teachers. For example, in Sean's fourth year, he was asked by the principal to serve as a community of learners

(COL) leader of three other teachers. The goal of the COLs that year was to provide all teachers the opportunity to co-plan with their peers and be coached where appropriate. Sean used this platform as a way to engage his teachers in the planning and classroom teaching practices of the GR teacher, including working solely from RME designed instructional sequences. He often used a coaching template (Appendix D) that Stephan had used with him to structure his planning meetings with teachers. In this way, Sean became a mentor who created activities and resources to mentor other teachers new to the GR teaching approach. Coaching others (in essence serving as a GR teaching mentor for others) provided another level of activity that strengthened his continued learning and classroom teaching practices as well as grew a new field of GR teachers.

Conclusion

In this chapter, we have described the guided reinvention approach to teaching that has grown out of decades of classroom-based research informed by the instructional design theory of Realistic Mathematics Education. The GR teaching approach differs sharply from many current inquiry approaches by framing teachers' work as supporting their students' reinvention of important mathematical ideas. Not only is instruction grounded in realistic scenarios, but attempts are made to help students build on their informal, concrete work with real-world settings to create abstract mathematical strategies.

We have argued that a guided reinvention approach to teaching requires knowledge of hypothetical learning trajectories and familiarity with research on students' conceptual development in the topic area being taught. Therefore, both the mathematical content and the ways of supporting students' progressive development are brought more to the forefront of teachers' practices. Teachers must develop the ability to use formative assessments to select, modify, and sequence learning activities that will guide students to reinvent increasingly sophisticated mathematical understandings. A teacher may draw upon problems and activities in a textbook in the course of creating, implementing, and revising instructional sequences, but guided reinvention teaching involves much more than simply following a textbook and asking students, "Why?"

We have also argued that a GR teaching approach is contingent upon the constitution of certain taken-as-shared social and sociomathematical norms that influence both small group interactions and whole-class discourse. Further, the teacher must be able to introduce notation, pose questions, and highlight student contributions that will support her students' thinking and move them along a learning trajectory. In other words, GR teaching is a system of interactions among the instructional sequence, the teacher's practice (including norm building, notational support, and formative assessment), and the students' participation. If we have made GR teaching sound complex, that is because it is. It involves social and sociomathematical *norm*-building and specific attention to students' *mathematics,* the nature of the instructional materials, teacher-led discourse and questioning, and student strategies that best support student learning.

In the next part of our chapter, we elaborated on the classroom teaching and planning practices of an expert, guided reinvention teacher. We then outlined five learning goals that can be used by mentor GR teachers in their efforts to support aspiring GR teachers. As a starting point, the mentor may begin by engaging the teacher in the act of listening to his students hermeneutically rather than evaluating his current teaching practice. We argued that learning to listen in this way prepares the teacher for the remaining learning goals involving assessing students cognitively to inform instruction, incorporating the planning and classroom practices into one's current teaching, and coaching oneself and others. Given the complex learning goals and practices involved in learning the GR teaching approach, we argue that it may take up to 5 years of working in a close mentoring program with an expert GR teacher or researcher. Building GR teacher capacity is then crucial so that they can then serve as GR mentors to new teachers within the profession.

In retrospect, this chapter outlined a hypothetical learning trajectory for a type of *teacher professional development* that has been over 25 years in the making. We believe that this chapter can provide mathematics educators with a framework for mathematics professional development that utilize a variety of mentoring activities to support aspiring GR teachers. We suggest that mathematics educators draw upon the learning goals in this chapter to develop their own hypothetical learning goals for their work with teachers.

Appendix A: Integer Hypothetical Learning Trajectory (HLT)

Phase	Tool	Imagery	Activity/ taken-as-shared interests	Possible topics of mathematical discourse	Possible gesturing and metaphors
One	Net worth statements	Assets and debts are quantities that have opposite effect on net worth	Learning finance terms	Conceptualizing an asset as something owned, a debt as something owed Conceptualizing a net worth as an abstract quantity (not tangible)	
Two	Net worth statements (vertical number line)	Differences in collections of assets and collections of debts	Determining a person's net worth Who is worth more?	Different strategies for finding net worths	Pay off

(continued)

(continued)

Phase	Tool	Imagery	Activity/ taken-as-shared interests	Possible topics of mathematical discourse	Possible gesturing and metaphors
Three	Symbols (+ and −)	+ means asset and − means debt	Determining and comparing net worths	Different strategies for finding net worths / Creating additive inverses as objects	Pay off
Four		Good decisions increase net worth / Bad decisions decrease net worth	Which transactions have good and bad effects on net worth?	When taking away an asset, is this good or bad? / When taking away a debt, is this good or bad? / Judging the results of transactions and therefore direction to move on a number line	Arms moving up and down to indicate good or bad movements
Five	Vertical number line (VNL) *Model of to model for transition*	Empty number line to express (+ and −) movements	Transactions Reasoning with number line to find a net worth after a transaction has occurred	How do various transactions affect net worth? / Going through zero / The effect of different transactions / Different strategies for finding net worths	Arms moving up and down to indicate good or bad movements / Pay off
Six	Unknown transaction/ net worth problems		Determining different possible transactions	Inventing integer rules / $+(+)=+$ / $-(-)=+$ / $+(-)=-$ / $-(+)=-$	Pay off

Appendix B: Sample of Cognitive-Based Interview Task

Ellen, Jim, and Steve bought three helium-filled balloons and paid $2.00 for all three. They decided to go back to the store and get enough balloons for everyone in their class. How much did they have to pay for 24 balloons?

$2.00

Appendix C: A Resource for Transforming GR Classroom Practices

	Teacher evidence	Student evidence
Teacher practice: *social norms*		
• T encourages Ss to explain		
• T encourages Ss to ask questions		
• T encourages Ss to ask questions *to other Ss*		
• T encourages Ss to understand other Ss solutions		
• T encourages Ss to use mistakes as learning opportunities		
• T encourages Ss to indicate agreement or disagreement		
• T encourages Ss to take responsibility/ownership for their learning		
Teacher practice: *discourse*		
• T restates Ss explanation in clearer language		
• T restates Ss explanation in a more advanced way		
• T introduces vocabulary when students have invented an idea		
• T asks Ss to repeat other Ss solutions		
• T asks questions that promote higher-level thinking (e.g., comparing, analyzing, synthesizing)		
• T uses Ss solutions effectively to engineer his/her summary		
Teacher practice: *mathematical*		
• T encourages conjecturing		
• T encourages proving		
• T encourages different solutions		
• T encourages efficient solutions		
• T encourages sophisticated solutions		
Teacher practice: *imagery*		
• T encourages Ss to record their thinking		
• T encourages Ss to model their thinking		
• T encourages Ss to draw on previous images when they are stuck		
• T "cements" Ss ideas on board or in display around the room		
Teacher practice: *small group*		
• T encourages Ss to ask each other for help		
• T collects data, not fix Ss mistakes		
• T asks Ss how they solved problems		
• T encourages Ss to draw on previous images when they are stuck		

Appendix D: Coaching Template

Mathematical Idea(s) of Lesson
Launch
Explore: Anticipated Student Thinking
Whole-Class Discussion
Assessment: What Evidence Shows Mathematical Ideas Are/Are Becoming Realized

References

Akyuz, D. (2010). *Supporting a standards-based teaching and learning environment: A case study of an expert middle school mathematics teacher.* Unpublished doctoral dissertation, University of Central Florida, Orlando, FL.

Akyuz, D., Stephan, M., & Dixon, J. K. (2013). Improving the quality of mathematics teaching with effective planning practices. *Teacher Development Journal, 17*(1), 92–106.

Ball, D. L. (1991). What's all this talk about discourse? *Arithmetic Teacher, 39*, 44–48.

Campbell, P. F., & Malkus, N. N. (2010). *The impact of elementary mathematics coaches on teachers' beliefs and professional activity.* Paper presented at the annual meeting of the American Educational Research Association, Denver, CO.

Cobb, P., & Yackel, E. (1996). Constructivist, emergent, and sociocultural perspectives in the context of developmental research. *Educational Psychologist, 31*, 175–190.

Cobb, P., Wood, T., Yackel, E., Wheatley, G., & Merkel, G. (1988). Research into practice: Creating a problem solving atmosphere. *Arithmetic Teacher, 36*(1), 46–47.

Cobb, P., Yackel, E., & Wood, T. (1989). Young children's emotional acts while doing mathematical problem solving. In D. B. McLeod & V. M. Adams (Eds.), *Affect and mathematical problem solving: A new perspective* (pp. 117–148). New York: Springer.

Cobb, P., Wood, T., Yackel, E., & McNeal, B. (1992). Characteristics of classroom mathematics traditions: An interactional analysis. *American Educational Research Journal, 29*, 573–604.

Cobb, P., Gravemeijer, K., Yackel, E., McClain, K., & Whitenack, J. (1997). Mathematizing and symbolizing: The emergence of chains of signification in one first-grade classroom. In D. Kirschner & J. A. Whitson (Eds.), *Situated cognition theory: Social, semiotic, and neurological perspectives* (pp. 151–233). Hillsdale: Erlbaum.

Cobb, P., Stephan, M., McClain, K., & Gravemeijer, K. (2001). Participating in classroom mathematical practices. *The Journal of the Learning Sciences, 10*(1&2), 113–163.

Costa, A. L., & Garmston, R. J. (1994). *Cognitive coaching: A foundation for renaissance schools.* Norwood: Christopher-Gordon.

Davis, B. (1997). Listening for differences: An evolving conception of mathematics teaching. *Journal for Research in Mathematics Education, 28*(3), 355–376.

Freudenthal, H. (1973). *Mathematics as an educational task.* Dordrecht: Riedel.

Gravemeijer, K. (1994). Educational development and developmental research in mathematics education. *Journal for Research in Mathematics Education, 25*(5), 443–471.

Gravemeijer, K. (2004). Learning trajectories and local instruction theories as means of support for teachers in reform mathematics education. *Mathematical Thinking and Learning, 6*(2), 105–128.

Gravemeijer, K., & Stephan, M. (2002). Emergent Models as an instructional design heuristic. In K. P. E. Gravemeijer, R. Lehrer, B. v. Oers, & L. Verschaffel (Eds.), *Symbolizing, modeling and tool use in mathematics education* (pp. 145–169). Dordrecht: Kluwer Academic Publishers.

Inoue, N., & Buczynski, S. (2011). You ask open-ended questions, now what? Understanding the nature of stumbling block in teaching inquiry lessons. *Mathematics Educator, 20*(2), 10–23.

Kowal, J., & Steiner, L. (2007). Instructional coaching. *The Center for Comprehensive School Reform and Improvement*, September Issue Brief (pp. 1–8).

McCombs, B. (1995). *Teacher survey*. Aurora: Mid-Continent Regional Educational Laboratory.

Murray, S., Ma, X., & Mazur, J. (2009). Effects of peer coaching on teachers' collaborative interactions and students' mathematics achievement. *Journal of Educational Research, 102*(3), 203–212.

Neufeld, B. (2002). *Using what we know: Implications for scaling up implementation of the CCL model*. Cambridge, MA: Education Matters, Inc.

Richards, J. (1991). Mathematical discussions. In E. von Glasersfeld (Ed.), *Radical constructivism in mathematics education* (pp. 13–52). Dordrecht: Kluwer.

Schoenfeld, A. (2000). Models of the teaching process. *Journal of Mathematical Behavior, 18*(3), 243–261.

Simon, M. A. (1995). Reconstructing mathematics pedagogy from a constructivist perspective. *Journal for Research in Mathematics Education, 26*(2), 114–145.

Steffe, L., & Thompson, P. (2000). Teaching experiment methodology: Underlying principles and essential elements. In R. Lesh & A. Kelly (Eds.), *Research design in mathematics and science education* (pp. 267–307). Hillsdale: Erlbaum.

Stephan, M., & Akyuz, D. (2012). A proposed instructional theory for integer addition and subtraction. *Journal for Research in Mathematics Education, 43*(4), 428–464.

Stephan, M., & Whitenack, J. (2003). Establishing classroom social and sociomathematical norms for problem solving. In F. Lester (Ed.), *Teaching mathematics through problem solving: Prekindergarten-Grade 6* (pp. 149–162). Reston: NCTM.

Stephan, M., Bowers, J., Cobb, P., & Gravemeijer, K. (Eds.). (2003). Supporting students' development of measuring conceptions: Analyzing students' learning in social context. *Journal for Research in Mathematics Education Monograph Series* (No. 12). Reston: NCTM.

Stephan, M., Underwood-Gregg, D., Weller-Weinhold, M., & Millsap, G. (2012). *Reinvention teaching*. The annual meeting of the International Group for the Psychology of Mathematics Education, Kalamazoo, MI.

Thompson, A. G., Philipp, R. A., Thompson, P. W., & Boyd, B. (1994). Calculational and conceptual orientations in teaching mathematics. In *1994 yearbook of the National Council of Teachers of Mathematics* (pp. 79–92). Reston: National Council of Teachers of Mathematics.

Underwood-Gregg, D. (2002). Building students' sense of linear relationships by stacking cubes. *Mathematics Teacher, 95*(5), 330–333.

Underwood-Gregg, D., & Yackel, E. (2002). Helping students make sense of algebraic expressions: The candy shop. *Mathematics Teacher, 7*(9), 492–497.

West, L., & Staub, F. C. (2003). *Content-focused coaching: Transforming mathematics lessons*. Portsmouth/Pittsburgh: Heinemann/University of Pittsburgh.

Wood, T., & Yackel, E. (1990). The development of collaborative dialogue in small group interactions. In L. P. Steffe & T. Wood (Eds.), *Transforming early childhood mathematics education: An international perspective* (pp. 244–252). Hillsdale: Lawrence Erlbaum Associates.

Yackel, E. (2003). Listening to children: Informing us and guiding our instruction. In F. K. Lester (Ed.), *Teaching mathematics through problem solving: Prekindergarten-grade 6* (pp. 107–121). Reston: National Council of Teachers of Mathematics.

Yackel, E. (2008). Theoretical analyses and practice—Making theoretical analyses relevant to practice. *Panama-Post—Reken-wiskundeonderwijs: Onderzoek, ontwikkeling, praktijk, 27*(3/4), 69–80.

Yackel, E., & Cobb, P. (1996). Sociomathematical norms, argumentation, and autonomy in mathematics. *Journal for Research in Mathematics Education, 27*, 458–477.

Yackel, E., Cobb, P., & Wood, T. (1991). Small group interactions as a source of learning opportunities in second grade mathematics. *Journal for Research in Mathematics Education, 22*, 390–408.

Yackel, E., Cobb, P., & Wood, T. (1999). The interactive constitution of mathematical meaning in one second grade classroom: An illustrative example. *Journal of Mathematical Behavior, 17*, 469–488.

Yackel, E., Rasmussen, C., & King, K. (2000). Social and sociomathematical norms in an advanced undergraduate mathematics course. *Journal of Mathematical Behavior, 19*, 275–287.

Challenging Mathematics with Multiple Solution Tasks and Mathematical Investigations in Geometry

Roza Leikin

Abstract In this chapter, I analyze multiple solution tasks (MSTs) and mathematical investigations (MIs) and the interplay between them. I argue that MSTs and MIs are effective instructional tools for balancing the level of mathematical challenge in the mathematics classroom and, thus, for realizing students' mathematical potential at different levels. Additionally, these tasks lead to the development of mathematical knowledge, mental flexibility, and critical thinking. They also deepen mathematical understanding since they promote the design of mathematical connections of different types. I present several examples of MSTs and MIs and analyze these mathematical tasks from the perspective of their conventionality, the mathematical connections embedded in the tasks, and their potential for developing learners' mathematical creativity. MIs will be presented in this paper in connection to MSTs. Particular emphasis is placed on analyzing the relationships between production of multiple solutions, mathematical investigations, and varying levels of mathematical challenge.

Keywords Mathematical challenge • Geometry • Problem solving • Multiple solution strategies • Investigation in dynamic geometry • Task transformations

Introduction

This chapter will rely on several basic assumptions:

1. The main purpose of mathematical instruction is to provide learning opportunities that enable the realization of learners' intellectual potential.

R. Leikin (✉)
Faculty of Education, University of Haifa, Haifa 31905, Israel
e-mail: rozal@edu.haifa.ac.il

Y. Li et al. (eds.), *Transforming Mathematics Instruction: Multiple Approaches and Practices*, Advances in Mathematics Education, DOI 10.1007/978-3-319-04993-9_5, © Springer International Publishing Switzerland 2014

2. Mathematical challenge is a core factor in mathematical instruction that promotes the realization of learners' mathematical potential.
3. Along with developing mathematical knowledge and skill, mathematics education should be directed toward developing learners' mathematical creativity.

In this paper, I will analyze multiple solution tasks (MSTs) and mathematical investigations (MIs) as effective tools that promote the realization of students' mathematical potential. I will explore relationships between MSTs and MIs and will argue that a combination of MSTs and MIs mutually strengthens their instructional power.

Background

Mathematical Potential

Based on the definition of mathematical promise (NCTM 1995; Sheffield 1999, 2009), I use a construct of a student's *mathematical potential*, which is a complex function of four variables: mathematical ability (*both analytical and creative*), affective characteristics, individual personality traits, and learning opportunities which the person encounters in his/her life (Leikin 2009a). The variables are inter-related, and each clearly plays an important role in the realization of the mathematical potential of a student. The construct of mathematical potential acknowledges the dynamic (developmental) nature of the human intellectual potential, meaning that abilities can be developed and beliefs may be altered if the opportunities provided to students match their potential.

It is quite obvious that mathematical potential varies in different students from low to high (even extremely high) levels. This variability determines heterogeneous nature of the mathematics classes that constitutes one of the central common challenges in teachers' practice. Each class, even those in which students are selected according to their ability level, is heterogeneous and requires teachers to devolve to their students' mathematical tasks that will allow each and every student to realize his/her mathematical potential to the maximal level.

According to the construct of students' mathematical potential (including the students' abilities, affective characteristics, and personality), mathematical tasks introduced to the students should, first of all, match their mathematical abilities and knowledge. The tasks should secondly be directed toward the promotion of positive affects, at both global and local level (Goldin 2009). The global affect includes stable structures such as beliefs, motivation, and attitudes toward mathematics, whereas the local affect includes, for example, contentment or dissatisfaction associated with progress in solving a particular problem. Students' commitment to task performance and their persistence in achieving the goal are personal characteristics that are definitely important for the realization of their potentials and should be encouraged by the task.

Creativity and Mathematical Potential

Creativity is a personal and social trait that fosters human progress at all levels and at all points in history. In school mathematics, students' creativity can be expressed in production of mathematical ideas/solutions in a new situation (to a new mathematical problem that was not learned previously) or production of original solutions to problems previously learned (Leikin and Pitta-Pantazi 2013). Leikin (2009b) suggested that creativity in school students is relative creativity, since this creativity is usually regarded with respect to their own individual educational history and in comparison with other students. This is in contrast to absolute creativity, which is evaluated in terms of high achievements in the creator's field and whose significance is evaluated by the professional community that regards it as a meaningful creation from a historical perspective.

Developing creative mathematical thinking was ignored for many years by different school curricula, as well as in mathematics education research. However, in the past decade more attention has been given to the creative component of mathematics education. Starting with Haylock (1987) and Silver (1997), Sriraman (2005), Sheffield (2009), and Leikin (2009b) emphasized the possibility of developing mathematical creativity in all students.

Research literature acknowledges the relationship between knowledge and creativity: On the one hand, being creative in a field requires a person to have a certain knowledge base that allows him to be creative. On the other hand, creativity is one of the mechanisms of knowledge development. The former view is based on Vygotsky's (1930/1984, 1930/1982) argument that creativity (imagination) is one of the basic mechanisms that allows new knowledge to develop. A child activates his/her imagination when connecting new and previously known concepts, when elaborating the known constructs, and when developing abstract notions. Thus, imagination (or creativity) is a basic component of knowledge construction.

Researchers in mathematics education explicitly connect development of mathematical creativity with implementation of MSTs (Silver 1997; Leikin 2009a, b; Levav-Waynberg and Leikin 2012a) and with problem posing (Silver 1997) and MIs (Yerushalmy 2009). This paper presents an analysis of MSTs and MIs as instructional tools in mathematics education and mathematics instruction directed toward the development of mathematical creativity and varying levels of mathematical challenge that suit different ability levels.

Yerushalmy (2009) argues that *Proofs and Refutations* by Lakatos (1976) is the ultimate example of creativity in mathematics. It demonstrates the creative process of conjecturing, in which even definitions should be created by the shared effort of a teacher and a group of learners. In Lakatos's essay, a problem that seemed to have been already solved on the first page led to a mathematically rich, creative discussion. This paper presents several examples of simple mathematical problems which, by means of different requirements, are transformed into tasks with different levels of mathematical challenge.

Mathematical Challenge

In my view, *a mathematical challenge is an interesting and motivating mathematical difficulty that a person can overcome* (Leikin 2007, 2009a). Mathematical challenge is a core element of mathematical instruction aimed at fulfillment of the learners' mathematical potential through integration of mathematical difficulty and positive affect in the learning process (Barbeau and Taylor 2009). The importance of the construct of challenge is rooted in Vygotsky's (1978) notion of ZPD (zone of proximal development) and Leontiev's (1983) theory of activity and Davydov's (1996) principles of "developing education."

The importance of mathematical challenges in mathematics education strengthens the meaningful distinction between mathematical problems and exercises. An exercise is a mathematical task a student can solve using a readily available algorithm. Sheffield (2009) maintains that teachers must challenge students who are ready to move to a higher level and provide hints to students who may be frustrated. Thus, exercises can be solved without the teacher's involvement, but mathematical challenges aimed at developing students' mathematical knowledge usually entail scaffolding provided by a teacher. A challenging problem must meet four conditions: First, the person who performs the task has to be motivated to find a solution. Second, the person has to have no readily available procedures for finding a solution. Third, the person has to make an attempt and persist to reach a solution. Fourth, the task or a situation has several solving approaches (Leikin 2004, compiled from Polya 1981; Schoenfeld 1985; Charles and Lester 1982).

A mathematical challenge is *subjective* because it depends on the learner's abilities and knowledge. A mathematical challenge is also *relative*: Whereas a task that is challenging for student A might be too easy and thus unchallenging for student B, the same task might be too difficult and thus too challenging for student C. Mathematical tasks introduced to learners in the presence of a teacher should be challenging, while exercises should be assigned for homework – especially for students with high mathematical potential.

Challenging mathematical tasks can require solving mathematical problems, proving, posing new questions and problems, and investigating mathematical objects and situations (Barbeau and Taylor 2009). Investigation tasks are the most inclusive tasks that take into consideration different mathematical situations, conjecturing, examining the conjectures, proving, and posing new questions. Some variables, like the length of the logical or manipulative chain of a solution and the conceptual density of a task (Silver and Zawodjewsky 1997), can determine the task's complexity. However, the length of a solution and the conceptual density do not raise the interest of a student in solving a problem and thus do not affect the degree of its challenge.

Conventionality of a task or of its solution is an additional variable (and the main one, in my opinion) that determines the level of mathematical challenge embedded in the task. Conventional solutions are those generally recommended by the curriculum, displayed in textbooks and taught by the teachers. By contrast, unconventional solutions are based on strategies usually not prescribed by the school curriculum or those which the curriculum recommends with respect to a different type of problem. From the Vygotskian perspective, unconventional tasks require imagination in connecting students' existing knowledge to the new ideas constructed while approaching the tasks (Vygotsky 1930/1984). From this perspective, mathematical challenge is determined by the level of the learners' familiarity with the strategies (ways) that may be used to approach a problem and, thus, by the level of autonomy in solving an unconventional task. When solving unconventional problems or proving new theorems, students must make connections with previously learned material, connections that require creative thinking. Mathematical challenges should allow mathematically promising students to experience activities in which professional mathematicians are involved:

> Felix Klein (1924) came out strongly against the practice of presenting mathematical topics as completed axiomatic-deductive systems, and instead argued for the use of the so-called *bio-genetic* principle in teaching. [According to this approach] learners should be exposed to or engaged with the typical mathematical processes by which new content in mathematics is discovered, invented and organized. (De Villiers 1998)

Finally, the level of mathematical challenge can be determined by mathematical tasks devolved to the students and can be enhanced by the didactical setting in which the tasks are introduced to the students.

In the next section, I define and briefly exemplify different types of challenging mathematical tasks. In the section entitled "From Multiple Proofs to Investigation and Back to Multiple Proofs," I present one particular geometry problem that is transformed into MST and IT as performed by prospective teachers at a "theory and practice in teaching school geometry" course. I explain the mutual relationships between multiple proofs and investigations. In the last section of this paper, I return to the construct of mathematical challenge and explain how tasks presented in this paper facilitate students with different levels of mathematical potential in overcoming mathematical challenges.

Examples of Different Types of Mathematically Challenging Tasks

Defining Tasks

De Villiers (1998) argues that defining activities allow bridging school mathematical activities with those of professional mathematicians. These activities can be introduced to students at a stage when a concept has not yet been learned, and they can be asked to provide a new definition for the concept. Figure 1 illustrates a task in which students are required to define midlines in a quadrilateral in different ways that determine different numbers of the midlines.

a   Define midlines in a quadrilateral so that a quadrilateral would have exactly two midlines.
b   Define midlines in a quadrilateral so that a quadrilateral would have exactly four midlines.
c   Define midlines in a quadrilateral so that a quadrilateral would have exactly six midlines.

Fig. 1 Defining midlines in a quadrilateral

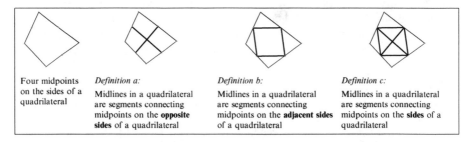

Four midpoints on the sides of a quadrilateral

Definition a:
Midlines in a quadrilateral are segments connecting midpoints on the **opposite sides** of a quadrilateral

Definition b:
Midlines in a quadrilateral are segments connecting midpoints on the **adjacent sides** of a quadrilateral

Definition c:
Midlines in a quadrilateral are segments connecting midpoints on the **sides** of a quadrilateral

Fig. 2 Definitions of midlines in a quadrilateral

In such an activity, students are creators of their mathematical world. They deepen both their understanding of a concept of a midline and the meaning of a metamathematical notion of a definition. This defining task is challenging; it is both difficult and interesting. The difficulty is related to the requirement for rigorous use of mathematical language – changing just one word in a sentence changes the objects defined (see Fig. 2). Additionally, challenge is related to the unconventional nature of the task associated both with involving the students in creation of their mathematical world and with unfamiliarity of the mathematical concept: Though the midline of a trapezoid is one of the central concepts of school geometry, the "midline of a quadrilateral" is not part of the curriculum. The outcomes are surprising and the activity is joyful and gratifying.

Investigation Tasks

In the last two decades, the mathematics education community has strongly emphasized the importance of investigation-based learning environments (Da Ponte 2007; Yerushalmy 2009). Yerushalmy (2009) argued that the *objectives of any curriculum* include encouraging the personal growth and development of individuals, preparing people for work, and transmitting the culture from one generation to the next (Schwartz 1999). However, *in practice*, most mathematics curricula are organized along a set of techniques and procedures, adhering to a specific order and way of viewing the concepts to be learned (Yerushalmy 2009). Here I demonstrate techniques in which mathematical investigations can become a routine in mathematics classroom.

Investigation tasks require students to consider a particular situation, object, or group of objects, identify their properties, and prove them. The main component

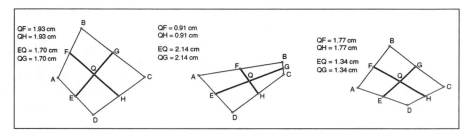

Fig. 3 Midlines connecting opposite sides in a quadrilateral bisect each other

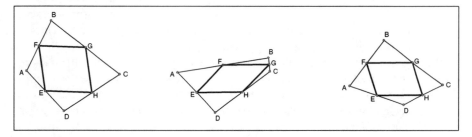

Fig. 4 Midlines connecting adjacent sides in a quadrilateral form a parallelogram

of an investigation activity in mathematics is conjecturing, which means "putting forward a proposition about objects and operations on them that suggests unexpected relationships" (Yerushalmy 2009, p. 103). Furthermore, investigation activities require refining the conjectures, refuting or proving them, and, consequently, monitoring the proof. Thus, investigation activities both require and develop students' creative and critical reasoning. Figures 3 and 4 illustrate some possible results of investigation of the properties of midlines in quadrilaterals.

The properties that students identify in activities of this kind are usually not new to professional mathematicians; however, they are new and surprising to students. "At the K–12 level, one normally does not expect works of extraordinary creativity; however, it is certainly feasible for students to offer new insights" (Sriraman 2005).

Proof Tasks

The central role of proofs in mathematics education is widely agreed upon among mathematicians, educational researchers, and mathematics educators (Lin et al. 2009). Proof tasks are among the most challenging in school mathematics. The challenge embedded within proof tasks can be associated with procedures that are not readily available for students, with the requirements of rigorous justifications, and with (in geometry) auxiliary constructions that must be performed. This paper demonstrates that the order in which proof problems are presented to the students can also determine the level of mathematical challenge of a task.

For students to prove that midlines connecting opposite sides in a quadrilateral bisect each other before proving that midlines connecting adjacent sides in a quadrilateral form a parallelogram is a real challenge (Figs. 3 and 4). On the other hand, proving that midlines in a quadrilateral that connect opposite sides of a quadrilateral bisect each other after proving that midlines in a quadrilateral connecting adjacent sides form a parallelogram can be trivial.

Note that in the classroom, no explicit requirement for multiple proofs was presented to the students with respect to the six midlines in quadrilaterals, the internal quadrilaterals, or their diagonals. However, different proofs were produced by different students. These student-generated proofs serve as the basis of classroom discussion on the clarity of the solutions, their elegance, and level of difficulty. Through observation of multiple proofs, students focus on the connections between different mathematical concepts and different mathematical properties that enable them to produce a variety of solutions. The emphasis is also made here on the sequence in which the proofs are performed and the different challenges posed by the different sequences.

I present additional examples of how the order in which proof problems are introduced to students can vary the level of a mathematical challenge, by means of Problem 3.

From Proof to Investigation and Back to Proof

One of the ways to discover a challenge embedded in a proof problem is to transform a proof problem into an investigation task (Leikin 2004; Leikin and Grossman 2013). All the tasks and their solutions presented in this section are borrowed either from school mathematics classrooms or from workshops for prospective mathematics teachers.

Problem 1

Problem 1a: The Original Proof Problem

In the isosceles trapezoid ABCD, the diagonals are perpendicular (AC⊥BD). Prove that the altitude of the trapezoid is equal to the midline joining the midpoints of the two sides of the trapezoid. Prompt: Build the altitude through O [the point of intersection of the diagonals].

This proof problem, according to its placement in the textbook, clearly requires from the students the application of the midline of a trapezoid theorem. The drawing is presented, and the prompt, which is given in the text of the problem, simplifies the solution and directs it toward one particular solving approach. An intended solution of the original tasks is depicted in Fig. 5.

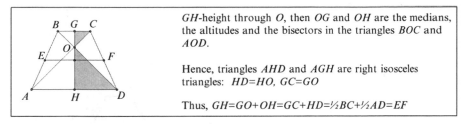

GH-height through O, then OG and OH are the medians, the altitudes and the bisectors in the triangles BOC and AOD.

Hence, triangles AHD and AGH are right isosceles triangles: HD=HO, GC=GO

Thus, GH=GO+OH=GC+HD=½BC+½AD=EF

Fig. 5 A solution of the original task

In the lesson described here (conducted several times with prospective mathematics teachers), the following investigation Problem 1b transformed from Problem 1a and clearly related to the defining task presented earlier in this paper.

Problem 1b: The New Investigation Problem

In the isosceles trapezium ABCD, the diagonals are perpendicular (AC⊥BD). Find possible relationships between two midlines of the trapezoid, which join midpoints of the opposite sides of the trapezoid.

Replacement of "the altitude" in the original problem by the "second midline" makes the problem more elegant. The students cope with an open question: It becomes clear that the altitude is perpendicular to the midline; however, the relationship between the two midlines is not obvious.

This formulation of the problem leads first to the challenge of constructing the isosceles trapezoid with perpendicular diagonals (see more details in Leikin 2012a, b). Requirement of such a construction leads to the precise analysis of the properties of an isosceles trapezoid whose diagonals are perpendicular. This analysis includes thinking about necessary and sufficient conditions of the geometric figure.

Several different strategies for construction of the equilateral trapezoid with perpendicular diagonals can be performed. Figure 6 depicts two of these constructions.

Perpendicular diagonals that are congruent and are divided into two pairs of congruent segments by the intersection point serve a sufficient condition for construction of the given figure. The different constructions include either two pairs of congruent segments on the two perpendicular straight lines or completing a right isosceles. Within each big strategy, there are several variations, and the different ways in which the given trapezoid can be constructed are usually surprising for both teachers and students.

Let me note here that in advanced-level mathematics classes or in courses for prospective mathematics teachers, students are required to perform the construction, whereas, in mid-level or low-level mathematics classes, students are presented with various constructions performed by the teacher. After the figure construction stage, mathematical discussion is based on the properties used by either the students or the teacher for constructing the figure. The discussion is focused on those

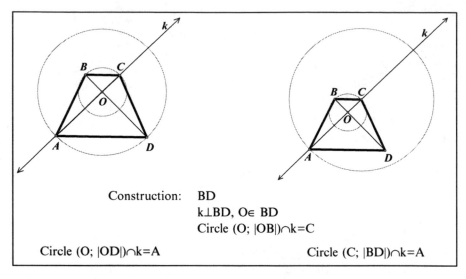

Construction: BD

k⊥BD, O∈ BD

Circle (O; |OB|)∩k=C

Circle (O; |OD|)∩k=A   Circle (C; |BD|)∩k=A

Fig. 6 Two different constructions

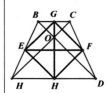

The internal quadrilateral with vertexes in the midpoints of the given trapezoid is a square (a parallelogram with equal and perpendicular sides since the diagonals in the trapezoid are equal and perpendicular). Thus the midlines that join midpoints of the opposite sides of the trapezoid are equal to each other and perpendicular to each other as the diagonals of the square.

Fig. 7 The alternative proof that follows from the trapezoid construction

properties of the figure which constitute sufficient conditions for the figure's construction that guarantee immunity of the figure's properties under dragging in dynamic geometry environment (DGE).

By dragging the figure (in DGE), and by measuring and comparing, the participants realize that the two midlines connecting opposite sides of an equilateral trapezoid with perpendicular diagonals are equal and perpendicular. As in the case presented in the previous section, students are not explicitly required to produce multiple proofs; however, the alternative proof follows from the way in which the trapezoid was constructed (see Fig. 7).

Multiple Solution Tasks

Multiple solution tasks are tasks that contain an explicit requirement for solving a problem (or proving a theorem) in multiple ways. The differences between the solutions can be based on using (a) different representations of a mathematical concept (e.g., proving the formula of the roots of a quadratic function using graphical representation, symbolic representation in canonic form, or symbolic representation in a polynomial form), (b) different properties (definitions or theorems) of mathematical concepts from a particular mathematical topic (Fig. 5), (c) different mathematical tools and theorems from different branches of mathematics, or (d) different tools and theorems from different subjects (not necessarily mathematics) (Leikin 2007, 2009b).

The requirement for multiple solutions (or proofs) transforms a conventional (routine) problem into a challenging and unconventional one. A problem for which a solution strategy is algorithmic can require insight when it must be solved in multiple ways. For example, a symmetric system of linear equations ($3x+2y=5 \wedge 2x+3y=5$) can be solved algorithmically by the substitution of variables or by linear combinations. But if asked to find an additional solution, students become more attentive and can argue that $x=y$ and because the system "has special coefficients, they are the same but inverse in the two equations" (cited from an interview with a student).

In other cases, the challenge is related to the large number of proofs that can be produced to solve one particular problem. The requirement for production of multiple proofs requires mental flexibility (Elia et al. 2009) that determines the level of mathematical challenge.

There are two main types of MST and MI implementation in the classroom: teacher-initiated and student-initiated implementation (Leikin and Levav-Waynberg 2008). In a *teacher-initiated implementation*, the teacher creates a didactical situation in which students are required to produce multiple solutions (for MSTs) or discover new mathematical facts (for MIs). These requirements become a part of a didactical contract between the teacher and the students. Teacher-initiated MSTs and MIs may differ with respect to their openness. A teacher can plan either a *guided instruction*, in which his/her outlines several directions in which solutions or investigations might be performed and the students have to perform these MSTs or MIs, or *non-guided solutions*, in which the students have to find directions for solving the problems while also being expected to produce solutions using them. In *student-initiated situations*, the teacher does not plan MSTs as a part of the planned learning trajectory; therefore, the way the lesson develops depends on student ideas and teacher flexibility. The possibility of solving a problem in more than one way can be raised by the students themselves. This happens either when they don't understand the first solution offered or when they find an alternative solution and want to share it with the teacher and their classmates. In this chapter, I address a setting in which the teacher initiates production of multiple solutions and mathematical investigations. This setting is challenging for a teacher himself/herself, as it cannot be precisely planned and it requires variability of scaffolding methods.

There are clear mutual relationships between MSTs and MIs: Multiple solutions (proofs) lead to investigations of the applicability of different proofs to different mathematical objects and the existence of additional properties that can be proven in similar but different ways. Figure 8 demonstrates an MST with seven different proofs, which all were generated by the students during a 90-min mathematics lesson. Most of the students produced one or two proofs, while the collective solution space appeared to be much richer and exposed students to different mathematical

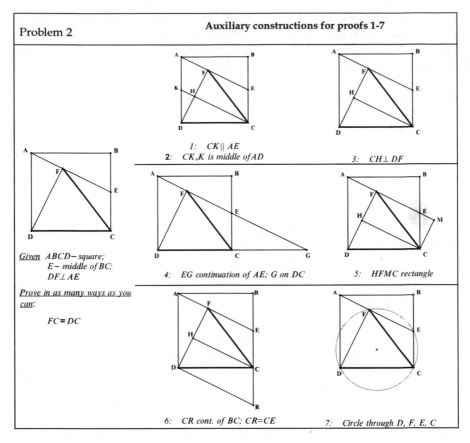

Fig. 8 Example of MST with seven different solutions

tools and different ways of thinking. In this way, the implementation of an MST led the teacher to an IT in the "what if not" manner, which included an exploration of the object's properties, of the proofs, of the connections between them, and of their applicability with respect to other mathematical objects. The setting leads to learning geometry by the students and their teacher, alike.

Problem 2

MSTs in geometry are among the effective didactical approaches that lead to the development of geometry knowledge (Levav-Waynberg and Leikin 2012a, b). Figure 8 demonstrates an example of an MST in geometry that has 7 different proofs. Six proofs (proofs 1, 3, 4, 5, 6, 7) are based on different auxiliary constructions, while Proof 2 is based on the same auxiliary construction as Proof 1 but refers to the same element of mathematical figures in different ways (e.g., while HC is a median, an altitude, and a height in the triangle CDF, it is a midline in the trapezoid). The challenge in this MST is embedded in the requirement of producing multiple proofs,

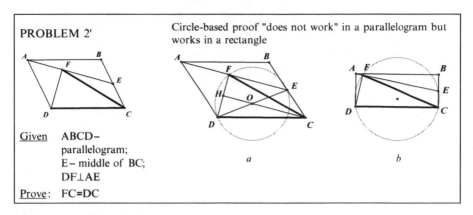

PROBLEM 2'	Circle-based proof "does not work" in a parallelogram but works in a rectangle

Given   ABCD–
         parallelogram;
         E– middle of BC;
         DF⊥AE
Prove: FC=DC

a   b

Fig. 9 Proof which are specific for a square

while the variability of mathematical tools from different geometry topics requires mental flexibility and connectedness of mathematical knowledge.

Problem 2 is equivalent to a problem in which the givens are identical, but participants are asked to prove that FC=BC. This property does not exist in rectangles which are not squares and is more challenging since it requires the solvers to discover that in order to prove that FC=BC, they must prove that FC=DC.

Back to Investigation

Some of the central questions to consider when producing multiple solutions to a problem are the following: "Which mathematical concepts are common to all the solutions? Which additional properties of the objects follow from these solutions? Which mathematical objects, different from the one given in the problem, also fulfill these properties?" For example, through investigation, students discovered that a property proved for a square in Problem 2 exists in any parallelogram. In this case, the challenge is in choosing proofs that are specific to a square and cannot be applied to a new problem without examining all the proofs produced for a square.

Proof 7 (Fig. 8) is only one proof that makes use of the property of the square BCD=90°. It does not hold for a parallelogram (Fig. 9a); however, it works in a rectangle (Fig. 9b).

From Multiple Proofs to Investigation and Back to Multiple Proofs

This section focuses on one geometry problem (Problem 3a), borrowed from a standard textbook, that was transformed into an integrative task (Problem 3b) including

Problem 3a	Given: AB – diameter in circle (O, R) AD, BC, DC – tangent segments Prove: DOC = 90°	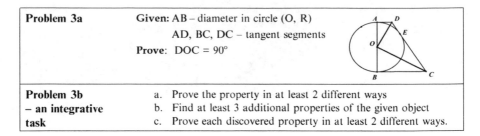
Problem 3b – an integrative task	a. Prove the property in at least 2 different ways b. Find at least 3 additional properties of the given object c. Prove each discovered property in at least 2 different ways.	

Fig. 10 Integrative task based on Problem 3

production of multiple proofs and mathematical investigations. The integration of multiple proving and investigation activities allows varying levels of mathematical challenge so that each student can fulfill the task requirements; however, they may perform the task at different levels, as will be presented below. All the proofs and discoveries described below are taken from the works of prospective mathematics teachers performed as a homework assignment. The richness of the discoveries and the proofs demonstrates that teachers are able to develop their proficiency in generating MIs for their students.

Problem 3

Multiple Proofs for Problem 3

Problem 3 is of an integrative nature that includes proving a geometric property in multiple ways, investigating a geometric object given in the problem for additional properties (experimenting, conjecturing, testing), discovering of (relatively) new properties, proving or refuting the discovered properties, and formulating new multiple proofs and investigation problems. Figure 10 presents four proofs for Problem 3. Proofs 3.1, 3.2, and 3.3 use properties of the segments OD and OC: Proof 3.1 uses properties of segments OD and OC to be bisectors of angles ADC and DCB and the sum of angles in quadrilateral. Proof 3.2 is based on the ability of OD and OC to bisect angles AOE and EOB and the value of a flat angle. Proof 3.3 uses the property that the segments OD and OC are perpendicular to chords AE and EB, and the property of the inscribed angle AEB relies on the diameter. Proof 3.4 uses the property of the midline OM in the trapezoid ADCB (OM is half of the sum AD + BC) and the property of the tangent segment from a point to a circle (AD + BC = DE + EC); OM is a median in the triangle DOC and OM = $\frac{1}{2}$DM. Thus, DOC is a right angle (Fig. 11).

I now turn to the mathematical investigation (performed by students in DGE) and analyze proofs and investigations and the varying levels of mathematical challenge embedded in the task.

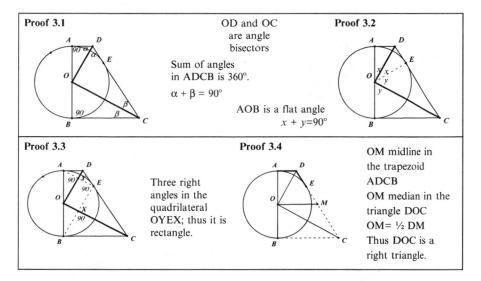

Fig. 11 Four proofs for Problem 3

Discovering New Properties

Once students started investigating the given geometric object (with DGE), they searched for additional properties of the given geometric object. They chose elements of the given object, performed additional constructions, performed measurements, compared different measures, and searched for the invariants under dragging. Once some conjectures were raised, they were tested by the participants again and were proven. The requirement for the performance of multiple proofs was very important here, since these proofs led to the discovery of additional properties of the given geometric object. Figure 12 illustrates eight properties that students discovered when performing investigations and proofs.

The discovered properties vary in their complexity. Property 1 follows immediately from Proof 3.2, and Property 2 is an element of Proof 3.3. Thus, these properties are trivial. Properties 3 and 4 are slightly less trivial since Property 1 serves as proof for Property 3 and Property 4 follows Property 2. Properties 3 and 4 are more challenging when discovered without knowing Properties 1 and 2. Properties 5, 6, 7, and 8 are more challenging for discovery since all of them introduce new geometric objects and their proofs are more complex, as they require auxiliary constructions.

Proving the Discovered Properties

Proving Properties 1 and 2 is a trivial task, since these proofs were performed within Proofs 3.2 and 3.3. Proving Properties 3 and 4 is trivial once Properties 1

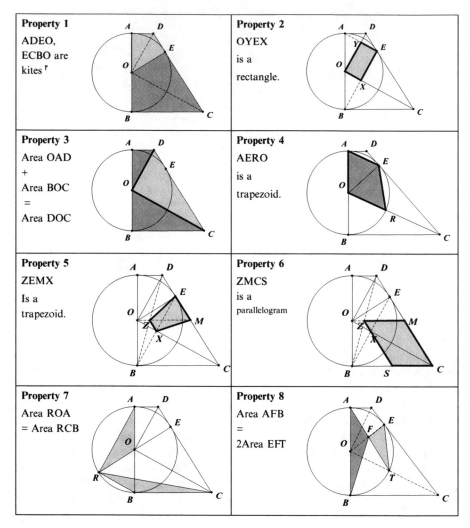

Fig. 12 Eight discovered properties

and 2 are proven. However, these proofs are less trivial if Properties 3 and 4 have to be proven before Properties 1 and 2. Once again, the sequence of proving activities determines challenge embedded in the proving task.

Proving Properties 5–8 appeared to be more challenging. Figure 13 depicts outlines of proofs for these properties. All the proofs require auxiliary constructions, continuous visual and analytical decomposition of the geometric objects into composing elements, and composition of the elements into a whole picture (cf. Duval 2012). One of the challenges of these proofs is the identification of the common elements in different geometric figures (e.g., segment ZX is one of the bases in the trapezoid ZXME and a midline in the triangle DBE) and their different

Properties 5 and 6: ZEMX is a trapezoid, ZMCS is a parallelogram.

Proof outline			
OM midline in trapezoid ADCB ZM‖BC BZ=ZD BX=XE			ZX is a midline of the triangle DBE ZX‖DE ZS‖MC ZX‖EM

Property 7: Area ROA = Area RCB

Proof a - outline			Proof b - outline
WOSR and WCLR are rectangles A(AOR)= ½ AR*WO =WR*RS A(RCB)= ½ RB*CL= =RS*WR			AOR ≅ EOB OB-Median in REB A(AOR)=½ A(REB) CL=½ EB A(RCB)= ½ A(REB)

Property 8: Area AFB = 2Area EFT

Proof outline			
FO median in AFB A(AFB)= 2A(AOF) We can prove A(AFO)=A(EFT)			
According to Property 4 AETO is a trapezoid; thus A(AFO)=A(EFT)			**Note:** *One should know this property of the trapezoid; otherwise it should be proven.*

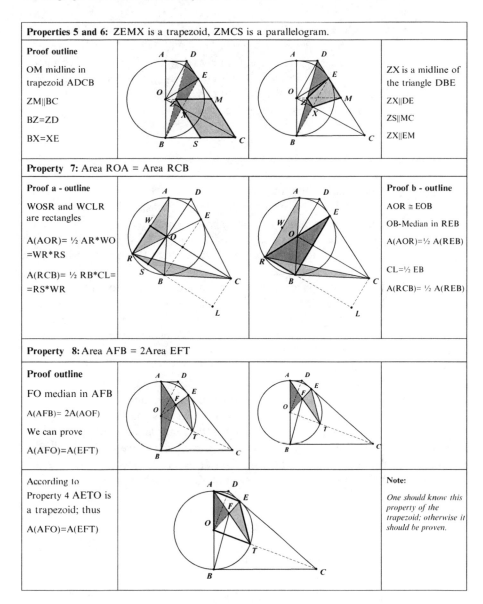

Fig. 13 Proof outlines – eight discovered properties (see Fig. 12)

functions as related to the different figures. Once one of the properties (5 or 6) is proven, the other becomes less challenging. Figure 13 depicts two different proofs for Property 7. The proofs themselves include additional properties of the given geometric object. Proof of Property 8 is based on one of the basic properties of trapezoid (equality between the areas of "side triangles"). However, this property is not a part of the school curriculum and not used in geometry problem solving; thus, the proof can be considered a difficult one. Moreover, preceding steps of this proof also require decomposition of the big triangle into two "halves" and composing a trapezoid from the vertices of the two equivalent triangles. The level of challenge can be reduced by connecting Property 8 with Property 4, if proven earlier. All of the proofs depicted in Fig. 13 require deep, broad, and connected knowledge from different topics within the school geometry course.

Summary: Multiple Proving and Investigation Activity

Each participant in this activity produced several proofs. Some proofs were similar (e.g., 3.1 and 3.2), while others differed in auxiliary constructions and theorems used for proving the property (e.g., 3.1 and 3.4). Each participant discovered "new" properties and proved them. Collectively, all of the participants were presented with 4 proofs for Problem 3, and additionally, after discovering new properties, produced proofs of "new" geometric properties.

The whole-group discussion touched on issues that in the usual "one proof for each problem" setting were irrelevant. Among the focal issues for discussion were sameness and differences between the proofs and between the discovered properties, the elegance of the proofs and surprise embedded in the discovered properties, the clarity and complexity of proofs, and the preciseness and completeness of the proofs.

Not less important for this activity is the essentiality of communicative and collective elements of knowledge construction. The clear evolution of the knowledge development in this task started from the individual mathematical production (proving and discovering) based on individual knowledge skills and understanding, then turning to collective production in which each of the participants was exposed to the individual outcomes, advancing to collaborative production which involved comparing and connecting different individual products and ultimately resulting in a shared product that broadens and promotes individual production, knowledge, and understanding.

Discussion

Challenge Embedded in MSTs and MIs

At the beginning of this chapter, I presented the construct of students' mathematical potential which comprises students' abilities (both analytical and creative) and their affective characteristics and individual personality traits. I presented examples of MSTs and MIs, in which challenge is embedded and their common characteristics including newness, which leads to discovery, surprise, and enjoyment; difficulty, which requires coping and persistence; and pleasure associated with surprise and the satisfaction of overcoming the difficulty.

I argue that many textbook problems can be transformed into MSTs and MIs. Problems 1, 2, and 3 in this paper demonstrate such transformations. While the requirement to solve (prove) a problem in multiple ways commonly transforms a problem into an MST, transformation of a proof problem into an investigation task is more complex (for complexity of the transformation, see Leikin 2012a). Problems 1, 2, and 3 in this paper lead to investigation in different ways. Problem 1 is reformulated so that the main elements of the problems were renamed; Problem 2 leads to investigation in the "what if not" manner; and Problem 3 was transformed into an IT by a simple requirement: "find additional properties of the given figure." Geometric construction of the given object can serve as a pitfall in such an activity, and teachers can provide students with construction guidance in order to reduce the level of complexity.

Barbeau (2009) argues that "mathematical challenges in a classroom can equip students for facing future challenges in life by fostering desirable attributes such as patience, persistence and flexibility" (ibid., p. 6). The teachers' main role in any mathematical classroom is devolution of good mathematical tasks to the students. These include the teachers' expectations regarding the students' level of mathematical knowledge, understanding, and rigorousness in mathematical performance, as well as the level of autonomy granted to students in their mathematical activities and the use of tasks that require creative and critical thinking. This learning should "cultivate *a sense of satisfaction in personal mathematical development* in each student" (Goldin 2009, p.192) and take place in an atmosphere of mutual respect and support between the teacher and the students. Students must "sign" this contract and endeavor to comply with its provisions. Mathematical challenge in this chapter is presented and analyzed as being at the core of such a contract, from both teachers' and students' perspectives.

Challenge and Creativity: Two Sides of the Coin

The relative nature of a mathematical challenge and that of mathematical creativity become obvious when employing MSTs and MIs. The tasks described in this chapter demonstrate that MSTs and MIs allow varying levels of mathematical challenge in one particular mathematics class. Once a teacher presents such a task to a class, the students have freedom to cope with a task at an appropriate level of difficulty and to be satisfied with his/her individual mathematical products (proofs, discoveries, etc.). Thus, by means of MSTs and MIs, a mathematical challenge can be monitored by a teacher by using varying levels of uncertainty, identifying mathematical similarities and differences, developing a critical view on proofs and proving, rethinking mathematics, and learning from other students' thinking. The examples presented in the chapter demonstrate that by changing the order in which mathematical statements should be proven by students, a teacher can change the level of the mathematical challenge. Thus, when dealing with problems related to the same mathematical object, the teacher allows different students to cope with challenges at different levels. The individual activities lead to common discussions in which students can participate independently of the task with which students coped individually.

Clearly, MSTs and MIs are creativity related. These tasks require and develop mathematical flexibility. As being flexible is defined as being "different from one-self," students can be flexible when discovering different properties and producing different proofs. The students should activate their critical reasoning to evaluate the differences between their products. Since the products vary in their sameness and differences, the flexibility can also be considered as a relative construct. The MSTs do not necessarily require originality. However, it becomes a real challenge for students with high abilities to produce an original proof which is "different from others' proofs." In turn, MIs require students to be original since they involve discovery of properties which are "new for the students." This newness is relative in most cases. However, my practice demonstrates that sometimes classroom activities related to MSTs and MIs and their integration lead to discoveries at the absolute level (see Leikin 2012b).

Concluding Remark

I would like to challenge the reader by asking you to solve Problem 4 and find mathematical connections between Problems 1, 3, and 4.

Problem 4

Is it possible to inscribe a circle into an isosceles trapezoid with perpendicular diagonals?

References

Barbeau, E. (2009). Challenging: A human activity. In E. Barbeau & P. Taylor (Eds.), *ICMI study-16 volume: Mathematical challenge in and beyond the classroom* (pp. 53–96). New York: Springer.

Barbeau, E., & Taylor, P. (Eds.). (2009). *ICMI study-16 volume: Mathematical challenge in and beyond the classroom*. New York: Springer.

Charles, R., & Lester, F. (1982). *Teaching problem solving: What, why and how*. Palo Alto: Dale Seymour Publications.

Da Ponte, J. P. (2007). Investigations and explorations in the mathematics classroom. *ZDM Mathematics Education, 39*, 419–430.

Davydov, V. V. (1996). *Theory of developing education*. Moscow: Intor (in Russian).

de Villiers, M. (1998). An alternative approach to proof in dynamic geometry. In R. Lehrer & D. Chazan (Eds.), *Designing learning environments for developing understanding of geometry and space* (pp. 369–393). Hillsdale: Lawrence Erlbaum.

Duval, R. (2012). The first crucial point in geometry learning: Visualization. How to see figures mathematically and not perceptually for becoming able to solve problems by oneself? *The Plenary Lecture presented at the 7th Mediterranean Conference on Mathematics Education -* Section of the East-Meets-West on Innovation and Entrepreneurship - Congress and Exhibition. Nicosia, Cyprus.

Elia, I. V., den Heuvel-Panhuizen, M., & Kolovou, A. (2009). Exploring strategy use and strategy flexibility in non-routine problem solving by primary school high achievers in mathematics. *ZDM, 41*, 605–618.

Goldin, G. A. (2009). The affective domain and students' mathematical inventiveness. In R. Leikin, A. Berman, & B. Koichu (Eds.), *Creativity in mathematics and the education of gifted students* (pp. 149–163). Rotterdam: Sense Publishers.

Haylock, D. W. (1987). A framework for assessing mathematical creativity in schoolchildren. *Educational Studies in Mathematics, 18*, 59–74.

Lakatos, I. (1976). In J. Worrall & E. Zahar (Eds.), *Proofs and refutations*. Cambridge/New York: Cambridge University Press.

Leikin, R. (2004). Towards high quality geometrical tasks: Reformulation of a proof problem. In M. J. Hoines & A. B. Fuglestad (Eds.), *Proceedings of the 28th international conference for the psychology of mathematics education* (Vol. 3, pp. 209–216). Bergen: Bergen University College.

Leikin, R. (2007). Habits of mind associated with advanced mathematical thinking and solution spaces of mathematical tasks. *The fifth Conference of the European Society for Research in Mathematics Education – CERME-5* (pp. 2330–2339). Available on-line: http://ermeweb.free.fr/Cerme5.pdf

Leikin, R. (2009a). Bridging research and theory in mathematics education with research and theory in creativity and giftedness. In R. Leikin, A. Berman, & B. Koichu (Eds.), *Creativity in mathematics and the education of gifted students* (pp. 383–409). Rotterdam: Sense Publishers.

Leikin, R. (2009b). Exploring mathematical creativity using multiple solution tasks. In R. Leikin, A. Berman, & B. Koichu (Eds.), *Creativity in mathematics and the education of gifted students* (pp. 129–145). Rotterdam: Sense Publishers.

Leikin, R. (2012a). What is given in the problem? Looking through the lens of constructions and Dragging in DGE. *Mediterranean Journal for Research in Mathematics Education, 11*(1–2), 103–116.

Leikin, R. (2012b). Creativity in teaching mathematics as an indication of teachers' expertise. Research Forum on "Conceptualizing and developing expertise in mathematics instruction". In T. Y. Tso (Ed.), *The proceedings of the 36th international conference for the psychology of mathematics education* (Vol. 1, pp. 128–131). Taiwan: PME.

Leikin, R., & Levav-Waynberg, A. (2008). Solution spaces of multiple-solution connecting tasks as a mirror of the development of mathematics teachers' knowledge. *Canadian Journal of Science, Mathematics, and Technology Education, 8*(3), 233–251.

Leikin, R., & Pitta-Pantazim, D. (2013). Creativity and mathematics education: The state of the art. *ZDM – The International Journal on Mathematics Education, 45*(4), 159–166.

Leontiev, L. (1983). *Analysis of activity. Vol. 14: Psychology*. Vestnik MGU (Moscow State University).

Levav-Waynberg, A., & Leikin, R. (2012a). The role of multiple solution tasks in developing knowledge and creativity in geometry. *Journal of Mathematical Behavior, 31*(1), 73–90.

Levav-Waynberg, A., & Leikin, R. (2012b). Using multiple solution tasks for the evaluation of students' problem-solving performance in geometry. *Canadian Journal of Science, Mathematics, and Technology Education, 12*(4), 311–333.

Lin, F. L., Hsieh, F. J., Hana, G., & De Villiers, M. (Eds.). (2009). *The proceeding of the 19th ICMI study conference: Proofs and Proving in Mathematics Education*. Taiwan: National Taipei University.

National Council of Teachers of Mathematics (NCTM). (1995). *Report of the NCTM task force on the mathematically promising*. NCTM News Bulletin, 32.

Polya, G. (1981). *Mathematical discovery*. New York: Wiley.

Schoenfeld, A. H. (1985). *Mathematical problem solving*. New York: Academic.

Schwartz, J. L. (1999). Can technology help us make mathematics curriculum intellectually stimulating and socially responsible? *International Journal of Computers for Mathematical Learning, 4*, 99–119.

Sheffield, L. J. (Ed.). (1999). *Developing mathematically promising students*. Reston: National Council of Teachers of Mathematics.

Sheffield, L. J. (2009). Developing mathematical creativity – Questions may be the answer. In R. Leikin, A. Berman, & B. Koichu (Eds.), *Creativity in mathematics and the education of gifted students* (pp. 87–100). Rotterdam: Sense Publishers.

Silver, E. A. (1997). Fostering creativity through instruction rich in mathematical problem solving and problem posing. *ZDM, 3*, 75–80.

Silver, E. A., & Zawodjewsky, J. S. (1997). *Benchmarks of students understanding (BOSUN) project*. Technical guide. Pittsburgh: LRDC.

Sriraman, B. (2005). Are giftedness & creativity synonyms in mathematics? An analysis of constructs within the professional and school realms. *The Journal of Secondary Gifted Education, 17*, 20–36.

Vygotsky, L. S. (1930/1984). Imagination and creativity in adolescent. In D. B. Elkonin (Ed.), *The collected works of L. S. Vygotsky* (Child psychology, Vol. 4, pp. 199–219). Moscow: Pedagogika (in Russian).

Vygotsky, L. S. (1978). *Mind in society: The development of higher psychological processes*. Cambridge, MA: Harvard University Press. (Published originally in Russian in 1930)

Yerushalmy, M. (2009). Educational technology and curricular design: Promoting mathematical creativity for all students. In R. Leikin, A. Berman, & B. Koichu (Eds.), *Creativity in mathematics and the education of gifted students* (pp. 101–113). Rotterdam: Sense Publishers.

Transforming Professional Practice in Numeracy Teaching

Merrilyn Goos, Vince Geiger, and Shelley Dole

Abstract The development of numeracy, sometimes known as quantitative literacy or mathematical literacy, requires students to experience using mathematics in a range of real-world contexts and in all school subjects. This chapter reports on a research study that aimed to help teachers in ten schools plan and implement numeracy strategies across the middle school curriculum. Teachers were introduced to a rich model of numeracy that gives attention to real-life contexts; application of mathematical knowledge; use of representational, physical, and digital tools; and positive dispositions towards mathematics. These elements are grounded in a critical orientation to the use of mathematics. Over one school year, the teachers worked through two action research cycles of numeracy curriculum implementation. The professional development approach included three whole-day workshops that supported teachers' planning and evaluation and two rounds of school visits for lesson observations, teacher and student interviews, and collection of student work samples. During workshops, teachers also completed written tasks that sought information about their confidence for numeracy teaching and how they were using the numeracy model for planning. Drawing on data collected during workshops and school visits, we demonstrate how teachers' instructional practices changed over time as they progressively engaged with the numeracy model.

Keywords Numeracy • Mathematical literacy • Quantitative literacy • Teacher development • Instructional practice • Contexts • Dispositions • Tools • Critical orientation

M. Goos (✉) • S. Dole
School of Education, The University of Queensland, St Lucia,
QLD 4072, Australia
e-mail: m.goos@uq.edu.au; s.dole@uq.edu.au

V. Geiger
School of Education, Australian Catholic University, P.O. Box 456,
Virginia, QLD 4014, Australia
e-mail: Vincent.Geiger@acu.edu.au

Y. Li et al. (eds.), *Transforming Mathematics Instruction: Multiple Approaches and Practices*, Advances in Mathematics Education, DOI 10.1007/978-3-319-04993-9_6,
© Springer International Publishing Switzerland 2014

Numeracy is a term used in many English-speaking countries, such as the UK, Canada, South Africa, Australia, and New Zealand, whereas in the USA and elsewhere, it is more common to speak of *quantitative literacy* or *mathematical literacy*. Steen (2001) described quantitative literacy as the capacity to deal with quantitative aspects of life and proposed that its elements included confidence in mathematics, appreciation of the nature and history of mathematics and its significance for understanding issues in the public realm, logical thinking and decision-making, use of mathematics to solve practical everyday problems in different contexts, number sense and symbol sense, reasoning with data, and the ability to draw on a range of prerequisite mathematical knowledge and tools. The OECD's (2004) PISA program offers a similarly expansive definition of mathematical literacy as:

> an individual's capacity to identify and understand the role mathematics plays in the world, to make well-founded judgments, and to use and engage with mathematics in ways that meet the needs of that individual's life as a constructive, concerned and reflective citizen. (p. 15)

Steen (2001) maintains that, for numeracy to be useful to students, it must be learned in multiple contexts and in all school subjects, not just mathematics. Although this is a challenging notion, a recent review of numeracy education undertaken by the Australian government (Human Capital Working Group, Council of Australian Governments 2008) concurred, recommending:

> That all systems and schools recognise that, while mathematics can be taught in the context of mathematics lessons, the development of numeracy requires experience in the use of mathematics beyond the mathematics classroom, and hence requires an across the curriculum commitment. (p. 7)

The cross-curricular importance of numeracy is endorsed by the recently introduced national curriculum for Australian schools, which identifies numeracy as a general capability to be developed in all subjects (Australian Curriculum, Assessment and Reporting Authority 2012).

This chapter reports on a yearlong research study that investigated approaches to help teachers plan and implement numeracy strategies across the curriculum in the middle years of schooling (grades 6–9). The study was informed by a rich model of numeracy that was introduced to the teachers as an aid for their curriculum and instructional planning. The chapter addresses two of the research questions that guided the project:

1. To what extent did teachers' instructional practices change over time as they progressively engaged with the numeracy model?
2. How effective was the professional development approach in building teachers' confidence in numeracy teaching?

The first section of the chapter outlines the theoretical framework for the study, which comprises the numeracy model and the professional development approach for working with teachers. The second section describes the research design and methods. In the third section, we describe how teachers developed new strategies for numeracy instruction, drawing on an analysis of the whole group's developmental trajectories through the numeracy model and a case study of one individual teacher. The final section evaluates the effectiveness of the professional development approach in terms of changes in teachers' confidence in numeracy teaching.

Theoretical Framework

Numeracy Model

Current definitions of numeracy, quantitative literacy, and mathematical literacy share many common features and may usefully inform curriculum development and national or international assessments of students' educational achievement. However, they do not provide direct guidance to teachers on how to plan instruction with a rich numeracy focus. Goos (2007) has also argued that a description of numeracy for new times is needed to better acknowledge the rapidly evolving nature of knowledge, work, and technology. She developed the model shown in Fig. 1 to represent the multifaceted nature of numeracy in the twenty-first century. This model was intended to be readily accessible to teachers as an instrument for planning and reflection.

According to this model, numeracy development requires attention to real-life *contexts*; the application of *mathematical knowledge*; the use of representational, physical, and digital *tools*; and positive *dispositions* towards the use of mathematics. A further important and overarching element of the model is a *critical orientation* to the use of mathematics. Table 1 provides a succinct summary of the elements of the numeracy model, each of which is elaborated below.

A numerate person requires *mathematical knowledge*. In a numeracy context, mathematical knowledge includes not only concepts and skills but also problem-solving strategies and the ability to make sensible estimations (Zevenbergen 2004).

A numerate person has *positive dispositions* – a willingness and confidence to engage with tasks, independently and in collaboration with others, and apply their mathematical knowledge flexibly and adaptively. Affective issues have long been held to play a central role in mathematics learning and teaching (McLeod 1992), and the importance of developing positive attitudes towards mathematics is emphasized in national and international curriculum documents (e.g., National Council of Teachers of Mathematics 2000; National Curriculum Board 2009).

Being numerate involves using *tools*. Sfard and McClain (2002) discuss ways in which symbolic tools and other specially designed artifacts "enable, mediate, and shape mathematical thinking" (p. 154). In school and workplace contexts, tools may be representational (symbol systems, graphs, maps, diagrams, drawings, tables, ready reckoners), physical (models, measuring instruments), or digital (computers, software, calculators, Internet) (Noss et al. 2000; Zevenbergen 2004).

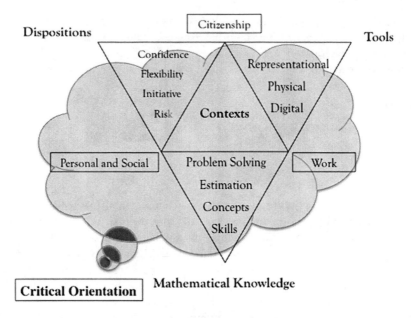

Fig. 1 A model for numeracy in the twenty-first century (Goos 2007)

Table 1 Descriptions of the elements of the numeracy model

Element	Description
Mathematical knowledge	Mathematical concepts and skills, problem-solving strategies, and estimation capacities
Contexts	Capacity to use mathematical knowledge in a range of contexts, both within schools and beyond school settings
Dispositions	Confidence and willingness to engage with tasks and apply mathematical knowledge flexibly and adaptively
Tools	Use of physical (models, measuring instruments), representational (symbol systems, graphs, maps, diagrams, drawings, tables), and digital (computers, software, calculators, Internet) tools to mediate and shape thinking
Critical orientation	Use of mathematical information to make decisions and judgments, add support to arguments, and challenge an argument or position

Because numeracy is about using mathematics to act in and on the world, people need to be numerate in a range of *contexts* (Steen 2001). All kinds of occupations require numeracy, and many examples of work-related numeracy are specific to the particular work context (Noss et al. 2000). Informed and critical citizens need to be numerate citizens. Almost every public issue depends on data, projections, and the kind of systematic thinking that is at the heart of numeracy. Different curriculum contexts also have distinctive numeracy demands, so that students need to be numerate across the range of contexts in which their learning takes place at school (Steen 2001).

This model is grounded in a *critical orientation* towards numeracy since numerate people not only know and use efficient methods, they also evaluate whether the results obtained make sense and are aware of appropriate and inappropriate uses of mathematical thinking to analyze situations and draw conclusions. In an increasingly complex and information-drenched society, numerate citizens need to decide how to evaluate quantitative, spatial, or probabilistic information used to support claims made in the media or other contexts. They also need to recognize how mathematical information and practices can be used to persuade, manipulate, disadvantage, or shape opinions about social or political issues (Jablonka 2003).

Professional Development Approach

In working with teachers, we integrated four professional development strategies recommended by Loucks-Horsley et al. (2003). The first strategy involved formation of *collaborative partnerships* between participating teachers, university researchers, and curriculum support officers from the state Department of Education, which commissioned the study. Collaborative structures provide opportunities for professional learning around topics negotiated and agreed upon by the group, thus ensuring common goals. Collaborations are more contextualized to the teachers' setting than most other forms of professional learning. The emphasis on collegiality and communication provides a forum for teachers to discuss specific issues related to their classrooms in an environment in which the discussion is valued by their colleagues.

The second strategy was to *examine teaching and learning* using action research. We conducted a series of project workshops and school visits to support teachers through two action research cycles of plan, act, observe, and reflect in order to replan and continue through the next cycle. Additional elements of this strategy included inviting teachers to contribute to or formulate their own questions, linking teachers with sources of knowledge and stimulation from outside their schools, and documenting and sharing the learning from research.

Third, we provided teachers with *immersion experiences* that included numeracy-based learning opportunities and examples of numeracy investigations and assessment tasks. Successful use of immersion experiences as a strategy for professional learning requires two key elements: qualified facilitators and long-term experiences. Both of these elements were embedded in the design of the project. The research team has extensive mathematical and numeracy knowledge, many years' experience as classroom teachers, and in-depth understanding of the goals and challenges of implementing numeracy pedagogy. In addition, unlike one-off professional development models, the immersion experiences occurred at every teacher meeting. Hence many of the drawbacks of immersion experiences – lack of time and resources, mismatch with individual teachers' learning sequence, and lack of connection to direct classroom practice – were reduced.

Fourth, we expected *curriculum implementation* by requiring teachers to develop and implement units of work that targeted numeracy demands of the diverse curriculum areas from which they were drawn. Most short-term workshops that demonstrate innovative materials do not provide support (or even the expectation) for the teachers to trial these ideas in their own classrooms. As a result, the ideas provided in these one-off workshops are rarely put to use in the classroom (Cohen and Hill 2001). By including the requirement of implementation of the units as part of the project, we were able not only to ensure that the teachers would use the ideas with their students but also to allow them critical support and time for reflection on the experience. In addition, because the teachers completed at least two cycles of curriculum implementation, they were able to put into practice elements that were learned and refined after the first attempt.

Research Design and Methods

Teachers were recruited from ten schools with diverse demographic characteristics: four primary schools (kindergarten–grade 7), one secondary school (grades 8–12), four smaller schools in rural areas (grades 1–12), and one school that combined middle and secondary grades (grades 6–12). Each school nominated two teachers, thus ensuring that participants were able to connect with a colleague from their own school. They included generalist primary school teachers who taught across all curriculum areas as well as secondary teachers qualified to teach specific subjects (mathematics, English, science, social education, health and physical education, design studies).

There were three elements to the research design: (1) an audit of the middle years curriculum to identify the numeracy demands inherent in all curriculum areas (see Goos et al. 2010); (2) three whole-day professional development workshops that brought together all participants to *examine teaching and learning* and provide *immersion experiences*; and (3) two daylong visits to each school to evaluate *curriculum implementation* via lesson observations, collection of planning documents and student work samples, and audio-recorded interviews with teachers and students. The overall research plan is summarized in Table 2 to show the timeline for the project, key activities in the professional development approach, and data sources that informed our research into changes in teachers' instructional practices.

At the first project workshop, teachers were introduced to the numeracy model and the action research approach, and the findings of the curriculum audit were shared and discussed. The aim of the audit was to draw teachers' attention to the numeracy demands within all curriculum areas and hence to encourage them to accept responsibility for developing students' numeracy capabilities in the subjects they taught. We provided immersion experiences that were designed as cross-curricular numeracy investigations suitable for use with middle year students. These included investigations of Barbie dolls' physical proportion (with direct links to the health and physical education curriculum; see Fig. 2), the occurrence of the Golden

Table 2 Research design

Time	Activity	Data sources
February	Curriculum audit: identify numeracy demands in all curriculum areas	
March	Professional development workshop: introduce numeracy model; share findings from curriculum audit; try out numeracy teaching strategies and tasks; plan for implementation	Survey of numeracy teaching confidence
June	School visits: observe and evaluate implementation	Lesson observations, interviews with teachers and students, collection of teaching materials
August	Professional development workshop: evaluate implementation; share teaching resources and strategies; plan for implementation	
October	School visits: observe and evaluate implementation	Lesson observations, interviews with teachers and students, collection of teaching materials
November	Professional development workshop: evaluate implementation; reflect on professional learning	Survey of numeracy teaching confidence
		Map trajectories through the numeracy model

Rectangle in art, design, and nature (linked to the arts and design studies curricula), and planning for participation in the Tour Down Under, a bicycle race similar to the Tour de France (with links to the social education curriculum). At the end of this day, teachers were also asked to complete a survey that asked them to assess their confidence in various aspects of numeracy teaching.

The focus of the second workshop was on evaluating the implementation of the initial numeracy unit from the perspective of participating teachers and students and on setting goals and planning for the second action research cycle. All teachers were asked to bring evidence of one idea, activity, or unit they had tried with their class, to describe to the whole group how well (or not) it had worked, and to explain what they learned from this experience and how they would use this evaluation to plan subsequent lesson sequences. Time was also allocated to revisiting the numeracy model and the curriculum audit and to provide feedback on observations from the first round of school visits. We found very little evidence of a critical orientation in any of the lessons we had observed in the first round of school visits, despite opportunities in these lessons for including critique of real-life situations or actions. In interviews with teachers, it emerged that they were unsure about how to embed this element of the numeracy model into their planning and practice. Therefore, at the second workshop, we presented a range of stimulus materials drawn from print and digital media sources and asked teachers to work together to develop these into lessons that would promote a critical orientation in their students, without losing sight of the other elements of the numeracy model. (See Fig. 3 for an example of stimulus material.)

Barbie and Body Measurements

1. Measure your:
- height
- arm span
- length of index finger
- length of nose (bridge to point)
- head circumference
- wrist circumference.

(Work in pairs or small groups to make the measuring easier.)

2. Record females' personal measurements in the left column of the table below.

Name:			Barbie		
Body part	**Measurement**	**% of Height**	**Body part**	**Measurement**	**% of Height**
height			height	30.0 cm	
arm span			arm span	24.0 cm	80.0%
index finger			index finger	1.0 cm	3.3%
nose			nose	0.5 cm	1.7%
head			head	10.0 cm	33.3%
wrist			wrist	2.0 cm	6.7%

3. Now calculate and record the **ratio** of each measurement to height, and convert this to **percentage** of height. **Record** this personal information in the "% of height" column.

4. Compare the % of height data for female members of your group.

5. We will also use **spreadsheet formulae** to calculate **ratios** of body parts to heights for the whole class (using decimal or percentage representation).

6. Now we'll use **spreadsheet formulae** to find the **mean** (average) of each body ratio for the class. What similarities and any differences do you notice? What is the physical meaning of these?

7. Make similar **measurements** for **Barbie** and record these in the table above. Calculate her body **ratios** (express also as percentage of height) and record these. **Compare** her proportions with the average proportions of human females calculated from our class set of data.

Is Barbie a realistic representation of human proportions?

What would Barbie look like if she were scaled up to human height?

Fig. 2 Barbie activity used in first teacher workshop

At the third workshop that concluded the project, the research team began by reporting on students' perceptions of numeracy (taken from interviews with students on school visits); how well they liked mathematics (or not); where they saw numeracy in other learning areas, outside school, and in future careers; what advice they would give mathematics teachers to make learning mathematics more effective and enjoyable; and what they thought their teachers learned through

Readers of the *Courier-Mail* newspaper are invited to write in with questions such as the one below for the cookery expert (a well known chef).

> **Q. I am planning to make a small Christmas cake in a six-inch tin (15 cm) and would like to know how to calculate the quantities of ingredients needed if my recipe is for a larger tin.**
>
> A. Just break down the recipe accordingly; for example, if your cake recipe is for a 12-inch tin (30cm), then halve the recipe.

Is this answer good advice? What questions could you ask to help your students take a critical orientation to this information?

Fig. 3 Critical orientation stimulus material used in second teacher workshop

participation in this project. We next provided teachers with copies of the numeracy model and asked them to map their trajectory through the model throughout the project. They did this by identifying the element of the model that represented their entry point to the project, together with other elements of the model that became more meaningful or significant to them over time. As a result of our analysis of school visit data, we invited four teachers who exemplified different types of professional learning trajectories to report on their experiences. (One of these is the teacher whose case study is reported in a later section of this chapter.) We also immersed the teachers in a final numeracy investigation that used temperature data we had collected from inside a car at 10-min intervals over 2 h. Teachers were asked to sketch out a numeracy activity driven by questions that would support a critical orientation to the data and the contexts in which it might be collected and interpreted. At the end of the workshop, we readministered the numeracy self-assessment survey to enable us to track any changes in confidence in numeracy teaching.

The data used in this chapter are drawn from the following sources:

1. Field notes from lesson observations and interviews with teachers (research question 1)
2. Annotated copies of the numeracy model that were made by teachers at the last project workshop to map their developmental trajectory (research question 1)
3. Teachers' responses to the numeracy confidence survey that was administered at the first and last project workshops (research question 2)

The data were analyzed using qualitative and quantitative methods. To address research question 1, changes in teachers' instructional practices were analyzed by identifying how teaching plans and actions aligned with the elements of the numeracy model as the project progressed. For research question 2, concerning teacher confidence, Likert-style responses to the survey were converted to scores, and the score totals were compared at the beginning and end of the project to identify any changes in confidence levels.

New Numeracy Teaching Strategies

This section discusses the developmental trajectories of all teachers in terms of the numeracy model that guided the study and illustrates new numeracy teaching strategies via a teacher case study.

Teacher Trajectories Through the Numeracy Model

At the final project workshop, teachers were provided with a copy of the numeracy model and asked to annotate it in a way that indicated their changing understanding of numeracy over the duration of the project (Geiger et al. 2011). For example, Karen annotated her copy of the numeracy model as shown in Fig. 4.

Karen's annotations show that her initial entry point to promoting students' numeracy was to improve their mathematical knowledge, or specifically their skills. However, her annotations show her growing awareness of elements of numeracy through her participation in the project. Following her annotations counterclockwise appears to reflect her trajectory: she wanted to develop mathematical knowledge but also increase links to real-world contexts. For example, she came to recognize the importance of using real data. She also noticed increased student confidence and initiative in relation to dispositions. Her note about taking a risk reflects her own change in perspective in relation to students having confidence in their mathematical skills rather than just being able to demonstrate the skills. Her comment at the top of the diagram is an overall reflection on the growth of her own conceptualization of numeracy.

Of the 20 teachers involved in the project, 18 completed the mapping task in the way we requested. We examined every annotated copy of the model to identify the entry point or starting element indicated by each teacher and then the sequence of elements in which they claimed to have developed interest and understanding as the project progressed. The resulting teacher trajectories are shown in Table 3.

Of the 18 valid responses, 8 people indicated that they had entered the project with a concern for students' *dispositions*. Their annotations suggested that they were uneasy with students' negative feelings towards mathematics and wanted to devise units of work that would have a positive impact on dispositions. Seven teachers indicated that their starting point had been students' *mathematical knowledge* and skills, and their annotations suggested that they believed that if students had appropriate mathematical knowledge and skills, they would be successful in applying these as required in context. Only three teachers indicated that they started the project with an emphasis on *contexts*, stating that through contexts, students could apply their mathematics knowledge in meaningful situations. None of the teachers indicated that they came to the project with a primary interest in the use of *tools* or a *critical orientation*.

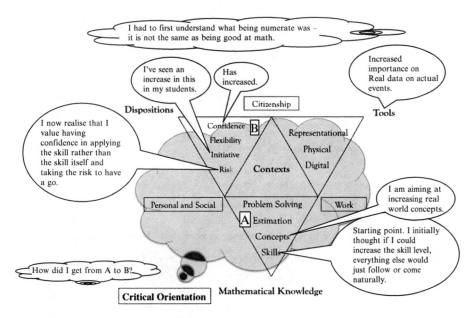

Fig. 4 Karen's trajectory through the numeracy model

Table 3 Teacher's self-identified trajectories through the numeracy model

Starting element	Trajectories		
Dispositions (D)	D → K/T/C	D → C	
	D → K/T → C	D → C → T	
	D → K/T → C/CO	D → C → K (2 teachers)	
	D → K/T/C → CO		
Knowledge (K)	K → D (2 teachers)	K → T → D (2 teachers)	K → C → D
	K → D/C		
	K → D → T		
Context (C)	C → K → CO	C → All	
	C → K → D → T		

D dispositions, *K* knowledge, *T* tools, *C* context, *CO* critical orientation

Although varied, teachers' trajectories through the model showed some patterns of similarity (see Table 3). *Knowledge* to *dispositions* (K → D) and *dispositions* to *knowledge* (D → K) were common patterns, possibly indicating teachers' beliefs about the connection between success in using mathematical knowledge and a positive disposition. Only four teachers indicated that they considered the *critical orientation* aspect of the numeracy model, and this was their end point. Although the teachers identified different starting points and trajectories through the numeracy model, at least half of the valid responses to the mapping task indicated they had attended to four of the model's five components during the life of the project: 16 teachers annotated *knowledge*, 16 *dispositions*, 13 *contexts*, and 9 *tools*.

Challenge: The Roman Colosseum

Ancient Rome was said to be founded in 753BC.

1. How long after Rome was founded was the Colosseum commissioned?

2. How long after Rome was founded was the Colosseum finished?

3. How long after the Colosseum was finished was the Arch of Constantine built?

The Colosseum is elliptical in shape. The area of an ellipse is given by the formula $A = \pi ab$, where a is the "long radius" and b is the "short radius".

4. What is the area of the Colosseum?

5. Would the Colosseum fit into the Melbourne Cricket Ground (MCG)?

"It cost more to visit the Colosseum today than to see the football at the MCG!", said a disgruntled Australian visitor.

7. Is this statement true, or is he just grumpy because his football team won the wooden spoon again this year?

Fig. 5 The Roman Colosseum challenge

Case Study of a Secondary School Mathematics Teacher

Maggie was one of the teachers in the project who explored every aspect of the numeracy model as she developed new numeracy teaching strategies. She taught mathematics and science at a large secondary school in a rural town. She was an early career teacher only in her second year of teaching. The class with which she worked for this project was a grade 8 mathematics class.

First School Visit

Initially, Maggie struggled to come to grips with how to highlight the *numeracy* within mathematics, but she decided to focus on teaching mathematics in real-life contexts that would be of interest to her students. She was supported in her planning by the school's mathematics coordinator, who was an experienced teacher. Together they planned an investigation based on the television program *The Amazing Race*. They decided that students would need 2–3 weeks in the computer laboratory to complete the investigation, which was based on organizing an adventure holiday around the world, given an itinerary and a budget of $10,000. Along the way students had to complete a number of challenges for which they earned an additional $2,000 each. The challenges, which included *Diving with Sharks* in Cairns, *Skiing* in Switzerland, and visiting *The Roman Colosseum*, focused on using directed number in context, a topic that students had studied in the previous weeks. In *The Roman Colosseum* challenge, students were also required to use formulas in the context of comparing areas of the Colosseum and the Melbourne Cricket Ground, as well as looking at exchange rates and converting between currencies (see Fig. 5). Students were expected to use the Internet to find information about flights, accommodation, and places they would be visiting. Maggie felt nervous about the first lesson because she was unsure of how the class would react. At first students seemed somewhat daunted by the size of the investigation, but Maggie and the mathematics coordinator decided that it was well structured enough to be tackled in small chunks.

Members of the research team observed the second lesson of this unit. The lesson took place in the computer laboratory that Maggie had booked for the duration of this numeracy investigation. Students entered the room and went straight to work without any prompting by Maggie. Although there were enough computers for each student, most collaborated with a partner on the tasks. Students appeared motivated and well prepared, and they were able to explain the investigation to us when we questioned them. Maggie noted that some previously disengaged students were interested in the investigation, while a few others remained aloof. Some students seemed so engaged in the task that they acted as though it was real; for example, when Maggie asked one boy "Where are you up to?," he replied, "I'm on my way to Paris!"

This lesson placed mathematics in the real-life *context* of an adventure holiday. It targeted *mathematical knowledge* of directed numbers and operations with integers (formulae, money calculations), using digital (Internet) and representational (charts, tables) *tools*. We did not observe teacher actions that promoted positive *dispositions* towards numeracy, but students were clearly motivated and confident in tackling the investigation and trying out different combinations of flights and accommodation bookings that would fit within their budget. A *critical orientation* does not seem to have been built into this investigation. However, this orientation could be promoted via teacher questioning, such as that we observed when Maggie helped a student compare advantages and disadvantages of booking cheap backpackers' accommodation.

At this stage of the project, Maggie thought she had changed the way she approached teaching numeracy in mathematics by placing more emphasis on using "bigger" tasks without a purely mathematical focus. She also realized that tasks she thought were routine, such as extracting data from tables, posed numeracy challenges for students that she had previously taken for granted.

Second School Visit

Since our first visit, Maggie had been reflecting on what she had learned as a teacher from her previous investigation – *The Amazing Race*. She observed that any student who had attempted the task had done something well, but overall the performance by students on the task was uneven. Maggie attributed this unevenness to absenteeism, for some students, who found it difficult to catch up on the work they had missed and so lost momentum with the larger task, and, for other students, difficulty with maintaining focus on the task for its 3-week duration.

Maggie used *The Amazing Race* experience when planning her next task – an investigation into the relationship between the heights and walking speeds of

Does your height influence your walking speed?

In this activity you will investigate whether there is any relationship between a person's height and their walking speed.

Using Microsoft Excel and the data we have collected, construct a scatterplot for our class data, with height in cm on the horizontal axis and speed on the vertical axis. Also construct scatterplots for the male data and the female data separately.

Comment on whether there is a trend in the data. Compare all three graphs. What are the similarities and differences?

Based on your findings is it possible to predict the walking speed of the following people?

Staff Member	Teaching Area	Height (cm)	Predicted Speed
Miss G	Mathematics	156	
Mr D	Science	196	
Mr M	Principal	180	
Miss J	English	178	

If so, explain the process you have used to make the predictions. If not, explain your reasons for not being able to make a prediction.

Fig. 6 Predicting walking speeds

students in her class, which was part of a bigger theme titled *Approaches to a Healthy Lifestyle*. Within this theme, Maggie included many smaller tasks that she hoped would make it easier for students to maintain interest and to catch up if they were absent.

The mathematics embedded in the *height versus walking speed* investigation included elements of collecting, representing, reducing, and analyzing data. Students were required to learn how to calculate the mean, median, and mode of a data set, represent data using line and scatterplots, and use representational tools such as graphs to make predictions about an individual's walking speed, given their height (see Fig. 6 for part of this activity). As part of the preparation for the task, Maggie had explicitly taught the underlying mathematical concepts and skills required by the task.

In the lesson we observed, students were to make scatterplots using Excel in order to determine whether there was a pattern in the data they had collected on height and walking speed. In earlier lessons, they had collected height data and calculated the mean, median, and mode. In another lesson, students had marked out a 40 m section of a 100 m running track and then found the time it took to walk this distance. With this information, students had calculated their walking speeds in meters per second, meters per minute, and kilometers per hour.

Students worked in the computer room in much the same way as we had previously observed. All appeared engaged with the task and each group or individual produced a scatterplot, although the appearance of the graphs varied between each group and individual depending on the scales chosen or on the choice of variable for the x and y axes. Most students were able to describe a general trend in the data and use this to make a prediction about what might be Maggie's (Miss G's) or the school principal's walking speeds, based on their heights (see Fig. 6). Interestingly, many students gave most attention to their own data point within the scatterplot with comments such as "This is me" (pointing at the appropriate data point) and "This is how tall I am and how fast I walk." Using personal data seemed to be effective for engaging students with the task. From a student's perspective, the activity was about them and how they compared to the rest of the class.

Students expressed surprise that the scatterplot was not linear, so that taller people did not necessarily walk faster. Maggie spoke to each group and challenged them to explain why this should be the case. Some groups suggested that alternative variables – with associated alternative hypotheses – should be explored, including, for example, the relationship between walking speed and leg length or between walking speed and stride rate. One group suggested there might be a stronger relationship between a person's height and their maximum walking pace rather than their natural walking pace.

Maggie chose an engaging *context* that made use of students' personal details to introduce the *mathematical knowledge* that was used in this lesson. The use of personal data encouraged positive *dispositions* towards involvement in and completion of the task. This task required knowledge of how to produce a scatterplot from a data set using Excel and the capacity to make predictions from trends in the data. Maggie asked students to use *representational tools* such as scatterplots and *digital tools* in the form of computers and Excel. By challenging students to explain the variance in their data from the anticipated linear relationship, Maggie introduced a *critical orientation* to the task.

Maggie's Trajectory Through the Numeracy Model

When we asked what the key factors in developing Maggie's new understanding of teaching numeracy were, she said she began with a desire to improve her teaching by increasing her focus on embedding student learning in engaging *contexts*. She believed this was a vital precondition to helping students understand why they needed to gain *mathematical knowledge*. Through the course of the project, Maggie noticed her increased focus on developing activities that provided a *critical orientation* towards the use of mathematics. Only later did she realize the role that *dispositions* played in encouraging students to try approaches to solving a problem for themselves rather than expecting her, as the teacher, to simply provide solutions. By the end of the project, Maggie said she had also increased her use of digital *tools* because she could see there were advantages in using these to explore and analyze authentic contexts.

When Maggie reflected on how she had changed and what she had learned during the course of the project, she identified her readiness to make use of more extended tasks when teaching mathematics. However, she tempered this view by arguing that tasks needed to be made up of self-contained subtasks that allowed students to move towards smaller achievable goals. Structuring tasks in this way also meant that students who had been absent were not intimidated by what they needed to do to cover work that took place while they were away.

In the future, Maggie aims to implement two extended units per semester like *The Amazing Race* and *Approaches to a Healthy Lifestyle*. For her, the level of engagement she observed while students were working on thematic activities was a compelling case for their inclusion within mathematics classes. Together with her teaching partner in this project, she was invited to speak at a staff meeting about her involvement in the project. She hopes that once other teachers understood the benefits for students of working with context-driven, extended tasks, there might be opportunity to work across a broader range of subject areas.

Effectiveness of the Professional Development Approach

Changes in teachers' confidence in numeracy teaching provide an indicator of the effectiveness of the professional development approach that was used in this project.

At the first and last project meetings, teachers completed a survey that asked them to assess their confidence in various aspects of numeracy teaching. The survey was based on the *Numeracy Standards for Graduates of Pre-Service Teacher Education Programs* published by the Queensland Board of Teacher Registration (2005). Two sets of standards were published: one for teachers of mathematics (early years and primary teachers, specialist mathematics teachers in the middle and senior years of schooling) and another for teachers of disciplines other than mathematics (specialist teachers in the early and primary years, as well as teachers of subjects other than mathematics in the middle and senior years of schooling). Participating teachers were asked to identify themselves as belonging to one of these two categories in order to complete the relevant survey.

The Numeracy Standards draw on the *Standards for Excellence in Teaching Mathematics in Australian Schools* formulated by the Australian Association of Mathematics Teachers (2006). They address three domains:

1. Professional knowledge: knowledge of students, of numeracy, and of students' numeracy learning
2. Professional attributes: personal attributes, personal professional development, and community responsibility
3. Professional practice: learning environment, planning, teaching, and assessment

Standards statements were available for each domain and sub-domain. These were turned into survey items for which teachers were asked to indicate their level of confidence, using a 5-point Likert scale, where a score of 1 corresponded to very unconfident, 2 to unconfident, 3 to unsure, 4 to confident, and 5 to very confident.

At the first and last project meetings, 15 and 12 teachers, respectively, completed the self-assessment as teachers of mathematics, while 4 and 5, respectively, completed the self-assessment as teachers of disciplines other than mathematics. Some teachers were present at only the first or last meeting, while two changed the way they identified themselves (as teachers of mathematics or other disciplines) between the first and last meetings. Because we are interested in change over time, we report only on data obtained from teachers who attended both the first and last project meetings and who completed the same version of the survey on both occasions. These respondents included nine teachers of mathematics and three teachers of disciplines other than mathematics.

To analyze survey responses, score totals were first calculated for each survey item for both groups of teachers who completed the surveys at the first (pre) and last (post) project meetings. To examine changes in confidence between the beginning and end of the project, shifts in the total scores of at least 4.5 and 1.5 were considered to be of interest for the two groups, respectively, because this was equivalent to half the group changing their level of confidence by 1 point on the Likert scale (e.g., from unsure to confident). The magnitude of score totals was also of interest, with score totals of at least 36 or 12 indicating confidence (i.e., an average score of 4) across the respective groups.

The complete data set is provided in Table 4 for teachers of mathematics and in Table 5 for teachers of disciplines other than mathematics. The tables also provide the results of the pre-post analysis using the criteria described above: score totals on items for which teachers indicated they felt confident are presented in bold type, while items signaling a change in confidence over the duration of the project are identified by shaded cells.

Table 4 indicates that at the start of the project, the teachers of mathematics (primary teachers as well as specialist teachers of mathematics in the middle and senior years of schooling) felt confident that they possessed the personal attributes and commitment to professional learning required for numeracy teaching, which vindicated their selection as participants. They also had confidence in some aspects of their professional knowledge (knowledge of the diversity of students' numeracy needs, of the pervasive nature of numeracy, of numeracy learning opportunities across the curriculum). However, they lacked confidence in their ability to establish an appropriate numeracy learning environment, plan for numeracy learning, and demonstrate effective numeracy teaching and assessment strategies. By the end of the project, these teachers felt confident in almost every aspect of numeracy teaching, apart from their ability to foster risk taking and critical inquiry in numeracy learning and to cater for the diversity of mathematical abilities and numeracy needs of learners. According to the analysis criteria identified earlier, their confidence levels had risen substantially on 16 of the 32 survey items, most notably on those in the domains of professional knowledge and professional practice. We were also interested to note increased confidence in areas not explicitly targeted by the project, such as theories of how students learn mathematics and the use of multiple representations of mathematical ideas.

Table 5 suggests that the small group of teachers of disciplines other than mathematics expressed greater confidence in numeracy teaching than their colleagues at the start

Table 4 Confidence scores for teachers of mathematics (pre-post); $n=9$

Domain	Standard statement	Score totals	
Professional knowledge	**Teachers will**	Pre	Post
Students	Understand the diversity of mathematical abilities and numeracy needs of learners	38	38
Numeracy	Exhibit sound knowledge of mathematics appropriate for teaching their students	35	37
	Understand the pervasive nature of numeracy and its role in everyday situations	37	40
	Demonstrate relevant knowledge of the central concepts, modes of inquiry, and structure of mathematics	32	36.5
	Establish connections between mathematics topics and between mathematics and other disciplines	35	41
	Recognize numeracy learning opportunities across the curriculum	36	42
Students' numeracy learning	Understand contemporary theories of how students learn mathematics	29	36
	Possess a repertoire of contemporary, theoretically grounded, student-centeredteaching strategies	33	36
	Demonstrate knowledge of a range of appropriate resources to support students' numeracy learning	32	36.5
	Integrate ICTs to enhance students' numeracy learning	29	36.5
Professional attributes	**Teachers will**		
Personal attributes	Display a positive disposition to mathematics and to teaching mathematics	40	42
	Recognizethat all students can learn mathematics and benumerate	37	42.5
	Exhibit high expectations for their students' mathematics learning and numeracy development	37	40
	Exhibit a satisfactory level of personal numeracy competence for teaching	40	40
Personal professional development	Demonstrate a commitment to continual enhancement of their personal numeracy knowledge	40	41
	Exhibit a commitment to ongoing improvement of their teaching of mathematics	41	44
	Demonstrate a commitment to collaborating with teachers of disciplines other than mathematics to enhance numeracy teaching and learning	38	37
Community responsibility	Develop and communicate informed perspectives of numeracy within and beyond the school	34.5	36
Professional practice	**Teachers will**		
Learning environment	Promote active engagement in numeracy learning	35.5	39
	Establish a supportive and challenging numeracy learning environment	33.5	37
	Foster risk taking and critical inquiry in numeracy learning	32.5	31
Planning	Highlight connections between mathematics topics and between mathematics and other disciplines	34	38.5
	Cater for the diversity of mathematical abilities and numeracy needs of learners	34	35
	Determine students' learning needs in numeracy to inform planning and implementation of learning experiences	31.5	36
	Embed thinking and working mathematically in numeracy learning experiences	28.5	36
	Plan for a variety of authentic numeracy assessment opportunities	31.5	36
Teaching	Demonstrate a range of effective teaching strategies for numeracy learning	32.5	37
	Utilize multiple representations of mathematical ideas in mathematics and in other curriculum areas	28.5	34
	Sequence mathematical learning experiences appropriately	35.5	39.5
	Demonstrate an ability to negotiate mathematical meaning and model mathematical thinking and reasoning	30.5	36
Assessment	Provide all students with opportunities to demonstrate their numeracy knowledge	31	39
	Collect and use multiple sources of valid evidence to make judgmentsabout students' numeracy learning	30	36

Table 5 Confidence scores for teachers of disciplines other than mathematics (pre-post); $n = 3$

Domain	Standard statement	Score total	
Professional knowledge	**Teachers will**	Pre	Post
Students	Recognize the numeracy knowledge and experiences that learners bring to their classrooms	12	12
	Understand the diversity of numeracy needs of learners	12	12
Numeracy	Understand the pervasive nature of numeracy and its role in everyday situations	13	13
	Understand the meaning of numeracy within their curriculum area	12	13
	Recognize numeracy learning opportunities and demands within their curriculum area	8	14
Students' numeracy learning	Demonstrate knowledge of a range of appropriate resources and strategies to support students' numeracy learning in their curriculum area	11	12
Professional attributes	**Teachers will**		
Personal attributes	Display a positive disposition to supporting students' numeracy learning within their curriculum area	13	13
	Recognize that all students can be numerate	11	10
	Exhibit high expectations of their students' numeracy development	12	11
	Exhibit a satisfactory level of personal numeracy competence for teaching	13	13
Personal professional development	Demonstrate a commitment to continual enhancement of personal numeracy knowledge	13	14
	Exhibit a commitment to ongoing improvement of their teaching strategies to support students' numeracy learning	13	14
	Demonstrate a commitment to collaborating with specialist teachers of mathematics to enhance their own numeracy learning and numeracy teaching strategies	13	14
Community responsibility	Develop and communicate informed perspectives of numeracy within and beyond the school	12	13
Professional practice	**Teachers will**		
Learning environment	Promote active engagement in numeracy learning within their own curriculum context	13	13
	Establish a supportive and challenging learning environment that values numeracy learning	13	12
Planning	Take advantage of numeracy learning opportunities when planning within their own curriculum context	13	14
	Display willingness to work with specialist teachers of mathematics in planning numeracy learning experiences	13	14
	Determine students' learning needs in numeracy to inform planning and implementation of learning experiences	11	13
Teaching	Demonstrate effective teaching strategies for integrating numeracy learning within their own curriculum context	12	14
	Model ways of dealing with numeracy demands of their curriculum area	12	14
Assessment	Provide all students with opportunities to demonstrate numeracy knowledge within their curriculum area	12	13

of the project (score totals equivalent to "Confident" on 18/22 items). Yet, despite this high starting point, reasonable gains in confidence over the life of the project were recorded on items related to recognizing the numeracy learning opportunities and demands in their own curriculum areas, determining students' numeracy learning needs to inform planning, demonstrating effective numeracy teaching strategies, and modeling ways of dealing with the numeracy demands of their curriculum area.

Expressions of increased confidence provide indirect evidence of the effectiveness of the professional development program and need to be interpreted in the light of observations of classroom practice and other data collected from teachers, such as the trajectories through the numeracy model discussed in a previous section. Teachers reported feeling confident about many aspects of numeracy teaching before the project started, and so we were surprised to see endorsement of even higher confidence levels at the end of the project. However, the responses to the confidence survey are consistent with other data in that we observed changes in teachers' planning and classroom instruction as well as changes in their understanding and use of the numeracy model.

Conclusion

In highlighting the positive outcomes of this project, we do not wish to imply that all participating teachers made significant changes to their practice, even though most claimed to have gained more confidence in numeracy teaching and a better understanding of what numeracy means. We have not reported here on our observations of the varying levels of commitment to the project displayed by the teachers with whom we worked. Many became fully immersed in exploring and implementing the numeracy model to the extent that some commented that the model had changed the way they thought about teaching. However, a few teachers, according to their students, only made an effort to incorporate numeracy into their lessons on occasions when the researchers were visiting their schools. There are many possible reasons why teachers might engage with, ignore, or even resist changes in instructional practice promoted by teacher educators. Pedagogical beliefs, planning skills, and constraints within the school environment that limit access to resources or support for new ideas are all factors that need to be considered when designing research that aims to transform teaching practice.

There are many challenges in planning for and promoting numeracy learning across the school curriculum. This study demonstrated that it is possible to plan for numeracy learning, but teachers also need to be alive to serendipitous moments for promoting numeracy as opportunities occur during lessons, for example, by "seeing" the numeracy embedded in current events or students' personal experiences. Effective numeracy teaching also requires that teachers have a rich conception of numeracy themselves. The numeracy model provided a framework for attending to and valuing numeracy in a holistic way. Teachers seemed most comfortable with incorporating the *knowledge*, *dispositions*, and *contexts* components of the model into their thinking about numeracy. Development of a *critical orientation* occurred to a lesser extent, and in general teachers continued to express low confidence in this aspect of their practice. Even those individuals who eventually incorporated a critical orientation into their planning did so only after exploring and becoming comfortable with the other elements of the numeracy model. Perhaps teachers still lacked a clear understanding of how a critical orientation could be embedded into numeracy teaching, or they may not have felt ready to address this aspect of the model until their understanding of other components was secure. Further research is needed to explore how teachers can be supported in developing personal conceptions of numeracy, as well as numeracy teaching practices, that value a critical orientation, since this perspective is vital to educating informed and aware citizens.

References

Australian Association of Mathematics Teachers. (2006). *Standards for excellence in teaching mathematics in Australian schools*. Retrieved June 5, 2012, from http://www.aamt.edu.au/content/download/499/2265/file/standxtm.pdf

Australian Curriculum, Assessment and Reporting Authority. (2012). *General capabilities in the Australian Curriculum*. Retrieved March 24, 2012, from http://www.australiancurriculum.edu.au/GeneralCapabilities/Overview/

Board of Teacher Registration, Queensland. (2005). *Numeracy in teacher education: The way forward in the 21st century*. Brisbane: Author.

Cohen, D., & Hill, H. (2001). *Learning policy: When state reform works*. New Haven: Yale University Press.

Geiger, V., Goos, M., & Dole, S. (2011). Teacher professional learning in numeracy: Trajectories through a model for numeracy in the 21st century. In J. Clark, B. Kissane, J. Mousley, T. Spencer, & S. Thornton (Eds.), *Mathematics: Traditions and (new) practices* (Proceedings of the 23rd biennial conference of the Australian Association of Mathematics Teachers and the 34th annual conference of the Mathematics Education Research Group of Australasia, pp. 297–305). Adelaide: AAMT & MERGA.

Goos, M. (2007). *Developing numeracy in the learning areas (middle years)*. Keynote address delivered at the South Australian Literacy and Numeracy Expo, Adelaide.

Goos, M., Geiger, V., & Dole, S. (2010). Auditing the numeracy demands of the middle years curriculum. In L. Sparrow, B. Kissane, & C. Hurst (Eds.), *Shaping the future of mathematics education* (Proceedings of the 33rd annual conference of the Mathematics Education Research Group of Australasia, pp. 210–217). Fremantle: MERGA.

Human Capital Working Group, Council of Australian Governments. (2008). *National numeracy review report*. Retrieved January 7, 2011, from http://www.coag.gov.au/reports/docs/national_numeracy_review.pdf

Jablonka, E. (2003). Mathematical literacy. In A. Bishop, M. A. Clements, C. Keitel, J. Kilpatrick, & F. Leung (Eds.), *Second international handbook of mathematics education* (pp. 75–102). Dordrecht: Kluwer.

Loucks-Horsley, S., Love, N., Stiles, K., Mundry, S., & Hewson, P. (2003). *Designing professional development for teachers of science and mathematics* (2nd ed.). Thousand Oaks: Corwin Press.

McLeod, D. (1992). Research on affect in mathematics education: A reconceptualization. In D. Grouws (Ed.), *Handbook of research on mathematics teaching and learning* (pp. 575–596). New York: Macmillan.

National Council of Teachers of Mathematics. (2000). *Principles and standards for school mathematics*. Reston: NCTM.

National Curriculum Board. (2009). *Shape of the Australian curriculum: Mathematics*. Retrieved June 5, 2012, from http://www.acara.edu.au/verve/_resources/Australian_Curriculum_-_Maths.pdf

Noss, R., Hoyles, C., & Pozzi, S. (2000). Working knowledge: Mathematics in use. In A. Bessot & J. Ridgeway (Eds.), *Education for mathematics in the workplace* (pp. 17–35). Dordrecht: Kluwer.

Organisation for Economic Cooperation and Development. (2004). *Learning for tomorrow's world: First results from PISA 2003*. Paris: OECD.

Sfard, A., & McClain, K. (2002). Analyzing tools: Perspectives on the role of designed artifacts in mathematics learning. *The Journal of the Learning Sciences, 11*(2&3), 153–161.

Steen, L. (2001). The case for quantitative literacy. In L. Steen (Ed.), *Mathematics and democracy: The case for quantitative literacy* (pp. 1–22). Princeton: National Council on Education and the Disciplines.

Zevenbergen, R. (2004). Technologising numeracy: Intergenerational differences in working mathematically in new times. *Educational Studies in Mathematics, 56*, 97–117.

Exploratory Activity in the Mathematics Classroom

João Pedro da Ponte, Neusa Branco, and Marisa Quaresma

Abstract In this chapter, we show that mathematical explorations may be integrated into the core of the daily classroom mathematics activities instead of just being a peripheral activity that is carried out occasionally. Based on two episodes, one on the initial learning of the rational number at grade 5 and the other on the learning of algebraic language at grade 7, we show how teachers may invite students to get involved and interpret such tasks and how they may provide students with significant moments of autonomous work and lead widely participated collective discussions. Thus, we argue that these tasks provide a classroom setting with innovative features in relation to conventional education based on the exposition of concepts and procedures, presentation of examples, and practice of exercises and with much more positive results regarding learning.

Keywords Explorations • Teaching practice • Tasks • Classroom communication • Rational numbers • Algebraic thinking

Introduction

In problems and exploration tasks, the students do not have a readymade procedure to obtain a solution. Therefore, they need to understand the question, formulate a strategy to solve it, carry out this strategy, and review and reflect on the results.

J.P. da Ponte (✉) • M. Quaresma
Instituto de Educação, Universidade de Lisboa,
Alameda da Universidade, 1649-013 Lisboa, Portugal
e-mail: jpponte@ie.ulisboa.pt; mq@campus.ul.pt

N. Branco
Escola Superior de Educação de Santarém and Instituto de Educação,
Universidade de Lisboa, Alameda da Universidade, 1649-013 Lisboa, Portugal
e-mail: neusacvbranco@gmail.com

Y. Li et al. (eds.), *Transforming Mathematics Instruction: Multiple Approaches and Practices*, Advances in Mathematics Education, DOI 10.1007/978-3-319-04993-9_7, © Springer International Publishing Switzerland 2014

Mathematics problems and explorations have much in common – the main difference is that problems indicate what is given and what is asked in a concise way, whereas explorations contain elements of uncertainty or openness, requiring students to undertake a significant work of interpreting the situation and often of reworking the questions (Ponte 2005).

In this chapter, we argue that these tasks may be used to create a productive classroom environment in contrast to the more common classroom based on exposition of concepts and procedures, presentation of examples, and practice of exercises. Our goal is to show how such tasks can be presented to the students, providing significant moments of autonomous work and leading to widely participated whole-class or collective discussions, and that such environment has positive implications for students' learning. We illustrate these ideas with two situations based on exploratory work at grade 5 (on rational numbers) and grade 7 (addressing algebraic reasoning).

The Exploratory Classroom

In an exploratory classroom we identify two key elements: (1) tasks proposed to the students and (2) ways of working, with associated roles of teacher and students and communication patterns.

Tasks

The tasks are important, not in themselves, but because of the activity of the students while solving them. What students learn in a mathematics classroom mainly results from the activities that they undertake and by reflecting on this activity (Christiansen and Walther 1986). The development of a rich and productive mathematics activity may stand on different kinds of tasks such as problems, investigations, explorations, and even exercises (Ponte 2005). Exercises are tasks with a precise formulation of givens, conditions, and questions, aimed at the clarification of concepts and consolidation of procedures that the student already knows. Problems are tasks aimed at the creative application of knowledge also already held by the student. In contrast, explorations are tasks aimed at the construction of new concepts, representations, or procedures, and investigations are even more challenging tasks aimed at the development of new concepts or at a creative use of concepts already known by the student. The teacher needs to select the tasks according to the objectives set for each class, paying attention to their suitability to the targeted students.

The nature of the context (mathematical or real life) is a very important aspect of a task. Students may find useful hints to solve tasks in aspects of the context.

However, as Skovsmose (2001) points out, many supposedly real-life contexts are basically artificial – this author calls them "semi-real" contexts. At the same time, it should be noted that it makes a significant difference whether we work in mathematical contexts with which we have some familiarity or in mathematical contexts that are new to us.

The representations involved are another important aspect on a task. Bruner (1966) distinguishes between enactive (objects, body movements), iconic (pictures), and symbolic representations. Often, alongside the formal representations or even before these representations, students profit from working with informal representations or even from constructing their own representations. Naturally, the teaching materials used, including manipulative materials, daily life objects, digital technologies, etc., determine the representations that students will use to work on a given task to a large extent.

We must note that problems include moments of exploration. We may formulate hypotheses, analyze the given conditions or make conjectures about possible solutions, and test their consequences. In many problems, it is possible to generate data and explore regularities in such data. However, exploratory tasks are distinctive in that they always require a careful interpretation of the situation, then the creation or reformulation of more precise questions to investigate, and, often, the construction of new concepts and representations. In this way, besides enabling the application of already learned concepts, explorations may promote the development of new concepts and the learning of new representations and mathematical procedures.

Problem solving is an important curriculum orientation, especially since the publication of *An agenda for action* (NCTM 1980). This document proclaimed that "problem solving should be the focus of school mathematics" (p. 1). Later, other curriculum documents kept emphasizing problem solving (e.g., NCTM 2000). As a consequence, problem solving won a positive connotation among textbook authors and mathematics teachers, as corresponding to a necessary and important activity in the mathematics class. However, the place of problem solving in mathematics teachers' professional practice proved to be problematic. Some teachers hold initiatives such as the "problem of the week" or "problem of the month." The classroom work still went on as before, with the only difference being that, from time to time, at a special moment, a problem was proposed, often with little relation to the current topic that the class was studying. On the other hand, particularly in primary school, teachers kept using traditional word problems, sometimes feeling that these tasks were just disguised exercises requiring students to make a simple computation. The difficulties in achieving a productive classroom implementation led to an impasse, prompting mathematics educators to recognize that problem solving as a curriculum orientation was not matching the expectation (Schoenfeld 1991). Therefore, it becomes necessary to better understand the types of problems that could be useful in the classroom and, most especially, how teachers might use them.

The increasing availability of digital technology tools, such as computers and calculators, is probably the main factor that led to the increasing acceptance of exploration and investigation tasks. These technologies easily allow the simulation of complex situations that would otherwise be difficult to study (Papert 1972). However, even without digital technology, it is possible to explore many situations in a mathematical way. In fact, explorations have much to do with modeling – requiring the creation of representations that may be used to construct a mathematical model of a situation. But they also have important aspects of mathematical work such as using definitions, classifying objects, and relating properties. The two terms, explorations and investigations, are increasingly used, and it is difficult to establish a clear dividing line between them – we talk about "investigations" when the tasks involve mathematical situations with a considerable degree of challenge for most students and talk of "explorations" when the situations allow the easy involvement of most of them.

Ways of Working, Roles, and Communication Patterns

In the classroom, students may work in many different ways. In collective mode, the teacher interacts with all students at the same time. In group work and in pairs, the students are encouraged to share ideas among themselves. Working individually, the students may find the required concentration to deal with abstract ideas. In all these cases, the students may participate in two kinds of classroom discourse – collective, with all class mates and the teacher, and private, with a few colleagues or directly with the teacher.

An exploratory class usually unfolds in three phases (Ponte 2005): (1) presentation of the task and its interpretation by students (whole class), (2) development of work by students (in groups, pairs, or individually), and (3) discussion and final synthesis (whole class). As Bishop and Goffree (1986) indicate, the last phase is the most appropriate occasion to expose connections, allowing students to relate ideas on various topics and showing how mathematical ideas are naturally intertwined. In addition, discussion moments are opportunities for the negotiation of mathematical meanings and the construction of new knowledge. As the NCTM (2000) indicates, "[l]earning with understanding can be further enhanced by classroom interactions, as students propose mathematical ideas and conjectures, learn to evaluate their own thinking and that of others, and develop mathematical reasoning skills" (p. 21). Therefore, each task always ends with a collective discussion in order to allow the students to reflect, contrast ideas, processes, and come to final conclusions.

Classroom discourse is univocal, when it is dominated by the teacher, or dialogic, when the students' contribution is valued as important (Brendefur and Frykholm 2000). Usually, the role of the teacher is to propose the tasks to carry out, to establish working modes, and to direct the classroom discourse. However, the teacher may assume the role of the single mathematical authority or share it with the students, in which case he/she seeks to stimulate their reasoning and argumentation ability. The role of the students is always working on the proposed tasks. However, this role may vary widely in many respects – for example, as the students assume that they must intervene only when they are asked or, on the contrary, that they must intervene, at group or collective level, always when they have a significant contribution to make.

Unlike the conventional collective classroom, which is strongly controlled by the teacher and where the students' possibilities of intervention were very limited, in an exploratory classroom, students are provided with significant opportunities for participation. In exploratory classes, Lampert (1990) shows how students are encouraged to present their strategies and solutions as well as to question the solutions and strategies of others, seeking to understand or to refute them. Also in these classes, Wood (1999) highlights the learning potential in valuing justifications and exploring disagreements among students, for the construction of shared meanings.

For Stein et al. (2008), the starting point for collective discussions must be the students' work. They state that a productive mathematics discussion has two fundamental characteristics: (1) it is based on students' thinking; and (2) it puts forward important mathematical ideas. These authors underline the complexity of the work of the teacher in conducting a mathematical discussion, pointing out that the students' strategies are often very different from each other and largely unpredictable. They indicate that the teacher needs to give coherence to the diversity of the students' ideas, relating them to established mathematical knowledge, at the same time that students' authority and accountability are enhanced. Focusing on the conduction of classroom collective discussions, Cengiz et al. (2011) identify a set of instructional actions through which the teacher may seek to create opportunities to promote pupils' mathematical thinking: eliciting actions that lead students to present their methods, supporting actions to help children to understand the mathematical ideas, and extending actions to help students to move forward in their thinking.

The next two sections present selected episodes taken from teaching experiments (Branco 2008; Quaresma 2010) of students working on tasks and of classroom discussions, indicating how the features of the exploratory work were important for students' learning. Given the aim of this paper, the episodes are analyzed according to four main features of classroom exploratory work: (1) designing tasks and classroom organization, (2) promoting the involvement of students in interpreting and carrying out the tasks, (3) students' work including and negotiation of meanings, and (4) collective discussions.

Exploring Representations of Rational Numbers

Task and Classroom Organization

The first situation is taken from a study aiming to understand how the work on an exploratory teaching unit using different representations and different meanings of rational numbers, with grade 5 students, may contribute to the understanding of these numbers and of order, comparison, and equivalence of rational numbers (Quaresma 2010). The task "folding and folding again" is taken from the supporting materials of the new mathematics curriculum for grades 5–6 (Menezes et al. 2008) and was proposed in the first lesson to this class dedicated to the study of rational numbers. It should be noted that in grades 3–4, these students had already studied decimal numbers as well as fractional operators, but did not use the fraction representation.

Folding and Folding Again

1. Find three paper strips geometrically equivalent. Fold them in equal parts: the first in two, the second in four, and the third in eight.
   After you fold each strip, represent in different ways the parts that you got.

2. Compare the parts of the three strips that you got by folding. Record your conclusions.
3. In each strip, find the ratio between the length of the parts that you got after folding and the length of the strip. Record your conclusions.

The purpose of this task is to introduce the language associated with rational numbers in different representations and meanings. Specifically, the teacher aimed for students to learn: (1) to represent a rational number as a fraction, decimal, and percent; (2) to understand and use rational numbers as part-whole relations and measures; and (3) to compare numbers represented in different forms. The task involves the meanings of part-whole, measure, and ratio, with continuous magnitudes (rectangular segments) and is presented in the context of paper strips. The information is given through active representations (paper strips), and the answers may be given in verbal, pictorial, decimal, or fraction representations or as percentages. The first question gives the "whole," a strip of paper, and asks the students to represent three different parts of it. Question 2 asks the students to compare the three parts thus obtained. The students may use whichever representation that they wish; however, it is expected that they use the information obtained in the previous question to make the comparisons. Question 3 asks the students to determine the ratio between the length of the strip and the length of each of the parts obtained by folding.

This task provides an opportunity for students to get involved in an exploratory activity. Question 1 begins as an exercise asking students to do several folds but then assumes a more open nature by asking them to represent it in "different ways," something that most students have difficulty interpreting as an indication to use fractions, decimals, pictorial, verbal, or other representations of rational numbers. Question 2 asks them to compare different strips and to "draw conclusions," which is a very open statement, allowing for diverse interpretations. Finally, question 3 involves a term whose meaning is not obvious for these students ("reason"), as well as a new indication to draw further conclusions.

The teacher organizes the students in six groups of four to five students and gives each of them a sheet of paper with the proposed questions. First, she reads aloud questions 1 and 2, gives about 30 min for the students to work, and then promotes a collective discussion for about 25 min. Then, she distributes question 3 and gives students about 20 min to solve it. It is then discussed by the whole class for about 15 min, after which the class ends. In a subsequent class, the teacher promotes a new discussion to recall important ideas and to summarize the work carried out. Therefore, there are several cycles with three different moments – presentation and negotiation of the task, students' autonomous work, and collective discussion.

Getting Involved and Negotiating the Task

As the teacher reads aloud questions 1 and 2, the students start working with no difficulty, folding the strips, and painting the parts that they get. The situation changes when they face the indication to "represent in different ways" which they have great difficulty in interpreting. This leads the teacher to promote a moment of collective discussion to negotiate the meaning of various terms. In question 1, the teacher holds a strip and folds it into two equal parts so that all students can see, thus making an active representation. Then, she draws the strip on the board, representing pictorially the part to consider and then asks students to state what part of the strip is painted. Using the verbal representation, many students say that "half of the strip" is painted. Then, the teacher continues to insist on other ways to represent that part, and from the verbal representation "half," some students suggest the decimal representation "0.5." The teacher asks for other forms of representation and two students indicate the fraction "one of two." Finally, as the students do not indicate any further representation, the teacher questions: "What if I wanted to represent it as a percent? It would be possible?" Immediately, most students say that "it is 50 %." This whole-class discussion represents the first collective negotiation of a part of the first question, which allows the continuation of the work.

Students' Work

The initial discussion helps the students to get an understanding of the situation. They readily engage in working on the remaining points of question 1. The teacher moves around the room, observing the work of the different groups, paying attention to the new discoveries and questions that arise. Taking into account the previous situation, the students do not show difficulty in indicating various representations of $\frac{1}{4}$ of the strip and conclude that $\frac{1}{4} = 0.25$. However, they have noticeable difficulty in finding a decimal representation for $\frac{1}{8}$, because they have trouble finding half of 0.25, showing some insecurity in the use of the decimal number system.

After the students solved question 1, the teacher asks them to stick their responses on the board to present their discoveries to the whole class. Thus, active representations (paper strips) become pictorial representations and are the basis for solving questions 2 and 3. Solving question 2 also requires an explanation of the work to carry out, as students show difficulty understanding what "compare the parts of the three strips that you got by folding" means. The teacher begins by showing the first two strips ($\frac{1}{2}$ and $\frac{1}{4}$) and asks the students to compare them. The visualization leads the students to conclude that $\frac{1}{4}$ is half of $\frac{1}{2}$ and this is the starting point for the group work. Later, in question 3, the teacher also feels the need to help students to understand the statement. As the paper strips have different measures, she chooses to ask them to consider that all measure 20 cm and, from this, the students easily come to recognize some relationships.

Collective Discussions

At the beginning of the whole-class discussion of question 1, to support the participation of students, the teacher asks each group to post their work on the board. Then she asks the first group to present their work to the class. Diana, the spokeswoman, says "In Figure B we wrote: fourth part, 1 by $4\left[\frac{1}{4}\right]$; 1 divided by 4, 25 %, and 0.4."

The students do not realize the error of her colleague when she says "0.4." The teacher decides to go on to the presentation of another group (Fig. 1):

Tiago: So we have: fourth part, one of four $\left[\frac{1}{4}\right]$, 1 divided by 4, 25, and 0.25 %.
Teacher: (…) Do you agree Diana?
Diana: Yes…?
Class: No! That is wrong…
Teacher: What is wrong?
Rui: It's 0.25…
Teacher: Why?
Rui: Because is the fourth part.
Daniel: It is 0.25 because it is a half of the first. The first was 50; if we make half is 25.
André: Oh teacher! I think it is because 0.25 is the fourth part of 100. Because 25 times 4 gives 100.

One must note that after the teacher's question "Why?," several students (Rui, Daniel, André) present successively more refined explanations. Out of the six groups, only that of Diana makes the mistake of "transforming" the denominator of the fraction into a decimal number. The remaining groups obtained the decimal number by comparing the previous value and 100 %.

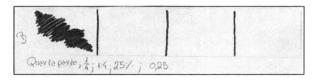

Fig. 1 Solution of question (1a) by Leonor, Rui, Henrique, and Tiago

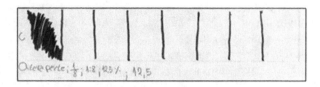

Fig. 2 Solution of the question (1c) by Leonor, Rui, Henrique, and Tiago

In the third strip, all groups correctly use verbal representations, fractions, quotients, and percent. However, in general, they show difficulties in the decimal representation. There are essentially two types of errors. One, as we saw, appeared in Diana's group that writes the decimal numeral by transforming the denominator of the fraction. Another error made by some groups originates in the difficulty in determining one-half of 0.25. The students begin by seeking to determine half of 25 % and get 12.5 %, but they have difficulty in obtaining half of 0.25. The students know that $\frac{1}{4}$ is 0.25, but when making half of 0.25, they get 12.5 (Fig. 2). This result creates a conflict because they believe that it does not make sense, as the half of 0.25 should be a smaller number and, in this case, 12.5 is greater. The students also show difficulty in understanding the decimal number system and do not remember that they may add a zero to get 0.250 and, from there, easily find 0.125.

However, during the discussion of the task, the students get the correct answer:

Daniel: It is 12.5 % because C is half of B.
Teacher: If B is 25 %, is C…
Daniel: It is the half, that is, 12.
Teacher: It is 12 %?
Luís: No teacher, it is 12.5 %. Because 12.5 + 12.5 is 25.
Teacher: So how is it in decimals?
Tiago: It is 0.125.
(…)
André: It is 0.125.
Teacher: Why?
André: It is 0.125 because 0.125 × 8 gives a whole unit.

Tiago indicates the right answer, but it is André that justifies it by establishing the relationship with the unit.

> b) is the half of a).
> c) is the fourth "half" of a)
> a) is twice b).
> a) is four times c).
> c) is half of b)
> b) is twice c).

Fig. 3 Solution of question 4 by André, Francisco, Rodrigo, and Miguel

In question 2, all groups establish some relationships between the parts, but only a few compare all of the strips. All groups use only verbal language to express these relationships. An example is given in Fig. 3.

André's group, besides the simple relationships of "half" and "double," establishes more complex relationships such as "quadruple" (based on the "double of the double") and "fourth part" ("fourth half," as they say, to mean "half of half"). Identical formulations were presented by the Mariana's group. In discussing this question, the teacher asks each group to indicate the relationships that they found. Since the students only use the verbal representation, the teacher asks them to use the mathematics language:

Daniel: The relationship between the first and second is that the second is a half of the first.

Teacher: How can I write that using numbers? How do I make a half?

André: Divide by 2.

Rui: "One of four" is equal to a half divided by two.

André: b is the double of c.

Teacher: How do I write that?

André: One of four is the double.

Teacher: How is it the double?

André: Two times…

Teacher: Two times what?

André: One dash eight.

Teacher: One-eighth. One-fourth is the double of one-eighth.

Alexandre: The first is the double of the second.

Teacher: How do I write that?

Alexandre: One-half is the double of one over four.

One must note that the students use a spontaneous language to speak of fractions ("one of four," "one mark eight"), language that the teacher tries to improve whenever possible.

Notwithstanding several difficulties, the students are able to find the main relationships among $\frac{1}{2}$, $\frac{1}{4}$, and $\frac{1}{8}$ essentially using the strips as active representations. The students are able to compare the three fractions presented by themselves, which aids them in understanding rational numbers, especially in regard to the meaning of part-whole and understanding the magnitude of a rational number. They express these relationships in verbal language and show difficulties in using mathematical

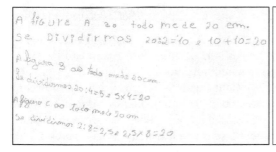

A figure A ao todo mede 20 cm. Se Dividirmos 20:2=10 e 10+10=20 A figura B ao todo mede 20cm Se dividirmos 20:4=5 e 5x4=20 A figura C ao todo mede 20 cm Se dividirmos 2:8=2,5 e 2,5x8=20	Picture A is 20 cm in all. If we divide 20:2=10 and 10+10=20. Picture B is 20 cm in all. If we divide 20:4=5 and 5x4=20. The picture C is 20 cm in all. If we divide 20:8=2.5 and 2.5x8=20

Fig. 4 Solution of question 3 by Carolina, Diana, and Filipe

language. This was the first class where they met this topic in a formal way, so it is natural that they show difficulties with the language of fractions.

Question 3 aims to develop the students' understanding of ratio. To facilitate the solution the teacher provides a "friendly" size for the strip, 20 cm. The students build upon the relationships among the parts of the strip, discussed in the previous question, to find the length of each part, which they represent as shown in Fig. 4.

Although the students were able to establish relationships between the total length of the strips and the length of the parts, they do not use the symbolic representation of a ratio as a fraction. Instead, they express it in verbal language:

Teacher: So let's see what conclusions you reached. What relationship did you found between the length of the strip and the length of the first part?

Luís: The half measures 10 cm. That is, if the strip is 20, the half is 10. That is 20 divided by 2.

Teacher: So, what is the relationship between the length of part and whole?

Several students: It's the half.

We must note the teacher's questioning style in the collective discussion, marked by open questions ("come to explain…," "agree…," "what is wrong?," "why?," "and then what happens to the decimal?"). Note, also, that the classroom culture integrates the notion that the students may contribute with different responses as well as disagree and argue with each other.

Synthesis

In the final synthesis, the teacher poses several questions to summarize the aspects where students showed more difficulty. Thus, referring to question 1, she points to the decimal number system, so that students understand why $0.25:2=0.125$. It is concluded that that fraction bars correspond to the operation of division, in this case, $\frac{1}{8} = 1 : 8 = 0.125$. Based on the students' work, the teacher asks them to state a "rule" for converting a decimal into a percent. The students, analyzing the examples discussed, conclude that they may "move" the decimal two "places" to the right, which the teacher explains as related to a multiplication by 100.

Returning to question 2, some equivalent fractions are analyzed, and it is concluded that a given part may be represented by an infinite number of fractions. The representation of the unit is also discussed and it is concluded that when the numerator and the denominator are the same, there is a unit which we may represent, for example, by $\frac{4}{4} = 1$. A student also verifies that $\frac{4}{8} = \frac{1}{2}$ because 4 is half of 8, leading the class to conclude that there are several fractions that represent the same as $\frac{1}{2}$, all of them with a numerator that is half of the denominator. Although the equivalence of fractions was not explicitly addressed, this was a first move toward this notion. The terms related to fractions (numerator, denominator) and their relationship were also explained, especially in the part-whole meaning. To confirm students' understanding, the teacher asks them to order the three fractions obtained, and they easily indicate that $\frac{1}{2} > \frac{1}{4} > \frac{1}{8}$ and conclude that "as we fold the strip, the parts become increasingly small."

The work on question 3 confirmed that students did not know about fractions, but had an intuition for fraction relationships. Therefore, the teacher used this mainly to collect information and later prepare the approach of the concept of ratio.

Developing Algebraic Thinking

Task and Classroom Organization

The second situation arises from a study aiming to understand how a teaching unit for grade 7, based on the study of patterns, contributes to the development of students' algebraic thinking, particularly for their understanding of variables and equations (Branco 2008). This is consistent with the curriculum recommendations that stress the development of algebraic thinking through promoting students' generalizations and representations (Blanton and Kaput 2005), working with pictorial and numerical sequences, and emphasizing a structural interpretation of equations (Kieran 1992). The task "crossing the river" (adapted from Herbert and Brown 1999) was proposed to students after they had already undertaken some work with pictorial sequences, supporting a first contact with the algebraic language, and before the formal study of equations.

Crossing the River

1. Six adults and two children want to cross a river. The small boat available may only take an adult or one or two children (that is, there are three possibilities: 1 adult in the boat; 1 child in the boat; 2 children in the boat). Any person may conduct the boat. How many trips the boat needs to make, crossing the river, so that everybody is on the order bank?
2. What happens if the river is to be crossed by:

   - 8 adults and 2 children
   - 15 adults and 2 children
   - 3 adults and 2 children

3. Describe in words how you will solve the problem if the group of people is constituted by two children and an unknown number of adults? Verify if your rule works for 100 adults?
4. Write a formula for a number of *A* adults and two children.
5. A group of adults and two children made 27 trips to cross the river. How many adults were in this group?
6. What happens if the number of children changes? In the following examples, verify what changes in your formula:

   - 6 adults and 3 children
   - 6 adults and 4 children
   - 8 adults and 4 children
   - *A* adults and 7 children

The aims of this task are to promote the students' ability to (1) find regularities and generalize them, (2) use and interpret the algebraic language, and (3) analyze how different problem conditions yield different solutions. This section describes and analyzes several episodes of students working on the task and moments of classroom discussion, indicating how the features of the exploratory class were important to promoting their learning.

The students had worked previously with pictorial sequences, formulating generalizations about the underlying rules and representing them algebraically. However, this task involves a new kind of situation. In fact, the task is formulated in natural language and its solution depends on finding an appropriate representation to be able to design a suitable strategy and interpret the results obtained. So, this task provides an opportunity for an exploration activity. First, it requires a careful interpretation of the situation and to carry out simulations satisfying the given conditions (How may an adult pass to the other bank? And a child?). During this exploration, the regularities may be expressed in different representations. The identification of regularities in the movements of adults and children allows students to generalize the situation and to represent it algebraically, as they have done in previous classes. This situation also requires the students to do a careful interpretation of the results that they obtained. The consideration of a fixed number of children and a variable number of adults leads to the exploration of a sequence (1 adult, 2 adults, and so on). The consideration of a variable number of children and a variable number of adults gives rise to a family of sequences, making this exploration even more complex.

As in the previous case, the work on this task involves different patterns of classroom work – with presentation of the task and negotiation of ideas, students' autonomous work (in pairs), and collective discussions. Every moment of autonomous work is followed by a whole-class discussion, in successive cycles. The realization of the task ends with a final synthesis.

Getting Involved and Negotiating the Task

The teacher organizes the students into pairs to discuss the situation among them and to formulate strategies to solve it. As she presents the task, she highlights the conditions given for the trips. The students begin simulating the first trip and discussing various possibilities among their groups. However, the situation appears to be quite confusing and they pose many questions to the teacher regarding the given conditions and presenting hypotheses. This leads to a somewhat agitated environment.

At this point the teacher realizes that a more extended collective discussion is necessary to help the students to understand the conditions of the situation. So, she requests the students' attention and, following the suggestion of a student pair, she asks what happens if, in the first trip, the boat is driven by an adult. The students realize that the first trip must be done by two children in order to allow the boat to return to the starting point, driven by a single child. The teacher asks students to think about who can go on the boat on the subsequent trips. She alerts students that it is sought the minimum number of trips and thus trips back by adults returning with the boat must be avoided.

Students' Work

The students try several possibilities. Some of them create situations where the adult returns with the boat without an adult passing effectively to the other bank. Some student pairs try to put an adult and two children on a trip or an adult and a child. The following dialogue between Diana and the teacher shows how the students at this stage are still struggling to understand the conditions of the problem:

Diana: If the two children go to there, then another comes.
Teacher: Yes. Two go to there and then one stay there and the other comes.
Diana: But an adult cannot go with a child?
Teacher: No. An adult has to go it alone, isn't it?
Diana: I get it. Go two children there, then one comes. Then she stays there and an adult comes.

1 – first crossing 2 children
2 → 1 childreturns
3 → 1 adult goes
4 → 1 child return
5 → 2 children go
6 → 1 child returns
7 → 1 adult goes
8 → 1 child return
9 → 2 children go
10 → 1 child returns
11 → 1 adult goes
12 → 1 child return
13 → 2 children go
14 → 1 child returns
15 → 1 adult goes
16 → 1 child return
17 → 2 children go
18 → 1 child returns
19 → 1 adult goes
20 → 1 child return
21 → 2 children go
22 → 1 child returns
23 → 1 adult goes
24 → 1 child return
25 → In the end 2 children go

Fig. 5 Representation of Beatriz and Andreia's answer for question 1

Teacher: Right.
Diana: Then, the other child comes and goes another adult.
Teacher: Yes. And will stay here two adults. Who will take the boat to there?
Diana: So!?

Diana and Mariana simulate the trips and, like other student pairs, they end up with a correct indication of the first four trips. However, they suggest that the fifth trip is made by an adult, leading to the situation in which an adult returns with the boat. For some time, the students continue their exploration in an autonomous way, closely observed by the teacher. After some time, all student pairs find that the fifth trip must be done again by the two children and keep thinking about the trips required until everyone is on the other bank. The students use different representations. Some describe all trips in natural language (Fig. 5), while others produce schemes or combine iconic and symbolic representations (Fig. 6).

Diana and Mariana identify the regularity in the trips, but they do not indicate the total number of trips and they do not say what happens at the end. These students do not represent 25 trips but only the 4 trips necessary for each adult to cross the river (Fig. 7).

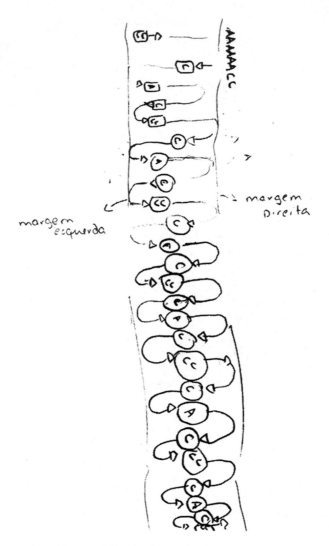

Fig. 6 Representation of Joana and Catarina in question 1

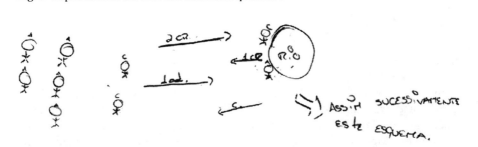

Fig. 7 Representation of Diana and Mariana in question 1 [They write: "Thus this scheme successively"]

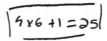

Fig. 8 Representation of the number of trips by Diana and Mariana in question 1

Discussing with the teacher, Diana and Mariana conclude that this set of four trips must be repeated 6 times, with two children staying on the first bank. They find that in addition to the 24 trips, a last trip is necessary to move the two children to the place where the adults are, making a total of 25 trips. They write this in a rather abstract language (Fig. 8).

As the student pairs complete the solution of this first question, the teacher, moving around the room, finds that, although all of the groups found the correct number of trips, some did not identify the pattern of trips required for an adult to change to the other bank.

The students move on to question 2, which involves a constant number of children and a varying number of adults. Having found the regularity in the previous question, the students easily respond to the three points. With 8 adults and 2 children, for example, some students represent the total number of trips by the expression $8 \times 4 + 1 = 33$ showing that they understood the regularity and are able to apply it to new situations. Other students, like Joana and Catarina, give an answer in a mixture of symbolic and natural language: "If there are 8 adults and 2 children, we add 2 sets of 4 trips, so we add 8 trips to 25, $25 + 8 = 33$; therefore, 33 trips are required." These students arrive at their answer starting from the previous situation with 6 adults and 2 children.

Collective Discussions

When most students finish question 2, the teacher promotes a moment of collective discussion to assess their understanding of the situation and contrast their different representations. Some representations enable a quick identification of the pattern of trips, such as those indicated in Figs. 5, 6, and 7. The presentation and discussion of strategies are important for students to understand the situation in a deeper way, clarify meanings, and realize the importance of the efficient use of representations. This discussion also creates the conditions for students to make further generalizations.

In the case of 8 adults and 2 children, Susana shows a rather abstract reasoning when she writes the symbolic expression $8 \times 4 + 1 = 33$. Going to the board, she explains its meaning to her colleagues:

> We make eight adults times the number of trips that they have to do in order to take an adult to the other bank. And we do one more, that is, the number that the children do in returning.

Students' Further Work and Discussions

Based on this discussion and on the conclusions that they reached, the students continue to work autonomously on Questions 3, 4, and 5, which they solve quickly. Question 3 asks that they describe what happens for any number of adults. Most students give their answer in natural language. But some associate natural and symbolic language like Joana and Catarina who say "It is the number of adults × 4 + 1." During the collective discussion of this question, Susana presents her rule to determine the total number of trips, using her own words: "It is the number of adults times the four trips plus a trip of the children." She indicates once more the meaning that she ascribes to the different elements of the expression.

In question 4, when the students write the required expression, they give very concrete meanings to its terms. In the discussion, they present several algebraic expressions, such as $A \times 4 + 1$, $4 \times A + 1$, and $4A + 1$, promoting a discussion about the commutative property of multiplication and the omission of the signal "×." The meanings of terms and coefficients are also discussed – the coefficient 4 is the sequence of 4 trips that is repeated, the term $4A$ indicates the number of trips required for an adult to change to the other bank, and the term 1 represents the last trip made by two children. The teacher asks the students how they can calculate the number of trips for different numbers of adults, using the algebraic expression and taking into account the meaning of the terms and correlation coefficients:

Teacher: If A is equal to 26, what does it mean?
Joana: That there are 26 adults.
Teacher: If A is equal to 26, I say that there are 26 adults. How must I do?
Susana: It is 26 times 4 plus 1.

Question 5 indicates the number of trips and asks the number of adults in the group, without any adults repeating a trip. The students suggest carrying out the inverse operation, but not everyone is clear on what operation should come first. They use an arithmetic approach, which is natural since they had not yet started the study of equations. Some divide 27 by 4 but verify that in such a case it does not make sense to remove the last trip. During the collective discussion, Joana indicates her response "From 27 one subtracts 1 and then divides by 4" and identifies that this cannot be possible because the value of 6.5 is not a natural number. This question allows the discussion of the adequacy of the result and of the response to give taking into account the context and promoting the interpretation of the mathematical result obtained. The teacher proposes the analysis of a new situation that is not indicated in the task: trying to verify whether the students understand and solve it and interpret their results. She questions how many adults are in a group that makes 81 trips, keeping the 2 children. The students show that they understand the Joana's strategy and can use it in new situations.

Question 6 introduces a new issue. The students are asked to explore the influence of variation in the number of children in the number of trips. Analyzing this new situation, they note that this does not change the set of 4 trips needed for an adult to change to the other bank. With two children, beyond the set of four trips per adult, there is a trip at the end to carry a child. If there are three children, they realize that only changes the number of trips at the end but note that it is necessary to make two more trips for the third child to also change the bank. They answer to each situation based on the particular schemes, without establishing a generalization. As some students show difficulty in understanding, the teacher promotes a collective discussion to solve this last question:

Teacher: When I have 2 children, it is this here [$8 \times 4 + 1$]. How many children are missing?
Batista: Two.
Teacher: And how many trips I have to do to get them?
Susana: Four more.
Teacher: Every time I get one more child, it is two trips [conclusion of the previous questions]. If there are 8 adults and 4 children…say, Filipe.
Xico: Eight times four plus one plus four.
Teacher: And now, if you have A adults e 7 children? [No one answers.] For 2 children, the expression is that [$4A + 1$]. But now I don't have two, I have how many more?
Andreia: Five.
Teacher: I'll have five more. How many trips do I have to do for each one?
Diana: Two.
Andreia: Five times two.
Teacher: So, how is it? How do I simplify the expression?
Susana: $4A$ plus…
Diana: Two times five gives ten.
Batista: Eleven.

In the discussion of this last question, the students analyze the influence of changing the number of children in the expression they initially wrote. They note that the sequence of four trips required to put an adult on the other bank is the same and that, besides at the end of the trip carried out by the two children, there are two trips for each additional child.

Synthesis

At the end of the lesson, the pattern identified in the first question is made explicit and the meaning of the algebraic expression that generalizes the situation whatever the number of adults holding two children is revised. The impossibility of simplifying the expression $4A + 1$ is recognized. The students find that this expression is not equivalent to $5A$, both based on the context and in the use of the distributive property. The interpretation of the terms of the expression according to the context is thus remembered by students that identify its importance for a proper analysis of the results obtained in the last two questions. In question 5, the students realize that a given number may be the number of trips made by a group of adults and two children if, after subtracting one to the number obtained, it is divisible by 4. In the last question, the fact one may use the answer to question 1 to understand what happens when the number of children increases, as well as the use of the expression $4A + 1$ to determine the number of trips to A adults and different number of children, is highlighted.

Discussion and Conclusion

The classes that we described based on exploration tasks were aimed at promoting significant learning. In solving the task "folding and folding again" the students use strategies based on visualization and supported on active and pictorial representations. Doing this task, the students develop their ability to recognize and use various types of representations of rational numbers, especially fractions and associated verbal language and recall the percent representation. They also use one-half as a reference point (Post et al. 1986) to relate the different parts of the strip, showing they understand the pattern in question and they use that knowledge to reach other representations without always starting from the unit. Further, they conclude that, as the number of parts increases, the sections become smaller and smaller. Thus, they establish various multiplicative relationships between $\frac{1}{2}$, $\frac{1}{4}$, and $\frac{1}{8}$ which supports them in developing rational number sense. The students recognize multiple representations of rational numbers and state rules to convert decimal numerals into percents, although sometimes they do not apply them in the subsequent questions. They compare rational numbers in various active and pictorial representations and establish simple multiplicative relationships (double, half) and more complex relationships (four times, fourth). They show some sense of equivalent fractions and compare the three presented fractions, although, as expected, they did not come to represent the ratio as a fraction.

The overall results of this teaching experiment (Quaresma 2010) show that students improved their understanding of fractions and percents, as well as of decimals. In addition, they developed their understanding of comparing and ordering rational numbers, using mainly the decimal representation. The understanding that students show of rational numbers, realizing that a rational number can be represented in different ways and showing flexibility in choosing the most appropriate representation with which they can solve the proposed tasks, supports the teaching and learning hypothesis.

The work developed on the task "crossing the river" also reaches the goals set by the teacher. The initial exploration carried out by the students and collective discussions were critical for solving all the questions of the task. This exploitation that arises in an informal way provides the emergence of different representations and leads them to formulate a generalization and, subsequently, to study the situation more formally. In this way, the students rebuild their representations of the situation and make a natural use of letters as variables. The presentation of the findings by the students, using their own words, diagrams, and symbols, allows a better understanding of the situation and the ascribing of meaning to the generalization that they later express in algebraic language. The students also develop the capacity to interpret the algebraic language from their analysis of the different expressions, in particular as regards the use of properties of operations. This interpretation of language algebraic allows them to reason backward to determine the number of adults given the total number of trips. Based on the algebraic expression that gives the total number of trips for a group with A adults and 2 children, $4A + 1$, identify the inverse operations to carry out and the correct order to undertake them. Finally, they analyze the effect of varying the number of adults and children in the number of required number of trips. They generalize this situation by using natural language and mathematical symbols, identifying the need for two trips per child in addition to a group of A adults and 2 children. The moments of autonomous work of student pairs allow them to progress in the interpretation of the situation and in searching for answers and in discussing in detail several opportunities. In the interactions with the students, the teacher poses questions to ascertain students' understanding of the concepts and their ability to use them, as well as to help students' further understanding and mastery of concepts. The collective discussions in an early stage of solving the task help the students to understand the situation, at an intermediate stage allow for the sharing of representations and the identification of regularities so that everyone can get along on the following questions, and at the end favor the systematization of the results and conclusions obtained and the analysis of more complex situations.

The overall results of this teaching experiment (Branco 2008) show that the students developed some aspects of algebraic thinking, including the ability to generalize and use algebraic language to express their generalizations, also supporting the teaching and learning hypothesis. However, the evolution of the students is not equally significant in all domains considered. In problem solving involving equations, they favor arithmetic strategies that do not always prove effective and exhibit some difficulty in using the algebraic language to represent the proposed situations. They show development in the understanding of the algebraic language concerning the different meanings of the symbols in various contexts and the meaning and manipulation of expressions, but in many specific aspects, this understanding is still fragile, suggesting that they have a long way to go in developing their algebraic thinking.

It should be noted that, in addition to the open nature of exploration tasks that require extensive students' effort in interpreting, representing, and simulating cases, such learning also results from the structure of the class and the communication style promoted by the teachers. Both classes were held in cycles composed of moments for presentation and interpretation of tasks, moments of autonomous work in student pairs or groups, and moments of collective discussion. The work was completed with a summary of the main ideas. The communication style promoted by the teachers sought to value the contributions of students, highlighting the arguments and counterarguments they provided. This kind of exploratory class has been increasingly used in Portugal, under the new basic education mathematics curriculum, with a positive influence on students' learning (Ponte 2012).

The situations presented show that the exploration tasks may form the basis of everyday work in the classroom, providing a suitable environment for learning the concepts, representations, and procedures that constitute the core of the mathematics curriculum. Such tasks also constitute a favorable ground for the development of transversal skills such as mathematical reasoning and communication. Unlike other kinds of tasks that tend to assume a peripheral role in teachers' practice, we find that explorations can be naturally integrated into teaching and learning of various mathematical topics. The development of the suitable conditions for implementing them at different educational levels poses interesting challenges to teachers and mathematics educators.

Acknowledgment This work is supported by national funds by FCT – Fundação para a Ciência e Tecnologia – through the project Professional Practices of Mathematics teachers (contract PTDC/ CPE-CED/098931/2008).

References

Bishop, A., & Goffree, F. (1986). Classroom organization and dynamics. In B. Christiansen, A. G. Howson, & M. Otte (Eds.), *Perspectives on mathematics education* (pp. 309–365). Dordrecht: Riedel.

Blanton, M. L., & Kaput, J. J. (2005). Characterizing a classroom practice that promotes algebraic reasoning. *Journal for Research in Mathematics Education, 36*(5), 412–446.

Branco, N. (2008). *O estudo de padrões e regularidades no desenvolvimento do pensamento algébrico,* Dissertação de mestrado, Universidade de Lisboa. Available at: http://repositorio.ul.pt

Brendefur, J., & Frykholm, J. (2000). Promoting mathematical communication in the classroom: Two preservice teachers' conceptions and practices. *Journal of Mathematics Teacher Education, 3,* 125–153.

Bruner, J. (1966). *Toward a theory of instruction.* Cambridge, MA: Harvard University Press.

Cengiz, N., Kline, K., & Grant, T. J. (2011). Extending students' mathematical thinking during whole-group discussions. *Journal of Mathematics Teacher Education, 14,* 355–374.

Christiansen, B., & Walther, G. (1986). Task and activity. In B. Christiansen, A. G. Howson, & M. Otte (Eds.), *Perspectives on mathematics education* (pp. 243–307). Dordrecht: Reidel.

Herbert, K., & Brown, R. (1999). Patterns as tools for algebraic reasoning. In B. Moses (Ed.), *Algebraic thinking, grades K-12* (pp. 123–128). Reston: NCTM.

Kieran, C. (1992). The learning and teaching of school algebra. In D. A. Grouws (Ed.), *Handbook of research on mathematics teaching and learning* (pp. 390–419). New York: Macmillan.

Lampert, M. (1990). When the problem is not the question and the solution is not the answer: Mathematical knowing and teaching. *American Educational Research Journal, 27*(1), 29–63.

Menezes, L., Rodrigues, C., Tavares, F., & Gomes, H. (2008). *Números racionais não negativos: Tarefas para 5.º ano.* Lisboa: DGIDC. Available at: http://repositorio.ul.pt

National Council of Teachers of Mathematics (NCTM). (1980). *An agenda for action.* Reston: NCTM.

National Council of Teachers of Mathematics (NCTM). (2000). *Principles and standards for school mathematics.* Reston: NCTM.

Papert, S. (1972). Teaching children to be mathematicians vs. teaching about mathematics. *International Journal of Mathematical Education and Science Technology, 3*(3), 249–262.

Ponte, J. P. (2005). Gestão curricular em Matemática. In GTI (Ed.), *O professor e o desenvolvimento curricular* (pp. 11–34). Lisboa: APM.

Ponte, J. P. (2012). What is an expert mathematics teacher? In T. Y. Tso (Ed.), *Proceedings of the 36th conference of the international group for the psychology of mathematics education* (Vol. 1, pp. 125–128). Taipei: PME.

Post, T., Behr, M., & Lesh, R. (1986). Research-based observations about children's learning of rational cumber concepts. *Focus on Learning Problems in Mathematics, 8*(1), 39–48.

Quaresma, M. (2010). *Ordenação e comparação de números racionais em diferentes representações: uma experiência de ensino*, Dissertação de mestrado, Universidade de Lisboa. Available at: http://repositorio.ul.pt

Schoenfeld, A. H. (1991). What's all the fuss about problem solving? *ZDM, 91*(1), 4–8.

Skovsmose, O. (2001). Landscapes of investigation. *ZDM, 33*(4), 123–132.

Stein, M. K., Engle, R. A., Smith, M., & Hughes, E. K. (2008). Orchestrating productive mathematical discussions: Five practices for helping teachers move beyond show and tell. *Mathematical Thinking and Learning, 10*, 313–340.

Wood, T. (1999). Creating a context for argument in mathematics class. *Journal for Research in Mathematics Education, 30*(2), 171–191.

The Affordances of Using Visibly Random Groups in a Mathematics Classroom

Peter Liljedahl

Abstract Group work has become a staple in many progressive mathematics classrooms. These groups are often set objectives by the teacher in order to meet specific pedagogical or social goals. These goals, however, are rarely the same as the goals of the students vis-à-vis group work. As such, the strategic setting of groups, either by teachers or by students, is almost guaranteed to create a mismatch of goals. But, what if the setting of groups was left to chance? What if, instead of strategic grouping schemes, the assignment of groups was done randomly? In this chapter, I explore the implementation of just such a strategy and the downstream effects that its implementation had on students, the teacher, and the way in which tasks are used in the classroom. Results indicate that the use of visibly random grouping strategies, along with ubiquitous group work, can lead to: (1) students becoming agreeable to work in any group they are placed in, (2) the elimination of social barriers within the classroom, (3) an increase in the mobility of knowledge between students, (4) a decrease in reliance on the teacher for answers, (5) an increase in the reliance on co-constructed intra- and intergroup answers, and (6) an increase in both enthusiasm for mathematics class and engagement in mathematics tasks.

Keywords Collaboration • Group work • Social barriers • Integration • Mobilization of knowledge • Randomization

P. Liljedahl (✉)
Faculty of Education, Simon Fraser University, 8888 University Drive, Burnaby, BC, Canada
V5A 1S6
e-mail: liljedahl@sfu.ca

Y. Li et al. (eds.), *Transforming Mathematics Instruction: Multiple Approaches and Practices*, Advances in Mathematics Education, DOI 10.1007/978-3-319-04993-9_8,
© Springer International Publishing Switzerland 2014

Introduction

Group work has become a staple in the progressive mathematics classroom (Davidson and Lambdin Kroll 1991; Lubienski 2000). So much so, in fact, that it is rare to not see students sitting together for at least part of a mathematics lesson. In most cases, the formation of groups is either a strategically planned arrangement decided by the teacher or self-selected groups decided by the students—each of which offers different affordances. The strategically arranged classroom allows the teacher to maintain control over who works together and, often more importantly, who doesn't work together. In so doing she constructs, in her mind, an optimal environment for achieving her goals for the lesson. Likewise, if the students are allowed to decide who they will work with, they will invariably make such decisions strategically in the pursuit of achieving their goals for the lesson. In either case, the specific grouping of the students offers different affordances in the attainment of these, often disparate, goals.

But, what if the selection of groups was not made strategically—by either party? What if it was left up to chance—done randomly—with no attention paid to the potential affordances that specific groupings could offer either a teacher or a learner? In this chapter, I explore a different set of affordances that result from the use of randomly assigned collaborative groupings in a high school mathematics classroom.

Group Work

The goals for strategically assigning groups can be broken into two main categories: educational and social (Dweck and Leggett 1988; Hatano 1988; Jansen 2006). Each of these categories can themselves be broken into subcategories as displayed in Fig. 1. When a teacher groups her students for pedagogical reasons, she is doing so because she believes that her specific arrangement will allow students to learn from each other. This may necessitate, in her mind, the need to use homogenous groupings or heterogeneous groupings where the factor that determines homo- or heterogeneous groupings can range from ability to thinking speed to curiosity. When she groups students in order to be productive, she is looking for groupings that lead to the completion of more work. This may, for example, require there to be a strong leader in a group for project work. It may also mean that friends or weak students do not sit together, as such pairings may lead to less productivity. Groupings designed to maintain peace and order in the classroom would prompt the teacher to not put "troublemakers" together, as their antics may be disruptive to the other learners in the class.[1] Interestingly, students may self-select themselves into

---

[1] From a researcher's perspective, each of these goals, and the accompanying use of group work, may be predicated on an underlying theory of learning and the role that peer interaction plays in said theory. From the teacher's perspective, however, these decisions are less likely to be made based on theory and more likely to be made according to what they believe about the teaching and learning of mathematics in coordination with their beliefs about the utility of group work (Liljedahl 2008).

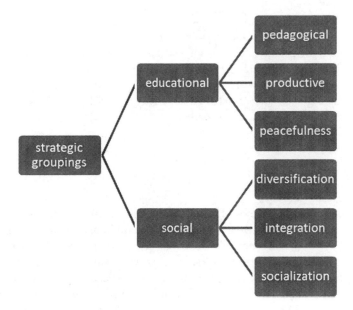

Fig. 1 Goals for strategic groupings

groupings for the same aforementioned reasons (Cobb et al. 1992; Webb et al. 2006; Yackel and Cobb 1996).

More commonly, however, students group themselves for social reasons (Urdan and Maehr 1995)—specifically to socialize with their friends. Teachers too sometimes form their groups to satisfy social goals. They may feel that a particular group of students should work together specifically because of the diversity that they bring to a setting. Sometimes, this is simply to force a gender mix onto the collaborative setting. Other times, it is more complex and involves trying to get students out of their comfort zone, to collaborate with, and get to know, students they don't normally associate with. A teacher may choose to create a specific grouping to force the integration of an individual student into a group that they are not yet a part of—for example, the integration of an international student into a group of domestic students. Finally, and less likely, a teacher may specifically wish for their students to work with their friends—often as a reward for positive performance or behaviour in the classroom.

Regardless of the goals chosen, however, there is often a mismatch between the goals of the students and the goals of the teacher (Kotsopoulos 2007; Slavin 1996). For example, whereas a teacher may wish for the students to work together for pedagogical reasons, the students, wishing instead to work with their friends, may begrudgingly work in their assigned groups in ways that cannot be considered collaborative (Clarke and Xu 2008; Esmonde 2009). These sorts of mismatches arise from the tension between the individual goals of students concerned with themselves, or their cadre of friends, and the classroom goals set by the teacher for everyone in the room. Couple this with the social barriers present in classrooms and a teacher may be faced with a situation where students not only wish to be with certain classmates but also disdain to be with others. In essence, the diversity of potential goals for group work and the mismatch between educational and social goals in a classroom almost ensures that, no matter how strategic a teacher is in her groupings, some students will be unhappy in the failure of that grouping to meet their individual goals. How to fix this? One way would be to remove *any* and *all* efforts to be strategic in how groups are set.

Random Groupings

Over the last 6 years, I have done research in a number of classrooms where I have encouraged the teachers to make group work ubiquitous, where new groups are assigned every class, and where the assignment of these groups is done randomly. In every one of these classrooms, the lesson begins with the teacher generating random groups for the day. The specific method for doing this varies from teacher to teacher. Some give out playing cards and have students group themselves according to the rank of the card they have drawn. Others have students assigned a permanent number and then draw groups of three or four numbered popsicle sticks or numbered disks randomly from a jar. In other classes, the students watch the teacher randomly populate a grid with numbers wherein each row of the grid then forms a group. One teacher I worked with had this grid placement done automatically by a program displayed on an interactive whiteboard. Another teacher I worked with had laminated photographs of all of the students and distributed these into groups by shuffling and then randomly drawing three or four photos at a time. Regardless of the particulars of the method, however, the norm that was established in each of the classes that I worked in was that the establishment of groups at the beginning of class was not only random, but visibly random. Once in groups, students were then universally assigned tasks to work on, either at their tables or on the whiteboards around the room. The students stayed in these groups throughout the lesson, even if the teacher was leading a discussion, giving instructions, or demonstrating mathematics.

Although often met with resistance in the beginning, within 3–4 weeks of implementation, this approach has consistently led to a number of easily observable changes within the classroom:

- Students become agreeable to work in any group they are placed in.
- There is an elimination of social barriers within the classroom.
- Mobility of knowledge between students increases.
- Reliance on the teacher for answers decreases.
- Reliance on co-constructed intra- and intergroup answers increases.
- Engagement in classroom tasks increases.
- Students become more enthusiastic about mathematics class.

Ironically, these are often the exact affordances that teachers' strategic groupings of students are meant, but often fail, to achieve. How is this possible? What is it about the use of visibly random groups that allows this to happen? Drawing on data from one classroom, this chapter looks more closely at these aforementioned observed changes as well as what it is about visibly random groupings that occasion these changes.

Methodology

The data for this study was collected in a grade 10 (ages 15–16) mathematics classroom in an upper-middle-class neighbourhood in western Canada. The students in the class were reflective of the ethnic diversity that exists within the school at large. Although there are students from many different cultures and backgrounds in the school, and the class, the majority of students (>90 %) are either first- or second-generation immigrants from China or Caucasian Canadians whose families have been in Canada for many generations. These two dominant subgroups are almost equal in representation. This, almost bimodal, diversity is relevant to the discussion that will be presented later.

The classroom teacher, Ms. Carley (a pseudonym), has 8 years of teaching experience, the last six of which have been at this school. In the school year that this study took place, Ms. Carley decided to join a district run learning team facilitated by me. This particular learning team was organized around the topic of group work in the classroom. As the facilitator, I encouraged each of the 13 members of the learning team to start using visibly random groups on a daily basis with their classes. Ms. Carley had joined the team because she was dissatisfied with the results of group work in her teaching. She knew that group work was important to learning but, until now, had felt that her efforts in this regard had been unsuccessful. She was looking for a better way, so when I suggested to the group that they try using visibly random groups, she made an immediate commitment to start using this method in one of her classrooms. This, in turn, prompted me to conduct my research in her class.

The data was collected over the course of a 3-month period of time from the beginning of February to the end of April. The time frame is significant because it highlights that this was not something that was implemented at the beginning of a school year when classroom norms (Yackel and Cobb 1996) are yet to be established and students are more malleable. The fact that the change occurred mid-year allowed me the unique opportunity to compare classroom discourse, norms, and patterns of participation before and after implementation. Initially, I was present for every class. This included three classes prior to implementation as well as the first 3 weeks (eight classes) after initial implementation. After this, I attended the classes every 2 or 3 weeks until the end of the project.

I became a regular fixture in the classroom and acted not only as an observer but also as a participant (Eisenhart 1988), interacting with the students in their groups and on the tasks set by the teacher. The data consists of field notes from these observations, interactions, and conversations with students during class time interviews with Ms. Carley and interviews with select students. Interviews were conducted outside of class time and audio recorded. Over the course of the study, Ms. Carley was interviewed, if only briefly, after every observed lesson. During this time frame, 12 students were also interviewed, with two of them being interviewed twice. These data were coded and analysed using the principles of analytic induction (Patton 2002). "[A]nalytic induction, in contrast to grounded theory, begins with an analyst's deduced propositions or theory-derived hypotheses and is a procedure for verifying theories and propositions based on qualitative data" (Taylor and Bogdan 1984, p. 127 cited in Patton 2002, p. 454). In this case, the a priori proposition was that the changes that I had observed in other classrooms were linked to the use of a visibly random grouping scheme. This proposition became the impetus for the collection of data in that it drove what I was looking for and how I was looking. It became the lens for my observations and it motivated my interview questions. It also pre-seeded the themes that I was looking for in the coding of the data.

This is not to say that my data collection and analysis were blind to the emergence of new themes. As a participant/observer in the classroom, I was aware of, and deliberately looking at, a great many things going on around me. During the coding and analysis of the data, I was looking for nuances in the relationship between visibly random grouping schemes and the changes I had observed. So, despite the fact that I had a priori themes in mind, I still coded the data using a constant comparative method (Creswell 2008). This recursive coding allowed for the emergence of not only nuanced themes but also new themes.

Results and Discussion

Similar to the other classes wherein I have observed the implementation of random grouping schemes, Ms. Carley's class exhibited the same observable changes. In what follows, I explore each of these changes more thoroughly, illuminating the nuances of each with results from the data.

Students Become Agreeable to Work in Any Group They Are Placed In

Group work is not something that is foreign to the students in Ms. Carley's class. From time to time, she allows the students to sit in pairs or threes to work on their homework, and the class had already done one group project on graphing where the students were allowed to self-select who they worked with. When Ms. Carley decided to implement a more ubiquitous approach to group work in general and the use of random groups in particular, she chose to use a standard deck of playing cards to generate the groups. She had 30 students in the class and she had decided to have the students work in groups of three. So, she selected from the deck 3 cards of each rank (ace—ten). These were shuffled and then the students were allowed to each select one card. Although she experimented with the number of students per group, and had to make adjustments based on absences, this is a grouping scheme that she stayed with for the duration of the study.

On the first day, the students were not told what was going on but just presented with the cards as described. Later, I learned that many of the students had thought that "it was a magic trick". When every student had a card, Ms. Carley announced that these would be the groups that they would be working in and assigned a "station" for each group depending on their card. This was an interesting time. Many of the students went dutifully to their stations. However, there were a few students who I observed were trying to fix it so that they were with their friends. I will elaborate on two of these cases in particular.

Hunter, despite his card, went directly to the station where his friend Jackson was sitting. This did not go unnoticed as Ms. Carley immediately noticed that this group now had four members instead of three. When she dealt with this she immediately challenged Hunter to see his card. When I asked her about this later she said that "it had to be Hunter. It is always Hunter. He is a bit of a scammer and he likes to be with Jackson". In the flurry of the first few minutes of class, Ms. Carley had to perform a similar check on one other group of four.

Unnoticed by Ms. Carley, however, was the situation that unfolded immediately in front of me. Jasmine approached a group of three and took the card out of one of the group members' hand replacing it with her own card and said, "you're over there", gesturing towards one of the corners of the room. From my initial observations of the class and my conversations with Ms. Carley, I knew that Kim, Samantha, and Jasmine are very close friends, are part of the "in" crowd within their grade, and tend to stick very close together during free time and when allowed in their other classes. The group that Jasmine approached had Samantha in it.

In general, this sort of jockeying behaviour was observed for the first three classes after implementation. Hunter did try it again but Ms. Carley intervened even before he got to Jackson, and on the third day, Hunter and Jackson legitimately ended up together—much to the chagrin of Ms. Carley. Jasmine, however, was successful each time she tried to switch groups using the same strategy. After the first week, however, the behaviour stopped for both Hunter and Jasmine. At this point, I interviewed both Hunter and Jasmine about their antics:

Researcher So, I noticed that last week you tried a few times to sit with Jackson. Are you still trying to do so?
Hunter   No.
Researcher Why not?
Hunter   At first I thought that the teacher was trying to keep us apart. Then, on Friday, we got to work together.
Researcher So, do you still think the teacher is trying to keep you apart?
Hunter   No. I don't think she likes us working together, but when the cards came up the way they did she didn't change it. I guess it's up to the cards now.
Researcher I saw what you did last week.

Jasmine	What do you mean?
Researcher	I saw how you switched groups.
Jasmine	Oh that. That's nothing.
Researcher	But you didn't do it this week. Why not?
Jasmine	I guess it doesn't matter so much. I mean, it is just for one class and then the groups change again.
Researcher	What does that have to do with it?
Jasmine	At first I was worried that I was going to be stuck with that group for a long time, like when we worked on the project or in my other classes.
Researcher	What happens in the other classes?
Jasmine	My English teacher changes the seating plan every month and then you're stuck there forever.

For Hunter, the defining quality of Ms. Carley's grouping scheme was the random nature of it. Once he came to see that it was both random and that the random outcomes would be respected, he became more relaxed about it. For Jasmine, however, the defining quality was the short-term commitment that the grouping strategy demanded. When I had first observed Jasmine's antics, I had assumed that it had to do with trying to be close to her friends when, in reality, she was trying to avoid being "stuck" with a group she didn't like. Once she became confident that the groups were temporary, she stopped trying to manipulate the groups.

I also interviewed Jennifer in the third week after implementation. I selected Jennifer because she had shown no overt objections to the grouping schemes used in the class:

Researcher	I'm wondering what you think about all this grouping stuff that is going on.
Jennifer	It's ok I guess. It doesn't matter what I think though, it looks like it's here to stay.
Researcher	What do you mean by "it's here to stay"?
Jennifer	Well, when the teacher started class last Monday, the same way I knew that this is the way it was going to be. When she started class today [Monday of the third week], I was sure of it.

Jennifer's observation coincides perfectly with the subsiding of any residual visible opposition to the random groupings. Although she was not overtly opposed to the groupings in the first week, her mention of the practice continuing in the second and third weeks and how that was a sign that "it's here to stay" indicates a resignation to the new classroom norm (Yackel and Cobb 1996) that is likely shared by many of her peers. This is a different phenomenon from Hunter, who saw the randomness in the cards, or Jasmine, who focused on the temporariness in each grouping. These three themes occurred and reoccurred in many of the conversations I overheard, conversations I was part of, and in interviews. Sometimes they occurred in isolation as in the excerpts presented above. Other times they were present in combination with each other.

More interestingly, resignation to a new norm became the only thing commented on by the third week. That is, regardless of what the students thought about the introduction of visibly random groups, the residual effect was that "it is how we do things in this class". Even in the last week of the study when I asked specific students to recall the early days of the use of the playing cards, their recollections of it were that it was just the introduction of a new way to do things. That is, although the randomization being visible, the cards being respected, and the groups being only for one class were of great importance in the first weeks, what endured to the end was just the norm. This is in alignment with Yackel and Cobb's (1996) observation that norms are not something that are imposed on a class, but are negotiated between the teacher and the students. The grouping scheme being visibly random and the groups being only for one period were important elements in these negotiations.

There Is an Elimination of Social Barriers Within the Classroom

As mentioned earlier, there is an almost bimodal diversity in both the class and the school where the study took place. My observations of this "split" are exemplified in the conversations that I had with Ms. Carley prior to her implementation of random groups:

Researcher   Can you think of any problematic situations that you think will prevent this [random groupings] from being successful?
Ms. Carley   The obvious one is the split between the Asian and Caucasian students.
Researcher   What do you mean *split*?
Ms. Carley   It's almost as though we have two distinct cultures in this school with almost no overlap. The Caucasian students have their own social groupings, not all together. And the Asian students have their own. And there is almost no mixing between the two. In fact, it's almost as though they aren't even aware of each other.
Researcher   I have noticed that. Is that normal you think?
Ms. Carley   I don't know about normal but it is certainly not unique to this school. I have a good friend who teaches in Surrey and she has seen the same thing but with different groups of students. We talk about it often and what we can do about it.

What Ms. Carley describes is a situation that is easily observable in both the hallways and in the classroom. When Ms. Carley allowed the students to self-select who they wanted to work with, the selections were always guided by this "split". This is not to say that there were any racial tensions in the group. I observed no evidence of dislike or disdain for each other. It really was just as Ms. Carley had described—two distinct social groupings. We both saw this as a formidable challenge and were simultaneously anxious and hopeful about how the random groupings would play out.

It is quite possible that some of Jasmine's antics (described in the previous section) were motivated by this social dichotomy. On both the first and second day of implementation, she was randomly assigned to a group that had two Asian students in them. The second time that she "stole" someone else's card, she took it from the sole Asian girl in the group where she wanted to be in. But, as stated in the previous section, these sorts of behaviours by Jasmine and others in the class ceased after the first 2 weeks of implementation as the students settled into the new norm. This is not to say that the social divide had disappeared yet.

After 3 weeks of implementing visibly random groups, some interesting phenomena began to emerge. Whereas in the first few days after implementation there was an awkwardness present in the first few minutes of group work, now there was an "at ease*ness*" about the way the students came together. This was more than comfort with a process, however. It was more akin to a familiarity between students. This can be seen in the interview with Melanie:

Researcher	Tell me about how your group work went today?
Melanie	Fine.
Researcher	Who were you with?
Melanie	I was with Sam and … um … the guy … I don't know his name.
Researcher	Frank?
Melanie	That's it. Frank!
Researcher	Can you tell me a little bit about Sam and Frank?
Melanie	Ok. Sam is smart. I worked with her one time before. She really knows what is going on so I try to listen carefully to her when she has something to say. She's in my Science class as well and her sister is in my English class.
Researcher	How do you know that Sam's sister is in your English class.
Melanie	Sam told me today.
Researcher	What about Frank?
Melanie	I don't know Frank that well, but my friend worked with him last week and he said that Frank is a really nice guy.

To help orient this conversation, it is useful to know that Melanie is Caucasian and that both Sam and Frank are Asian. What is remarkable about this is that there is an awareness about each other that is forming. Sam is aware that Melanie is in her sister's English class and Melanie is aware that her friend worked with Frank last week. These are both strong indicators that the two groups are now seeing each other—aware of each other—in a way that Ms. Carley (and I) had observed was not happening prior to implementation. Further, Melanie's interview reveals that the two groups are not only talking to each other, they are talking about each other.

This is not to say that race was the only social barrier at play within this classroom prior to implementation. As in any school, there was also a more subtle, but very real, social hierarchy at play. There were students who were "in" and students who were "out". As already mentioned, Jasmine, Kim, and Samantha were part of the "in" crowd. Prior to implementation they always sat together, and as seen, Jasmine worked hard to maintain this together*ness* at initial implementation. For Jasmine, this was eased by the realization that the groups were short-lived. For Samantha, it was eased by the fact that the nature of the group work had changed:

Researcher   It's been six weeks now since Ms. Carley started moving you around. What do you think about it?
Samantha   It's ok.
Researcher   I know that you used to like to sit with Jasmine and Kim a lot. How is it being away from them?
Samantha   I'm not away from them. I still see them all the time and I did sit with Kim and Charles the other day. But it's different now. Before we would just sit and talk. Now we are working on stuff at the boards and stuff. There isn't a lot of time to just socialize anyway.
Researcher   How do you think Jasmine and Kim feel?
Samantha   Jasmine is ok with it now. She wasn't at first. And Kim never cared. She is really easy going.

It is obvious from this transcript that Kim is also at ease, and always was, with the random grouping scheme. More subtle, however, is the mention of Charles. Charles is an Asian boy definitely not in the "in" crowd. I'm pretty sure that prior to implementation Samantha did not know his name. Now she mentions him in passing. This points to what I was observing at this point in the study—Ms. Carley's class had jelled into a cohesive whole, absent of any social divides.

There is a lot to be seen and to be discussed in regard to the breaking down of social barriers, both racial and non-racial, and my naïve treatment of it is not meant to diminish the rich traditions of such research (c.f. DeVries et al. 1978). I merely wanted to highlight the role that the visibly random grouping scheme played in the breaking down of some of these barriers.

Mobility of Knowledge Between Students Increases

As mentioned, prior to implementation, group work in Ms. Carley's class was something students did as they worked on their homework or on a project. After implementation, group work became ubiquitous. The main activity in these groups was to work through a series of tasks that Ms. Carley set during her lessons. These were originally "try this one" tasks that followed direct instruction. But as the study went on, Ms. Carley began to also use tasks as a way to initiate discussions. The tasks also became more challenging, requiring the students to do more than just mimic the examples already presented on the boards. This "ramping up" of the use of tasks was accompanied by a number of easily observable changes in the way in which the groups worked, with the most obvious of which was the way in which the knowledge moved around the room.

Immediately after implementation, group work looked very much like it did prior to implementation—the students worked largely independent of each other, interacting only to check their answers with their group members or to ask one or another to explain how to do something. After 4 weeks, however, group work looked very different. Students now spent almost no time working independently. Instead, they spent their time working collaboratively on the tasks set by Ms. Carley. This collaboration consisted of discussion, debate, and the sharing and demonstration of ideas. In part this was due, of course, to the increasing demand and frequency of the tasks set by the teacher. But it was also due to the coalescing of the groups into collaborative entities:

Researcher So, the students seem to be working well together.

Ms. Carley Yes ... I'm still amazed at exactly how well.

Researcher We've talked a lot about the tasks you are using and how you are using them. Do you think the tasks are responsible for the group work we are seeing now?

Ms. Carley You know, I've thought a lot about that lately. At first I thought it was all due to the tasks. In fact, I was talking to a colleague who was asking about my class. She was asking for a copy of the tasks so she could start using them with her students and that's when I realized that it's sort of a chicken and egg thing. If we spring the tasks on the students before they know how to work in groups, then it won't work. At the same time, if we try to teach them how to work in groups without having something to work on, then it won't work either.

Researcher So, how did you manage it in this class? What came first?

Ms. Carley I think the random groups came first. That broke the mould on what group work had looked like in the past and gave me room to introduce a new way of working.

Ms. Carley's synopsis aligns well with my observations. Prior to implementation, group work had a well-defined set of actions and behaviours associated with it. These norms were not conducive to the collaborative skills and affordances necessary to increase the demand on students vis-à-vis the ubiquitous use of tasks. The introduction of random groups into the classroom shattered the existing norm and allowed for a new set of classroom norms to be established that were more conducive to collaboration.

The collaboration now visible in the room went beyond the intra-group activity, however. Intergroup collaboration also became a natural and anticipated part of every class. This often took one of three forms: (1) members of a group going out to other groups to "borrow an idea" to bring back to their group, (2) members of a group going out to compare their answer to other answers, (3) two (or more) groups coming together to debate different solution or a combination of these as exemplified in my observations of Kevin's group in week four of the study:

Researcher Good problem today, huh? I didn't get a chance to sit with you today. Can you tell me how you guys solved it?

Kevin   Yeah, that was a tough one. We were stuck for a long time.

Researcher We were too [referring to the group I was working with]. What did you eventually figure out?

Kevin   Well, we saw that the group next to us was using a table to check out some possibilities and we could see that there was a pattern in the numbers they were using so we tried that. That sort of got us going and we got an answer pretty quickly after that.

Researcher   Was it the right answer?

Kevin   It was, but we weren't so sure. The group next to us had a different answer and it took a long time working with them before we figured out which one was correct.

Kevin's recollection of the day's activities is reflective of what I observed between these two groups and, in fact, many groups on a daily basis. When I asked Sam (who was in the other group) about this, she had some interesting insights about why this coming together of the two groups worked so seamlessly:

Researcher   Your group worked pretty closely with another group today. How did you feel about the fact that they copied from you?

Sam   Did they? I didn't notice. But it isn't really copying. We are all just working together.

Researcher   In other classes I have been in, I don't see that happening. You know, groups sharing with each other.

Sam   That's probably because they don't work together as much as we have. I mean, we are always together with different people. I think I have worked with everyone in this room now. If you asked me who I worked with yesterday I'm not sure I could tell you. And if you asked the teacher to tell you who was in which group today, I don't think she could tell you either. When we were trying to figure out which answer was correct, we were like one big group.

What Sam is describing is what I have come to call the *porosity* of groups. Although group boundaries are defined for the period, these boundaries are clearly temporary and arbitrary. This allows for them to also be seen as open and allowing for the free movement of members from one group to another to extend the collaborative reach of the group. When asked about this, many students mention that they feel that they are free to move around the room as necessary to "get the job done".

Along with this mobility of groups and group members comes *mobility of knowledge*— the movement of ideas, solution strategies, and solutions around the room. In fact, it is the need to move knowledge that prompts the movement of individuals as they go out "to borrow an idea". The free and easy mobility of knowledge results in a marked decrease in the students' reliance on the teacher as the knower:

Researcher   Have you noticed anything else that has changed over the last five weeks?

Ms. Carley   I've noticed that I'm not answering as many questions anymore.

Researcher   Are you not answering them or are you not being asked them?

Ms. Carley   Both, I think. I know there was a point where I was deliberately trying to not answer questions, trying to push the students back into the groups to figure it out. But now that is not a problem. They just don't ask me questions as much anymore. It's like that chicken and egg thing again.

Similar to the relationship between the use of random groups and the use of more challenging tasks, the relationship between the teacher not answering questions and the students not asking questions seems to be in some sort of symbiosis. That is, in order for the group work to become effective and meaningful, the teacher needs to stop answering questions and, as the group work becomes effective and meaningful, the students stop needing to ask questions. Ms. Carley's class has become a collective making use of both intra- and inter-group collaborations.

This is not to say that the role of the teacher is diminished. Ms. Carley still sets the tasks, the groups, and the expectations. More importantly, however, she monitors the flow of knowledge around the room:

Researcher I noticed that you were forcing some groups together today. What were you trying to achieve?

Ms. Carley It depends. Sometimes I am trying to crash ideas together. Other times I am trying to help a group get unstuck. Which groups do you mean?

Researcher I mean when you sent one whole group from over there to over here.

Ms. Carley Ah. Well, that group over there had gotten an answer pretty quickly. As it turned out, it was the right answer, but I didn't think they had done enough work checking their answer so I sent them over to that group to shake their confidence a little bit.

Researcher How so?

Ms. Carley Well, that group had a different answer and that would force the two groups to figure out what was going on.

Not only is Ms. Carley monitoring the flow of knowledge in the room, she is manipulating it—forcing it to move in certain directions and moving it for a variety of different reasons. In so doing, her role in the classroom has changed.

Researcher So, how are you liking your classroom these days?

Ms. Carley I'm loving it. I feel like the students are completely different. I'm completely different. It's like I have a new job and its WAY better than my old one.

Students Become More Enthusiastic About Mathematics Class

Ms. Carley is not the only one who is enjoying her new role, however. Many of the students I either talked to as part of my classroom participation or in interviews alluded to the fact that Ms. Carley's mathematics class is *now* an enjoyable place to be:

Frank I like this class *now*.

James Math is *now* my favourite subject.

In the fifth week of the study, I spoke with Jasmine about how she was enjoying this class:

Researcher	So, it's been a while since that day where you were trying to switch groups. How are you enjoying things now?
Jasmine	I love this class. I mean, math isn't my favourite subject. But I love coming here.
Researcher	Why is that? What is it about this class that you love?
Jasmine	I'm never bored. There is always something going on and time passes so quickly.
Researcher	I looked at Ms. Carley's attendance book. For the last four weeks, you have never missed a class or even been late. I only looked at four weeks, what would I have seen if I looked further back?
Jasmine	You would have seen some absences and lots of lates. I mean, it's not like I skipped class. I don't skip. It's just that there were reasons to be away. I guess I now try not to let there be reasons.
Researcher	What about lates?
Jasmine	I'm often late for my classes. Not just math.
Researcher	But you haven't been late at all lately.
Jasmine	Hmm … I guess I don't want to be.

Jasmine didn't like mathematics the subject, but she loved mathematics the class. The changes that had occurred, which began with the random groupings, had transformed the Ms. Carley's class into something that she didn't want to miss out on.

This was a trend that I observed in many students. In terms of attendance, absences and lates were down across the board. Prior to implementation, Ms. Carley had an average of 3.2 absences per class and an average of 6.7 lates per class. Between week 4 and week 7 after implementation, the averages were 1.6 and 2.2, respectively. Ms. Carley's class became a place where students wanted to be. Conversations with other students echoed Jasmine's sentiments. In my conversations with Chad, Stacey, and Kendra, I decided to push a little further by asking them to draw comparisons:

Researcher	So, how is this class different from other classes?
Stacey	I like this one.
Researcher	Ha … do you not like other classes?
Stacey	I do. But not like this one. This one is way more dynamic. We are always doing something new and …
Kendra	And the beginning of every class is a bit of an adventure when we get to find out who we work with.
Researcher	It's been six weeks. Hasn't it gotten old yet … the thing with the random groups?
Chad	No. It's still fun.
Researcher	I want to continue with Stacey's comments. In what ways is this class different from other classes?

Chad   Hmm ... we need to think in this class. There really is no other way
              around it. In other classes, you can sort of just tune out, but not in here.
Kendra   And you have to collaborate. There is no way I could get by just doing
              it on my own, even if Ms. Carley would let us.
Researcher   It sounds like a lot of hard work.
Stacey   It is, but in a good way. I mean, like I'm never bored.

These comments speak not just to enjoyment but also engagement. The students need to be engaged in Ms. Carley's class and they seem to enjoy this engagement. The comments of these students confirm what both Ms. Carley and I had observed in the class as a whole.

Researcher   So, what do you think? How is it going?
Ms. Carley   My sense is that it is going really well. This week all of the students really
              seem to be into it. Everyone shows up ready to go, and then we go. There
              are no complaints, everyone is smiling, and we get a lot done.

Conclusions

I stated at the outset that the changes that I observed in Ms. Carley's class are reflective of the changes I had seen in many of the other classes in which I had been privileged to participate as teachers made the decision to start using visibly random grouping schemes. But, in the past, these had just been observations. My more focused approach to studying Ms. Carley's class confirmed my prior (and subsequent) observations and also informed and enlightened them. As in the other classroom, I had observed that the introduction of random groupings was pivotal in producing broad changes in the classroom. However, these changes were more than just changes to the way the class was run. The introduction of random groupings led to, and allowed for, changes in the students, the teacher, and what was possible in this new setting.

The students became open to working with anyone. The social barriers that existed in the classroom came down and the classroom became a collaborative entity that was not defined by, or confined to, the boundaries set by the teacher. As these barriers came down and the class coalesced into a community, their reliance on the teacher as the knower diminished and their reliance on themselves and each other increased. Their enjoyment of mathematics (the class, if not necessarily the subject) increased as well as their engagement.

Figure 1 (above) showed how neatly the strategic educational and social goals could be partitioned. When nonstrategic grouping methods were used, the resulting behaviours cannot be so easily partitioned into educational and social affordances. For example, the increased mobility of knowledge is a direct result from the students' increased reliance on intra- and intergroup generated results. However, this cannot be separated out from the fact that social barriers in the room have come down. Taken together, the data showed that the use of visibly

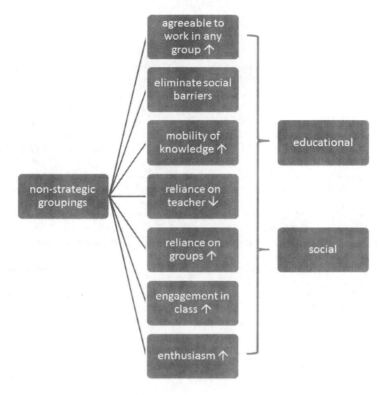

Fig. 2 Results of nonstrategic groupings

random groupings produces student behaviour that can be seen as being both educational and social in nature (see Fig. 2). As such, the nonstrategic use of visibly random groupings turned out to be a better strategy than the aforementioned strategic grouping schemes.

Student change aside, Ms. Carley altered the way she used tasks as well as the way she answered questions. She found that she no longer needed to be the knower or the teller in the room. She changed the timing and the method of her direct instruction, and she began to rely much more on her ability to manipulate groups and move ideas around the room. Tasks, too, took on a new life in the class. Their role changed from "try this one" to objects around which group work was organized. They increased in frequency and difficulty, and they became the objects and objectives of lessons.

The introduction of visibly random groupings was the impetus that both allowed for and necessitated the many other changes that I observed. Through the renegotiation of classroom norms (Yackel and Cobb 1996), the students could not continue to behave as they had earlier, Ms. Carley could not continue being the same teacher she had been prior to implementation, and tasks could not have avoided evolving. Change begot change.

References

Clarke, D., & Xu, L. (2008). Distinguishing between mathematics classrooms in Australia, China, Japan, Korea and the USA through the lens of the distribution of responsibility for knowledge generation: Public oral interactivity and mathematical orality. *ZDM, 40*(6), 963–972.

Cobb, P., Wood, T., Yackel, E., & McNeal, B. (1992). Characteristics of classroom mathematics traditions: An interactional analysis. *American Educational Research Journal, 29*(3), 573–604.

Creswell, J. W. (2008). *Educational research: Planning, conducting, and evaluating quantitative and qualitative research* (3rd ed.). Upper Saddle River: Pearson Education, Inc.

Davidson, N., & Lambdin Kroll, D. (1991). An overview of research on cooperative learning related to mathematics. *Journal of Research in Mathematics Education, 22*(5), 362–365.

DeVries, D., Edwards, K., & Slavin, R. (1978). Biracial learning teams and race relations in the classroom: Four field experiments using Teams-Games-Tournament. *Journal of Educational Psychology, 70*(3), 356–362.

Dweck, C. S., & Leggett, E. L. (1988). A social-cognitive approach to motivation and personality. *Psychological Review, 95*, 256–273.

Eisenhart, M. A. (1988). The ethnographic research tradition and mathematics research. *Journal for Research in Mathematics Education, 19*(2), 99–114.

Esmonde, I. (2009). Mathematics learning in groups: Analyzing equity in two cooperative activity structures. *Journal of the Learning Sciences, 18*(2), 247–284.

Hatano, G. (1988). Social and motivational bases for mathematical understanding. *New Directions for Child Development, 41*, 55–70.

Jansen, A. (2006). Seventh graders' motivations for participating in two discussion-oriented mathematics classrooms. *Elementary School Journal, 106*(5), 409–428.

Kotsopoulos, D. (2007). Investigating peer as "expert other" during small group collaborations in mathematics. In *Proceedings of the 29th annual meeting of the North American Chapter of the International Group for the Psychology of Mathematics Education*. Lake Tahoe: University of Nevada, Reno.

Liljedahl, P. (2008). Teachers' insights into the relationship between beliefs and practice. In J. Maaß & W. Schlöglmann (Eds.), *Beliefs and attitudes in mathematics education: New research results* (pp. 33–44). Rotterdam: Sense Publishers.

Lubienski, S. T. (2000). Problem solving as a means towards mathematics for all: An exploratory look through a class lens. *Journal for Research in Mathematics Education, 31*(4), 454–482.

Patton, M. Q. (2002). *Qualitative research and evaluation methods*. Thousand Oaks: Sage.

Slavin, R. E. (1996). Research on cooperative learning and achievement: What we know, what we need to know. *Contemporary Educational Psychology, 21*, 43–69.

Urdan, T., & Maehr, M. (1995). Beyond a two-goal theory of motivation and achievement: A case for social goals. *Review of Educational Research, 65*(3), 213–243.

Webb, N. M., Nemer, K. M., & Ing, M. (2006). Small-group reflections: Parallels between Carley discourse and student behavior in peer-directed groups. *Journal of the Learning Sciences, 15*(1), 63–119.

Yackel, E., & Cobb, P. (1996). Sociomathematical norms, argumentation, and autonomy in mathematics. *Journal for Research in Mathematics Education, 27*(4), 458–477.

Part II
Transforming Mathematics Instruction with School Curriculum Changes

Preface to Part II

Edward A. Silver

Amid a vast array of variations in language, culture, and educational traditions, some commonalities pertain to school mathematics across the globe. One is the centrality of textbooks to school mathematics teaching and learning. Mathematics textbooks vary greatly across countries and grade levels in their organization and display of content and the support provided to students or to teachers. Moreover, the historical trajectories of curriculum development reflected in textbooks develop in ways that reflect varying influences across countries (Jones 1970; Stanic and Kilpatrick 1992). Yet their pivotal importance to classroom instruction in almost all settings of compulsory schooling in the world is undeniable. They serve both as teaching/learning tools and as tangible representations of expectations for mathematics instruction in the educational context in which they are used.

A second commonplace of mathematics instruction is that teachers tend to be more successful in assisting students to learn facts and procedures than they are in helping students gain proficiency with mathematical problem solving and reasoning. Even in high-performing countries on international comparative assessments of mathematics attainment, there is usually dissatisfaction with the performance of students on cognitively demanding tasks.

The chapters in this part offer fascinating glimpses at the complex interaction between curriculum and instruction, with particular attention to the role that curriculum might play in nudging mathematics classroom instruction to be more ambitious and more effective in helping students become adept with mathematical problem solving and reasoning. Complementing the approaches suggested in others parts of the volume, these chapters explore the role that curriculum and curriculum materials (e.g., textbooks) might play in efforts to reform mathematics instruction.

E.A. Silver (✉)
School of Education, University of Michigan,
610 E. University Ave., Ann Arbor, MI 48109, USA
e-mail: easilver@umich.edu

Y. Li et al. (eds.), *Transforming Mathematics Instruction: Multiple Approaches and Practices*, Advances in Mathematics Education, DOI 10.1007/978-3-319-04993-9_9, © Springer International Publishing Switzerland 2014

The examples treated in these chapters come from four different countries—China, Japan, the Netherlands, and Portugal—with different languages, cultures, and education traditions. The examples vary with respect to the scope and complexity of the curriculum change undertaken or instructional reform being sought. What the chapters have in common is a focus on how curriculum changes might leverage changes in instruction, and they provide some measure of hope that this strategy might be useful in efforts to promote more ambitious mathematics instruction.

Why Curriculum as a Tool for Reform?

Derived from the Latin word *currere*—meaning "to run"—the word curriculum referred initially to the course that runners followed in a competition. Today, it is a word with multiple meanings, including the sequence of courses that a student may complete, the topics that are contained in a given grade, or the specific expectations regarding content, skills, competencies, and habits of mind that are deemed necessary for educational or societal reasons. These varied meanings all focus on the content of the curriculum as it appears in textbooks or official documents such as syllabi, frameworks, and catalogues. There are other distinctions pertaining to curriculum that may be even more critical for our understanding of how curriculum might play a role in instructional reform.

More than two decades ago, Travers and Westbury (1989) suggested an important distinction between curriculum as planned and curriculum as enacted. In the Second International Mathematics Study (SIMS), the *intended curriculum* (as represented in official documents and textbooks) was contrasted with the *implemented curriculum* (measured through questionnaires given to teachers). These were, in turn, related to the *attained* curriculum, as reflected in students' performance on SIMS test items. The distinction among these three different "versions" of curriculum draws attention to the variation that was found in SIMS and in many other studies when the official curriculum of a country or school system is compared to the topics taught and emphasized in classrooms in that country or school system, and then to the proficiency obtained by the students taught in those classrooms.

The tripartite distinction offered by Travers and Westbury suggests both the promise and peril of pinning one's hopes for instructional reform on curriculum change. Because official curriculum documents and textbooks can be viewed as blueprints for school mathematics instruction, they can serve as tools to influence classroom instruction. If one were intent on making mathematics instruction more ambitious, for example, one might alter the official (i.e., intended) curriculum or textbooks to place more emphasis on problem solving and reasoning. If the official curriculum were deterministic of school mathematics, changes in classroom instruction (i.e., the implemented curriculum) would follow directly and lead to corresponding changes in student outcomes (i.e., the attained curriculum). Alas, the picture is decidedly more complicated and perilous. As we know, teachers are not merely obedient servants of other people's intentions, nor are they superheroes possessing the power to deal effortlessly with the challenges of classroom instruction, especially when it is oriented toward more ambitious goals.

The effects of curriculum changes are mediated by a number of factors and actors, among which are teachers and students. The implemented curriculum is largely a function of the actions and reactions of teachers and students in classrooms, and it is constrained by a complex array of cultural, historical, political, and social factors. Yet, it is the implemented curriculum that affords students' opportunities to learn and thus influences quite directly the attained curriculum as reflected in what students actually learn. A reform effort that uses curriculum change to generate instructional change requires that teachers, students, and mathematical content interact in ways that may run counter to dominant cultural, historical, political, and social forces. Because ambitious teaching is difficult, and because proficiency with mathematical problem solving, reasoning, and other cognitively demanding performances is also challenging, the probability is small that a change in the intended curriculum in the direction of more ambitious practices and outcomes will be faithfully and successfully implemented in classroom instruction unless careful attention and support are provided to teachers and students.

In his chapter, Gravemeijer summarizes a number of reasons for caution in expecting curriculum reform to yield instructional innovation, yet he also suggests why these might not be fatal flaws in this strategic approach to the goal of more ambitious mathematics instruction. In their chapter, Oliveira and Mestre illustrate how teachers and students might be supported to overcome perceived and actual obstacles in the enactment of innovative curriculum materials that promote ambitious mathematics teaching and learning.

Toward More Ambitious Mathematics Teaching: Changing Curriculum to Change Instruction

Over several decades, a body of research evidence has amassed pointing to the benefits of ambitious teaching (sometimes called by various other names, including authentic instruction, teaching for understanding, higher-order instruction, problem-solving instruction, and sense-making instruction) in the mathematics classroom (e.g., Boaler 2002; Bransford et al. 1999; Brownell and Moser 1949; Carpenter et al. 1996; Fawcett 1938; Hiebert et al. 1996; Newmann and Associates 1996; Schoenfeld 2005; Silver and Lane 1995; Stein and Lane 1996). Many questions remain unanswered about precisely how ambitious teaching practices are linked to students' learning to solve problems and reason mathematically or to exhibit mathematics learning with understanding (see, e.g., Hiebert and Grouws 2007), but there has been increasing interest among mathematics educators in making student engagement with cognitively complex mathematics tasks and processes a regular feature of classroom instruction (e.g., Fennema and Romberg 1999; Hiebert and Carpenter 1992). In his chapter in this volume, Gravemeijer provides a contemporary line of argument for more ambitious mathematics teaching, updating some of the classic themes.

Despite growing evidence of its efficacy, ambitious instruction has not become the norm in mathematics classrooms anywhere in the world, though typical classroom teaching in some countries is certainly relatively more oriented toward ambitious instruction than in many other countries. Similarly, comparative analyses of the intended mathematics curriculum across countries have typically reported that the curriculum represented in official documents and in textbooks in some countries is more ambitious than in many other countries. Notwithstanding the caveats noted above, such findings are suggestive of a reform strategy that would use curriculum change as a lever for instructional change. In his chapter, Gravemeijer fills in some details of this argument as sketched in this chapter.

Several of the chapters in this part offer additional evidence that it may be possible to use curriculum to influence mathematics instruction to be more attentive to mathematical processes, such as problem solving and communication. For example, Watanabe examined Japanese school mathematics textbooks to discern changes over time that might be associated with perceived changes in Japanese classroom instruction. He notes a trend in the treatment of problem solving in the textbooks that appears to be consistent with a trend in mathematics teaching in Japan toward more use of structured problem solving as a core feature of classroom instruction. He is not able to identify a causal relationship from his data, but he does offer a plausible argument for a relationship between the curriculum changes and the instructional changes.

Another example is provided by Ni and colleagues who report two studies examining how curriculum changes affected classroom instruction in Chinese mathematics classrooms. In one study, they contrasted the tasks used in classrooms where a reform curriculum was implemented with those used in classrooms where a traditional curriculum was in place. They reported finding greater use of cognitively demanding tasks in the classrooms implementing the reform curriculum. In a subsequent study, they investigated how the use of such tasks influenced classroom discourse. The findings of their study mirror those of other similar research, suggesting that cognitively demanding tasks are not self-enacting and that teachers may need assistance to learn to use them well to orchestrate productive classroom conversations that advance students' mathematics learning.

Two other chapters focus on the teaching and learning of specific content. Oliveira and Mestre treat algebraic thinking in grade four mathematics. They describe how curriculum revisions were undertaken in Portugal to draw attention to relational thinking in the teaching of fourth-grade mathematics topics, such as computation strategies and problem solving. They also describe the issues that arose when the materials were implemented in a classroom. In another chapter, Huang and Li discuss the design features of the so-called exemplary lessons, focusing on an example tied to the mathematical topic of algorithms. They trace the learning of the teacher who developed the lesson and illustrate how the development of exemplary lessons is an approach that appears to be a feasible way to influence instruction in Chinese secondary schools.

Viewed individually, the chapters in this part offer useful cases to assist us in understanding the complex space of interaction between curriculum and instruction. Taken collectively, these chapters suggest some reasons for optimism that curriculum reform might be a successful strategy to employ as a means to achieve instructional change. They also remind us of the myriad issues that need to be considered and addressed in any such undertaking.

References

Boaler, J. (2002). *Experiencing school mathematics: Traditional and reform approaches to teaching and their impact on student learning*. Mahwah: Lawrence Erlbaum Associates.

Bransford, J. D., Brown, A. L., & Cocking, R. R. (1999). *How people learn: Brain, mind, experience, and school*. Washington, DC: National Academy Press.

Brownell, W. A., & Moser, H. E. (1949). *Meaningful vs. mechanical learning: A study in grade III subtraction* (Duke University Research Studies in Education, No. 8). Durham: Duke University Press.

Carpenter, T. P., Fennema, E., & Franke, M. (1996). Cognitively guided instruction: A knowledge base for reform in primary mathematics instruction. *Elementary School Journal, 97*(1), 3–20.

Fawcett, H. P. (1938). *The nature of proof: A description and evaluation of certain procedures used in a senior high school to develop an understanding of the nature of proof*. New York: Teachers College, Columbia University.

Fennema, E., & Romberg, T. A. (Eds.). (1999). *Mathematics classrooms that promote understanding*. Mahwah: Lawrence Erlbaum Associates.

Hiebert, J., & Carpenter, T. P. (1992). Learning and teaching with understanding. In D. A. Grouws (Ed.), *Handbook of research on mathematics teaching and learning* (pp. 65–97). New York: Macmillan.

Hiebert, J., & Grouws, D. A. (2007). The effects of classroom mathematics teaching on students' learning. In F. K. Lester (Ed.), *Second handbook of research on mathematics teaching and learning* (pp. 371–404). Charlotte: Information Age Publishing.

Hiebert, J., Carpenter, T. P., Fennema, E., Fuson, K., Human, P., Murray, H., et al. (1996). Problem solving as a basis for reform in curriculum and instruction: The case of mathematics. *Educational Researcher, 25*(4), 12–21.

Jones, P. S. (Ed.). (1970). *A history of mathematics education in the United States and Canada* (32nd Yearbook). Reston: National Council of Teachers of Mathematics.

Newmann, F. M., & Associates. (1996). *Authentic achievement: Restructuring schools for intellectual quality*. San Francisco: Jossey-Bass.

Schoenfeld, A. H. (2005). On learning environments that foster subject-matter competence. In L. Verschaffel, E. De Corte, G. Kanselaar, & M. Valcke (Eds.), *Powerful environments for promoting deep conceptual and strategic learning* (pp. 29–44). Leuven: Studia Paedagogica.

Silver, E. A., & Lane, S. (1995). Can instructional reform in urban middle schools help students narrow the mathematics performance gap? Some evidence from the QUASAR project. *Research in Middle Level Education, 18*(2), 49–70.

Stein, M. K., & Lane, S. (1996). Instructional tasks and the development of student capacity to think and reason: An analysis of the relationship between teaching and learning in a reform mathematics project. *Educational Research and Evaluation, 2*(1), 50–80.

Stanic, G., & Kilpatrick, J. (1992). Mathematics curriculum reform in the United States: A historical perspective. *International Journal of Educational Research, 17*(5), 407–417.

Travers, K. J., & Westbury, I. (1989). *The IEA study of mathematics I: Analysis of mathematics curricula*. New York: Pergamon Press.

Transforming Mathematics Education: The Role of Textbooks and Teachers

Koeno P.E. Gravemeijer

Abstract In this chapter, we discuss the question of how we can encourage mathematics education to shift towards more inquiry-oriented practices in schools and what role textbooks and teachers play in such a reform. The stage is set by an exposition on the need for curriculum innovation in light of the demands of the twenty-first century. This points to a need to address goals in the area of critical thinking, problem solving, collaborating, and communicating. However, previous efforts to effectuate a change in mathematics education in that direction have not been very successful. This is illustrated by experiences in the Netherlands. In relation to this, the limitations of transforming education using textbooks and problems with up-scaling are discussed. To find ways to address these problems, an inventory is made of what can be learned from decades of experimenting with reform mathematics education while trying to achieve the very goals that are discerned as crucial for the twenty-first century. On the basis of this inventory, suggestions are made for shaping textbooks in such a manner that they may better support this kind of transformation. At the same time it is pointed out that the latter requires a complementary effort in teacher professionalization and a well-considered alignment of both efforts.

Keywords Textbooks • Curriculum innovation • Reform mathematics • Realistic mathematics education (RME)

K.P.E. Gravemeijer (✉)
Eindhoven School of Education, Eindhoven University of Technology,
Rijnsburgerweg 47, 2334BG Leiden, The Netherlands
e-mail: koeno@gravemeijer.nl

Y. Li et al. (eds.), *Transforming Mathematics Instruction: Multiple Approaches and Practices*, Advances in Mathematics Education, DOI 10.1007/978-3-319-04993-9_10,
© Springer International Publishing Switzerland 2014

Introduction

The issue of how to transform mathematics education is more urgent than ever. In order to prepare the students for the twenty-first century, a transformation of mathematics education is needed. This calls for a change towards a form of mathematics education that fosters abilities such as critical thinking, problem solving, collaborating, and communicating. In this chapter we address how such a radical change—which given its scope may truly be called a transformation—can be brought about. We will look at the role textbooks can play, and we will argue that changing the textbooks will not be sufficient but will have to be complemented with extensive teacher education. We will discuss those issues on the basis of the history of RME in the Netherlands. To counter these difficulties, we will inventory what can be learned from decades of experimenting with reform mathematics. Next, we will discuss how this can be worked out in textbooks and teacher professionalization. We will show that this requires a different kind of textbook; it calls for textbooks that offer more information about intended learning processes and the means by which these processes can be supported. We will further argue that adaptations of the underlying domain-specific instruction theory will be called for. Still, textbook changes will not be sufficient. A large part of the critical points for successfully enacting reform mathematics will have to be addressed in teacher professionalization. Following Fullan (2006), we will argue that this calls for a setup in which teachers collectively work on improving their own practice. This in turn calls for a well-considered alignment of textbook design and teacher learning. We will start by illuminating the need for transformation by discussing the demands of the twenty-first century.

The Need to Transform Mathematics Education

Today's schools must prepare their students' participation in the society of the twenty-first century. However, they are currently failing in this endeavor. According to Tony Wagner (2008), there is a gap between what schools (in the USA) teach and what students will need to succeed in today's global knowledge economy. He argues that "students are simply not learning the skills that matter most for the twenty-first century" (ibid, 8–9). And he goes on to say that "Our system of public education—our curricula, teaching methods, and the tests we require students to take—were created in a different century for the needs of another era. They are hopelessly out-dated" (ibid, 8–9). The skills that current and future jobs require differ significantly from what our current education system offers. New requirements emerge, inter alia, from the informatization of our society and the globalization of our economy—today's workers have to compete with other workers from all over the world. Wagner interviewed numerous CEOs of large companies and he found a strong communality in what they look for in new employees; as one of them phrases it: "First and foremost, I look for someone who asks good questions" (ibid, 2). The underlying rationale is that these employees will have to function in dynamic organizations. Employees today continuously have to learn new things. From this perspective, asking the right questions is an important skill. In this respect, there is a huge gap between what society demands and what schools offer. Schools, Wagner (ibid) goes on to say, are not designed to teach students how to think. The reason for that, he argues, is that we as a society never asked schools to teach students to think. Prevailing mathematics and language education, for instance, focuses on skills, instead of understanding. This is reflected in national tests that are not designed to assess the student's ability to reason and analyze. Instead there is a tendency to limit tests even further to the so-called basics. Such is the case in the No Child Left Behind initiative in the USA, with detrimental effects (Ravitch 2010).

Along with the increase of the dynamics of the modern workplace, there is also a shift in the type of work people do. Empirical research by the economists Levy and Murnane (2006) shows that employment involving cognitive and manual routine tasks in the USA dropped between 1960 and 2000, while employment involving analytical and interactive nonroutine tasks has grown in the same period. This change especially concerned industries that rapidly automatized their production. Parallel to the development in industry, similar changes occurred in other areas where strong computerization took place. This change happened on all levels of education. Jobs with a high routine character are disappearing. Jobs that will be offering good prospects for the future are jobs which concern nonroutine tasks: tasks that require flexibility, creativity, problem-solving skills, and complex communication skills. Autor et al. (2003) refer to examples such as reacting to irregularities, improving a production process, or managing people. The jobs of the future are the ones that ask for flexibility, creativity, lifelong learning, and social skills. The latter are jobs that require communication skills, or face-to-face interaction— such as selling cars or managing people. These changes do not only affect the decline or rise specific jobs; existing jobs are changing as well. Secretaries and bank employees, for instance, have gotten more complex tasks since word processors and ATMs have taken over the more simple tasks.

The effects of computerization and globalization overlap and reinforce each other (Friedman 2005). Routine tasks can easily be outsourced, since information technology enables a quick and easy worldwide exchange of information. Another effect of globalization is that it forces companies to work as efficient as possible. This requires companies to immediately implement computerization and outsourcing when it is economically profitable and strengthens the market position of the company. It also demands that the company be on the lookout for opportunities to improve efficiency. As a consequence, working processes will have to be adapted continuously. This, in turn, puts high demands on workers, who have to have a certain level of general and mathematical literacy to be able to keep up.

In summary, we may conclude that schools will have to change to comply with the requirements imposed by a rapidly changing society.

Wagner (2008) is not alone in his observations. Many initiatives evolved around twenty-first century skills (see Voogt and Pareja Roblin 2010, for a review[1]). The frameworks that emerged from these projects all appear to strongly agree on the need for skills in the areas of communication, collaboration, ICT literacy, and social/cultural awareness. We may take Wagner's (2008) list of "new survival skills" as an example:

1. Critical thinking and problem solving
2. Collaborating and leading by influence
3. Agility and adaptability
4. Initiative and entrepreneurism
5. Effective oral and written communication
6. Accessing and analyzing information
7. Curiosity and imagination

We may also follow Wagner (ibid) in arguing that the twenty-first century skills are not just about employability. They will also have to include broader goals, such as becoming a responsible, active, and well-informed citizen. Wagner (ibid) typifies this broader goal by asking if the students would eventually be well equipped for acting as a member of a jury within the US legal system: "Would they know how to distinguish fact from opinion, weigh evidence, listen with both head and heart, wrestle with the sometimes conflicting principles of justice and mercy, and work to seek the truth with their fellow jurors?" (Wagner 2008, xvi–xvii).

Attempts to Transform Mathematics Education

We may observe, however, that calls for more emphasis on critical thinking, problem solving, collaborating, communicating, and so forth, are not new. Especially not in mathematics education (e.g., National Council of Teachers of Mathematics 1980; Freudenthal 1973). But attempts to change educational practices in schools in this direction have not been very successful. This also holds for the Netherlands and the approach that became known as Realistic Mathematics Education (RME). RME appears to offer a worked out theory of how to reconcile problem solving, communicating, and so forth with the need to achieve conventional goals in mathematics education.

---

[1] This concerned: the "Partnership for 21st century skills" (Partnership for 21st Century Skills 2008), "EnGauge" (North Central Regional Educational Laboratory and the Metiri Group 2003), "Assessment and Teaching of 21st Century Skills" (ATCS) (Binkley et al. 2010), "National Educational Technology Standards" (NETS) (Roblyer 2000), and "Technological Literacy for the 2012 National Assessment of Educational Progress" (NAEP).

RME came into being as a reaction to the failures of traditional mathematics education. In the 1960s, the students mainly learned rules, which they mixed up and could not apply properly. As an alternative, Freudenthal's (1973) inspiring ideas about "mathematics as a human activity" and "guided reinvention" were elaborated as a long-term program of design research and educational development—with (what later became known as) the Freudenthal Institute at its center. Thanks to consistent government funding, the Freudenthal Institute was able to work on a coherent educational program for more than three decades. The instruction theory of realistic mathematics education, RME, has become well known internationally. At the moment, however, there is a critical discussion about the role of RME in Dutch schools (see, for instance, van den Heuvel-Panhuizen 2010). The discussion centers on the "what" and the "how" of mathematics education. Critics claim that there is not enough attention to the basic skills. They also disapprove of the guided reinvention approach that is employed, which is ineffective and confusing in their view. Protagonists of RME and their opponents seem to be trapped in a very unproductive deadlock. What is worse, this controversy has turned into a political battle, which stands in the way of a much needed discussion about how mathematics education should prepare students for the future.

How could RME become the object of rather fierce attacks, after so many years of praise?

RME gained recognition in the international mathematics education community on the basis of both scientific publications and the dissemination of prototypical courses and textbooks. A significant drawback for this innovation in the Netherlands, however, was the lack of funding for in-service teacher education and the weakening of the position of mathematics education in the institutes for teacher education. This resulted in significant discrepancies between RME theory and how teachers understood and enacted RME ideas (Gravemeijer et al. 1991). Over time, some in-service teacher education was granted by the government (van den Heuvel-Panhuizen and de Goeij 2007) but its scope was limited. Because of the limitations in preservice and in-service teacher education, the focus shifted towards the textbooks. Design research and professional instructional design led to increasingly more refined (prototypical) instructional sequences and corresponding local instruction theories. These smoother, more refined, instructional sequences—in which there was less need for problem solving—were worked into the textbooks in one form or another. The results of all this was put into question when a decline in the results of tests on multiplication and division was reported in a national survey at the end of primary school (Janssen et al. 2005). These results lead to publications in the media which criticized schools, today's mathematics education, and the realistic approach. Then, even though the results on other topics in the same survey showed improvement, and Dutch students still ranked rather high in international surveys such as TIMSS (Mullis et al. 2004) and PISA (OECD 2010), it must also be acknowledged that we did not see the overall improvement which was expected. We may argue that the Dutch experience underscores the fact that there are serious limitations to conveying instructional approaches via textbooks, which is an issue that we will explore in more detail below.

Limits to Transforming Education by Textbooks

We may start by observing that there are various limitations to the effectiveness of teacher guides. In the 1980s, Westbury (1983) already pointed to the following obstacles:

- Teachers have to read the teacher guides.
- They have to understand what they read.
- They have to be willing to do what they understand.
- They have to be able to do what they have understood.

In more modern terms, we may say that teacher guides are boundary objects (Akkerman and Bakker 2011). They are constructed in one community of practice (Wenger 1998), that of the instructional designers, and are to be used by teachers, who are part of a different community of practice. In this sense, the teacher guides cross the boundary between these two communities of practice, which have different goals, different languages, and different frameworks of reference. The teacher guides are to convey knowledge constructed in the community of instructional designers, to teachers who are not part of that community and who were not involved in its development process. This creates the risk of misinterpretation.

We may argue that this problem has become more pressing in recent years. Whereas in the past, experienced teachers or headmasters could design textbooks on their own, drawing on years of practice, such experience is lacking in reform mathematics. Reform mathematics is rooted in the innovative ideas of scholars, which are elaborated on in experimental classrooms, or schools. Such experiments often form the basis for textbook design, in which teachers may participate but where the researchers usually take the lead—as is the case in the Netherlands and with the so-called NSF curricula in the USA. Consequently, the design of textbooks has become the work of experts, who have their background in educational research or teacher education. Moreover, the role of textbooks as boundary objects has become more problematic, since teacher guides have become conveyers of curriculum innovation, as the teacher guides have to convey to the teachers how to enact innovative ways of teaching. However, the complexity of interactive, problem-centered mathematics education, and the corresponding teaching skills, is overwhelming. Teachers have to find a way to cope with, and productively use, a variety of solutions and other input of students. They have to reconcile the tension between consolidating and expanding while keeping an eye on the long-term goals that transcend their own classroom. In the light of the above, it may not come as a surprise that the RME innovation in Dutch schools was not as successful as one hoped for—especially since the necessary teacher education was failing.

Pitfalls of Curriculum Innovation

In sum, we may conclude that the innovators at the Freudenthal Institute underestimated the difficulty of curriculum innovation. In this respect, we may hark back to the admonition of Dewey, which was repeated by Ann Brown (1992, 172):

> To say the least, it is a cautionary note for contemporary designers that Dewey (1901) a century ago warned that educational reform would not be easy to engineer. Dewey's description of cycles of innovation and resistance sounds uncannily like Cunban's (1984, 1990) contemporary Cassandra bulletins. First comes unrest concerning the schools and how they operate, followed by fervent claims and promises from reformers. Intensive research by the converted is then carried out in a small set of classrooms rich with human and, today, technological resources. "The victory is won and everybody—unless it is some already overburdened and distracted teacher—congratulates everybody else that such steps can be taken" (Dewey 1901, p. 334). But then come the frustrated attempts by ordinary teachers to adopt the new methods in absence of support, followed by the inevitable decline in use, and the eventual abandonment of the program. As Dewey argued, "within a short time, complaints are heard that children do not read well," "or a public outcry calls for the reforms to be rescinded in favor of the status quo." One major question facing contemporary designers is how to avoid repeating the Cuban-Dewey cycle: exhilaration, followed by scientific credibility, followed by disappointment and blame.

What Does It Take to Transform Mathematics Education?

In reflecting on the challenge posed by the "Cuban-Dewey cycle," we may ask ourselves what one could do to make the envisioned reform in mathematics education more successful. In doing so, we want to broaden the discussion to what we may call "reform mathematics." From the 1970s onwards, we have seen a shift in thinking about education in the educational research community, from "instruction" towards "construction." The accepted view today is that knowledge cannot be transmitted but that students have to play an active role in constructing their own knowledge. It is this idea of students constructing their own knowledge that calls for problem-centered interactive mathematics education, of which RME is an example and which we will refer to as "reform mathematics," or "inquiry mathematics" in the following.

When considering the question, "How to make the reform in mathematics education more successful?" it may be argued that the research literature on "reform mathematics" offers many useful insights. In the following, we will list what we believe are the most critical aspects, in order to create a basis for considering what role textbooks and teachers may play in transforming mathematics education. In this respect, we discern the following critical points concerning the enactment of reform mathematics (Gravemeijer 2012):

- Social norms and socio-mathematical norms
- Task orientation
- Mathematical interest

- Topics for discussion
- Hypothetical learning trajectories
- Local instruction theories
- Symbolizing and modeling
- Vertical mathematization

Social Norms and Socio-mathematical Norms

Research shows that students do not easily engage in problem solving and reasoning in regular classrooms (Desforges and Cockburn 1987). Cobb and Yackel (1996) argue that this is not surprising, because students are often familiar with a classroom culture in which the classroom social norms are that the teacher has the right answers, the students are expected to follow given procedures, and correct answers are more important than the student's own reasoning. In this type of classroom, teachers usually ask questions to which they already know the answer. Apart from being used to this situation, students have learned what to expect and what is expected from them. In relation to this, Brousseau (1988) speaks of an implicit "didactical contract." It is significant, however, that the students have learned this by experience, not from a teacher who told them so. The basis of the traditional school-math social norms is that the students have to come to grips with knowledge the teacher already has. The teacher's role is to explain and clarify; the students' role is to try to figure out what the teacher has in mind. The reform mathematics social norms are completely different; here, the students have to figure out things for themselves, and instead of giving them answers, the teachers may ask them new questions. Students in these classrooms are expected to work together as a research—annex learning—community. To make this happen, the students have to adopt classroom social norms that fit an inquiry-oriented classroom culture. These encompass the obligation to explain and justify one's solutions, to try and understand other students' reasoning, and to ask questions if one does not understand, and challenge arguments one does not agree with.

Since the aforementioned classroom norms are not specific to mathematics, the teacher also has to establish socio-mathematical norms (Cobb and Yackel 1996), which relate to what mathematics is. This is expressed in norms about issues such as what counts as a mathematical problem, what counts as a mathematical solution, and what counts as a more sophisticated solution. In regard to the latter, we may argue that socio-mathematical norms lay the basis for the intellectual autonomy of the students (Kamii et al. 1993), as it enables them to decide for themselves which solutions are more sophisticated—and thus represent mathematical progress. Mark that this does not mean that the teacher has no authority at all. On the contrary, the teacher is the one who determines what it means to learn mathematics in this classroom. The teacher determines what mathematics is, what mathematical arguments are, and so forth. In addition, the teacher guides and supports the process by posing tasks, framing topics for discussion, orchestrating discussions, and, when needed, making connections with the mathematical conventions and practices of the wider community.

The shift from school-math norms towards inquiry-math norms takes some conscious effort. Just telling the students that the expectations and obligations have changed will not bring the change about. The students have (unconsciously) appropriated the school-math norms from experiencing school-math classrooms. It is therefore important that they experience that other behaviors are valued (Yackel 1992). To establish new social norms, the teacher has to convince the students that what is valued and what is rewarded has changed. One way to do so is to use concrete instances of infringements on the new norms or exemplary behavior as opportunities to clarify the norms.

Task Orientation

In addition to appropriating inquiry-based norms, students also have to be willing to invest effort in solving mathematical problems, discussing solutions, and discussing the underlying ideas. Students may engage in learning activities for different reasons. The attitude of students in a mathematics classroom can be broadly divided in two categories, *ego orientation* and *task orientation* (Jagacinski and Nicholls 1984). Ego orientation implies that the student is very conscious of the way he or she might be perceived by others. Ego-oriented students are afraid to fail, or to look stupid in the eyes of their fellow students, or the teacher. As a consequence, they may choose not to even try to solve a given problem in order to avoid embarrassment. Task orientation on the other hand implies that the student's concern is with the task itself and on finding ways of solving that task. Mark that task orientation and ego orientation can be influenced by teachers. Research done by Cobb et al. (1989) shows that a classroom culture that emphasizes individual growth, on the one hand, and the development of mathematical understanding as a collaborative endeavor, on the other hand, may foster the task orientation of the students.

Mathematical Interest

In connection with student motivation, we may add that next to "pragmatic interest," which realistic problems appeal to, students will also have to develop "mathematical interest" (Gravemeijer and Van Eerde 2009). This concerns the preparedness of the students to investigate solution procedures, concepts, and so on, from a pure mathematical perspective. This is a necessary condition for construing more sophisticated mathematics. Mathematical interest will rarely come naturally but instead has to be cultivated by the teacher via questions such as the following: What is the general principle here? Why does this work? Does it always work? Can we describe it in a more precise manner? We may assume that the teacher can foster the students' mathematical interest by making mathematical questions a topic of conversation and by showing a genuine interest in the students' mathematical reasoning. We may add that mathematical interest is not only a prerequisite for reinvention on the part of the students but also is an important goal in and of itself. If we succeed in helping students develop mathematical interest, they may be much better prepared for further education and for participating in the society of the twenty-first century.

Topics for Discussion

Another essential role of the teacher concerns the orchestration of productive whole-class discussions. In doing so, the teacher has to build on the input of the students. Cobb (1997) argues that this should not take the form of working towards the fastest or most sophisticated solution. Instead, the teacher has to identify the differences in mathematical understanding which underlie the variation in student responses. Next, he or she has to frame these underlying mathematical issues as topics for whole-class discussions. Then, he or she must orchestrate a productive whole-class discussion on those topics in order to foster higher levels of mathematical understanding.[2]

Hypothetical Learning Trajectory

Planning instruction in reform mathematics is rather complicated since it is assumed that teachers can influence their students' knowledge construction only in an indirect manner. To design instructional activities that may foster the intended learning processes, the teacher has to try to anticipate how the students might think. In this manner, the teacher can plan instructional activities which may foster the mental activities of the students that fit his or her pedagogical agenda. In relation to this, Simon (1995) speaks of a hypothetical learning trajectory, which encompasses a consideration of the mental activities the students might engage in as they participate in the envisioned instructional activities and how these mental activities relate to the chosen learning goal. Complementary to anticipation, the hypothetical learning trajectory also requires evaluation. The teacher has to investigate whether the thinking

---

[2] In a similar feign, Stein et al. (2008) discern practices for promoting productive disciplinary engagement, which are related to identifying, framing, and discussing mathematical issues. Although a difference may be that Stein et al. (2008) seem to try to address both mathematical ideas and the solution strategies of the students, Cobb (1997) emphasizes the mathematical issues that underlie student solutions and tries to steer away from a focus on solution strategies as such.

of the students actually evolves as the conjectured learning trajectory predicted. On the basis of this investigation, the teacher has to decide on the continuation, which may involve adjusting or revising the learning trajectory.

Local Instruction Theory

To support teachers in designing, evaluating, and adapting HLTs, textbooks may offer a set of exemplary instructional activities that can be used to teach a certain topic (such as, for instance, fractions, long division, or data analysis) and a rationale or local instruction theory (Gravemeijer 2004) that underpins it. In recent years, ideas similar to that of a local instruction theory have received growing attention as means for supporting teachers. Simon's (1995) notion of a hypothetical learning trajectory has been expanded by several authors. Nowadays, the appellatives, learning trajectory, and learning progressions are used to describe the trajectory for a given topic (Clements and Sarama 2004; Confrey et al. 2009; Daro et al. 2011)—which reflects the fact that the work on developing learning trajectories, learning progressions, or local instruction theories is much broader than that of the RME community. The different names come, of course, with subtle differences in meaning, but we will not elaborate upon this here. In this chapter we will take the way the idea of a local instruction theory worked out in RME as our framework of reference. In this respect, we discern three levels, the level of the domain-specific instruction theory for a given domain, such as mathematics; the level of the local instruction theory for a given topic, such as multiplication of fractions or addition and subtraction up to 100; and the level of the hypothetical learning trajectory, concerning one or two lessons. The local instruction theory then consists of a theory about a possible learning process for a given topic and theories about the means of supporting that process. The latter also encompasses the required classroom culture. The local instruction theory may be used by a teacher as framework of reference when designing HLTs tailored to his or her classroom at a given moment in time. Mark that local instruction theories differ significantly from the content of conventional teacher guides. The local instruction theories do not comprise scripted lessons. Instead, local instruction theories offer frameworks of reference for designing hypothetical learning trajectories. For—even with local instruction theories available—teachers will still have to construe their own hypothetical learning trajectories. Each hypothetical learning trajectory will have to be tailored to the actual situation of *this* teacher, *these* students, and at *this* moment in time.

Significant teacher learning will be required to support teachers in getting a handle on how to design hypothetical learning trajectories for their own classrooms. This was one of the stumbling blocks in the Netherlands; the limited opportunities for teacher professionalization pushed textbook authors into trying to translate local instruction theories into detailed series of instructional activities and extensive teacher guides—which, in effect, impeded the reform.

Symbolizing and Modeling

From the perspective of teachers and instructional designers, it makes perfect sense to try to develop "transparent" models that make abstract mathematical knowledge apprehensible for students. They see their mathematical knowledge reflected in the models. They see their knowledge of the decimal system, for instance, reflected in base-ten MAB blocks. For students, however, the MAB blocks are just wooden blocks (see for instance Labinowics 1985). We cannot expect the students to see more sophisticated mathematics in such concrete models than the mathematics they have already acquired. This raises the question of *how* students are to learn abstract mathematics from concrete external representations. This problem is known as the "learning paradox" (Bereiter 1985), which Cobb et al. describe as:

> (T)he assumption that students will inevitably construct the correct internal representation from the materials presented implies that their learning is triggered by the mathematical relationships they are to construct before they have constructed them. (…) How then, if students can only make sense of their worlds in terms of their internal representations, is it possible for them to recognize mathematical relationships that are developmentally more advanced than their internal representations? (Cobb et al. 1992, p. 5)

We may try to circumvent the learning paradox by aiming at a dynamic process of symbolizing and modeling, within which the process of symbolizing and the development of meaning are reflexively related (Meira 1995). This approach is elaborated in the so-called emergent-modeling design heuristic (Gravemeijer 2004). The idea is that students start with modeling their own informal mathematical activity. Then, in the process that follows, the character of the model is meant to change for the students. Initially the students think in terms of the context within which the problem is posed. Under the guidance of the teacher, their attention should shift towards the mathematical relations involved. Then the students may begin to construct a network of mathematical relations, which can give new meaning to the model: on the basis of which the model can become a model for more formal mathematical reasoning. Mark that the model we are referring to is more an overarching concept than one specific model. In practice, "the model" in the emergent-modeling heuristic is actually shaped as a series of consecutive *sub-models* that can be described as a cascade of inscriptions or a chain of signification (Whitson 1997). From a more global perspective, these sub-models can be seen as various manifestations of the same model. It may be added that due attention should be given to whether the actions with a new sub-model signify earlier activities with earlier sub-models for the students.

We may observe, however, that advancing learning processes in which symbolizing and meaning coevolve is not on the agenda of textbook authors and teachers. While we argue such an effort is needed, textbook authors will have to lay out the routes along which a dialectic processes of symbolizing and developing meaning may be brought about, whereas teachers will have to develop the skills needed to guide such processes effectively.

Vertical Mathematization

The presumption of reform mathematics is that students will be able to construct more abstract, conventional mathematics, when they are supported in building upon their informal situated knowledge. In relation to this, we speak of vertical mathematization, which may evolve on different levels. Tzur and Simon (2004) recently showed how abstracting new mathematical conceptions can be understood on a microlevel as a mental mechanism of reflection on activity-effect relationships. On a macrolevel, we may speak of progressions from informal situated knowledge to more formal mathematical knowledge in which mathematical processes are reified (Sfard 1991).

Recent research in the Netherlands, however, showed that, even though such long-term vertical mathematizating processes are a core element of RME, they are in fact not supported by Dutch textbooks. A number of studies revealed that informal solution procedures were treated as end goals in Dutch textbooks in the case of subtraction up to 100 (Kraemer 2011), multiplication of fractions (Bruin-Muurling 2010), and linear equations (van Stiphout 2011), and the shift towards more formal mathematics was neglected. We may take this as a warning that we, as mathematics educators, run the risk of taking the progression towards higher levels of mathematics for granted too easily. Helping students in generalizing over informal solution procedures may take substantial effort. On the one hand, informal solution procedures have to be grounded in the students' experiential reality, while, on the other hand, students have to transcend the specificity of the informal solution procedures to construct more general, more formal, ways of thinking. Moreover, students may spontaneously generalize in directions which are at odds with the intended mathematization towards more abstract mathematics (Magidson 2005). Students will have to be supported in reflecting on the mathematical coherence that underlies the various solution procedures. Investigating how they relate mathematically may help them to construct mathematical conceptions on a higher level. Surely the aforementioned strategies such as cultivating mathematical interest and framing mathematical issues as topics for discussion will come into play here.

Revisiting Textbooks as Means of Support for Transforming Math. Ed.

The critical points we identified above may be addressed in teacher education and instructional design.[3] Especially important are establishing inquiry-oriented social norms and socio-mathematical norms, fostering task orientation, cultivating

---

[3] In relation to this we may point to a study by Tarr et al. (2008), which showed that NCTM Standards-based learning environments positively impact achievement on performance assessments tests that measure mathematical reasoning, problem solving, and communication, as well as proficiency in skills and procedures, but only when coupled with a curriculum that is designed to embody this pedagogical orientation. In particular, when teachers of NSF-funded curricula were enacting the curriculum as intended by the authors, student achievement was compelling.

mathematical interest, identifying and framing topics for discussion, orchestrating productive whole-class discussions, and designing and evaluating hypothetical learning trajectories, typically belonging to the domain of teacher education. Local instruction theories, however, may be addressed in instructional design. This will require a new way of arranging textbooks. The scripted character and the ready-made tasks of conventional textbooks limit teachers in adapting to their students' reasoning. Instead, textbooks will have to inform teachers about local instruction theories and explicate what mental activities hypothetical learning trajectories have to focus on. Mark that in our conception, local instruction theories are tied to a domain-specific instruction theory, such as RME. We may add that there is a reflexive relation between the domain-specific instruction theory and the local instruction theories. In fact, the RME theory was initially construed on basis of a reflection on many local instructional designs (Treffers 1987). Thus, the local instruction theories inform the domain-specific instruction theory, and the domain-specific instruction theory informs the design of local instruction theories. This also implies that the domain-specific instruction theory is dynamic, and we may argue that the original RME theory has to be adapted to tailor it to the goals of the twenty-first century—a process which is already under way.

RME originates from the 1970s and was designed to fit the then contemporary curriculum goals in the Netherlands, in which basic skills and algorithms formed the core. The bulk of the design work concerned the reinvention of the written algorithms and routines for operations with fractions, decimals, and percentages. In relation to this, progressive mathematizing is often transformed into progressive schematizing (Treffers 1987). A curriculum that is tailored to the twenty-first century will not only have to address the so-called twenty-first century skills but will also have to aim at other mathematical goals. Flawless execution of the written algorithms will be of less importance, since we may leave this kind of work to machines. Having a good understanding of how and why these algorithms work will stay important, however. Moreover, the students will have to be flexible with number relations, approximations, and applications. Furthermore, students will have to understand the mathematical processes involved in the way computers transform everyday-life phenomena into quantitative information in order to get a handle on what computers and computerized appliances do and how they can be put to use. What is important here is a conceptual understanding of variables, covariation, graphs, measuring, and statistics (Gravemeijer 2010; Hoyles et al. 2010). Apart from the change in content, this also implies a shift from routine, procedural skills to mathematical reasoning on a more general level. This has consequences for RME theory.

We may illustrate this with the view of modeling. In the approach of Treffers (1987), the emphasis is on schematizing and stepwise shortening solution procedures. In a twenty-first century approach, more attention will be given to the conceptual aspects of modeling. In this respect, the emergent modeling design heuristic may be seen as exemplary (Gravemeijer 2004). Here, the goals are cast in terms of a framework of mathematical relations. Students are expected to construct some new mathematical realities, in a process in which the means of symbolizing they use and the meaning of what these symbolizations signify for them coevolve.

This implies that, rather than the efficiency of the solutions, the underlying mathematical issues should be framed as topics for whole-class discussion.

It may be noted that this increased emphasis on conceptual aspects, in and of itself, calls for textbooks in which more information is given about the underlying theories than is common in current textbooks. In addition, textbooks will have to contain exemplary instructional activities. In this respect, information technology may be used to create tasks which can be adjusted by the teacher. Further, the textbooks may be accompanied by computers (and other) tools.

Mindful of the warnings of Dewey (1901), however, we have to acknowledge that disseminating new textbooks will surely not be sufficient. Thus, the introduction of new textbooks will have to be accompanied by fitting preservice or in-service teacher education. Given the fact that the inflow of new teachers is relatively small compared to the total number of teachers, the bulk will have to be in in-service teacher education, or teacher professionalization. Given what we know of the latter, special care will have to be taken on this aspect as well.

Enactment and Teacher Professionalization

History shows that curriculum innovation is very hard. Fullan (2006), who spent several decades on studying curriculum innovation, observes that most curriculum innovations leave very few traces. In his view, the main reason for this lack of effect is that in-service teacher education usually does not affect what teachers do in their own classrooms. In-service teacher education courses are usually given in classes at the university, and teachers may try to enact what they have learned in their own classrooms. The problem, however, is that teachers do not get feedback on what they do in their own classrooms. Thus, when teachers try to enact what they have learned from the in-service courses in their own classroom, there is no way they can know if what they do corresponds with what was intended. In Fullan's (ibid) eyes, the lack of feedback is not only a problem with in-service courses but is a more broad obstacle for teacher professionalization or innovation. Since, in general, teachers are not visited in their classrooms, they do not get feedback on their teaching practice. This does not only mean that they are not corrected; it also means that they also do not get positive feedback on what they do well.

> "The problem [is that] there is almost no opportunity for teachers to engage in continuous and sustained learning about their practice in the settings in which they actually work, observing and being observed by their colleagues in their own classrooms and classrooms of other teachers in other schools confronting similar problems of practice. This disconnect between the requirements of learning to teach well and the structure of teachers' work life is fatal to any sustained process of instructional improvement." (Elmore cited by Fullan 2006, p. 12)

Fullan (2006) therefore advocates the creation of a culture of collective professional learning, within which teachers can individually and collectively work on the process of improving their way of working in the classroom. This could be done by creating professional communities of teachers that aim to investigate their teaching and improve their instructional practice. Here we may think of the Japanese lesson-study model that is promoted by Hiebert and Siegler (Hiebert et al. 2002).

The professional learning that will be needed encompasses pedagogical content knowledge (Shulman 1987), beliefs (Thompson 1984), and the ability to enact the intended pedagogy. In respect to the first, one of the challenges will be to enable (prospective and practicing) teachers to design hypothetical learning trajectories on the basis of (externally developed) local instruction theories and resource materials. Ideally, teachers should be given the opportunity to experience the learning process that the designer/researcher of the local instruction theory went through by some form of reinvention. Solving sequence related problems, anticipating solutions of primary or secondary school students, analyzing student work and teaching episodes, and such could be the constituents of such a reinvention process (Fosnot 2003). Moreover, the combination of reflection on your own solution procedures in connection with what Stephan et al. (2014) call, "engaging in the act of listening hermeneutically" to students may have a profound influence on their ideas about how students learn, which may be a catalyst for influencing teachers' beliefs. Building on that, teachers will have to be made familiar with the overall educational philosophy that underlies the local instruction theories and come to grips with key principles—which for RME concern mathematics as an activity, guided reinvention, didactical phenomenology, and emergent modeling (Gravemeijer 2008).

Following the aforementioned reasoning of Fullan (2006), it is clear that developing knowledge and adopting new beliefs will not be sufficient. In order to reorganize their instructional practices, teachers need feedback when they try to enact those practices. If we want to be successful in fostering a substantial innovation of the actual educational practice in schools at a scale, we will have to look for ways of facilitating and supporting groups of teachers who collectively work at improving their teaching practice. Here we may build on work that has been done with the lesson-study model by Hiebert and Stiegler (Hiebert et al. 2002) and on experiences with individual approaches, such as cognitive apprenticeship (Stephan et al. 2014) and coaching (Hoek and Gravemeijer 2011). As a last caveat, we want to point to another layer of complexity, which concerns the larger scale of schools and school systems. Improving the quality of mathematics education on scale requires, among others, a shared, coherent vision of high-quality instruction throughout the whole system (Cobb and Jackson 2011).

In light of the above, we may argue that we may have to take the adaptation of textbook design even further and start thinking about how resources such as textbooks may function within a professional learning community of teachers and even about designing resources for supporting such communities.

Conclusion

In order to prepare today's students for the twenty-first century we will have to transform mathematics. The change that is needed concerns a shift towards general educational goals such as critical thinking, problem solving, collaborating, and communicating, which fit the changes that are advocated for in mathematics education. However, this type of innovation proved to be very hard to achieve, while the power of textbooks to support educational change is limited. Thus, a combination of textbook design and teacher professionalization will have to be employed to achieve the necessary transformation of mathematics education. Based on the inventory we made of what can be learned from decades of experiments with reform mathematics, we conclude that textbooks will have to be adapted to include information about learning processes and means of supporting those learning processes. That is to say, textbooks will have to convey information about local instruction theories, which are embedded in a domain-specific instruction theory. RME may function as such a domain-specific instruction theory, although RME theory itself has to evolve to fit the goals of the twenty-first century. These textbooks will have to be accompanied by teacher professionalization, in which teachers collectively invest in improving their own teaching. Here, the lesson-study model may function as a paradigm. Issues that will have to be addressed are establishing inquiry-oriented social norms and socio-mathematical norms, fostering task orientation, cultivating mathematical interest, identifying and framing topics for discussion, orchestrating productive whole-class discussions, designing and evaluating hypothetical learning trajectories on the basis of local instruction theories, guiding symbolizing and modeling, and carrying vertical mathematization through until the level of more sophisticated mathematics is reached. Given the complexity of such an operation, it may be argued that textbook design and professionalization will have to be carefully aligned to be successful. As a final note, we stress that the teacher has a pivotal role in this process and that teacher ownership is crucial to teacher learning. This points to a third requirement for transforming mathematics education, getting the teachers on board. And given the position of teachers and schools in our society, this means that one of the preparatory steps we as mathematics educators will have to take is to try to convince the wider society of the need to transform mathematics education.

References

Akkerman, S., & Bakker, A. (2011, June). Boundary crossing and boundary objects. *Review of Educational Research, 81*(2), 132–169.

Autor, D., Levy, F., & Murnane, R. (2003). The skill content of recent technological change: An empirical exploration. *Quarterly Journal of Economics, 118*(4), 1279–1333.

Bereiter, C. (1985). Towards a solution of the learning paradox. *Review of Educational Research, 55*(2), 201–226.

Binkley, M., Erstad, O., Herman, J., Raizen, S., Ripley, M., & Rumble, M. (2010). *Defining 21st century skills*. Retrieved from http://atc21s.org/wp-content/uploads/2011/11/1-Defining-21st-Century-Skills.pdf

Brousseau, G. (1988). Le contrat didactique: le milieu. *Recherche en didactique des mathématiques, 9*(3), 33–115.

Brown, A. L. (1992). Design experiments: Theoretical and methodological challenges in creating complex interventions in classroom settings. *Journal of the Learning Sciences, 2*(2), 141–178.

Bruin-Muurling, G. (2010). *The development of proficiency in the fraction domain. Affordances and constraints in the curriculum*. Ph.D. thesis, Eindhoven School of Education, Eindhoven University of Technology, Eindhoven.

Clements, D., & Sarama, J. (2004). Learning trajectories in mathematics education. *Mathematical Thinking and Learning, 6*(2), 81–89.

Cobb, P. (1997). Instructional design and reform: Locating developmental research in context. In M. Beishuizen, K. P. E. Gravemeijer, & E. C. D. M. van Lieshout (Eds.), *The role of contexts and models in the development of mathematical strategies and procedures*. Utrecht: Cdß Press.

Cobb, P., & Jackson, K. (2011). Towards an empirically grounded theory of action for improving the quality of mathematics teaching at scale. *Mathematics Teacher Education and Development, 13*(1), 6–33.

Cobb, P., & Yackel, E. (1996). Constructivist, emergent, and sociocultural perspectives in the context of developmental research. *Educational Psychologist, 31*, 175–190.

Cobb, P., Yackel, E., & Wood, T. (1989). Young children's emotional acts while doing mathematical problem solving. In D. McLeod & V. M. Adams (Eds.), *Affect and mathematical problem solving: A new perspective* (pp. 117–148). New York: Springer.

Cobb, P., Yackel, E., & Wood, T. (1992). A constructivist alternative to the representational view of mind in mathematics education. *Journal for Research in Mathematics Education, 23*(1), 2–33.

Confrey, J., Maloney, A. P., Nguyen, K. H., Mojica, G., & Myers, M. (2009). *Equipartitioning/splitting as a foundation of rational number reasoning using learning trajectories.* Paper presented at the Exploratory Seminar: Measurement Challenges Within the Race to the Top Agenda Center for K – 12 Assessment & Performance Management. 33rd conference of the International Group for the Psychology of Mathematics Education, Thessaloniki, Greece.

Cuban, L. (1984). *How teachers taught: Constancy and change in American classrooms, 1890–1980.* New York: Longman.

Cuban, L. (1990). Reforming again, again and again. *Educational Researcher, 13*, 3–13.

Daro, P., Mosher, F., & Corcoran, T. (2011). *Learning trajectories in mathematics* (Research report No. 68). Madison: Consortium for Policy Research in Education.

Desforges, C., & Cockburn, A. (1987). *Understanding the mathematics teacher, a study of practice in first school.* London: The Falmer Press.

Dewey, J. (1901). The situation as regards the course of study. *Journal of Proceedings and Addresses of the Fortieth Annual Meeting of the National Education Association*, 332–348.

Fosnot, C. T. (2003, June). *Teaching and learning in the 21st century.* Plenary address, AMESA conference, Capetown, South Africa.

Freudenthal, H. (1973). *Mathematics as an educational task.* Dordrecht: Riedel.

Friedman, T. L. (2005). *The world is flat* (pp. 5–12). London: Penguin Books.

Fullan, M. (2006, November). Leading professional learning, *The School Administrator, 63*(10), 10–14. http://www.michaelfullan.ca/Articles_06/Articles_06b.pdf

Gravemeijer, K. (2004). Learning trajectories and local instruction theories as means of support for teachers in reform mathematics education. *Mathematical Thinking and Learning, 6*(2), 105–128.

Gravemeijer, K. (2008). RME theory and mathematics teacher education. In D. Tirosh & T. Wood (Eds.), *International handbook of mathematics teacher education: Vol.1. Knowledge and beliefs in mathematics teaching and teaching development* (pp. 283–302). Rotterdam: Sense Publishers.

Gravemeijer, K. (2010). Mathematics education and the information society. In A. Araújo, A. Fernandes, A. Azevedo, & J. F. Rodrigues (Eds.), *Educational interfaces between mathematics and industry, conference proceedings* (pp. 243–252). Bedford: Comap, Inc.

Gravemeijer, K. (2012). Aiming for 21st century skills. In S. Kafoussi, C. Skoumpourdi, & F. Kalavassis (Eds.), *Proceedings of the Commission Internationale pour l' Etude et L'Am´elioration de l'Enseignement des Math´ematiques (CIEAEM 64): Mathematics education and democracy: Learning and teaching practices* (pp. 30–43). Greece: Rhodes.

Gravemeijer, K., & Van Eerde, D. (2009). Design research as a means for building a knowledge base for teachers and teaching in mathematics education. *Elementary School Journal, 109*(5), 510–524.

Gravemeijer, K., van Heuvel-Panhuizen, M., van den Donselaar, G., Ruesink, N., Streefland, L., Vermeulen, W., te Woerd, E., & van der Ploeg, D. (1991). *Methoden in het reken-wiskundeonderwijs, een rijke context voor vergelijkend onderzoek.* Utrecht: OW&OC/ISOR.

Hiebert, J., Gallimore, R., & Stigler, J. W. (2002). A knowledge base for the teaching profession: What would it look like and how can we get one? *Educational Researcher, 31*(5), 3–15.

Hoek, D., & Gravemeijer, K. (2011). Changes of interaction during the development of a mathematical learning environment. *Journal of Mathematics Teacher Education, 14*, 393–411.

Hoyles, C., Noss, R., Kent, P., & Bakker, A. (2010). *Improving mathematics at work, the need for techno-mathematical literacies* (TLRP's Improving learning series). New York: Routledge.

Jagacinski, C. M., & Nicholls, J. G. (1984). Conceptions of ability and related affects in task involvement and ego involvement. *Journal of Educational Psychology, 76*(5), 909–919.

Janssen, J., van der Schoot, F., & Hemker, B. (2005). *Balans van het reken- wiskundeonderwijs aan het einde van de basisschool 4.* Arnhem: Cito.

Kamii, C., Lewis, B. A., & Livingstone Jones, S. (1993). Primary arithmetic: Children inventing their own procedures. *Arithmetic Teacher, 41*(4), 200–203, Columbia: Teacher College Press.

Kraemer, J.-M. (2011). *Oplossingsmethoden voor aftrekken tot 100.* Ph.D. thesis, Eindhoven School of Education, Eindhoven University of Technology, Eindhoven.

Labinowics, E. (1985). *Learning from children.* Amsterdam: Addison-Wesley.

Levy, F., & Murnane, R. J. (2006). *How computerized work and globalization shape human skill demands.* Downloaded November 2, 2006.

Magidson, S. (2005). Building bridges within mathematics education: Teaching, research, and instructional design. *Journal of Mathematical Behavior, 24*, 135–169.

Meira, L. (1995). The microevolution of mathematical representations in children's activities. *Cognition and Instruction, 13*(2), 269–313.

Mullis, I. V. S., Martin, M. O., Gonzalez, E. J., & Chrostowski, S. J. (2004). *TIMSS 2003 international mathematics report: Findings from IEA's Trends in International Mathematics and Science Study at the fourth and eighth grades.* Boston: Boston College, International Study Center.

National Council of Teachers of Mathematics. (1980). *An Agenda for action: Recommendations for school mathematics of the 1980s.* Reston: National Council of Teachers of Mathematics.

North Central Regional Educational Laboratory and the Metiri Group. (2003). *enGauge, 21st century skills: Literacy in the digital age.* Naperville: NCREL.

OECD. (2010). *PISA 2009 results: What students know and can do – Student performance in reading, mathematics and science* (Vol. 1). Paris: PISA, OECD Publishing.

Partnership for 21st Century Skills. (2008). *21st century skills education & competitiveness. A resource and policy guide.* Downloaded October 19, 2010, from http://www.p21.org/documents/21st_century_skills_education_and_competitiveness_guide.pdf

Ravitch, D. (2010). *Death and life of the Great American school system. How testing and choice are undermining education.* New York: Basic Books, 283 blz. € 24,95.

Roblyer, M. D. (2000). The National Educational Technology Standards (NETS): A review of definitions, implications, and strategies for integrating NETS into K-12 curriculum. *International Journal of Instructional Media, 27*(2), 133–146.

Sfard, A. (1991). On the dual nature of mathematical conceptions: Reflections on processes and objects as different sides of the same coin. *Educational Studies in Mathematics, 22*(1), 1–36.

Shulman, L. S. (1987). Knowledge and teaching: Foundations of the new reform. *Harvard Educational Review, 57*, 1–22.

Simon, M. A. (1995). Reconstructing mathematics pedagogy from a constructivist perspective. *Journal for Research in Mathematics Education, 26*, 114–145.

Stein, M. K., Engle, R. A., Smith, M. S., & Hughes, E. K. (2008). Orchestrating productive mathematical discussions: Five practices for helping teachers move beyond show and tell. *Mathematical Thinking and learning, 10*, 313–340.

Stephan, M., Underwood-Gregg, D., & Yackel, E. (2014). Guided reinvention: What is it and how do teachers learn this teaching approach? In Y. Li (Ed.), *Transforming mathematics instruction: Multiple approaches and practices.* Cham, Switzerland: Springer.

Tarr, J. E., Reys, R. E., Reys, B. J., Chávez, O., Shih, J., & Osterlind, S. J. (2008). The impact of middle-grades mathematics curricula and the classroom learning environment on student achievement. *Journal for Research in Mathematics Education, 39*(3), 247–280.

Thompson, A. G. (1984). The relationship of teachers' conceptions of mathematics and mathematics teaching to instructional practice. *Educational Studies in Mathematics, 15*(2), 105–127.

Treffers, A. (1987). *Three dimensions. A model of goal and theory description in mathematics education* (The Wiskobas project). Dordrecht: Riedel.

Tzur, R., & Simon, M. (2004). Distinguishing two stages of mathematics conceptual learning. *International Journal of Science and Mathematics Education, 2*(2), 287–304.

van den Heuvel-Panhuizen, M. (2010). Reform under attack – Forty years of working on better mathematics education thrown on the scrapheap? No way! In L. Sparrow, B. Kissane, & C. Hurst (Eds.), *Shaping the future of mathematics education: Proceedings of the 33rd annual conference of the Mathematics Education Research Group of Australasia* (pp. 1–25). Fremantle: MERGA.

van den Heuvel-Panhuizen, M., & de Goeij, E. (2007). Offering primary school teachers a multi-approach experience-based learning setting to become a mathematics coordinator in their school [CD-ROM]. In *Proceedings of the 15th ICMI study, The Professional Education and Development of Teachers of Mathematics*, Águas de Lindóia, Brazil, 15–21 May 2005. Unesp.

van Stiphout, I. (2011). *The development of algebraic proficiency in Dutch secondary education.* Ph.D. thesis, Eindhoven School of Education, Eindhoven University of Technology, Eindhoven.

Voogt, J., & Pareja Roblin, N. (2010). *21st century skills – Discussion paper.* Enschede: University of Twente.

Wagner, T. (2008). *The global achievement gap, why even our best schools don't teach the survival skills our children need – And what we can do about it.* New York: Basic Books.

Wenger, E. (1998). *Communities of practice: Learning, meaning, and identity.* Cambridge: Cambridge University Press.

Westbury, I. (1983). How can curriculum guides guide teaching? Introduction to the symposium. *Journal of Curriculum Studies, 1*(1), 1–3.

Whitson, J. A. (1997). Cognition as a semiotic process: From situated mediation to critical reflective transcendence. In D. Kirschner & J. A. Whitson (Eds.), *Situated cognition theory: Social, semiotic, and neurological perspectives* (pp. 97–150). Hillsdale: Erlbaum.

Yackel, E. (1992). *The evolution of second grade children's understanding of what constitutes an explanation in a mathematics class.* Paper presented at the Seventh International Congress of Mathematics Education, Quebec City.

Opportunities to Develop Algebraic Thinking in Elementary Grades Throughout the School Year in the Context of Mathematics Curriculum Changes

Hélia Oliveira and Célia Mestre

Abstract This chapter intends to illustrate and discuss one developmental project in the context of basic education curriculum changes concerning the early introduction of algebraic thinking on classroom instruction in one fourth grade class. From a more general point of view, this discussion centers on the relationship between the official, planned, enacted, and learned curriculum. Different aspects of these dimensions of the curriculum are exemplified from the analysis of some mathematical tasks and instances of the mathematical communication processes that took place in the classroom throughout one school year.

The progress made by the students reveals that the curricular guidelines have several characteristics that altogether contribute to accomplish the general curriculum goal of students' algebraic thinking development: conceiving early algebra as the development of a way of thinking that links arithmetic to algebra, underlying the need to work with valuable mathematical tasks in the classroom, and fostering the students' mathematical communication. However, we contend that the learned curriculum was possible by the project characteristics, where the enacted curriculum reflects the specificity of the class we have been working with.

Keywords Algebraic thinking • Curriculum changes • Classroom instruction • Dimensions of the curriculum • Mathematical communication • Mathematical tasks • Elementary grades

H. Oliveira (✉)
Institute of Education, University of Lisbon, Alameda da Universidade,
1649-013 Lisboa, Portugal
e-mail: hmoliveira@ie.ulisboa.pt

C. Mestre
Research Unity of the Institute of Education, University of Lisbon,
Alameda da Universidade, 1649-013 Lisboa, Portugal
e-mail: celiamestre@hotmail.com

Y. Li et al. (eds.), *Transforming Mathematics Instruction: Multiple Approaches and Practices*, Advances in Mathematics Education, DOI 10.1007/978-3-319-04993-9_11,
© Springer International Publishing Switzerland 2014

Introduction

Algebra has been traditionally conceived in the mathematics curriculum of several countries as a theme that is introduced to students by the age of 12 or 13. The basic education curriculum (grades 1–9) that began to be implemented in some Portuguese schools in the 2009/2010 school year and in every school around the country in the subsequent year brought different perspectives on what algebra is, how should it be taught, and when to start its teaching. This mathematics curriculum (ME 2007) introduces the idea of algebraic thinking as a main goal for students, favoring the connection between arithmetic and algebra, starting in the first 4 years of schooling.

Another significant innovation in this curriculum (ME 2007) is the integration of three learning objectives, designated as transversal capacities: problem solving, mathematical reasoning, and mathematical communication. To develop these capacities, the curriculum materials emphasize the need to present challenging mathematical tasks and to develop new approaches in the classroom, namely, giving students the opportunity to communicate and discuss their ideas with the teacher and with their peers.

An important movement in mathematics education has been advocating a view of algebra as a strand in the curriculum (NCTM 2000) starting in the early years. Often referred to as *early algebra*, this vision for the curriculum has the potential to unify the existing mathematics curriculum into a more connected mathematical experience for students (Kaput et al. 2008). These ideas stimulated us to develop a project with one fourth grade class that seeks to find new ways for "students to work with several layers of awareness of generality in all areas of their mathematics curriculum prior to any formal introduction to algebra" (Britt and Irwin 2011, p. 153). This project intends to promote the development of students' algebraic thinking, and at the same time to contribute to the improvement of students' number sense, which is a main learning objective for the first 4 years of schooling (ME 2007).

These are important curriculum goals that represent a great challenge to teachers of these grades who are generalists and for whom these are relatively far-flung ideas in contrast to their current practices. In fact, the class in this study had supposedly started to work according to these new curriculum perspectives in the previous year, and yet, in the beginning of the project, it was evident that the promotion of algebraic thinking was not present in students' previous mathematical activities.

The objective of this chapter is to discuss the impact of the basic education curriculum changes concerning the early introduction of algebraic thinking on classroom instruction in one fourth grade class, through a collaborative developmental project for one school year. From the analysis of the project's development, centered on some mathematical tasks' examples proposed to primary students and the subsequent classroom activity, we discuss the relationship between the official, planned, enacted, and learned mathematics curriculum.

Different Dimensions of the Curriculum

There is a growing interest in mathematics education in understanding the relationship between the official curriculum and the implemented curriculum or enacted curriculum: for instance, how teachers interpret and adapt the curriculum materials and its implications for students' learning (Lloyd et al. 2009). According to Remillard and Heck (2010), the mathematics curriculum can be regarded "as a plan for the experiences that learners encounter and the actual experiences designed to help them reach specified learning goals" (p. 2). When curriculum reforms take place, the "plan" might change dramatically, compelling the teachers to design new "actual experiences" for students. In effect, the learning that takes place in the classroom is mediated by the actions of the teacher and the curricular materials that are provided.

In this chapter, we consider the curriculum in a broad sense to include the following dimensions: the official or written curriculum as well as other materials that have been produced in association with the designated curriculum to assist teachers in its implementation; the intended curriculum, which includes the teacher's planning (written and/or mental) of the lessons, as well as the resources he/she prepares for the class; the *enacted* curriculum, the one that effectively takes place, by the interaction between the teacher and the students and between the students and the resources; and finally, the *learned* curriculum, what the student effectively learns.

This way of conceiving the curriculum, which recognizes its different dimensions, brings to the forefront the role of the teachers in relation to the curriculum. In particular, we may consider three main perspectives of the teachers' role: as primary "implementers" of the curriculum materials, as experimenters who constantly modify curriculum materials, and as collaborators who take part in the production and testing of curriculum materials (Ziebarth et al. 2009). However, these authors recognize that each teacher may assume different roles in the curriculum development and that these should be better regarded "as points on a continuum" (p. 173). In fact, in different moments or contexts, the teacher may have different levels of participation in the development of the intended curriculum: for instance, by the type of utilization he/she does of curriculum materials.

In respect to the recent curriculum in Portugal (ME 2007), some materials were produced in articulation with the official curriculum, to support teachers in its implementation. The materials produced to support the curriculum ideas in algebra explain the foundation to the big ideas in this theme and propose mathematical tasks to use with students. However, that document does not have a textbook style, as it leaves to the teacher the task of defining the intended curriculum, especially in a transversal theme like algebraic thinking in the first grades.

By the other side, in general, there is a strong adherence to textbooks by the teachers. Each textbook entails a particular perspective concerning the program and therefore displays different versions of the intended curriculum: but even then it is not clear how the teacher will interpret it. The discussion of these issues is relevant for understanding the context where the present reform of the Portuguese mathematics curriculum occurred, and the possibilities for a real impact on classroom instruction.

The Mathematics Curriculum for Basic Education

In different countries such as China, Singapore, Turkey, or the USA, the mathematics curriculum has been changing, establishing new focuses on the mathematical content to be taught and learned as well as on the instructional approaches to be developed (Hirsch and Reys 2009; Fan and Zhu 2007; Kulm and Li 2009; Zembat 2010). This has also happened in Portugal, where the previous mathematics curriculum dated back to 1991. The new curriculum (ME 2007), introduced as a reformulation of the previous, actually presents important new ideas about the teaching and learning of algebra, specifically the notion of algebraic thinking that is presented as a capacity to be developed in students from the early years of schooling. This curriculum also presents new perspectives concerning the development of students' capacities, besides the mathematical content knowledge, and suggests methodological approaches to teaching in order to fulfill the learning objectives. We will expand these ideas in the following Sections.

Algebra in the Curriculum

The mathematics curriculum for basic education in Portugal (ME 2007) presents four main axes for mathematics teaching and learning: working with numbers and operations, algebraic reasoning, geometric thinking, and working with data. In the first 4 years of schooling (First Cycle), there is a big emphasis on the work with numbers and operations in the perspective of developing students' number sense and mental computation. There are suggestions for teachers to explore with students different computational strategies based on the composition and decomposition of numbers, in the properties of the operations and in the relationships between numbers and between operations.

In close connection with these views about the development of students' number sense and mental computation, the curriculum assumes that students in these grades should start to develop algebraic thinking, considering the algebra learning as a form of mathematical thinking from the early years of schooling. The document assumes that students start to deal with algebraic ideas as they establish general relationships between numbers and study certain properties of numbers and operations. However, the topic Regularities, namely, the study of sequences by investigating numerical regularities, is explicitly the entry point to the algebraic reasoning in the official document: "The work with generalizable regularities, according to rules that the students may formulate by themselves, for instance in figurative sequences, helps them to develop the capacity of abstraction and contributes to the development of algebraic reasoning" (ME 2007, p. 14).

Other curriculum materials, produced in articulation with the official curriculum, contend that, as students begin to contact with sequences in the First Cycle, there is an opportunity to begin to work informally the concept of function, in the first years

(Ponte et al. 2009). The official curriculum also establishes a link between the work on numerical sequences and the early study of proportional reasoning: for instance, from tables. Following these curriculum orientations, students should start to explore the notion of joint variation in these school grades. In the Second Cycle (grades 5 and 6), the curricular goals establish that students should further develop those notions, working with them in a more formalized manner, and begin to use algebraic symbolism.

Therefore, the general orientation for the First Cycle concerning students' algebraic thinking is in some way quite fluid coming close to the perspective of the principles and standards (NCTM 2000) which stresses that it should be understood as a way of thinking that brings meaning, depth, and coherence to other subjects' learning. The question is: How is this official curriculum interpreted by the teachers concerning the development of students' algebraic thinking since these are news perspectives that they are not acquainted to? The curricular materials produced to support the process of curriculum transformation develop further these ideas and present instances of possible mathematical tasks to propose to students and, in some cases, also provide examples from the students' work. Even then, it may be difficult to teachers to conceive by their own the intended curriculum to foster the development of algebraic thinking, by anticipating how to construct a path that supports students in that direction. Without professional experience in this domain, teachers will also feel the need to learn from examples of the enacted curriculum that show the students' evolution.

Mathematical Communication

This mathematics curriculum also presented, as learning goals, the development of three transversal capacities: problem solving, mathematical reasoning, and mathematical communication (ME 2007). Choosing from these, we focus our argument on the last point, as it has a strong connection with the work that has been done in the project presented in this chapter. The curricular document stresses that students' mathematical communication plays an essential role in mathematics learning, since it helps them to organize, clarify, and consolidate their thinking. The students develop this capacity as they explain, share, and discuss ideas, strategies, and reasoning. This general learning goal is subdivided into four more specific categories: interpretation, representation, expression, and discussion. Among these, representations assume a paramount importance since mathematical ideas to be understood, explained, or discussed have to be represented in some way. For instance, the curriculum refers, for the First Cycle of schooling, that the teacher should use different types of representations such as drawings and words to represent mathematical ideas and progressively introduce schemes, tables, symbols, and graphs, as well as relate the symbols and schemes created by students to the conventional notation. These mathematical representations are at the heart of algebraic thinking.

This perspective about mathematical communication is fundamental to promote students' algebraic thinking. In fact, the students are able to progress from informal language to a more formal one as they express themselves and analyze other forms of representation of strategies and generalizing processes. Therefore, they need to have opportunities to express their mathematical ideas and exchange their different perspectives and ways of conceiving the mathematical ideas.

Methodological Approaches

The official curriculum makes several suggestions concerning the methodological approaches teachers may adopt in their teaching. There are two aspects we want to stress: the role of the mathematical tasks and of the classroom environment or culture in the learning process. In fact, the curriculum assumes an active role of the students in mathematics learning and that their work is "significantly structured by the tasks the teacher proposes" (ME 2007, p. 8). Globally, the document stresses that the mathematical tasks should provide students one coherent path of learning. Specifically for the First Cycle, the document points out the importance of the tasks' contexts, referring that these are models that support the student's thinking.

This document also assumes the development of transversal capacities as a main goal, as we mentioned before. Accordingly it stresses that the classroom environment "should be favorable to communication, encouraging students to express orally their reasoning and also to express their doubts and difficulties, to pose questions and to comment their own mistakes or those of their colleagues" (p. 30). It also recognizes that it is fundamental to create moments for discussion and reflection, since students "learn not only from the activities they develop but mainly from the reflection they do upon those activities" (p. 11). According to this document, the teacher has a central role in questioning and stimulating the students for these processes.

The Developmental Project

The developmental project that was prepared and carried out by the authors is based on the mathematics curriculum presented (ME 2007) and on recent research on algebraic thinking in the early grades. Taking into account the novelty of the idea of developing students' algebraic thinking in the early grades, this project intends to (1) explore how to construct sequences of mathematical tasks that assist students in that goal and (2) investigate how that development takes place.

Rationale: Algebraic Thinking

The notion of algebraic thinking adopted in this project follows the one defined by Blanton and Kaput (2005) "as a process of generalization of mathematical ideas from a set of particular instances, establish those generalizations through the discourse of argumentation, and express them in increasingly formal and age-appropriate ways" (p. 413). As generalization is at the center of this process, we draw on different authors to go deep in this concept (e.g., Britt and Irwin 2011; Carraher et al. 2008; Dörfler 2008; Ellis 2007; Mason et al. 2009; Russell et al. 2011). Two key domains of algebraic thinking for the early years are the generalized arithmetic and functional thinking (Blanton 2008). The first domain has to do with the use of arithmetic to develop and express generalizations, and the second one with the exploration of numerical and figurative patterns to describe functional relationships. This perspective is in line with the one we find in the Portuguese curriculum, as presented in the previous section. This project intends to show how such orientations can be put into practice.

These two interrelated aspects of early algebraic thinking (relational and functional thinking) are targeted in the project. We focus especially on tasks and contexts that promote the development of quasi-variable thinking (Britt and Irwin 2011), as these seem to be a promising pathway for students to develop the concept of variation and the capacity to generalize (Mestre and Oliveira 2012). Following the perspective of Warren and Cooper (2005), functional thinking may be considered as the relational thinking that focuses on the relations between two or more quantities that change simultaneously. As the notions of relation and transformation are fundamental for the concept of function, the notion of variation should be explored early in school (NCTM 2000) and that can be accomplished through the work, for instance, with numeric and figurative sequences.

The Project: The Intended Curriculum

This project was designed by both authors for one fourth grade class and the lessons were taught by the second author (from now on the "teacher-researcher"). As mentioned above, the main goal was to develop students' algebraic thinking, by looking transversally to the different mathematical topics in the designated curriculum and finding ways to promote "awareness of generality" (Britt and Irwin 2011).

The class has 19 students, 7 girls and 12 boys, with an average age of 9 years. The new mathematics curriculum (ME 2007) was introduced in this school in the previous school year, in the third grade, and the class was taught by a different teacher. However, in the beginning of the school year, when the teacher-researcher proposed the first mathematical tasks from the project to the students, they revealed many difficulties in the questions that involved number sense, exploring regularities, or generalizing processes. They manifested a strong tendency to focus exclusively on the use of algorithms for solving the tasks, but revealed some lack of understanding in its use. We also observed some frailties in their learning when they were exploring numerical relations. For example, when we began to work on numerical sequences with the class, several students were very surprised to notice that the expression 11×3 appeared as a part of the multiplication table, arguing that "The three times table ends with 10×3." Therefore, these first tasks in the project allowed us to understand that the expected number sense and relational thinking were not learned curriculum for the class, and consequently neither was algebraic thinking. This forced us to go back and work on the fundamental ideas that we expected to be developed in the previous year. The sequences of tasks were then constructed on the basis of what the research team evaluated as being the students' learned curriculum, namely, what they already were able to do, and what aspects of the curriculum seemed to us still underdeveloped.

Taking into account the potential algebraic treatment of each of the mathematical topics of the annual class planning, we created five sequences of tasks (Table 1), throughout the school year, according to the new curriculum themes, topics, and specific goals, targeting the aspects of the algebraic thinking that are stressed by the research on this theme.

The mathematical tasks were introduced in the classroom with an average of two per week, lasting from 90 to 120 min. A total of 42 tasks were explored and grouped in the five sequences referred in the previous table.

The paramount importance of the mathematical tasks, which should be cognitively demanding, and the teacher's support to "students' productive engagement with them [the tasks]" (Silver 2009, p. 830) was also present in the project's intended curriculum. The development of the tasks and the way the teacher explores them with the students are grounded on the notion of learning as a sociocultural activity, adopting a dialogic inquiry stance, and anchored on the following perspectives (Wells 2000): curriculum is a means, not an end; outcomes are both aimed for and emergent; activities must allow diversity and originality; and activities are situated and unique. Accordingly, one important aspect of the teacher-researcher's approach is the attention she gives to the moments of whole-class discussion and systematization, since sense-making and communication have been regarded as fundamental mathematical activities (Lloyd 2009) and that it is also a central orientation of this mathematics curriculum (ME 2007), as we mentioned before.

Research Methods

The teacher-researcher has worked in this school for several years as a generalist teacher, but as she had a leave to do research during this school year, she developed these lessons with a class who had another generalist teacher daily. The

Table 1 Sequences of tasks according to the curriculum goals and the project's intended curriculum

Curriculum goals			Project's intended curriculum	
Themes	Topics/subtopics	Specific goals	Algebraic thinking aspects	Sequences of tasks
Numbers and operations	Natural numbers Numerical relationships Multiples and divisors	To identify and give examples of multiples and divisors of a natural number To understand that the divisors of one number are divisors of its multiples (and that multiples of one number are multiples of its divisors)	To explore: Regularities on multiples and divisors Numerical relations The relation of equality The proprieties of operations To express the generalization in natural language	I
	Operations with natural numbers Multiplication	To use computation strategies (mental or written) for the four operations, applying their proprieties To understand the effects of operations on numbers	To explore: Numerical relations The equality relation The proprieties of operations The inverse operations Different representations To express the generalization in different representations	II
			To explore: The proprieties of operations The equality relation The study of variation To express the generalization in different representations	III
Measure	Length and area Perimeter Area	To solve problems involving perimeter and area concepts	To explore: Variation and covariation Functional relations Different representations (natural language, tables, diagrams, graphs, symbolic language)	IV
Numbers and operations	Regularities Sequences	To investigate numerical regularities To solve problems involving proportional reasoning	To explore: Numerical relations Functional relations Relations using different representations (natural language, tables, diagrams, symbolic language)	V

teacher-researcher was present in the classroom from one to three times each week and taught most of the project's lessons.

The project unfolds as a teaching experiment in the classroom and adopts a research design perspective (Gravemeijer and Cobb 2006), involving the planning of sequences of mathematical tasks, teaching, and data collection and analyses, followed by the planning of a new sequence of tasks that takes into consideration the impact of the previous tasks on the students' learning. All lessons were video-taped, and the students' written work on every task was collected. This data collection had two purposes: to analyze the students' progress in order to adjust and plan the following tasks (the developmental project) and to understand how students develop their algebraic thinking (the research project).

Implementing the Project: The Enacted Curriculum

In this chapter, we present instances from the students' activity in three mathematical tasks to illustrate the enacted curriculum in two main dimensions from the intended curriculum for this class: relational reasoning and functional thinking. The chosen tasks focus on important aspects of the algebraic thinking that were explored with the students.

Exploring Computational Strategies

Taking as point of departure for planning the lessons some difficulties concerning students' number sense, a sequence of tasks on computational strategies was developed, targeting the relational thinking. The one we will elaborate on is the fourth task of the second sequence (Fig. 1). Its intention is that students interpret the situation as one where the double and the half relationships were used, explain it, and then generalize the strategy.

In their strategy explanation, the different pairs of students recognized the relations of double and of half between the multiplication tables of four and of eight. The figure above (Fig. 2) shows that these two students were able to identify the relation of double used in the computational strategy. They represent the double relation through numerical expressions, to each one of the examples presented in the task, clearly identifying the products of the eight times table as the double of the products of the four times table.

The answer of the next pair of students illustrates how they recognize the relation of double and half used in the computation strategy (Fig. 3). These students use other examples besides the ones presented in the task, showing the procedure they used to obtain the products of the eight times table using the double of the products from the four times table, even though they did not register them

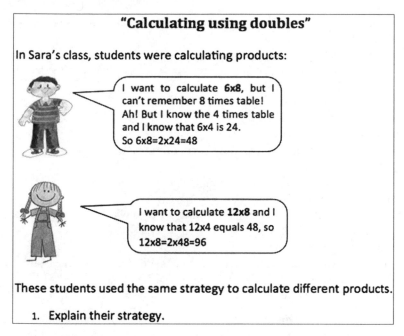

Fig. 1 Task "Calculating using the double"

Fig. 2 António and
Carolina's written work

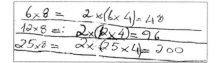

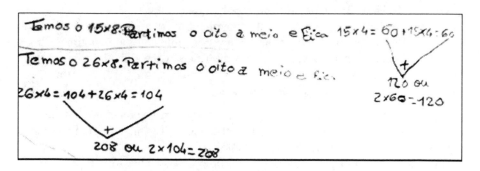

Fig. 3 Joana and Gonçalo's written work

correctly. The students show that they are able to understand the strategy beyond the given examples.

In the collective exploration of the task with the class, some particular cases of the computational strategy were presented. After that, the teacher-researcher conducts the discussion with the goal of helping the students to generalize the strategy beyond the studied cases.

Teacher – Okay. We have three examples, but this strategy only fits those examples?
Several students – No.
Fábio – The strategy we used is good for all computations.
Teacher – And how can we synthesize that strategy in a clear way? What strategy
        was that?
Diogo – We made the double computation.
Teacher – The double of what?
Diogo – Double of the result.
Teacher – Can you explain better? Develop it a little more…?
(Diogo does not answer)
Teacher – What was the multiplication table that we want to work with?
Several students – The eight.
Teacher – And to work with the eight times table, we used which multiplication table?
Several students – The fourth's.
Rita – We can use the halves.
Teacher – And what did we find out? I can make the eight times table using
        which one?
Several students – The fourth's.

Subsequently, another student, Rita, was able to express the computational strategy of generalization beyond the particular cases, but still used confusing and repetitive language. With this in mind, the teacher-researcher asks for a simpler but more general expression, advancing the students in the process.

Rita – If we go to the four times table, the multiply four by the number that we
        wanted from the eight times table, if we multiply twice, we will have the
        result from the eight times table.
Teacher – How can I say that in a simpler way?
Carolina – To know 25×8 we do from 25×4.
Teacher – You are using a particular example. But what if it's more general?
        We were talking about the eight times table and the four times Table.
        I can say that in a very simple way. To know the eight times table, what
        do I do?
Several students – Double the four times table.

From this moment on, one student proposes the generalization of the computation strategy in natural language and writes it on the board: "To find the eight times table, we do the double ($\times 2$) of the four times table."

In these illustrations we can see that students were able to comprehend the structure underlying the computational strategy used in the numerical expressions presented. Therefore, the students identified the double and half relations in the four and the eight times tables from the presented examples. More than that, students were able to use that strategy with other examples. During the collective exploration of the task, students could express the generalization of that computational strategy in natural language, in the context of the multiplication tables they knew.

"Ana and Bruno's stickers"

Ana and Bruno are doing a stickers collection. On last the Sunday, their grandmother gave them the same amount of stickers to paste on their books of stickers. Ana pasted 18 stickers on her book and kept the remaining on the box A. Bruno pasted 20 stickers on his book and kept the remaining on the box B.

We can represent the **amount of Ana's stickers** in this way:

$$18 + Ⓐ$$

Number of stickers pasted on Ana's book   Number of stickers kept on box A

We can also represent the **amount of Bruno's stickers** in this way:

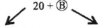

Number of stickers pasted on Bruno's book   Number of stickers kept on box B

As the two kids have the same amount of stickers, we can make this equality:

$$18 + Ⓐ = 20 + Ⓑ$$

a) How many stickers might Ana have in box A and how many stickers might Bruno have in box B?

b) Find if there are other values for the number of stickers in boxes A and B, in way that the total amount of stickers of the two kids is the same.

c) What is the relationship between the numbers you used in box A and box B?

d) If the equality is as it follows, what is the relationship between the numbers in boxes A and B?

$$226 + Ⓐ = 231 + Ⓑ$$

Fig. 4 Task "Ana and Bruno's stickers"

From Quasi-variable Thinking to the Notion of Variation

The task to be presented here (adapted from Stephens and Wang 2008) also focuses on relational thinking and introduces numerical equalities with two unknown quantities in relation, in a realistic context with meaning for students (Fig. 4). It concerns one arithmetic compensation situation, involving addition and subtraction. It was the fifth task of the third sequence that was explored with these students.

This situation was created in order for students to explore quasi-variables (Fujii 2003), as they attend to the structure of the equality, and also to promote algebraic generalization, since they are asked to express the relationship between the unknown quantities and to extend this kind of reasoning to other expressions involving bigger numbers.

In the first question, the students were asked to say how many stickers there were in boxes A and B so that the equality was kept. In the next question, the students

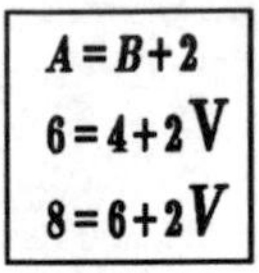

Fig. 5 Exploration of
the representation suggested
by Rita during the collective
discussion

$$A = B + 2$$
$$6 = 4 + 2\,V$$
$$8 = 6 + 2\,V$$

were confronted with the situation of using other possible values for boxes A and B, in order to keep the equality. In that answer, every student presented more than one pair of possible values that kept the equality.

For the third question, regarding the expression of the relation between the values used for boxes A and B, five of the nine pairs of students were able to show, in a very clear way, the relation between boxes A and B with explicit references of the used relationship. For example, one pair of students gave the following answer: "The relationship that exists between the numbers that I used in boxes A and B is that in box A there is always plus two stickers than in box B. Because twenty is two stickers more than eighteen, so it is always plus two stickers." These students show that they recognize the numerical relationship used in the equality, including the numerical value and the direction of the arithmetical compensation. They also recognize and explain that the existing relation between the values given to boxes A and B was dependent on the relation between the initial ones (20 and 18).

In the collective discussion, one of the students, Fábio, spontaneously suggested that the generalization could also be written in mathematical language and proposed the expression "$B - 2 = A$." To facilitate the expressions' discussion presented by Fábio, the teacher-researcher proposed that the students build a table on the board with possible pairs of values for A and B. After that, another student, Rita, suggested that the correct representation should be $A = B + 2$ (Fig. 5). That representation was written on the board, and students experimented with different values of A and B to confirm that the symbolic representation was correct.

In the following lesson, one continuity task, "Find A and B," was explored (Fig. 6). This task was also adapted from Stephens and Wang (2008), but without a modeling context, and also presented a situation of arithmetical compensation, now involving multiplication and division operations.

In the second question, eight of the nine pairs were able to identify the relationship between the numbers in boxes A and B in a very clear way. One pair, João and Lawry, wrote it this way: "The relation that exists between numbers that I put in the Boxes A and B is that $6 \times 2 = 12$, and because 12 is the double ($\times 2$) of the number 6, so every numbers that I put in box A are the double ($\times 2$) of [those] in box B."

The solution shows that students were able to represent symbolically, through two different expressions, the relationship between the values of A and B (like the double or the half) (Fig. 7). They also presented a table, evidencing the recognition of A and B as variable values and some sense of covariation. However, possibly influenced by the addictive nature of the compensation present in the previous task, they defined inaccurately the third pair of values, assuming that "the difference is two."

---

1. **Think about the following mathematical sentence:**

$$6 \times Ⓐ = 12 \times Ⓑ$$

a) Put numbers in box Ⓐ and box Ⓑ to make three correct sentences like the one above.

b) What is the relationship between the numbers in box Ⓐ and box Ⓑ?

c) If the mathematical sentence is the following one, what is the relationship between numbers in box Ⓐ and box Ⓑ?

$$15 \times Ⓐ = 5 \times Ⓑ$$

Fig. 6 Task "Find A and B"

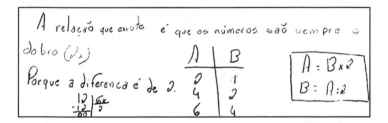

Fig. 7 António and Fábio's written work

In the collective discussion, the students present, without difficulty, the relation between the numbers of box A and the box B and vice versa. Some students' statements show that, besides comprehending the numerical relation between the unknown values, they are able to reach a generalization of the values that satisfy the present equality and identify the variable concept. The following excerpts are instances of that:

João – The numbers of the box A will always be the double of what is in the box B.

Matilde – The box A can be any number, but it always has to be the double of the box B.

Keeping in mind the work done with the symbolic expressions in the previous task, the teacher asks for another way to write A and B. Matilde goes to the board and correctly writes: $A = 2 \times B$ and $B = A:2$.

In the last question of this task, involving more complex relations of the triple and the third part, all students were able to express the relation between A and B

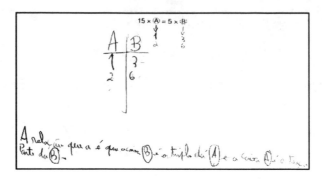

Fig. 8 João and Marco's written work

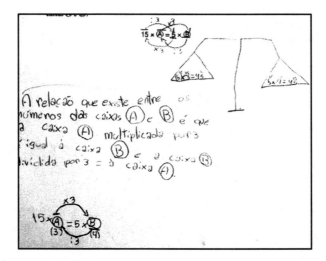

Fig. 9 Gonçalo and Joana's written work

values in a more or less explicit way. None of the pairs used only one form of representation, completing the explanation of the relation in natural language with another form of representation, like a table or an arrow diagram. For example, in the solution of one pair of students (Fig. 8), we observe the double use of a structured table and of a *proto-table* formed by two columns with two pairs of values. These students were able to express the relation between the values given to boxes A and B in natural language and in a clear way: "The relationship is that box B is the triple of box A and box A is one third of box B."

Another pair of students used different ways to express the relation between the numbers in boxes A and B (Fig. 9). The arrows diagram shows the kind of relations between *A* and *B* values, and also the dependency relation with 15 and 5. These students also use the scale representation to illustrate an example of the equality.

In the collective discussion, we observed that the majority of students understood the numerical relationships portrayed by this question and could also explain it in

---

Cubes with Stickers

Joana is building a game with cubes and stickers. She connects the cubes through one of its faces and forms a queue of cubes. Then she glues a sticker in each of the cube's faces. The figure shows the construction that Joana did with two cubes. In that construction she used 10 stickers.

1. Find out how many stickers Joana used in a construction with:
1.1. Three cubes; 1.2. Four cubes; 1.3.Ten cubes; 1.4. Fifty two cubes.

2. Can you find out what is the rule that allows you to know how many stickers Joana used in a construction with any given number of cubes? Explain how you thought.

Fig. 10 Task "Cubes with Stickers" (Adopted from Moss et al. 2005)

natural language, for instance, when they say that "B could be any number, but must be the triple of A," and in symbolic language through mathematical expressions such as "$B = 3 \times A$" and "$A = B:3$."

The analysis of the students' activity shows that they are able to recognize the structure of the numerical equality presented and express the compensation involved, attributing correct values and recognizing the direction of that compensation. The work developed by students also presents strong evidence of the use of the equal sign in a relational mode, an important aspect of relational thinking. The students also begin to use the notions of variation and covariation, even in an incipient way, and expressing those notions by the use of several forms of representations.

Exploring Functional Thinking in Figurative Sequences

Our third example comes from one of the last lessons in the project (sequence V), illustrating how the work on sequences helped students to consolidate their understandings of variation and how symbolizing is becoming a form of communication with meaning to them. This task was intended to help students further explore the functional thinking by identifying the variables presented in the situation and how they relate to each other. Different forms of representations were expected to appear in students' written work.

The proposed task "Cubes with Stickers" had two parts, but here we discuss only the first one (Fig. 10). Students had worked on different numerical or figurative sequences in other lessons throughout the year, but this one was more difficult since they had to grasp the pattern in three-dimensional objects.

The teacher-researcher used concrete materials to model the situation before students started working on the task autonomously. The students, in general, easily found the general expression for the sequence, expressing it in words and/or in symbols, and some of them also fell back to drawings and tables for depicting the

Fig. 11 João and Henrique's written work

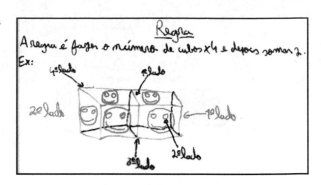

Fig. 12 André, Joana, and Gonçalo's written work

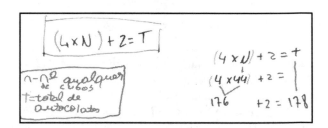

situation. All of the students understood in this moment that what they were supposed to do was finding a "general rule" (as they expressed it) for the number of stickers in any cube. As a matter of fact, when they started to solve the task they immediately searched for a relationship between two variables and did not look for the relationship between consecutive terms of the sequence, since they no long accepted a recursive generalization as a desirable output of their work.

Effectively, all groups of students were able to explain the direct relation between the general term and its respective order. A few of them expressed that relation just in a word sentence, but showed that they know how to determine the number of stickers for any required number. In the case of João and Henrique (Fig. 11), they explained that the rule ("regra") is obtained by "doing the number of cubes multiplied by four and then adding two." They also drew one figure in the sequence to explain why they multiply by four.

One of the many pairs of students that expressed the direct relation in algebraic symbols, writing down a formula, also specialized for a certain number of cubes to illustrate how to use that expression (Fig. 12). They also explained the meaning of the variables they use: "n- any number of cubes" and "T=total of cubes."

The two examples show that students were not only able to understand the structure of the sequence – what is constant and what changes – and correctly realized the variation of the involved quantities, but also expressed it in a general form. The emergence of functional thinking is also evident, since students used tables to represent the two variables involved in the situation: the number of cubes in each construction and the respective number of stickers. In the following example, the students also establish a relationship between each element in the right column

Fig. 13 André and
Carolina's written work

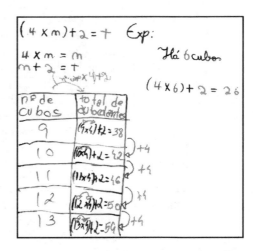

Fig. 14 Beatriz, Diogo,
and Rita's written work

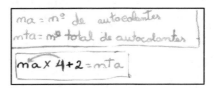

and the previous one, which has to do with the direct relation they found for each
term of the sequence (Fig. 13). These different ways of looking at the variation
between the quantities involved in the situation strengthen the development of
students' functional thinking; therefore, the teacher-researcher selected this as one
of the students' strategies to be discussed with the whole class.

In the moment when students present and discuss their work with the whole
class, we gather evidence that they are using the algebraic symbolism with personal
meaning to communicate their mathematical ideas. Students make an effort to
understand their colleagues' ideas because they want to verify its correctness and
also to address the teacher-researcher's common question for analyzing which of
those strategies or expressions they consider to be simpler or more efficient according
with the task's purposes. In the next example (Fig. 14), when Rita presents her
group's solution, some students question their option for the independent variable:
"na = number of stickers."

João – It's very complicated because [you use] "na," number of stickers, [it means
        that] you should already know the number of stickers…
Gonçalo – It's the same thing to know the number of stickers and to do times four.
João – But then she already knew the number of stickers!
Rita – No, we don't. For example, we have this square, we have one sticker on top,
        you do one times four, but I don't know the total number of stickers.
Teacher – Explain that using the cubes.

Rita – We have all these stickers, we are not counting anything, we only count the ones on top that are two … there are two stickers, you do two times four plus two.

Carolina – But why don't you put the number of cubes? It's easier to understand…

(…)

Teacher – I would like to hear what Matilde thinks about this issue.

Matilde – I think that what Rita said was right. I understood that she was explaining that it can be three or four cubes or 100, it can be any number. On top you have the stickers, then all you have to do is to multiply those stickers by four and then doing plus two.

In the class there are two groups of students with different opinions: those who think that Rita's group is correct and that their solution is similar to those presented before, as they recognize that the variable is the same and that the apparent difference only has to do with the label they used, and those who do not accept their colleagues' choice for the independent variable. After arriving at a consensus mediated by the teacher-researcher, the class is further pushed to look carefully into the description of the label used by Rita's group.

Teacher – Now I think that… we need to be careful when we use "any given number of smiles," or "any given number of stickers," I think we need to be especially careful there…

Gonçalo – In there she said the one on top, but if it is the one on the front it is also 3 stickers and 3 cubes.

Diogo – It's the same.

Teacher – And if it is the total of stickers isn't it also the number of stickers?

Several students – Yes.

Teacher – So what is missing to be said there? Number of stickers…

Diogo – And cubes.

Fábio – No, "Number of stickers on top."

Teacher – "On top, of one cube face…" because if not, I can't…

João – If not it can be any cube face and not the "side" ones…

These episodes coming from the last part of this teaching experiment show that these students are developing very important aspects of the intended algebraic thinking. The level of symbolism that some students used indicates that they are not simply reproducing formalized symbols introduced by the teacher but that symbolizing is becoming a form of communication with meaning for them.

Concluding Remarks

Reforms in mathematics curriculum often do not produce the desired outcome in the learned curriculum, especially when innovative and challenging ideas are presented to teachers who have limited knowledge and experience concerning these new perspectives. We consider the development of algebraic reasoning in the early grades to be one of those cases, at least in our country. In this chapter we illustrate and discuss the impact of basic education curriculum changes concerning the early introduction of algebraic thinking on classroom instruction in one fourth grade class and reflect, from a more general point of view, upon the relationship between the official, the planned, the enacted, and the learned curriculum.

From the implementation of the project, we conclude that according to the designated curriculum, it is possible to implement a trajectory for teaching algebraic thinking development throughout the school year and that students are starting exhibiting that kind of thinking effectively. In line with what has been described, for instance, in the case of Chinese or Singaporean elementary students (Cai et al. 2011), we also found for these Portuguese elementary students that an earlier emphasis on algebraic ideas contributes to the development of algebraic thinking. For us, this is possible to be done in the context of the mathematics curriculum (ME 2007) as it integrates three important dimensions: *a developmental perspective of algebraic thinking, the promotion of mathematical communication*, and *valuable mathematical tasks*.

One main concern for teachers, in the context of curricular reforms, is the possibility of the inclusion of new topics in an already crowded curriculum (Russell et al. 2011). The progress of this project allows us to demystify this obstacle, since students have learned the designated curriculum as well as developed new understandings and capacities, during 1 year of implementation of the new curriculum. Certain characteristics of the curriculum were expanded by the project, according to the research in this field, namely, (1) bringing out the generalized character of arithmetic, (2) exploring relational thinking in different situations, and (3) using the work with regularities and sequences to promote the emergence of students' functional thinking. The link between arithmetic and early algebra is made through the generalization of relationships and properties, and the *development of algebraic ideas is regarded as a form of thinking*.

Concerning the development of *students' mathematical communication* considered as a capacity in the mathematics curriculum (ME 2007), two main ideas seem very promising to the way they were explored and expanded in the project: the promotion of the use of different representations and the quest for students to explain and discuss their ideas. These provided the means for the further development of generalization in the classroom's discourse and for the students' progress in the use of algebraic symbolism.

New methodological approaches recommended by the mathematics curriculum included classroom management issues as well as the nature of the mathematical tasks proposed to students. The work that has been carried out in the project following the curriculum methodological approaches shows evidence of what Murray (2010) describes as being an essential ingredient of early algebraic instruction: "the focus on student reasoning and the discourse that allows students to identify connections among concepts, and then build on these connections to form generalizations" (p. 73). This is possible when the teacher organizes the classroom activities while assuming the sharing and discussion of students' ideas as part of the learning process. For that to happen, the *mathematical tasks* also have to be judiciously chosen in order to (1) motivate students to the activity by the challenging them, (2) potentiate relevant elements of algebraic thinking, and (3) establish connections with previous work. We believe that the tasks in the project possess these characteristics, as the enacted and learned curriculum went together.

As the mathematics curriculum for basic education in Portugal (ME 2007) proposed general orientations concerning the development of algebraic thinking, this project reveals the possibility of effectively developing an intended and an enacted curriculum that serves the purposes of the official one. The enacted curriculum that unfolded from this project may help teachers to see how to plan for algebraic thinking and how the curriculum can be implemented. This is a very important step since it seems to be a challenging goal in mathematics education, one that raises many difficulties even for teachers with a strong mathematical preparation (Oliveira 2009).

In the context of the implementation of this curriculum (ME 2007), several initiatives have taken place: for instance, the production of materials according to the ideas of the official document, as well as some in-service courses for teachers that assume different forms (Ponte 2012). Therefore, we envision three important dimensions in the implementation of some new big ideas in the context of a curricular transformation (in this case, for algebraic thinking): one path for curriculum development, supportive curriculum materials, and the envisioned teacher development.

Although the field of research on teachers' use of curriculum materials is growing, it is still underdeveloped (Lloyd et al. 2009). Therefore, projects as this one that seek to integrate the official curriculum and accompanying materials as well as the results from the research in the field may bring new understandings about this issue. In fact, the present project elucidates the complex relationship between the intended and the enacted knowledge in classes where the teacher's instructional approach assumes a dialogic inquiry stance (Wells 2000), and consequently the role of the students in defining the enacted dimension of the curriculum is highly noteworthy.

In this context the teacher-researcher assumes an active role in the production of the curriculum materials assuming simultaneously the character of experimenter and collaborator (Ziebarth et al. 2009). In fact, collaboration settings between teachers and researchers may be a favorable context to help teachers to have confidence in implementing new approaches (Ponte et al. 2003). The work done by the research team gave the teacher-researcher the necessary intellectual and emotional confidence to carry on such a demanding endeavor of planning and developing five sequences of tasks with one class for 1 year.

This project exemplifies one possible path for primary students' development of algebraic thinking according to the mathematics curriculum (ME 2007). We believe that the replication of such mathematical experience in other classes with other teachers is not a simple endeavor. The discussion of projects that center on the development of teaching units may be inspiring for teachers. In this case, we illustrate that it was possible to assist students to develop algebraic thinking, even when they seemed far from having achieved the intended curriculum when the project begun. This is quite promising, because if students start earlier and continue after this school grade to work in this way, they will be in a very good position to overcome many of the difficulties that research has identified in algebra learning. The gap between the intended and the learned curricula is most often a matter of the enacted curriculum. In this developmental project, at the same time that we adopted the curriculum orientations including intended mathematics topics, capacities, and ways of working in the classroom, we assume a perspective of learning where outcomes are both aimed for and emergent and where activities are situated and unique (Wells 2000). Therefore, the enacted curriculum reflects the specificity of the class we have been working with. The ecological elements present in each context have to be taken into consideration when new curriculum proposals arrive at schools, and those include both the students and the teachers.

Acknowledgment This work is supported by national funds through FCT – *Fundação para a Ciência e Tecnologia* – in the frame of the Project *Professional Practices of Mathematics Teachers* (contract PTDC/CPE-CED/098931/2008).

References

Blanton, M. L. (2008). *Algebra and the elementary classroom. Transforming thinking, transforming practice*. Portsmouth: Heinemann.

Blanton, M., & Kaput, J. (2005). Characterizing a classroom practice that promotes algebraic thinking. *Journal for Research in Mathematics Education, 36*(5), 412–446.

Britt, M. S., & Irwin, K. C. (2011). Algebraic thinking with or without algebraic representation: A pathway for learning. In J. Cai & E. Knuth (Eds.), *Early algebraization: A global dialogue from multiple perspectives* (pp. 137–159). New York: Springer.

Cai, J., Ng, F. S., & Moyer, J. (2011). Developing students' algebraic thinking in earlier grades: Lessons from China and Singapore. In J. Cai & E. Knuth (Eds.), *Early algebraization: A global dialogue from multiple perspectives* (pp. 21–41). New York: Springer.

Carraher, D. W., Martinez, M. V., & Schliemann, A. D. (2008). Early algebra and mathematical generalization. *ZDM – The International Journal on Mathematics Education, 40*, 3–22.

Dörfler, W. (2008). En route from patterns to algebra: Comments and reflections. *International Journal on Mathematics Education, 40*, 143–160.

Ellis, A. B. (2007). A taxonomy for categorizing generalizations: Generalizing actions and reflection generalizations. *The Journal of the Learning Sciences, 16*, 221–262.

Fan, L., & Zhu, Y. (2007). From convergence to divergence: The development of mathematical problem solving in research, curriculum, and classroom practice in Singapore. *ZDM – The International Journal on Mathematics Education, 39*, 491–501.

Fujii, T. (2003). Probing students' understanding of variables through cognitive conflict problems: Is the concept of a variable so difficult for students to understand? In N. A. Pateman, B. J. Dougherty, & J. T. Zilliox (Eds.), *Proceedings of the 27th conference of the International Group for the Psychology of Mathematics Education* (pp. 49–65). Honolulu: PME.

Gravemeijer, K., & Cobb, P. (2006). Design research from a learning design perspective. In J. van den Akker, K. Gravemeijer, S. McKenney, & N. Nieveen (Eds.), *Educational design research* (pp. 45–85). London: Routledge.

Hirsch, C. R., & Reys, B. J. (2009). Mathematics curriculum: A vehicle for school improvement. *ZDM – The International Journal on Mathematics Education, 41*, 749–761.

Kaput, J., Carraher, D. W., & Blanton, M. L. (Eds.). (2008). *Algebra in the early grades* (pp. xvii–xxi). New York: Lawrence Erlbaum Associates & NCTM.

Kulm, G., & Li, Y. (2009). Curriculum research to improve teaching and learning: National and cross-national studies. *ZDM – The International Journal on Mathematics Education, 41*, 709–715.

Lloyd, G. M. (2009). School mathematics curriculum materials for teachers' learning: Future elementary teachers' interactions with curriculum materials in a mathematics course in the United States. *ZDM – The International Journal on Mathematics Education, 41*, 763–775.

Lloyd, G. M., Remillard, J. T., & Herbel-Eisenmann, B. A. (2009). Teachers' use of curriculum materials: An emerging field. In J. T. Remillard, B. A. Herbel-Eisenmann, & G. M. Lloyd (Eds.), *Mathematics teachers at work: Connecting curriculum materials and classroom instruction* (pp. 3–14). New York: Routledge.

Mason, J., Stephens, M., & Watson, J. (2009). Appreciating mathematical structure for all. *Mathematics Education Research Journal, 21*(2), 10–32.

Mestre, C., & Oliveira, H. (2012). From quasi-variable thinking to algebraic thinking: A study with grade four students. In *Pre-proceedings of the 12th International Congress on Mathematical Education* (pp. 2091–2098). Seoul: ICMI.

Ministério da Educação – ME. (2007). *Programa de Matemática do Ensino Básico* [Mathematics curriculum for basic education]. Lisboa: DGIDC.

Moss, J., Beaty, R., McNab, S. L., & Eisenband, J. (2005). *The potential of geometric sequences to foster young students' ability to generalize in Mathematics.* http://www.brookings.edu/gs/brown/algebraicreasoning.htm

Murray, M. K. (2010). Early algebra and mathematics specialists. *The Journal of Mathematics and Science: Collaborative Explorations, 12*, 73–81.

National Council of Teachers of Mathematics. (2000). *Principles and standards for school mathematics.* Reston: NCTM.

Oliveira, H. (2009). Understanding the teacher's role in supporting students' generalization when investigating sequences. *Quaderni di Ricerca in Didattica (Matematica), 19*(Supplemento 4), 133–143.

Ponte, J. P. (2012). A practice-oriented professional development programme to support the introduction of a new mathematics curriculum in Portugal. *Journal of Mathematics Teacher Education, 15*(4), 317–327.

Ponte, J. P., Segurado, I., & Oliveira, H. (2003). A collaborative project using narratives: What happens when pupils work on mathematical investigations? In A. Peter-Koop, V. Santos-Wagner, C. Breen, & A. Begg (Eds.), *Collaboration in teacher education: Examples from the context of mathematics education* (pp. 85–97). Dordrecht: Kluwer.

Ponte, J. P., Branco, N., & Matos, A. (2009). *Álgebra no Ensino Básico* [Algebra in basic education]. Lisboa: ME-DGIDC.

Remillard, J., & Heck, D. (2010) Influences on the enacted curriculum. *Conference presented at the CSMC Research Associates.* Accessed from http://mathcurriculumcenter.org/PDFS/RemillardHeck.pdf

Russell, S., Schifter, D., & Bastable, V. (2011). Developing algebraic thinking in the context of arithmetic. In J. Cai & E. Knuth (Eds.), *Early algebraization: A global dialogue from multiple perspectives* (pp. 43–69). New York: Springer.

Silver, E. A. (2009). Cross-national comparisons of mathematics curriculum materials: What might we learn? *ZDM – The International Journal on Mathematics Education, 41*, 827–832.

Stephens, M., & Wang, X. (2008). Investigating some junctures in relational thinking: A study of year 6 and year 7 students from Australia and China. *Journal of Mathematics Education, 1*(1), 28–39.

Warren, E., & Cooper, T. (2005). Young children's ability to use the balance strategy to solve for unknowns. *Mathematics Education Research Journal, 17*(1), 58–72.

Wells, G. (2000). Dialogic inquiry in education: Building on the legacy of Vygotsky. In C. D. Lee, & P. Smagorinsky (Eds.), *Vygotskian perspectives on literacy research* (pp. 51–85). New York: Cambridge University Press. Accessed from https://www.csun.edu/~SB4310/601%20files/dialogicinquiry.pdf

Zembat, I. O. (2010). A micro-curricular analysis of unified mathematics curricula in Turkey. *ZDM – The International Journal on Mathematics Education, 42,* 443–455.

Ziebarth, S., Hart, E. W., Marcus, R., Ritsema, B., Schoen, H. L., & Walker, R. (2009). High school teachers as negotiators between curriculum intentions and enactment: The dynamics of mathematics curriculum development. In J. T. Remillard, B. A. Herbel-Eisenmann, & G. M. Lloyd (Eds.), *Mathematics teachers at work: Connecting curriculum materials and classroom instruction* (pp. 171–189). New York: Routledge.

Transformation of Japanese Elementary Mathematics Textbooks: 1958–2012

Tad Watanabe

Abstract Quality of teaching is a major factor in students' mathematics learning. Stigler and Hiebert (1999) showed that mathematics teaching in Japanese schools is significantly different from what is typically observed in US classrooms. However, Japanese mathematics educators claim that Japanese mathematics teaching has transformed significantly over the last 50 years. Although teaching is influenced by a variety of factors, textbooks play a significant role in what mathematics is taught and how it is taught. In other words, textbooks may significantly influence students' opportunities to learn. Thus, six editions of a Japanese elementary school mathematics series since 1958 were analyzed to identify any change that might indicate the transformation of mathematics instruction in Japan. The analysis revealed that the features included in the series have changed over the years to support more explicitly the problem-solving-based mathematics instruction described by Stigler and Hiebert (1999).

Keywords Elementary school mathematics • Japan • Historical analysis • Textbook analysis • Problem-solving-based instruction

Introduction

There is a general consensus that teaching is the most critical in-school factor influencing students' learning (e.g., National Council for Accreditation of Teacher Education 2010). Therefore, continuously improving mathematics teaching is a major focus of mathematics educators, both practitioners and researchers.

T. Watanabe (✉)
Department of Mathematics and Statistics, Kennesaw State University,
1000 Chastain Rd. Mail Bag # 1601, Kennesaw, GA 30144, USA
e-mail: twatanab@kennesaw.edu

Y. Li et al. (eds.), *Transforming Mathematics Instruction: Multiple Approaches and Practices*, Advances in Mathematics Education, DOI 10.1007/978-3-319-04993-9_12, © Springer International Publishing Switzerland 2014

Mathematics teaching is, however, a complex activity and is influenced by many factors. It is unlikely that changes in one single factor would completely transform mathematics teaching either individually or collectively. On the other hand, the effects of changes in several factors may not be purely additive – the whole may be more than just the simple sum of the parts. Therefore, it is important that we continue to work on those factors we do know influence mathematics teaching.

One important factor that has been shown to influence teaching is textbooks. Shimahara and Sakai (1995) argued that elementary school teachers in both Japan and the United States heavily depend on their textbooks to teach mathematics. Textbooks are the essential bridge between the intended curriculum (such as a national course of study in Japan and the Common Core State Standards (CCSSI 2010) in the United States) and the implemented curriculum. Thus, textbooks influence both what and how mathematics teachers teach, which in turn influence students' opportunities to learn mathematics.

Stigler and Hiebert (1999) characterized Japanese mathematics instruction as "structured problem solving" (p. 27). In this form of teaching, a lesson starts with a teacher posing a problem without showing students how to solve it. After students tackle the problem independently for several minutes, the teacher will have them share their solutions, often both correct and incorrect. The teacher will then orchestrate a whole class discussion, carefully analyzing the shared ideas to lead the class to an understanding of new mathematics. The lesson ends with a brief period in which the teacher, often with the students, summarizes what was learned in the lesson. According to a survey conducted by the Japan Society of Mathematical Education (2001), more than 95 % of Japanese teachers surveyed felt that this style of mathematics teaching that centers on problem solving is a generally effective teaching model. In the same survey, about 60 % of the teachers responded that they either regularly or frequently utilize this style of teaching. An additional 37 % of the teachers responded that they occasionally implement problem-solving-based lessons.

Watanabe's (2001) examination of Japanese elementary school mathematics textbooks and the accompanying teacher's manuals revealed that the textbooks are organized to support structured problem solving. In the Japanese elementary mathematics textbooks, the beginning of a lesson is signified by a problem. The teacher's manual will often include anticipated students' responses, including common misconceptions. The manual also provides a mathematical evaluation of some of those responses, which may be useful as teachers orchestrate the whole class discussion. In addition, the teacher's manual includes *hatsumon* which are key questions teachers can pose to facilitate students' mathematical explorations.

Although the current Japanese elementary mathematics textbooks may be organized to support structured problem solving, some Japanese mathematics educators argue that the shift to the problem-solving-based mathematics instruction is a fairly recent event, strongly influenced by the publication of the NCTM's *Agenda for Action* in 1980 (e.g., A. Takahashi 2001, personal communication). Several other influential writings on problem solving, including George Polya's *How to Solve It*, were translated and published in Japan in the 1970s and 1980s, which Japanese mathematics educators examined and tested their ideas through lesson study to gradually transform their instruction.

Therefore, if the shift to structured problem solving is a recent event and textbooks are one of the critical influences of mathematics instruction, a natural question to ask is how Japanese mathematics textbooks have changed over the years. To explore that question, 6 editions of a Japanese elementary mathematics textbook series from 1958 to present were analyzed. This chapter reports the findings from the analysis of these editions and discusses the potential implications.

Methodology

Textbooks

Currently, there are six commercial publishers who produce elementary school (grades 1 through 6) mathematics textbooks. The textbook series examined for this study is published by Tokyo Shoseki. Historically, the series has been one of the two most widely used elementary mathematics textbooks in Japan. These two series are used in about 70 % of Japanese schools. The 1989 and 2008 editions have been translated into English. All textbooks used in Japanese schools must be reviewed and approved by the Ministry of Education, Culture, Sports, Science, and Technology to ensure their alignment to the national courses of study (COS). Since the original COS, which was published after the World War II, the COS has been revised eight times. Specifically, the editions examined in this study were approved for six different revisions – 1958, 1968, 1977, 1989, 1999, and 2008.[1]

Mathematical Focus of the Analysis

Examining the entirety of the textbooks was not feasible. Therefore, the analysis focused on two topics: area of triangles and quadrilaterals in grade 5 and multiplication and division by fractions in grade 6. These two topics were selected because they were two of the critical foundations for algebra identified by the National Mathematics Advisory Panel (2008). In addition, the grade-level placement of these topics remained constant across all revisions of the COS. By focusing on the topics that were consistently discussed at the same grade level, the difference in grade placement could be eliminated as a potential reason for modifications. Finally, these topics remain challenging both for teachers to teach and for students to learn. These topics can easily be taught by simply giving students the formulas or the

---

[1] Because some of the old editions obtained for the analysis did not include the publication years, in this manuscript these editions are referenced by the corresponding COS years.

algorithms. Yet, such a procedural focus is far from sufficient in light of recent recommendations and standards (e.g., NCTM 2000; CCSSI 2010). Therefore, understanding how Japanese textbooks transformed the teaching of these topics may be informative for teachers from other countries.

Textbook Analysis

Because the current study is examining the changes in Japanese elementary school mathematics textbooks in light of the structured problem-solving approach to mathematics teaching, the analysis needed to focus on the important features of this teaching approach. Those features include:

- A lesson focus on one (or a few) problem(s)
- An invitation for students to share their own ideas
- Critical examination of solution strategies by students to synthesize a new idea and/or a procedure (Stigler and Hiebert 1999; Takahashi 2011)

Thus, even though a lesson centers on a problem, the solution of the problem is not the focus. Rather, it is the reasoning process of solution strategies and collective critical reflection on those strategies that are the central features of instruction. Furthermore, visual representations play an important role for both teachers and students (Nunokawa 2012). Therefore, a decision was made to focus the analysis on problems and visual representations in these editions. In addition, we attempted to identify and examine any other features that might influence the way teachers might teach mathematics with these textbooks.

The analysis of these editions took place in two stages. In stage one, the focus was identifying features of the textbook. Thus, during this stage, all problems as well as their locations in these editions were marked. The problems were then counted and examined to determine their natures – for example, if the question was just asking for a specific numerical answer or asking for an explanation. The problem context for all word problems was also noted. Likewise, all visual representations in the units were marked, and their types were recorded.

In the second stage of the analysis, the findings identified in the first stage were compared and contrasted across different editions. For example, a probe was made into the use of the same problems, or problems in the same context but different numerical values, in different editions. If a problem found in one edition was not in other editions, the body of the textbook in other editions was examined to see if the same question, or a similar one, was being discussed in the narrative. Another example of the comparison made is the nature of worked-out solutions. If a complete solution to a problem was presented in one edition, the other editions were examined to see if a comparable problem was also worked out. As those worked-out problems were compared, it was also noted that some editions would attribute those solutions to hypothetical elementary school students and ask students who are using the textbook to think about the solution strategy. Yet, in another edition, alternative solutions were presented, and students were asked to compare them.

Similar comparisons were made with respect to the visual representations identified in the first stage. For example, if a particular type of visual representation was used in an edition, the other editions were checked to see if the same type of representation was also used with similar problems and what other representations preceded or followed the representation. For example, most editions used double number line diagrams to represent multiplication of fractions, but in some editions, the representation was presented later in the unit than in others. Finally, as different editions of the series were compared and contrasted, modifications of some features in these editions were noted.

Findings

Problems

Table 1 summarizes the number of problems in these 6 editions of the textbook series. As for the number of problems, the oldest edition (1958) appears to include a slightly smaller number of problems than the other five editions, both in terms of the total numbers and in terms of the average number per textbook page. This difference becomes more distinct when we consider where these problems are found. In a textbook chapter, whether we are looking at a Japanese textbook or a US textbook, we often find special sections that are composed of collections of problems. Those sections are often titled "Exercises," "Practices," "Unit Problems," etc. The 1958 edition differs from the other five editions in that it contains many more problems proportionally in those special sections than the other 5 editions do. Thus, when only the main body of the unit is considered, the 1958 edition contains, on the average, only one problem per page, much fewer than the other five editions, as it can be seen in Table 1.

On the surface, a fewer number of problems may appear to be more consistent with the problem-solving teaching often attributed to Japanese mathematics teaching. However, there is another difference in where problems appear in the 1958 textbook

Table 1 Number of problems and their distributions

COS year	1958	1968	1977	1989	2000	2008
Area
# of problems total	43	64	71	53	60	88
# of problems/page	3.1	4.6	4.4	3.3	4.3	4.2
# of problems in special sections	26	27	15	13	19	14
# of problems in the body/page	1.0	4.1	4.3	3.6	4.1	4.1
Fractions
# of problems total	68	115	147	80	82	86
# of problems/page	3.4	4.4	4.6	3.8	4.3	3.7
# of problems in special sections	44	48	45	16	25	19
# of problems in the body/page	2	3.7	4.1	3.8	3.8	3.5

Fig. 1 Three hypothetical students' ideas about how to find the area of the triangle (*shaded*) from the 1989 edition of the textbook (p. 73)

compared to the other edition. In the 1958 edition, problems often follow explanations. For example, in the area unit, the 1958 textbook opens with an explanation of how a parallelogram may be transformed into a rectangle by cutting and rearranging a triangular section from one end to the other. Then, the question is posed to find the area of this parallelogram. In contrast, starting with the 1968 edition, students are first presented with the task, "Let's think about ways to find the area of this parallelogram." Thus, although the 1958 edition may contain a fewer number of problems, the way those problems are posed in the textbook does not appear to be consistent with the structured problem-solving approach in which students are asked to tackle a problem without first being shown how such a problem may be solved.

Another way the 1958 edition is different from the other editions is the number of open-ended problems. Many – in fact, a majority – of the problems in all of these editions of the textbook series ask for one specific numerical answer, such as the area of a triangle with specific dimensions or how much 1 m of wire weighs when the weight of 1 1/3 m of the same wire is given. However, there are also questions that do not have a specific numerical answer. For example, in the area unit of the 1989 edition, students are asked to "explain ways 3 students found the area of the given triangle" (see Fig. 1).

In the multiplication of fractions unit of the same edition, students are asked to think about ways to calculate $4/5 \times 2/3$. For the purpose of this analysis, these types of problems were labeled "open" problems. As it can be easily seen in Table 2, the number of open problems dramatically increased starting in the 1968 edition. The increase in open problems is more drastic in the units on fraction multiplication

Table 2 Number of open problems found in the body of the textbooks across the six editions

COS year	1958	1968	1977	1989	2000	2008
Area						
# of open problems in the body of textbook	3 (18 %)	12 (32 %)	13 (23 %)	16 (40 %)	12 (29 %)	16 (22 %)
Fractions						
# of open problems in the body of textbook	0 (0 %)	12 (18 %)	9 (9 %)	15 (23 %)	20 (35 %)	27 (40 %)

% in the parentheses indicates the proportion of open problems in the body of textbooks

and division. In the 2000 and 2008 editions of the textbook, more than a third of problems in the body of the textbook are open problems.

Although the five editions – 1968, 1977, 1989, 2000, and 2008 – share many similarities that contrasted with the 1958 edition, the three most recent editions are different from the 1968 and 1977 editions in important ways. Although it is very common for textbooks to attribute an idea or a solution of a problem to a hypothetical student, starting in the 1989 edition, this series also began including cartoon drawings of those students. Moreover, for some problems, the textbook includes two (or more) students' ideas and asked students (readers) to examine, compare, and contrast those ideas. For example, Fig. 1 above shows a problem from the 1989 edition (5A p. 73) that asks students to explain how Yuji, Naoko, and Minoru thought about finding the area of the given triangle. Figure 2 comes from the fraction multiplication unit in the most recent (2008) edition. The textbook poses the following problem as the opening problem in the unit (translation is by the author throughout this chapter):

With 1 deciliter of paint, we can paint $4/5$ m^2 of boards. How many square meters of boards can we paint with $2/3$ deciliters of this paint?

Then, solutions by Yumi and Hiroki are shown, and students are asked to compare the final equations in these two solution approaches.

In the 1958, 1968, and 1977 editions, there are no instances in which the textbooks presented more than one student's ideas simultaneously to be examined. Having students examine multiple solutions to a given problem is a key step in the structured problem-solving instruction. Thus, starting with the 1989 edition, this series seems to include that step of instruction explicitly.

Representations

The analysis of representations used in these editions of the textbook focused on the fraction multiplication and division units in grade 6. The area units contained many drawings, but they are of the figures whose area must be determined. Therefore, they were not considered "representations."

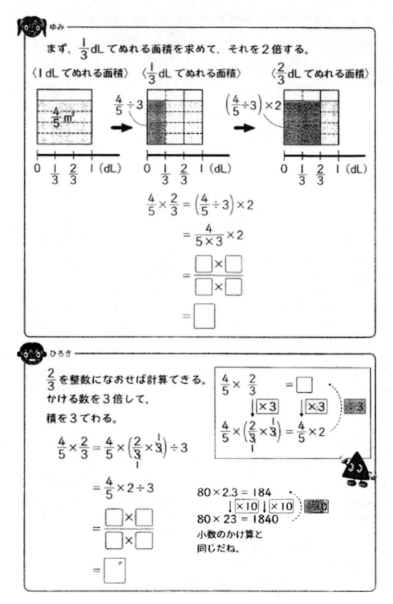

Fig. 2 Two hypothetical students' ideas about how to calculate $4/5 \times 2/3$ from the 2008 edition of the textbook (p. 25)

Once again, representations – both in types and how they are used – in the 1958 edition are different from the other five editions. In the 1958 edition, the unit on fraction multiplication and division opens with a story in which students are trying to determine the area of a flowerbed at their school. The rectangular flowerbed

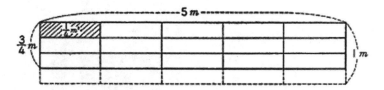

Fig. 3 Area model presented in the opening section of the 1958 unit on fraction multiplication and division (p. 5)

measures 5 m by 3/4 m. The book goes on to describe how a student, Yoshiko, thought of this situation as $5 \times 3/4$,[2] which is multiplying a fraction by a whole number, the idea they studied in grade 5. The textbook carries out the calculation and concludes that the area of the flowerbed is 3 3/4 m².

The textbook then presents the reasoning of another student, Tadashi. Tadashi, unlike Yoshiko, thought of the situation as $3/4 \times 5$, multiplication of a whole number by a fraction, something they had not yet studied. The book then presents the area model shown in Fig. 3 and explains how $3/4 \times 5$ can be calculated.

The textbook explains that, from the diagram, we can see that the flowerbed is made up of 15 small rectangles with areas of 1/4 m² each. Therefore, the total area of the flowerbed is 3 3/4 m². Thus, the 1958 edition uses the area model to illustrate multiplication by fractions, and the diagram is used as a tool for the authors to explain the procedure.

In the other five editions, unlike the 1958 edition, the unit opens with a problem. Although the problems in these five editions all involve area, the mathematical nature of the problems is different from the problem in the 1958 edition. The problems in the five later editions are as follows:

A tractor can plow 3/5 ha of fields in 1 h. How many hectares of fields can you plow in 3/4 h? (1968)

With 1 deciliter of paint, you can paint 3/5 m² of boards. How many m² can you paint with 3/4 deciliters of this paint? (1977)

With 1 deciliter of paint, you can paint 4/5 m² of boards. How many m² can you paint with 2/3 deciliters of this paint? (1989, 2000, and 2008)

Although these problems involve the area of a rectangular region, the factors are no longer the dimensions of the rectangle. Rather, these problems are rate problems. Therefore, these five editions use a slightly different representation which is a combination of the area model with a number line (see Fig. 4, from the 1977 edition).

---

[2] In the Japanese convention, the first factor in a multiplication expression represents the multiplier. In this textbook series, multiplication (and division) of fractions by whole numbers is discussed before the unit on multiplication by fractions, sometimes in grade 5 and sometimes in grade 6, depending on the COS. This is done so because students can continue to use the equal group interpretation as long as the multiplier is a whole number. When the multiplier becomes something other than a whole number, students must expand their interpretation of the multiplication operation, in addition to thinking about the calculation process.

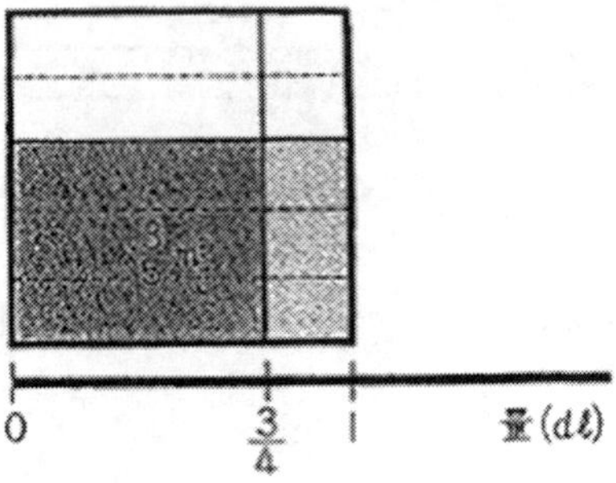

Fig. 4 Representation of the
opening problem in the fraction multiplication unit in the
1977 edition (p. 5)

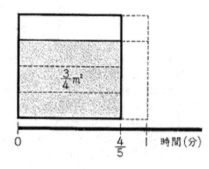

Fig. 5 Combined area-number
line representation for a partitive division problem from the
1977 edition

Fig. 6 The representation of
the opening division problem
in the 1958 edition (p. 11)

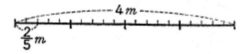

Although the end result may be similar to the typical area model representation, this combined area-number line representation may be used with partitive division problems. For example, in the 1977 edition, the unit on fraction division opens with the following problem:

It took 4/5 min for Akira's father to paint 3/4 m² of boards. How many m² can you paint in 1 min?

This problem is then represented as shown in Fig. 5.

An area model cannot truly represent this problem situation, as 4/5 is not the dimension of the rectangle. However, an area model may be used to represent the calculation, 3/4 ÷ 4/5 by drawing a rectangle with the area of 3/4 m² and 4/5 m as one of the dimensions. However, such a drawing is of little help to actually find the quotient. In fact, the 1958 edition, the division of fraction section starts with the situation in which a student cuts out 2/5 m segments from a 4 m tape, a quotitive division situation. The textbook then uses a segment model shown in Fig. 6 to represent the situation.

Another feature that is common in all but the oldest (1958) edition is the use of equations with words. In these 5 editions, after the problem is posed to the student, the initial emphasis is that the problem situation can be represented by a multiplication equation with a fraction multiplier. In order to help students understand

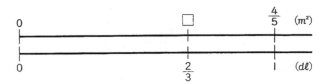

Fig. 7 A double number line representation for the introductory problem on multiplication by fractions in the 1989, 2000, and 2008 editions (Taken from the 2000 edition (p. 63))

that idea, these 5 editions use an equation with words. The problem situations for the 1989, 2000, and 2008 editions are identical, and the textbooks include the following equation:

$$[\text{Area of boards that can be painted with 1 deciliter}] \times [\text{Amount of paint (deciliter)}]$$
$$= [\text{Area of boards that can be painted}]$$

In each of these five editions, the textbook develops the idea that the problem can be solved by the calculation 3/5 × 3/4 (in the 1968 and 1977 editions) or 4/5 × 2/3 (in the 1989, 2000, and 2008 editions). Then, and only then, the textbook asks students to think about how this calculation may be completed.

Although the five editions since 1968 use the same combined area-number line representation and an equation with words to introduce multiplication and division by fractions, the three most recent editions (1989, 2000, and 2008) also use a double number line representation (see Fig. 7) that does not appear in the 1968 and 1977 editions. In fact, in these three editions, the double number line representation is presented immediately after the problem statement, before the combined area-number line model and the equation with words.

This model, unlike the area model or the combined area-number line model, does not necessarily help students find the product. Rather, it represents how the quantities in the problem situation are related. However, as Watanabe et al. (2010) noted, this form of representation is used to represent the multiplication and division of decimal numbers in grade 5. Thus, it appears that the intention of this model is also to help students understand the multiplicative nature of the problem situation based on the relationships of the quantities. In these three most recent editions, as well as the 1968 and 1977 editions, the combined area-number line model is used to illustrate how the calculation may be completed.

The 1968 and 1977 editions use a similar representation – double-sided number line – later in the units. For example, in these editions, after the calculation method for fraction multiplication is developed, special cases (e.g., multiplying mixed numbers) are considered. Then, the 1977 edition explores the relationship between the multiplier and the size of the product in relationship to the multiplicand through the following problem:

1 m of cloth costs 360 yen. What is the price of 1 1/3 m of the same cloth? What is the price of 2/3 m?

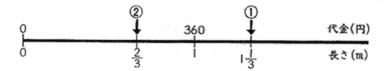

Fig. 8 A double-sided number line representation from the 1977 edition (p. 9)

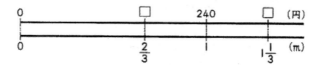

Fig. 9 A double number line representation of a similar problem from the 1989 edition (p. 11)

To illustrate this problem situation, the textbook includes the following model (Fig. 8).

Readers can easily see that the basic structure of this model is the same as that of a double number line. In the 1989 edition of the book, a similar problem (the price of 1 m of cloth is 240 yen) is represented as shown below (Fig. 9).

Thus, it is quite possible to include a double-sided number line representation with the introductory problem in the 1968 and 1977 editions, as the double number line is used in the 1989, 2000, and 2008 editions. However, it is clear that the authors of the 1968 and 1977 editions chose not to do so, while the authors of the 1989, 2000, and 2008 editions intentionally included it as the first model of the problem situation.

General Features

As we examined the general features of these six editions of the series, we noted that the three most recent editions (1989, 2000, and 2008) shared some similarities that are distinct from the previous three editions. For example, in the 1989 through 2008 editions, the opening problems in the units (for both area and multiplication and division of fractions) appear on the right-hand page of the book. All of these problems are worked out; however, because of this layout, the initial pages only show the problems, with the solutions on the following pages. The 1989 and 2000 editions include a 1-page review problem section so that the division of fraction units starts on the right-hand page. Since the units start on the left-hand page in the previous three editions, this choice appears to be intentional.

Another distinct feature of the three most recent editions is the inclusion of cartoonlike characters. The inclusion of cartoon drawings of hypothetical elementary school students was already discussed above. However, in addition to these cartoon- children characters, these three editions include various avatars offering comments and questions. Some of the comments offered by these avatars suggest possible ways of reasoning for the given problem. For example, in the fraction multiplication unit of the 1989 edition, an avatar comments, "What if the amount of the paint used were 2 deciliters…" beside the question asking students to write an equation to represent the problem situation. Thus, the avatar's comment leads students to think about what they have already learned. In the area unit of the 2000 edition, after the textbook asks students to consider ways of determining the area of a parallelogram, an avatar comments, "If we change the shape to something for which we already know how to calculate the area …." Once again, the avatar suggests thinking about ways to use prior knowledge.

Another type of comment offered by these avatars is summaries of mathematical explorations. For example, in the 1989 edition, after students explore the relationship between the multiplier and the size of the product in relationship to the multiplicand, a different avatar offers the summary in a balloon:

$$\text{Multiplier} > 1 \rightarrow \text{Product} > \text{Multiplicand}$$
$$\text{Multiplier} < 1 \rightarrow \text{Product} < \text{Multiplicand}$$

In the 2000 edition, after students discuss various ways to find the area of the given parallelogram by transforming it into rectangles, an avatar comments, "Even though the shapes have changed, their areas are the same, aren't they?"

Discussion

From these six editions of the series, we get the sense that problem solving has been an essential feature of each edition of the textbook. However, problem solving in the oldest edition (1958) appears to play a different role than it does in the other five editions. In the 1958 edition, each unit opens with an inquiry situation. For example, the unit on fraction multiplication begins with a question statement, "How many square meters is the area of a flowerbed at Tadashi's school if it is a rectangle with the length of 3/4 m and the width of 5 m?" However, this question is not marked as a question for students. Instead, the textbook immediately states that the area can be calculated using $5 \times 3/4$ (already learned) or $3/4 \times 5$ (not yet learned). Then, the book goes on to explain how $3/4 \times 5$ can be calculated utilizing the area model. Problems that are clearly marked for students follow the explanation. In contrast, in the 1968 through 2008 editions, each unit opens with a problem that is clearly intended for students. Thus, in the 1958 edition, problems are included to help students practice the ideas that have been explained. In contrast, in the other five editions, problem solving is an important step of mathematics learning.

Although each unit opens with a problem in the five more recent editions, the way the problem is handled is different in the three most recent editions (1989, 2000, and 2008) from how it is handled in the 1968 and 1977 editions. In the 1968 and 1977 editions, the opening problem is completely worked out and explained. For example, in the fraction multiplication unit of the 1977 edition (see above for the problem), the textbook explains that even when the amount of paint used becomes a fraction, like 3/4, we still use multiplication to find the total area painted. Then, they state, "Let's think about how we can calculate $3/5 \times 3/4$." However, this statement is immediately followed by an explanation: "We can determine the amount of area that can be painted with 3/4 deciliters by tripling the amount that can be painted with 1/4 deciliter." Then, the textbook presents the following two tasks to guide students to an answer for the original problem:

Determine the amount of area that can be painted with 1/4 deciliter by calculating $3/5 \div 4$.

Based on the amount of area that can be painted with 1/4 deciliter, determine the amount of area that can be painted with 3/4 deciliters.

The progression in the area unit is similar. After the opening problem, which asks students to think about ways to calculate the area of the given parallelogram, the book immediately instructs the students to change the given parallelogram to a rectangle, as shown in the figure. Thus, in the 1968 and 1977 editions, although the textbook starts with a problem for students, a solution is clearly specified and demonstrated.

On the other hand, the opening problems in the 1988, 2000, and 2008 editions are followed by another question or a less suggestive comment by an avatar. Thus, in these three editions, it is the students who must come up with the multiplication expression, $4/5 \times 2/3$, instead of being given the expression. Moreover, the inquiry task "Let's think about ways to calculate!" is posed clearly as a task to students. Similarly, in the area unit of the 1989 edition, an avatar asks, "How can we change the parallelogram into a rectangle?" Then, instead of the textbook presenting a way to transform the parallelogram into a rectangle, the 1989 edition includes two hypothetical students' ideas and asks students to explain how those two students might have thought about the problem.

Thus, the textbook series overall seems to be moving toward the expectation that students do more reasoning. Perhaps this trend is part of the reason that the average number of problems per page is about the same in the more recent editions compared to the 1968 or 1977 editions, even though the newer editions are dealing with fewer problem situations. Some of the questions worked out in the 1968 and 1977 editions are posed as tasks for students in the newer edition, thus increasing the number of problems.

Although the differences in the oldest edition to the most recent edition are striking, the changes between two successive editions seem to be relatively small in general. The exceptions are between the 1958 and 1968 editions and between the 1977 and 1989 editions. The shift between the 1958 and 1968 editions seems to suggest a significant shift in teaching philosophies. In the 1958 edition, the image of instruction presented in the textbook is that of teacher demonstration, followed by student practice. However, starting with the 1968 edition, this particular series seems to put more emphasis on students' problem solving as the main mechanism of teaching and learning instead of teacher (or textbook) explanation – an image of mathematics instruction more consistent with the structured problem-solving approach described by Stigler and Hiebert (1999).

Although the shift between the 1958 and 1968 editions may indicate the beginning of a shift in instruction, the images of mathematics teaching surmised from the textbook in the 1968 and 1977 editions are still different from structured problem solving. In those two editions, as discussed earlier, a particular approach to solve the given problem is often discussed immediately after the problems are presented. Although some of the ideas may be attributed to a hypothetical student, a mathematics lesson illustrated in the textbook does not include critical examination of a variety of solution processes, an essential component of the structured problem-solving style of teaching. In that perspective, the shift between the 1977 and 1989 editions may be more significant.

As discussed earlier, starting with the 1989 edition, this series began including more than one approach to the opening problem in a unit. Students are then asked to explain the reasoning – an important step in comparing and contrasting the various approaches. Those solution strategies seem to serve as possible examples of students' reasoning that teachers may expect from their students. Furthermore, subquestions and comments by avatars seem to suggest possible teachers' questions and comments spoken while students are solving the opening problem or during the class discussion. Thus, these features in the more recent editions are written just as much for teachers as for students, and the newer textbook seems to support the structured problem-solving approach to mathematics teaching much more explicitly than older editions do.

Even what appear to be superficial changes, like the presentation of the opening problem on the right-hand page, may be significant support for teachers in implementing a problem-solving-based lesson. Although Japanese teachers may rely on their textbooks to teach mathematics lessons, we have also witnessed many lessons in which teachers tell the students to put their books away at the beginning of the lesson. The teachers then present the problem from the textbook for students to think about. The presentation of the problem can be easily done with a document camera or an enlarged copy of the textbook page. If the page contains the solution, the teachers must make sure that the undesired part is covered up.

Although the newer edition of the series appears to be in alignment with the structured problem-solving approach described by Stigler and Hiebert (1999), there are still some aspects of such a style of teaching that is not fully present in the textbook series. For example, in a problem-solving-based lesson, students' incorrect reasoning plays a significant role. However, even the most recent edition of the series does not include incorrect solutions. For example, we know that many students think that the area of a parallelogram may be calculated by multiplying the lengths of two adjacent sides. Such a misconception may play an important and useful role during an actual lesson. However, because it is not included in the textbook, teachers are left to determine how to incorporate it productively in a lesson. Perhaps the teacher's editions provide some suggestions; they were, unfortunately, not available for this analysis.

Closing Remarks

The analysis of the textbook pages presented in this chapter generally supports the claim by some Japanese mathematics educators that the transition to more problem-solving-based mathematics teaching happened gradually over the years. However, the current study has several limitations. First, the analysis only examined units on area of polygons and fraction multiplication and division. Although these are two mathematically significant topics, they occupy only about 10 % of the textbook pages in those two grades.

Furthermore, both of these topics are discussed in the upper elementary level. Might there be differences in the way the textbook is organized in the primary grades versus in the upper elementary levels? A cursory glance through the 2008 edition of the 2nd grade textbook shows that most units start on the right-hand pages. Furthermore, there are a number of problems for which multiple ideas from hypothetical students are presented. Thus, the general patterns observed in this study may indeed be generalized to the whole textbook series. However, a more comprehensive analysis might be useful.

This chapter addresses the potential influences of curriculum, and textbooks in particular, on transforming mathematics instruction. However, the study reported in this chapter is limited in at least two ways. First, we do not really know whether Japanese mathematics instruction transformed over the last half century. The Japanese teaching described in Stevenson and Stigler (1992) was based on observations in the late 1970s and the 1980s. The description appears to be reasonably consistent with the description given in the Stigler and Hiebert (1999), based on the observations made in the 1990s, supporting the idea that teaching is a cultural activity and much of it remains constant across generations (Stigler and Hiebert 1998). Unfortunately, we do not have any data about what Japanese mathematics instruction was like in the 1960s, or earlier. However, we have heard from many Japanese mathematics educators that mathematics teaching in Japan in the 1960s was teacher centered and teacher driven – teaching that is much more consistent with the 1958 edition of the series.

Another obvious limitation is that this study does not involve analysis of actual instruction. Although textbooks may be an important bridge between the intended curriculum and the implemented curriculum, it is still not the implemented curriculum. However, we believe that textbooks do present a vision of mathematics instruction espoused by the authors. We can also anticipate what a lesson might look like if a teacher were to teach from the textbook.

In spite of these limitations, the findings of the study provide some insights into the transformation of mathematics instruction through school curriculum changes, particularly changes in textbooks. Although the current study did not examine actual instruction incorporating this textbook series, it is safe to conclude that the series continues to change to accommodate more and more of the vision of mathematics instruction espoused by Japanese mathematics educators (e.g., Takahashi 2011). For example, the newer editions include more alternative solution approaches to be compared and contrasted during the whole class discussion phase of structured problem solving. Sub-questions following the main problem help teachers establish students as, at least, cocreators of new knowledge. Reflective comments and suggestions offered by cartoon characters provide a model of mathematical habits of mind.

Brown (2009) points out that textbooks can influence teachers' actions through their affordances and constraints. The changes in this Japanese textbook series demonstrate how textbooks can incorporate affordances and constraints to promote a particular approach to mathematics teaching – namely, structured problem solving. These changes adopted by the publisher may be a contributing factor in the spread of this teaching approach, which is now spread to the point that a majority of Japanese teachers practice it frequently.

References

Brown, M. W. (2009). The teacher-tool relationship: Theorizing the design and use of curriculum materials. In J. T. Remillard, B. A. Herbel-Eisenmann, & G. M. Lloyd (Eds.), *Mathematics teachers at work: Connecting curriculum materials and classroom instruction* (pp. 17–36). New York: Routledge.

Common Core State Standards Initiative. (2010). *Common core state standards for Mathematics.* http://www.corestandards.org/assets/CCSSI_Math%20Standards.pdf

Japan Society of Mathematical Education. (2001). *Sansuujugyou no houhou ni kansuru chosa no kekka.* (Results of a survey of elementary school mathematics lesson format.) *83*(2), 31–42 (in Japanese).

National Council for Accreditation of Teacher Education. (2010). *Transforming teacher education through clinical practice: A national strategy to prepare effective teachers.* Report of the Blue Ribbon Panel on Clinical Preparation and Partnerships for Improved Student Learning. Washington, DC: The Council.

National Council of Teachers of Mathematics. (1980). *Agenda for action.* Reston: The Council.

National Council of Teachers of Mathematics. (2000). *Principles and standards for school mathematics.* Reston: The Council.

National Mathematics Advisory Panel. (2008). *Foundations for success: The final report of the National Mathematics Advisory Panel.* Washington, DC: U.S. Department of Education.

Nunokawa, K. (2012). Multi-relation strategy in students' use of a representation for proportional reasoning. *Eurasia Journal of Mathematics, Science, & Technology Education, 8*(4), 167–182.

Shimahara, N. K., & Sakai, A. (1995). *Learning to teach in two cultures: Japan and the United States.* New York: Garland Publishing.

Stevenson, H. W., & Stigler, J. W. (1992). *The learning gap: Why our schools are failing and what we can learn from Japanese and Chinese education.* New York: Summit Books.

Stigler, J. W., & Hiebert, J. (1998). Teaching is a cultural activity. *American Educator, 22*(4), 4–11.

Stigler, J. W., & Hiebert, J. (1999). *The teaching gap: Best ideas from the world's teachers for improving education in the classroom.* New York: The Free Press.

Takahashi, A. (2011). The Japanese approach to developing expertise in using the textbook to teach mathematics. In Y. Li & G. Kaiser (Eds.), *Expertise in mathematics instruction: An international perspective* (pp. 197–219). New York: Springer.

Watanabe, T. (2001). Content and organization of teachers' manuals: An analysis of Japanese elementary mathematics teachers' manuals. *School Science and Mathematics, 101*, 194–205.

Watanabe, T., Takahashi, A., & Yoshida, M. (2010). Supporting focused and cohesive curricula through visual representations: An example from Japanese textbooks. In B. Reys & R. Reys (Eds.), *Mathematics curriculum: Issues, trends, and future directions* (NCTM seventy-second yearbook, pp. 131–144). Reston: National Council of Teachers of Mathematics.

Changes in Instructional Tasks and Their Influence on Classroom Discourse in Reformed Mathematics Classrooms of Chinese Primary Schools

Yu-Jing Ni, Xiaoqing Li, Dehui Zhou, and Qiong Li

Abstract This chapter describes two studies that show the impact of China's new mathematics curriculum on classroom instruction. The first study examined the cognitive features of instructional tasks implemented in primary-level mathematics classrooms adopting the new curriculum in comparison to those using the conventional curriculum. The results indicated that the reform-oriented classrooms used more tasks with *high cognitive demand, multiple representations*, and *multiple solution methods* than the non-reform classrooms did. The second study looked into how *cognitive demands, multiple representations*, and *multiple solution methods* were related to the nature of student-teacher discourse in the reformed classrooms. It was found that tasks of high cognitive demand were associated with teachers' high-order questioning which, in turn, was related to students' highly participatory responses. It was also found that tasks of high cognitive demand as well as teachers' high-order questions were associated with the teacher's authority in evaluating students' answers. In contrast, tasks of *multiple*

Y.-J. Ni (✉)
Ho Tim Building, Faculty of Education, The Chinese University of Hong Kong, Shatin, NT, Hong Kong, China
e-mail: yujing@cuhk.edu.hk

X. Li
Rm B432, Department of Psychology, Normal College, Shen Zhen University, Nanshan, Shenzhen, Guangdong 518052, China
e-mail: xiaoqingligd@hotmail.com

D. Zhou
Department of Counseling and Psychology, Hong Kong Shue Yan University, Hong Kong, China
e-mail: dhruthzhou@gmail.com

Q. Li
Teacher Education Research Center, School of Education, Beijing Normal University, No. 19, XinJieKouWai St., HaiDian District, Beijing 100875, People's Republic of China
e-mail: qiongli@bnu.edu.cn

Y. Li et al. (eds.), *Transforming Mathematics Instruction: Multiple Approaches and Practices*, Advances in Mathematics Education, DOI 10.1007/978-3-319-04993-9_13,
© Springer International Publishing Switzerland 2014

solution methods were showed to be related to teachers' simple questions, and teachers' simple questions led to more teacher-student joint authority in evaluating students' responses. Some implications of the findings from the studies are discussed in order to further our understanding of the current instructional practice in Chinese mathematics classrooms and to help formulate strategies to sustain and affect the desirable changes in the classrooms.

Keywords Primary mathematics • Instructional tasks • Classroom discourse • Chinese mathematics classrooms • Curriculum reform

The government of Mainland China put forth new curriculum standards in 2001 for their 9-year compulsory education (Ministry of Education 2001a). Meanwhile, the Ministry of Education also introduced and approved designated textbooks and teachers' guides to facilitate the implementation of the new curriculum. In the same year, on a voluntary basis, numerous schools in 38 cities (counties) from 27 provinces across the country adopted the new curriculum standards and new textbooks. By the fall of 2006, the implementation had become mandatory across the country.

The new mathematics standards (Ministry of Education 2001b) include three areas for Chinese students to develop: knowledge and skills, processes and methods, and affective demeanor and value. The objectives aim for students (1) to acquire important knowledge and the basic problem-solving skills in mathematics that are important for their lifelong learning; (2) to apply knowledge of mathematics and related skills to observe, analyze, and solve problems in daily life and in other subjects by using mathematical methods; and (3) to appreciate the close relationship among mathematics, nature, and society. While maintaining the acquisition of basic mathematics knowledge and skills as the foundation for the compulsory mathematics education, the objectives are intended to highlight the goal of mathematics education to provide students the learning experience of how mathematics knowledge is established and advanced by observation, reflection, and communication and how to use mathematical tools to observe, analyze, and solve problems, which was neglected in the previous curricula.

To develop the mathematics achievement attributes in students that are desired by the new curriculum, a change in the kinds of instructional tasks used for classroom instruction is required, because instructional tasks serve as the proximal source for students to learn from instruction (Doyle 1983; Stein et al. 1996, 2000). The nature of instructional tasks, therefore, is considered to potentially affect students' views about the subject matter and their competence in its execution. To align with the new curriculum, instructional tasks should be more problem oriented to afford students the opportunity to observe, communicate, and reason about mathematics. Also, the instructional tasks should provide students with the opportunity to put knowledge and skills to use in solving mathematics problems. Furthermore, the instructional tasks should help students develop an interconnected understanding of concepts, procedures, and principles through the use of knowledge and skills in problem solving (Cai 1995; Schoenfeld 1992). Finally, the use of such instructional tasks is expected to help create the learning environment in which students are guided to engage in a more dialogic classroom discourse and thus to develop their sense of authority over learning and knowledge.

The new mathematics curriculum had been implemented for 5 years before our studies were carried out between 2005 and 2008 (Ni et al. 2009). There was a serious concern about the efficacy of the new curriculum, as well as a lack of systematic empirical studies to evaluate the impact of the new curriculum on classroom instruction. The focus of our studies was to assess whether or not the new changes were taking place in instructional tasks in mathematics classrooms and how the new changes in the instructional tasks, if there were any, were related to teacher-student discourse in mathematics classrooms. Li and Ni (2011) reported the results of the comparative study of instructional tasks being implemented in reformed classrooms and conventional classrooms, respectively. Ni et al. (2012) then documented the way in which task features such *as high cognitive demand*, *multiple representations*, and *multiple solution strategies* that are promoted by the reformed curriculum might influence classroom discourse behaviors of Chinese teachers and students in the reform classrooms. Below, we first describe the two studies and then discuss some implications of the findings to expand our understanding of the current instructional practice in Chinese mathematics classrooms and formulate strategies to sustain and affect the desirable changes in classrooms.

Study 1: Changes in Instructional Tasks in Reformed Classrooms

A collection of instructional tasks make up a curriculum, and those tasks form the basic treatment units in classroom instruction. Doyle (1983) divides academic instructional tasks into three major classes: memory tasks, procedural or routine tasks, and comprehension/understanding tasks. By building on Doyle's framework (1983, 1988) and the ideas of reformed mathematics curriculum in the USA (NCTM 1989, 1997), Stein and her colleagues (Stein et al. 1996, 2007) developed a conceptual framework to characterize the cognitive features of mathematics instructional tasks. The system contains three dimensions: (1) cognitive levels of instructional tasks, which refers to whether a learning task requires merely memorization, routine procedure, or relating a procedure to its underlying concepts; (2) single or multiple representations (e.g., symbolic, visual, hands-on manipulation) involved in the tasks; and (3) single or multiple solution methods encouraged in the tasks. Findings in cognitive psychology have indicated that the nature of learning tasks influences learners by directing their attention to particular aspects of content and by specifying ways of processing information (Anderson 2000; Doyle 1983; Marx and Walsh 1988; Ni and Zhou 2005). The three cognitive dimensions of mathematics learning tasks as identified by Stein et al. are suggested to influence student learning favorably in different grade levels (Hiebert and Wearne 1993; Stein and Lane 1996; Stigler and

Hiebert 2004). This line of research has provided the impetus for the current mathematics curriculum reform in many countries, including China. Recommendations for the curriculum reform emphasize the importance of exposing students to meaningful and challenging mathematical tasks, because meaningful and cognitively demanding tasks are considered to be more likely provide authentic opportunities for students to explore mathematical ideas. As a result of being exposed to more challenging tasks, students are expected to become competent in mathematics (e.g., Stein et al. 1996; Schoenfeld 1992). The purpose of this study was to examine whether or not the recent curriculum reform in China has influenced classroom practice as reflected in the implemented instructional tasks.

In the study, 58 fifth grade mathematics teachers were randomly recruited from 20 schools in two school districts in Zhengzhou of the Henan province in central China to take part in the study. Thirty-two teachers from ten schools were from one district using the new curriculum, whereas the other 26 of them were from ten schools in another district using the conventional curriculum. All of the reform classes had been taught with the reformed curriculum since the students were in first grade, and likewise the conventional classes taught with the conventional curriculum since the first grade. The students were assigned to the schools by the proximity of the school to where they lived. The teachers from the two groups were comparable in terms of educational level and teaching experience. The average class size for the reform group was 57 students per class and 56 students per class for the non-reform group. Such large class sizes were due to the fast urbanization phenomenon which has taken place in China since the end of the last century, during which more and more families have been migrating from rural areas to cities in the country. For more details about the characteristics of the teachers and students, see Ni et al. (2009, 2011).

Each of the 58 classrooms had three mathematics lessons for three consecutive school days videotaped. All of the videotaping was completed within 1 month, between November and December 2006. The teachers were informed of their respective observation schedules 1 week before the observation took place. They were told that the goal of the study was to see what would typically happen in Chinese mathematics classrooms. Therefore, they should teach in the usual way and with no extra preparation. Of the obtained 171 valid videotaped lessons, there were 146 lessons on new knowledge, 15 review lessons, and 10 exercise lessons. Considering any plausible influence of lesson type on types of instructional tasks to be used, our analysis was restricted to the 146 lessons on new knowledge. This included 87 lessons from the reform classrooms and 58 lessons from the non-reform classrooms.

According to Doyle (1983) and Stein et al. (1996, 2007), a mathematical task is defined as a classroom activity or a segment of classroom work of which the purpose is to focus the attention of students on a particular mathematical idea. In our study, any self-contained mathematics problem, activity or exercise that involved the students during a lesson was counted as a learning task. Among a total of 986 instructional tasks that were identified via an observation of the videotaped lessons, 518 were from the reform group and 478 from the non-reform group (Li and Ni 2011).

These identified instructional tasks were then coded along the following three dimensions (Stein et al. 1996, 2000; Renkl and Helmke 1992; Stigler and Hiebert 1999): (1) type of cognitive process that is required for students to engage in solving the task, (2) the existence of multiple solution strategies, and (3) the extent to which the task lends itself to multiple representations. In terms of cognitive processes, "memorization" tasks involve either reproducing or committing to memory previously learned facts, rules, formulae, or definitions. Tasks that are described as "procedures without connections" are algorithmic, and they have little or no connection to the concepts or meaning that underlie the procedures being used. "Procedures with connections" are tasks that focus students' attention on the use of procedures for the purpose of developing mathematical concepts. For example, the task *Do 1/4, 0.25, and 25 % stand for the same amount?* would be an example of a memory task. An example of procedural or routine task would be *Transform 3/8 into a decimal and percentage*. A task which relates procedure to its underlying concepts would be comparable to the following example:

Shade the area which stands for 3/5 of a 10 × 10 grid and explain.

Three kinds of presentations were coded, including numerical symbols, graphic illustrations, and hands-on manipulations. When a teacher used not only an arithmetical form but also a graphic form, other visual illustrations, or hands-on manipulations to present an instructional task, it was considered a task of multiple representations. An instructional task also was coded based on whether or not the teacher encouraged students to think about multiple solution methods toward a given task.

The study showed that the reform classrooms implemented more learning tasks of *high cognitive demands* than the non-reform classrooms. In the reform classrooms, 49.9 % of the tasks were *procedure with connections*, whereas these accounted for only 22.8 % of the tasks in the non-reform classrooms. The reform classes also used a higher proportion of *instructional tasks that involved visual illustrations*—37.3 % of the learning tasks compared to 10.5 % in the non-reform classrooms. In addition, the reform classrooms adopted more instructional tasks involving *hands-on manipulation* (10.5 % compared to 5.4 %) and *multiple solution methods* (35.9 % compared to 15.7 %). These results suggest that the changes in instructional tasks were taking place in the Chinese classrooms adopting the new mathematics curriculum.

Study 2: Influence of the Instructional Tasks on Classroom Discourse in the Reformed Classrooms

Instructional tasks and classroom discourse are two of the most important features of classroom instruction. These are considered to be key factors that define the links between teaching and learning (Hiebert and Wearne 1993; Li and Ni 2011; Stein et al. 1996). The use of instructional tasks with *high cognitive demands*, *multiple representations*, and *multiple solution methods* is expected to help create a more dialogic classroom discourse between the teacher and the students. Instructional tasks and classroom discourse usually occur simultaneously and interweave with each other in classroom. Consequently, one common assumption is that changes in the type of learning tasks would bring about changes in classroom discourse. That is, change the substance of what is being taught, i.e., instructional tasks, in order to influence how teaching and learning occur, i.e., classroom discourse (e.g., Ministry of Education 2001a, b; National Council of Teachers of Mathematics 1989). However, several studies suggest that their links are more complicated than this, because the relations between the nature of instructional task and the nature of classroom discourse are constrained by various factors.

Henningsen, Stein, and their colleagues (Henningsen and Stein 1997; Stein et al. 1996) demonstrated that many other classroom-based factors, such as classroom norms, teachers' instructional dispositions, and students' learning dispositions, can either provide support or, alternatively, inhibit the implementation of the intended high cognitive demand tasks. It has been observed that high cognitive demand tasks involve more ambiguity and higher levels of personal risk for both teachers and students. The mutual constraint of instructional tasks and classroom discourse can become more acute and complex with implementation of high cognitive demand tasks within the context of Chinese culture and traditions.

In Mainland China, the education system is highly centralized and, as such, can make changes in instructional tasks mandatory. This can be accomplished by merely changing the existing curriculum standards and textbooks. However, the government has no effective mechanism with which to bring about mandatory changes to classroom discourse. The inherent nature of classroom discourse is determined by the behaviors of individual teachers and individual students. Therefore, it was no surprise to observe that the Chinese classrooms using the reform curriculum and those utilizing a conventional curriculum differed significantly in what kinds of instructional tasks were implemented. Nevertheless, the two groups of classrooms did not differ very much with regard to the nature of classroom discourse, whether dominated by the teacher or shared together by the teacher and the students (Li and Ni 2011). Therefore, changes in instructional tasks do not necessarily bring about changes in classroom discourse, because classroom discourse is also influenced by other factors, not merely by changes in instructional tasks.

Therefore, we conducted Study 2 to examine the way that the new features of instructional tasks influenced elements of classroom discourse and how the instructional tasks with the antecedent elements of classroom discourse, e.g., teacher questions, affected later elements, such as classroom authority in evaluating students' answers. The study (Ni et al. 2012) utilized the data of 90 videotaped class sessions from the reform classrooms only in Study 1 and examined how the measured features of instructional tasks affected the classroom discourse behaviors of the Chinese teachers and students. The class lessons were analyzed along the following four aspects of classroom discourse: *questions from teachers, answers from students, the teachers' reactions to the responses of students,* and *the nature of authority*—teacher authority or teacher-student joint authority for evaluating a student's response. We coded the classroom discourse based on the assumption that teachers and students contribute to teacher-student and student-student interactions (Cobb et al. 1992;

Hamm and Perry 2002; Li 2004; Stigler et al. 1996; Stigler and Hiebert 1999; Williams and Baxter 1996).

The coding category of *teachers' questions* refers to the way in which teachers use questions to stimulate students' specific mathematical thinking (Perry et al. 1993). Four types of teacher questions were observed: (1) *Memory recall questions* require students to repeat facts, procedures, or mathematical rules that were previously taught in the class. (2) *Procedural questions* ask students to describe the procedure that leads to an answer. (3) *Explanatory questions* require students to explain their contemplations in selecting strategies and procedures for solving problems or why a certain procedure works. (4) *Analytic and comparative questions* lead students to consider the nature of a problem or a certain strategy or ask students to compare two students' solution methods. The last two types of teacher questions require students to make reasonable connections of knowledge and skills, and therefore, the questions are referred to as "higher-order questions." In contrast, memory recall questions and questions that describe procedures are regarded as "lower-order questions."

Student answers were coded into these five categories. (1) A *simple answer* is to provide just a "Yes" or "No" answer. (2) A *descriptive answer* is to describe a procedure taken to achieve an answer. (3) An *explanatory answer* is to explain why a certain strategy is applied. (4) A *commentary answer* is to evaluate different solution approaches or comment on others' answers. (5) A *student raising a new question* provides new opportunities to explore a given topic further. In the study, *simple answering* and *descriptive answering* were grouped as *simple answers. Students' explanatory answering, commentary answering*, and *raising new questions* were regarded as *highly participatory answers*.

The coding category of *teachers' responses* was concerned with how the teachers reacted to students' answers. According to Hamm and Perry (2002), a teacher may have four different reactions to students' answers: (1) The teacher abandons or ignores the student's idea. (2) The teacher acknowledges the student's reply but does not follow through to incorporate it into the lesson. (3) The teacher repeats the student's idea to express approbation. (4) The teacher examines, utilizes, and clarifies the student's idea.

The coding category of *the evaluation authority* designates the source of authority in classroom dialogue (Hamm and Perry 2002; Li 2004). The question remains as to whether the correctness of an answer is determined solely by the teacher or by both the teacher and the students. (1) Teacher authority is determined by the correctness that is assessed by the teacher through verbal or nonverbal reactions to students' answers. (2) Teacher-student joint authority indicates that the teacher and students are working together to establish correctness.

Regression analyses were conducted to investigate the relationship between the measured features of instructional tasks and the elements of classroom discourse. Consistent with the existing literature, the results showed that teachers tended to ask more higher-order questions when using instructional tasks high in cognitive demand. Students showed a high level of *participatory responses*, such as explaining an answer, commenting the other's response, and raising a question, which appeared to be influenced directly by teachers' higher-order questioning, but not directly by the tasks of *high cognitive demand* themselves. However, it was puzzling that in teachers' pursuit of *multiple solution methods* toward a task with their students, they were more inclined to ask memorization and procedural lower-order questions. Also unexpected was that instructional tasks high in cognitive demand or teachers' higher-order questions were associated more with teacher authority in evaluating students' answers. Also, none of the three cognitive features of instructional tasks was found to promote teacher-student joint authority in teacher-student discourse of the classrooms.

Discussion

Interpretation of the Findings

The findings from Study 1 showed that the Chinese reform classroom used more learning tasks with *higher cognitive demand*, involving *multiple representations* and *multiple solution methods*, than the non-reform classrooms did. The differences in the examined instructional tasks between the reform classrooms and the conventional classrooms were considered to reflect more the curricular influences than individual differences between the two groups of teachers. A further analysis indicated that only the curricular factor, not the teachers' demographic characteristics, showed an effect on the observed difference (Li and Ni 2011). Also, the teachers of the reform classes had different years of experience with using the new curriculum, and the years of experience had an effect on the difference in types of instructional tasks implemented in their classrooms (Ni et al. 2009). These suggest that curriculum materials, particularly textbooks and teacher manuals, are the main instructional resources that teachers rely on to make decisions concerning content selection and teaching methods (Stylianides 2009; Tarr et al. 2006). While assuming the influence of the curriculum materials (particularly the textbooks) on the observed differences in instruction practice between the groups, we did not directly investigate this source and its actual influence on the implemented tasks. This was a major limitation of the study. Nevertheless, the results about the differences in kinds of instructional tasks used between the reform classrooms and the conventional classrooms showed an expected effect of the reform curriculum on the classroom instruction.

The results of Study 2 reveal a complicated picture depicting the dynamics between the features of instructional tasks and the nature of classroom discourse in the Chinese classrooms that were in the first 5-year stage of enacting a new mathematics curriculum. The three cognitive features of instructional tasks (*high cognitive demands*, *multiple representations*, and *multiple solution methods*) were shown to have various relationships with the sequential elements of classroom discourse. This is consistent with the previous findings that high cognitive demand tasks link procedures to underlying concepts and elicit higher-order questions from teachers that encourage students to provide explanations and analysis (Ball 1993; Nystrand et al. 2003). However, the task feature of *high cognitive demands* did not display a direct link to students' highly participatory responses, but teachers' high-order questions did. This observation complements the findings by Stein et al. (1996) and Henningsen and Stein (1997) that the way a teacher orchestrates classroom communication constraints intended utilities of high cognitive demand tasks.

It was unexpected that the task feature of *multiple solution methods* was related to teachers' lower-order questions. A further inspection of the videotaped lessons showed that the teachers did encourage students to think about alternative solution methods but seldom guided the students to compare the solution methods proposed by students. This might in part explain why the task feature of *multiple solution methods* was associated with teachers' lower-order questions. Baxter and Williams (2010) made a similar observation in their study of American mathematics classrooms. They explained that the teachers asked students to come up with different solution methods more for the purpose of social scaffolding, to encourage students talk more in classroom, than for the purpose of cognitive scaffolding, to guide students for acquiring specific mathematics knowledge. To elaborate on this reasoning, we consider the association of *multiple solution methods* with a teacher's lower-order questioning to be a reflection of the dual influences on the teacher's behavior. One stems from the teacher's effort to manage adhering to the new curriculum requirement to engage students into a more dialogic classroom discourse. The other stems from the challenge posed for the teacher to foster a greater degree of discourse, which demands both the skill from the teachers to orchestrate classroom discourse and the considerable domain knowledge and pedagogical content knowledge. When students present different ideas, or even the same ideas using different expressions, the teacher is faced with the task of figuring out how to assist students in experiencing the regularity, preciseness, and logicality of mathematics without discouraging their participation.

It was also unexpected that both the task feature of *high cognitive demands* and teachers' higher-order questions tended to be associated with teacher authority in evaluating students' responses. This result suggests that the new features of instructional tasks do not necessarily result in a shift in the norms of classroom discourse, especially in Chinese classrooms where teachers and teaching have been very directive and students are used to it (Ni et al. 2010). On the other hand, the teacher-student shared authority over evaluation of student responses was related to students' highly participatory answers. Meanwhile, students' highly participatory answers were predicted by teachers' higher-order questions that were in turn promoted by the task feature of *high cognitive demands*. Therefore, it is probable that the task feature of *high cognitive demands* indirectly influenced students to produce more highly participatory answers via teachers' higher-order questions in classroom discourse and students' highly participatory responses were then beneficial to the creation of teacher-student joint authority over classroom discourse.

These findings support the conceptualization of instructional tasks at the three levels, as represented in the curriculum materials, as selected by teachers, and as implemented in the classroom (Stein et al. 2007). The multiple representations of instructional tasks entail no linear relationship between types of instructional tasks and ways of classroom discourse because the factors constraining the different levels are different. Therefore, the specific characteristics of instructional tasks could not determine the nature of classroom authority, teacher authority, or teacher-student shared authority over knowledge (Hamm and Perry 2002). Instructional tasks with the features of *high cognitive demands*, *multiple representations*, and *multiple solution methods* certainly provide a richer and more demanding content that encourages discussions between teachers and students. However, the discourse can either be dominated by the teacher or can evolve in a way that the teacher and students all share the authority over knowledge.

Implications of Findings for Informing Mathematics Classroom Instruction

The results of these studies provide evidence-based descriptions of the impact of the new curriculum on the features of instructional tasks and classroom discourse in Chinese classrooms. They raise expectations and also pose challenges for sustaining the desirable changes as a result of curriculum reform. One challenge is to align the three levels of unitizing high-level instructional tasks, as they are chosen in curriculum materials, selected by teachers, and implemented in the classroom (Stein et al. 2007). As the results of the studies demonstrated, at the implementation level, the teachers had the difficulty to guide productive classroom discourse with the high-level instructional tasks. The difficulty lies in the multiple requirements put on the teachers, such as (1) to understand how students make senses of the tasks, (2) to manage to align students' disparate ideas and approaches to the disciplined understanding of mathematics, and (3) to hold the students accountable to the classroom learning community to gain the authority over learning and over knowledge (e.g., Ball 2001; Engle and Conant 2002; Stein et al. 2008). The teachers need to be provided more professional support in this regard. It was understood that Chinese teachers were required to attend mandatory training on the new curriculum for a minimum of 48 h every year (Guan and Meng 2007). One emphasis of the professional training and development is to assist the Chinese teachers in developing the pedagogical expertise and tools to guide whole-class discussions for a more dialogic classroom discourse on learning worthwhile and important mathematics.

An example of the tools for professional training is the four principles for fostering productive disciplinary engagement that have been proposed by Engle and Conant (2002). The principles are *problematizing subject matter* to encourage students to raise questions to the learning tasks, *giving learners the authority* to address the questions and to come up with their own ways to solve them, *holding learners accountable* to other learners and to shared disciplinary norms by supporting the students be responsive to the discussed content, and *providing students with relevant resources*, e.g., time and intellectual tools, to carry out the above three. The principles are considered an abstract of the underlying regularities to explain and inform the moment-by-moment decisions of classroom teachers as they engage students in disciplinary learning.

A second example of the tools is the five key classroom practices synthesized by Stein and her colleagues (Stein et al. 2008) to guide effective whole-classroom discussions and to support the principles of productive disciplinary engagement to be implemented gradually and reliably in classroom. The key practices are *anticipating*, *monitoring*, *selecting*, *sequencing*, *and connecting*. The first practice is for the teacher to anticipate likely student responses to a given demanding instructional task based on an understanding of the students' prior knowledge. The second practice is to monitor students' responses to the task in order to identify the mathematical learning potential from particular student responses. The third practice, based on the first two, is to select the identified strategies or representations provided by the students and present them to the class to make it more likely that important mathematical ideas coming from the students can be discussed by the class. The fourth is to sequence the selected student responses in such a way that can help more effectively illustrate, emphasize, and generalize the important mathematical ideas. The last practice is to make connections between selected student responses and between student responses and the key mathematics ideas to be learned. The five practices and the four principles were developed to address the challenges to substantialize constructivist pedagogy by incorporating instructional content and dialogic interaction in classroom.

It is understood that an emphasis on teachers' training and professional development concerning how to guide productive whole-class discussions on learning important mathematics cannot be done by merely handing the teachers a set of identified tools. Instead, the emphasis can only be realized through an understanding of how the teachers comprehend the new curriculum and through continuous professional, dialogic reflection by individual teachers and the teaching community on the tools in relation to their classroom practice. Fortunately, one organizational feature of Chinese schools can provide the infrastructure to support such professional training and development. In most Chinese schools, teachers are organized into teaching research groups or lesson preparation groups by school subject and grade level. The lesson preparation/teaching research groups have regular meetings to discuss general issues of teaching, to study curriculum materials, to make lesson and unit plans, and to observe and analyze instruction for one another (Han and Paine 2010; Paine and Ma 1993; Wang and Paine 2003). The lesson preparation/ teaching research groups probably need to pay more attention on how to make use of and invent the tools of constructivist pedagogy to promote productive disciplinary engagement by students in classroom.

Han and Paine (2010) conducted a fine ethnographic documentation of the process required to prepare public lessons[1] by a teaching research group of first grade mathematics teachers in China. From the documentation, it was observed that the teaching research group was studying the textbook and teacher manual intensively on how teaching subtraction with word problems such as "There are 10 boys and

---

[1] Public lessons refer to the lessons that are conducted by the teachers whom are considered by respective school districts to be exemplary on teaching and are open to teachers in and outside of the schools. Public lessons are a regular part of teacher professional development activity in China. It also helps to efficiently disseminate socially and culturally favored teaching methods. Han and Paine (2010) documented the processes of preparing public lessons by a group of Chinese mathematics teachers.

7 girls in a class. How many more boys are there than the number of girls?" The group made sure that the lesson would be in line with the teacher manual's advice on the importance of teaching children to use the one-to-one correspondence principle, to compare two quantities, and to be able to address and overcome the possible misconception in students who think 10 minus 7 for the word problem as removing seven girls from the group of ten boys. The documentation did not show that the teaching group had planned how to make the lesson more open to students' ideas and incorporate them into the lesson. The Chinese teachers' study of the curriculum materials in an attempt to capture the essence of the mathematics topic to be taught reflects the respectable Chinese school mathematics tradition of teaching foundational mathematics knowledge and skills. The analysis of the curriculum materials will also provide the content basis for classroom discussion to focus on the basic and important mathematics. However, a content analysis of curriculum materials is necessary, but not sufficient, for fostering productive disciplinary engagement in mathematics teaching and learning. It is in this connection that tools like the four principles and five practices of constructivist pedagogy could be useful references for Chinese teachers to complement their command of knowledge for teaching mathematics (Ma 1999; Han and Paine 2010).

Acknowledgement The authors wish to thank the two anonymous reviewers for their constructive comments on an earlier version of the paper. The two studies described in the article were supported by the Research Grant Council of Hong Kong Special Administration Region, China (CERG-4624/05H; CERG-449807; CUHK Direct Grant-4450199), Hong Kong Institute of Educational Research at the Chinese University of Hong Kong (#6900840), and also the National Center for School Curriculum and Textbook Development, Ministry of Education of the People's Republic of China. However, the findings and opinions expressed in the article do not necessarily reflect the positions of the funding agencies.

References

Anderson, J. R. (2000). *Cognitive psychology and its implications*. New York: Worth.

Ball, D. L. (1993). Halves, pieces, and twoths: Constructing and using representational contexts in teaching fractions. In T. P. Carpenter, E. Rennena, & T. A. Romberg (Eds.), *Rational numbers: An integration of research* (pp. 157–195). Hillsdale: Erlbaum.

Ball, D. L. (2001). Teaching, with respect to mathematics and students. In T. Wood, B. S. Nelson, & J. Warfield (Eds.), *Beyond classical pedagogy: Teaching elementary school mathematics* (pp. 11–22). Mahwah: Erlbaum.

Baxter, J. A., & Williams, S. R. (2010). Social and analytic scaffolding in middle school mathematics: Managing the dilemma of telling. *Journal of Mathematics Teacher Education, 13*(1), 7–26.

Cai, J. (1995). *A cognitive analysis of U. S. and Chinese students' mathematical performance on tasks involving computation, simple problem solving, and complex problem solving*. Reston: National Council of Teachers of Mathematics.

Cobb, P., Wood, T., Yackel, E., & McNeal, B. (1992). Characteristics of classroom mathematics traditions: An international analysis. *American Educational Research Journal, 29*, 573–604.

Engle, R. A., & Conant, F. C. (2002). Guiding principles for fostering productive disciplinary engagement: Explaining an emergent argument in a community of learners classroom. *Cognition and Instruction, 20*, 399–483.

Doyle, W. (1983). Academic work. *Review of Educational Researcher, 53*, 159–199.

Doyle, W. (1988). Work in mathematics classes: The context of students' thinking during instruction. *Educational Psychologists, 23*, 167–180.

Guan, Q., & Meng, W. J. (2007). China's new national curriculum reform: Innovation, challenges and strategies. *Frontiers of Education in China, 2*, 579–604.

Hamm, J., & Perry, M. (2002). Learning mathematics in first grade classrooms: On whose authority? *Journal of Educational Psychology, 94*, 126–137.

Han, X., & Paine, L. (2010). Teaching mathematics as deliberate practice through public lessons. *The Elementary School Journal, 110*(4), 519–541.

Henningsen, M., & Stein, M. K. (1997). Mathematical tasks and student cognition: Classroom-based factors that support and inhibit high-level mathematical thinking and reasoning. *Journal for Research in Mathematics Education, 28*, 524–549.

Hiebert, J., & Wearne, D. (1993). Instructional tasks, classroom discourse, and students' learning in second-grade arithmetic. *American Educational Research Journal, 30*(2), 393–425.

Li, Q. (2004). *Elementary school mathematics teachers' subject matter knowledge and pedagogical content knowledge: Their relationship to classroom instruction*. Unpublished doctoral dissertation, The Chinese University of Hong Kong, Hong Kong.

Li, Q., & Ni, Y. J. (2011). Impact of curriculum reform: Evidence of change in classroom practice in the Mainland China. *International Journal of Educational Research, 50*, 71–86.

Ma, L. (1999). *Knowing and teaching elementary mathematics: Teachers' understanding of fundamental mathematics in China and the United States*. Mahwah: Erlbaum.

Marx, R. W., & Walsh, J. (1988). Learning from academic tasks. *Elementary School Journal, 88*(3), 207–219.

Ministry of Education. (2001a). <基础教育课程改革纲要(试行)>. 北京:北京师范大学出版社 [The curriculum reform guidelines for the nine-year compulsory education (trial version)]. Beijing: Beijing Normal University Press (in Chinese).

Ministry of Education. (2001b). <全日制义务教育数学课程标准(实验稿)>. 北京: 北京师范大学出版社 [Curriculum standards for school mathematics of nine-year compulsory education (trial version)]. Beijing: Beijing Normal University Press (in Chinese).

National Council of Teachers of Mathematics. (1989). *Curriculum and evaluation standards for school mathematics*. Reston: Author.

National Council of Teachers of Mathematics. (1997). *Improving student learning in mathematics and science: The role of national standards in state policy*. Reston: Author.

Ni, Y. J., & Zhou, Y. D. (2005). Teaching and learning fraction and rational numbers: The origin and implications of whole number bias. *Educational Psychologist, 40*, 27–52.

Ni, Y. J., Li, Q., Cai, J., & Hau, K. T. (2009). *Has curriculum reform made a difference? Looking for change in classroom practice*. Hong Kong: The Chinese University of Hong Kong.

Ni, Y. J., Chiu, C. C., & Chan, Z. J. (2010). Chinese children learning mathematics: From home to school. In M. H. Bond (Ed.), *The handbook of Chinese psychology* (pp. 143–154). Oxford: Oxford University Press.

Ni, Y., Li, Q., Li, X., & Zhang, Z.-H. (2011). Influence of curriculum reform: An analysis of student mathematics achievement in mainland China. *International Journal of Educational Research, 50*, 100–116.

Ni, Y. J., Zhou, D. H., Li, X., & Li, Q. (2012, April). *Influence of instructional tasks on student/teacher discourse in mathematics classrooms of Chinese primary schools*. Paper presented at the annual conference of American Educational Research Association, Vancouver, Canada.

Nystrand, M., Wu, L. L., Gamoran, A., Zeiser, S., & Long, D. A. (2003). Questions in time: Investigating the structure and dynamics of unfolding classroom discourse. *Discourse Processes, 35*(2), 135–198.

Paine, L., & Ma, L. (1993). Teachers working together: A dialogue on organizational and cultural perspectives of Chinese teachers. *International Journal of Educational Research, 19*, 675–697.

Perry, M., VanderStoep, S. W., & Yu, S. L. (1993). Asking questions in first-grade Mathematics classes: Potential influences on mathematical thought. *Journal of Educational Psychology, 85*, 31–40.

Renkl, A., & Helmke, A. (1992). Discriminate effects of performance-oriented and structure-oriented mathematical tasks on achievement growth. *Contemporary Educational Psychology, 17*, 47–55.

Schoenfeld, A. H. (1992). Learning to think mathematically: Problem solving, metacognition, and sense making in mathematics. In D. A. Grouws (Ed.), *Handbook of research on mathematics teaching and learning* (pp. 334–371). New York: Macmillan.

Stein, M., & Lane, S. (1996). Instructional tasks and the development of student capacity to think and reason: An analysis of the relationship between teaching and learning in a reform mathematics project. *Educational Research and Evaluation, 2*, 50–80.

Stein, M. K., Grover, B. W., & Henningson, M. (1996). Building student capacity for mathematical thinking and reasoning: An analysis of mathematical tasks used in reformed classrooms. *American Educational Research Journal, 33*(2), 455–488.

Stein, M., Smith, M., Henningsen, M., & Silver, E. (2000). *Implementing standard-based mathematics instruction: A case book for professional development*. New York: Teacher College Press.

Stein, M. K., Remillard, J., & Smith, M. S. (2007). How curriculum influences student learning. In F. Lester (Ed.), *Second handbook of research on mathematics teaching and learning* (pp. 319–369). Greenwich: Information Age Publishing.

Stein, M. K., Engle, R. A., Smith, M. S., & Hughes, E. K. (2008). Orchestrating productive mathematical discussions: Helping teachers learn to better incorporate student thinking. *Mathematical Thinking and Learning, 10*, 313–340.

Stigler, J. W., & Hiebert, J. (1999). *The teaching gap: Best ideas from the world's teachers for improving education in the classroom*. New York: Free Press.

Stigler, J. W., & Hiebert, J. (2004). Improving mathematics teaching. *Educational Leadership, 61*, 12–16.

Stigler, J. W., Fernandez, C., & Yoshida, M. (1996). Traditions of school mathematics in Japanese and American elementary classrooms. In L. P. Steffe, P. Nesher, P. Cobb, G. A. Goldin, & B. Greer (Eds.), *Theories of mathematical learning* (pp. 149–175). Mahwah: Lawrence Erlbaum.

Stylianides, G. J. (2009). Reasoning-and-proving in school mathematics textbooks. *Mathematical Thinking and Learning, 11*, 258–288.

Tarr, J. E., Chávez, Ó., Reys, R. E., & Reys, B. J. (2006). From the written to the enacted curricula: The intermediary role of middle school mathematics teachers in shaping students' opportunity to learn. *School Science and Mathematics, 106*(4), 191–201.

Wang, J., & Paine, L. (2003). Learning to teach with mandated curriculum and public examination of teaching as contexts. *Teaching and Teacher Education, 19*, 75–94.

Williams, S. R., & Baxter, J. A. (1996). Dilemmas of discourse-oriented teaching in one middle school mathematics classroom. *The Elementary School Journal, 97*, 21–38.

Improving Mathematics Classroom Instruction through Exemplary Lesson Development: A Chinese Approach

Rongjin Huang and Yeping Li

Abstract In this chapter, we aim to examine a popular approach to improving mathematics classroom instruction through exemplary lesson development in China. Features of a content-focused exemplary lesson are analyzed in detail, and a practicing teacher's experience participating in the development of the exemplary lesson is also examined. The case study suggests that pursuing instruction excellence is a process of negotiating culturally valued teaching traditions and reform-oriented notions. The process of developing an exemplary lesson is of the features of deliberate practice, and the product of developing exemplary lesson forms a type of high-leverage practice. Finally, the implications of developing exemplary lessons for improving mathematics classroom instruction in China are discussed.

Keywords Curricular content changes • Exemplary lesson • Mathematics instruction • Master teacher • Deliberate practice • High-leverage practice

This chapter is built upon an article that formally appeared in ZDM: Huang, R. and Li, Y. (2009). Pursuing excellence in mathematics classroom instruction through exemplary lesson development in China: A case study. *ZDM - The International Journal on Mathematics Education, 41*, 297–309.

R. Huang (✉)
Department of Mathematical Science, Middle Tennessee State University,
MTSU Box 34, Murfreesboro, TN 37132, USA
e-mail: hrj318@gmail.com

Y. Li
Department of Teaching, Learning and Culture, Texas A&M University,
MS 4232, College Station, TX 77843-4232, USA
e-mail: yepingli@tamu.edu

Y. Li et al. (eds.), *Transforming Mathematics Instruction: Multiple Approaches and Practices*, Advances in Mathematics Education, DOI 10.1007/978-3-319-04993-9_14, © Springer International Publishing Switzerland 2014

Background

A multitude of reform efforts have occurred in mathematics education in the past two decades (National Council of Teachers of Mathematics [NCTM] 1991, 2000; Martin 2007). One major focus of these efforts is to prompt ambitious instruction, which includes the following features: (1) cognitively challenging instructional tasks (Stein and Lane 1996; Stigler and Hiebert 2004; Weiss and Pasley 2004); (2) task implementation, or opportunities for students to engage in high-level thinking and reasoning throughout an instructional episode (Stein and Lane 1996; Stigler and Hiebert 2004); and (3) opportunities for students to explain their mathematical thinking and reasoning in mathematical discussions (Boaler and Staples 2008; Cobb et al. 1997). Despite some success in this endeavor, traditional models of instruction still dominate the educational landscape (Jacobs et al. 2006; Stigler and Hiebert 1999). Teachers find it very challenging to implement "ambitious teaching" (Silver et al. 2009). Recently, researchers have emphasized the importance of using high-leverage practices in helping prospective and novice teachers learn to teach (Ball and Forzani 2011; Ball et al. 2009; Grossman and McDonald 2008; Hatch and Grossman 2009). According to Ball and colleagues (2009), high-leverage practices "are those that, when done well, give teachers a lot of capacity in their work. They include activities of teaching that are essential to the work and that are used frequently, ones that have significant power for teachers' effectiveness with pupils" (pp. 460–461). Specifically, they include patterns of students' thinking in specific content areas, misconception of particular contents (Ball and Forzani 2011), and comparison of approaches to teaching of group discussion in different classrooms (Hatch and Grossman 2009). Yet, less attention has been given to the development of those high-leverage practices.

Coincidently, professional developments in China and Japan have focused on developing public lessons (Han and Paine 2010; Huang and Bao 2006) or study lessons (Lewis et al. 2006). In particular, one of the latest Chinese efforts to develop exemplary lessons has demonstrated its power in improving classroom instruction and promoting teachers' expertise growth and developing transferable instructional products (Huang and Li 2009; Huang et al. 2011). Some exemplary lessons have focused on implementing certain teaching strategies (Huang and Bao 2006), while others have aimed to effectively teach particular contents (e.g., Zhang et al. 2008). The model carries a focus on teachers' learning through participating in the process of developing an exemplary lesson (Hiebert and Morris 2012). Nevertheless, much remains to be understood about the characteristics of exemplary lesson instruction that are valued and how to pursue such classroom instruction excellence. Thus, this study is designed to answer the following questions:

1. What is the process utilized to develop the exemplary lesson in discussion?
2. What are the characteristics of the exemplary lessons currently valued in China?
3. What may the practicing teachers learn from exemplary lesson development?

To address these questions, the paper is organized into four sections. First, the characteristics of mathematics classroom instruction currently valued in China will be identified based on a literature review. Then, the approach to pursue mathematics instruction excellence through exemplary lesson development, as adapted in a nationwide research project in China, will be briefly described. After that, a particular exemplary lesson developed in the project will be examined in great details. Finally, some implications of pursuing mathematics instruction excellence through exemplary lesson development will be discussed.

Some Features of Mathematics Classroom Instruction Valued in China

Although no universal agreement of what effective mathematics teaching is exists (e.g., Krainer 2005; Li and Shimizu 2009), studies have documented indications of certain characteristics of effective teaching practices in China. In particular, a number of comparative studies on mathematics classroom teaching reveal several key features of Chinese mathematics instruction. For example, in contrast to US classrooms, Stigler and Perry (1988) found that Chinese students were more involved in mathematics tasks posed by the teacher. In addition, Chinese mathematics lessons were more polished and structured than mathematics instruction in the USA (Stevenson and Lee 1995). Recently, Chinese mathematics classroom instruction was found to have the following features: lecture-dominated whole classroom instruction, explaining new topics carefully, conducting a lesson coherently, emphasizing mathematical reasoning and connections, and practicing with variation problems (e.g., Chen and Li 2010; Huang et al. 2006; Leung 2005).

Through examining the teaching of Pythagoras' theorem over three decades, Tang et al. (2012) found that "two basics" teaching, which emphasizes the development of students' basic knowledge and basic skills, has been evolved in terms of its formats and essence. Although some key elements of "two basics" teaching including developing new knowledge based on previous knowledge with small pace incrementally, teachers' telling dominantly, and practicing with variation problems are still prominent, some reform-oriented features such as connections of knowledge, multiple perspectives of proof, and students' engagement (Ministry of Education, China 2001, 2003) have been incorporated. From a historical perspective, Shao et al. (2012) confirmed that "laying a sound foundation for all students is the first priority" in China legitimizes "two basics" teaching. By assimilating some Western notions of mathematics instruction, the current reform of mathematics classroom instruction in China is aimed to make the following balances: extensive practice vs. conceptual understanding, variant embodiments vs. invariant mathematical essence, teacher guidance vs. student self-exploration, explanative analysis vs. exploratory trial, and logical deduction vs. inductive synthesis (Shao et al. 2012).

In sum, rooted in Chinese cultural traditions and influenced by Western reform notions, Chinese mathematics classroom instruction seem to have the following features: (a) developing students' mathematical knowledge and mathematics reasoning, (b) emphasizing knowledge connections and instructional coherence,

(c) strengthening students' new knowledge acquisition with systematic variation problems, (d) striving for a balance between the teachers' guidance and students' self-explorations, and (e) summarizing key points in due course. These features of effective teaching in China will be used as references in analyzing instructional improvements in this study.

The Case Study of Developing an Exemplary Lesson

In this section, we first introduce a currently used approach to pursue excellent classroom instruction through joint development of exemplary lessons. Then, a particular nationwide project that focuses on the teaching of core concepts through exemplary lesson development will be described. Finally, a detailed analysis of an exemplary lesson will be presented.

Developing Exemplary Lessons: A Promising Approach to Improve Teachers' Knowledge and Teaching Practices

In China, there is a coherent in-service teachers' professional system, within which teachers have been immersed in observing experienced teachers' classroom instruction and being observed by others (Stewart 2006; Wong 2010). Huang, Peng, and colleagues (2010) further described some other popular practices for teachers' professional development such as mentorship scheme, school-based and/or city-based teaching research activities, and municipal and national teaching skill competitions (lesson explaining and lesson teaching). Meanwhile, a teacher promotion system provides a supporting mechanism and incentive for teachers to engage in these activities (Li et al. 2011). Within this promotion system, secondary teachers can be promoted from primary via intermediate to senior positions through a systematic and strict appraisal procedure. It is a critical competence for teachers to design and deliver exemplary lessons in order to be promoted to a higher level (e.g., Huang et al. 2010).

This teacher promotion system also provides a platform for teachers to value and pursue mathematics classroom instruction excellence. Through this promotion system, master teachers who hold senior or above positions have played a crucial role in fostering teachers' professional development. Master teachers not only take responsibility for routinely mentoring junior teachers, but also develop and demonstrate exemplary lessons for others, particularly in the context of implementing reform-oriented curriculum (Li et al. 2011).

Recently, in order to facilitate the implementation of new curriculum, many in-service teacher-training programs have been introduced. Joint efforts to develop exemplary lessons to demonstrate how to handle paradoxical teaching problems such as how to integrate certain innovative teaching ideas into classroom instruction, or how to teach certain newly added content, are common elements of these various programs. Considering the roles played by master teachers (senior or above) during exemplary lesson development, we will describe how a master teacher develops an exemplary lesson within a nationwide project and analyze what unique features the exemplary lesson may have and how the master teacher may learn from developing the exemplary lesson.

The Content-Focused Lesson Development: A Nationwide Research Project

A longitudinal and nationwide project entitled "Structuring Mathematics with Core Concepts at Secondary School Level and Its Experimental Implementation" has been in action since early 2006 (Zhang et al. 2008). The aims of this project are to (1) help teachers recognize and understand the logical development and internal relationship among the core concepts and demonstrate how to effectively teach these core concepts and (2) help students better understand and master mathematics core concepts and know the mathematical ideas and methods underlying these concepts in essence. To achieve these goals, the project suggested a uniform lesson design framework, which includes the following aspects: (1) profound understanding of mathematics concepts, (2) accurate identification of teaching objectives, (3) deep analysis of student difficulties in understanding the concepts, (4) problem-oriented teaching procedure, (5) practicing new knowledge effectively and in time, and (6) assessing students' achievement.

Developing an instructional design of a core concept usually includes the following cyclic procedures: collaborative design of lesson, implementing lesson, reflecting, and revision and reteaching. The process will end when a satisfactory design is achieved within the group of project members. Finally, a case study on the development of the exemplary lesson of teaching core concepts (video, lesson design, and reflection of the development) is constructed for nationwide exchanges and sharing in journal papers or multiple media materials (see Zhang et al. 2008).

More than 300 team members in different fields, such as mathematics educators at universities, secondary mathematics textbook developers, secondary mathematics teaching researchers, and secondary school teachers from more than seven provinces in China, have participated in this project. This project is organized hierarchically. At the national level, all of the members are university professors, senior researchers, and secondary master teachers from different provinces and cities. At the local (provincial or municipal) level, all of the members are voluntarily recruited by national members at each setting. These members consist of master teachers and junior teachers from different types of schools. Moreover, the project may extend its influence to other teachers beyond this project through the following ways: One is to invite all the interested teachers to attend public demonstrating lessons both at national and local levels. The other is to distribute exemplary lessons with relevant videos and documents for teachers' scrutiny.

A sub-team headquartered in a southeastern city, with about ten members, developed a lesson on algorithms, a newly added content topic in high school mathematics curriculum. The team members include master teachers and junior teachers from both key and normal schools. As one of three teachers who had been taking an active role in designing and teaching the lesson, Ms. Chen was a senior mathematics teacher at a key school (a highly prestigious high school at the provincial level) in the city. She has a bachelor's degree and a masters' diploma in mathematics and about 20 years of teaching experience. She had participated in several teacher professional development programs, such as the new curriculum training and provincial key teacher training. Ms. Chen also won the first-class award of junior teacher instruction competition and teaching mastery at the municipal level.

Developing a Particular Exemplary Lesson

In this part, we introduce features of the content and the process of developing this particular exemplary lesson.

The Content of This Exemplary Lesson

This exemplary lesson focuses on algorithms. Algorithms are part of the newly added content in compulsory mathematics 3 at grade 11. The reasons for adding this content are the importance of algorithmic thinking method, its fundamental role in computer science, its broad applications, and its embodiment in many different mathematics contents such as solving systems of equations, finding common factors, etc. The chapter includes three sections: algorithms and programming flow charts (two lessons), basic algorithmic sentences (three lessons), algorithmic cases studies (six lessons), and a summary (one lesson). Through the learning of this chapter, students are expected to preliminarily experience algorithmic thinking methods, the power of using a programming flow chart to solve problems through mathematical cases studies, learn how to use a programming flow chart to present the process of solving problems, experience the basic thinking method of algorithms and its importance and efficiency, and further develop reasoning, thinking, and expression. The content of the exemplary lesson, *introduction to algorithms*, is the first lesson of this chapter, which is arranged for a standard 45-min duration.

The Process of Developing the Exemplary Lesson

First of all, the teacher individually developed a lesson plan of selected topic (several teachers in this sub-team are requested to design lesson plans for the same content), and the different designs were reviewed within the team at the city level. Based on the comparison and analysis of different designs, and the comments of team members, the teacher developed a new design for teaching the content. Then, the teacher gave a public lesson in her own class for team members and other experts at the city level to observe and comment on. Based on post-lesson feedbacks and self-reflections, the teacher revised the design of the lesson for further public observation (referred to as the original design in this study). Then, a public lesson was conducted in another city for demonstration and study with the team members at the national level. Although the teacher was satisfied with her performance in the public lesson, the experts in the national team gave her many criticisms. Based on this public lesson and the expert suggestions, she made a fundamental revision of the lesson design (called the revised design): giving up previous contextual problems and only using the mathematical problems provided in the textbook (10 of 11 problems are directly copied from or adapted from the textbook) for introducing and developing relevant concepts. After that, she gave a public lesson in her own school, but not with her own class, which was also videotaped for demonstration in a teacher-training program at the provincial level. After that, she gave two public demonstrations of the lesson based on the same design with minor adjustments at the provincial and national levels.

Data Source and Analysis

In order to answer research question 2, we collected the following data: two lesson plans (the original and revised ones) and two videotaped lessons, five master teachers' (these master teachers were from another city, so they did not know Ms. Chen personally) written comments on this revised lesson, and Ms. Chen's reflection report and a semi-structured interview with her. The five master teachers were asked to provide their written comments based on the following questions: (1) What are the main features of the lesson? What parts are most impressive to you? Please explain your opinions in detail. (2) If rating this lesson with a five-point scale (1 presents the lowest, while 5 presents the highest), please give your rating and rationale. What kinds of exemplary roles do you think it may have, and why? In addition, the five types of questions guided our interviews with Ms. Chen, namely, background, the topic selection, the process of developing the lesson, experience and attainment, and notions of teaching and learning in general.

By analyzing the revised lesson plan and videotaped lesson from different perspectives, we aim to capture the characteristics of this lesson. With regard to master teachers' comments, we developed a coding system based on previous framework (Huang and Li 2008). Two raters coded all the five teachers' written comments separately. The inter-rater agreement was 81 %, and all the differences were resolved through discussions. On Ms. Chen's reflection report and interview transcripts, we identify main stages of changes and gains through participating in the process of developing exemplary lesson.

The Exemplary Lesson Design

In this part, we will describe the main segments of the exemplary lesson which includes the following phases: (1) introduction of the topic, (2) introduction to the concept of algorithms through solving problems, (3) forming the concept through analyzing and synthesizing, (4) fostering the understanding of the concept and learning to express with daily language through solving deliberately selected problems, and (5) classroom exercise and homework.

Introduction of the topic. Through showing pictures of counting chips, an abacus, and computers from the textbook, a common method is induced underlying those instruments, namely, algorithm. The background of those pictures is one masterpiece of mathematics developed by Mr. Zhu Shiji in the Song dynasty (960–1279), which included the great mathematics achievement by ancient Chinese mathematicians. Through posing the question: What are the algorithms, which related to all these instruments? The topic is induced naturally.

Introduction to algorithms through problem-solving. At this stage, several internally connected problems are discussed. Problem 1: Can you find the procedures to solve a system of linear equations with two unknowns, namely, $x-2y=-1$ and $2x+y=1$?

It is intended that recalling the steps needed to solve a system of linear equations will motivate students to explore general methods of solving many systems of linear equations, which will further provide foundation and experience for forming algorithm concepts.

Problem 2: What are the differences between your answer and the answer in the textbook? What are the characteristics of the answer provided by the textbook? This problem aims to draw students' attention to the solution procedures in general situation, and the logical structure of the solution.

Problem 3: Write the procedures of solving a system of linear equations

$$\begin{cases} a_1x + b_1y = c_1 & (1) \\ a_2x + b_2y = c_2 & (2) \end{cases} \quad (a_1b_2 - a_2b_1 \neq 0).$$

This problem led to students' further review of the procedures of solving general systems of linear equations with two unknowns, which aimed to help students know that an algorithm is a method for solving a group of problems that can be generalized. This idea is the base for generating the concept of algorithms.

Forming the concept of algorithms through analyzing and summarizing. The teacher asked the following questions: What does algorithm mean? How do you express an algorithm? (Problem 4) This problem led students to acquire preliminary knowledge about algorithms, although they are unable to express the concept comprehensively based on previous examples. By questioning and answering, students are involved in the process of generating the concept.

Fostering students' understanding of the concept of algorithms and learning how to express algorithms by natural language through solving problems. Three more abstract problems were posted for students to solve and discuss. Problem 5: Write down the procedures to judge whether 7 is a prime number. This problem is intended to help students realize there is a certain recursive structure in the procedures of solving the problem. It provides students with the condition to recognize the features of algorithms and to learn how to express an algorithm with natural language. Problem 6: Given a whole number n ($n>2$), can you design an algorithm to judge whether it is a prime number or not? Students were invited to solve this problem by themselves on the basis of Problem 5. Thus, they can further understand algorithms, realize the functions and strengths, and learn how to express algorithms with natural language. Meanwhile, students may realize that there is a certain structure in the algorithms.

Problem 7: Write down algorithms for finding the approximate solution of equation $x^2-2=0$ ($x>0$) by the bisection method. This problem is intended to review the bisection method, which is a classic method of algorithms, demonstrating the sequence and operation clearly. Solving this problem is expected to help students further recognize the logical structure of algorithms, comprehend the algorithmic thinking and characteristics, and further consolidate how to express algorithms by natural language.

Summarization. Through thinking about and answering the following questions, the content taught was reviewed and summarized. These questions are as follows: (1) Can you express more algorithm examples? (Problem 8) (2) Compared to the process of solving general problems, what are the most important features of algorithms? (Problem 9).

Exercise and homework. Exercises and homework were arranged. Two problems were for classroom exercise. One is from the textbook (Problem 10), and the other is a counterexample (Problem 11). Moreover, two problems were assigned as the homework.

Features of This Exemplary Lesson

In this part, we examine and identify some unique features of this exemplary lesson. First, we identify what kinds of learning opportunities the teacher created in this lesson from a perspective of teaching for understanding (Carpenter and Lehrer 1999). Then, based on five master teachers' comments on this lesson, we try to capture what aspects are valued in this exemplary lesson by master teachers.

An Analysis from the Perspective of Teaching for Understanding

According to the framework by Carpenter and Lehrer (1999), the five forms of mental activities that are conducive to developing mathematics understanding in classrooms include (a) constructing relationships, (b) extending and applying mathematical knowledge, (c) reflecting about experiences, (d) articulating what one knows, and (e) making mathematical knowledge one's own. In this study, constructing relationships refers to building the new knowledge based on previous knowledge and building interconnected concepts and representations. Extending and applying learned knowledge means to apply knowledge to solve problems and build a foundation for further study. Reflecting mainly refers to summary. Articulating includes group discussion and public sharing. Making mathematics knowledge one's own refers to making mathematics interesting in the context of daily life and exploring knowledge by students themselves. In this lesson, the teacher tried to help students construct the concept of algorithms with understanding through presenting systematic, interconnected problems for students to explore and share. We can identify the following evidence that benefits students' understanding of the concept.

Building the new concept through reviewing and solving problem progressively. The teacher paid close attention to building the new concept upon previously learned concepts and methods. At the beginning of the lesson, the teacher presented some pictures on Chinese chips, abacuses, and computers from the textbook. This was intended to relate the new topics to those concepts and methods implicitly. Then, the teacher deliberately presented two problems with regard to a system of equations with two unknowns from numerical coefficients to symbolic ones for students to explore and discuss. Through this process, some features of the new concept— algorithm such as general procedures to solve a group of problem, in sequent procedures—were progressively exposed. Finally, the formal concept was stated explicitly and clearly based on student's contributions as follows:

T: Please read the expression on blackboard, what are the salient features of this expression compared to your own?

S: Consecution (*tiaoli*)

T: What does it mean?

S: Uh

T: Can you use other words?

S: Sequence (*shunxue*)

T: Expressing in sequence procedures, is it right ?

S: Right

T: Thus, based on the previous problem, can we solve a group of problems? We project the procedure of solving this group of problems by following sequent steps, and these steps consist of an algorithm. Do you agree?

S: (Confirmation with nod)

T: Good. Sit down please (Writing down: the concept of algorithms)

T: Regarding algorithms, there is an expression in the textbook as follows (shown on the blackboard): In mathematics, algorithms usually refer to definite, finite procedures by following certain roles for solving a group of problems. Nowadays, algorithms can be programmed and implemented on a computer to solve problems.

After presenting the definition of algorithm, the teacher reemphasized the characteristics (definite, finite, and sequent) and its relationship with methods to solve a particular system equation.

Consolidating the concept through applying the concept systematically. The teacher presented two sets of problems for applications. One was to judge whether a whole number is a prime number or not, and the other was to find the approximate solution of a set of equations. With regard to the judgment of prime numbers, the teacher presented different numbers from 7, to 35, to 1997, and guided students to find and articulate the procedures of the algorithm. The recursive structure of an algorithm was experienced, which is crucial for further programming. Take one episode for example. Within this interaction, the teacher guided students to express the algorithm to judge whether 7 is a prime number or not:

T: Then, can you design an algorithm to judge whether the whole number 7 is a prime number or not?

S: (Student's discussion)

T: Keep silence. Listening to her explanation.

S: First, 7 is divided by 1

T: Can you answer what prime number is?

S: Oh. 7 is divided by 2 first.

T: Right. Do not need to divide by 1. Because a prime number means the number that does not include any factorization numbers except 1 and itself. Thus, she changed to divide 7 by 2 first.

S: If 7 is divided by 2, there is a remainder. Then 7 is divided by 3, there is a remainder... 7 is divided by 6, there is a remainder. Thus, we can conclude that 7 is a prime number.

T: Very good. She expressed by using first, then, after that. In fact, we replace these words with first, second, third. So, we can say: first, 7 is divided by 2, there is a remainder. How can we tell computer to judge a number is divided by another number?

S: To see the remainder is zero

T: Right. Just see the remainder. Now, can we write these procedures more precisely? (Write down on the blackboard: First, 7 is divided by 2, what is the remainder?

S: Remainder is 1.

T: First, 7 is divided by 2, the remainder is 1.

T: (Writing down) Because remainder is not zero.

T: (Writing down) Thus, 2 cannot divide 7 completely.

T: Very good. In fact, we have to express each step definitely and clearly. Now, I express what she said just now as shown on the screen. She just said: first step, 7 is divided by 2 and the remainder is 1. Because the remainder is not zero, so 7 can't be divided completely.

T: How about the second step?

S: Second step, 7 is divided by 3, the remainder is 1. Because the remainder is not zero, so 7 cannot be divided by 3.

Through questioning and answering, the students developed and expressed the algorithm regarding how to judge whether 7 is a prime number or not. Moreover, students were asked to develop an algorithm to judge whether 1997 is a prime number or not.

Clarifying the concepts through encouraging student's articulation. As demonstrated in previous episodes, during the process of solving problems, the teacher tried her best to encourage students to express what they know, as shown in the previous episode.

Reflecting on the concept through summarizing. Once they learned something new, the teacher paid attention to applying this concept and summarizing the key points of the concept in due course. Before closing the lesson, the teacher invited students to summarize the lesson as follows:

T: Class. In this lesson, we have learned the concept of algorithms. You should realize that we emphasize the definite and finite procedures to solve a class of problems by following certain rules. Moreover, we can program to implement the algorithm in a computer. What are the salient features of algorithms?

S and T: Sequent, finite, definite.

T: Very good. In fact, an algorithm has three important features: sequence, definiteness, and finiteness. Through solving different problems, you should experience there are some structures in algorithms. For example, in solving the system of equations, there is main sequence structure. While in solving the last two problems, we realize the recursive structure and conditional structure. Now, let us look at the next problem.

In summary, according to current particular perspective, the teacher provided many opportunities for students to form, consolidate, apply, and express the concept, which are conducive to students' understanding of the concept taught.

An Analysis from Master Teachers' Perspectives

All five of the master teachers were knowledgeable, with an average of 20 years of teaching experience (ranging from 11 to 30 years). Four of them [denoted as T1 to T4] taught mathematics at key high schools, while the last [denoted as T5] was a teaching researcher at the municipal level and the local coordinator of this project. The average rating of this lesson was a 4.5 ranging from 3.5 to 5, which means this lesson was judged as a good one. Through detailed reading and an analyzation of the entirety of the five master teachers' comments, their opinions were classified into three broad categories, namely, instruction objectives, instructional designs, and instructional processes. *Instruction objectives* consist of three items concerning the intended and achieved goals in knowledge and skills, mathematical thinking, and cultural value and attitudes. *Instructional designs* include the aspects of

Table 1 Frequency of items used by the master teachers

Category	Items	T1	T2	T3	T4	T5	Total
				Teacher			
Instructional objectives	Knowledge and skill		1	1	1	1	4
	Mathematical thinking		1	1	1	1	4
	Attitude and values		1	1	1	1	4
Instructional designs	Focusing the essence of the concept	1	1	1	1		4
	Dealing with important and difficult point		1		1		2
	Development of topics progressively	1	1	1	1	1	5
	Problem-based teaching methods	1	1				3
	Properly using textbook		1			1	2
Instructional processes	Students' participation	1	1	1		1	4
	Teacher' guidance	1	1	1		1	4
	Stimulating students' thinking		1		1		2
	Students' induction and abstract	1	1	1	1		4

teaching planning such as focusing on the essence of the concept, dealing with important and difficult knowledge points, organizing and developing knowledge progressively, readiness of students' knowledge and cognition level, appropriateness of the textbook use, and selection of teaching methods (e.g., problem-based teaching method). *Instructional processes* refer to the classroom interactions and contributions made by the teacher and students such as the teacher's guidance, students' participations, student's self-exploratory learning, and so on. Table 1 shows the frequency of relevant items used by these teachers.

Table 1 indicates that all five teachers appreciated the lesson's good organization and full development of the concept progressively. For example, T2 explained as follows:

> To achieve teaching objectives, the teacher purposely drew students' attention from the solution of a system of equations to its process and method. Meanwhile, the teacher steered students to express the process and method using their own language. Thus, the structure of solving system of equations and its natural language expression were connected. During the process, the teacher implicitly emphasized the features of [algorithms] such as, certain rules, a set of problems, and definite procedures, which makes good preparation for introducing the concept.

The second set of impressive aspects are how the teacher tried to balance the teacher's guidance and the students' participations and make comprehensive teaching objectives focus on the mathematical essence of the concept while enlightening students' observations, inductions, and abstractions. Four master teachers gave positive comments on the teacher's guidance and students' participations. For example, T3 appreciated that "the teacher made a proper balance between the teacher's guidance [*zhudao*] and students-centered instruction [*zhuti*]." Four of them emphasized the importance of setting and achieving three dimensions of teaching objectives (suggested in national curriculum standards), while another four focused on the mathematical essence of the concept. For example, T5 emphasized the importance of achieving a comprehensive teaching objective as follows:

> This lesson achieves three dimensions of teaching objectives: (1) during the process of forming the concept of algorithms, students understood what is an algorithm so that the knowledge aim was achieved; (2) during the process of achieving knowledge aims, students mastered several algorithms of solving problems, thus ability objective was achieved; (3) from ancient abacus to modern computer, algorithm thinking has played a fundamental role, thus, the affection, mathematical thinking, and cultural value were reflected to a certain extent.

Four of them appreciated the teacher's focus on the mathematics content in essence. For example, T2 highlighted the salient feature of the lesson as "unfolding this lesson surrounding the concept of algorithms and focusing on the essence of the problem in question." The critical aspects of the concept are "solving a set of problems," "certain rules to follow," "definite and finite procedures," and so on. He further explained the importance of inducing and abstracting as follows: "by adopting the concept development from special cases to the general situation, the teacher continuously enlightens students to induce and abstract."

Also, three of the five master teachers emphasized the importance of problem-based teaching and learning. Moreover, two of them mentioned the following aspects: a problem-based teaching method, the full use of the textbook, and stimulating students' thinking.

In responding to the question of what kinds of exemplary aspects the lesson may have, these master teachers recommended the following aspects: (1) guiding students in developing and constructing the mathematical concept, (2) achieving three dimensions of teaching objectives, (3) focusing on the core concept formation and relevant mathematical thinking, and (4) profound understanding and appropriate use of the textbook.

In addition, they also provided some improvement suggestions: (1) enlightening students' self-learning and thinking, (2) reducing the amount of content, (3) proper dealing of logical structure difficulties, and (4) using precise teaching language and less telling.

Taken together, these master teachers agreed that this is a good lesson, and it has some demonstration aspects, which include (1) guide students to develop and construct the mathematical concept progressively, (2) achieve three dimensions of teaching objectives, (3) focus on core concept formation and relevant mathematical thinking, (4) have a profound understanding and proper use of the textbook, and (5) make a balance between the teachers' guidance and students' participations. However, there were some suggestions on the improvements of this lesson which include paying due attention to students' self-exploration, the quantity and difficulty of content, and use of classroom instruction language.

The Growth of Ms. Chen

In order to understand Ms. Chen's changes during the process of developing the exemplary lesson, we analyze Ms. Chen's reflection report and a semi-structured interview. In her *reflection report*, she revealed her personal journey through developing the exemplary lesson from satisfaction at the first demonstration to some regrets in the follow-up demonstrations over the five teaching trials for *introduction to algorithms*. The following parts describe her main changes to the development of this exemplary lesson.

Daily situation oriented design. She spent 1 month to collect relevant materials, analyze, and prepare an instructional design after accepting the task to develop a study lesson on algorithms, which was a totally new concept for her. Then, she gave a public lesson for the members of the research group at the city level at her school. Based on an extensive discussion within the research group, she revised the design for a further demonstration lesson at the city level. In this design, she used two interesting problems to introduce the concept. The first problem is as follows:

> A farmer wants to bring a wolf, a goat, and a basket of vegetables over a river with a small ship. On the board, the farmer can only bring each of them one time. When the framer is on spot, wolf, goat, and vegetable are safe. However, when the framer is not present, the wolf will eat goat and the goat will eat vegetables. Please give a design for the farmer to bring all of them over the river safely.

The second problem is a famous Chinese "chicken and rabbit staying in the same cage" problem as follows:

> There are some chickens and rabbits staying in the same cage. If there are 35 heads and 94 legs, how many chickens and rabbits are there?

With the support of multimedia, there was a warm atmosphere on the surface with frequent interactions between the teacher and students, and many practicing teachers liked this lesson also. However, during the post-lesson reflection session, many experts at the nationwide level criticized this design and denied the daily life-learning situation that focused on contexts too much and ignored the mathematical essence of the concept. She realized that it is crucial to have a deep understanding of the textbook in terms of its representations, examples, and exercise problems, which is fundamental for a good lesson design.

Developing a mathematics concept-oriented design. Once she realized the weakness of the previous design, she developed a new design based on experts' suggestions and self-reflection, and the teacher gave a third public lesson that was also videotaped as a demonstration lesson for teacher training at the provincial level. This lesson design, as shown in previous section, paid great attention to forming, developing, and consolidating the concept in the essence through exploring a series of deliberately selected problems. However, she did not like that lesson. On the one hand, the classroom she gave the lesson to was not her own class, so the students were not willing to participate in the public lesson. Thus, the classroom atmosphere was relatively tedious. On the other hand, since she worried about students' understanding of the recursive structure and its expression, she explained more with a lot of superfluous words. On the reflection of this lesson, she realized that when delivering a good lesson, a teacher should pay close attention to students' readiness and tries her/his best to fully motivate students' enthusiasm and initiative. It is crucial for a mature teacher to use precise language to enlighten and guide students to focus on important and key points of the concept being taught.

Mathematical concept formation and students' participation balanced design. After that, she delivered the public lesson twice, at the provincial and national levels. Building on the previous teaching practice and reflections, she was more successful in formatting a mathematics concept, motivating and engaging students, and achieving a better classroom instruction performance overall. However, some new regrets were also created. For example, in the fifth public lesson, an interesting and historical situation got students excitedly and actively engaged in forming and developing the concept, she enjoyed the process so much that she forgot time control. It raised other critical issues: How to properly deal with the relationship between students' self-exploration and teacher's guidance? How to effectively manage classroom time? In a well-prepared lesson, if a competent teacher cannot manage the classroom effectively, how can junior teachers deal with these relationships properly in their daily lessons? She has thought and tried to find solutions to these questions in her subsequent teaching practices.

Multiple effective teaching methods but not a fixed teaching method. In her summary, she said "through the whole process of developing this exemplary lesson, I've got a considerable gain. I not only have experienced and realized many problems and updated my own ideas and learned how to do teaching research but also improved my basic classroom teaching skills, reflection ability in and after the lesson, and significantly fostered my ability in dealing with teaching problems. I realized that there are certain teaching principles but no fixed method to all kinds of situations and there are endless opportunities to learn."

In her interview, she confirmed relevant opinions on her feelings and attainment as follows:

> Overall, I had suffered from high stress and heavy workload, but I had learned a lot. So, it is worthwhile and it really helps me understand the new curriculum. Through this project, I had gained in terms of the following aspects: First, it advanced my understanding of the new curriculum: from repulsion at the beginning to acceptance later on. Second, through the process of design, implementation, reflection, and revision, it fostered my understanding of the textbook and ability in dealing with the textbook properly. Third, it gave me a lot of enlightenment through sharing different teaching designs and participating in exchange activities, particularly comparing different designs and observing lessons and listening to other master teachers' comments and so on.

The joint development of exemplary lessons reflects some common points about how to teach core mathematics concepts. The design and delivery of this exemplary lesson lay great emphasis on the following aspects: (1) achieving three dimensions of teaching objectives (knowledge, ability and mathematical methods, culture value and affection); (2) focusing on the formulation, development, and consolidation of the concept through exploring a series of purposely selected problems; (3) better understanding and appropriate use of the textbook; and (4) making a balance between teachers' guidance and students' self-learning and thinking.

Moreover, Ms. Chen learned a lot from participating in the process of developing an exemplary lesson, including deepening the understanding of content knowledge, optimizing the design of teaching the content, and ability to deal with the textbook in general. And most importantly, she learned to pose problems and solve problems consciously, which enhanced her reflection awareness and ability.

Discussion and Conclusion

Exemplary lesson development has demonstrated its impact on helping teachers not only to understand new content but also to figure out effective ways of teaching them. This exemplary lesson shows a problem-based teaching approach. Solving a series of deliberately selected problems is intended to stimulate students' learning interests, connect the new topic to previous knowledge, form the new concept, clarify and consolidate the concept, and apply the concept in different contexts. Particular emphasis was placed on forming and understanding the essence of the concept and the underlying mathematical ideas, through exploring and solving a series of mathematically worthwhile problems. The lesson successfully exemplified the following aspects: (1) setting comprehensive and feasible teaching objectives; (2) focusing on the essence of core concept (connotation and extension); (3) guiding students to form, develop, and consolidate the mathematics concept progressively; and (4) profound understanding and proper use of the textbook.

In their study, Huang et al. (2012) depicted how a teacher developed an exemplary lesson of teaching a topic in geometry. They made quite similar observations regarding the improvement of teaching: appropriately identifying comprehensive instructional objectives, coherently developing knowledge, effectively dealing with difficult content points, and strategically organizing problem sequences. Thus, we are certain that participating teachers have benefited from their efforts to pursue excellence in mathematics classroom instruction. Through developing exemplary lessons, they developed a better understanding of the new curriculum content and the process of designing and developing an effective lesson, and more importantly, they have learned how to raise paradoxical problems in teaching and find ways to handle those problems.

Instruction Excellence as a Balance Between Culturally Valued Traditions and Reform-Oriented Notions

The characteristics of the exemplary lesson identified in the previous sections partly reflect certain culturally valued features of mathematics instruction in China, such as instruction coherence, well-developed knowledge, practicing knowledge with systematic problem variations, demonstrating some innovative efforts in exposing mathematical thinking and cultural value with regard to the concepts to be learned, and encouraging students' participation and self-exploration. In particular, the flexible use of systematic problems with variations for introducing and practicing new content and developing students' problem-solving ability is a cultural belief of mathematics teaching in China (Li 2006) and a popular strategy in effective teaching (Cai and Nie 2007; Gu et al. 2004; Huang et al. 2006). The national project explicitly suggested adopting a problem-oriented teaching procedure as one of the principles for lesson design. We can see how the team members' notions on mathematical instruction impacted the development of the design of the particular exemplary lesson. As a result, the design of the lesson shifted from focusing on the superficially contextual situations, which were used mainly for motivating students' interest and participation but were not pertinent to developing mathematical concepts in essence, to focusing on mathematically worthwhile problems, which were used effectively for developing mathematical concepts. It is the deep understanding and proper use of the textbook and the joint reflection on experiment teaching that make this shift happen. Meanwhile, teachers' guidance is still in place to a certain extent; although, participating teachers realized the need to provide students with self-exploratory opportunities as much as possible. The legitimation of teachers' guidance is rooted deeply in the Chinese conception of teachers, which emphasizes teachers' roles in transmitting, instructing, and disabusing knowledge (Li et al. 2008; Shao et al. 2012).

Pursuing Instruction Excellence as a Participation in Deliberate Practice

The dynamic process of developing an exemplary lesson, namely, multiple cycles of design, teaching, reflection, and revised design, is crucial. During the process, not only does understanding of the content to be taught become more and more profound, but the ways to teach the content also get more and more feasible and effective. There is no doubt that the case presents an important approach that is undertaken in China to make good use of master teachers' experiences and team joint efforts. During the past couple of years, the approach has been popularized and has resulted in extensive influences on in-service teacher professional development in China (Huang and Li 2009).

Ericsson and his colleagues (Ericsson 2008; Ericsson et al. 1993) have emphasized the importance of participation in special activities, *deliberate practice,* for continued improvement and the attainment of expert performance. A deliberate practice has the following features: Teachers are given a task with a well-defined goal, motivated to improve, provided with feedback, and provided with ample opportunities for repetition and gradual refinements of their performance (Ericsson 2008). Thus, this study revealed that exemplary lesson development provides a kind of "deliberative practice" for experienced and senior teachers to continuously develop their expertise because of "the provision of immediate feedback, time for problem-solving and evaluation, and opportunities for repeated performance to refine behavior" (Ericsson 2008, p. 988). Unlike *deliberate practice* for musicians to practice a piece of "classic music" repeatedly to improve their performance, delivering a lesson to different students who the teacher does not know is quite challenging. The teacher has to learn about the students and adjust her/his teaching to cater to students' diversity as soon as possible during the class. Although this kind of *deliberate practice* is not comfortable for practicing teachers (as Ms. Chen said), it may be critical in order to draw teachers' attention to their students and persuade them to teach mathematics for all students.

Product of Instruction Excellence as a Kind of High-Leverage Practice

Researchers made hypermedia lesson cases that consist of clips of the exemplary lesson, participant teachers' reflections, experts' comments and students' feedback (Bao and Huang 2007). The instructional products based on the development of exemplary lesson (lesson designs, teachers' self-reflection report, experts' comments on lessons, and videotaped lessons) are practical, insightful, and changeable, which provide alternative approaches to improving teaching (Morris and Hiebert 2011). Positive roles of video clips in teachers' learning have been widely documented (Borko et al. 2008; Sherin and Han 2004; Sherin and van Es 2009). Thus, the instructional products (video case studies) could serve as a kind of high-leverage practice for teachers learning to teach. Beyond "micro" high-leverage practices such as effectively dealing with students' thinking in specific content areas and misconceptions of particular contents (Ball and Forzani 2011), the Chinese approach focuses on developing exemplary lessons teaching specific content topics repeatedly over years (Huang et al. 2012), or even over decades (Tang et al. 2012). As such, these well-developed exemplary lessons that include "micro" high-leverage practices, could be adapted for teachers to use or learn.

In summary, the Chinese approach to pursuing instruction excellence has demonstrated its power and uniqueness. As a process of deliberate practice, exemplary lesson development provides a mechanism that enables participating teachers to improve their teaching continuously; as a product of high-leverage practice, exemplary lesson development creates opportunities for others to learn to teach from using the instructional products. Compared with the Japanese lesson study (Lewis et al. 2006), the commonalities are to focus on teachers' practical needs and issues, to emphasize reflecting on or being in action, revising design, and enacting new action. However, the Chinese model pays much attention to upgrading teaching/ learning notions pertinent to the new curriculum standards and teachers' joint creation of cases of class teaching and sharing of their exemplary lessons (Huang and Bao 2006; Huang et al. 2011).

Limitations

In this chapter, we examined how a teacher improved her teaching through direct involvement in the development of an exemplary lesson. However, developing an exemplary lesson is a joint effort made by teachers and teacher researchers. We speculate that all those who participate in developing exemplary lessons (teachers who participate in the process of developing exemplary lessons and/or teachers who merely watch public exemplary lessons, and teaching researchers who supervise the process of developing exemplary lessons) could learn something. The findings of this case study should not be applied to those who are not directly involved in teaching exemplary lessons. It would be meaningful to explore how different participants benefit from being involved in exemplary lessons development. In addition, it is important to examine the interactions among teachers and teaching researchers to see how they might learn from each other. Nonetheless, this study provides a vivid description of how practicing teachers can continuously improve their classroom instruction through exemplary lesson development in this context. Cross-culturally, when reflecting whether the practice in China can be adapted to other education systems, it is crucial to note the differences in cultural values, teaching traditions, education systems, and teacher preparation systems.

Acknowledgments We would like to thank Dr. Jianyue Zhang from the People's Education Press in China for allowing us to use the exemplary lesson from their project. Thanks also go to Mr. Xuejun Li at Hangzhou Teaching Research Institute for helping collect relevant data. We are grateful to those participating master teachers for their time and views. We appreciate the editors and reviewers' constructive suggestions on improving the paper. However, all the ideas presented in the paper, including inappropriate opinions, belong to the authors.

References

Ball, D. L., & Forzani, F. M. (2011). Teaching skillful. *Educational Leadership, 68*(4), 40–45.

Ball, D. L., Sleep, L., Boerst, T., & Bass, H. (2009). Combining the development of practice and the practice of development in teacher education. *Elementary School Journal, 109*, 458–474.

Bao, J., & Huang, R. (2007, June). Hypermedia video cases for in-service mathematics teacher professional development in China (regular lecture). In C. S. Lim, S. Fatimah, G. Munirah, S. Hajar, & M. Y. Hashimah (Eds.), *Proceeding of 4th East Asia regional conference on mathematics education* (pp. 47–53). Malaysia: Universiti Sans Malaysia.

Boaler, J., & Staples, M. (2008). Creating mathematical futures through an equitable teaching approach: The case of Railside School. *Teachers College Record, 110*, 8–9.

Borko, H., Jacobs, J., Eiteljorg, E., & Pittman, M. E. (2008). Video as a tool for fostering productive discussions in mathematics professional development. *Teaching and Teacher Education, 24*, 417–436.

Cai, J., & Nie, B. (2007). Problem solving in Chinese mathematics education: Research and practice. *ZDM – The International Journal on Mathematics Education, 30*, 459–473.

Carpenter, T. P., & Lehrer, R. (1999). Teaching and learning mathematics with understanding. In E. Fennema & T. A. Romberg (Eds.), *Mathematics classroom that promote understanding* (pp. 19–32). Mahwah: Lawrence Erlbaum.

Chen, X., & Li, Y. (2010). Instructional coherence in Chinese mathematics classroom – A case study of lesson on fraction division. *International Journal of Science and Mathematics Education, 8*, 711–735.

Cobb, P., Boufi, A., McClain, K., & Whitenack, J. (1997). Reflective discourse and collective reflection. *Journal for Research in Mathematics Education, 28*, 258–277.

Ericsson, K. A. (2008). Deliberate practice and acquisition of expert performance: A general overview. *Academic Emergency Medicine, 15*, 988–994.

Ericsson, K. A., Krampe, R., & Tesch-Romer, C. (1993). The role of deliberate practice in the acquisition of expert performance. *Psychological Review, 100*, 363–406.

Grossman, P., & McDonald, M. (2008). Back to the future: Directions for research in teaching and teacher education. *American Educational Research Journal, 45*(1), 184–205.

Gu, L., Huang, R., & Marton, F. (2004). Teaching with variation: An effective way of mathematics teaching in China. In L. Fan, N. Y. Wong, J. Cai, & S. Li (Eds.), *How Chinese learn mathematics: Perspectives from insiders* (pp. 309–348). Singapore: World Scientific.

Han, X., & Paine, L. (2010). Teaching mathematics as deliberate practice through public lessons. *The Elementary School Journal, 110*, 519–541.

Hatch, T., & Grossman, P. (2009). Learning to look beyond the boundaries of representation: Using technology to examine teaching (Overview for a digital exhibition: Learning from the practice of teaching). *Journal of Teacher Education, 60*, 70–86.

Hiebert, J., & Morris, A. K. (2012). Teaching, rather than teachers, as a path toward improving classroom instruction. *Journal of Teacher Education, 63*(3), 92–102.

Huang, R., & Bao, J. (2006). Towards a model for teacher professional development in China: Introducing Keli. *Journal of Mathematics Teacher Education, 9*, 279–298.

Huang, R., & Li, Y. (2008). Challenges and opportunities for in-service mathematics teacher professional development in China. *Journal of Mathematics Education, 17*(3), 1–7.

Huang, R., & Li, Y. (2009). Examining the nature of effective teaching through master teachers' lesson evaluation in China. In J. Cai, G. Kaiser, B. Perry, & N. Wong (Eds.), *Effective mathematics teaching from teachers' perspectives: National and international studies* (pp. 163–182). Rotterdam: Sense Publishers.

Huang, R., Mok, I., & Leung, F. K. S. (2006). Repetition or variation: "Practice" in the mathematics classrooms in China. In D. J. Clarke, C. Keitel, & Y. Shimizu (Eds.), *Mathematics classrooms in twelve countries: The insider's perspective* (pp. 263–274). Rotterdam: Sense Publishers.

Huang, R., Peng, S., Wang, L., & Li, Y. (2010). Secondary mathematics teacher professional development in China. In F. K. S. Leung & Y. Li (Eds.), *Reforms and issues in school mathematics in East Asia* (pp. 129–152). Rotterdam: Sense Publishers.

Huang, R., Li, Y., Zhang, J., & Li, X. (2011). Developing teachers' expertise in teaching through exemplary lesson development and collaboration. *ZDM – The International Journal on Mathematics Education, 43*(6–7), 805–817.

Huang, R., Li, Y., & Su, H. (2012). Improving mathematics instruction through exemplary lesson development in China. In Y. Li & R. Huang (Eds.), *How Chinese teach mathematics and improve teaching* (pp. 186–203). New York: Routledge.

Jacobs, J., Hiebert, J., Givvin, K., Hollingsworth, H., Garnier, H., & Wearne, D. (2006). Does eighth-grade mathematics teaching in the United States align with the NCTM *Standards?* Results from the TIMSS 1995 and 1999 video studies. *Journal for Research in Mathematics Education, 36*, 5–32.

Krainer, K. (2005). What is "good" mathematics teaching, and how can research inform practice and policy? (Editorial). *Journal of Mathematics Teacher Education, 8*, 75–81.

Leung, F. K. S. (2005). Some characteristics of East Asian mathematics classrooms based on data from the TIMSS 1999 video study. *Educational Studies in Mathematics, 60*, 199–215.

Lewis, C., Perry, R., & Murata, A. (2006). How should research contribute to instructional improvement? The case of lesson study. *Educational Research, 35*(3), 3–14.

Li, S. (2006). Practice makes perfect: A key belief in China. In F. K. S. Leung, K. D. Graf, & F. J. Lopez-Real (Eds.), *Mathematics education in different cultural traditions: A comparative study of East Asia and the West* (pp. 129–138). New York: Springer.

Li, S., Huang, R., & Shin, Y. (2008). Mathematical discipline knowledge requirements for prospective secondary teachers from East Asian perspective. In P. Sullivan & T. Wood (Eds.), *Knowledge and beliefs in mathematics teaching and teaching development* (pp. 63–86). Rotterdam: Sense Publishers.

Li, Y., Huang, R., Bao, J., & Fan, Y. (2011). Facilitating mathematics teachers' professional development through ranking and promotion practices in the Chinese mainland. In N. Bednarz, D. Fiorentini, & R. Huang (Eds.), *International approaches to professional development of mathematics teachers* (pp. 72–87). Ottawa: Ottawa University Press.

Li, Y., & Shimizu, Y. (2009). Exemplary mathematics instruction and its development in selected education systems in East Asia. *ZDM – The International Journal on Mathematics Education, 41*(3), 257–262.

Martin, T. S. (2007). *Mathematics teaching today: Improving practice, improving student learning* (2nd ed.). Reston: National Council of Teachers of Mathematics.

Ministry of Education, P. R. China. (2001). *Mathematics curriculum standard for compulsory education stage (experimental version).* Beijing: Beijing Normal University Press.

Ministry of Education, P. R. China. (2003). *Mathematics curriculum standard for high schools.* Beijing: People's Education Press.

Morris, A. K., & Hiebert, J. (2011). Creating shared instructional products: An alternative approach to improving teaching. *Educational Researcher, 40*(1), 5–14.

National Council of Teachers of Mathematics. (1991). *Professional standards for teaching mathematics.* Reston: Author.

National Council of Teachers of Mathematics. (2000). *Principles and standards for school mathematics.* Reston: Author.

Shao, G., Fan, Y., Huang, R., Li, Y., & Ding, E. (2012). Examining Chinese mathematics classroom instruction from a historical perspective. In Y. Li & R. Huang (Eds.), *How Chinese teach mathematics and improve teaching* (pp. 11–28). New York: Routledge.

Sherin, M. G., & Han, S. Y. (2004). Teacher learning in the context of a video club. *Teaching and Teacher Education, 20,* 163–183.

Sherin, M. G., & van Es, E. A. (2009). Effects of video club participation on teachers' professional vision. *Journal of Teacher Education, 60,* 20–37.

Silver, E. A., Mesa, V., Morris, K., Star, J., & Benken, B. (2009). Teaching for understanding: An analysis of mathematics lessons submitted by teachers seeking NBPTS certification. *American Educational Research Journal, 46,* 501–531.

Stein, M. K., & Lane, S. (1996). Instructional tasks and the development of student capacity to think and reason: An analysis of the relationship between teaching and learning in a reform mathematics project. *Educational Research and Evaluation, 2,* 50–80.

Stevenson, H. W., & Lee, S. (1995). The East Asian version of whole class teaching. *Educational Policy, 9,* 152–168.

Stewart, V. (2006). China's modernization plan: What can US learn from China? *Education Week, 25*(28), 48–49.

Stigler, J. W., & Hiebert, J. (1999). *The teaching gap: Best ideas from the world's teachers.* New York: Free Press.

Stigler, J. W., & Hiebert, J. (2004). Improving mathematics teaching. *Educational Leadership, 61,* 12–16.

Stigler, J. W., & Perry, M. (1988). Mathematics learning in Japanese, Chinese, and American classrooms. *New Directions for Child Development, 41,* 27–54.

Tang, H., Peng, A., Chen, B., Kung, K., & Song, N. (2012). Characteristics of "two basic" teaching in secondary mathematics classroom in China. In Y. Li & R. Huang (Eds.), *How Chinese teach mathematics and improve teaching* (pp. 28–43). New York: Routledge.

Weiss, I. R., & Pasley, J. P. (2004). What is high quality instruction? *Educational Leadership, 61,* 24–28.

Wong, J. L. N. (2010). What makes a professional learning community possible? A case study of a mathematics department in a junior secondary school of China. *Asia Pacific Education Review, 11,* 131–139.

Zhang, J., Huang, R., Li, Y., Qian, P., & Li, X. (2008, July 6–13). *Improving mathematics teaching and learning with a focus on core concepts in secondary school mathematics: Introducing a new nation-wide effort in Mainland China.* Paper presented at 11th international congress on Mathematical Education (ICME 11), Monterrey, Mexico.

Part III
Transforming Mathematics Instruction with Different Approaches in Teacher Education

Preface to Part III

Peter Sullivan

In his chapter in this part, Yang reports on Smith and Stein proposing that "if a teacher sets up a low level demands task … it has no possibility to be implemented as a … doing mathematics task". This raises an interesting and perhaps challenging perspective related to the overall focus and intent of the chapters in this part that are grouped under the heading "Transforming Mathematics Instruction with Different Approaches in Teacher Education".

One of the delightful aspects of the TIMSS and PISA studies is the development among mathematics educators of an orientation to learning about approaches to teaching mathematics through examining practices in other countries. The chapters in this part are drawn from projects and initiatives in the USA and in China, and it is interesting to identify some similarities and differences. There are two reports of teacher learning in China: one focusing on school-based and teacher-led Mathematics Teaching Research Groups (MTRGs); and the other reporting on teaching competitions. The four reports from US initiatives are all substantial and focused. One of the three reports from the USA describes the use of case methods, which are widely used in professional education in fields other than education, and one uses sample student responses to a task as a prompt to teacher learning, while the other two draw on data from large and presumably well-funded teaching development projects. The following six chapters in this part connect teacher learning with reflective consideration of classroom exemplars, they all use examples of practice to reinforce or articulate theoretical perspectives, all see teacher improvement as central to enhancing student opportunity to learn mathematics, and all

P. Sullivan (✉)
Faculty of Education, Monash University, Clayton 3800, Australia
e-mail: peter.sullivan@monash.edu

Y. Li et al. (eds.), *Transforming Mathematics Instruction: Multiple Approaches and Practices*, Advances in Mathematics Education, DOI 10.1007/978-3-319-04993-9_15,
© Springer International Publishing Switzerland 2014

identify the choice of tasks as a critical component of quality teaching. Indeed, it is worth reading all the chapters even if just for the task examples and the descriptions of ways the tasks can be used and interpreted.

There are, though, important differences between the approaches. The chapters from the USA rely on substantial input from researchers: for one, it was the creation of the cases; for another, it was the gathering and analysis of student work; and for the others, it was the development of the resources and teacher learning programmes. In contrast, the two examples from China both focus on the work of practitioners who are implementing their everyday approaches to teaching. Teacher-driven approaches are arguably more sustainable and more readily connected to everyday classroom practice.

It is interesting to consider underlying cultural factors that may have led to such differences. One of these may be the apparent willingness of Chinese teachers to allow others not only to observe their practice but also for the observers to "argue" with each other about those practices. Another possible cultural difference is that both the MTRGs and the teaching competitions illustrate an expectation that teaching approaches of individual teachers can be transformed through studying the practice of others. In one case, the teaching being observed is expert, with even the losing entries in the teaching competition being arguably expert. But in the MTRGs, the teachers are classroom practitioners, and there is presumably no expectation that the teaching being observed is expert. On the other hand, in the US examples, at least some of the cases are written to act as models for the prospective teachers, and the tasks and approaches in the two initiatives, the *Implementing the Problem-Solving Cycle* and the *Learning and Teaching Geometry* projects, have been developed by teams, trialled and presented to teachers with substantial background information. These differences in approaches also have implications for the sustainability of initiatives, their potential for transfer to other contexts and the generalisability of the approaches to teachers not in the projects.

An interesting aspect for me (being neither from the USA nor China) is the lack of consideration within the chapters of the differences in readiness of students. While the USA and China have quite different profiles, in both contexts, the differences in achievement of students of the same age are substantial. If students of the same age are grouped by their achievement, even noting that there is still a diversity of ability with those classes, this has implications for the teaching style adopted. On the other hand, if students are not grouped by achievement, the range of achievement levels within a class may well facilitate rather than inhibit drawing out the types of generalisations being sought in all five of the chapters. In other words, the nature of class composition has major implications for the approaches to teaching, and therefore teacher education, irrespective of how students are grouped. It would be helpful if what the approaches have to say about addressing the diversity of student readiness to learn is made more explicit.

To return to the proposition about the connection between the nature of the task and the quality of the teaching, it is arguable that this connection presents some sort of paradox. On the one hand, the tasks presented in the US chapters, specifically the *sticky gum* task, *looking for a square number*, the *wheelchair* task, the *apples* task and *Frank's fresh farm produce,* are all innovative, they connect important mathematical ideas, they allow students opportunities for decision making, and they create the potential for student problem-solving and reasoning. In contrast, the tasks presented in the Chinese chapters are everyday exercises by comparison, one dealing with well-established approaches to the theorem of Pythagoras and the other to index laws. The paradox being that the threat to the US tasks is actions teachers might take to minimise the challenge to the students, whereas the Chinese tasks create the potential for teachers to extend the tasks beyond the obvious. For example, it is arguable that index laws, as explained by Li and Li, offer the first real instances for students to generate mathematical results for themselves. Indeed, it seems to have been the main characteristic of the prize-winning teacher that he was able to interact with students in ways that motivated them to derive the laws from the examples that he presented and the patterns in the responses to exercises he set. This seems to be an example of how the procedurally focused exercises were turned by the teacher into "doing mathematics".

It is clear that we all still have much to learn from each other about approaches to transforming mathematics instruction. These chapters make an important contribution to that learning.

Facilitating Video-Based Professional Development: Planning and Orchestrating Productive Discussions

Hilda Borko, Jennifer Jacobs, Nanette Seago, and Charmaine Mangram

Abstract Video has become increasingly popular in professional development (PD) to help teachers both learn subject matter for teaching and systematically analyze instructional practice. Like other records of practice, video brings the central activities of teaching into the PD setting, providing an opportunity for teachers to collaboratively study their practice without being physically present in the classroom. In this chapter, we explore how video representations of teaching can be used to guide teachers' inquiries into teaching and learning in an intentional and focused way. We draw primarily from our experiences developing and field-testing two video-based mathematics PD programs, Learning and Teaching Geometry (LTG) and the Problem-Solving Cycle (PSC), and preparing PD facilitators using those programs to lead video-based discussions. On the basis of evidence from these projects, we argue that PD leaders can guide teachers to examine critical aspects of learning and instruction through the purposeful selection and use of video footage. Furthermore, we use data from the LTG and PSC projects to build a chain of evidence demonstrating that video-based PD can support improvements in teachers' mathematical knowledge for teaching, their instructional practices, and, ultimately, student learning.

H. Borko (✉) • C. Mangram
Graduate School of Education, Stanford University, 485 Lasuen Mall,
Stanford, CA 94305-3096, USA
e-mail: hildab@stanford.edu; cmangram@stanford.edu

J. Jacobs
Institute of Cognitive Science, University of Colorado Boulder,
1099 Fairway Ct., Boulder, CO 80303, USA
e-mail: jenniferj@davidslane.com

N. Seago
WestEd, 400 Seaport Court, Suite 222, Redwood City,
CA 94063-2767, USA
e-mail: nseago@wested.org

Y. Li et al. (eds.), *Transforming Mathematics Instruction: Multiple Approaches and Practices*, Advances in Mathematics Education, DOI 10.1007/978-3-319-04993-9_16, © Springer International Publishing Switzerland 2014

Keywords Mathematics professional development • Video-based professional development • Teacher learning • Teacher professional development • Mathematics education • Teacher knowledge • Teacher leader development • Teaching practice

Video has become increasingly popular in professional development (PD) to help teachers both learn subject matter for teaching and systematically analyze instructional practice. Video—like other records of practice, such as examples of student work and instructional materials—brings the central activities of teaching into the PD setting, providing an opportunity for teachers to collaboratively study their practice without being physically present in the classroom (Ball and Cohen 1999; Borko et al. 2010; Little et al. 2003; Putnam and Borko 2000). Video records capture the complexity of the classroom, including aspects of classroom life that a teacher might not notice in the midst of carrying out a lesson. By creating a shared experience, video can serve as a focal point for PD participants' collaborative exploration of classroom interactions. Clips from videotaped classroom episodes can be viewed repeatedly and from multiple perspectives, enabling teachers to closely examine one another's instructional strategies and students' reasoning, as well as the content addressed in the lessons, and to discuss ideas for improvement.

As Brophy (2004) cautioned, however, teachers "usually do not gain many new insights or ideas about improving their teaching from simply watching classroom videos. If they do not have a clear purpose and agenda for viewing the video, they are likely to watch it passively, much as they might watch a television program" (p. x). Without skillful guidance, what teachers attend to when they watch classroom video and how they interpret what they notice are likely to be guided by their existing conceptions of effective instruction. An important question, then, is: *How can PD programs capitalize on the power of video representations of teaching to guide teachers' inquiries into teaching and learning in an intentional and focused way, so that the video becomes an effective tool for their learning?*

Our chapter seeks to provide some initial responses to this question. We draw primarily from our experiences developing and field-testing two video-based mathematics PD programs, Learning and Teaching Geometry (LTG) and the Problem-Solving Cycle (PSC), and preparing PD facilitators using those programs to lead video-based discussions. On the basis of evidence from these projects, we argue that PD leaders can guide teachers to examine critical aspects of learning and instruction through the purposeful selection and use of video footage. Furthermore, we use data from the LTG and PSC projects to build a chain of evidence demonstrating that video-based PD can support improvements in teachers' mathematical knowledge for teaching (MKT; Ball et al. 2008), their instructional practices and, ultimately, student learning.

Planning and Orchestrating Productive Video-Based Discussions in Teacher Professional Development

Facilitation is a critical factor in the successful use of video in many PD models, including the LTG and PSC projects. There are numerous parallels between facilitating productive classroom discussions and facilitating productive discussions in PD workshops. The literature on facilitating classroom discussions is much more extensive than the comparable literature on PD discussions, and we find it to be a useful starting point in conceptualizing the work of PD leaders. Orchestrating classroom mathematics discussions that build on student thinking in an intentional manner is one of the more challenging pedagogical tasks for K-12 teachers. To successfully lead such discussions requires that teachers have deep knowledge of the relevant content, of student thinking about that content, and of instructional moves that are likely to guide the discussion in fruitful directions. They must be able to draw upon this knowledge in the moment, in response to specific student contributions. PD facilitators make similar moment-to-moment decisions as they seek to build on teachers' ideas and guide conversations, while ensuring that the environment is supportive and inclusive.

Skillful facilitation of classroom discussions has been characterized as disciplined improvisation, in which teachers must balance structure and flexibility in order to scaffold student learning (Sawyer 2011). This analogy to improvisation appears applicable to PD facilitation as well. Like improvisational actors, teachers and facilitators need to listen actively, acknowledge ideas that are shared and incorporate them into subsequent questions, be open to allowing responses to modify the direction of the discourse, and redirect the conversation when appropriate (Barker and Borko 2011). By using improvisational tenets such as "yes, and," teachers and facilitators can purposefully take up relevant contributions in order to simultaneously build on the contributor's thinking while guiding the class toward a deep understanding of important mathematical ideas. Masterful facilitation of discussions, like masterful improvisation, requires thoughtful planning. By anticipating the likely moves of others and considering possible responses to those moves teachers and facilitators, like improvisational actors, can be prepared to guide the conversation in directions that they desire.

Smith, Stein, and colleagues (Stein et al. 2008; Smith and Stein 2011) identified five pedagogical practices that can help mathematics teachers use students' responses during discussions to further their mathematical agenda for the lesson. These practices, designed for leading whole-class discussions that occur after students have worked on cognitively challenging mathematics tasks, are intended to help teachers manage both what content will be discussed and how it will be discussed. The practices are organized in the manner they are likely to occur in the classroom and labeled as follows: *anticipating* student responses, *monitoring* their thinking, *selecting* approaches for the class to explore, *sequencing* students' shared work, and *connecting* student responses to one another and to key mathematical ideas. All five practices can, to some extent, be planned for in advance. Thus, they provide teachers "with some control over what is likely to happen in the discussion as well as more time to make instructional decisions by shifting some of the decision making to the planning phase of the lesson" (Smith and Stein 2011, pp. 7–8).

Elliott et al. (2009) proposed that Stein et al.'s (2008) five practices, understood somewhat flexibly, also have important implications for the work of teacher educators and PD leaders. They argued that by applying these practices in their PD workshops, facilitators can be more intentional in leading conversations around rich mathematical tasks. In a similar vein, we suggest that there are specific practices facilitators can engage in to purposefully use classroom video during PD, especially as they strive to engage teachers in productive conversations around that video.

Inspired by the analogy to improvisation and the five practices for successfully managing classroom mathematics discussions, in this chapter we posit a framework for facilitating video-based discussions during PD workshops. Our framework includes three practices for planning discussions and three for orchestrating them. These practices are intended to promote high-quality conversations during which teachers deeply explore mathematical concepts, students' mathematical reasoning, and teachers' instructional behaviors.

The framework we propose is motivated by our experiences developing and studying the LTG and PSC mathematics PD programs. Two features of classroom video are central to our conceptualization of this framework—that the video clips are minimally edited segments of naturally occurring classroom lessons and that they are "examples," not "exemplars." That is, we are referring to video that is expected to serve as a springboard for analysis and discussion about mathematics teaching and learning, not as a model of "expert practice." The video may come from lessons taught by the participating teachers (as in the PSC program) or from lessons taught by other teachers (as in the LTG program). Further, although the framework may be relevant to other content areas, in this chapter we present it as specific to mathematics PD efforts, reflecting our experiences in that content area.

Planning Video-Based Discussions

Our framework includes three decision points that are central to planning a video-based discussion for a mathematics PD workshop: (1) determining the goals for the discussion and selecting video clips, (2) identifying features of the video clip that are important for meeting the goals, and (3) crafting questions to guide the discussion. These planning decisions are specific to the use of video and do not preclude many other planning decisions that apply to leading mathematics PD in general, such as the selection of the mathematics domain and tasks and the development and maintenance of a supportive community.

Identifying goals for the video-based discussion and selecting appropriate video clips are interrelated decisions, and either decision might precede the other in the planning process. That is, a decision about the mathematical and pedagogical goals for the discussion will naturally impact the choice of video clips.

Conversely, facilitators may select a goal for the discussion because they identify particularly interesting moments in a videotaped lesson that warrant careful unpacking and deep exploration. In either case, the facilitators' decisions about goals for a PD workshop depend on the intended audience and the overall goals of the PD program.

Video clips used in the LTG and PSC programs are intended to capture teachers' attention, focus them in particular directions, and be both challenging and accessible to the participating teachers. They show a period of time during the lesson from which the teachers can learn something about the mathematics content, students' thinking, or pedagogy that is valuable and related to the goals for the workshop (Borko et al. 2011). In the PSC program, we have found that using videos to highlight student thinking rather than teachers' practice helps decrease teachers' initial anxiety over being videotaped or having their videos watched and analyzed by their colleagues. Once a supportive community has been established and teachers have developed their analytic skills, facilitators typically choose clips that capture potentially problematic moments in a classroom or mathematically or pedagogically challenging content.

A critical component of planning for productive video-based discussions is identifying features of the video clip that are important for teachers to notice and discuss. By identifying in advance the features of the video clip that they would like the group to analyze and crafting questions to focus the teachers' attention on these features, PD leaders can increase the likelihood that they will engage in productive discussions about the detailed aspects of student thinking and the effects of teachers' actions on student learning.

Once the facilitator has identified these relevant features of the video, the next step is crafting questions that will guide the discussion. Coming to the workshop with questions to guide the viewing of the videos and launch the discussions is essential. Equally important and more likely to be neglected in the planning process are "back-pocket questions" that the leader can pull out to enliven the discussion or shift its direction. By engaging in a planning process that includes consideration of what teachers are likely to notice in the video, what they are likely to miss, and the range of comments they might offer, facilitators can more readily craft effective launching and back-pocket questions and ensure that the conversation goes down an intentional path and remains productive.

Orchestrating Video-Based Discussions

Our framework also includes three practices that are central to orchestrating productive video-based discussions: (1) eliciting teachers' thinking about the lesson segment, (2) probing for evidence of their claims, and (3) helping the group to connect their analyses to key mathematical and pedagogical ideas. Together, these practices encourage the teachers to focus on key features of the mathematics content, student thinking, and/or pedagogy portrayed in the video and to analyze these features with respect to the goals of the workshop. Carefully attending to the planning practices described above can support PD leaders to more readily engage in these three orchestrating practices. For example, by identifying important features of the video clip and crafting launching and back-pocket questions, the leader will be prepared to elicit teachers' responses to the clip and probe for evidence in the video to support their claims.

The initial elicitation of teachers' thinking about the video clip may produce a relatively straightforward description of the events or ideas it contains. However, by scaffolding teachers' responses and probing for evidence-based reasoning, facilitators can foster a more in-depth analysis of the mathematics content, student reasoning, or instructional practices that are the intended focus of the clip. This process of encouraging teachers to move from description to analysis matches the developmental trajectory of "learning to notice" that van Es (2011) identified. Thus, starting off by requesting a descriptive commentary may be a fruitful strategy for making the clip accessible, drawing teachers into the conversation, and guiding them to elaborate on their ideas and draw inferences from their observations. As teachers enter into a richer discussion about the clip, facilitators can gradually prompt them to make relevant connections to important mathematical and pedagogical topics.

The facilitator's prepared guiding questions can serve a variety of functions, including moving the teachers through a discussion of the clip in a purposeful manner and helping the teachers to understand the facilitator's goals in selecting the clip as a learning opportunity. Facilitators may find it useful to share their prepared questions with the group, either orally or in writing, prior to showing the video. This strategy makes it more likely that teachers will attend to elements that are relevant to the focus of the workshop. At the same time, understanding facilitation as skilled improvisation suggests that there must be some degree of flexibility, allowing room for the facilitator to listen carefully to teachers' ideas and adapt questions responsively, as well as creating space for teachers to take ownership of the conversation within selected boundaries.

Illustrating Approaches to Facilitating Video-Based Professional Development

The following sections of this chapter focus on the two mathematics PD projects in which the authors currently are engaged: Learning and Teaching Geometry and the Problem-Solving Cycle. The two projects have similar goals of increasing teachers' mathematical knowledge for teaching, improving their instructional practices, and promoting student achievement, and as we discuss in the chapter, the projects show initial evidence of meeting these goals. Additionally, classroom video plays a central role in the PD models used within both projects.

One reason we include a discussion of these two projects in the chapter is that they illustrate different approaches to the design and enactment of PD, both of which make use of the framework we propose. We have described these programs as being located at different places along a continuum of adaptability (Borko et al. 2011). At one end of the continuum are highly specified approaches to PD, in which the goals, resources, and facilitation materials are specified for a particular, predetermined set of PD experiences. At the other end are approaches that are highly adaptive; that is, they have goals and resources derived from the local context and facilitation based on general guidelines. LTG is an example of highly specified PD, whereas the PSC is an adaptive PD program.

In the following sections, we provide an overview of each PD program and data regarding its impact. For both programs, the evidence suggests that they have the potential to affect substantial changes in the participating teachers. We also present vignettes in our discussions of the two programs, as illustrations of the role that video-based conversations can play in fostering teacher learning. The vignettes and accompanying analyses highlight how the design of each program incorporated the proposed framework for preparing and leading video-based PD discussions.

Learning and Teaching Geometry

Overview of the LTG Project

The Learning and Teaching Geometry[1] (LTG) project is currently creating modular, sequenced PD materials for middle school mathematics teachers, with a focus on classroom geometry lessons. LTG will produce commercially available materials that outline in advance a particular set of goals and activities and will include video clips and questions to be used for facilitating those activities. The LTG materials are intended to initiate inquiry into key content and pedagogical issues with respect to teaching and learning the concept of mathematical similarity. A core component of the materials is a set of videocases highlighting teachers' and students' experiences working with similarity problems in their classrooms.

The LTG PD Materials

The LTG materials contain 54 h of PD that support the teaching and learning of mathematical similarity, in alignment with the Common Core State Standards for Mathematics (Seago et al. 2010, 2013). These materials include a Foundation Module and several Extension Modules. The Foundation Module guides teachers through a series of ten, 3-hour sessions (see Fig. 1). The sessions follow a learning trajectory that is designed to enrich teachers' knowledge as well as their ability to support students' understanding of similarity. The Extension Modules offer options

---

[1] The LTG project is funded by the National Science Foundation (Award number DRL 0732757).

Session 1	Session 2	Session 3	Session 4	Session 5	Session 6	Session 7	Session 8	Session 9	Session 10
A geometric, transformations-based view of congruence	A geometric, transformations-based view of similarity	Relationship between dilation and similarity	Properties of dilation	Preservation of angles & proportional lengths through dilation	Ratios within & between similar figures	Ratios within & between similar figures, part 2	Connections between similarity, slope & graphs of linear functions	Area of similar figures	Closure and re-capping of big ideas
Defining Congruence and Similarity			Relationships and Attributes of Similar Figures				Connections		Closure

Fig. 1 The foundation module: ten 3-hour sessions

for further exploration of related topics, such as justifying claims related to similarity, exploring definitions of similarity, using representations and tools in the study of similarity, and supporting English Language Learners to learn the language and concepts central to similarity.

The nature of each LTG session is largely predetermined and specified as part of the package of materials. These materials contain extensive resources for facilitators using the modules with teachers. For example, for each video clip, there is a time-coded transcript, a lesson graph, guiding questions to ask, and detailed notes related to the clip (e.g., optional "back-pocket" questions to pose, mathematical support, and cautionary notes). These materials support facilitators in maintaining the intended mathematical and pedagogical storyline, as they lead discussions about the video clips that highlight content issues, students' geometric thinking, and/or instructional moves.

The information contained within the session resources reflects the planning practices specified in our framework. A primary planning task for LTG facilitators, then, is to gain familiarity with the goals and resources for each session. Planning for a given session largely involves reviewing the materials and becoming knowledgeable about the content of the videocases, the guiding questions, the surrounding mathematical tasks, etc. As is illustrated in the vignette below, gaining familiarity with these resources is essential to orchestrating productive video-based discussions.

Impact of the LTG Materials

A field test of the LTG Foundation Module was conducted in eight sites throughout the USA in order to generate both formative and summative evaluation data. The field test took place over the 2010–2011 and 2011–2012 school years and involved 126 participants (87 treatment teachers and 39 comparison teachers),[2] including

---

[2] It is important to note that participants were not randomly assigned to condition. Comparison teachers were recruited with the intent of comparability to treatment teachers.

in-service and preservice teachers, teacher leaders, and mathematics coaches. Three pre/post instruments were used to examine the impact of the Foundation Module on teachers' mathematical knowledge for teaching related to geometric similarity: a content assessment and two sets of embedded assessments.

The content assessment is a multiple-choice test that includes 25 items related to similarity and geometric transformations. The items were compiled and modified from released items used by state, national, and international assessment sources. On this assessment, teachers in the treatment group demonstrated an average gain of 8.73 percentage points from the pretest (mean of 63.66) to posttest (mean of 72.39), which was significantly larger than the average gain of 1.68 percentage points made by comparison group, where the pretest mean was 65.79 and the posttest was 67.47 $(F = 9.65, p < .05)$.

The embedded assessments incorporate tasks and activities that exist within the Foundation Module as part of the PD; they include an open-ended mathematics task (three questions) and a video analysis task (three questions). Both tasks address content knowledge and pedagogical content knowledge related to teaching and learning similarity. The mathematics task asks teachers to examine a group of four rectangles and describe the ones that are mathematically similar (Question 1), generate a different method students might use to solve the problem correctly (Question 2), and generate an incorrect method (Question 3). The two administrations of the mathematics task were the same, except for the specific set of rectangles that was given. For the treatment group, on average, there was a significant improvement in the scores on Questions 1 and 2 from pre- to posttest (Wilcoxon Signed Ranks Tests; p values $<.05$). The comparison group, on average, did not demonstrate significant changes on any of the questions.

The video analysis task is based on a video clip of a seventh grade student who uses dilation to solve a similarity problem. After watching the clip, teachers are asked to describe the student's method (Question 1) and then explain how a student might apply that same approach to solve two associated problems (Questions 2 & 3). The treatment group, on average, showed significant improvement in their scores for all three questions (Wilcoxon Signed Ranks Tests; p values $<.05$). The comparison group, on average, did not demonstrate significant changes on any of the questions.

The student sample included 266 students (162 treatments and 104 controls) across 20 classrooms from two of the field test sites. Students completed a 20-item multiple-choice test that covered the same topics and was drawn from the same sources as the teacher content assessment. Students of teachers in the treatment group, on average, demonstrated greater improvement in the percent of items they solved correctly compared to students of teachers in the comparison group $(t = 2.31, p < .05)$.

Overall, the LTG PD materials were shown to significantly impact the treatment teachers' knowledge as well as their students' geometry knowledge. Thus the field test data offer evidence of the promise of LTG for achieving the intended learning outcomes.

Michael's Pilot of the LTG Materials

In this section, we focus on a field test of the Foundation Module facilitated by Michael, a codeveloper of the LTG PD materials. Michael worked with a group of nine teachers, most of whom were middle school mathematics teachers, during the 2011–2012 academic year. All of the sessions were attended by another member of the project team and videotaped.

In the vignette, we draw on a portion of Michael's facilitation of Session 2, in which the teachers are first introduced to a dynamic view of similarity. The goals of the session are (1) to explore and represent static and dynamic ways of thinking about similar figures and (2) to examine students' conceptions of similarity. In terms of planning, Michael relied on the resources in the LTG materials, including the videos and the accompanying session agenda. As a codeveloper of the materials, Michael was very familiar with these resources; however, he carefully reviewed each video and made notes to himself throughout the agenda prior to conducting the session. Michael specifically considered the session goals, what features of the video clips to highlight, the facilitation questions intended to guide the discussion, and likely teacher responses.

Vignette: Foundation Module Session 2

In Session 1, which was held about a month prior to Session 2, the teachers explored congruent figures and were introduced to the terminology "static" and "dynamic." A static view of similarity refers to a numeric focus on the relationships between corresponding parts of similar Figures. A dynamic view of similarity refers to a focus on geometric transformations and, in particular, on enlarging or reducing figures proportionally. In Session 2, the teachers examine students' conceptions of similarity, and they continue to investigate and differentiate static and dynamic views of similarity. To this end, Session 2 includes a video clip in which a class of 6th grade students discusses their ideas and questions about what makes figures similar.

In the beginning of the clip, a student, Jenny, tries to clarify a question that her classmate, Ryan, just asked. Jenny says, "I think what Ryan was trying to say is that if you had two triangles—and one of them was really fat and one of them was skinny but really tall—would they both be similar." The LTG materials encourage facilitators to ask a series of questions that unpack Jenny's statement, along with a variety of statements made by other students in the class. The session agenda suggests that facilitators ask teachers (1) about the ideas or questions each student raises, (2) to create a visual representation of the student's thinking, and (3) to consider whether the students were thinking about similarity from a static or dynamic perspective.

Armed with an engaging video clip, guiding questions on the session agenda, and a deep understanding of both the mathematical content and the central aims of the LTG materials, Michael was able to foster a conversation in which the teachers discussed all of the suggested topic areas. In the vignette that follows, we highlight portions of this conversation and identify moments where Michael listened attentively, elicited and built on teachers' ideas, encouraged teachers to provide evidence for the claims they wanted to make, and helped the teachers connect their analyses of the video clip to key mathematical topics:

After showing the clip, Michael has the group focus on Jenny's idea. The teachers are still relatively new to the convention of watching and discussing video clips in a professional learning environment, and Michael is intentionally casual in his demeanor. He starts by asking the teachers what they heard Jenny say. This question seems simple enough, and a few teachers provide short answers.

One teacher offers that she heard Jenny say they had to be the same shape. Michael reiterates, "Okay, so this idea that they're the same shape." Another teacher claims that Jenny said "same polygon." Although Jenny was actually talking about triangles, Michael reacts in a nonjudgmental but deliberate manner. He repeats, "Same polygon. She used the words 'same polygon'?" At this point, a third teacher responds, "No, I heard same triangle." The teachers all have a printed transcript of the video clip in front of them, and they appear to be scanning over it, looking back at what Jenny actually said.

Launching the discussion of a video clip by asking a non-evaluative, straightforward question provides time for teachers to process what happened in the clip and read over the transcript. It also helps to establish a safe, trusting community by establishing that wrong answers are acceptable. Depending on the nature of the clip, facilitators may find it helpful to ask questions about what someone in the video said (as Michael did in this case) or to restate the idea verbalized (or shown) in the video. In some clips, when the students are solving a problem in a unique way, facilitators might request that the teachers attempt the problem in the same way as the students. While such activities may initially seem simple, they ensure that viewers understand precisely what took place in the video, highlight nuances that might initially be missed, and promote a more objective and accurate interpretation of the ideas and events observed in the video:

Next Michael moves to a more challenging question, asking, "So is that a static or dynamic way of thinking?" Several teachers quickly answer, "static." Michael presses the group to say more about this response, probing for evidence and encouraging the teachers to think deeply about some of the key mathematical terminology intended to be highlighted in the session.

Michael asks, "Why static?" and Teacher 1 responds, "Because she was just comparing two static figures." Unsatisfied with this answer, Michael continues to probe, "What do you mean?" Teacher 1 considers and says somewhat hesitantly, "Well, she wasn't stretching one of them." Another teacher agrees, noting "that's true." Here, Michael employs the strategy of repeating the teacher's answer back to the group and he comments, "Ok, so it's static if there's no stretching." Upon hearing her argument phrased this way, Teacher 1 laughs and appears uncertain about how to respond.

Teacher 2 steps in to make the counter argument that Jenny was, in fact, talking about stretching the triangle. This teacher argues, "One [triangle] was really fat and one was really skinny. So she must have stretched the skinny one out to make it fatter.... There must be some stretching and shrinking going on somewhere." Teacher 3 disagrees, "I thought she was thinking about two distinct figures that didn't have anything to do with each other." Not willing to concede, Teacher 2 continues to argue that Jenny must have been thinking about stretching and repeats, "But one was really fat and one was really skinny."

As they strive to determine whether Jenny's idea should be classified as a static way of thinking, the three teachers are attempting to make sense of both what Jenny was saying as well as the mathematical definitions of the terms static and dynamic. By trying to determine whether Jenny was talking about the corresponding features of two distinct triangles, or some sort of geometric transformation taking place around one of the triangles, they are hitting on exactly the key distinctions between these perspectives. Michael's rephrasing of Teacher 1's comment that "It's static if there's no stretching" was a cause for laughter but, in fact, highlighted the notion that "static" implies there is no motion. His rephrasing led Teacher 2 to argue that there was indeed motion in Jenny's idea. Regardless of which teacher was correct, this connection of the terms to whether or not there is movement is a critical one mathematically and links explicitly to the learning goals of the session:

Michael uses this disagreement as an opportunity to encourage the teachers to visually represent Jenny's idea, a facilitation move suggested in the session agenda. He walks over to an easel prepared with large chart paper and asks the group, "What might the picture look like, of what Jenny is referring to?"
A teacher responds, "Like an equilateral triangle and a tall isosceles triangle that's not equilateral," and Michael begins drawing the triangles shown below.

Several teachers tell him to make sure the base of one triangle is "skinnier" than the other. As they sit looking at these two triangles, the teachers begin to clarify what they think the terms "static" and "dynamic" mean in this context.
The conversation begins when one teacher poses the question, "If static usually compares sides, she wasn't comparing sides. So would that be static?" Michael remains silent and several other teachers attempt to answer. One teacher suggests that a static view has to involve numbers, whereas a dynamic view involves pictures and stretching.
Michael listens attentively while the teachers talk, occasionally rephrasing what they are saying or adding small pieces of relevant information. When the conversation winds down, he steps in to summarize the group's understanding of the terms static and dynamic, and in doing so, moves them toward a central mathematical

concept within the professional development: dilation. Michael's summary does more than revoice what the teachers have already said; he explicitly connects Jenny's idea to relevant terminology, definitions, and visual representations. At the same time, during his summary, Michael assumes a non-definitive manner, as if to be sure the teachers understand that the topic is not yet closed.

Pointing to the triangles he has drawn Michael remarks, "So this might be static. Like [Jenny is] imagining those two triangles sitting there. And maybe they are doing something visual, like looking at bases compared to sides. Versus a dynamic [approach]… This is starting to get into dilation. [Michael draws a picture like the one below of a triangle being dilated or scaled to create a larger triangle.]. It's transforming into the other shape, dynamically. What do we think about that?"

The session continues with the teachers exploring this idea of shapes transforming and constituting a continuous family. As they move into a discussion of what other students in the video clip had to say about similar triangles, the teachers have more opportunities to revisit and refine their ideas about static and dynamic ways of thinking.

As previously noted, LTG facilitators work within a highly specified PD model. They are given all of the materials they will need for each PD session in advance and are expected to follow a relatively scripted path. That is, the materials have a defined mathematical trajectory; there are specific goals, video clips, and guiding questions within each session. These detailed facilitation resources support the facilitator to implement our recommended planning and orchestrating practices. At the same time, the analogy of facilitation as improvisation implies there are important "in the moment" decisions that PD leaders must make throughout each session. Being mindful of the practices we outlined earlier in the chapter and remaining intentional about each facilitation move are essential tools for orchestrating productive discussions around video.

The Problem-Solving Cycle

Overview of the Problem-Solving Cycle and Teacher Leadership Preparation

The Problem-Solving Cycle (PSC) is an iterative, long-term approach to mathematics professional development that entails multiple cycles of three interconnected PD workshops, all organized around a rich mathematics task (Jacobs et al. 2007;

Koellner et al. 2007). Each cycle involves a different mathematics task and highlights specific topics related to student learning and instructional practice. Which tasks to use and which topics to address are determined by the facilitator, in an effort to best meet the needs and interests of the participating teachers.

During Workshop 1 of a given cycle, teachers collaboratively solve the selected mathematics task and develop plans for teaching it, taking into consideration the needs and mathematical abilities of their students. The goals of this workshop are to help teachers develop a deeper knowledge of the subject matter and strong planning skills. After the first workshop, each teacher implements the task with his or her own students and the lessons are videotaped. The facilitators then carefully choose video clips that highlight key moments in the instruction and in students' thinking about the task. Workshops 2 and 3 of the cycle focus on the teachers' classroom experiences and rely heavily on the clips selected from their videotaped lessons. The goals of these two workshops are to help teachers learn how to elicit and build on student thinking and to explore a variety of pedagogical strategies for teaching with rich problems based on targeted learning goals.

The Teacher Leader Preparation approach to preparing PSC facilitators was developed in our current project, *Toward a Scalable Model of Mathematics Professional Development: A Field Study of Preparing Facilitators to Implement the Problem-Solving Cycle* (iPSC).[3] The approach is designed to provide ongoing, yet gradually decreasing, support to full-time mathematics teachers, to prepare them to lead PSC workshops in their schools. The goal of the Teacher Leader Preparation is for the teacher leaders to gain the understanding and skills needed to effectively plan and lead PSC workshops. That is, by a designated point in time, they should be able to engage in the practices for planning and orchestrating PSC workshops without external support from the PSC research/development team.

As enacted in the iPSC project, the Teacher Leader Preparation involved two major components: a summer leadership academy and at least two cycles of structured guidance for facilitating the PSC. All of the teacher leaders participating in the iPSC project attended a summer leadership academy focused on explicating the core principles and practices for the facilitation of PSC workshops. During the academy, they participated in PSC simulations (mini-cycles) using the mathematics tasks selected for the upcoming academic year PSC cycles. In addition, members of the project team provided ongoing structured guidance as the teacher leaders began facilitating the PSC workshops in their schools. As an initial activity in each PSC cycle, the teacher leaders taught the selected task in one of their classes and videotaped their lessons. Then, prior to conducting each PSC workshop, teacher leaders attended a full-day Mathematics Leader Preparation meeting (MLP) led by the project team. These meetings were designed to assist the teacher leaders in planning and conducting all aspects of their upcoming PSC workshops.

The second and third MLP meetings focused specifically on helping the teacher leaders prepare to lead video-based discussions during Workshops 2 and 3. With the

---

[3] The iPSC project is funded by the National Science Foundation (Award number DRL 0732212).

support of the MLP leaders (i.e., the PSC research/development team), teacher leaders engaged in the practices for planning video-based PD discussions recommended in this chapter. MLP leaders worked with the teacher leaders to decide on goals for their workshops, select video clips from the available recorded PSC lessons, identify examples of instructional moves and students' mathematical reasoning in the video clips, develop launching and back-pocket questions aligned with the video clips, and anticipate possible teacher responses to the video and guiding questions. Through role-playing, the teacher leaders then practiced the facilitation of these discussions and received feedback from their peers and ISM leaders. The role-playing simulations enabled them to fine-tune their questions and gain additional insights into likely teacher responses.

Impact of the PSC and Teacher Leadership Preparation

In the iPSC project, we collected extensive qualitative and quantitative data on the nature of the support provided to the teacher leaders, the quality of their PSC workshops, and the impact of the program on the teacher leaders and teachers with whom they worked. These data include video records of all MLP meetings and PSC workshops, interviews with the teacher leaders conducted at the conclusion of each PSC iteration, and a pre/post mathematical knowledge assessment given to the teacher leaders and teachers with whom they worked. We used parallel forms of the *Mathematical Knowledge for Teaching* (MKT-MS) assessment for middle school teachers, developed by the Learning Mathematics for Teaching (LMT) Project (Hill et al. 2004) in order to document changes in teachers' mathematical knowledge for teaching over the course of their participation in the iPSC study. Additionally, we used an observation protocol created by the LMT researchers, the *Mathematical Quality of Instruction* (MQI) instrument (Hill et al. 2008), to analyze the teachers' classroom instruction over a 1½-year period. Here, we briefly summarize our analyses of changes in teacher leaders' and teachers' knowledge and instructional practices.

We analyzed pre-post differences in the MKT-MS scores to measure the impact of the iPSC on teacher leaders' and teachers' knowledge of mathematics for teaching (Borko 2012; Koellner et al. 2011). Sixty-two participants (10 teacher leaders and 52 teachers) completed both the pre- and post-administration of the MKT-MS. The participants overall showed significant knowledge gains, as measured by the change in their MKT-MS scores. The teacher leaders had an average pretest score of 72.4 % correct and an average posttest score of 78.1 %, whereas the teachers had an average pretest score of 65.4 % correct and an average posttest score of 70.7 %. Paired *t*-tests indicate significant gains for the participants as a whole and for the teachers as a subgroup. It is important to note that there was no comparison sample of teachers in the iPSC project, so these findings should be interpreted with caution.

We applied the MQI to 51 videotaped lessons from 13 participants and analyzed the changes in their PSC and typical lessons over a 1½-year period (Jacobs et al. 2014). The MQI captures four dimensions related to the mathematical quality of instruction of a given lesson: (1) richness of the mathematics, (2) working with students and mathematics, (3) errors and imprecision, and (4) student participation in meaning-making and reasoning. The instrument also includes two overall lesson ratings, for "whole-lesson mathematical quality of instruction (overall MQI)" and "lesson-based guess at mathematical knowledge for teaching (overall MKT)." Teachers who participated in the iPSC study—including both teacher leaders and the teachers with whom they worked—experienced increases in instructional quality on both their PSC and typical lessons on some of the dimensions included in the MQI instrument. Furthermore, their overall MQI and MKT ratings generally increased over time. Especially notable were the consistent increases within the dimension of "working with students," suggesting that teachers are more attentive to their students' thinking after participating in PSC workshops. Instructional improvements were more often evident in teachers' PSC lessons as compared to their typical lessons. This finding suggests that the participants were capable of providing increasingly high-quality instruction even if they did not do so on an everyday basis (For a more in-depth discussion of the project's impact on teachers and teacher leaders, please see Jacobs et al. 2014).

Vignette from Mandy's Fuel Gauge Workshop 3

The vignette below is drawn from a video-based discussion that Mandy, one of the teacher leaders, facilitated during Workshop 3 of a PSC cycle that used the Fuel Gauge task. The Fuel Gauge task is a rate and ratio task, adapted from Jacob and Fosnot (2008) (see Fig. 2). A significant feature of this task is that it can be solved in multiple ways.

During Workshop 1 of this PSC cycle, the teachers in Mandy's group solved the Fuel Gauge task using a variety of solution strategies (some working primarily with miles and some primarily with fractions of the tank of gas) and shared their strategies with the group. Mandy facilitated a discussion in which the teachers explored the mathematical connections between the different solution strategies, anticipated solution strategies their students were likely to use and errors they might make, and identified possible adaptations to the task and questions to scaffold students' learning. Workshop 2 began with the teachers sharing reflections on their teaching of the Fuel Gauge task. They then watched and discussed a video clip of a small group of students from Mandy's class working together on the problem.

During the MLP meeting that preceded her Workshop 3, Mandy identified two video clips and two goals that she had for the workshop, and she developed several guiding questions to help frame and carry out the discussion about the clips.

Frank runs a business called Frank's Fresh Farm Produce. Once a week he drives north of the city to farms where he buys the best possible fresh produce for his customers. Frank can travel 600 miles (965.6 km) on a full tank of gas. His truck has a fancy, accurate fuel gauge.

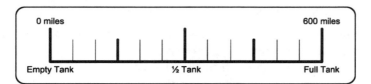

Usually Frank has time to visit only one farm on each trip, but one week he decides to visit both Stan's and Louisa's farms. When Frank drives from his store to Stan's farm and back, he knows he uses 5/12 of a tank of gas. When he drives to Louisa's farm and back, he uses 1/3 of a tank. From a map of the area, he learns that there is a road from Stan's farm to Louisa's farm that is 120 miles. (193.1 km) long. He realizes that he can drive from his store to Stan's farm, then to Louisa's farm, and then back to his store in one loop.

Frank can tell by looking at the fuel gauge that he has 5/8 of a tank of gas. Can he drive this loop without having to stop for fuel? Or should he buy gas before he starts his trip?

Fig. 2 The fuel gauge task

Mandy's two distinct but related goals were (1) to help the teachers identify and understand the mathematical misconceptions behind a student error and (2) to help the teachers identify pedagogical strategies that might enable the videotaped students to move to a deeper level of mathematical understanding.

The video clips Mandy selected both show a small group of students working together to solve the Fuel Gauge task. In the second clip, a student explains how she determined the portion of the fuel tank Frank used to travel from Stan's farm to Louisa's farm. There are two mathematical errors in her explanation. The first error is that she incorrectly divided 600 by 120 rather than dividing 120 by 600. The second is that she "dropped" the zeros from both numbers yielding 60 divided by 12, but then she added one zero back to the quotient to get 50 miles:

Mandy begins the video watching activity by providing some context for the teachers in her workshop. She tells them that the videotaped class is 7th grade advanced Algebra. According to Mandy, "One student is going to have a pretty extreme mathematical error." At this time, Mandy points to the student on the screen to whom the group of teachers should pay close attention. Then, she provides a set of questions to guide the video watching: "What are the students' mathematical misconceptions? What are their understandings? What are the teacher's instructional moves? Where do we go from here?"

In preparing the teachers for watching video, Mandy enacted two especially notable facilitation moves. First, she set the goals for the day—as a way of anchoring the various activities. Second, by providing guiding questions and asking teachers to focus on a particular student, she provided a structure to the video watching. Mandy's guiding questions established a purpose for the activity by specifying a mathematical and pedagogical lens through which teachers should view the clips:

The group watches the first video clip and engages in a brief discussion about the students' mathematical understandings. The teachers agree that the students seem to have a good understanding of equivalent fractions. Before they watch the second video clip, Mandy provides further context by stating, "The teacher leaves the group, the students work alone for about 10 minutes, and they decide that they are stuck."

Mandy then shows the second clip, in which a student indicates that she is solving for the fraction of the fuel tank required to travel between Stan's and Louisa's farms. She sets up the problem as 600 divided by 120. She then converts the problem to 60 divided by 12 and correctly performs the division. However, she adds a zero to the quotient and comes up with the answer 50. Following the video clip, Mandy opens the discussion, "We need to figure out what she is doing." One teacher says: "She wants to compute 120 divided by 600 but she's doing 600 divided by 120." Another teacher focuses on a second error: "She's doing 600 divided by 120 and converting it to 60 divided by 12. But you don't just magically take away the zeros. You divide them out and they don't come back." Focusing again on the first error, a third teacher explains: "She's looking for a fraction of a gas tank, but she's coming up with the opposite of that because she's using the numbers in the wrong order, the reciprocal."

At this point in their discussion of the video clip, the teachers have identified the two errors. To guide them to focus on one error at a time and to unpack the student's thinking, Mandy places a large sheet of paper in the center of the table and suggests that the teachers begin to collaboratively recreate the students' strategy. As they are working, the teachers discuss how the student has set up the ratio in the problem and what the numbers in the ratio represent.

Mandy asks, "We know the 120 is the miles, so what's the 600?" Several of the teachers respond in unison, "Total miles." Teacher 1 quickly clarifies, "Total miles in a tank." Mandy continues, "What's the 5?" Teacher 1 suggests that the student was trying to find 1/5 of a tank of gas. Teacher 2 provides a different way of interpreting the 5. She suggests that the student may have been trying to determine the number of trips between Stan's and Louisa's farms that Frank can take on a full tank of gas. Not sure that she understands Teacher 2's interpretation, Mandy asks, "Can you explain that one more time?" Teacher 2 elaborates, "Frank can make 5 one way trips—2 and a half round trips—if he has a full tank of gas."

By asking Teacher 2 to repeat her interpretation of the 5, Mandy is encouraging the teachers to carefully unpack and understand the student's strategy, instead of staying focused on the "right way" to solve the problem. This facilitation move places the emphasis on analyzing student thinking rather than critiquing the correctness of a given answer:

The teachers shift their attention to the second error. One teacher speculates that the student "took the zeros away to make the division easier.... thinking 'I know I took the zeros away so I need to put them back on.'" Another teacher reflects, "I think that's one thing that confuses kids is when you start saying add zeros or take off zeros, rather than saying you are dividing both numbers by 10. The students don't really know when to do what." Teacher 2 adds, "I agree. Instead of saying 'drop the zeros', you have to say 'divide them both by 10.'"

When Mandy is confident that each of the teachers understands the mathematical strategies the student is using and the misconceptions underlying her errors, she pushes the group to think about the pedagogical implications. Mandy's focus on both understanding students' thinking and considering possible pedagogical moves to make in response to students' misconceptions is typical of her facilitation of video-based discussions:

Mandy questions the group, "What is our concern with them just dropping the zeros? How are we going to address that?" Teacher 2 offers, "I would ask, 'What is 50 divided by 10? How many 10s are there in 50? And what is 500 divided by 100?' to show that you get the same answer. Then I would ask, 'So, what happens to the zero?'" Teacher 4 proposes another line of questioning related to the reasonableness of the student obtaining 50 and 120 as factors of 600. She poses the question, "Does it make sense that 120 goes into 600 fifty times?" Teacher 1 suggests, "Count by 50s and see how long it takes to get to 600. It is not going to be 120 times. "Following up on both comments, Mandy points to the group math paper and suggests, "Or just count by 120. That might be faster."

Mandy's posing of the two related questions, "What is our concern with them just dropping the zeros?" and "How are we going to address that?" serves to frame the students' misconception as a teachable moment. Not only is it important for teachers to be able to identify what students do and do not understand, it is also important that they gain facility in determining appropriate next steps. Lastly, Mandy connects the teachers' discussion to larger pedagogical issues, namely, that there may be students in the classroom who have not mastered mathematical concepts that are foundational to the lesson:

Mandy inquires, "How do we use this information from our kids—the kids we have in our classrooms? What do we do as teachers to continue to make sure that this student is understanding?" Teacher 3 responds, "I think one thing you have to understand is whether the student's error is a simple mistake or a complete misconception. If they write it out and realize 'Oh, it's not 50. It's 5.' I think that's one place you have to ask yourself, 'Is this something that they really don't understand?'" Looking back at the student's paper, Teacher 3 continues, "I don't understand what she did there so I would talk her through that. I would try to figure that out. Was it that she did this mental math and made the mistake?" Another teacher agrees and suggests additional questions that might help to understand the student's strategy. He says, "I don't think we've listened to her enough. I don't think we know enough about what she was thinking. I mean, we know what she [the student] said, but she [the teacher] did not ask, 'What is the 600?' And 'What is the 120?' And 'Why are you dividing it?' So, I really don't think we know enough to know how far off she is."

Although Mandy provides some opportunity for teachers to speculate about what the teacher in the video might have done subsequent to the portion of the lesson shown on the video clip, she quickly moves the conversation back to identifying pedagogical moves that could be made in response to the student misconception by redirecting with questions and statements:

Mandy agrees, "Yes, and some of that is what we are talking about here. What are our instructional moves? What would we do as the teacher? Our goal is to understand where the student is in these types of situations. When you are in the classroom listening to students, you get those red flags. You say to yourself, 'I really need to make sure I go back to this student next class or next time or put something like this on the test to double-check and see.'"

Mandy then summarizes the central themes that her group addressed throughout this iteration of the PSC—including instructional moves to encourage students to collaborate and explain their mathematical thinking, as well as ways of listening to students to assess their mathematical reasoning. Mandy concludes the workshop by asking the group to reflect on how they have been impacted by their participation in the PSC throughout the year.

This vignette and analysis of a portion of a video-based discussion are intended to portray the skillful use of video in a PSC workshop. As we have seen, Mandy posed two questions to frame teachers' viewing of the video clips and then used a series of probing questions and comments to guide their analysis of the student errors, the misconceptions underlying them, and instructional practices that could be used to address these errors. Her planning for this discussion during the preceding MLP meeting included determining the workshop goals, selecting the video clips, and developing launching and probing questions. In addition to using these planned questions, Mandy listened carefully to the teachers and, at several points during the conversation, asked questions to clarify or extend their ideas. We do not know whether Mandy attempted to anticipate teachers' likely responses when planning the workshop, although her skillful use of planned and improvised questions and comments suggests that she was very familiar with both the videotaped lesson and what the teachers in her group were likely to notice and comment on.

Conclusion and Future Directions

Ensuring the productivity of video-based conversations in mathematics professional development workshops is a tremendously challenging endeavor (e.g., Givvin and Santagata 2010; Santagata 2009). To help manage the complexity of this task, in this chapter we have suggested specific practices that are likely to be useful for facilitators as they engage in both planning and orchestrating such conversations. We provided examples from our experiences developing and field-testing the LTG and PSC PD programs to illustrate how these practices look in two different contexts. The LTG and PSC projects represent different models of video-based mathematics PD, in which the goals and processes range from highly specified (LTG) to much more adaptable (PSC). That is, LTG facilitators follow a more scripted approach to PD; they are given the video clips to show, along with detailed session agendas containing guiding questions and mathematical support. By contrast, PSC facilitators follow a more organic path in which they designate their own workshop goals and select video clips from their participants' lessons. In considering facilitation practices to highlight in this chapter, our aim was to be broad enough to pertain to a wide range of PD models, yet detailed enough to be meaningful, particularly for novice PD facilitators.

By presenting some of the data on the positive impact of both the LTG and PSC projects, our goal was to demonstrate that video-based mathematics PD efforts can be effective, particularly when led by a knowledgeable and well-prepared facilitator who engages in the planning and orchestrating practices we have suggested. The results from these two projects would, quite likely, have looked very different if the facilitation had been less skillful.

In the field of mathematics, most PD facilitators are in the beginning stages of honing their leadership skills (Zaslavsky and Leikin 2004). In order to provide high-quality learning opportunities for teachers, there is an urgent need to prepare facilitators to successfully carry out PD. The suggestions and illustrations offered in this chapter may also be useful for facilitator educators in this relatively new line of work.

Additional research that includes a close inspection of effective facilitation practices would be helpful to either refine or add to the framework we put forth in this chapter. It would also be beneficial to learn from researchers working outside of mathematics about which practices, if any, are applicable to PD facilitation in other content areas. More broadly, we encourage researchers to attend to the education of PD facilitators, in particular by documenting the knowledge base they draw on, best practices for leading effective PD workshops, and the supports they require to become increasingly skillful.

References

Ball, D. L., & Cohen, D. K. (1999). Developing practice, developing practitioners: Toward a practice-based theory of professional education. In L. Darling-Hammond & G. Sykes (Eds.), *Teaching as the learning profession: Handbook of policy and practice* (pp. 3–32). San Francisco: Jossey-Bass.

Ball, D. L., Thames, M. H., & Phelps, G. (2008). Content knowledge for teaching: What makes it special? *Journal of Teacher Education, 59*, 389–407.

Barker, L., & Borko, H. (2011). Presence and the art of improvisational teaching. In K. Sawyer (Ed.), *Structure and improvisation in creative teaching* (pp. 279–298). New York: Cambridge University Press.

Borko, H. (2012). Designing scalable and sustainable professional development: The Problem-Solving Cycle and teacher leader preparation. In M. Glaser-Zikuda, T. Seidel, C. Rohlfs, A. Groschner, & S. Ziegelbauer (Eds.), *Mixed methods in empirical educational research* (pp. 259–271). Munster: Waxmann.

Borko, H., Jacobs, J., & Koellner, K. (2010). Contemporary approaches to teacher professional development. In P. Peterson, E. Baker, & B. McGaw (Eds.), *International encyclopedia of education* (Vol. 7, pp. 548–556). Oxford: Elsevier.

Borko, H., Koellner, K., Jacobs, J., & Seago, N. (2011). Using video representations of teaching in practice-based professional development programs. *Zentralblatt für Didaktik der Mathematik: International Reviews on Mathematical Education, 43*(1), 175–187. doi:10.1007/s11858-010-0302-5.

Brophy, J. (Ed.). (2004). Advances in research on teaching. In *Using video in teacher education* (Vol. 10). Oxford: Elsevier.

Elliott, R., Kazemi, E., Lesseig, K., Mumme, J., Carroll, C., & Kelley-Petersen, M. (2009). Conceptualizing the work of leading mathematical tasks in professional development. *Journal of Teacher Education, 60*, 364–379. doi:10.1177/0022487109341150.

Givvin, K. B., & Santagata, R. (2010). Toward a common language for discussing the features of effective professional development: The case of a US mathematics program. *Professional Development in Education, 37*(3), 439–451.

Hill, H. C., Schilling, S. G., & Ball, D. L. (2004). Developing measures of teachers' mathematics knowledge for teaching. *Elementary School Journal, 105*, 11–30. doi:10.1086/428763.

Hill, H. C., Blunk, M., Charalambous, C., Lewis, J., Phelps, G. C., Sleep, L., & Ball, D. L. (2008). Mathematical knowledge for teaching and the mathematical quality of instruction: An exploratory study. *Cognition and Instruction, 26*, 430–511.

Jacob, B., & Fosnot, C. T. (2008). *Best buys, ratios, and rates: Addition and subtraction of fractions*. Portsmouth: Heinemann.

Jacobs, J., Borko, H., Koellner, K., Schneider, C., Eiteljorg, E., & Roberts, S. A. (2007). The problem-solving cycle: A model of mathematics professional development. *Journal of Mathematics Education Leadership, 10*(1), 42–57.

Jacobs, J., Koellner, K., John, T., & King, C. (2014). The impact of the Problem-Solving Cycle professional development on mathematics knowledge and instruction. In Y. Li, E. A. Silver, & S. Li (Eds.), *Transforming mathematics instruction: Multiple approaches and practices*. Berlin/Heidelberg: Springer.

Koellner, K., Jacobs, J., Borko, H., Schneider, C., Pittman, M., Eiteljorg, E., Bunning, K., & Frykholm, J. (2007). The problem-solving cycle: A model to support the development of teachers' professional knowledge. *Mathematical Thinking and Learning, 9*(3), 271–303.

Koellner, K., Jacobs, J., & Borko, H. (2011). Mathematics professional development: Critical features for developing leadership skills and building teachers' capacity. *Mathematics Teacher Education and Development, 13*(1), 115–136.

Little, J. W., Gearhart, M., Curry, M., & Kafka, J. (2003). Looking at student work for teacher learning, teacher community, and school reform. *Phi Delta Kappan, 85*, 185–192.

Putnam, R. T., & Borko, H. (2000). What do new views of knowledge and thinking have to say about research on teacher learning. *Educational Researcher, 29*(1), 4–15.

Santagata, R. (2009). Designing video-based professional development for mathematics teachers in low-performing schools. *Journal of Teacher Education, 60*(1), 38–51. doi:10.1177/0022487108328485.

Sawyer, K. (2011). What makes good teachers great? The artful balance of structure and improvisation. In K. Sawyer (Ed.), *Structure and improvisation in creative teaching* (pp. 1–24). New York: Cambridge University Press.

Seago, N., Driscoll, M., & Jacobs, J. (2010). Transforming middle school geometry: Professional development materials that support the teaching and learning of similarity. *Middle Grades Research Journal, 5*(4), 199–211.

Seago, N., Jacobs, J., Driscoll, M., Nikula, J., Matassa, M., & Callahan, P. (2013). Developing teachers' knowledge of a transformations-based approach to geometric similarity. *Mathematics Teacher Educator, 2*(1), 74–85.

Smith, M. S., & Stein, M. K. (2011). *Five practices for orchestrating productive mathematics discussions*. Reston: National Council of Teachers of Mathematics.

Stein, M. K., Engle, R. A., Smith, M. S., & Hughes, E. K. (2008). Orchestrating productive mathematical discussions: Five practices for helping teachers move beyond show and tell. *Mathematical Thinking and Learning, 10*(4), 313–340. doi:10.1080/10986060802229675.

van Es, E. A. (2011). A framework for learning to notice student thinking. In M. G. Sherin, V. Jacobs, & R. Philipp (Eds.), *Mathematics teacher noticing: Seeing through teachers' eyes* (pp. 134–151). New York: Routledge.

Zaslavsky, O., & Leikin, R. (2004). Professional development of mathematics teacher educators: Growth through practice. *Journal of Mathematics Teacher Education, 7*, 5–32.

Professional Development for Secondary School Mathematics Teachers Using Student Work: Some Challenges and Promising Possibilities

Edward A. Silver and Heejoo Suh

Abstract Organizing teacher learning around the study of mathematical tasks and associated student work is a version of practice-based professional development that has been used effectively with preservice teachers and inservice elementary school teachers of mathematics. In this chapter, we examine the research evidence regarding the use of student work in teacher education and professional development, and we consider the potential impediments to using such an approach with inservice secondary school teachers, given many facets of their work and their preparation that appear to mitigate against the effectiveness of such an approach. To explore the feasibility of this approach with secondary school mathematics teachers, we consider in some detail the use of student work on one mathematics task, adapted from the PISA mathematics assessment, within a particular professional development initiative involving teachers in grades 7–11. Our examination of this experience indicates that although student work is not a self-enacting tool for teacher learning, professional developers can engage secondary school mathematics teachers with student work in ways that afford powerful and potentially transformative learning opportunities.

Keywords Teacher professional development • Secondary mathematics teachers • Examining student work • PISA • Algebra • Teacher education

E.A. Silver (✉)
School of Education, University of Michigan,
610 E. University Ave., Ann Arbor, MI 48109, USA
e-mail: easilver@umich.edu

H. Suh
College of Education, Michigan State University,
301e Erickson Hall 620 Farm Lane, East Lansing, MI 48824, USA
e-mail: suhhj@msu.edu

Y. Li et al. (eds.), *Transforming Mathematics Instruction: Multiple Approaches and Practices*, Advances in Mathematics Education, DOI 10.1007/978-3-319-04993-9_17,
© Springer International Publishing Switzerland 2014

Teacher educators, professional developers, and researchers have recently shown great interest in the design and facilitation of an approach to mathematics teacher education that is often called practice-based professional development. Ball and Cohen (1999) suggested that the everyday work of teachers could be a rich source for the development of a curriculum for professional learning grounded in the tasks, questions, and problems of practice. To accomplish this goal, they argued that records of authentic practice (e.g., tasks used in instruction or assessment, samples of student work) should become the core of professional education, providing a focus for sustained teacher inquiry and investigation. Other scholars have also pointed to the potential benefits of having teachers learn in and through professional practice (e.g., Ball and Bass 2002; Lampert 2001; Little 1999; Smith 2001; Stein et al. 2000; Wilson and Berne 1999). Several manifestations of this approach are evident in other chapters in this volume, including the use of narrative and video cases of teaching practice and the formation of professional learning communities of teachers around lesson planning and reflection on lessons.

In this chapter, we consider yet another opportunity for practice-based professional learning: examination of student work. Organizing teacher learning around the study of mathematical tasks and associated student work is one version of practice-based professional development. We begin with a brief overview of some ways that student work is used as an element of professional learning, after which we consider what has been learned from studies of the use of student work in teacher education and professional development settings. Next we turn our attention to the challenges of using this professional development approach with secondary school mathematics teachers, after which we consider in some detail how student work was used in a professional development initiative involving teachers of mathematics in grades 7–11. In so doing, we draw some observations that may generalize beyond the boundaries of that initiative and that we hope will be useful to others wishing to incorporate into their work with secondary mathematics teachers the examination of student work.

Examining Student Work

The examination of student work is an arguably ubiquitous aspect of mathematics teaching practice. In mathematics classrooms across the entire spectrum from kindergarten through advanced calculus at the university, teachers examine their students' work—the answers they give, the methods they employ, the justifications they offer, and the explanations they provide regarding process and product. Sometimes the examination involves listening carefully to what students say; more often it involves perusing their written responses to textbook exercises or problems posed by the teacher. Whether a teacher is engaging in homework review, quickly checking for comprehension of a new topic just introduced, or evaluating pupil attainment of recently taught ideas through performance on a quiz or test, the examination of student work is a robustly evident feature of mathematics teaching practice.

Many practice-based approaches to professional development include the examination of student work as an embedded component. For example, the examination of student work is a component of case-based approaches to professional development in mathematics (e.g., Schifter et al. 1999; Stein et al. 2000). Examining student work is also a key component of many resources intended to assist teachers to improve their knowledge and practices related to assessment of mathematics (e.g., Blume et al. 1998; Brown and Clark 2006; Parke et al. 2003; Stylianou et al. 2000) or to the effective planning and delivery of classroom lessons, as in Japanese Lesson Study and its American variants (e.g., Fernandez 2002; Fernandez et al. 2003; Lewis 2002; Silver et al. 2006).

Given the apparent ubiquity of examining student work as a feature of mathematics teaching, as well as its centrality to the practice of teaching mathematics for understanding, it is not surprising that teacher educators and scholars would view the use of student work as a tool for practice-based professional development. Some scholars have argued that the use of student work has the potential to influence professional discourse about teaching and learning, to engage teachers in a cycle of experimentation and reflection, and to shift teachers' focus from one of general pedagogy to one that is particularly connected to their own students (e.g., Ball and Cohen 1999; Little 1999). Whether these opportunities are realized, however, depends on how student work is used in professional activity. Also implicated is the inherent difficulty of understanding and interpreting appropriately what students are saying in their speech or written work (Wallach and Even 2005).

Research on the Use of Student Work in Professional Development

In a recent review of more than 25 published reports of empirical research on the use of student work in teacher professional development (primarily in the areas of literacy, science, and mathematics) in the United States, Little (2004) concluded:

> The available evidence does provide support for professional development activity in which looking at student work occupies a prominent place. Although the body of relevant research is small, findings from the available studies indicate that the collective examination of student work, where it is designed to focus teachers' attention closely on children's learning, may have a positive effect on outcomes of interest: teacher knowledge, teaching practice and (in some cases) student learning (pp. 104–105).

Nevertheless, if student work were an "automatic" source of teacher learning, then teachers would be learning all the time and improving their practice with great regularity. Alas, that does not appear to be the case. As Ball and Cohen (1999) noted, "simply looking at students' work would not ensure that improved ways of looking at and interpreting such work will ensue" (p. 16). Indeed, some studies reviewed by Little included detailed observational records of teacher interactions around student work, and they suggest that simply bringing together teachers to "look at student work" did not necessarily open up opportunities for teacher learning. Learning appeared to hinge on what the teachers were asked to do with the student work and how they were asked to interact with the student work and with each other.

Some studies have examined the effects of using student work with teachers of mathematics, and they offer insights into how this approach might be used effectively to promote teacher professional development. For example, Saxe et al. (2001) (see also Gearhart et al. 1999) contrasted the effects of three professional development approaches on teachers of upper elementary school mathematics. One approach made extensive use of student work to illustrate student thinking and conceptual development in the domain of fractions; the other two approaches did not. The findings of this study indicated significant effects on teaching practice and student performance on assessments of conceptual understanding and problem-solving proficiency in the classrooms of the teachers who received the form of professional development that included extensive experience with student work. The study design, however, did not permit attribution of the effects directly to the student work feature of the professional development.

Kazemi and Franke (2004) traced the evolution of 11 teachers at one elementary school as they met in monthly workgroups across a 1-year period to examine their students' responses to mathematical tasks and activities. Prior to each workgroup meeting, the teachers posed a similar mathematical problem to their students. The workgroup discussions centered on the collective scrutiny of the student work those problems generated. The researchers used a *transformation of participation* perspective to examine *what* teachers learned through collective examination of student work and *how* teacher learning was evident in shifts in participation in discussions centered on student work. The researchers documented shifts in teachers' participation across the year, and they identified two critical transformative moments. The first shift in participation occurred when teachers as a group learned to attend to the details of children's thinking. A second shift in participation occurred as teachers began to develop possible instructional trajectories in mathematics.

Kazemi and Franke noted that teachers in this study initially seemed comfortable making inferences about what students "must have been thinking" from the written records of student work. But these inferences were challenged when the teachers were encouraged to elicit students' verbal explanations of what they had done and how they were thinking and to report those classroom conversations to their colleagues in the workgroup along with the written work that students produced. Kazemi and Franke report that teachers' understanding of mathematics teaching and learning deepened, and their classroom practices shifted, when they attended to the details of student thinking and problem-solving practice as those were revealed in a combination of student work samples and narrative accounts of classroom interaction.

Crespo (2000) offers another example of using student work for teacher development, in this case with individuals preparing to become teachers. She engaged a group of 13 preservice elementary school teachers in an exchange of letters with grade 4 students to provide a context in which the preservice teachers could investigate students' ways of thinking and communicating in mathematics. The preservice teachers wrote and received six letters regarding the grade 4 students' work on three mathematics problems. Crespo noted that the preservice teachers initially were quick to make conclusive claims about students' understanding and their interest (or lack of interest) in mathematics on the basis of the students' written work, and they focused extensively on correctness of the students' answers, to the exclusion of considerations of nuances in student thinking. Over time the preservice teachers in Crespo's study came to revise their approach to examining student work. In particular, they became more open to stating provisional claims and revising them based on further consideration of evidence, and they began to focus on the meaning revealed in students' answers rather than simply the correctness.

Crespo used Davis's (1994, 1996, 1997) distinction between evaluative and interpretive discourse to frame her examination of changes that the preservice teachers in her study exhibited. Davis contrasted two distinctive orientations that a teacher may have toward listening to her students' thinking in the classroom. A teacher using an evaluative orientation tends to listen to students' ideas in order to judge them correct or incorrect and to diagnose and correct misunderstandings. With this orientation, the teacher sees the students' work in light of how she herself would approach the problem or in a manner consistent with the teacher's hypothesized learning trajectory for her students. In contrast, a teacher using an interpretive orientation tends to listen to students' ideas in order to understand rather than assess them. Teachers who display an interpretive orientation listen to their students' ideas with the aim of accessing their understandings, seeking information through more elaborated responses, and asking for demonstrations or explanations. Crespo noted that her preservice teachers moved from a predominantly evaluative orientation to a more interpretive orientation through successive iterations of engaging with challenging mathematical tasks, reflecting on their own ideas, and interacting with students' work.

Looking across these and a few other studies examining teachers' use of student work (e.g., Crockett 2002; Jansen and Spitzer 2009; Krebs 2005; Little et al 2003), we see indications that the use of student work can be a powerful element of effective professional development for teachers of mathematics. For example, Crockett (2002) worked with teachers of upper elementary grade mathematics in a teacher inquiry group and found that analyzing student thinking appeared more influential than other activities (solving open-ended problems, discussing videos of mathematics teaching, and common lesson planning) in provoking teachers to reconsider the teaching and learning of mathematics.

The research base discussed thus far consists entirely of studies involving preservice or inservice teachers of elementary school mathematics. What insights do we have into the ways in which examination of student work might be used with teachers of secondary school mathematics? Though the use of student work with secondary mathematics teachers remains largely unexamined, a few investigations have been undertaken.

Doerr (2006) reported a fairly detailed analysis of one teacher's shift in classroom practice from evaluator of student ideas to supporting students as self-evaluators of their emerging ideas. Doerr attributes this shift to the teacher's participation in a professional development project that made available extensive opportunities for teachers to examine the development of students' conceptual models of exponential growth in the context of their own classrooms. Doerr's analysis indicated that as the teacher attended to her students' thinking, she developed a more sophisticated schema for understanding the diversity of their ideas. The actions of the teacher supported extensive student engagement with the task and supported the students to revise and refine their own mathematical thinking.

Hughes (2006) studied the planning practices of ten preservice secondary mathematics teachers enrolled in a university teacher education program. Among her several research questions was ascertaining the extent to which attention to students' mathematical thinking was evident in preservice secondary mathematics teachers' written lesson plans or lesson planning process prior to and immediately after participation in a course that emphasized students' mathematical thinking as a key element of planning. Hughes found that the preservice teachers demonstrated significant growth on pre- to post-course measures in their ability to attend to students' thinking when planning a lesson on demand and for a university assignment. Furthermore, teachers continued to be able to apply these ideas when planning on demand and for university assignments several months later.

When Hughes traced the teachers into their first year of teaching to investigate whether they would apply the ideas they had learned when planning in their own practice, she found that teachers were more likely to attend to students' thinking when planning a lesson that used a high-level task compared to a lesson that used a low-level task, and their attention to students' thinking when planning lessons in their own classrooms around tasks with a high level of cognitive demand was similar to their preservice planning for lessons. Though the examination of student work was a key component of the teacher preparation experiences of the teachers in the Hughes study, it was only one of the many formative influences on the teachers, and so the study design did not permit specific attributions regarding the effects of that type of experience in comparison to other types (e.g., analyzing narrative and video cases of mathematics instruction, reading articles that summarized research on children's thinking and learning).

Taken together, the research with preservice elementary teachers, and the two examinations of secondary teachers discussed above, suggests the potential value of teacher professional development that involves having teachers examine student work. Despite this optimistic view, however, there are some good reasons to be skeptical that this approach could be successful with secondary mathematics teachers. The need for caution is clear if we examine closely the work of teachers of mathematics in secondary schools, their experiences in preparation to do that work, and what research has suggested about their views of mathematics, teaching, and learning. Some research suggests that secondary school teachers of mathematics differ from their elementary school counterparts in ways that might make it less likely that the use of student work would be a successful element of professional development for secondary teachers.

Secondary Mathematics Teachers and Teaching

The first thing that might be noted about secondary school mathematics teachers is that they typically have taken many more university mathematics courses than their elementary school teacher counterparts. The teaching in those mathematics classes, and especially in courses intended for mathematics majors at the college level, is likely to have emphasized the *coverage* of mathematics content through teacher lecture, textbook exercises, and student memorization and practice (Brown et al. 1990; Frykholm 1999; Thompson 1992). Typically in these prior experiences, mathematics proficiency would have been demonstrated through accurate, rapid recall of facts and correct execution of rehearsed procedures. Thompson et al. (1994) characterized this as a *calculational* rather than *conceptual* orientation to teaching.

Because secondary school mathematics teachers are likely to have succeeded (at least to the extent of passing the courses) in the mathematics classes they took in high school and college, they have little reason as individuals to question either the appropriateness or efficacy of the mathematics teaching approach they encountered. This so-called apprenticeship of observation and experience supports a reproductive stance rather transformative stance toward mathematics instruction (Brown and Borko 1992; Lortie 1975). This situation contrasts with that of most teachers of mathematics in elementary school, who are likely both to have taken fewer mathematics courses and to have a less favorable impression of their experiences in the courses they have taken.

Secondary mathematics teachers are generally organized within a departmental structure, so they tend to associate with others who have had similar experiences and hold similar views. Thus, an orientation toward reproduction of dominant patterns of mathematics instruction—patterns that do not encourage deliberate attention to individual student thinking—is likely to prevail among secondary school mathematics teachers (Little 2002).

A heavy emphasis in secondary school on content coverage rather than on the development of individual student understanding supports classroom assessment practices aimed at quick grading of correctness to assign grades rather than detailed examination of responses to uncover individual student ideas. A tendency, noted earlier in our discussion of Crespo's study, for teachers to focus almost exclusively on correctness when examining student work is closely associated with what Otero (2006) called a "get it or don't" conception of formative assessment.

It is important to note that this tendency among secondary teachers may also arise from the demands of the work of teaching secondary school mathematics. Whereas an elementary teacher will likely have 20–25 students to whom she teaches mathematics as one of multiple subjects across an entire year, a secondary teacher of mathematics likely to be responsible for teaching mathematics to more than 100 students each day and may have twice that number across an academic year if the school calendar is organized into semester courses. This striking difference in the number of different students encountered in instructional settings makes it likely (and arguably quite reasonable) that secondary teachers would be less inclined than elementary teachers toward considering student work in a more nuanced fashion.

Research also suggests that high school mathematics teachers tend to view verbal problem solving as a competency that follows mastery of symbolic computation, which may combine with other features of secondary school mathematics teaching—such as reliance on typical textbook presentation of content that places problem solving and applications after the presentation of symbolic rules and procedures, a stress on content coverage and "getting through the book," and a tendency to focus on correctness in evaluating student work—to encourage excessive attention on the teaching and learning of symbolic procedures with correspondingly less attention to complex problem-solving tasks that might yield insights into student thinking.

Nathan and Koedinger (2000a) asked more than 100 elementary, middle, and high school mathematics teachers to rank a set of mathematics problems based on expectations of their relative problem-solving difficulty. An earlier analysis of students' problem-solving processes performed by Nathan and Koedinger (2000b) showed that verbal problems were easier for students to solve than symbolic problems because verbal problems were more likely to elicit informal strategies such as guess and test. However, the teachers predicted the opposite, based apparently on a view that arithmetic reasoning develops prior to algebraic reasoning and symbolic problem solving develops prior to verbal reasoning. Nathan and Koedinger found that high school teachers were most likely to hold this view that the researchers called *symbol-precedence*. Secondary school teachers made the poorest predictions of students' performances, whereas middle school teachers' predictions were most accurate. Moreover, Nathan and Koedinger noted:

> Data from the belief instruments indicated that high school teachers in our sample—those most centrally charged with algebra instruction—were least aware of the efficacy of students' invented algebra solution strategies. Because high school teachers tend to have greater expertise in their content areas, they are personally more distant from the difficulties of their novice students. This may make high school teachers more susceptible to a kind of "expert blindspot" that prevents them from being made aware of certain aspects of learning such as alternative interpretations of symbolic equations. (p. 229)

Although secondary school mathematics teachers are typically legally authorized through their teacher certificate or license to teach any mathematics course offered in secondary schools, they usually become specialists in teaching one particular course (e.g., Geometry or Algebra 2). Such specialization has some advantages to an individual teacher in reducing preparation time and allowing for the refinement of lessons over time. Unfortunately, this tendency also has at least one potential deficiency; namely, a teacher of one course, say Algebra 2, may know surprisingly little about what students might have experienced and learned in classes taken prior to their arrival in Algebra 2.

In an examination of secondary mathematics teachers' knowledge and beliefs, Heid and colleagues (1999) reported that secondary mathematics "teachers expected that students would not know mathematics which they were not explicitly taught" (p. 239). On the face of it, this belief may seem quite sensible, but embedded within is a view that appears discordant with the notion of new knowledge being constructed by building on prior knowledge. The power of informal and prior knowledge in building sound understanding of mathematical ideas is a hallmark of decades of research on student learning (Bransford et al. 1999). The use of prior knowledge in teaching mathematical ideas does appear to have gained some attention at the elementary school level (Kilpatrick et al. 2001). Yet, the view among secondary mathematics teachers that students "don't know it until I teach it" would make it unlikely that they would want to inquire into student thinking to satisfy a curiosity about what students might already know that could be related to and built upon as they learn a subsequent curriculum topic.

These observations about secondary school mathematics teachers are intended neither to depress the readers of our paper nor to reflect a deterministic stance on our part. Rather they are intended to draw attention to impediments that one might reasonably expect to encounter in using student work in professional development with inservice secondary school mathematics teachers. To illustrate how these challenges might manifest themselves and how they might be overcome, we discuss next a professional development initiative for teachers of mathematics in grades 7–11, paying close attention to how student work was used and what happened when it was used.

Mathematics Teachers' Use of Student Work in Professional Development: A Close Look at the Apples Task

DELTA (Developing Excellence in Learning and Teaching Algebra) was a 3-year, multifaceted professional development initiative intended to support teachers of mathematics in the middle and secondary grades (grades 7–11) in Oakland County, Michigan, with a particular focus on ensuring strong student preparation in algebra. DELTA involved approximately 150 teachers from 13 different school districts, including 13 high schools and 20 feeder middle schools, serving approximately 19,000 students. The DELTA participants were drawn from school districts that were demographically quite variable; for example, the percent minority enrollment in these 13 districts ranged from lows of 3 and 5 % to highs of 84 and 94 %. To address the diverse needs of the districts and teachers, DELTA had multiple components, including courses for teachers regarding content and teaching strategies for basic algebra, classroom-based coaching, two algebra-related summits for administrators, algebra support seminar, administrator training, school improvement coaching, and a series of sessions focused on curricular coherence.

In this chapter, we draw on a slice of work undertaken during the first 2 years by the teachers and professional development specialists involved in DELTA's curricular coherence component (*Who's On First? Building Coherence and Connections Across Grade Levels*). The goal of this component of DELTA was to offer teacher teams from participating districts an opportunity to develop a *coherent* vision of algebra concepts, skills, and reasoning. The plan was that this would be done by drawing their attention to how algebraic proficiency might develop over several years of mathematics instruction rather than viewing it *atomistically* as discrete topics taught at specific time points. DELTA sought to provide an alternative to the atomistic perspective that appeared to be consistent with the array of individual curriculum objectives promulgated by the state of Michigan in its Grade Level Content Expectations (GLCE for grades K-8) and High School Content Expectations (HSCE for grades 9–12).

The plan was that teams would work together to cluster and sequence GLCE and HSCE expectations into teaching/learning trajectories that depict growth in major algebraic themes across grades 7–11. In constructing the trajectories, teachers would work to identify what is and is not taught in each grade, where to focus on building concepts, and where to build symbolic fluency by drawing on conceptual understanding. Proposed topics for algebra-related trajectories included proportionality, linear (and nonlinear) relations, relative and absolute change, and function.

Almost 100 teachers of middle grades and high school mathematics participated in at least a portion of the curricular coherence component of DELTA during the 2-year period of interest in this paper. There were 56 participants in year 1 and 92 in year 2 (including 26 continuing from year 1 and 66 new participants). The teachers were drawn from 13 different school districts. As is typical of such professional development, some of the participants enthusiastically volunteered their participation, and others attended because they were directed to do so by school or district leadership. In a survey administered to project participants during year 2, 57 % indicated that they were participating because they wished to learn strategies to help their students, and 43 % indicated that they were attending at directive of an administrator.

The Apples Task

The Apples task and related student work used in the DELTA project was an adapted version of an item [M136: Apples] that originally appeared on the mathematics assessment portion of the Programme for International Student Assessment (PISA) and was one of 50 mathematics tasks publicly released in 2006 (OECD 2006). PISA is a collaborative effort of member countries of the Organisation for Economic Co-operation and Development (OECD). The main objective of PISA is to provide policy-relevant data on the *yield* of education systems. The assessed population is 15-year-olds, an age that marks the end of compulsory schooling in most OECD member countries.

PISA assesses how well 15-year-old youth are able to use the knowledge and skills they have acquired in school to meet the literacy-related challenges they are likely to face outside of school as adult citizens. PISA focuses on literacy—the ability to use and apply knowledge and skills to real-world situations encountered in adult life—in the key subject areas of reading, mathematics, and science. The frameworks guiding the PISA assessments reflect a consensus across the OECD countries regarding the skills and abilities that demonstrate literacy in these areas. For the 2003 assessment, PISA defined mathematical literacy as follows:

> Mathematical literacy is an individual's capacity to identify and understand the role that mathematics plays in the world, to make well-founded judgements and to use and engage with mathematics in ways that meet the needs of that individuals' life as a constructive, concerned and reflective citizen. (OECD 2003, p. 24)

Compared to the original Apples task, the DELTA version (see Fig. 1) incorporated two variations. One was minor: replacing the word conifer with the

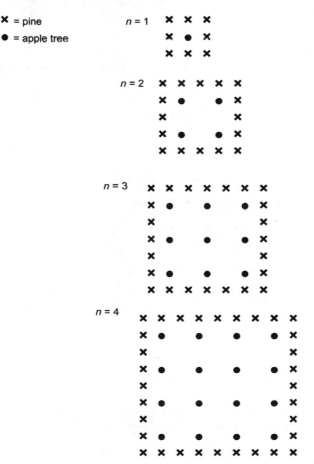

Fig. 1 The Apples task used in the DELTA project

Adapted from Mathematics Sample Tasks
OECD's 2009 PISA Assessment

Question 3.1

Complete the table:

n	Number of apple trees	Number of pine trees
1	1	8
2	4	
3		
4		
5		

Question 3.2 [Note: different wording than in original PISA task]
Describe the pattern (words or symbols) so that you could find the number of apple trees
for any stage in the pattern illustrated on the previous page:

Describe the pattern (words or symbols) so that you could find the number of pine trees for
any stage in the pattern illustrated on the previous page:

For what value(s) of n will the number of apple trees equal the number of pine trees. Show
your method of calculating this.

Question 3.3
Suppose the farmer wants to make a much larger orchard with many rows of trees. As the
farmer makes the orchard bigger, which will increase more quickly: the number of apple
trees or the number of pine trees? Explain how you found your answer.

Fig. 1 (continued)

word pine, a substitution thought to be more familiar to students in Michigan.
The other was a major revision of the wording of Question 3.2 in the original
Apples task:

> There are two formulae you can use to calculate the number of apple trees and the number
> of conifer trees for the problem described above:
> Number of apple trees $= n^2$
> Number of conifer trees $= 8n$
> Where n is the number of rows of apple trees.
> There is a value of n for which the number of apple trees equals the number of conifer trees.
> Find the value of n and show your method of calculating this.

The task was modified in this way for use in the DELTA project because the
project leaders thought that the revised version of question 3.2 would both allow

for a more diverse set of solution approaches and be more accessible to middle school students.

The DELTA professional development team viewed PISA items as good candidates for use in the curricular coherence component of the project for several reasons. First, PISA tasks typically call upon the use algebra skills, concepts, and processes. The Apples task, for example, involves legitimate algebraic content, including both linear and nonlinear relationships, and encompasses a range of algebraic thinking processes, as a solver analyzes, generalizes, and compares two different patterns, one linear and one quadratic.

Second, PISA tasks often involve multiple forms of representation. The Apples task, in particular, involves a verbal representation of a situation, associated with a corresponding visual representation. Tabular and symbolic representations are used in questions, and the last question asks students to explain their reasoning verbally.

Third, because PISA tests the residual, usable knowledge gained by 15-year-old students, the tasks tend to involve applications of knowledge to problems that are embedded in real-world contexts and are not tied to specific formats and exercise types associated with particular curriculum topics in mathematics courses. In the case of the Apples task, there is a contextual embedding, though it is not as interesting or authentic as in many PISA tasks, but the task exemplifies well the way that PISA tasks often step outside curriculum boundaries. In particular, the task involves both linear and quadratic relationships, and the third part of task moves beyond simple equations to consider rates of change in a manner that approaches topics taught in calculus.

Occasion 1: Teachers Solve Apples Task and Predict Student Solutions

The Apples task was first introduced in the first year of the curriculum coherence component at the third professional development session for teacher leaders held in January 2010. Prior to this session, participants had examined the state curriculum objectives (GLCEs and HSCEs) for grades 7–11 with attention to proportionality, linear and quadratic relations, and functions. They had also begun to formulate teaching/learning trajectories for these topics.

Teachers were given the Apples task and the following instructions:

1. Individually complete the Apples task.
2. Compare your thinking with a partner from your grade-alike small groups and resolve any differences.
3. Work with a grade-alike partner to consider what you would anticipate students at your grade level are likely to do in generating an appropriate solution for each part of the task.
4. Join others at your grade level to record your predictions on a poster.

After the grade-level groups had completed their work, the posters recording their anticipated student solutions were displayed in the room to facilitate a large group discussion that ensued. A summary of the information written on the posters by the four grade-level groups (grade 7, Algebra 1, and beyond Algebra 1) is shown in Fig. 2.

In the large group discussion, some high school teachers expressed skepticism regarding whether a typical middle school student, especially one in grade 7, would be able to solve questions 3.2 and 3.3. In their view, these questions required algebraic skills not likely to be available to students prior to Algebra 1 instruction. But the middle grades teachers pointed out that question 3.2 could be solved using a variety of approaches, including graphing. One middle school teacher referred to the graphing approach that some teachers used to solve question 3.2c earlier in the session, and she used that as an example to argue that seventh-grade students could solve the problem:

> Going back to the place where we were graphing the data points, especially if you did them in different colors, the red dots for the apple trees, the dots for the apple trees are going to start below the dots for the pine trees. And then pretty soon the red dots are going to be the ones that are up above the ones for the pine. So you could even do that in the seventh grade when you're using the data points on a graph rather than the function plots.

As a homework assignment following the January session, the participants were asked to administer the Apples task to at least one class of students, if that was feasible for them; to solicit colleagues who might also be willing to administer the task to one of their classes; to examine the solutions produced by the students; and to meet with a grade-level colleague to examine the student responses at your grade level and identify what the responses reveal about what students appear to understand, what they appear not to understand, and what the instructional implications appear to be.

Student Work on the Apples Task

Not all participants collected student work on the task, but many did. More than 30 participants from 22 schools in 13 different districts administered the Apples task to their students, and in some cases also to other classes at their schools, and collected the students' solution attempts. This yielded a set of more than 900 student responses from students in classrooms ranging from grades 5 through 12 and enrolled in a variety of mathematics courses (e.g., grade 7, Algebra 1, Algebra 2, precalculus).

Because the circumstances of task administration were likely quite varied in the DELTA case and different from that employed in the PISA assessment, it is not possible to make a valid comparison of performance. Nevertheless, we were curious to see how students in the DELTA sample performed, and we expected that the DELTA teachers would also want to know. The PISA performance information provided a convenient benchmark. Therefore, a research team (including the authors of this paper) working under the auspices of an NSF-funded project, *Using PISA to Develop Activities for Teacher Education (UPDATE)*, undertook a careful examination of the student work collected by

Who's on First? The Apple Task Solution Strategy Expected Trajectory

7th Grade Apple Task	8th Grade Apple Task
Question 3.2a and b • Use the table/pictures to extend pattern • Use words (starting with <u>pictures</u>) to develop expressions • After Moving Straight Ahead (CMP Unit) $y = mx + b$ for pine tree pattern Question 3.2c • 1 Solution plotting points from table Question 3.3 • Use graph and discuss "Steepness" "Red dots will catch up"	Question 3.2a and b • Use <u>table</u> to develop expression • Be able to write both expressions symbolically (linear and quadratic) Question 3.2c • 2 solutions for 8th when graphed (may not get both solutions algebraically) Question 3.3 • Rate of change or slope use vocabulary of "linear" and "quadratic"
Algebra I	**Beyond Algebra I**

Question 3.2a and b
• Generalize based on function class
 	
Question 3.2c
• Make set expressions equivalent to one another
  ○ $a = n^2$
  ○ $p = 8n$
 	
$$n^2 = 8n$$
$$n^2 - 8n = 0$$
$$n(n-8) = 0$$
$$\frac{n^2}{n} = \frac{8n}{n}$$
$$n = 8$$
Note: Division by 0 is problematic but students may not notice
 	
• Solve algebraically and get 2 solutions
 	
Question 3.3
	Question 3.2
	• Connection to other polynomials (Zeros) + intervals
	• Connection to domain and range (discrete vs. continuous)
	• Link linear to arithmetic sequences
	
	Question 3.3

Fig. 2 Teachers' anticipations regarding Apple task student solutions

the DELTA teachers. We used the PISA scoring rubric to evaluate the students' responses to questions 3.1 and 3.3.

The student work in the DELTA sample compared favorably to the US national sample of 15-year-olds for PISA in 2003. On question 3.1, 80 % of the DELTA sample received full credit, as opposed to 53 % in the US national sample and an average of 49 % for all the countries participating in PISA in 2003. In fact, the DELTA sample performance on this question was equivalent to that of Japan, the highest performing country in the PISA assessment on this question. On question 3.3, the performance of the DELTA sample was about 10 % correct, almost identical to that of the US national sample on this question in the 2003 PISA assessment.

Occasion 2: Teachers Analyze and Discuss Student Work

The Apples task was again considered at the next professional development session (the fourth of five sessions in year one) held in March 2010. This time, participants' attention was directed to the student work that was collected through their administration of the Apples task in their schools. In the portion of the session in which the Apples task was used, participants met in grade-alike groups to consider and discuss what they noticed when they examined the work produced by students at their grade level, with particular attention to what the work suggested about what students appear to understand, what they appear not to understand, and what the instructional implications appear to be. Their observations were recorded on poster paper and displayed in the room to facilitate a large group discussion that ensued.

What was striking about the poster displays and the discussions on this occasion, both in grade-alike groups and in whole group, was the almost exclusive focus on what the students did incorrectly in their work. The posters recording what the work revealed to teachers about what students understood were largely blank, whereas posters related to what the work revealed about what students did not understand had numerous entries, and at two of the grade levels, there were several "don't understand" posters filled with claims. For example, middle school teachers noted that few students employed graphical or symbolic representations or used the notion of "growth" to describe the patterns in the problem and that many appeared to apply the notion of exponential growth erroneously in the case of the quadratic. The Algebra 1 teachers observed that many students had difficulty setting up the equation to solve to find the solution in 3.2c, missed 0 as a solution, mistakenly rendered the repeated addition of 8 as $n + 8$ rather than as $8n$, and confused quadratic and exponential.

Some participants noted that many students attempted to use recursive reasoning to solve questions 3.2a and 3.2b. This was somewhat surprising to the participants given that their predictions, as summarized in Fig. 2, were that students would express generalized patterns using explicit forms.

Though the professional development leaders were disappointed in the extensive focus on mistakes and misunderstandings, to the near exclusion of attention to students' understandings or instructional implications, they decided to follow their plan for the day, which called for a lunch break and then moving on to another task they had planned for the afternoon session. The DELTA leadership was certain that the student work would yield much more useful information than had been evident in that morning discussion, but they saw that they needed to devise a more productive way to focus the participants' attention on the student work.

Interlude: Detailed Analysis of Student Work on the Apples Task

After the year one sessions concluded the UPDATE, research team (including the authors of this paper) undertook a careful examination of the student work, paying particular attention to student work on questions 3.2 and 3.3. We developed an analytic coding process that blended and adapted the original PISA scoring guide with Lannin's (2005) classification scheme used to characterize students' strategies for solving mathematics problems involving pattern generalization.

Our goal was to identify in the students' responses facets of algebraic thinking that might provoke a fruitful conversation among teachers. We looked specifically at students' use of recursive or explicit approaches to characterizing the generalization and the extent to which their generalization was expressed using equations or verbal descriptions. Two general observations emerged from our examination of the student work that we judged to have potential to engage the DELTA participants:

- Students in upper grades and more advanced mathematics classes (Algebra 2; precalculus) tended to use mathematical symbolism and equations, whereas their counterparts in middle school and in lower level mathematics classes relied more often on verbal descriptions. Yet, even the students in upper level classes used verbal descriptions rather than symbolic expressions fairly often to express a generalization.
- Some students at all grade levels used recursive strategies to solve questions 3.2a and 3.2b, with more using recursion for question 3.2b; students using recursion used only verbal descriptions rather than symbolic expressions to express their generalizations.

The first observation was consistent with the predictions of the teachers (see Fig. 2). That is, students in higher-level courses (e.g., Algebra 2; precalculus) were more likely to use mathematical symbolism and equations than were their counterparts in lower grades. Students in higher grades were also more successful than those in lower grades, which also reflected a normative expectation. Yet even within this predicted and predictable finding, there was a surprise: A substantial portion of the students in higher grades used verbal descriptions (e.g., about 30 % of the Algebra 2 and precalculus students used words rather than symbols to express the generalization for question 3.2a, and the percent was slightly higher for question 3.2b).

The second observation, however, was definitely not anticipated: Students in the DELTA sample used recursive reasoning frequently, and they did so at all grade levels. For example, on question 3.2a, 15 % of the grade 7 students used recursive reasoning in their work, and the same percent of Algebra 2 students used recursive reasoning in their work. On question 3.2b, about one-third of the grade 7 students used recursion, and nearly one-half of the Algebra 1 and Geometry students did so! Interestingly, *recursion appeared nowhere in the teachers' predictions* noted in Fig. 2 at any grade level. Moreover, students employed verbal descriptions almost exclusively to express their recursive generalizations, apparently because they lacked formalisms (e.g., Now/Next notation) to assist in expressing recursive generalizations.

Following our analysis of the student work, we created packets of student responses that contained specific examples to reflect the major strategies and representations evident in the full sample of student work: recursive description, recursive equation, explicit description, and explicit equation. Then we met with the DELTA professional development leaders and discussed with them the findings from our analysis. We also shared the packets of sample student responses and discussed how these might be used in a subsequent session with the DELTA participants.

Occasion 3: Teachers Revisit Student Work on Apples Task

The Apples task, particularly the work generated by students in their attempt to solve the task, was the focus of attention again during the second year of the project. In the March 2011 session, the participants (including some who continued from the first year and a large number of new participants) began by reviewing the Apples task and the predictions generated by participants in year 1. This allowed the new participants to familiarize themselves with the task and the prior work that had been done.

Teachers were then given the packets of student responses described above, and they were asked to examine the responses to questions 3.2a and 3.2b and to sort them into groups. Initially the teachers tended to sort the responses into two piles: correct or incorrect. Some had a third pile for responses that might be considered partially correct. Then the professional development session leader instructed the teachers to sort the responses for each question into the following categories: Describe recursive pattern in words, (try to) express a recursive pattern using symbolic notation, describe an explicit pattern using words, and express an explicit using symbolic notation (see Fig. 3 for an example of each type). Teachers were also asked to predict the percent of students who would be likely to produce each type of response at the grade level they teach (i.e., 15 % of grade 8 students will use words to describe a recursive pattern in question 3.2a). Teachers worked individually at first, then in pairs, and finally in grade-level groups to compare and refine their sorting and predictions.

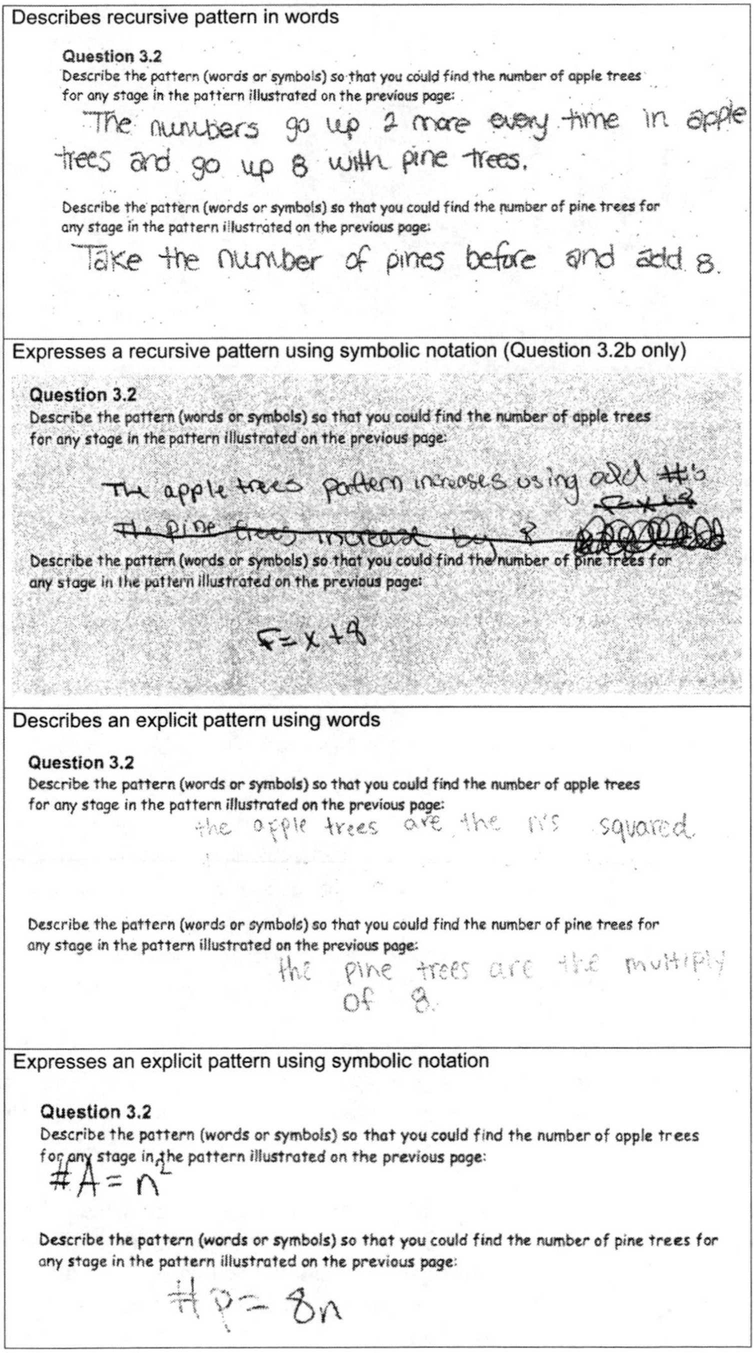

Describes recursive pattern in words

Question 3.2
Describe the pattern (words or symbols) so that you could find the number of apple trees
for any stage in the pattern illustrated on the previous page:

The numbers go up 2 more every time in apple trees and go up 8 with pine trees.

Describe the pattern (words or symbols) so that you could find the number of pine trees for
any stage in the pattern illustrated on the previous page:

Take the number of pines before and add 8.

Expresses a recursive pattern using symbolic notation (Question 3.2b only)

Question 3.2
Describe the pattern (words or symbols) so that you could find the number of apple trees
for any stage in the pattern illustrated on the previous page:

The apple trees pattern increases using odd #'s

The pine trees increase by 8

Describe the pattern (words or symbols) so that you could find the number of pine trees for
any stage in the pattern illustrated on the previous page:

$$P = x + 8$$

Describes an explicit pattern using words

Question 3.2
Describe the pattern (words or symbols) so that you could find the number of apple trees
for any stage in the pattern illustrated on the previous page:

the apple trees are the #'s squared

Describe the pattern (words or symbols) so that you could find the number of pine trees for
any stage in the pattern illustrated on the previous page:

the pine trees are the multiply of 8.

Expresses an explicit pattern using symbolic notation

Question 3.2
Describe the pattern (words or symbols) so that you could find the number of apple trees
for any stage in the pattern illustrated on the previous page:

$$\#A = n^2$$

Describe the pattern (words or symbols) so that you could find the number of pine trees for
any stage in the pattern illustrated on the previous page:

$$\#P = 8n$$

Fig. 3 Example student responses in the four categories

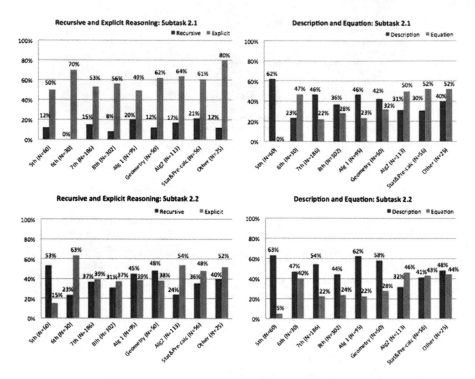

Fig. 4 Graphs depicting student response rates by type and grade

Grade-level predictions were shared and discussed briefly in a whole group session. In general, the predictions were that, as students progressed across the grades and through mathematics courses, they would become far more likely to express generalizations explicitly rather than recursively and they would also be far more likely to use symbolic expressions and equations rather than verbal descriptions.

The UPDATE team then explained how it had coded and analyzed the set of more than 900 student responses. For questions 3.2a and 3.2b, graphs were displayed to depict the frequency of student responses that expressed the generalization explicitly or recursively and that used verbal descriptions or symbolic expressions (see Fig. 4).

The graphical displays made vividly apparent the ways in which the student work deviated from the teachers' predictions. In particular, though the graphs revealed a trend toward expressing generalizations explicitly and with symbolic expressions, they also showed the surprising persistence of both recursive reasoning and verbal descriptions across the grades.

The findings of the UPDATE analysis were discussed briefly in whole group, and then the participants met in grade-alike groups to discuss the findings and graphs as they pertained to their grade level. Teachers were encouraged to identify instructional issues raised by these findings—issues that pertained within grade level and issues that might pertain across grade level. The number of responses in some groups (e.g., 6th grade, other) was so small that it was not possible to determine if the responses were in any sense representative, but aggregations of pre-algebra, algebra, and post-algebra tended to support firmer generalizations.

Lively group discussions ensued, as participants discussed and debated the findings and possible implications, moving fluidly between the graphs of general findings and the specific student responses that were available to them in the packets examined earlier in the day. Following the discussion in grade-alike groups, the participants moved into cross-grade groups that intentionally mixed middle school and high school teachers. In these groups, participants discussed what the findings of this analysis suggested about what students were and were not learning from their mathematics instruction at each grade level. The teachers also examined the teaching/learning trajectories for proportionality, function, linear and quadratic relations, and other topics to see how and where they might be revised to address the issues revealed by this examination of student work in order to increase curricular coherence.

In written reflections at the end of the session, some teachers noted that the examination of student work in that day's session provoked them to think about student work in deeper ways that went beyond right/wrong and multiple strategies. Several commented on the value of the Apples task activity in focusing their attention not only on what they are expected to teach at a grade level but also on how this ties to what is taught before and after. Other participants noted that the session had highlighted for them the limitations of right/wrong evaluations of student work when compared to a more nuanced consideration of strategies and representations. Several teachers mentioned recursion as a specific strategy that they had not previously valued, but that they now needed to reconsider in light of the clear tendency of students to use recursive reasoning in analyzing patterns. A teacher noted the importance of "bridging" recursive and explicit expressions for generalizations to help students make a smooth transition, and another teacher pointed to the need to provide students with specific instruction in using Now/Next notation to express their recursive observations.

Discussion

The Apples task experience described here embodies several points raised earlier in this paper in our review on literature regarding the use of student work in teacher professional development. The secondary teacher participants in the DELTA project exhibited a number of the characteristics identified earlier—an evaluative rather than interpretive orientation when examining student work, a symbol-precedence view when predicting the trajectory of student performance, a skepticism about the ability of students to be able to solve difficult problems prior to specific instruction regarding those problems, and a corresponding faith that students would be apt to use sophisticated solution methods to solve problems after receiving instruction in those methods. Each of these was challenged by their experience in examining the Apples task student work. In fact, the DELTA professional development team felt that the participants' experience with the Apples task, particularly the third occasion, was a key point in the project that triggered a shift in the orientation of many of the participants.

Though our presentation here has been largely descriptive, and our data do not allow us to make definitive claims regarding effects, several observations appear to be in order regarding the way teachers engaged with the Apples task and associated student work in the DELTA project context. We discuss here three that may have sufficient generality to be of use to others who wish to use the examination of student work as a central feature of teacher professional development.

The Mathematical Task

The Apples task was a challenging mathematical task that treated concepts and skills that were viewed as legitimate by all the teachers from grades 7–11. The modification that was made when the task moved from PISA to DELTA appears to have been critical for two reasons. First, it made the task more accessible to middle school students who had not yet been taught to write and solve algebraic equations. Second, the modification opened the door to students' use of recursive reasoning to express the generalization. Our hunch is that recursion would have been far less likely to appear in the student work if the original PISA version of question 3.2 had been used. In fact, recursive thinking is only mentioned briefly in the PISA scoring rubric as an element of a possible response to question 3.3 that should receive partial credit. Similarly the DELTA participants did not anticipate students' use of recursive reasoning to express generalizations, and they were surprised by its robust appearance in the student work. The salience of recursion in the student work turned out to be a source of surprise for the teachers and thus an opportunity for their learning.

The modification did not, however, reduce or alter the mathematical character of the original PISA task. And as a task derived from PISA, the Apples task was both accessible to and challenging for the entire range of students from middle grades to upper secondary school.

The Teacher/Student Grade Span

The mixing of middle school and high school teachers in the participant group appeared to have several desirable consequences for the work with the Apples task. First, a range of perspectives on how students might solve the task were available for consideration. Specifically, the Algebra 1 teachers were provoked to consider how students might solve such a problem prior to instruction in an Algebra 1 course. Second, the range of teachers and grades supported participants' consideration of curricular coherence issues as they considered in cross-grade groups the evidence from the student work. The consideration of student work in this case was embedded within a larger project focus on curricular coherence and was undertaken within a stream of professional activity related to teaching/learning trajectories that reflected attention to the development of algebraic ideas and understandings across the grades. Third, the range of grades taught by the teachers ensured that the student work collected on the task would similarly reflect that range. This allowed the group of participants to make predictions regarding typical responses at particular grade levels and also regarding trajectories across grades—predictions that were challenged when the participants examined the student work, thereby creating a learning opportunity for the teachers.

The Professional Learning Task

We have identified desirable aspects of the Apples task and the wide grade span of the DELTA participants as important elements in the story. Yet these were not sufficient to ensure teacher learning from examining the student work. As we saw in the account of the second occasion in DELTA when project participants examined the student work collected in their schools, the teachers did not move far from a right/wrong consideration of student work. It was not until the third occasion when a major shift in orientation appeared to occur.

What was different about the third occasion? Participants were directed to examine student responses with particular criteria in mind that drew attention to strategy and representation and drew attention away from considerations of correctness. Participants attended to specific examples of student responses that had been chosen in advance to be representative of certain strategies and representations. This careful attention to particular examples of student work was juxtaposed in the session with the presentation of a comprehensive analysis of student responses with respect to key features of strategy and representation, and the depiction of those findings in graphical displays that focused participants' attention on those considerations with respect to the totality of responses.

These features of the professional learning task on the third occasion appear to have been critically important, but the experience of project participants in solving the tasks and predicting student solutions on prior occasions is also likely to have played an important role in creating the learning opportunities that were manifested on the third occasion. For example, the predicted solutions seemed to be important in provoking surprise (and an opportunity for learning) when they were compared to the actual student work. Also, the inadequacy of sorting student responses into piles of correct and incorrect responses became more apparent when the participants reflected on how much more was learned by considering strategies and representations.

Further affirmation of the importance of these features of the professional learning task is provided by subsequent examples of project activity in which the professional development team used a similar approach with other tasks, with a transfer of responsibility to the teacher participants to perform the analysis of student strategies and representations and with careful scaffolding of participants' analytic work through questions designed to draw attention to key issues. Moreover, several of the participants adopted a similar approach in their work with colleagues in district-level and school-level professional development sessions that they led.

Conclusion

We began by noting that organizing teacher learning around the study of mathematical tasks and associated student work is one version of practice-based professional development. Our review of research examining the use of student work in teacher education and professional development settings suggested the potential efficacy of such approaches, particularly with preservice teachers and inservice elementary school teachers. We asked whether this approach might also work with inservice secondary school teachers, especially given many facets of their work and their preparation that appear to mitigate against the effectiveness of such an approach. To explore the feasibility of this approach with secondary school mathematics teachers, we considered in some detail the use of student work on one mathematics task, adapted from the PISA mathematics assessment, within a particular professional development initiative involving teachers in grades 7–11. Our examination of this experience indicated that student work is not self-enacting as a tool for teacher professional learning, but that professional developers can engage secondary school mathematics teachers with student work in ways that create powerful and potentially transformative learning opportunities.

Acknowledgements We thank Valerie Mills, Dana Gosen, and Geraldine Devine—leaders of the DELTA project in Oakland Schools—for allowing us to witness their skillful practice as teacher professional developers. They graciously agreed to use the PISA Apples task in their project, and they made available to us detailed session records and artifacts. We also thank Patricia Kenney for her assistance in identifying the PISA Apples task as a fruitful candidate for use in this work and Rachel Snider for her assistance with data collection, analysis, and interpretation. This research was supported by the National Science Foundation under Grant No. 1019513 [Using PISA to Develop Activities for Teacher Education] and the Michigan Department of Education for its grant to Oakland Schools [Developing Excellence in Learning and Teaching Algebra]. Any opinions, findings, conclusions, or recommendations expressed here are those of the authors and do not necessarily reflect the views of the National Science Foundation and Michigan Department of Education, nor those of any of the folks acknowledged above.

References

Ball, D. L., & Bass, H. (2002). Toward a practice-based theory of mathematical knowledge for teaching. In *Proceedings of the annual meeting of the Canadian Mathematics Education Study Group* (pp. 3–14). Kingston: CMESG.

Ball, D., & Cohen, D. (1999). Developing practice, developing practitioners: Toward a practice-based theory of professional education. In L. Darling-Hammond & G. Sykes (Eds.), *Teaching as the learning profession: Handbook of policy and practice* (pp. 3–32). San Francisco: Jossey-Bass.

Blume, G. W., Zawojewski, J. S., Silver, E. A., & Kenney, P. A. (1998). Focusing on worthwhile mathematical tasks in professional development: Using a task from the national assessment of educational progress. *Mathematics Teacher, 91*, 156–170.

Bransford, J. D., Brown, A. L., & Cocking, R. R. (1999). *How people learn: Brain, mind, experience, and school*. Washington, DC: National Academy Press.

Brown, C. A., & Borko, H. (1992). Becoming a mathematics teacher. In D. A. Grouws (Ed.), *Handbook of research on mathematics teaching and learning* (pp. 209–239). New York: Macmillan.

Brown, C. A., & Clark, L. V. (Eds.). (2006). *Learning from NAEP: Professional development materials for teachers of mathematics*. Reston: National Council of Teachers of Mathematics.

Brown, S., Cooney, T., & Jones, D. (1990). Mathematics teacher education. In W. R. Houston (Ed.), *Handbook of research on teacher education* (pp. 639–656). New York: Macmillan.

Crespo, S. (2000). Seeing more than right and wrong answers: Prospective teachers' interpretations of students' mathematical work. *Journal of Mathematics Teacher Education, 3*, 155–181.

Crockett, M. D. (2002). Inquiry as professional development: Creating dilemmas through teachers' work. *Teaching and Teacher Education, 18*, 609–624.

Davis, B. A. (1994). Mathematics teaching: Moving from telling to listening. *Journal of Curriculum and Supervision, 9*, 267–283.

Davis, B. A. (1996). *Teaching mathematics: Toward a sound alternative*. New York: Garland Publishing.

Davis, B. A. (1997). Listening for differences: An evolving conception of mathematics teaching. *Journal for Research in Mathematics Education, 28*, 355–376.

Doerr, H. M. (2006). Examining the tasks of teaching when using students' mathematical thinking. *Educational Studies in Mathematics, 62*, 3–24.

Fernandez, C. (2002). Learning from Japanese approaches to professional development: The case of lesson study. *Journal of Teacher Education, 53*, 393–405.

Fernandez, C., Cannon, J., & Chokski, S. (2003). A US–Japan lesson study collaboration reveals critical lenses for examining practice. *Teaching and Teacher Education, 19*, 171–185.

Frykholm, J. A. (1999). The impact of reform: Challenges for mathematics teacher preparation. *Journal of Mathematics Teacher Education, 2*, 79–105.

Gearhart, M., Saxe, G. B., Seltzer, M., Schlackman, J., Ching, C. C., Nasir, N., Fall, R., Bennett, T., Rhine, S., & Sloan, T. F. (1999). Opportunities to learn fractions in elementary mathematics classrooms. *Journal for Research in Mathematics Education, 30*, 286–315.

Heid, M. K., Blume, G. W., Zbiek, R. M., & Edwards, B. S. (1999). Factors that influence teachers learning to do interviews to understand students' mathematical understandings. *Educational Studies in Mathematics, 37*, 223–249.

Hughes, E. K. (2006). *Lesson planning as a vehicle for developing pre-service secondary teachers' capacity to focus on students' mathematical thinking*. Doctoral dissertation, University of Pittsburgh, Pittsburgh.

Jansen, A., & Spitzer, S. M. (2009). Prospective middle school mathematics teachers' reflective thinking skills: Descriptions of their students' thinking and interpretations of their teaching. *Journal of Mathematics Teacher Education, 12*, 133–151.

Kazemi, E., & Franke, M. L. (2004). Teacher learning in mathematics: Using student work to promote collective inquiry. *Journal of Mathematics Teacher Education, 7*, 203–235.

Kilpatrick, J., Swafford, J., & Findell, B. (2001). *Adding it up: Helping children learn mathematics.* Washington, DC: National Academies Press.

Krebs, A. S. (2005). Analyzing student work as a professional development activity. *School Science and Mathematics, 105,* 402–411.

Lampert, M. (2001). *Teaching problems and the problems of teaching.* New Haven: Yale University Press.

Lannin, J. K. (2005). Generalization and justification: The challenge of introducing algebraic reasoning through patterning. *Mathematical Thinking and Learning, 7,* 231–258.

Lewis, C. (2002). *Lesson study: A handbook for teacher-led improvement of instruction.* Philadelphia: Research for Better Schools.

Little, J. W. (1999). Organizing schools for teacher learning. In L. Darling-Hammond & G. Sykes (Eds.), *Teaching as the learning profession: Handbook of policy and practice* (pp. 233–262). San Francisco: Jossey-Bass.

Little, J. W. (2002). Professional community and the problem of high school reform. *International Journal of Educational Research, 37,* 693–714.

Little, J. W. (2004). "Looking at student work" in the United States: A case of competing impulses in professional development. In C. Day & J. Sachs (Eds.), *International handbook on the continuing professional development of teachers* (pp. 94–118). Buckingham: Open University Press.

Little, J. W., Gearhart, M., Curry, M., & Kafka, J. (2003). Looking at student work for teacher learning, teacher community, and school reform. *Phi Delta Kappan, 83,* 184–92.

Lortie, D. (1975). *Schoolteacher.* Chicago: University of Chicago Press.

Nathan, M. J., & Koedinger, K. R. (2000a). An investigation of teachers' beliefs of students' algebra development. *Cognition and Instruction, 18,* 209–237.

Nathan, M. J., & Koedinger, K. R. (2000b). Teachers' and researchers' beliefs about the development of algebraic reasoning. *Journal for Research in Mathematics Education, 168–190.*

OECD. (2003). *The PISA 2003 assessment framework – Mathematics, reading, science and problem solving knowledge and skills.* Retrieved June 23, 2013, from http://www.oecd.org/edu/school/programmeforinternationalstudentassessmentpisa/33694881.pdf

OECD. (2006). *PISA released items: Mathematics.* Retrieved June 23, 2013, from http://www.oecd.org/pisa/38709418.pdf

Otero, V. K. (2006). Moving beyond the "get it or don't" conception of formative assessment. *Journal of Teacher Education, 57,* 247–255.

Parke, C., Lane, S., Silver, E. A., & Magone, M. (2003). *Using assessment to improve mathematics teaching and learning: Suggested activities using QUASAR tasks, scoring criteria, and student work.* Reston: National Council of Teachers of Mathematics.

Saxe, G., Gearhart, M., & Nasir, N. (2001). Enhancing students' understanding of mathematics: A study of three contrasting approaches to professional support. *Journal of Mathematics Teacher Education, 4,* 55–79.

Schifter, D., Bastable, V., Russell, S. J. (with Yaffee, L., Lester, J. B., & Cohen, S.). (1999) *Developing mathematical ideas, number and operations. Part 2: Making meaning for operations casebook.* Parsippany: Dale Seymour.

Silver, E. A., Mills, V., Castro, A., & Ghousseini, H. (2006). Blending elements of lesson study with case analysis and discussion: A promising professional development synergy. In K. Lynch-Davis & R. L. Ryder (Eds.), *The work of mathematics teacher educators: Continuing the conversation teaching* (AMTE Monograph Series No. 3, pp. 117–132). San Diego: Association of Mathematics Teacher Educators.

Smith, M. S. (2001). *Practice-based professional development for teachers of mathematics.* Reston: National Council of Teachers of Mathematics.

Stein, M. K., Smith, M. S., Henningsen, M. A., & Silver, E. A. (2000). *Implementing standards-based mathematics instruction: A casebook for professional development.* New York: Teachers College Press.

Stylianou, D. A., Kenney, P. A., Silver, E. A., & Alacaci, C. (2000). Gaining insight into students' thinking through assessment tasks. *Mathematics Teaching in the Middle School, 6,* 136–144.

Thompson, A. G. (1992). Teachers' beliefs and conceptions: A synthesis of the research. In D. Grouws (Ed.), *Handbook of research on mathematics teaching and learning* (pp. 127–146). New York: Macmillan.

Thompson, A. G., Philipp, R. A., Thompson, P. W., & Boyd, B. A. (1994). Calculational and conceptual orientations in teaching mathematics. In D. B. Aichelle & A. F. Coxford (Eds.), *Professional development for mathematics teachers* (pp. 79–92). Reston: National Council of Teachers of Mathematics.

Wallach, T., & Even, R. (2005). Hearing students: The complexity of understanding what they are saying, showing, and doing. *Journal of Mathematics Teacher Education, 8*, 393–417.

Wilson, S. M., & Berne, J. (1999). Teacher learning and the acquisition of professional knowledge: An examination of research on contemporary professional development. *Review of Research in Education, 24*, 173–209.

Cases as a Vehicle for Developing Knowledge Needed for Teaching

Margaret S. Smith, Justin Boyle, Fran Arbaugh, Michael D. Steele, and Gabriel Stylianides

Abstract In this chapter, we describe a practice-based curriculum for the professional education of preservice and practicing secondary mathematics teachers that (1) focuses on reasoning-and-proving, (2) has narrative cases as an integrated component, and (3) supports the development of knowledge of mathematics needed for teaching. We first provide an argument for the importance of reasoning-and-proving in the secondary curriculum and the unique role that cases can serve in providing opportunities to develop teachers' knowledge of mathematics, students learning, and teaching practices. We then provide an overview of the practice-based curriculum and discuss the overarching questions that have guided its design and development. We conclude with a discussion of what teachers appeared to learn from their experiences with the curriculum, with a particular emphasis on what the narrative cases appear to have contributed to their learning.

M.S. Smith (✉)
Department of Instruction and Learning, School of Education,
University of Pittsburgh, 230 S. Bouquet Street, Pittsburgh, PA 15260, USA
e-mail: pegs@pitt.edu

J. Boyle
College of Education, University of New Mexico,
Hokona Hall, Albuquerque, NM 87131, USA

F. Arbaugh
Department of Curriculum and Instruction, Pennsylvania State University,
259 Chambers Building, University Park, PA 16802, USA
e-mail: efa2@psu.edu

M.D. Steele
Department of Curriculum and Instruction, School of Education,
University of Wisconsin-Milwaukee, Milwaukee, WI, USA

G. Stylianides
Department of Education, University of Oxford, 15 Norham Gardens, Oxford OX2 6PY, UK
e-mail: gabriel.stylianides@education.ox.ac.uk

Y. Li et al. (eds.), *Transforming Mathematics Instruction: Multiple Approaches and Practices*, Advances in Mathematics Education, DOI 10.1007/978-3-319-04993-9_18,
© Springer International Publishing Switzerland 2014

Keywords Narrative cases • Knowledge needed for teaching • Teacher learning • Reasoning-and-proving

Ball and her colleagues (2001, 2005, 2008) have argued that mathematics teachers are a special class of users of mathematics and that what they need to teach mathematics effectively goes beyond what is needed by other well-educated adults, including mathematicians. Ball et al. (2008) describe *domains of knowledge of mathematics for teaching* as including subject matter knowledge (common content knowledge and specialized content knowledge) and pedagogical content knowledge (knowledge of content and students and knowledge of content and teaching).

In addition to identifying the kind of knowledge that teachers need for their work, a complimentary and equally important question is how to best foster this knowledge. Specifically, the more practical question that surfaces is: How can opportunities for teacher learning be designed so as to foster a knowledge base for teaching mathematics that is broad, integrated, and connected to practice? University mathematics courses, designed for professional mathematicians and technical users of mathematics, do not seem to meet the needs of teachers (Howe 1999). According to Ball (1990), "even successful participation in traditional math classes does not necessarily develop the kinds of understanding needed to teach if, as is often the case, success in these classes derives from memorizing formulas and performing procedures" (p. 27). Such university mathematics courses might support the development of common content knowledge for a wide range of mathematics users, but are not equipped to support the unique needs of teachers.

In a seminal paper, Ball and Cohen (1999) laid a foundation of a promising approach to the professional education of teachers. They argue that "teachers' everyday work could become a source for constructive professional development" (p. 6) through the development of a curriculum for professional learning that is grounded in the tasks, questions, and problems of practice. Their proposal is that teachers' professional practice be seen both as a site for professional learning and also as a stimulus for developing inquiry into practice from which many teachers could learn. To accomplish this goal, they argue that records of authentic practice – curriculum materials, narrative or video summaries of teachers planning for and/ or engaging in instruction, and samples of student work – should become the core of professional education, providing a focus for sustained teacher inquiry and investigation. Finally, Ball and Cohen caution designers of professional development experiences to avoid "simply reproducing the kind of fragmented, unfocused, and superficial work that already characterizes professional development" (p. 29).

The purpose of this chapter is to provide a detailed description of a practice-based curriculum for secondary mathematics teachers and discuss the potential of the curriculum for developing knowledge needed for teaching and, ultimately, for transforming mathematics instruction. The particular instantiation of a practice-based curriculum discussed herein focuses on reasoning-and-proving and has narrative cases as an integrated component. We begin with an argument for the importance of reasoning-and-proving in the secondary curriculum and the unique role that cases (which are the centerpiece of the curriculum) can serve in providing opportunities to develop teachers' knowledge of mathematics, students' learning, and teaching practices. We then provide an overview of the curriculum framed by the overarching questions that have guided its design and development, with particular emphasis on the construction of the narrative cases. We conclude with a discussion of what teachers with whom we have worked appeared to learn from their experiences with *Case of Reasoning-and-Proving in Secondary Mathematics* (CORP), with a particular emphasis on what the narrative cases appear to have contributed to their learning.

Background

Why Reasoning-and-Proving?

Although reasoning-and-proving represents a mathematical practice that transcends mathematical content areas (Hanna 1989, 1991, 1995; NCTM 2000; Schoenfeld 1994) in secondary mathematics classrooms, proof has been traditionally conceptualized as a particular type of exercise exemplified by the two-column format and found primarily in a single high school geometry course. Research shows that proof construction is a difficult activity for students (e.g., Bell 1976; Chazan 1993; Healy and Hoyles 2000; Lannin 2005; Senk 1985; Smith 2006), prospective teachers (e.g. Morris 2002; Selden and Selden 2003), and practicing teachers (e.g. Bieda 2010; Furinghetti and Morselli 2009; Knuth 2002a, b; Kotelawala 2009; Martin et al. 2005; Steele and Rogers 2012). Chazan (1993) reports that the 9th- and 10th-grade students had difficulty understanding the role of proof, particularly in distinguishing between proof and empirical evidence. Similar results were noted for secondary teachers (Knuth 2002a, b). Many teachers favored the empirical arguments over the proofs, finding them more convincing or easier to follow (Knuth 2002a). Secondary mathematics teachers tend to view proof largely as a specific topic of study rather than as a tool for doing mathematics or as a stance toward mathematics in general (Furinghetti and Morselli 2009; Knuth 2002b; Kotelawala 2009). This view stands in sharp contrast with the practice of mathematicians, where proof is used to justify new results and verify the results of others (Hanna 1995), and is the culmination of a series of activities (e.g., Lakatos 1976).

Teachers' current understanding of proof and its value in the secondary curriculum are of particular concern in light of the growing consensus that secondary mathematics programs need a greater emphasis on mathematical reasoning and proof. For example, the Common Core State Standards Initiative (National Governors Association Center for Best Practices, Council of Chief State School

Officers 2010) identifies reasoning abstractly and quantitatively and constructing viable arguments as key mathematical practices that students need to develop across a breadth of content areas. The authors of *Focus in High School Mathematics: Reasoning and Sense Making* (NCTM 2009) argue that reasoning and sensemaking "should occur in every mathematics classroom everyday" (p. 5). Making reasoning-and-proving a central feature of classroom instruction will require helping teachers understand both the role these mathematical processes can and should play in secondary mathematics and instructional approaches for developing their students' abilities to engage in a broad range of reasoning-and-proving activities.

Why Cases?

Materials that can effectively support teachers as they develop their pedagogical practice must assist teachers in developing a capacity for connecting the specifics of real-time, deeply contextualized teaching moments with a broader set of ideas about mathematics, about teaching, and about learning. Cases can play a key role by serving as prototypes (Shulman 1992) that instantiate a larger set of ideas about mathematics and classroom instruction. As with all good cases, prototype cases provide elaborate detail about a situation, allowing readers to experience its complexity, including teachers' thinking processes and the accompanying affect. In addition, prototype cases are theoretically specified; that is, they are situated within a larger theoretical framework that teachers can ultimately come to apprehend and utilize to make sense of new situations that they encounter. Toward this end, case discussions are crucial. They highlight the question, "What is this a case of?," thus stimulating learners "to move up and down, back and forth, between the memorable particularities of cases and the powerful generalizations and simplifications of principles and theories" (Shulman 1996, p. 201). Through reading and discussing cases, teachers can connect the events depicted in cases to their knowledge of mathematics, learning, and teaching and to their own practice.

While there is considerable enthusiasm for using cases in teacher education, and many claims regarding the efficacy of this approach (e.g., Merseth 1991; Sykes and Bird 1992), establishing an empirical basis for these claims has been a slow process. In 1999, Merseth noted "the conversations about case-based instruction over the last two decades has been full of heat, but with very little light" (p. xiv). Although much more work is needed, research on the use of cases does provide evidence that they can be used to enhance teachers' pedagogical thinking and reasoning skills (e.g., Barnett 1991), reason through dilemmas of practice (e.g., Harrington 1995; Markovits and Even 1999; Markovits and Smith 2008), support inquiry into classroom practices (e.g., Broudy 1990), learn key pedagogical practices that support student learning (e.g., Hillen and Hughes 2008), and facilitate the development of content knowledge (e.g., Merseth and Lacey 1993).

Cases of Reasoning-and-Proving: A Curriculum for Secondary Teacher Learning

The development of the curriculum, *Cases of Reasoning-and-Proving in Secondary Mathematics* (*CORP*), was guided by three overarching questions: (1) What is reasoning-and-proving? (2) How do secondary students benefit from engaging in reasoning-and-proving? (3) How can teachers support the development of students' capacity to reason-and-prove? Across six units (as shown in Table 1), teachers explore these questions through engagement in a variety of activities that include solving and discussing challenging mathematical tasks; analyzing narrative cases that make salient the relationship between teaching and learning and the ways in which student learning can be supported; examining and interpreting student work that features a range of solution strategies, representations, and misconceptions; and making connections to their own teaching practice.

Table 1 Overview of the six units in the CORP curriculum

Unit	Title	Description
1	Motivating the Need for Proof	In this unit, we focus on the limitations of empirical arguments and create an "intellectual need" (Harel 1998, 2013) for proof. Work centers around solving the task sequence (shown in Fig. 3), developed in a 4-year design experiment in an undergraduate mathematics course for prospective teachers (see Stylianides and Stylianides 2009), and analyzing two narrative cases in which high school teachers enacted the same task sequence with different outcomes.
2	Exploring the Nature of Reasoning-and-Proving	In this unit, we focus on developing criteria for proof that can be used to scrutinize arguments, to make decisions about the relative mathematical rigor of arguments, and to decide whether or not an argument counts as proof. The reasoning-and-proving framework (Stylianides 2008) is used to make salient the range of practices that support the ability to write proofs and to classify tasks (in terms of the practices they target). Work centers around solving the odd and even task – *prove that the sum of two odd numbers is always even* – and analyzing a set of student solutions to the task.
3	Supporting Students' Development of the Capacity to Reason-and-Prove	In this unit, we focus on how three dimensions of classrooms that promote understanding (Carpenter and Lehrer 1999; Hiebert et al 1997) – tasks, tools, and talk – shape students' opportunities to develop the capacity to reason-and-prove and how the teacher plays a central role in this effort. Work centers around the analysis of two narrative cases – one which features the odd and even task introduced in unit 2 and the other that focuses on the relationships between pairs of angles formed by two intersecting lines.

(continued)

Table 1 (continued)

Unit	Title	Description
4	Modifying Tasks to Increase the Reasoning-and-Proving Potential	In this unit, we focus on the limited availability of reasoning-and-proving tasks in typical textbooks (Thompson et al. 2012) and the ways in which mathematical tasks found can be modified in order to increase their reasoning-and-proving potential. Work centers around analyzing pairs of tasks and their modifications, abstracting general principles that could be used to modify tasks more broadly, and using the modification principles to alter additional tasks.
5	Making Connections: Using the Problem Context to Explain a Generalization	In this unit, we focus on how the context of the problem can help in making sense of mathematics. The five different representations of mathematical ideas – pictures, written symbols, language, real-world situations (i.e., context), and manipulative models (Clements 2004; Lesh et al. 1987) – are introduced as tools for building meaning and understanding the connections that can be made between the context and other representational forms. Work centers on solving the Sticky Gum task (shown in Fig. 2), analyzing a set of student solutions to the task, and analyzing two narrative cases in which teachers enacted the same task in their high school classrooms.
6	Making Connections: Using Visual Representations of Proofs to Explain Mathematics	In this unit, we focus on how pictures or diagrams can be a particularly compelling way to represent a proof because the visual images can help the viewer gain insight into why the conjecture is correct by "seeing" how the idea is illustrated geometrically or diagrammatically (Bell 2011; Knuth 2002c; Nelson 1993). The five representations of mathematical ideas discussed in Unit 5 are used again here to consider connections between "pictures" and other representation forms. Work centers on solving the number patterns task – *prove the claim that the difference of the squares of two consecutive whole numbers is equal to the sum of the two numbers* – and analyzing a narrative case in which a teacher enacts the same task in his high school classroom.

The map of a course built around these materials (see Fig. 1[1]) shows the range and sequence of CORP activities. For example, teachers always have an opportunity to engage in a mathematical task as a learner (rectangle) before analyzing either a case (oval) or student work samples (hexagon) based on the same task. There are several reasons for this sequencing: (1) teachers go on to read the case with much more interest and confidence; (2) engaging in the tasks allows misconceptions that the teachers themselves may have to surface and be

---

[1] The particular iteration of the course depicted in Fig. 1 was conducted over 12 sessions, each of which is represented by a column in the figure. Across different iterations of the course, what remains constant is the sequence of activities.

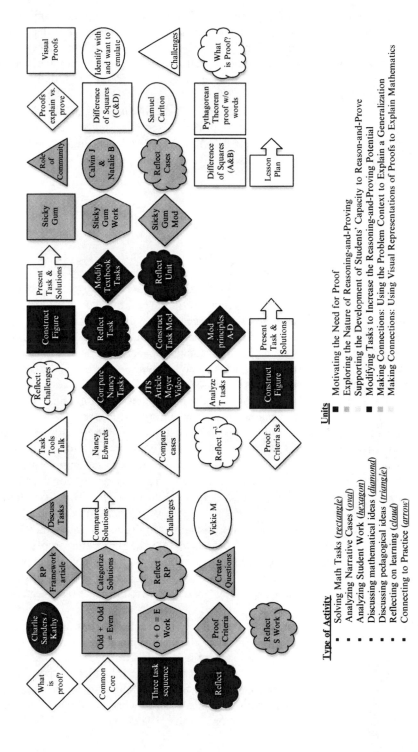

Fig. 1 The configuration of ideas and activities in the CORP materials

discussed; and (3) teachers are "primed for" and able to recognize many of the solution strategies put forth by students. Finally, Steele (2008) argues that working on the task and then engaging in a discussion of the case provide teachers with the opportunity to integrate their subject matter and pedagogical content knowledge and "create a more powerful learning experience than either activity might have afforded individually" (p. 15). Toward this end, it is critical that teachers engage in a mathematical discussion, based on a specific mathematical task that is connected to a particular case or set of student responses, that serves to support *their* learning. The goal of the course is to develop teachers understanding of reasoning-and-proving and their capacity to support their students' engagement in these practices.

Overarching Question 1: What Is Reasoning-and-Proving?

Our conceptualization of reasoning-and-proving is based on the view that while generalized deductive arguments establishing mathematical truth (i.e., proofs) are the ultimate goals of proving in mathematics, there are a number of other mathematical activities in which students can engage that will build their capacity to produce proofs. The work in which mathematicians themselves engage that culminates in a proof involves searching mathematical phenomena for patterns, making conjectures about those patterns, and providing informal arguments demonstrating the viability of the conjecture (e.g., Lakatos 1976). These activities aid any doer of mathematics in exploring the mathematical landscape associated with the phenomenon under examination, connecting the phenomenon to established mathematical ideas, and building a foundation for the development of a more formalized and general deductive argument. The heavy focus on the finished product in secondary classrooms (the proof, often in the 2-column form) does not afford students the same level of scaffolding used by professional users of mathematics to establish mathematical truth (Chazan 1990). Thus, we define *reasoning-and-proving* to encompass the breadth of the activity associated with identifying patterns, making conjectures, providing proofs, and providing non-proof arguments (Stylianides 2008, 2010). Further, we take the stance that proofs can be of different types including generic examples and demonstrations (e.g., direct proofs, proofs by exhaustion, mathematical induction, counterexample), take different forms (e.g., two-column, paragraph, flow chart), and use different representations (e.g., symbols, pictures, words).

The CORP materials provide the opportunity for teachers to explore reasoning-and-proving tasks, to analyze cases (detailed classroom episodes) in which a teacher is enacting the same reasoning-and-proving task with secondary students, and to analyze sets of student solutions for a subset of the tasks. While these activities have the potential to support the development of teachers' capacity to construct proofs, the main purpose is for teachers to broaden their view of what constitutes reasoning-and-proving. For example, as the participants solve *A Sticky Gum Problem* in Unit 5

A Sticky Gum Problem

Ms. Hernandez came across a gumball machine one day when she was out with her twins. Of course, the twins each wanted a gumball. What's more, they insisted on being given gumballs of the same color. The gumballs were a penny each, and there would be no way to tell which color would come out next. Ms. Hernandez decides that she will keep putting in pennies until she gets two gumballs that are the same color. She can see that there are only red and white gumballs in the machine.

1. Why is three cents the most she will have to spend to satisfy her twins?

2. The next day, Ms. Hernandez passes a gumball machine with red, white, and blue gumballs. How could Ms. Hernandez satisfy her twins with their need for the same color this time? That is, what is the most Ms. Hernandez might have to spend that day?

3. Here comes Mr. Hodges with his triplets past the gumball machine in question 2. Of course, all three of his children want to have the same color gumball. What is the most he might have to spend?

4. Generalize this problem as much as you can. Vary the number of colors. What about different size families? Prove your generalization to show that it always works for any number of children and any number of gumball colors.

Adapted from "A Sticky Gum Problem" in Aha! Insight by Martin Gardner, W. H. Freeman and Company, New York City / San Francisco, 1978. Interactive Mathematics Program www.mathimp.org

Fig. 2 A Sticky Gum Problem

(see Fig. 2), they are expected to engage in the full range of activities that are often part of developing a proof: identifying a pattern, making a conjecture, and then developing an argument to justify their conjecture. Other tasks, such as the Sum of Two Odds Task in Unit 2 (*prove that when you add any 2 odd numbers your answer is always even*), ask participants to engage only in the final activity of providing a proof.

The tasks also provide an opportunity for teachers to examine strong assumptions they may have regarding what counts as proof. For example, the Unit 1 sequence of three tasks (shown in Fig. 3) is intended to make salient that empirical arguments are not proofs (i.e., checking a proper subset of all the possible cases in a generalization is not enough to show that the generalization is always true), a misconception that is held by students and teachers alike (Knuth 2002a, b) and also encouraged in many mathematics textbooks. In addition, the analysis of student work samples that show a range of proofs and non-proof arguments lead teachers to begin to consider that it is the alignment with the criteria needed for proof rather than its form that determines its validity. Finally, the cases provide teachers with the opportunity to consider what reasoning-and-proving "looks like" in secondary classrooms (i.e., what is it students are doing and saying in classrooms where reasoning-and-proving is targeted).

Task 1 – The Squares Problem

1. How many different 3-by-3 squares are there in the 4-by-4 square below?
2. How many different 3-by-3 squares are there in a 5-by-5 square?
3. How many different 3-by-3 squares are there in a 60-by-60 square? Are you sure that your answer is correct? Why?

Task 2 - The Circle and Spots Problem
Place different numbers of spots around a circle and join each pair of spots by straight lines. Explore a possible relation between the number of spots and the greatest number of non-overlapping regions into which the circle can be divided by this means. When there are 15 spots around the circle, is there an easy way to tell for sure what is the greatest number of non-overlapping regions into which the circle can be divided?

Task 3 – Looking for a Square Number Problem
Does the expression $1 + 1141n^2$ (where n is a natural number) ever give a square number?
Stylianides & Stylianides (2009)

Fig. 3 Sequence of three tasks in Unit 1

Overarching Question 2: How Do Secondary Students Benefit from Engaging in Reasoning-and-Proving?

Reasoning-and-proving supports the development of a habit of mind that is useful in mathematics and beyond. The authors of *Focus in High School Mathematics: Reasoning and Sense Making* (NCTM 2009) explain that reasoning and sensemaking (which includes proof) will "enhance students' development of both content and process knowledge they need to be successful in their continued study of mathematics and in their lives" (p. 7). In particular, reasoning and sensemaking skills support informed decision-making, promote quantitative literacy, support civic engagement, and position graduates to lead in an increasingly technological economy and workforce (American Diploma Project 2004; NCTM 2009).

In CORP, teachers have the opportunity to consider the benefits of engaging secondary students in reasoning-and-proving through two types of activities: (1) the analysis of narrative cases that feature secondary school teachers and their students engaged in reasoning-and-proving activities and (2) through their implementation of and reflection on reasoning-and-proving tasks in their own classrooms. In Unit 3, for example, teachers analyze two narrative cases in which students are engaged in tasks that are intended to develop their capacity to reason-and-prove. Through their careful analysis of what students are being asked to do, how the case teachers support students' work, and what students appear to learn from the experience, teachers come to see the ways in which students can grow mathematically and begin to develop useful habits of mind with appropriate support and nurturing. In other narrative cases, such as in Unit 1, teachers will learn that students engaging in appropriate tasks without sufficient teacher support is not enough to develop reasoning-and-proving skills.

Overarching Question 3: How Can Teachers Support the Development of Students' Capacity to Reason-and-Prove?

In order for students to have increased opportunities to engage in the range of activities associated with reasoning-and-proving, classrooms must be transformed so that understanding and justifying why things work as they do becomes commonplace. Reasoning-and-proving cannot be learned in classrooms where teachers demonstrate how to do procedures and students practice applying learned procedures with no emphasis on sensemaking – the current practice in far too many classrooms where proof has become a ritual to be performed rather than a process through which learning and understanding are developed.

The CORP materials identify three dimensions of classrooms as essential to this transformation: (a) the set of tasks or activities in which students engage should be high level (Stein et al. 1996) and provide opportunities for students to look for patterns, make conjectures, and develop arguments (Stylianides 2008); (b) tools should be available to support students' reasoning and sensemaking as they engage with challenging tasks (Hiebert et al 1997); and (c) productive classroom talk must support powerful discourse about mathematics and enable students to share and refine their ideas (Herbel-Eisenmann et al. 2013). While tasks, tools, and talk have been identified as critical dimensions of classrooms that promote understanding (Carpenter and Lehrer 1999; Hiebert et al 1997), we argue that they are of paramount importance in classrooms that promote reasoning-and-proving. Tasks, tools, and talk work in concert to create an environment that supports students' growth and development as mathematical thinkers and learners. Across the CORP units, teachers have the opportunity to investigate how the tasks, tools, and talk in classrooms featured in a set of narrative cases afford and constraint students' opportunities to develop the capacity to reason-and-prove and how the teachers play a central role in the outcome of this instruction. In particular, the cases provide teachers with the opportunity to grapple with the complexities of supporting students' learning and engagement in reasoning-and-proving and to begin to identify ways in which teachers can, through their actions and interactions, support and inhibit student learning.

Development the CORP Cases and Related Materials

The first step in developing the CORP materials was to create a research-based framework that identified aspects of reasoning-and-proving and pedagogical strategies that we wanted to target in the materials. In particular, the framework (shown in Table 2) highlights what teachers need to know and be able to do related to reasoning-and-proving in order to transform current classroom practices and pedagogy that has been documented as supporting student learning.

The next step in the process involved identifying tasks that could make salient specific aspects of reasoning-and-proving (shown in Table 2, column 1) and classrooms in which the tasks were being used that would provide instantiations of a subset of the pedagogical strategies (shown in Table 2, column 2). Identifying secondary school classrooms where teachers were engaged in enacting high-level reasoning-and-proving tasks in their classrooms was a challenge, however, since the practice we were trying to capture did not represent the instruction found in most secondary schools (e.g., we were trying to document the very nonnormative practice that our materials were trying to promote). To address this issue, two different methods were used to generate the cases: (1) we selected a reasoning-and-proving task, provided a group of teachers with whom we were working with professional development focused on the task and its implementation (e.g., solving and discussing the task, considering different solution paths students might take), video recorded their enactment of the task in teachers' own classroom, and interviewed teachers following the lesson; and (2) we identified teachers implementing promising curricula and video recorded a series of instructional episodes over time. The video recordings and related material collected from this effort were reviewed and classroom episodes that were aligned with the development framework were identified.

At this point, the team developed the first drafts of the narrative cases[2]. Each case portrays the events that unfolded in a secondary school mathematics classroom as a teacher engaged students in solving a challenging mathematical task that requires them to use the processes of reasoning-and-proving. Each case begins with a description of the teacher, the students, and the school, so as to provide a context for understanding and interpreting the portrayed episode. A description of the teacher's goal for the lesson follows this description. The unfolding of the actual lesson is next, communicated in a fairly detailed way; this description of the lesson constitutes the largest portion of the case overall. The cases illustrate authentic practice – what really happens in a mathematics classroom when teachers endeavor to teach mathematics in ways that challenge students to reason-and-prove. As such they are not intended as exemplars of the best practice to be emulated, but rather as examples to be analyzed so as to better understand the relationship between tasks, tools, and talk and students' opportunities to engage in reasoning-and-proving practices. (See Table 3 for details about each of the cases in CORP.)

In particular, each case highlights the ways in which the teachers' selection of a "task" frames the work students do, the "tools" that they make available to assist

---

[2] While the cases are based on real events, they have been enhanced at times in order to bring out specific aspects of instruction we wish to highlight.

Table 2 The framework used to guide material development

Aspects of reasoning-and-proving	Pedagogical strategies
• Identifying a pattern, making a conjecture, forming a generalization, proving a claim is always true	• Selecting and implementing cognitively challenging tasks
• Using counterexamples to (dis)prove a claim	• Developing an sequence of instructional tasks that moves students along a learning trajectory
• Recognizing the limitations of empirical arguments	• Enacting a set of norms and practices that facilitate reasoning-and-proving
• Understanding the role of definition and assumptions in proof	• Orchestrating a productive discussion
	• Using a variety of tools to support learning
• Evaluating a collection of arguments in terms of their power to prove	• Asking questions that clarify, probe, and extend student thinking
• Using different methods (e.g., mathematical induction, contradiction, exhaustion) to prove a claim	• Modifying tasks so as to provide more opportunities for reasoning-and-proving
	• Encouraging problem posing
• Representing a proof in different ways (e.g., 2-column, visual diagram, flow chart)	• Assessing student learning
	• Reflecting on teaching and learning

students in sensemaking, and the classroom "talk." Specifically, while all of the teachers featured in the cases selected a task that has the potential to engage students in aspects of reasoning-and-proving, they are differentially successful in their efforts to develop students' reasoning-and-proving capacity. For example, in the case of Charlie Sanders (Unit 1), students' use of Geometer's Sketchpad to solve the Circle and Spots Problem (Task 2 of the sequence shown in Fig. 3) interfered with the task's goal of identifying the limitations of extending patterns. Charlie Sanders' students were more concerned about generating examples than looking for patterns across examples. By contrast, Nancy Edwards' (Unit 3) suggestion that students use square tiles to model odd numbers – specifically what it means to have "one left over" when you divide by two – allowed them to make progress on proving that the sum of two odd numbers is even. Some of the featured teachers (i.e., Charlie Sanders in Unit 1 and Samuel Carlson in Unit 6) did too much of the talking, telling, and thinking during the class, thereby providing limited opportunities for students' sensemaking and limiting the teacher's insight into what students were thinking. Other teachers (i.e., Kathy in Unit 1 and Vickie Mansfield and Nancy Edwards in Unit 3) used tasks, tools, and talk in ways that supported students' learning. The continuum shown in Fig. 4 situates each of the seven case teachers in terms of their success in supporting students learning and their ability to engage in reasoning-and-proving.

We find Charlie Sanders and Samuel Carlson at the low end of the continuum. Neither of these two teachers attended to student thinking and appeared to be more interested in students providing specific answers to routine questions. However, Charlie did allow time for students to work in groups, and some student groups without Charlie's support were still able to make progress in their understanding of reasoning-and-proving. Calvin Jensen and Natalie Boyer both attended more to what their students were saying than Charlie and Samuel did, but were unable to make progress in

Table 3 A Summary of the cases that appear in the CORP units

Unit	Title of case	Mathematical task	Professional learning task	What it is a "case of"
1	Developing in Students a Need For Proof: The Case of Charlie Sanders	See the three task sequence in Fig. 1	*Discussion* Consider the ways in which Kathy's implementation of the task sequence is similar to or different from Charlie's implementation of the same sequence. *Be sure to cite evidence to support your claims.*	Throughout the lesson, Charlie failed to draw students' attention to what they should be getting out of each task in the sequence. As a result, he negatively impacted students' opportunities to reflect on how each task in the sequence was challenging specific misconceptions they had about empirical arguments being proofs.
	Breaking the Equation "Empirical Argument = Proof" (The Case of Kathy)[a]		*Reflection* Did the instructional differences identified in Kathy and Charlie's classrooms matter with respect to student learning outcomes? Explain your position.	Kathy structured the lesson so that by the time students had completed the third task they realized they needed to learn about a more secure validation method – which is the purpose of the task sequence.

3

Writing and Critiquing Proofs: The Case of Vicky Mansfield

In the diagram, suppose the lines intersect so that $m\angle DBA = m\angle CBD$
Draw and prove conclusions about pairs of angles[b]

Pressing Students to Prove It: The Case of Nancy Edwards

Prove that the sum of two odd numbers is always even

Discussion

- What did the students in Vicky Mansfield's class appear to be learning and how did she support their learning?
- Identify the ways in which Nancy Edwards used tasks, tools, and talk to support her students' capacity to reason-and-prove. Keep track of evidence (i.e., line numbers) from the case to support your claims.

Reflection

- What lessons have you learned from your analysis of the two cases – Vicky Mansfield and Nancy Edwards – that apply to teaching reasoning-and-proving more broadly?
- Some math educators argue that the tasks used by both Nancy Edwards and Vicky Mansfield are too easy for high school students. What is your reaction to this claim? How do the teachers use the tasks to make them problematic for their students? What learning residue do you believe students leave each of these classes with?

Nancy and Vicky's use of appropriate tasks, the availability of different tools to encourage sense making, and their facilitation of both small and whole discussions that focused on the work of students supported their learning of what proof entails.

(continued)

Table 3 (continued)

Unit	Title of case	Mathematical task	Professional learning task	What it is a "case of"
5	Making Sure that All Students Understand: The Case of Calvin Jenson	A Sticky Gum Problem shown in Fig. 2	*Discussion* What does each teacher do to support (or inhibit) his/her students learning? Pay particular attention to the ways that tasks, tools, and talk supported or inhibited student learning. Be sure to list line numbers to support your claims.	Calvin may have spent too much time drilling students on the first part of the task and therefore made limited progress during the lesson on the more challenging aspects of the task.
	Helping Students Connect Pictorial and Symbolic Representations: The Case of Natalie Boyer		*Reflection* What lessons have you learned from the set of "Sticky Gum" experiences (i.e., solving the task, analyzing student work, analyzing cases) that you could apply to teaching more broadly?	Natalie used the context to help students make sense of the situation. However, her revision of the problem – eliminating exploring triplets – may have made it more difficult for students to generalize the situation.

| 6 | Using Visual Diagrams to Help Students "See It": The Case of Samuel Carlton | Explore the difference of the squares of two consecutive whole numbers, identify a pattern, and prove that the pattern of differences is certain to continue as the sequence of squares is extended[b] | *Discussion*
• What did the students in Samuel Carlton's classroom appear to be learning? *Be sure to provide evidence (line numbers) to support your claims.*
• What did Samuel Carlton do to support or inhibit his students' learning? What specific role did tasks, tools, and talk play in the outcome of the lesson? *Be sure to provide evidence to support your claims.*

Reflection
What did the case of Samuel Carlson contribute to your understanding of reasoning-and-proving and how to teach it? | Samuel does most of the talking in this class, and therefore we have limit insight into what students know and can do. The task may have been too structured – steering students thinking in a particular direction and leaving limiting the opportunity to explore the situation in different ways. |

[a]This case is excerpted from A. Stylianides (2009)

[b]These are abbreviated versions of the tasks that actually appear in the case

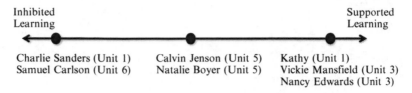

Fig. 4 The continuum of case teachers' success at supporting student learning

moving students' thinking toward the mathematical goals of the lessons, and Calvin purposely slowed students' progress so that every student was at the same part of the task at the same time. Finally, Kathy, Nancy Edwards, and Vickie Mansfield each facilitated their students' thinking toward the mathematical goal, but it was more evident in Nancy's case how all students were making reasoning-and-proving progress. By engaging teachers in the analysis of cases along the continuum, teachers have the opportunity to consider effective vs. ineffective pedagogy and what it might take to transform an unsuccessful lesson in to one that is more productive. In addition, teachers begin to identify with particular teachers in terms of where they are now in their teaching practice vs. where they would ultimately like to be and to consider how to get there.

In addition to the cases themselves, we also created professional learning tasks in which teachers engage as they explore the cases (see Column 4 of Table 3). In general, the discussion questions engage teachers in analyzing the particulars of each case and the reflection questions ask teachers to think more broadly about what is learned from the case and what it means more generally. Through their analysis and discussion of a case, teachers have the opportunity to develop knowledge of content and students (e.g., develop ability to predict what students are likely to do with specific tasks, anticipate student errors) and knowledge of content and teaching (e.g., how to sequence instruction, how to support student's ability to reason about mathematical relationships and develop proofs that support their conjectures, how to use student's approaches to advance the mathematics learning of the group).

The final step in creating the CORP materials was to sequence the activities within each unit and across units so as to ensure that later experiences in the curriculum built on earlier ones, that key ideas were revisited in different times in different ways, and that as a whole the ideas articulated in the development framework (Table 2) were sufficiently addressed.

Discussion

The purpose of this chapter was to provide a description of a practice-based curriculum and discuss the potential of the curriculum for developing knowledge needed for teaching and, ultimately, for transforming mathematics instruction. Through carefully designed sequences of activity (i.e., solving mathematical tasks, analyzing narrative cases, and examining student work samples), teachers have the opportunity to better understand what reasoning-and-proving is, the role of reasoning-and-proving

Table 4 Participants' responses to interview questions

Question	Categories	No. of participants
1. How has the course influenced your thinking about reasoning-and-proving or about teaching reasoning-and-proving?	Course provided tools for *how* to support learning of reasoning-and-proving	13 of 18
	Students need to learn how to construct proofs. Explicit attention is needed	12 of 18
	A valid argument does not need to follow a particular form or structure	8 of 18
	Constructing proofs can build students' understanding of mathematics	8 of 18
2. What specific activities do you believe have influenced your thinking about reasoning-and-proving or about teaching reasoning-and-proving?	Reading and discussing the cases	12 of 18
	Modifying tasks in order to increase the opportunities to reason-and-prove	12 of 18
	Analyzing student solutions to reasoning-and-proving tasks	10 of 18
	Solving mathematical tasks that engaged us in reasoning-and-proving	9 of 18

in mathematics and the secondary curriculum, and ways to support the development of students' capacity to engage in reasoning-and-proving through the use of appropriate tasks, tools, and talk.

We argued that the cases at the heart of the CORP play a critical role in supporting teacher learning by providing teachers with authentic contexts for considering mathematics content, pedagogy, and students as learners *and* how teachers' actions and interactions can support or inhibit what students learn about mathematics. As Lee Shulman (1992, p. 28) noted,

> ...cases integrate what otherwise remains separated. Content and process, thought and feeling, teaching and learning are not addressed theoretically as distinct constructs. They occur simultaneously as they do in real life, posing problems, issues, and challenges for new teachers that their knowledge and experiences can be used to discern.

Our use of the CORP materials with practicing and preservice teachers to date provides some evidence to suggest that the materials in general, and the cases in particular, can influence teachers' knowledge and beliefs related to reasoning-and-proving, a first step in influencing classroom practice. For example, the results of an analysis of the interview data collected from 18 teachers at the end of a course built around the CORP materials (outlined in Fig. 1) suggest that cases played an important role in shaping teachers understanding of reasoning-and-proving and the ways in which they can support the development of these practices in their own students. As shown in Table 4, teachers' responses suggest that their thinking about reasoning-and-proving had been influenced in important ways. They claimed to have acquired tools that would aid them in supporting students learning, and they indicated that they had come to realize that explicit instruction regarding proof was needed. As Karen explained,

> I think I just want to start from the beginning of the year, talking about how important it is to provide justification and to be thinking about how you can support your answers, so like to say, "Is that enough to convince a skeptic?" or whatever. I want to start with that right off the bat, saying things like that, to get students in the mindset of "How am I supporting what I'm saying? How do I know my answer's always going to work?" It's strange because that's something you have to start from at the very, very beginning. I really can't just start it in the middle of the year and expect everything to be perfect. It's definitely a process.

In addition, teachers came to understand that valid arguments could take different forms and that constructing proofs was not just an end but rather a means for developing understanding of mathematics more generally. This perspective stands in sharp contrast to the findings of earlier research (e.g., Knuth 2002b).

Participants' responses to interview question 2 make salient the activities in which teachers engaged that they felt most impacted their thinking about reasoning-and-proving. Of particular note in this discussion is the fact that 12 of the 18 participants (67 %) indicated that reading and discussing the cases were a contributing factor to their learning. As two participants explained,

> I have to say all of the [case] studies. Like Nancy Edwards…'Cause that really gave us a means to talk about what is good reasoning proving instruction and what isn't. And then like to see like where we are if we are able to like compare ourselves to what we thought was good and bad and then help us figure out what we might need to do to help us. (Brittany)
> I like the class discussions [in the cases] since they [the students] were thinking on their own. It was kind of refreshing to see that because every high school and college class I have been in math is just the teacher talking, so I thought it was really cool in these cases the students were talking where the teacher was just kind of back seat driver most of the time, and I thought that was cool. (Meredith)

Further evidence of the potential of the cases to influence teachers' thinking and learning comes from the final course activity in which participants were asked to reflect on the seven cases they had read and indicate: (1) the teacher with which they most identified and (2) the teacher they most want to emulate. First, all of the course participants aspired to be like Kathy, Vickie, and Nancy, the three teachers who we identified as best supporting student learning (see Fig. 3). Second, 12 of the course participants (67 %) indicated that they were currently most like one of the less effective teachers. These two findings suggest that course participants were able to recognize good instruction, distinguish from less effective instruction, and recognize limitations in their own practices related to reasoning-and-proving.

Additional research is needed to confirm these early findings and to determine the extent to which the knowledge gained through experiences with the CORP curriculum impacts classroom instruction and, ultimately, improves student knowledge and ability with respect to these important mathematical practices. Toward this end, members of the CORP development and evaluation teams are currently studying a subset of the preservice and practicing teachers who engaged with the CORP materials in courses or professional development initiatives to determine the impact of their experiences on their actual practice. Research such as this will provide additional support regarding the efficacy of using cases in teacher education and in using the CORP materials to develop teacher knowledge related to reasoning-and-proving.

Acknowledgement The Cases of Reasoning-and-Proving in Secondary Mathematics (CORP) project was supported by the National Science Foundation under award no. DRL 0732798. The views expressed are those of the authors and do not necessarily represent the views of the supporting agency. The authors which to acknowledge the contributions of James Greeno, Amy Hillen, Gaea Leinhardt, and Michelle Switala who collaborated in conceptualizing, designing, and/or creating the materials described herein.

References

American Diploma Project. (2004). *Ready or not?* Washington, DC: Achieve, Inc.

Ball, D. L. (1990). The mathematical understandings that prospective teachers bring to teacher education. *Elementary School Journal, 90*, 449–466.

Ball, D. L., & Cohen, D. K. (1999). Developing practice, developing practitioners: Towards a practice-based theory of professional education. In L. Darling-Hammond & G. Sykes (Eds.), *Teaching as the learning profession: Handbook of policy and practice* (pp. 3–32). San Francisco: Jossey-Bass.

Ball, D. L., Lubienski, S. T., & Mewborn, D. S. (2001). Research on teaching mathematics: The unsolved problem of teachers' mathematical knowledge. In V. Richardson (Ed.), *Handbook of research on teaching* (4th ed., pp. 433–456). New York: Macmillan.

Ball, D. L., Hill, H. C, & Bass, H. (2005). Knowing mathematics for teaching: Who knows mathematics well enough to teach third grade, and how can we decide? *American Educator, 29*(1), 14–17, 20–22, 43–46.

Ball, D. L., Thames, M. H., & Phelps, G. (2008). Content knowledge for teaching: What makes it special? *Journal of Teacher Education, 59*(5), 389–407.

Barnett, C. (1991). Building a case-based curriculum to enhance the pedagogical content knowledge of mathematics teachers. *Journal of Teacher Education, 42*(4), 263–272.

Bell, A. (1976). A study of pupils' proof – Explanations in mathematical situations. *Educational Studies in Mathematics, 7*, 23–40.

Bell, C. J. (2011). A visual application of reasoning and proof. *Mathematics Teacher, 104*(9), 690–695.

Bieda, K. (2010). Enacting proof-related tasks in middle school mathematics: Challenges and opportunities. *Journal for Research in Mathematics Education, 41*(4), 351–382.

Broudy, H. S. (1990). Case studies – Why and how. *Teachers College Record, 91*, 449–459.

Carpenter, T. P., & Lehrer, R. (1999). Teaching and learning mathematics with understanding. In E. Fennema & T. A. Romberg (Eds.), *Mathematics classrooms that promote understanding* (pp. 19–32). Mahwah: Lawrence Erlbaum Associates.

Chazan, D. (1990). Quasi-empirical views of mathematics and mathematics teaching. *Interchange, 21*(1), 14–23.

Chazan, D. (1993). High school geometry students' justification for their views of empirical evidence and mathematical proof. *Educational Studies in Mathematics, 24*(4), 359–387.

Clements, L. (2004, September). A model for understanding, using, and connecting representations. *Teaching Children Mathematics, 11*, 97–102.

Furinghetti, F., & Morselli, F. (2009). Teachers' beliefs and the teaching of proof. In F. Lin, F. Hsieh, G. Hanna, & M. de Villiers (Eds.), *Proceedings of the 19th international commission on mathematical instruction: Proof and proving in mathematics education* (ICMI Study Series 19, Vol. 1, pp. 166–171). Taipei: National Taiwan Normal University. Springer.

Hanna, G. (1989). More than formal proof. *For the Learning of Mathematics, 9*(1), 20–23.

Hanna, G. (1991). Mathematical proof. In D. Tall (Ed.), *Advanced mathematical thinking* (pp. 54–61). Dordrecht: Kluwer.

Hanna, G. (1995). Challenges to the importance of proof. *For the Learning of Mathematics, 15*, 42–49.

Harel, G. (1998). Two dual assertions: The first on learning and the second on teaching (or vice versa). *American Mathematical Monthly, 105*, 497–507.

Harel, G. (2013). Intellectual need. In K. Leatham (Ed.), *Vital directions in mathematics education research*. New York: Springer Science+Business Media.

Harrington, H. (1995). Fostering reasoned decisions: Case-based pedagogy and the professional development of teachers. *Teaching and Teacher Education, 11*(3), 203–221.

Healy, L., & Hoyles, C. (2000). A study of proof conceptions in algebra. *Journal for Research in Mathematics Education, 31*, 396–428.

Herbel-Eisenmann, B. A., Steele, M. D., & Cirillo, M. (2013). Developing teacher discourse moves: A framework for professional development. *Mathematics Teacher Educator, 1*(2), 181–196.

Hiebert, J., Carpenter, T. P., Fennema, E., Fuson, K. C., Wearne, D., Murray, H., Olivier, A., & Human, P. (1997). *Making sense: Teaching and learning mathematics with understanding*. Portsmouth: Heinemann.

Hillen, A. F., & Hughes, E. K. (2008). Developing teachers' abilities to facilitate meaningful classroom discourse through cases: The case of accountable talk. In M. S. Smith & S. Friel (Eds.), *Cases in mathematics teacher education: Tools for developing knowledge needed for teaching* (Fourth monograph of the Association of Mathematics Teacher Educators). San Diego: AMTE.

Howe, R. (1999). A review of knowing and teaching elementary mathematics. *Journal for Research in Mathematics Education, 30*(5), 579–589.

Knuth, E. J. (2002a). Teachers' conceptions of proof in the context of secondary school mathematics. *Journal of Mathematics Teacher Education, 5*(1), 61–88.

Knuth, E. J. (2002b). Secondary school mathematics teachers' conceptions of proof. *Journal for Research in Mathematics Education, 33*(5), 379–405.

Knuth, E. J. (2002c). Proof as a tool for learning mathematics. *The Mathematics Teacher, 95*(7), 486–490.

Kotelawala, U. (2009). A survey of teacher beliefs on proving. In F. Lin, F. Hsieh, G. Hanna, & M. de Villiers (Eds.), *Proceedings of the 19th international commission on mathematical instruction: proof and proving in mathematics education* (ICMI Study Series 19, Vol. 1, pp. 250–255). Taipei: National Taiwan Normal University. Springer.

Lakatos, I. (1976). *Proofs and refutations: The logic of mathematical discovery*. Cambridge: Cambridge University Press.

Lannin, J. K. (2005). Generalization and justification: The challenge of introducing algebraic reasoning through patterning. *Mathematical Thinking and Learning, 7*(3), 231–258.

Lesh, R., Post, T., & Behr, M. (1987). Representations and translations among representations in mathematics learning and problem solving. In C. Janvier (Ed.), *Problems of representations in the teaching and learning of mathematics* (pp. 33–40). Hillsdale: Lawrence Erlbaum.

Markovits, Z., & Even, R. (1999). The decimal point situation: A close look at the use of mathematics-classroom-situations in teacher education. *Teaching and Teacher Education, 15*, 653–665.

Markovits, Z., & Smith, M. S. (2008). Case as tools in mathematics teacher education. In D. Tirosh & T. Wood (Eds.), *International handbook of mathematics teacher education: Vol. 2: Tools and processes in mathematics teacher education*. Rotterdam: Sense Publishers.

Martin, T. S., McCrone, S. M. S., Bower, M. L. W., & Dindyal, J. (2005). The interplay of teacher and students actions in the teaching and learning of geometric proof. *Educational Studies in Mathematics, 60*, 95–124.

Merseth, K. K. (1991). *The case for cases in teacher education*. Washington, DC: American Association of Colleges of Teacher Education.

Merseth, K. K. (1999). A rationale for case-based pedagogy in teacher education. In M. A. Lundeberg, B. B. Levin, & H. L. Harrington (Eds.), *Who learns what from cases and how?: The research base for teaching and learning with cases* (pp. ix–xv). Mahwah: Lawrence Erlbaum.

Merseth, K. K., & Lacey, C. A. (1993). Weaving stronger fabric: The pedagogical promise of hypermedia and case methods in teacher education. *Teaching and Teacher Education, 9*(3), 283–299.

Morris, A. K. (2002). Mathematical reasoning: Adults' ability to make the inductive-deductive distinction. *Cognition and Instruction, 20*(1), 79–118.

National Council of Teachers of Mathematics. (2000). *Principles and standards for school mathematics*. Reston: Author.

National Council of Teachers of Mathematics. (2009). *Focus in high school mathematics: Reasoning and sense making*. Reston: Author.

National Governors Association Center for Best Practices, Council of Chief State School Officers. (2010). *Common core state standards mathematics*. Washington, DC: Authors.

Nelson, R. B. (1993). *Proof without words: Exercises in visual thinking*. Washington, DC: Mathematical Association of America.

Schoenfeld, A. H. (1994). What do we know about mathematics curricula? *Journal of Mathematical Behavior, 13*(1), 55–80.

Selden, A., & Selden, J. (2003). Validations of proofs considered as texts: Can undergraduates tell whether an argument proves a theorem? *Journal for Research in Mathematics Education, 34*, 4–36.

Senk, S. L. (1985). How well do students write geometry proofs? *Mathematics Teacher, 78*(6), 448–456.

Shulman, L. S. (1992). Towards a pedagogy of cases. In J. Shulman (Ed.), *Case methods in teacher education* (pp. 1–30). New York: Teachers College Press.

Shulman, L. S. (1996). Just in case: Reflections on learning from experience. In J. Colbert, K. Trimble, & P. Desberg (Eds.), *The case for education: Contemporary approaches for using case methods* (pp. 197–217). Boston: Allyn & Bacon.

Smith, J. C. (2006). A sense making approach to proof: Strategies of students in traditional and problem-based number theory courses. *Journal of Mathematical Behavior, 25*, 73–90.

Steele, M. D. (2008). Building bridges: Cases as catalysts for the integration of mathematical and pedagogical knowledge. In M. S. Smith & S. N. Friel (Eds.), *Cases in mathematics teacher education: Tools for developing knowledge needed for teaching* (Association of Mathematics Teacher Educators monograph series, Vol. 4, pp. 57–72). San Diego: AMTE.

Steele, M. D., & Rogers, K. A. C. (2012). Relationships between mathematical knowledge for teaching and teaching practice: The case of proof. *Journal of Mathematics Teacher Education, 15*, 159–180.

Stein, M. K., Grover, B., & Henningsen, M. (1996). Building student capacity for mathematical thinking and reasoning: An analysis of mathematical tasks used in reform classrooms. *American Educational Research Journal, 33*, 455–488.

Stylianides, G. J. (2008). An analytic framework of reasoning-and-proving. *For the Learning of Mathematics, 28*(1), 9–16.

Stylianides, A. J. (2009). Breaking the equation "empirical argument = proof. *Mathematics Teaching, 213*, 9–14.

Stylianides, G. J. (2010, September). Engaging secondary students in reasoning-and-proving. *Mathematics Teaching, 219*, 39–44.

Stylianides, G. J., & Stylianides, A. J. (2009). Facilitating the transition from empirical arguments to proof. *Journal for Research in Mathematics Education, 40*, 314–352.

Sykes, G., & Bird, T. (1992). Teacher education and the case idea. In G. Grant (Ed.), *Review of research in education* (Vol. 18, pp. 457–521). Washington, DC: American Educational Research Association.

Thompson, D. R., Senk, S. L., & Johnson, G. J. (2012). Opportunities to learn reasoning and proof in school mathematics textbooks. *Journal for Research in Mathematics Education, 43*(3), 253–295.

The Process of Instructional Change: Insights from the Problem-Solving Cycle

Jennifer Jacobs, Karen Koellner, Tyrone John, and Carolyn D. King

Abstract Breaking traditional instructional patterns is a notoriously challenging endeavor, particularly on a broad scale. However, a number of professional development (PD) efforts in mathematics have produced promising results, even within a relatively short time frame. In this chapter, we focus on the impact of one such effort and report on teachers' instructional changes after they participated in the Problem-Solving Cycle (PSC) model of PD. We discuss quantitative patterns from a dataset of 51 videotaped lessons obtained from 13 participants, highlighting changes in their PSC and typical lessons over a 1.5-year period. We also present a case study analysis to illustrate the specific nature of the classroom improvements made by one participant. Overall, teachers experienced the most change in their ability to work effectively with students' productions around meaningful mathematics. These findings add to the literature that demonstrates instructional growth potential among teachers who take part in PD for less than 2 years.

J. Jacobs (✉)
Institute of Cognitive Science, University of Colorado Boulder,
1099 Fairway Ct, Boulder, CO 80303, USA
e-mail: jenniferj@davidslane.com

K. Koellner
Department of Curriculum and Teaching, Hunter College, The City University of New York,
695 Park Ave, Ste 913W, New York, NY 10065, USA
e-mail: kkoellne@hunter.cuny.edu

T. John
Urban Education, Graduate Center, City University of New York,
201-15 Linden Blvd. St, Albans, NY 11412, USA
e-mail: tyronej@gmail.com

C.D. King
Queensborough Community College, City University of New York,
1336 E. 56th Street, Brooklyn, NY 11234, USA
e-mail: carolyndking@gmail.com

Y. Li et al. (eds.), *Transforming Mathematics Instruction: Multiple Approaches and Practices*, Advances in Mathematics Education, DOI 10.1007/978-3-319-04993-9_19, © Springer International Publishing Switzerland 2014

Keywords Mathematics teaching • Classroom practice • Instructional change • Professional development

What Do We Know About Instructional Change?

From a historical perspective, instructional change in the United States has taken place at what many describe as a frustratingly slow pace. Several decades ago, Hoetker and Ahlbrand (1969) contributed a review of the literature dating back to the late nineteenth century that detailed "the persistence of recitation" as the primary instructional script. Teachers following a recitation script are more likely to seek predictable, correct answers rather than probing students' ideas and encouraging them to explain their thinking. A more recent review by Hiebert and Grouws (2007) asserts that, in US mathematics classrooms, teachers continue their reliance on a recitation script that focuses on the development of routine skills and pays relatively little attention to supporting students' conceptual development of critical ideas and relationships.

Gallimore and Santagata (2006) maintain that it should not be particularly surprising that recitation has dominated US classrooms for more than a century. Teaching is a cultural activity and, as such, is highly resistant to change (Gallimore 1996; Tharp and Gallimore 1988). At the same time, reform efforts are currently in full force in the United States, which is striving to break traditional instructional patterns and replace them with a focus on student engagement and inquiry. The Common Core State Standards (NGACBP and CCSS 2010) not only suggest what content should be taught, but they highlight instructional practices that push strongly against a recitation script. For those educators who seek to promote the successful implementation of the CCSS and foster instruction more in line with developing students' conceptual understanding, it is essential to keep in mind just how difficult change can be.

Large-scale studies of mathematics instruction show that change is slow and largely "at the margins" of the reform movement, rather than at its core. For example, Jacobs et al. (2006) reported results from both the TIMSS 1995 and 1999 datasets showing that US teachers more often follow the traditional classroom patterns reported by Hoetker and Ahlbrand (1969) than the type of instruction recommended by the NCTM Standards (NCTM 2000). Weiss and colleagues (Weiss et al. 2003; Weiss et al. 2004) paint a similar portrait of US mathematics based on a nationally representative sample of mathematics lessons from the *Inside the Classroom* study. Their analyses reveal that the majority of lessons were low in quality, lacked intellectual rigor, and did not provide sensemaking appropriate for the needs of the students. Few lessons included teacher questioning that was likely to move students' understanding forward. Most commonly, teachers used low-level "fill-in-the-blank" questions, asked at a rapid pace, with an emphasis on obtaining correct answers and moving on.

Recently, Silver and colleagues engaged in an investigation of portfolios submitted by mathematics teachers seeking certification by the National Board for Professional Teaching Standards (Silver 2010; Silver et al. 2009). The researchers found that approximately half of the teachers in their sample submitted portfolios without including even one task that was judged to be cognitively demanding (Silver et al. 2009). In addition, few of the submitted tasks required students to provide explanations or reason mathematically, suggesting numerous missed opportunities to support students' conceptual development. The fact that these teachers were attempting to showcase their best practice in order to gain certification as highly accomplished teachers makes these findings especially disappointing and provides further evidence that teaching for understanding is not yet a regular feature of US mathematics classrooms.

Professional Development as a Vehicle for Promoting Change

Having a clear picture of what instructional practices currently look like versus what kind of practices are desired, along with a healthy respect for the difficulty of fostering immediate and meaningful change, is critical to the generation of effective PD. Professional development that treats teachers as lifelong learners and supports them as professionals can offer meaningful learning opportunities (Little 1993; Putnam and Borko 1997). In particular, PD can provide a forum in which teachers deeply consider students' thinking and generate ideas for planning and implementing instruction that supports and builds on students' knowledge.

A number of well-known PD efforts in mathematics have shown significant impacts on teachers' classroom instruction, teacher knowledge, and students' achievement. For example, Bell and colleagues (Bell et al. 2010) conducted a large-scale evaluation of the widely used Developing Mathematical Ideas (DMI) PD materials. They found that across multiple sites with multiple facilitators, participation in DMI (over a period of time that ranged from an intensive 1-week session to a more spread out 1-year period) significantly impacted teachers' knowledge of mathematics for teaching relative to a comparison group of teachers. Similar data come from a study of California's Mathematics Professional Development Institutes, which offered intensive summer workshops to elementary school teachers. Based on a sample of 398 teachers across 15 institutes, Hill and Ball (2004) report a significant increase in their knowledge of mathematics for teaching as a result of their participation.

Particularly compelling evidence of the potential of mathematics PD on an even larger scale comes from an evaluation of the Local Systemic Change through Teacher Enhancement program (LSC). The LSC program involved 88 mathematics and science PD projects across the United States, with the goal of providing high-quality learning experiences for large numbers of teachers. In-depth analyses of these projects suggest that, in aggregate, they positively impacted teachers' attitudes toward reform-oriented teaching, their content knowledge, the quality of the instruction in their observed lessons, and student achievement (Banilower et al. 2006; Heck et al. 2008). The evaluators concluded that the "LSCs were strong in creating a culture conductive to teacher learning, in the quality of preparation of professional development providers, and in preparing teachers to use high quality materials and appropriate pedagogy" (Banilower et al. 2006, p. 89). In another attempt to look at a relatively large set of data, Blank and de las Alas (2010) conducted a meta-analysis of 16 studies of PD programs and found that mathematics PD leads to consistent positive gains in student mathematics achievement (with a mean effect size of 0.21).

How Should We Measure Instructional Change?

Although there is a growing pool of instruments to objectively measure the impact of PD on pertinent aspects of teachers' knowledge (e.g., Hill et al. 2004, 2007b; Kersting et al. 2012), classroom instruction is still commonly measured via teachers' self-report (e.g., Boyle et al. 2004; Desimone et al. 2002; Huffman et al. 2003; Ingvarson et al. 2005; Supovitz et al. 2000). However, as Hiebert and Grouws (2007) caution, teachers tend to overreport features of teaching they believe are desired by the researchers, calling into question the validity of such reports.

Investigating changes in classroom practice through a more objective lens, such as from live observations or videotaped records, is a complex and demanding endeavor (Desimone 2009). We argue that more objective documentation is useful not only in determining the precise impact of a PD program but also for gaining an understanding of the specific manner in which teachers change their instructional practices over time. By gathering more nuanced data on the degree and nature of instructional change, researchers can predict the likelihood of changes in specific, key instructional practices. Likewise, future PD efforts could be structured to meet the targeted needs of teachers within a realistic time frame for improvements in practice.

Contrary to the hopes of researchers, funding agencies, and perhaps even teachers themselves, making dramatic, notable changes in practice requires a considerable amount of time (Weinstein et al. 1995). Classroom changes for most teachers tend to be gradual and accompanied by ideological shifts (Loucks-Horsley et al. 2010). Even when change does occur, it is often found to be uneven and takes root slowly (Richardson 1990). Expecting teachers to overhaul their instruction immediately subsequent to participation in a PD program is generally unrealistic. At the same time, certain PD programs hold promise for substantially impacting classroom practice within a 1- to 2-year time frame (e.g., Bell et al. 2010; Hill and Ball 2004).

The iPSC Study

The project *Toward a Scalable Model of Mathematics Professional Development: A Field Study of Preparing Facilitators to Implement the Problem-Solving* (iPSC) is investigating the scalability of the Problem-Solving Cycle (PSC) and its impact on teachers' knowledge, instructional practices, and student achievement. As part of the iPSC project, teacher leaders (TL) from a large, urban school district in the Western United States received several years of focused preparation as they began implementing the PSC in their schools (Koellner et al. 2011a). The participating TLs were all full-time middle school mathematics teachers. Elsewhere, we have described the nature and quality of PSC workshops led by the TLs (Borko et al. 2014b). A separate chapter in this book explores the preparation of the TLs, their facilitation practices, and the impact of the iPSC on the participants' knowledge (Borko et al. 2014a). Here, our focus is on the impact of the iPSC on the participating teachers' classroom instruction.

The PSC is intended to be an iterative, long-term approach to mathematics PD (Jacobs et al. 2007; Koellner et al. 2007). The PSC consists of a series of three interconnected workshops in which teachers engage in a common mathematical and pedagogical experience, organized around a rich mathematical problem. This common experience provides a framework upon which the teachers can build a supportive community that encourages reflection on mathematical understandings, student thinking, and instructional practices. The model is designed to be implemented by a knowledgeable facilitator, typically a teacher at the school who has suitable leadership qualities.

During the first workshop in a cycle, teachers collaboratively solve the selected mathematical problem and develop plans for teaching it to their students. After the workshop, teachers teach the problem to their own students, and the lesson is videotaped. This lesson is called the "PSC lesson." The next two workshops in a cycle focus on the group's collective experiences teaching the problem and rely on selected video clips from the PSC lessons to foster productive conversations. The broad goals of these two workshops are to help teachers learn how to elicit and build on student thinking and to explore a variety of instructional strategies to effectively respond to student thinking.

If we view PD as a career-long endeavor, we can similarly understand the improvement of classroom instruction as long-term undertaking. In this chapter, we explore instructional changes that were evident over the course of the teachers' participation in the iPSC project. Drawing on both quantitative coding and a qualitative case study analyses, we analyze patterns in the classroom data at two time points, looking at both PSC lessons and non-PSC lessons (i.e., typical lessons). Our goal is to investigate the nature of teachers' emerging changes, based on a view of instructional improvement as a gradual process, but one that can likely be detected within 1 year following an effective PD program.

Method

Participants

The iPSC project began as a university-district partnership, with the expectation that the university would provide 2½ years of professional development—using the PSC model—to the middle mathematics teachers in the district. The PD involved developing the leadership capacity of a select group of teachers, such that the researchers could eventually decrease their role and the TLs, with the support of the district

Table 1 Number of teachers who took part in the iPSC during the first 1.5 years

	Semester 1: Spring 2008	Semester 2: Fall 2008	Semester 3: Spring 2009
Teacher leaders	7	5	5
Case study teachers	0	8	8

Note: In a school where there were co-teacher leaders, we only recruited one pair of case study teachers

Table 2 Number of lessons videotaped for the participating teachers

	PSC lessons		Typical lessons	
	First	Last	First	Last
Teacher leaders (*n*=5)	5 – Spring 2008	5 – Spring 2009	4[a] – Spring 2008	5 – Spring 2009
Case study teachers (*n*=8)	8 – Fall 2008	8 – Spring 2009	8 – Fall 2008	8 – Spring 2009
Total	13	13	12	13

[a]Due to logistical difficulties, one of the TLs did not have a typical lesson filmed in Spring 2008

administration, could continue implementing the PSC in their schools indefinitely. This expectation has, in fact, been met; at the present time, the TLs are implementing the PSC in the vast majority of the middle schools in the participating district with no direct involvement by the research team (Jacobs et al. 2012).

The data reported in this chapter are from the initial 1.5 years of the project, during which the research team worked closely with a small group of TLs (see Table 1). In our first semester working with the district, the participants consisted of seven TLs from four schools. The following school year, five of these TLs (from three schools) began facilitating PSC workshops with the mathematics teachers at their schools. At this time, we recruited two teachers from each PSC group to serve as case study teachers. The TLs and case study teachers agreed to have two lessons videotaped each semester: their PSC lesson and a "typical lesson."

The 13 teachers that are the focus of this chapter (five TLs and eight case study teachers) had a range of teaching experience from 1 to 32 years, with a mean of approximately 8 years. They were roughly evenly divided as teachers of sixth- (46 %), seventh- (46 %), and eighth-grade (54 %) students, with some teaching at multiple grade levels. All had completed at least two college-level mathematics courses, with a mean of approximately five courses.

Data Collection and Measures

The analyses presented in this chapter focus on 51 videotaped lessons, as described in Table 2. Specifically, we examined the "first" and "last" PSC and typical lesson filmed for each teacher (within the first 1.5 years of the iPSC project). As previously noted, the TLs began participating in the project one semester prior to the case study teachers. Therefore, while the dates of their last lessons are the same (Spring 2009), the dates of their first lessons are a semester apart (Spring 2008 for the TLs and Fall 2008 for the case study teachers).

We analyzed this set of 51 lessons using the *Mathematics Quality in Instruction* (MQI) instrument (Hill et al. 2008) to investigate changes in the quality of the teachers' mathematics lessons. Hill and colleagues (2008) explain that the mathematical quality of instruction refers to "a composite of several dimensions that characterize the rigor and richness of the mathematics of the lesson" (p. 431). The MQI is derived from and aligned with the NCTM Standards (Hill et al. 2007b; Kilday and Kinzie 2009; NCTM 2000). Hill and colleagues have used the instrument in a number of studies and provided detailed information on its development—along with the establishment of its reliability and validity—in several published reports (Hill et al. 2007a, 2008; Learning Mathematics for Teaching Project 2011).

The MQI measures five dimensions of instruction: (1) classroom work is connected to mathematics, (2) richness of the mathematics, (3) working with students and mathematics, (4) errors and imprecision, and (5) student participation in meaning-making and reasoning. These dimensions fit well with the research goals of the iPSC project and the nature of the teaching the project tried to promote. Within the latter four dimensions, a series of three to six items are coded on a 3-point Likert-style rating scale (generally: low, mid, or high) for each 7.5-min lesson segment. In addition, there are two items that rate the overall lesson in terms of the mathematical quality of instruction and the teacher's estimated mathematical knowledge for teaching. For these two items, we adapted the MQI's 3-point rating scale and instead used a 5-point scale (poor, fair, good, very good, or excellent).

First, a team of four coders achieved inter-rater reliability of at least 80 % for all codes in the MQI. Then, members of the research team worked in pairs to code each lesson, coding individually and then discussing and reconciling their disagreements. Midway through the coding process, the two pairs coded the same two lessons to ensure that our application of the instrument remained consistent.

Results

Quantitative analyses based on the entire dataset of 51 videotaped lessons highlight the nature of the participants' PSC and typical lessons and how they changed over time. An illustrative case study analysis then serves to document the changes in one teacher's lessons during the course of her participation in the iPSC project. This analysis illustrates what changes in specific practices can look like and how the MQI ratings play out in particular lessons.

Quantitative Patterns

Dimension Averages

We provide a general overview of the quantitative data by examining the average ratings within the four main dimensions captured by the MQI.[1] The *math richness* dimension includes a series of items that capture the depth of mathematics offered to students, such as the degree to which there are accurate explanations, multiple solution methods, and fluent mathematical language in the lesson. The *working with students* dimension includes items that capture the degree to which teachers build on their students' mathematical productions or conceptually remediate their errors. Items in the *errors and imprecision* dimension capture the extent to which there are teacher errors, including language and notation errors, as well as the degree of clarity in the teacher's presentation of the content. The dimension *student participation* includes items that measure the extent to which students provide explanations, reason, and contribute to meaning-making.

Figure 1 shows the average ratings within each of the four dimensions for the teachers' first and last PSC and typical lessons. The largest improvement can be seen in the *working with students* dimension, for both the PSC and typical lessons. This finding suggests that, over time, the teachers were better able to build on their students' ideas and help them work through their errors in a conceptual manner.

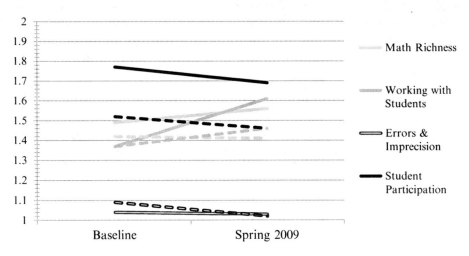

Fig. 1 Dimension averages for PSC and typical lessons (*Solid lines* = PSC lessons; *dashed lines* = typical lessons)

---

[1] The vast majority of lessons videotaped as part of the iPSC study were entirely or almost entirely "connected to mathematics"; therefore, our presentation of results does not include that dimension of the MQI.

The *math richness* dimension increased slightly for the PSC lessons (while remaining constant for the typical lessons), indicating that the teachers included more opportunities for students to engage in rich mathematics in their later PSC lessons. The *errors and imprecision* dimension decreased slightly for the typical lessons (while remaining constant for the PSC lessons), which means the error ratings for the later typical lessons fell to approximately the level of the PSC lessons. The *student participation* dimension decreased somewhat for both the PSC and typical lessons, suggesting that the teachers were less focused on ensuring that their students contributed to meaning-making in the lesson.

Looking at these patterns in another way, one might notice that *student participation* is actually the dimension that was consistently rated the highest across the lessons and time periods. Although the ratings did drop, it is possible that teachers were increasingly focused on ensuring that their lessons contained sufficient mathematical richness and conceptual work for students and they became somewhat less attuned to ensuring the same high levels of student participation.

Another pattern of interest is the fact that the teachers' PSC lessons were consistently rated higher than their typical lessons. This finding is not especially surprising, given the extensive PD work that teachers engaged in around the PSC problems prior to using them in their classrooms. In addition, the PSC problems were intentionally selected to be rich, open-ended tasks, and as such they are likely to be different from the tasks participants routinely used in their everyday practice. Furthermore, rich tasks can more readily lead to higher ratings on the MQI instrument, assuming that teachers implement them in the desired manner. At the same time, the fact that the PSC and typical lessons are not widely discrepant suggests that teachers are generally consistent in their instructional styles, and changes either within a time period (comparing PSC to typical lessons) or across time periods (comparing the first and last lessons) are relatively small on average.

Working with Students

We now take a closer look at the dimension that consistently showed the greatest improvement, *working with students*. There are three items within this dimension: (1) remediation of student errors and difficulties, (2) responding to students' mathematical productions, and (3) overall working with students and mathematics. As Fig. 2 shows, all three items increased to some extent over time, for both the PSC and typical lessons. Similar to the pattern in Fig. 1, the PSC lessons were almost always rated higher than the typical lessons. Teachers generally received the highest ratings for responding to students, indicating that they were attentive to students' productions and responded in mathematically appropriate ways, such as by weaving their ideas into the development of the lesson. Although their ratings for conceptual remediation were a bit lower, teachers were making strides in improving this aspect of their instruction. Higher ratings for conceptual remediation indicate that teachers addressed students' misunderstandings or difficulties with the mathematics in a conceptual manner, as opposed to addressing them procedurally or not at all.

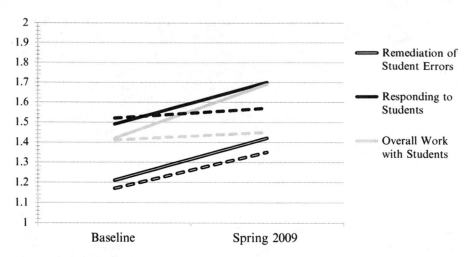

Fig. 2 Working with students categories for PSC and typical lessons (*Solid lines* = PSC lessons; *dashed lines* = typical lessons)

Overall Mathematical Quality of Instruction

As previously noted, the MQI instrument includes an overall lesson rating for the mathematical quality of instruction. This rating captures the degree to which the lesson included elements such as productive teacher-student interactions around the content, errors, mathematical richness, and a sharp mathematical focus that allowed students to develop the important ideas under consideration. Figure 3 shows that all of the PSC lessons were judged to be either "good" or "very good," with a pronounced increase in "very good" ratings over time. There was a wider range in the ratings of the typical lessons. The baseline typical lessons ranged from "poor" to "excellent." In Spring 2009, the typical lessons ranged from "fair" to "very good," with a notable increase in the number of "good" and "very good" lessons. In general, the PSC lessons were rated higher on overall quality of instruction relative to the typical lessons. At both time points, more PSC lessons were rated as "very good"; close to one third of the PSC baseline lessons and one half of the PSC Spring 2009 lessons were rated as "very good."

Qualitative Patterns: A Case Study Analysis of Yasmin

In this section, we illustrate the nature of classroom changes made by one iPSC participant, Yasmin, with a specific focus on changes in the *working with students* dimension of the MQI. Yasmin was selected for our case study analysis because she exhibited some of the largest increases in ratings on this dimension. Our aim, therefore, is to document what changes in practice in this area can look like, rather than

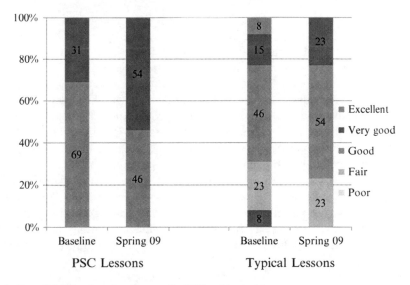

Fig. 3 Overall MQI ratings by category for PSC and typical lessons

to suggest that they are typical. While we can only speculate as to why Yasmin was willing to change her practice in a relatively dramatic manner, based on a series of interviews, we hypothesize that she was highly influenced by her involvement in the iPSC project and became increasingly motivated to provide deeper learning experiences for her students.

Yasmin was in her third year of teaching when the iPSC project began. Yasmin was teaching eighth grade at a relatively new middle school, built in a growing suburb in a predominantly middle class neighborhood. She was identified by her principal as willing and able to become a PSC facilitator, along with another mathematics teacher from her school. In her initial interview, Yasmin stated that she hoped participating in the iPSC would lead her mathematics department to use their PD time more productively. She lamented that the math teachers at her school rarely met as a department, and when they did they generally engaged in logistical endeavors, such as managing their budgets. She was especially interested in taking a leadership role to ensure they would become more cohesive as a department, focus on mathematics teaching and learning, and share ideas aimed at improving their instruction.

As a teacher leader and co-facilitator of the PSC workshops, Yasmin encouraged her colleagues to pursue the topic of teachers' questions, including brainstorming "good questions" and reflecting on how to use questioning as an alternative to telling students the answer. These topics were covered in the facilitator preparation workshops that Yasmin attended, where numerous strategies were discussed both with respect to leading PSC workshops that highlighted questioning and to improving classroom instruction by being mindful of one's questioning techniques. A focus on teacher questioning carried over into Yasmin's reflections on her own classroom practice. Prior to her participation in the iPSC project, Yasmin described her teaching style as mostly lecturing and then reviewing, with a strong emphasis on preparing students for their in-class exams. Approximately 1.5 years later, when she discussed her Spring 2009 PSC lesson, Yasmin reflected, "My whole goal was not to give away too much information. I didn't want to tell them, 'This is how you do it....' I was trying to have kids do critical thinking to come up with their own conclusions, rather than to have mine." During this same interview, Yasmin remarked that even when covering new material in her "typical" lessons, she is more careful not to give away too much information, striving instead for her students to determine how to solve a given problem by using their background knowledge.

Below we provide a case study analysis based on portions of two of Yasmin's videotaped lessons, her first typical lesson and her last PSC lesson. These two lessons depict notably different instructional styles and speak to Yasmin's growth as a teacher, particularly in the area of working with students. In her baseline lesson, Yasmin taught what would be considered a "traditional" textbook-based lesson, with an emphasis on procedures and following a prescribed strategy to obtain the correct answer. In this lesson, the students produced few "substantive productions" for Yasmin to build upon, there were no attempts to provide conceptual remediation, and the few errors that occurred were addressed quickly and procedurally. By contrast, during Yasmin's last PSC lesson, she encouraged her students to pursue multiple solution paths by building on the ideas they generated, pushing them to think conceptually, and using the students' own errors to guide their learning.

Yasmin's Baseline Typical Lesson

Yasmin's first videotaped lesson was an algebra lesson in which students were solving absolute value equations. They appeared to be practicing what they learned from a previous lesson, as there was no direct instruction and students were expected to know how to solve these equations with little guidance from the teacher. The lesson largely consisted of seatwork, and although Yasmin was attentive to her students' mathematical work, she offered little in the way of mathematical support, instead encouraging the students to turn to their peers when they requested assistance.

As they enter the classroom, Yasmin directs her students' attention to the review problems she has written on the overhead projector. While they work on these problems, Yasmin walks around the classroom and checks their homework. After this routine 10-minute opening, Yasmin introduces the main component of the lesson: working in designated groups of three to solve problems 19–22 on page 223 of their algebra textbook. Yasmin directs the students to talk in their groups about what they need to do and how to do it. Correspondingly, one student comments to her group of peers, "We need to solve the equation. First, we solve it regular and then we solve it using a negative."

Most students seemed to know how to go about solving the assigned problems. They were supposed to treat the absolute value component within each equation as two possible cases, one being positive and one being negative. However, the specific procedures for working with absolute values within equations appeared more solidified for some students than others. Due to the nature of the tasks, there were few opportunities for students to think conceptually or to pursue unique solution methods.

Yasmin walks over to a group that has their hands raised. When they ask her to confirm that their answer is correct Yasmin responds, "Why did you do it that way?" One student counters with a smile, "Because you said to." Yasmin continues to push him, "Why did I say to do it that way?" The student states that he combined like terms. Yasmin replies, "You need to first combine like terms, but only those terms that are not included in the absolute value sign. Here, the x is part of the absolute value so you will solve for x in both part one, which is positive, and part two, which is negative."

In the above episode, like many throughout the lesson, Yasmin's focus was on ensuring that her students approached equations containing an absolute value by obtaining two solutions. She called the positive solution "part one" and the negative solution "part two." By breaking down the mathematical procedures in this way, Yasmin's apparent goal was mastery and efficiency. As we see here, although Yasmin occasionally asked "why" questions of her students, they were not expected to produce true mathematical explanations, and, in general, the classroom dialogue never moved beyond statements of the steps that would lead to a correct solution.

Toward the end of the lesson, Yasmin tells the students to move out of their groups and go back to their original seats. She explains that she will call on one student at a time to come to the SMART board and share their responses to each of the four assigned equations. Dylan volunteers to do the first equation. Yasmin goes over her expectations for what students are to do when they come to the board, "When you are up there, you are not just writing the answer down. You need to explain what you did step by step." Dylan writes the equation on the board, $[3x + 6] - 7 = 3$, and begins talking through his solution method, "First, you need to get all of the numbers not in the absolute value sign over to one side. So first, you add 7 to both sides, and $7 + 3$ is 10." Yasmin steps in and reminds Dylan that he is only going to share the positive solution and the next person will share the negative solution. This interjection confuses Dylan and he asks, "What do I do?" Yasmin repeats, "Just the positive," but Dylan is now uncertain about how to proceed. A classmate tells Dylan that he should subtract 6 from each side and then solve for x. Dylan hesitates and asks, "Did I do it wrong?" Neutrally, Yasmin replies, "Ask the class." The class tells Dylan that he was doing it right but he was not done and to keep going. Someone says, "You still need to solve for x." Reassured, Dylan finishes the problem and states his solution, "$x = 4/3$."

The classroom discussion continued in this manner, with students coming up to the front of the room and sharing their answers to the remainder of the equations. It is perhaps not surprising that even after a long practice session, some students still struggled to recall what they were expected to do and did not fully understand why they set the equation first to a positive number and then to a negative number. Yasmin maintained a low profile throughout the lesson and often reflected questions back to the students or their classmates. Although this strategy appeared aimed at encouraging the

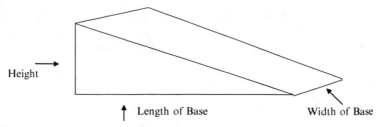

Here is your task:
- Compare each pair of ramps.
- Make an ordered list using all models (1–8), from the least steep to most steep.
- Provide a mathematical justification for how you ordered your list.
- Describe any patterns you notice in the data.

Ramp Model #	Height	Length	Width Base
A1	18	72	32
A2	19	73	34
B3	12	60	37
B4	18	90	41
C5	24	120	36
C6	28	215	36
D7	37	181	26
D8	43	215	38

Fig. 4 The wheelchair ramps problem (*Note*: These figures do not conform to actual construction codes for wheelchair ramps)

students to be more self-reliant, it meant that errors or misconceptions did not drive the instruction in any way and they were never tackled in a mathematically insightful or conceptual manner.

Yasmin's Spring 2009 PSC Lesson

Yasmin began her lesson by discussing the task, entitled wheelchair ramps (adapted from Lobato and Siebert 2002; See Fig. 4). She told the students that they were going to help a company that makes ramps for wheelchairs improve their upcoming catalog. Customers were complaining that the old catalog was confusing because they were not able to determine the steepness of each ramp. The new catalog would feature 8 models of wheelchair ramps and lists not only their dimensions of length, height, and width but also their steepness. Yasmin explained to her students that they needed to determine the steepness of each ramp and then order them from the least to most steep. After this introduction to the problem, the students started working in groups, sorting out their thinking regarding steepness. In the remainder of this vignette, we describe several excerpts from the lesson that illustrate how Yasmin remediated errors and responded to students' mathematical productions as they worked on the task.

A company that makes wheelchair ramps needs to revise their catalog to include the steepness of each ramp. Your company was given a subcontract to do this work. Within the current catalog of wheelchair ramps, there are eight models. You need to determine the steepness of each ramp and order them from the least steep to most steep in the catalog.

Yasmin comes over to a group and asks what they have figured out so far. One student asserts, "The lowest number is going to be the steepest ramp." Yasmin presses her for clarification, "You need to be clear on why a ramp is the most steep or the least steep and tell us how you are going to prove it." Other students in the group explain that they are multiplying the lengths and widths together to determine steepness. Taking up this (incorrect) line of thinking, Yasmin asks, "How does multiplying help?" One student responds, "If the ramp has a smaller number [i.e., product], then it means it would be the least [steep]. Yasmin challenges the group to prove their theory by trying more examples.

In this excerpt, Yasmin is engaging in brief conceptual remediation. After eliciting the students' thinking, she was able to understand their misconception and consider how the students might explore their idea further in a productive manner. Rather than telling the students that they were incorrect, Yasmin suggested a specific way for them to test their conjecture, with the expectation that they would be able to see for themselves the error in the strategy.

Yasmin moves to another group with their hands raised. One student says, "I am confused because, for finding the steepness, don't you just multiply the length and height and divide by 2?" Yasmin responds, "How is that steepness?" Another group member states, "That is area, not slope." Yasmin continues the conversations by asking, "So is area the same as slope?" "No," the group answers together. Yasmin probes to see if they really understand whether slope and area are different: "So, you are saying slope, but then you are doing the formula for area?" One boy declares, "What we are doing doesn't make sense." Yasmin pursues a line of questioning to ensure the students understand slope: "Then what is slope?" The boy replies, "Division." Yasmin prods him, "Division of what?" When she is greeted by silence, Yasmin gestures to the "word wall" which includes the term "slope," along with a definition and several examples. The students then answer cautiously, "Rise over run." Yasmin continues her questioning, "What is the rise?" After one student explains that rise would be the height, she asks, "What is the run?" "Length," the group says in unison.

Here, we see Yasmin continuing to support students in their initial stages of engaging in the task. She does not provide procedures or even suggestions for how to solve the task. Rather she helps the students determine whether they are on the right track by having them explain their mathematical ideas. As she went around to each group, Yasmin paid careful attention to where the students were in their mathematical thinking. Based on their oral and written productions, Yasmin encouraged the students to persist in the task, face their own misconceptions, and move forward in more productive ways.

As the lesson progressed, some students continued to struggle and groups explored various approaches to solve the problem. In the following excerpt, Yasmin returns to a group of students who are using a difference model to determine steepness (i.e., they are subtracting the heights from the lengths). Yasmin had encouraged this group to graph the ramps with the same differences to see if they also had the same steepness. Graphing the ramps—that is, plotting the given points (length, height) and connecting them to the origin (0,0)—allows for a visual inspection and comparison of steepness. Engaging in this suggestion challenged the students and provided enough cognitive dissonance that they began to consider other strategies. Producing a graph also provided some new opportunities for the students to conceptually grasp how height and length are related in the determination of steepness.

Yasmin asks the group what numbers they used in their graphs. One student replies, "4 and 8, and 3 and 6." Yasmin quickly counters, "I thought you were going to use two numbers with a difference of three to see if they had the same slope. Using those numbers, one has a difference of three and one has a difference of four. I wanted you to look at [ramps with] the same difference." Yasmin reminds the group, "You told me before that the smaller the difference, the steeper the ramp. If you are graphing this and you have two ramps that have the same difference [but different dimensions], do they have the same steepness too?" When she gets no response, Yasmin clarifies her request, "So this has a difference of three. Find two ramps that both have a difference of three, and see if you can tell if they are the same steepness." Yasmin waits while the students create the graph she requested. Yasmin then asks them to interpret the lines they have drawn: "Do they have the same steepness?" Pointing to one of the lines a student answers, "No, this one is more steep." Yasmin pushes them to reason through this finding, "But your theory says that they should have the same steepness, right?" When the students have difficulty answering, Yasmin encourages them to pursue the idea further. She points out two more ramps that have the same difference, but different slopes, and encourages them to think about how to modify their theory. As she leaves the table, one boy comments, "You are challenging us!" To which Yasmin replies, "Good!"

In the above excerpt, Yasmin initially notices that the group of students did not engage in the careful analysis of their subtraction method that she had anticipated. Yasmin uses this opportunity to help her students begin engaging in just such an analysis. She restates the question they were asking, watches as they graph the ramps, and then ensures that they recognize what the issue is. Yasmin's choice to push this group of students to graph the problem is especially interesting as a means of providing conceptual remediation. In creating the graph, the students are able to accurately apply the relationship between height and length to generate the slope of the ramp. This visual depiction of the problem helps to convince the students that their original method contains a critical flaw.

Yasmin comes back to this same group approximately five minutes later to check on their progress. She asks, "What did you find out? Are they the same steepness?" At first the students jokingly say the ramps are the same steepness, but then admit they are not and that their subtraction strategy does not work. One student wonders, "What should we do?" to which Yasmin responds, "I don't know. What do you think?" Another boy suggests, "Well, we could use fractions and reduce them, and the smallest fraction would be the steepest, right?" Yasmin remains neutral about this suggestion, but encourages the group to consider whether it would work. One of the boys notes that, in reduced form, one ramp is ¾ and another is 1/6. 1/6 is smaller so that ramp should be less steep. Agreeing with this approach, another student explains two more times how they could generate fractions, reduce them, and identify which ramp was less steep.

As this excerpt depicts, the students eventually generated an accurate strategy for determining steepness based on fractions. In fact, these "fractions" should be understood as ratios of height to length, but regardless of their label, it is clear that the students were beginning to think of the numbers in relative terms. Yasmin encouraged the students to work systematically down their own solution path. For example, she directed them to examine number pairs that had a difference of three and then make a graph to visually inspect the slopes. Analyzing the graph—a representation frequently used in their algebra class—eventually led the students to abandon their subtraction strategy and to consider creating "fractions" from the given measurements. Yasmin supported her students by building on their ideas, maintaining an appropriate level of mathematical challenge, and ensuring that they could claim ownership of the final solution.

Discussion

The findings presented in this chapter corroborate and expand on our earlier work examining the impact of the PSC on instructional practice (Koellner et al. 2011b) and further demonstrate the potential for growth among teachers who take part in the PSC. Teachers in the iPSC study experienced the most dramatic classroom improvements in the domain *working with students*. This domain, generally speaking, captures teachers' efforts to attend to their students' thinking and provide conceptual remediation. We hypothesize that strengthening teachers' capabilities in this area of teaching may be a first step toward improving the overall quality of their instruction on an everyday basis. In other words, the ability to work effectively with students' productions around meaningful mathematics may be an initial and robust change for teachers participating in the PSC. Longer-term investigations are needed to determine whether other aspects of instructional change, such as improvements in the richness of the mathematics and the students' participation in meaning-making, occur later in time and coincide with continued participation in the PSC.

Even within a group of teachers who participate in the same PD, their experiences as learners may vary greatly. Just as there are a myriad of conditions that mediate the effects of teaching on student learning (Hiebert and Grouws 2007), there are also numerous factors likely to mediate the effects of PD on teaching. Among those who are motivated to change their classroom teaching due to their PD experiences, the exact nature and time frame around such changes can influenced by a large number of individual and contextual factors (Farmer et al. 2003; Franke et al. 2001). For example, Yasmin may have been especially motivated to change not only due to her participation in the PSC but due to her experiences preparing for and facilitating PSC workshops. Perhaps linked to her newly established leadership role, Yasmin carefully attended to the impact that teachers' questioning can have on students' thinking and strove to modify her teaching so that student-generated ideas would play a greater role.

Kazemi and Hubbard (2008) argue that knowledge gained in PD should be understood as a tool that can help teachers think about instruction in new ways. Due to teachers' unique circumstances, including the nature of their resources, the school context, their students, and their own identity as teachers, the impact of any given PD is likely to play out in a variety of ways on the participants. Franke et al. (1998) propose that "teacher change may not be captured in the [professional development] experiences the teachers have engaged in but in the meanings they have constructed" (p. 68). Future research on this topic should further investigate the degree to which there are individual differences related to the impact of PD on classroom instruction and more clearly delineate the factors that underlie such differences.

Acknowledgements The professional development program featured in this paper was funded by the National Science Foundation (Award number DRL 0732212). The views shared in this article are ours and do not necessarily represent those of NSF.

We gratefully acknowledge the teachers who took part in the study, the mathematics coordinators who supported the project, and the district administrators.

References

Banilower, E. R., Boyd, S. E., Pasley, J. D., & Weiss, I. R. (2006, February). *Lessons from a decade of mathematics and science reform: A capstone report for the local systemic change through teacher enhancement initiative* (Research Monograph-Prepublication Copy). Chapel Hill: Horizon Research, Inc.

Bell, C., Wilson, S., Higgins, T., & McCoach, B. (2010). Measuring the effects of professional development on teacher knowledge: The case of developing mathematics ideas. *Journal of Mathematics Education, 41*(5), 479–512.

Blank, R. K., & de las Alas, N. (2010). *Effects of teacher professional development on gains in student achievement: How meta analysis provides scientific evidence useful to education leader.* Washington, DC: Council of Chief State School Officers. Retrieved from https://www.sree.org/conferences/2010/program/abstracts/233.pdf

Borko, H., Jacobs, J., Seago, N., & Mangram, C. (2014a). Facilitating video-based professional development: Planning and orchestrating productive discussions. In Y. Li (Ed.), *Transforming mathematics instruction: Multiple approaches and practices.* Cham, Switzerland: Springer.

Borko, H., Koellner, K., & Jacobs, J. (2014b). Examining novice teachers' facilitation of mathematics professional development. *Journal of Mathematical Behavior, 33*(8), 149–167.

Boyle, B., While, D., & Boyle, T. (2004). A longitudinal study of teacher change: What makes professional development effective? *Curriculum Journal, 15*(1), 45–68.

Desimone, L. M. (2009). Improving impact studies of teachers' professional development: Toward better conceptualizations and measures. *Educational Researcher, 38*(3), 181–199.

Desimone, L. M., Porter, A. C., Garet, M. S., Yoon, K. S., & Birman, B. F. (2002). Effects of professional development on teachers' instruction: Results from a three-year longitudinal study. *Educational Evaluation and Policy Analysis, 24*, 81–112.

Farmer, J. D., Gerretson, H., & Lassak, M. (2003). What teachers take from professional development: Cases and implications. *Journal of Mathematics Teacher Education, 6*, 331–360.

Franke, M. L., Carpenter, T. P., Fennema, E., Ansell, E., & Behrend, J. (1998). Understanding teachers' self-sustaining, generative change in the context of professional development. *Teaching and Teacher Education, 14*(1), 67–80.

Franke, M. L., Carpenter, T. P., Levi, L., & Fennema, E. (2001). Capturing teachers' generative change: A follow-up study of professional development in mathematics. *American Educational Research Journal, 38*, 653–689.

Gallimore, R. (1996). Classrooms are just another cultural activity. In D. L. Speece & B. K. Keogh (Eds.), *Research on classroom ecologies: Implications for inclusion of children with learning disabilities* (pp. 229–250). Mahwah: Erlbaum.

Gallimore, R., & Santagata, R. (2006). Researching teaching: The problem of studying a system resistant to change. In R. R. Bootzin & P. E. McKnight (Eds.), *Strengthening research methodology: Psychological measurement and evaluation.* Washington, DC: American Psychological Association.

Heck, D. J., Banilower, E. R., Weiss, I. R., & Rosenberg, S. L. (2008). Studying the effects of professional development: The case of the NSF's local systemic change through teacher enhancement initiative. *Journal for Research in Mathematics Education, 39*(2), 113–152.

Hiebert, J., & Grouws, D. A. (2007). The effects of classroom mathematics teaching on students' learning. In F. K. Lester Jr. (Ed.), *Second handbook of research on mathematics teaching and learning* (pp. 371–405). Charlotte: Information Age Publishing.

Hill, H. C., & Ball, D. L. (2004). Learning mathematics for teaching: Results from California's Mathematics Professional Development Institutes. *Journal for Research in Mathematics Education, 35*, 330–351. doi:10.2307/30034819.

Hill, H. C., Schilling, S. G., & Ball, D. L. (2004). Developing measures of teachers' mathematics knowledge for teaching. *Elementary School Journal, 105*, 11–30. doi:10.1086/428763.

Hill, H. C., Ball, D. L., Blunk, M., Goffney, I. M., & Rowan, B. (2007a). Validating the ecological assumption: The relationship of measure scores to classroom teaching and student learning. *Measurement: Interdisciplinary Research and Perspectives, 5*, 107–118.

Hill, H. C., Sleep, L., Lewis, J. M., & Ball, D. L. (2007b). Assessing teachers' mathematical knowledge: What knowledge matters and what evidence counts? In F. K. Lester Jr. (Ed.), *Second handbook of research on mathematics teaching and learning* (pp. 111–155). Charlotte: Information Age Publishing.

Hill, H. C., Blunk, M., Charalambous, C., Lewis, J., Phelps, G. C., Sleep, L., & Ball, D. L. (2008). Mathematical knowledge for teaching and the mathematical quality of instruction: An exploratory study. *Cognition and Instruction, 26*, 430–511.

Hoetker, J., & Ahlbrand, W. P. (1969). The persistence of the recitation. *American Educational Research Journal, 6*(2), 145–167.

Huffman, D., Thomas, K., & Lawrenz, F. (2003). Relationship between professional development, teachers' instructional practices, and the achievement of students in science and mathematics. *School Science and Mathematics, 103*(8), 378–387.

Ingvarson, L., Meiers, M., & Beavis, A. (2005). Factors affecting the impact of professional development programs on teachers' knowledge, practice, student outcomes and efficacy. *Education Policy Analysis Archives, 13*(10), 1–28.

Jacobs, J. K., Hiebert, J., Givvin, K. B., Hollingsworth, H., Garnier, H., & Wearne, D. (2006). Does eighth-grade mathematics teaching in the United States align with the NCTM standards? Results from the TIMSS 1995 and 1999 video studies. *Journal for Research in Mathematics Education, 37*(1), 5–32.

Jacobs, J., Borko, H., Koellner, K., Schneider, C., Eiteljorg, E., & Roberts, S. A. (2007). The problem-solving cycle: A model of mathematics professional development. *Journal of Mathematics Education Leadership, 10*(1), 42–57.

Jacobs, J., Koellner, K., & Funderburk, J. (2012). Problem solved: Middle school math instruction gets a boost from a flexible model for learning. *Journal of Staff Development, 33*(2), 32–39.

Kazemi, E., & Hubbard, A. (2008). New directions for the design and study of professional development: Attending to the coevolution of teachers' participation across contexts. *Journal of Teacher Education, 59*(5), 428–441.

Kersting, N. B., Givvin, K. B., Thompson, B. J., Santagata, R., & Stigler, J. W. (2012). Measuring usable knowledge: Teachers' analyses of mathematics classroom videos predict teaching quality and student learning. *American Educational Research Journal, 49*(3), 568–589.

Kilday, C. R., & Kinzie, M. B. (2009). An analysis of instruments that measure the quality of mathematics teaching in early childhood. *Early Childhood Education Journal, 36*, 365–372.

Koellner, K., Jacobs, J., Borko, H., Schneider, C., Pittman, M., Eiteljorg, E., Bunning, K., & Frykholm, J. (2007). The problem-solving cycle: A model to support the development of teachers' professional knowledge. *Mathematical Thinking and Learning, 9*(3), 271–303.

Koellner, K., Jacobs, J., & Borko, H. (2011a). Mathematics professional development: Critical features for developing leadership skills and building teachers' capacity. *Mathematics Teacher Education and Development, 13*(1), 115–136.

Koellner, K., Jacobs, J., Borko, H., Roberts, S., & Schneider, C. (2011b). Professional development to support students' algebraic reasoning: An example from the problem-solving cycle model. In J. Cai & E. Knuth (Eds.), *Early algebraization: A global dialogue from multiple perspectives* (pp. 429–452). New York: Springer.

Learning Mathematics for Teaching Project. (2011). Measuring the mathematical quality of instruction. *Journal of Mathematics Teacher Education, 14*, 25–47.

Little, J. W. (1993). Teachers' professional development in a climate of educational reform. *Educational Evaluation and Policy Analysis, 15*(2), 129–151.

Lobato, J., & Siebert, D. (2002). Quantitative reasoning in a reconceived view of transfer. *Journal of Mathematical Behavior, 21*(1), 87–116.

Loucks-Horsley, S., Stiles, K. E., Mundry, S., Love, N., & Hewson, P. W. (2010). *Designing professional development for teachers of science and mathematics* (3rd ed.). Thousand Oaks: Corwin Press.

National Council of Teachers of Mathematics (NCTM). (2000). *Principles and standards for school mathematics*. Reston: NCTM.

National Governors Association Center for Best Practices, Council of Chief State School Officers. (2010). *Common core state standards mathematics*. Washington, DC: National Governors Association Center for Best Practices, Council of Chief State School Officers.

Putnam, R. T., & Borko, H. (1997). Teacher learning: Implications of new views of cognition. In B. J. Biddle, T. L. Good, & I. F. Goodson (Eds.), *International handbook of teachers and teaching* (Vol. 2, pp. 1223–1296). Dordrecht: Kluwer.

Richardson, V. (1990). Significant and worthwhile change in teaching. *Educational Researcher, 19*, 10–18.

Silver, E. A. (2010). Examining what teachers do when they display their best practice: Teaching mathematics for understanding. *Journal of Mathematics Education at Teachers College, 1*, 1–6.

Silver, E. A., Mesa, V. M., Morris, K. A., Star, J. R., & Benken, B. M. (2009). Teaching mathematics for understanding: An analysis of lessons submitted by teachers seeking NBPTS certification. *American Educational Research Journal, 46*(2), 501–531. doi:10.3102/0002831208326559.

Supovitz, J. A., Mayer, D. P., & Kahle, J. B. (2000). Promoting inquiry-based instructional practice: The longitudinal impact of professional development in the context of systemic reform. *Educational Policy, 14*(3), 331–356.

Tharp, R. G., & Gallimore, R. (1988). *Rousing minds to life: Teaching, learning, and schooling in social context*. Cambridge: Cambridge University Press.

Weinstein, R. S., Madison, S. M., & Kuklinski, M. R. (1995). Raising expectations in schooling: Obstacles and opportunities for change. *American Educational Research Journal, 32*, 121–159.

Weiss, I. R., Pasley, J. D., Smith, P. S., Banilower, E. R., & Heck, D. J. (2003). *Looking inside the classroom: A study of k-12 mathematics and science education in the United States*. Chapel Hill: Horizon Research, Inc. Downloaded on July 18, 2012, from http://secure.horizon-research.com/insidetheclassroom/reports/looking/complete.pdf

Weiss, I. R., Heck, D. J., & Shimkus, E. S. (2004). Looking inside the classroom: Mathematics teaching in the United States. *NCSM Journal, 7*(1), 23–32.

How Classroom Instruction Was Improved in a Teaching Research Group: A Case Study from Shanghai

Yudong Yang

Abstract In mainland China, a school-based teaching research system has been in place since 1952, and a Teaching Research Group exists in every school. In this paper, three of the teacher's lessons and the changes in each lesson are described, which might show how the lessons were continuously developed in the Teaching Research Group. The Mathematical Tasks Framework, the Task Analysis Guide, and the Factors Associated with the Maintenance and Decline of High-level Cognitive Demands developed in the *Quantitative Understanding: Amplifying Student Achievement and Reasoning* project (Stein and Smith, Maths Teach Middle School 3(4):268–275, 1998; Stein et al. Implementing standards-based mathematics instruction. Teachers College Press, New York, pp 1–33, 2000) were employed in this study. Based on the mathematical task analysis, the changes in three lessons were described, and the author provided a snapshot for understanding how a Chinese teacher gradually improved his/her lessons in the TRG's activities.

Keywords Case study • Mathematical lessons • Pythagoras Theorem • Mathematical tasks • Teaching research activities

Introduction

Unlike western culture, the classroom instruction of Chinese mathematics teachers is open for colleagues' observation, studies, and discussion. A Mathematical Teaching Research Group (TRG) exists in each school in mainland China because of the

This chapter is built upon an article that formally appeared in *ZDM*: Yang (2009).

Y. Yang (✉)
Shanghai Academy of Educational Sciences, 21 Cha Ling Road (North),
Shanghai, 200032, People's Republic of China
e-mail: mathedu@163.com

requirement at the system level. The three-level teaching research network (province-level Teaching Research Office (TRO), county-level TRO, and school-level TRG) has more than 50 years of tradition behind it.

The TRG is the basic unit in the network, and its main responsibility is to carry out studies on teaching in order to solve the practical problems of teachers. Early in 1952, the Ministry of Education stipulated in the *Provisional Regulation for Secondary School (draft)* that "Teaching research groups should be set up in all subjects in secondary schools." A Teaching Research Group is formed by teachers who teach the same subject. In general, a teacher is often assigned to teach one subject for 2–3 classes of the same age group in a school in mainland China. The duty of the TRG is "to study and improve the way of teaching" (MOE 1952).

The *Pythagoras Theorem* is a difficult topic for teachers to cope with, especially younger teachers. In fact, in the following study, a young teacher's lessons experienced the improvement process in the TRG's activities. The TRG's activities are organized by the leader of the TRG. What changes occurred when a teacher developed his/her lesson in the TRG's activities? How did the TRG's activities influence a teacher's instruction? In this paper, a young teacher's three lessons and the changes in each lesson were described, which might show how classroom instruction was continuously developed by the TRG. Considering the unique educational background in mainland China, though the Shanghai case was very representative, the author wanted to point out that the discussion and conclusions in this paper only fit to the concrete Shanghai teacher and Shanghai lessons and it could not be arbitrarily generalized in all lessons or teachers in mainland China.

Background for Chinese Classrooms

Mathematical teaching in China emphasizes basic knowledge and skills (Zhang et al. 2004), which results in students' high achievements in certain large-scale international comparisons (Fan and Zhu 2004). As some scholars mentioned (Lopez-Real et al. 2004), the Chinese classroom has several typical characters, i.e., large classes, whole class teaching, examination-driven teaching, content rather than process oriented, emphasis on memorization, etc. Some scholars criticized that this overexercising and over-drilling ignored the learning of mathematical essence (Tsatsaroni and Evans 1994; Partners in Change Project 1997; Romberg and Kaput 1999; Uhl and Davis 1999). Likewise, some experts in China advocated that the teaching of mathematics should de-emphasize its appearance, reinforce its substance (Song and Chen 1996), and distinguish the educational mathematics from the academic mathematics (Zhang 2001; Zhang and Wang 2002). The *exploring* styles of learning and teaching have been advocated by Teaching Research Officers since the National Mathematics Curriculum Standards for Compulsory Education (Ministry of Education 2001) was issued.

Based on the current situation in China, mathematics teaching has placed more emphasis on mathematics essence (Yang and Li 2005). Instead of overemphasizing the acquisition of mathematics skills, teaching should be rooted in students' common sense and experience and go deep into the problems' mathematical substance. In this way, teachers should let students experience mathematics activities as mathematicians do, such as mathematical conjecturing, plausible reasoning, exploring, validating, and justifying. Then, students will be able to reorganize their new common sense and experiences progressively. For what mathematics students experience in school influences their recognition of mathematics in their future life (Dossey 1992).

Methodology

A Theoretical Perspective for Mathematical Task Analysis

Stein and Smith (1998) used the Mathematical Tasks Framework to analyze hundreds of teaching cases in the *Quantitative Understanding: Amplifying Student Achievement and Reasoning* (QUASAR) project from 1990 to 1995, which showed how a mathematical task was changed when it was carried out in three stages: (1) when a task appeared in curricular or instructional materials, it was an ideal task set up by a curriculum expert or textbook editor; (2) when a task appeared in classroom teaching, it was an operational task set up by teachers; (3) when a task appeared in students' learning, it was an implemented task worked by students. From stage 1 to stage 3, the mathematical task would not necessarily stay on the same level, and some changes occurred in the continuous process. What students achieved relied on these three stages.

In their analysis of hundreds of teaching cases, Stein and Smith found that a higher cognitive task was always translated as a lower cognitive task by teachers in classroom teaching. Only when a task was set up by teachers on a high cognitive level did it have the possibility to be implemented on a high cognitive level by students. Furthermore, they defined four types of tasks in two levels: *memorization tasks* and *procedures-without-connection tasks* were defined as low-level demands in cognition by a description of their features; *procedures-with-connection tasks* and *doing-mathematics tasks* were defined as high-level demands in cognition by a description of their features. These can be found in the *Task Analysis Guide* structured by Stein and Smith (1998).

Stein and Smith (1998; Stein et al. 2000) found that a high-level demands task might be kept on the same level or dropped to a lower level when implemented by students, but a lower-level task had no possibility to be implemented on a higher level by students. For example, when doing a mathematics task (which is a high-level demands task) after it was set up by a teacher in classroom teaching, it might yield one of the four kinds of results. It might be implemented by the students on the same level as a doing-mathematics task or might be implemented by the students as a procedures-with-connection task, or a procedures-without-connection task, or even a memorization task. However, if a teacher sets up a low-level demands task

Table 1 Factors associated with maintenance and decline of high-level cognitive demands (Stein and Smith 1998; Stein et al. 2000)

Factors of maintenance or decline		Explanations
Factors Associated with the *Maintenance* of High-level Cognitive Demands	M1	Scaffolding of students' thinking and reasoning is provided
	M2	Students are given the means to monitor their own progress
	M3	Teacher or capable students model high-level performance
	M4	Teacher presses for justifications, explanations, and meaning through questioning, comments, and feedback
	M5	Tasks build on students' prior knowledge
	M6	Teacher draws frequent conceptual connections
	M7	Sufficient time is allowed for exploration—not too little, not too much
Factors Associated with the *Decline* of High-level Cognitive Demands	D1	Problematic aspects of the task become routinized
	D2	The teacher shifts the emphasis from meaning, concepts, or understanding to the correctness or completeness of the answer
	D3	Not enough time is provided to wrestle with the demanding aspects of the task
	D4	Classroom-management problems prevent sustained engagement in high-level cognitive activities
	D5	Task is inappropriate for a given group of students
	D6	Students are not held accountable for high-level products or processes

(e.g., a procedure-without-connection task), it has no possibility to be implemented as a procedure-with-connection task or a doing-mathematics task. Stein and Smith concluded that the Factors Associated with the Maintenance and Decline of High-Level Cognitive Demands are as shown in Table 1.

The theoretical framework of this mathematical task analysis constructed by Stein and Smith (1998; Stein et al. 2000) will be used in this paper to show what is changed in each lesson and how mathematical tasks are set up by the teacher as well as how they are implemented by students.

Source of Data

The School and the Teacher

The school was an ordinary junior high school with a mid-level economy in the Qingpu District, which is located in west suburb of Shanghai city. The mathematics TRG consisted of seven full-time mathematics teachers employed by the school. Two of them had more than 15 years' mathematics teaching experience (T1 and T2 are used to substitute their names), three of them had 5–10 years' mathematics teaching experience (T3, T4, and T5 are used to substitute their names), and two of them had less than 5 years' teaching experience (T6 is used to substitute one of them).

Ms N was the youngest teacher in the mathematics TRG. She had graduated from Shanghai Teachers University and had 2 years and 3 months of teaching experience. In this paper, we will study three of her lessons on the Pythagoras Theorem.

In Shanghai, mathematics TRGs exist in every primary and high school. Mathematics, Chinese language, and English language are the main subjects in every school, and the teachers in these three TRGs usually teach 2 or 3 classes of the same age group. Every teacher in these three TRGs only teaches one subject: mathematics, Chinese language, or English language. Ms N, after her 4-year study of Mathematics Education at the Shanghai Teachers University, taught mathematics in 3 parallel classes from grade 6 to grade 8. When the lesson data was collected, Ms N had just been through 3 months of her third year's teaching journey.

The Lessons

Three lessons on Pythagoras Theorem that were taught by Ms N in three grade 8 classes were videotaped, and the related TRG's activities were also videotaped. In China, the TRG's activities are mainly pre-lesson discussion on lesson plans and post-lesson discussion on lesson contents and instruction methods.

The first lesson was prepared solely by Ms N, so there was no pre-lesson discussion. After the first lesson, all members of the TRG discussed the problems of the lesson. Then, the members of the TRG discussed how to improve the lesson next time, and Ms N made a new lesson plan after the post-lesson discussion. Similar discussion procedures happened after the second and third lessons. This improving process is a typical procedure in TRGs in Shanghai.

Data Analysis

Analysis of the Lessons

In Shanghai, most of the lessons were teacher centered and most of the mathematics instruction kept to a basic model for historical reasons. Review of old knowledge was usually the first part of a lesson, and summarization of what had been learned was always the last part of a lesson. For a theorem-instruction lesson, the middle part often had three steps: producing the theorem, justifying the theorem, and applying the theorem. However, different teachers emphasized different steps in the middle part of the lesson, which showed their different aims in teaching the same topic. So, in the analysis of the lessons, firstly the structure of the lesson is identified in order to show a whole picture of the lesson. Then, two key tasks are focused on in this paper: producing the theorem and justifying the theorem. Applying the theorem often involved doing exercises, which will not be analyzed in this paper.

The mathematical tasks that appeared in textbooks were set up by teachers and then implemented by students in lessons. In this paper, tasks set up by teachers and implemented by students are/were checked in detail.

The *Task Analysis Guide* (Stein and Smith 1998) was used to define the cognitive level of the tasks set up by teachers and the tasks actually implemented by students. *Memorization tasks* and *procedures-without-connection tasks* were defined as low-level demands, and *procedures-with-connection tasks* and *doing-mathematics tasks* were defined as high-level demands. By this analysis guide, the tasks which really happened in classrooms would be judged if they were high cognitive demands tasks or not, and the result would show us how the tasks should be changed among textbook, teacher, and students.

The *Factors Associated with the Maintenance and the Decline of High-level Cognitive Demands* (Table 1) was used to recognize the main factors that influenced the teacher's implementation of tasks in her instruction. In Table 1, seven common factors associated with the maintenance of high-level cognitive demands and six common factors associated with the decline of high-level cognitive demands are described. In this study, the maintenance factors were coded as M1–M7, and the decline factors were coded as D1–D6 in the key task analysis of the lessons.

Analysis of the Interview of the Teacher

After each of Ms N's lessons and the post-lesson discussion, an interview with the teacher was carried out. So there were three interviews to collect the teacher's opinions on the lesson and the discussion in the TRG's activity. There were two focuses in analyzing these three interviews: (1) what did the teacher see as important in the lesson? (2) What did the teacher feel about others' opinions during the discussion of the lesson in the TRG's activity?

Analysis of the TRG's Discussion

After the on-the-spot observation on each of Ms N's lessons, the TRG members talked about the problems in the lesson and the possible improvements in the next lesson, which was facilitated by the leader of the TRG. All of the discussions were videotaped and transcribed. The transcript's analysis focused on two questions: (1) what did the other teachers in the TRG see as important in the lesson? (2) What kind of opinions influenced Ms N's next lesson?

Results

The results of the three lessons' analysis are presented as three parts, and then the three lessons are analyzed by comparison in summary. In each analysis of the lesson, the lesson structure, two key tasks, and discussion are presented.

The First Lesson

The Lesson Structure

1. Producing the proposition by questions (8 min and 15 s). After asking students to draw two right-angled triangles and measure their sides, Ms N gave out the proposition: $a^2 + b^2 = c^2$.
2. Justifying the proposition by explaining and asking students to read the related content in the textbook (15 min and 51 s)
3. Applying the Pythagoras Theorem to solve four questions in the textbook (21 min and 2 s)
4. Summarizing what was learned in this lesson briefly (43 s)

The Two Key Tasks

Producing the Proposition

How did Ms N set up the task? Firstly, Ms N asked a question to inspire students: "if we know the two edges of a right angle in a triangle, how can we get the hypotenuse?" After introducing a history about Gou 3, Gu 4, and Xian 5, Ms N let the students draw the triangle. She then let the students draw another triangle (5, 12, 13) and calculate the three edges' square. From these two sets of data, she asked: "what is the relationship among [the] three sides of the triangle?" From the Task Analysis Guide, it was a very open question for students. It needed complex, non-arithmetic thinking to come up with a proposition, and there was not an exact way to achieve the answer. It also needed students' hard cognitive efforts to answer the question which had the characteristic of a doing-mathematics task. So, the task was set up by the teacher as a task with high cognitive demands.

How did the students implement the task? In Table 2, seven factors which influenced students' high cognitive implementation of the task are shown.

From the lesson segment in Table 2, the whole process of producing propositions had very limited cognitive demands. According to the characteristic of mathematical tasks described in the Task Analysis Guide, the task of producing propositions implemented by students was a procedures-without-connection task.

Justifying the Proposition

How did Ms N set up the task? Ms N didn't give students the chance to try to justify the proposition by themselves, but directly wrote the algebraic formula [$a^2 + b^2 = (a+b)^2 - 2ab = (a+b)^2 - 4 \times 1/2ab$] on the blackboard. Then Ms N asked students to read the proving process in the textbook and gave some explanations on how the proposition

Table 2 The associated factors influenced students' implementing

Segments of the lesson		Factors
T:	In a triangle, if the two right-angled edges are 3 cm and 4 cm, then the hypotenuse is 5 cm. Right? This is a conclusion. Well, now use your ruler to measure them to check. Ok, use your own paper. Draw a triangle; its two right-angled edges are 3 cm and 4 cm. Well, let us see if the hypotenuse is 5 cm. Right?	D1 (Ms N "took over" the thinking and told students how to validate the figure)
(Students began to draw pictures)		
T:	Ok, one edge is 3 cm, the other one is 4 cm, and then you can see how long the hypotenuse is	D2 (Ms N only took care of the correctness of the expected answer)
S (choral):	5 cm	
T:	Well, next triangle, please draw it. One of the right-angled edge is 5 cm (stop five seconds to wait for students' drawing), and the other right-angled edge is 12 cm, which is much longer. How long is the hypotenuse?	D1 (Ms N "took over" the thinking and told students how to validate the figure)
(Students drew the triangle and measured the hypotenuse)		
T:	How long?	
S1:	13	
T:	Ok, we got two sets of data just now: one is 3, 4, and 5; one is 5, 12, and 13. Let us guess, 3 and 4 are right-angled edges, and 5 is the hypotenuse, right? Here 5 and 12 are right-angled edges, and 13 is the hypotenuse. Then what is the relationship among three sides of the triangle? Please discuss the question in your group and guess what kind of conclusion that we may get	D5 (only 2 sets of data, students learning without scaffold)
(Every 4 students as a group talked for 2 minutes, and Ms N patrolled)		D3 (not enough time to finish a high cognitive demands task)
T:	If the two right-angled edges are 3 and 4, correspondingly, we can find that 3^2 plus 4^2 is equal to 5^2, isn't it?	
S (choral):	Yes	
T:	Well, let's see the second set of data. Is 5^2 plus 12^2 equal to 13^2?	D1 (the high cognitive demands task has been transferred as a computational question)
(No answer, in silence)		
T:	$5^2 = ?$	
S (choral):	25	
T:	$12^2 = ?$	
S (choral):	144	
T:	The sum?	
S (choral):	169	
T:	Right? It is $5^2 + 12^2 = 13^2$	
S (choral):	Yes	

(continued)

Table 2   (continued)

Segments of the lesson		Factors
T:	Ok, now I noticed someone had found something. Well, who would like to tell what you've found?	D1 (by the computational tasks above, the thinking process of producing a proposition had been suggested by the teacher's two sets of data: $3^2 + 4^2 = 5^2$ and $5^2 + 12^2 = 13^2$)
S2:	The first right edge's square plus the second right edge's square is equal to the bevel edge's square	
T:	Then we have such a conclusion. If we generalized the conclusion, what would we get? (Stopped for about 6 seconds, Ms N pointed the blackboard.) If we know the three edges in the right-angled triangle, a, b, and c, then what will we get according to the conclusion mentioned just now?	
S (choral):	$a^2 + b^2 = c^2$	
T:	Good, $a^2 + b^2 = c^2$. That is to say, the sum of the two right edges' square is equal to the bevel edge's square, isn't it? Ok, the proposition we have guessed out, now let's justify it	

was justified in the textbook. Therefore, the task of justifying the proposition was set up in a "telling" way, which had the characteristics of a procedures-without-connection task:

- The procedures of justifying the proposition had been arranged by the teacher (directly told students how to operate the algebraic formula).
- The cognitive challenge for students was much less, because the textbook stated everything about the justifying process.
- The teacher emphasized the outcome of justifying a correct proposition, but didn't care to develop students' ideas on how to justify the proposition.

How did the students implement the task? As Stein and Smith's study pointed out (1998; Stein et al. 2000), only if the teacher sets up a task with a high cognitive demands level is there a possibility for students to implement it on a high cognitive demands level. That is to say, there is no possibility for students to implement a task in a high cognitive demands level if a task was set up by the teacher on a low cognitive demands level. It was obvious that the task set up by Ms N in the lesson was a low cognitive demands task, and so it is unnecessary to discuss whether students implemented the task in a low or high cognitive demands level.

The Discussion in the TRG

What Should Be Taught in the Lesson?

From Ms N's lesson structure, applying the theorem was seen as the most important part of the teaching, but some teachers questioned this.

Ms N: *In my lesson plan, the key segment is applying the theorem. In my opinion, justifying the theorem is too difficult for students. Well, I think there are difficulties for students to find a way to justify it, so I let them read the justifying process in the textbook and I gave some explanations.*

T1:   *The Pythagoras Theorem seemed very simple, and even some students knew it when they were in the primary school. But how such a theorem was found and how it was proved, few one can speak it out. So I think the key tasks should be reconsidered: what should students learn in the lesson?*

T4:   *According to the new curriculum standard, mathematical teaching should pay attention to make students experience the mathematical activities as a mathematician. So the process of producing a proposition should be redesigned.*

T2:   *In mathematical lessons, logical thinking is very important, which is the core of mathematics. Justifying the theorem should be finished by students in teacher's enlightening.*

From the above discussion, we can see how they gradually reached a consensus as to what should be taught.

How Should the Process of Producing Propositions Be Reasonable?

When the TRG reached a consensus on what should be taught in the lesson, their discussion shifted to how Ms N produced the Pythagoras Theorem.

T2:   *Just by the two sets of data, (3, 4, 5) and (5, 12, 13), students smoothly "found" the theorem. That was because of Ms N's questions about these numbers' square. It was almost equal to telling students the outcome.*

T3:   *We cannot ignore that maybe some students have read the textbook before Ms N's lesson and they have known the theorem.*

T1:   *What is a reasonable supposal in mathematics? It should be based on enough supportive data. Mathematical supposal doesn't mean guess a riddle.*

Ms N: *Yes. After the lesson, a boy came to the dais and asked me, "Ms N, in the triangle of (3, 4, 5), may I get a relationship among three edges: $(3 + 5) \div 2 = 4$?" At that time I was thinking maybe it was too arbitrary to get the Pythagoras Theorem just by two special right-angled triangles.*

Then, the subsequent discussion moved on to how to redesign the scaffolds to support students' production of propositions. They decided to use graph paper to build the connections between $a^2 + b^2 = c^2$ and the corresponding squares' areas.

Should the Thinking Way of Justifying the Proposition Be Explored by
Students Themselves?

T2:   *Ms N directly gave students the operation of algebraic formula that was not appropriate. Why the algebraic formula was operated like that? The thinking way of justifying the proposition hasn't been revealed but just*

Fig. 1 Calculating the area of
a catty-cornered square

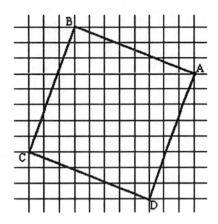

> let students do formula operation without any reasons. Well, that is to say, the
> key algebraic formula $(a+b)^2 = 4 \cdot 1/2ab + c^2$ was just given, maybe students
> just knew how to prove the proposition, but they didn't know why it was
> proved like that.

Ms N: *Indeed, that was the difficulty for me. How can I make students naturally
bethink of $a^2 + b^2 = (a+b)^2 - 4 \cdot 1/2ab$? In the reference book for teachers,
it was designed to use four right-angled triangles to make up, but it was
hard to be implemented by students. I don't know how to enlighten students; I don't know. Hope miracle happened? How to make students catch
it? That's the most difficult point for me in my preparation of the lesson.*

The follow-up discussion then moved ahead to how to overcome the difficult
points in teaching. The members of the TRG gave some suggestions on how
to relate the justifying process to the meaning of the figures of a^2, b^2, and c^2 on the
graph paper.

The Second Lesson

The Lesson Structure

1. Reviewing the method of area calculation (12 min and 32 s). By asking students
   to calculate a catty-cornered square (Fig. 1), the method of replenishing or partitioning four right-angled triangles to calculate the area was clarified.
2. Producing propositions by filling in a table (12 min and 57 s). Ms N asked
   students to fill in the values of four right-angled triangles (Fig. 2) in a datasheet
   (Fig. 3). When students finish filling in the datasheet, Ms N asked students to
   observe the datasheet and put forward what they've found and students found the
   proposition $a^2 + b^2 = c^2$.
3. Justifying the proposition by students themselves on the worksheet (27 min and 34 s)
4. Doing jigsaw games to verify the Pythagoras Theorem visually (10 min and 13 s)
5. Summarizing what was learned in this lesson briefly (37 s)

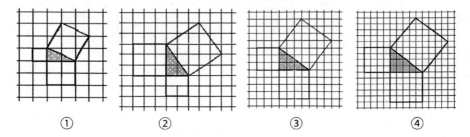

Fig. 2 Four right-angled triangles in the graph paper

Fig. 3 The datasheet

	①	②	③	④	...
a^2					
b^2					
ab					
c^2					

The Two Key Tasks

Producing the Proposition

How did Ms N set up the task? When Ms N set up the task, she firstly drew the squares of three edges of a right-angled triangle on the blackboard and gave some explanations on the geometrical meaning of a^2, b^2, and c^2. Then, she asked the students to calculate the value of a^2, b^2, ab, and c^2 and fill in the datasheet on the worksheet. Lastly, she asked the students to observe the datasheet and look for rules that might be there. Judging from the Task Analysis Guide, to find a rule needed students' complex and non-algorithmic thinking, though the datasheet was a scaffold. This task needed students to observe the datasheet and to understand the relationship of several algebraic values. Using these observations, it can be concluded that Ms N set up a doing-mathematics task.

How did the students implement the task? In Table 3, the factors which influenced students' implementation are coded.

From Table 3, the task implemented by students was high in cognitive demands. Firstly, the students' calculations and observations were built on the methods of area calculation and students' understanding of a^2, b^2, and c^2. Secondly, the datasheet was a scaffold which made the process of producing propositions reasonable for students. Thirdly, Ms N gave students enough time for the process of producing propositions. Though sometimes Ms N took over students' thinking and reasoning, the task was mostly implemented as a doing-mathematics task.

Table 3 The associated factors influenced students' implementing

Segments of the lesson		Factors
T:	Now there are four such figures on the No 2 worksheet; please calculate the value of a^2, b^2, c^2, and ab in each figure. Don't forget to fill the value in the data table	M1 (the teacher scaffold students' thinking and reasoning)
(Ms N walked around while students were doing the task)		
T:	Well, when you finished the data table, please observe the data table and do some comparisons to look for some rules. If you find something, write them down on the worksheet	
(Lasted 4 minutes and 38 seconds)		M7 (the teacher gave students proper exploration time)
T:	Ok. Now every four persons as a group to discuss what you've found. Firstly you should be sure that the values are correct. Then you may talk with your partners about the rules which you have found	
(Group discussion lasted 3 minutes and 26 seconds)		M7 (the teacher gave students proper exploration time)
T:	Ok, just now you've done calculation. Now let's see what you have found by observation of the data table. Who would like to tell us? Yang Ming, please	M5 (the teacher built the task on students' prior work)
S1:	$a^2 + b^2 = c^2$ (Ms N wrote it on the blackboard)	
T:	$a^2 + b^2 = c^2$. Something else? Li Hua?	
S2:	$\sqrt{(ab)^2} = ab$	
T:	$\sqrt{(ab)^2} = ab$. Well, sit down please. Anything else?	
S3:	when $a = 1, (ab)^2 = b^2$	
T:	Ok, anything else?	
T:	No more. Let's see the outcome here. When $a = 1, (ab)^2 = b^2$, this is a special outcome. From the figure, it seemed there is no meaning. Let's see the formula, $\sqrt{(ab)^2} = ab$. In fact, no matter what the values of a and b are, it is always right. It seemed no relationship with the figure which we are learning today. And then the formula $a^2 + b^2 = c^2$, what does a^2 mean?	D1 (without explanation from the students, the teacher took over the students' thinking and reasoning)
S (choral):	One of right edges' square	
T:	a means a right-angled edge, so is b. And $a^2 + b^2$ means the sum of two right-angled edges' square. How about c^2?	
S (choral):	The hypotenuse's square	
T:	This is the very topic what we will learn today. In a right-angled triangle, the sum of two right-angled edges' square is equal to the hypotenuse's square (while speaking, Ms N wrote it down on the blackboard)	

Justifying the Proposition

How did Ms N set up the task? When Ms N set up the task of justifying the proposition, she clued students "to use the method of calculating area to justify the proposition" which suggested a pathway to be followed explicitly. So it was a typical procedures-with-connection task.

How did the students implement the task? In Table 4, the factors which influenced students' implementation are given.

As can be seen from Table 4's analysis of the factors that influenced students' implementation, the task implemented by students was a procedures-without-connection task. Ms N reduced the complexity of the task by telling students to answer the question by "using the method of area calculation." So, the process of justifying was declined as a computational task, and the students focused on the correct calculation of the area of c^2 rather than mathematical understanding of the whole process of justifying a proposition.

The Discussion in the TRG

Do Students Need to Understand the Necessity of Justifying the Proposition?

T2:   *When students got the proposition, $a^2+b^2=c^2$, Ms N directly came to justify the proposition. If I were a student, I would have such a question: why does it need to be justified? The outcome is absolutely right according to the datasheet.*

Ms N: *Actually, I felt a little uncomfortable when I transferred to prove the theorem. But I didn't recognize that was a problem at that time.*

T4:   *I think, as a teacher, we should explain it to the students: in mathematics a potentially correct proposition should be proved generally. But what I am thinking is that, can students understand it?*

T1:   *It is necessary and important to create chances for students to understand the necessity of justifying a proposition. As you know, that's the very mathematical ideas in geometrical learning. You may ask students the question when they verified the proposition in the datasheet: how do you know it is always right in every right-angled triangle? Can you verify it by listing all examples of right-angled triangles?*

By discussion, the members of the TRG began to talk more on how to redesign the lesson to guide students' understanding of the necessity of justifying propositions.

Should the Logical Proof Be Done Strictly in Reasoning?

T5:   *I have a doubt. Why didn't Ms N take a tolerant way to admit student's reasoning in justifying the proposition? When the four congruent right-angled triangles were replenished or partitioned, why the big or small quadrangle was square hasn't been explained.*

Table 4 The associated factors influenced students' implementing

Segments of the lesson		Factors
T:	Now think it over. May we use the method of calculating area of c^2 to prove the proposition, $a^2 + b^2 = c^2$? That is to say the catty-cornered square. Try it on your worksheet	D1 (the teacher reduced the complexity of the task by telling how to do the problem)
(Students did it for 10 minutes and 30 seconds)		M7 (sufficient time is allowed for exploration)
T:	How did we calculate c^2? You may talk about it with your partners	
T:	Well, I noticed someone has finished it. Who would like to introduce your work? Li Yumin!	M3 (a capable student modeled high-level performance)
S1:	Draw a big square in which CB is an edge	
T:	Does it mean drawing a big square outside the right-angled triangle? Well, extend CB, and like this (Ms N draw the figure). Then how did you justify the proposition? (Fig. 4)	D6 (the teacher accepted students' unclear explanation)
S1:	Because of BC = AZ...	
T:	Because of BC = AZ, so the four right-angled triangles are congruent, right? And then?	D2 (the teacher took over the student's reasoning)
S1:	The area of quadrangle XYZC = $(AC + AZ)^2$	
T:	Using lowercase, it will be $(a+b)^2$ (Ms N wrote it down)	
S1:	The area of square ABDE = $(a+b)^2 - 4*1/2ab = (a+b)^2 - 2ab = a^2 + b^2$	
T:	And then?	
S1:	Because of the area of square ABDE = c^2	
T:	Yes, because the edge of square ABCD is c, its area is c^2. So we get $a^2 + b^2 = c^2$. Sit down please	D2 (the teacher took over the student's reasoning)
T:	Just now we justified the proposition by replenishing method. And the other method of calculating area, partitioning method, who would like to use it to justify the proposition? Zhang Wei!	D1 (the teacher reduced the complexity of the task by telling how to do the problem)
S2:	Intercept four congruent triangles in the square ABDE, and the area of each is equal to $\triangle$BCA	M3 (a capable student modeled high-level performance)
T:	Intercept? How to intercept (drew figures while speaking)? In the square ABDE, we partitioned it as four Rt$\triangle$ and one small square. And then? (Fig. 5)	D2 (the teacher took over the student's reasoning)
S2:	The area of square ABDE is equal to the area of square HIJK plus 4S$\triangle$BHA (while S2 was speaking, Ms N wrote it down on the blackboard)	
T:	Ok, and then?	
S2:	It is $(b-a)^2 + 4*1/2ab$	

(continued)

Table 4 (continued)

Segments of the lesson		Factors
T:	Well, the edge is b, and this edge is a. So the area of the small square is $(b-a)^2$. And then?	D2 (the teacher took over the student's reasoning)
S2:	$=b^2-2ab+a^2+2ab=b^2+a^2$. And because the area of square ABDE is c^2, $c^2=a^2+b^2$ (while S2 was speaking, Ms N wrote it down on the blackboard)	
T:	$c^2=a^2+b^2$, right? Yes, by these two methods, may we justify the proposition?	
S (choral):	Yes	
T:	Ok, here we got a very important theorem called the Pythagoras Theorem	

Fig. 4 Ms N's figure on the blackboard

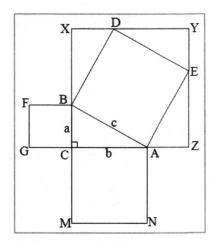

Fig. 5 Ms N's figure on the blackboard

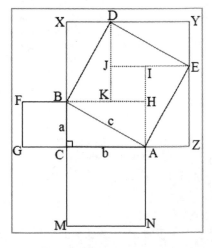

Ms N: *I thought it was too difficult for students. That was the reason why in my first lesson I didn't expect my students to prove the proposition. For example, when you replenished four congruent right-angled triangles on the catty-cornered square, you must explain why the three points are in the same line. That's too difficult for my students.*

T2: *As geometrical reasoning, the key steps should be explained by students.*

T1: *I don't think so. When students came to replenish four triangles, it was natural for them to "see" a big square. If the teacher stopped here and asked them to do explanations, firstly, maybe it might block students' wholly reasoning process in justifying the proposition, and secondly there is not enough time. The lesson overspent too much time.*

T2: *If it is too difficult for your students, I think at least the teacher should do explanations.*

T1: *Maybe, but for most students, they just began to learn geometrical reasoning, and the strict requirement may destroy their interest of further learning.*

This topic was quite controversial and the six teachers in the TRG quarreled about it for a long time. At last, considering the limited time in one lesson, most teachers consented that the strict reasoning should be required in the future learning. For the justification of the proposition, they thought the replenishing method should be communicated to in the whole class, because it was more understandable for most of the students. The partitioning method, though useful for a handful of students, would not be introduced to the whole class, and the teacher should instead encourage more students to try it after the lesson.

The Third Lesson

The Lesson Structure

1. Reviewing the method of area calculation (6 min and 36 s)
2. Producing propositions by filling in a table (20 min and 16 s). Ms N asked students to fill in the values of four right-angled triangles (same as Fig. 2 in the 2nd lesson) to a datasheet (Fig. 6). When students finished the datasheet, Ms N asked students to observe the datasheet and put forward some propositions.
3. Justifying of the proposition by students themselves on the worksheet (10 min and 21 s). Because of the hint of calculating a catty-cornered square on graph paper and Ms N's emphasis on the replenishing method, even with the blackout of the graph paper (Fig. 7), the students found the way to justify $c^2 = (a+b)^2 - 4 \times 1/2ab = (a+b)^2 - 2ab = a^2 + b^2$.
4. Doing jigsaw games to verify the Pythagoras Theorem visually (10 min and 49 s)
5. Summarizing what was learned in this lesson briefly (55 s)

Fig. 6 The datasheet

	I	II	III	IV	V
a					
b					
a^2					
b^2					
2ab					
c^2					

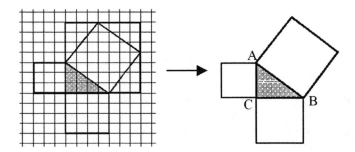

Fig. 7 Blackout of the graph paper

The Two Key Tasks

Producing the Proposition

How did Ms N set up the task? Ms N firstly drew the squares of the three edges of a right-angled triangle on the blackboard and gave some explanations on the geometrical meaning of a^2, b^2, and c^2. Then, she asked students to calculate the valuesv of a^2, b^2, $2ab$, and c^2 and fill them into the datasheet. Later, she asked students to observe the datasheet and look for rules that might be there. Judging from the Task Analysis Guide, the task needed students' complex and non-algorithmic thinking, though the datasheet was a scaffold. This task needed students to observe the datasheet and to understand the relationship between several algebraic values. Ms N set up a doing-mathematics task.

How did the students implement the task? In Table 5, the factors which influenced students' implementation are coded.

From the process of the students' production of propositions, students were required to access relevant knowledge and experiences and considerable cognitive effort to support or disprove what they have found. It was implemented by students as a typical doing-mathematics task.

Table 5 The associated factors influenced students' implementing

Segments of the lesson		Factors
T:	Ok, no problem with the data? Then carefully observe the data in the table please, and think about what inference we might get from the data. Well, see it. If you find one, don't stop there and try to find more	M1 (scaffolding students' thinking and reasoning)
(Students observed and discussed the datasheet for about 1 and a half minutes)		M7 (appropriate exploration time)
T:	Then please tell me what inference you have found? Li Dan!	
S1:	In my group, we found two conclusions: $2ab + 1 = c^2$ and $a^2 + b^2 = c^2$ (Fig. 8)	
T:	Oh? (S2 raised his hand) Well, Liu Yuyin, what do you think?	M4 (pressing explanation by questioning)
S2:	Ms N, I just drew a right-angled triangle, $a = 2$, $b = 4$. $2ab = 16$ and $c^2 = 20$, so $c^2 \neq 2ab + 1$	
T:	Pretty good! Liu Yuyin disproved it by a special example. It seemed that was very persuasive. So the proposition $c^2 = 2ab + 1$ doesn't come into existence. Oh, do you want to speak something?	M4 (pressing for meaning by comments and feedback)
S1:	We just found when $a - b = 1$, $2ab + 1 = c^2$ could come into existence	
T:	Sit down please. What you thought is reasonable and it seemed $c^2 = 2ab + 1$ was a conclusion with some conditions. Well, how about $c^2 = a^2 + b^2$? You, please	M4 (pressing for meaning by comments and feedback)
S3:	It is always right judging by all the examples in the worksheet. But I am thinking, if I give more examples... Even if one hundred of examples are right, but the one hundred and first example does not match it, how can I do? So if I want to be sure of its correctness, I must know that all of its examples are right. If there is only one example which doesn't match it, it would be still a conclusion with some conditions	
T:	Sit down please. If we want to know if it is a theorem, judging by several examples is not enough. Then what we should do?	M4 (pressing explanation by questioning)
S (choral):	Justification	

Justifying the Proposition

How did Ms N set up the task? When Ms N set up the task of justifying the proposition, like in the second lesson, she clued students to "think of the method to calculate the area of catty-cornered square," which suggested a pathway to follow explicitly. So it was a typical procedures-with-connection task.

How did the students implement the task? In Table 6, the factors which influenced students' implementation are coded.

From the process of implementing the task by students in Table 6, Ms N kept questioning and building connections between calculation and figures. Though it was not justified very strictly, students did get a whole understanding of the thinking way to justify the proposition. It was kept as a procedures-with-connection task.

Fig. 8 One of the datasheets

图表	I	II	III	IV	V
a	1	2	3	5	
b	2	3	4	6	
a²	1	4	9	25	
b²	4	9	16	36	
2ab	4	12	24	60	
c²	5	13	25	61	

Table 6 The associated factors influenced students' implementing

Segments of the lesson	Factors
T: Think of the method to calculate the area of the catty-cornered square to justify $a^2 + b^2 = c^2$. What is c^2 equal to?	D1 (telling how to do the problem)
(Students did it independently for 4 minutes and 50 seconds)	M7 (appropriate exploration time)
T: Well, let me ask somebody to tell us. Zhang Wen, try it	M3 (a capable student modeled high-level performance)
S1: Replenish three right-angled triangles around the catty-cornered square	
T: Replenish three right-angled triangles around the catty-cornered square (Ms N drew them on the blackboard). Next step? (Fig. 9)	D6 (the teacher accepted students' unclear explanation)
S1: The area of the biggest square is $(a+b)^2$	
T: What does c^2 mean? ... What is c^2 equal to?	M6 (keeping questioning the meaning) and M4 (building connection between figures and formula)
S1: So the biggest square subtracts four right-angled triangles. It is $(a+b)^2 - 4 \times 1/2ab$	
T: Subtract $4 \times 1/2ab$ and the area of each small right-angled triangle is $1/2ab$. Then we have got c^2; how do we justify the proposition?	
S1: Calculate out the square	
T: Well, let's calculate it	
S1: It is equal to $a^2 + 2ab + b^2 - 2ab = a^2 + b^2$	
(S1 said it and Ms N wrote it on the blackboard)	
T: We get $c^2 = a^2 + b^2$? May you explain the thinking way to justify it?	M4 (building connection between calculation and figures)
S: Yes. c^2 is the catty-cornered triangle and it is equal to that, the biggest square subtract four congruent right-angled triangles	
T: Good, sit down please. From the process of justification, we got the conclusion: the sum of two right-angled edges' square is equal to the hypotenuse's square. Now we verified its correctness and it is a true proposition, called Pythagoras Theorem	

The Discussion in the TRG

How Do the Teacher Deal with Students' Other Propositions?

T5:   *When I observed the lesson in the classroom, I noticed that several students produced other propositions in their worksheet. Like these: $c^2 = (a + b)^2 - 2ab$, $c^2 = (a - b)^2 + 2ab$ and $a + b + a^2 = b^2$. Though the first*

Fig. 9 Ms N's figure on the
blackboard

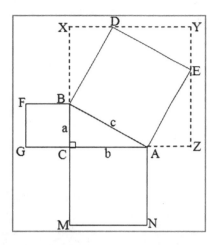

two could be simplified as $a^2 + b^2 = c^2$, *the last one wasn't understandable.
So I think Ms N should give such students chances to speak them out.*

T2: *Yes, I noticed them, too. The last one was created by one set of special
numbers. I suggest that Ms N should collect all the students' worksheets
to analyze students' thinking.*

T1: *After Ms N dealt with* $2ab + 1 = c^2$, *she should have asked such a question:
anybody else has other findings? Such question may inspire students' more
thoughts.*

Ms N: *Yes, I hurried up to move the lesson ahead. The second lesson overtimed
too much, so I felt that I did not have enough time.*

These teaching suggestions came from the teachers' classroom observations.
Ms N received some useful information which she hadn't noticed during the whole
class teaching process.

Is the Jigsaw Game Necessary for Students?

Though there was no possibility to have the fourth lesson, another new topic for the
redesign of the lesson was brought up.

T4: *For the jigsaw game, I don't understand its value in the lesson. The theorem has been justified by logical reasoning. Is it necessary for students to
manipulate it? To verify the theorem visually? (Fig. 10)*

Ms N: *I had the same doubt from the second lesson. Is the jigsaw game counted
as another kind of justification? Students have proved the theorem before
the game, so it is at most as a verifying activity. If I had the fourth lesson,
I would like use some problems to apply the theorem.*

T2: *The theorem has been justified. So the jigsaw game could be seen as an
applying problem. Students needed to change places of the four right-
angled triangles and presented that the area of the catty-cornered square
was the sum of two small squares. I think it was an applying problem.*

Fig. 10 Jigsaw game

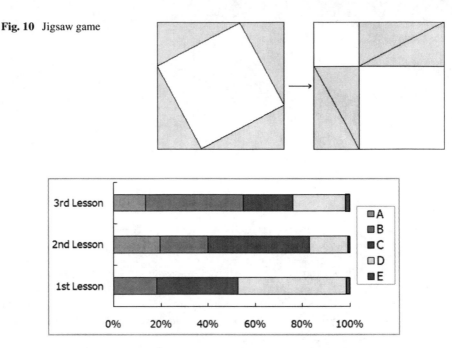

Fig. 11 Time percentage of segments in each lesson

In fact, the discussion on this topic reflected teachers' usual way of thinking: in the limited lesson time, what was the important part to be arranged in the lesson?

Summary and Discussion

What Was Changed?

If each lesson was divided into five common parts, reviewing the method of area calculation (segment A), producing propositions (segment B), justifying the proposition (segment C), applying the theorem/doing jigsaw games (segment D), and summarizing the learning (segment E), then the three lessons' segments could be compared. Figure 11 shows what the most important part of the lesson was, judging by the percentage of teaching time spent on each segment.

Ms N's three lesson structures (Fig. 11) reflected the change in her teaching behaviors. In the first lesson, applying the theorem was emphasized; in the second lesson, justifying the proposition; and in the third lesson, producing propositions.

The three lesson plans were also checked, and the change was listed in Table 7. From Ms N's lesson plans done by herself, what the teacher saw as important in the lesson might be reflected, too.

Table 7 The tasks set up by Ms N in each lesson plan

	Tasks set up by Ms N in each lesson plan	Features
The 1st lesson	To justify the theorem To apply it in exercises	Emphasis on the content of the theorem and its application
The 2nd lesson	To produce propositions To justify it and become a theorem	Emphasis on the process of producing propositions and the method of justifying it
The 3rd lesson	To produce propositions To understand the way of justifying it To verify the theorem visually by jigsaw games	Emphasis on the whole process of producing propositions, its justifying way, and understand it visually

Table 8 Producing propositions in three lessons

	As set up by teacher	As implemented by students	Maintenance or decline	Factors associated with maintenance or decline
The 1st lesson	Doing-mathematics task	Procedures-without-connection task	Decline	7 decline factors (4 D1, D2, D3, D5)
The 2nd lesson	Doing-mathematics task	Doing-mathematics task	Maintenance	4 maintenance factors (M1, M5, 2 M7) and 1 decline factor (D1)
The 3rd lesson	Doing-mathematics task	Doing-mathematics task	Maintenance	6 maintenance factors (M1, 4 M4, M7)

In the three lessons, two key topics were focused on and analyzed in this study: how the task was set up by the teacher and how it was implemented by students. The maintenance or decline of one high cognitive demand-type task per lesson is summarized in Tables 8 and 9.

Comparing the three lessons (Table 8), the task of producing propositions which was set up by the teacher and implemented by students declined to a low cognitive level in the 1st lesson, but maintained a high cognitive level in the 2nd and the 3rd lessons. Also, the maintenance factors increased and decline factors decreased gradually from the 1st lesson to the 3rd lesson.

As can be seen from Table 9, the tasks of justifying the proposition in these three lessons were set up by the teacher and implemented by students differently. In the 1st lesson, the task set up by the teacher was not a high cognitive one. In the 2nd lesson, the task set up by the teacher was a high cognitive one, but declined to become low cognitive. In the 3rd lesson, the task maintained high cognitive demands. Also, the maintenance factors increased and decline factors decreased gradually from the 2nd lesson to the 3rd lesson.

The change that took place in the three lessons might be contributed to the TRG's activities, which influenced Ms N's teaching behavior. The main topics in the three TRG's activities are summarized in Table 10.

Looking back on the three post-lesson discussions, which were often started by the problems in former lessons and ended with suggestions for the next lesson, some

Table 9 Justifying the proposition in three lessons

	As set up by teacher	As implemented by students	Maintenance or decline	Factors associated with maintenance or decline
The 1st lesson	Procedures-without-connection task	(No possibility to be implemented in a high cognitive level)	–	–
The 2nd lesson	Procedures-with-connection task	Procedures-without-connection task	Decline	3 maintenance factors (2 M3, M7) and 7 decline factors (2 D1, 4 D2, D6)
The 3rd lesson	Procedures-with-connection task	Procedures-with-connection task	Maintenance	5 maintenance factors (M3, 2 M4, M6, M7) and 2 decline factors (D1, D6)

Table 10 Discussion topics in the TRG

	Main topics in the TRG discussion	Features
The 1st lesson	What should be taught	Teaching aim centered
	Reasonable process of producing propositions	Focusing on key tasks
	Students' understanding of thinking a way of justification	Caring of students' actual learning
The 2nd lesson	Students' understanding of the necessity in justifying	
	Strictly logical proof in reasoning	
The 3rd lesson	Caring of students' other propositions	
	Jigsaw game's necessity for manipulation	

common features were noticed: the discussions were all teaching aim centered, focusing on key tasks, and finally caring of students' actual learning in lessons.

How Lessons Were Improved?

Learn from Other Teachers and Himself/Herself in the TRG

Because of the school-based teaching research system, it is very common for Chinese teachers to learn others' experience in the TRG's activities, which is called peer coaching. The value of peer coaching for teachers' professional development has been pointed out by various scholars (Anderson and Pellicer 2001; Lin et al. 1999).

After the study of teaching, especially the discussion, I think the way of teaching is clearer than that in the textbooks. I have known it well. Where a question should be given to students and where an emphasis is arranged, and the teaching details guided by master teacher in discussion, are more useful compared to my own lesson design (from Ms N's interview).

In Chinese school-based teaching research activities, teachers usually experience his/her own routine lesson and then the improved lesson, which integrates suggestions from the TRG's activity. When the research lesson teacher had a chance to teach three lessons repeatedly in parallel classrooms, he/she actually had a good opportunity to compare his/her own three lessons, which allowed him/her to learn from himself/herself.

After the second lesson, I thought it over a lot. Though I thought a lot about the design before the lesson, I cannot help thinking it again and again. If I restarted the lesson, I would rethink the conjunction among the four worksheets, the language to express every question, and the summarization after each activity (From Ms N's interview).

Construct Profound Understanding of Mathematics in the TRG

In Ma's study (1999), Chinese teachers didn't have high-level educational certificates, but they had a more profound understanding of mathematics than their US counterparts. In fact, the TRG members were teachers who taught the same subject and usually always taught that subject in 2 3 parallel classes in schools. So, the discussion in the TRG often related to their opinions on mathematics. When they talked about what should be taught and what should be learned, these kinds of questions were closely connected with their understanding of mathematics, and these teachers had constructed their understanding of mathematics gradually over a long teaching career.

A big idea about mathematics gave me deep impression. Let the students experience the process of justification and disproval. In my usual lesson I never thought about it. The mathematics examples, exercises, how to deal with them had been thought a lot before. From the discussion this time, I knew how to have such kind of lessons (From Ms N's interview).

Learn Teaching Theory in Actions

Since Chinese curriculum reform was carried out in the 1990s, teachers have faced more and more challenges from new ideas and teaching theories, and they have been required to attend many training courses. In these training courses, teachers learned new information and ideas from experts' lectures, but teaching theory is hard to practice in classrooms. Rather than that kind of "learning in listening," the TRG's activity was "learning in doing," in which teachers got grassroots professional development in their teaching practice (Paine and Fang 2006). In the three post-lesson discussions, the teachers tried to use graph paper as a scaffold to help students experience doing mathematics: from producing propositions to disproving or justifying them.

In my first lesson, I put emphasis on applying theorem to answer questions for I thought the theorem was too difficult to be justified. Actually, after I introduced the justification in the textbook, I myself felt guilty. Is that counted as a justification teaching? Now I knew the Scaffold Theory and understand how to use it in the teaching.

I never thought of graph paper and never expected it could be used in teaching a theorem (From Ms N's interview).

Though this was a single case from Shanghai, the three lessons' improving process was very representative, because the TRG's network generally exists on mainland China. Of course, not every lesson developed in a TRG can get honors in a nationwide competition of lessons. Actually, when a teacher's lesson wins a prize in China, it has often pooled a lot of collective wisdom, and all the members of the TRG see it as a boost for their team's reputation. This paper simply shows how a lesson was transformed, step by step, in the Shanghai case. In many Chinese teachers' minds, a good lesson is always a process and never an outcome.

References

Anderson, L. W., & Pellicer, L. O. (2001). *Teacher peer assistance and review: A practical guide for teachers and administrators.* Thousand Oaks: Corwin Press, Inc.

Dossey, J. A. (1992). The nature of mathematics: Its role and its influence. In D. A. Grouws (Ed.), *Handbook of research on mathematics teaching and learning* (pp. 39–48). New York: Macmillan.

Fan, L. H., & Zhu, Y. (2004). How have Chinese students performed in mathematics? A perspective from large-scale international comparisons. In L. Fan, N.-Y. Wong, J. Cai, & S. Li (Eds.), *How Chinese learn mathematics* (pp. 3–26). Singapore: World Scientific.

Lin, R. F., Yan, P. S., & Lin, Y. K. (1999). *Tongchai huzhu de guanke wenhua* [Observation culture of peer coaching]. Hong Kong: Hong Kong Association of Educational Assessment.

Lopez-Real, F., Mok, A. C. I., Leung, K. S. F., & Marton, F. (2004). Identifying a pattern of teaching: An analysis of a Shanghai teacher's lessons. In L. Fan, N.-Y. Wong, J. Cai, & S. Li (Eds.), *How Chinese learn mathematics* (pp. 382–412). Singapore: World Scientific.

Ma, L. P. (1999). *Knowing and teaching elementary mathematics.* Mahwah: Lawrence Erlbaum Associates, Publishers.

Ministry of Education. (1952). *Zhongxue Zanxing Zhangcheng* [Secondary school provisional regulation] (Chinese governmental document).

Ministry of Education. (2001). *Quanrizhi Yiwu Jiaoyu Kecheng Biaozhun (Shiyangao)* [National mathematics curriculum standards for compulsory education]. Beijing: Beijing Normal University Publishing House.

Paine, L. W., & Fang, Y. P. (2006). Reform as hybrid model of teaching and teacher development in China. *International Journal of Educational Research, 45,* 279–289.

Partners in Change Project. (1997). *The partners in change handbook—A professional development curriculum in mathematics* (p. 6). Boston: Boston University.

Romberg, T. A., & Kaput, J. J. (1999). Mathematics worth teaching, Mathematics worth understanding. In E. Fennema & T. A. Romberg (Eds.), *Mathematics classrooms that promote understanding* (pp. 3–17). Mahwah: Lawrence Erlbaum Associates, Inc.

Song, N. Q., & Chen, C. M. (1996). Zaitan "danhua xingshi, zhuzhong shizhi" [Re-discussion on desalt appearance and reinforce substance]. *Shu Xue Jiao Yu Xue Bao* [Journal for Mathematics Education], *59*(2), 15–18.

Stein, M. K., & Smith, M. S. (1998). Mathematics tasks as a framework for reflection: From research to practice. *Mathematics Teaching in the Middle School, 3*(4), 268–275.

Stein, M. K., Smith, M. S., Henningsen, M. A., & Silver, E. A. (2000). *Implementing standards-based mathematics instruction* (pp. 1–33). New York: Teachers College Press.

Tsatsaroni, A., & Evans, J. (1994). Mathematics: The problematical notion of closure. In P. Ernest (Ed.), *Mathematics, education and philosophy: An international perspective* (pp. 87–108). London: The Falmer Press.

Uhl, J., & Davis, W. (1999). Is the mathematics we do the mathematics we teach? In E. A. Gavosto, S. G. Krantz, & W. McCallum (Eds.), *Contemporary issues in mathematics education* (pp. 67–74). Cambridge/New York: Cambridge University Press.

Yang, Y. (2009). How a Chinese teacher improved classroom teaching in Teaching Research Group. *ZDM, 41*(3), 279–296.

Yang, Y. D., & Li, S. Q. (2005). Benyuanxing Wenti Qudong Ketang Jiaoxue [Driving classroom teaching by primitive mathematical ideas]. *Shu Xue Jiao Yu Xue Bao* [Journal for Mathematics Education], *14*(2), 59–63.

Zhang, D. Z. (2001). Guanyu shuxue zhishi de jiaoyu xingtai [Educational status on mathematical knowledge]. *Shu Xue Tong Bao* [Mathematical Bulletin], *5*, 2.

Zhang, D. Z., & Wang, Z. H. (2002). Guanyu shuxue de xueshu xingtai he jiaoyu xingtai [Educational and academic status on mathematical knowledge]. *Shu Xue Jiao Yu Xue Bao* [Journal for Mathematics Education], *11*(2), 1–4.

Zhang, D. Z., Li, S. Q., & Tang, R. F. (2004). The "two basics": Mathematics teaching and learning in Mainland China. In L. Fan, N.-Y. Wong, J. Cai, & S. Li (Eds.), *How Chinese learn mathematics* (pp. 189–207). Singapore: World Scientific.

Pursuing Mathematics Classroom Instruction Excellence Through Teaching Contests

Yeping Li and Jun Li

Abstract In this study, we focused on some of the teaching contests and features of mathematics classroom instruction excellence identified through teaching contests in the Chinese mainland. By taking a case study approach, we examined a prize-winning exemplary lesson that was awarded the top prize in a teaching contest at both the district and the city levels. The analyses of the exemplary lesson revealed important features of the lesson's content treatment, students' engagement, and the use of multiple methods to facilitate students' learning. These features are consistent with what the contest evaluation committees valued and what seven other mathematics expert teachers focused on in their comments. The Chinese teaching culture in identifying and promoting classroom instruction excellence through teaching contests is then discussed.

Keywords Chinese classroom • Classroom instruction analysis • Exemplary lesson • Instructional excellence • Mathematics instruction • Teaching contest

Introduction

It is commonly acknowledged that classroom teaching is key to the improvement of students' mathematics learning. Efforts to improve the quality of classroom instruction have led to the formation of diverse approaches and activities to improve the

This chapter is built upon an article that formally appeared in *ZDM*: Li and Li (2009).

Y. Li (✉)
Department of Teaching, Learning and Culture, Texas A&M University,
MS 4232, College Station, TX 77843-4232, USA
e-mail: yepingli@tamu.edu

J. Li
Faculty of Arts and Education, School of Education, Deakin University,
Geelong Waurrn Ponds Campus, Locked Bag 20000, Geelong Victoria 3220, Australia

Y. Li et al. (eds.), *Transforming Mathematics Instruction: Multiple Approaches and Practices*, Advances in Mathematics Education, DOI 10.1007/978-3-319-04993-9_21, © Springer International Publishing Switzerland 2014

quality of teachers in terms of their knowledge, skills, and performance (e.g., Li and Even 2011). Cross-nationally, such differences in approaches and activities can be dramatic, especially when teaching is viewed differently across cultural contexts (e.g., Li and Even 2011; Li and Li 2009). Li and Li specified such differences between the East and West in viewing and improving teaching as a professional practice. In the West, teaching is seen more as a professional activity that is unique to each classroom, and few teachers would sit in other's classrooms to observe and then discuss their classroom instruction. In contrast, China has a much different culture of teaching, where mathematics teaching is taken as a professional activity that is open to public scrutiny and evaluation (Li et al. 2011). It is a common practice for Chinese mathematics teachers not only to sit in others' classrooms and discuss teaching with fellow teachers but also to develop and polish lesson instruction together. Such cross-cultural differences suggest a special cultural context in China that promotes the development of different professional activities for the improvement of teachers and their teaching.

Mathematics classroom teaching in China has been a topic of interest to mathematics educators and researchers in many education systems over the years (Li and Huang 2013). Cross-cultural differences and similarities in viewing what contributes to high-quality classroom instruction call for a better understanding of Chinese classroom instruction that goes beyond the surface features. Because teaching is seen as a professional activity that is open to public scrutiny and evaluation in China, it becomes possible to learn what has been evaluated as exemplary mathematics classroom instruction through teaching contests, a unique professional activity that also helps promote teacher professional development in China.

In this chapter, we will thus focus on teaching contests, a popular yet singular professional activity that is often organized at different levels by the Chinese education administration and various professional organizations. Through teaching contests, excellent mathematics classroom instruction is identified and awarded, and participating teachers are given great opportunities to develop and improve their classroom teaching. Thus, teaching contests serve as a platform to promote mathematics classroom instruction excellence in China. In particular, we aim to present and discuss the teaching contest as an organized professional activity in China, the features of mathematics classroom teaching excellence identified and valued through the teaching contest, and the cultural values embedded in judging and promoting mathematics classroom instruction excellence in China.

Teaching Contest as a Professional Activity in China

General Description of Teaching Contest

Teaching contests are often organized by the education administration with different participation scopes in China. It can be a nationwide, province-wide, citywide, district-wide, or school-wide contest. A high-level teaching contest is often organized with contestants who were winners of the low-level contests. For example, the secondary mathematics education committee of the China Education Academy organizes one contest every 2 years on excellent mathematics classroom instruction (now called the national exemplary lesson demonstration). Participation in this nationwide contest (or exemplary lesson demonstration) requires one to first participate in a sequence of bottom-up contests that are organized at different administration levels. In general, the sequence of contests starts at the district level, which will select winning teachers to participate in the contest organized at the city or county level. Participants who are eligible to join the city or county level contest will all get an award, but the awards differ based on their performance in the contest at this level. The same process will be repeated for selecting contestants to join the contests organized at the provincial and then national levels.

In China, the teaching contest is a well-organized formal professional activity. It is organized and carried out with pre-specified procedures. The following is a sample procedure for organizing this type of teaching contest in a large southern city of China:

1. Form an organizing committee that will decide participants' eligibility, contest content and scope, organization format, general criteria, and ratio for prize winning.
2. Prepare the contest notice, then put an official stamp on the finalized notice, and distribute the notice to the districts and schools under direct administration of the city education bureau.[1]
3. Based on the official notice, every district will organize its own initial contest. Then the districts will submit the names of their contest winners together with their contest results, in a descending order of quality evaluated, to the city organizing committee for participation in the city-level contest.
4. For the schools that are under direct administration of the city's education bureau, participating contestants can join the city-level contest directly.
5. Within a predetermined period of time, the city organization committee will organize the city-level contest with contestants selected from its districts or schools. It is often organized into several subgroups. When the city-level contest is about halfway done, the evaluation committees for contest subgroups will exchange one or two members for the rest of the contest in each subgroup. The membership of the evaluation committee consists of three groups of professionals: mathematics instruction coordinators of the city education bureau, members of the standing committee of the city's school mathematics education association, and key mathematics teachers of the city's central groups for different grade levels.
6. All members of the evaluation committee then meet to exchange and discuss contest information and results. A consensus will be reached about contestants' performance and evaluation.

---

[1] In China, most schools are public schools. A few private schools have been established over the past years that are not administrated by the government.

7. Based on what is stated in the official notice and contest results, the organizing committee will decide the awards and then organize a ceremony to present the awards to contest winners.

Although there are some variations across different teaching contests in terms of contest focus and organization specifics, these contests are alike in that they view teaching as a professional activity that is open to public examination and evaluation. The detailed organization procedure, as presented above, reveals not only the formality of the teaching contests established by Chinese education administration but also the broad support and participation from teachers themselves.

Current teaching contests are often organized in different formats, including the traditional classroom instruction, as well as instructional design and lesson explaining. While instructional design is provided in a written form, the lesson-explaining contest is commonly carried out as an on-site oral presentation. Initiated about 20 years ago, lesson explaining was formally developed out of teacher group analysis of textbooks in China (Peng 2007). It has since developed into a popular professional activity that helps Chinese teachers to explain important features of their classroom instruction and their thinking, which may otherwise be unclear to others. Lesson explaining commonly contains a teacher's analysis of the textbook content, instructional objectives, consideration and design of teaching methods and procedure, and the teacher's consideration of students and their learning. Because lesson explaining promotes teacher reflective practice and discussion, it is used as an important activity in many schools in China to help improve teachers' mathematics knowledge and classroom instruction (Peng 2007).

Teaching contests can also be organized in conjunction with other professional contests for selecting key teachers. The selected key teachers are often required to provide instructional training to other teachers in the subject content area. For example, in a large southern city of China, a teaching contest is organized once every 3 years who's only participants are young mathematics teachers who are under the age of 40. The contest focuses on teachers' classroom teaching skills and is organized as part of a process to identify and select the ten best middle school mathematics teachers and ten best high school mathematics teachers in that city. In particular, contestants are required to be winners of at least the second-class awards in two other relevant contests: the mathematics teachers' problem solving contest and the mathematics teachers' education articles evaluation. In general, there are about 20 contestants for each level. The teaching contest will then generate the top ten winners for each school level. There are also some other contests that are organized with no regular schedule. For example, this same city once organized a competition of classroom instruction and lesson reflection under the new mathematics curriculum. This competition was also restricted to the winners selected or recommended from the district level.

In the following section, we will further discuss how the participating teachers' instructional competence is typically examined in the teaching contests in China.

Examining Videotaped Mathematics Classroom Instruction and Teaching Contests as Cultural Activities: A Case Study

Because the video captures well what goes on in classrooms, videotaped lessons have been widely used in China since the 1980s. At the beginning, video was mainly used to record master teachers' lesson instruction. Now, it is widely used in teacher education in order to demonstrate and discuss lesson instruction. In fact, videotaped lessons have also been used in teaching contests in China, especially in selecting good teachers at the district or city/county level. This method is different from the traditional, yet still commonly used approach in which contestants are asked to teach an unknown group of students with his/her planned lesson. Being aware of the possible limitations that a videotaped lesson instruction may carry, the teaching contest organizers often add additional requirements as parts of the contest. Depending on the theme of a contest, contestants may also be required to take part in mathematical problem solving contest, lesson instruction design contest, and/or lesson-explaining contest. Thus, results from other parts of the contest can provide a rich picture of a contestant's competence in focus.

In this study, we focused on a prize-winning videotaped lesson as an exemplary lesson from Mainland China. Through taking the case study approach, we aimed to examine the exemplary lesson that was identified and selected through several teaching contests. Moreover, it is also necessary for this study to go beyond the analysis of the videotaped exemplary mathematics lesson alone. In particular, by taking mathematics classroom teaching and teaching contests as cultural activities, we intended to collect rich data around the videotaped exemplary mathematics lesson and the teaching contest. Relevant documents were thus collected, and interviews with the prize-winning teacher and contest organizers were carried out to examine the process of the prize-winning lesson development and the contest evaluation. Finally, the prize-winning videotaped lesson was also shown to some other mathematics education experts and teachers in China to get their evaluation and views about excellence in mathematics classroom instruction.

To develop a better understanding of the exemplary classroom instruction that was identified and selected through the process of teaching contests, we will use both holistic and analytic approaches to describe and analyze the exemplary lesson in focus. While the holistic approach is used to depict a coherent picture of what was happening in the exemplary mathematics lesson, the analytic approach aims to provide a closer look at several different aspects of the lesson. As classroom instruction is a process that involves many different agents, cultural artifacts, and their interactions in the classroom setting, we thus focus on the aspects of content, student, and instruction. In particular, they include:

1. Content aspects: tasks used and connections made
2. Student aspects: students motivated to learn and students encouraged to reason, conjecture, and prove mathematical ideas carefully in a community of learners

and to conceptualize and solve mathematical problems through flexible use of various mathematical ideas and their connections
3. Instruction aspects: content introduction and activity arrangement, the use of different materials and class time and the teacher's instructional skills and his/her interactions with students

The specifications of these aspects also provide a framework for examining the interviews with the teacher, contest organizers, and other mathematics education experts and teachers in China.

Research Questions

In this study, we will examine features of mathematics classroom teaching excellence that are valued and were identified through the teaching contest and the cultural values embedded in judging and promoting such excellence in mathematics classroom instruction in China. In particular, we plan to take a case study approach to focus on a prize-winning mathematics lesson as an exemplary lesson. Through collecting data around the lesson case, this study is designed to address the following three questions:

1. What are the characteristics of the exemplary mathematics classroom instruction that was awarded through teaching contests in China?
2. What features in the exemplary lesson were valued and focused in the teaching contests in China?
3. What features in the exemplary lesson were identified and valued by other mathematics teachers and educators in China?

Methodology

Participants and Context of the Case

This study focused on a prize-winning exemplary lesson taught by a Chinese middle school mathematics teacher, Mr. Zhang.[2] We chose this lesson partly due to the convenience of obtaining this prize-winning videotaped lesson and the collaborations of the teacher and teaching contest organizers.

Like many other mathematics teachers in China, Mr. Zhang obtained a bachelor's degree in mathematics from a teacher preparation program at a normal university. He began to teach at a middle school in a large city of southern China upon his completion of the 4-year teacher preparation program study. According

---

[2] All the names used here or in the other places of this article are pseudonyms.

to Mr. Zhang, he also obtained the second-class instructor certificate of International Mathematical Olympiad issued in China right before he began to teach middle school. This suggests that Mr. Zhang had strong mathematical content preparation and was good at solving mathematics problems. At the time when he developed and taught this prize-winning mathematics lesson, Mr. Zhang was a junior teacher who had less than 3 years' teaching experience. Mr. Zhang, like other teachers in the school, was also a member of two different teaching research organizations in that school: (1) *the teaching research group* that is often a content subject-based organization contrived in a school and (2) *the lesson preparation group* for teachers teaching at the same grade level as a sub-organization of the teaching research group (e.g., Ma 1999; Wang and Paine 2003; Yang and Ricks 2013). According to Mr. Zhang, he received a lot of help and suggestions from his colleagues, especially from his mentor: who happened to be the head of the teaching research group that he belonged to.

Mr. Zhang participated in two teaching contests, one at the district level and the other at the city level. The school district that Mr. Zhang belonged to was a large school district, with 56 middle schools. The contest was organized as a two-level contest. The first level was carried out as an initial contest within the sub-districts of middle schools that were grouped in terms of geographical areas. In principle, all teachers were eligible to participate in the initial contest. The No. 1 winner at the sub-district level would be eligible to join the final contest at the whole district level. For the final contest, the contestant did not need to teach a lesson again, but simply let the district's evaluation committee watch the videotaped lesson made for the initial contest. Moreover, the final contest required the contestants to participate in the lesson-explaining contest in front of the district's evaluation committee and the instructional design contest. The contestants' performances were then evaluated in terms of these three different contests and summarized for an overall judgment. The contestants' performance summaries resulted in awards for three classes. There were two winners awarded for the first class and four winners awarded for each of the second and the third classes. Mr. Zhang won the first-class award at the whole district level and was actually the winner with the highest overall score in three contests of classroom teaching, lesson explaining, and instructional design.

The contests organized at the city level contained a "lesson-explaining contest" and a "videotaped lesson instruction contest under the new curriculum." The contest results from different school districts formed the base for the competition at the city level. With his contest result at the district level, Mr. Zhang joined these two contests at the city level. Similar to the final contest organized at the district level, the city-level contest also resulted in three classes of awards, with a ratio of awardees of 2:3:5. Mr. Zhang won a first-class award for the videotaped lesson instruction, as well as a second-class award for his lesson explaining at the city level.

Based on Mr. Zhang's own explanation, the process of generating the lesson was a process of continuous refinement that involved many others' help. Mr. Zhang developed the first version of the lesson plan and used it in teaching one of his two classes. As Mr. Zhang indicated, he was not happy with the instructional effects. After consulting with other members of his lesson preparation group, especially his mentor, he revised the lesson plan substantially and taught it again with another class that was not his own. He was almost satisfied the second time but felt that some minor changes were needed. Thus, he further revised the lesson plan through the next three versions and eventually had the fifth version as the final one. Based on the last version of the lesson plan, Mr. Zhang then taught the lesson with his one remaining class and also videotaped it for the teaching contest.

Types of Data Collected

The prize-winning lesson was a public lesson that was made available through the teaching contest organizers at the city level. After obtaining consent from all participants (including Mr. Zhang, two contest organizers at the district and the city levels, and other seven mathematics educators), further data collection was carried out to get relevant information concerning the lesson and teaching contests. All participants were informed that the data collection was for research purposes only. Because all of the participants were spread out across the country, it was almost impossible to collect all the data through face-to-face interviews. Moreover, we tended to provide participants ample time to think about relevant questions. In this way, the participants were able to write up detailed responses when they had free time. Thus, the method of mail surveys (Berends 2006) was used to collect relevant data in this study. When clarifications became necessary, we contacted the teacher and contest organizers again and collected all the information that was needed for the study. In particular, the following three types of data were collected in this study:

1. The mail survey from the teacher who designed and taught the prize-winning lesson in focus. A questionnaire was designed to collect relevant information about the prize-winning lesson directly from the teacher himself. In particular, we obtained the background information about the teacher himself, his thinking when he selected and structured the content topic for the lesson, the process of developing the prize-winning lesson, his lesson reflections, and his views about the value of teaching contests.
2. The mail surveys of the two contests' organizers who also served on evaluation committees. A questionnaire was also designed to collect information about the teaching contests at both the district and the city levels. The information collected included the procedure of organizing the teaching contest, any requirements for teachers' participation, evaluation components and criteria used in teaching contests, committee's evaluation of the prize-winning lesson in focus, and their views about the value of teaching contest in promoting classroom instruction excellence.
3. The mail survey of seven mathematics educators and expert teachers to obtain their views of the prize-winning lesson in focus. The videotaped lesson was provided to seven other mathematics educators and expert teachers in different cities

who were not part of the teaching contests. Without telling them that the videotaped lesson was a prize-winning lesson, these mathematics educators and teachers were asked to watch the videotaped lesson and then share their views about the lesson by filling out a specifically designed questionnaire. In particular, these mathematics educators and teachers were asked to comment on the lesson in terms of its strengths, weaknesses, and possible changes for improvement, if any. We intended to use open-ended questions in the questionnaire so that the respondents could comment on the lesson based on what they value. In this way, the respondents' comments help reveal not only their lesson evaluations but also the focal aspects in their evaluation. Moreover, the respondents were also asked to provide an overall evaluation score for the lesson (with 1 as the lowest score and 5 as the highest score) and explain their rationale.

Method of Data Analysis

All the data for this study was analyzed in the original language of Chinese. Selected data were translated to English to provide evidence in the later sections of this chapter. In particular, the lesson is transcribed verbatim, along with some contextual information and time recording for all the conversations that happened in the class. To address our first research question directly, we analyzed Mr. Zhang's prize-winning lesson both holistically and analytically (see, Stigler et al. 1996). While the holistic approach was used to provide an overview of what was happening in the exemplary mathematics lesson (see section "Overview of the exemplary lesson"), the analytic approach aimed to provide a closer look at several different aspects. Because the classroom instruction is a complex process that involves different agents, cultural artifacts, and their interactions in the classroom setting, we took a similar lens as the 1999 TIMSS video study to focus on the aspects of content, students, and instruction (Hiebert et al. 2003). In particular, they include (1) content aspects, the lesson's content treatment, tasks used, and connections made; (2) student aspects, students' learning and engagement in lesson activity; and (3) instruction aspects, the teacher's use of instructional methods and discourse in content introduction and activity arrangement, lesson coherence, and activity variations. The mail survey with the teacher was examined to supplement and triangulate the lesson analysis.

The mail surveys with the teaching contest organizers and seven other mathematics teachers were analyzed to highlight what features were identified and valued in the exemplary lesson. While the survey data were examined holistically, particular attention was also given to these three aspects: the mathematics content, students' learning and participation, and the teacher's classroom instruction. Through this analysis, we attempted to identify cultural values that were embodied in the contest evaluations and other mathematics teachers' views. Finally, the teacher and contest organizers' comments about teaching contest and its value were also discussed.

The following three sections are organized in an order corresponding to the three research questions. At first, we provide an overview of Mr. Zhang's prize-winning lesson and analyze its main features. Then, we discuss how the lesson was evaluated in the teaching contests. In the second section, we analyze and report the survey data collected from seven other mathematics educators and expert teachers to further our understanding of any possible cultural values that were embedded in judging the merit of mathematics classroom instruction in China. In the final section, we synthesize our findings and discuss the implications of this study.

The Exemplary Mathematics Lesson: The Computation of Powers

Because the contest organized in his district allowed the contestants to select their own content topics, Mr. Zhang selected the lesson's content topic for himself. When he learned about the initial teaching contest at the district level, Mr. Zhang was finishing a chapter on one-variable linear inequalities. The next chapter in the textbook was about the multiplication of integral expressions that include powers. Students had been introduced the concept of power, but not its computations. The first section of the chapter was "the computation of powers," and Mr. Zhang chose this as his content topic for the teaching contest.

In Mr. Zhang's class, 32 students were sitting in pairs at desks arranged in six rows facing a teaching podium at the front. The class was organized so as to have eight groups for possible group discussion when needed, with each group having two pairs of students seated in proximity to each other. Some teachers were also sitting in the classroom to observe the lesson.

Overview of the Exemplary Lesson

Taking a similar segmentation approach to the one used in the TIMSS video study (Hiebert et al. 2003), we identified and divided the lesson into three segments (see Table 1): (1) introducing the topic, presenting a problem in real-world context together with reviewing previous content that relates to solving the new problem; (2) developing rules of power computation, letting students solve sample problems and discussing their solutions; and (3) reinforcing and practicing, solving various sets of problems and sharing solutions. This sequence of lesson activity is common in China for lessons that introduce new content. The teacher often begins the lesson with a problem and/or content review, and the rest of the lesson is oriented toward developing new content and reinforcing students' learning through varying problems and the discussion of various solutions (e.g., Gu et al. 2004; Li and Huang 2013).

Table 1 Overview of the exemplary lesson on the computation of powers

Segment	Length	Description
1	6 min	Introducing the topic – showing a video clip to present a problem of computing a rocket traveling distance that involves power computations (4.5 min) and reviewing concepts of power, base, and exponent (1.5 min)
2	15 min	Developing rules of power computation – letting students solve several problems and the class discussing their solutions that lead to the formation of power computation rules (a combination of individual efforts and group sharing)
3	24 min	Reinforcing and practicing – letting students practice new content through solving problems that vary in several different ways and discussing their solutions (23 min) and having a summary (a bit less than 1 min)

Fig. 1 First two sets of computation problems

Computing and giving your result in the form of power:

Group A:

1. $5^3 \times 5^2 =$
2. $b^5 \cdot b^4 =$
3. $a^6 \cdot a^2 =$

Group B:

4. $(5^3)^2 =$
5. $(b^5)^4 =$
6. $(a^6)^2 =$

By showing the video clip of a Chinese rocket launching, Mr. Zhang began the lesson by recalling the event of launching the Chinese rocket, Shenzhou No. 6, into space and posing the problem "the rocket had flown at the speed of 7.9×10^3 m/s for almost 5 days; adding up about 4.1×10^5 s, how many meters had it flown in total?" After deliberating with the entire class, Mr. Zhang provided the formula on a computer's monitor in the form of PowerPoint slides for solving this problem and stated "We can write the expression for this problem, but it seems new for us to do the computations. In order to compute the distance that Shenzhou No. 6 traveled, we will need to learn the computation of powers today." Then, Mr. Zhang asked students to review how to write number multiplications using exponents. One is to write 2 as multiplied by itself 5 times; the other is to write a multiplied by itself m times. Then, Mr. Zhang reviewed the definition of power, base, and exponent.

After reviewing, Mr. Zhang asked students to try to solve two sets of computation problems (see problem groups A and B in Fig. 1) using previous knowledge by themselves first and then to discuss their solutions within their own groups.

One and half minutes later, Mr. Zhang chose one group's answers and showed their answers on an overhead projector for the whole class discussions, together with some explanations provided by that group. Then, Mr. Zhang asked the students to observe these answers and posed the following question: "Now we know that these answers are correct; please observe these two sets of the problem; can you tell me what changed and what did not change after the computations?" After getting responses from the class by chorus, Mr. Zhang concluded the students' answers: "Yes, we noticed that for both group A and group B, the base did not change and the exponents changed after the computation, right? How did they change? Group A is (with the class) to add the exponents together, and group B is (with the class) to multiply the two exponents."

Now, Mr. Zhang posed two other problems on a big screen using the symbolic representation (i.e., $a^m \cdot a^n = ?$ $(a^m)^n = ?$). He worked together with the students to come up with $a^m \cdot a^n = a^{m+n}$ on the blackboard, and called it *multiplying two powers with the same base*. After providing this guidance, Mr. Zhang asked students to use the same process to find the computation formula for another problem $(a^m)^n$. Students worked individually or in their groups for a few minutes. Mr. Zhang later chose an answer from one group and put it on the OHP for discussion. Then, Mr. Zhang summarized the process to the students: "In this case, the base is a^m, and we have a total of n times of a^m. We can use *two powers with the same base* to add the powers together. There are n of m; therefore, it should be a^{mn}." Mr. Zhang then asked whether there is another way to solve this problem. Another group of students brought their answer to the platform and one student explained to the whole class. The answer is $(a \cdot a \cdots a)(a \cdot a \cdots a)(a \cdot a \cdots a) \cdots (a \cdot a \cdots a)$. Mr. Zhang then summarized the rule for computing *the power of powers*. He further pointed out that "we can see the computation here; if it is to multiply the powers with the same base, we change the multiplication to addition, and if it is the power of powers, we change the power to the multiplication. This reflects a transforming thinking in mathematics. That is, we transform a high-level computation to a lower-level one."

For the next 24 min, Mr. Zhang provided three more sets of computation problems that vary in performance requirements (see Fig. 2). For the first set of computation problems, Mr. Zhang asked each group in turn to answer one of these questions. The second set of problems was to find errors and Mr. Zhang asked students to compete with each other for speed (*qiangda*) in providing their

---

I. Computing and giving your result in the form of power:
   1. $a \cdot a^5 =$ 2. $(y^2)^5 =$
   3. $(3^3)^4 =$ 4. $b^3 \cdot b^3 =$
   5. $10^{2004} \times 10^{2005} =$ 6. $(x^3)^3 =$
   7. $c^x \cdot c^2 =$ 8. $(b^y)^3 =$

II. Judging whether the following computations are correct, and explaining why.
   1. $a^4 \cdot a^4 = a^{16}$ 2. $a^2 + a^2 = a^4$
   3. $(a^3)^5 = a^8$ 4. $4a^2 - a^2 = 4$
   5. $a + a^2 = a^3$

III. Computing:
   1. $a^2 \cdot a \cdot a^4$ 2. $(y^3)^2 \cdot (y^2)^3$
   3. $(m^2)^3 \cdot (m^2)^2$ 4. $(a^3)^3 + a^8 \cdot a$

Two open-ended problems
   1. Fill-in blanks:
      $a^{12} = a \cdot a^{(\ )} \cdot a^5 = (a^2)^4 \cdot a^{(\ )} = (a^3)^2 \cdot (a^2)^{(\ )}$
   2. Please use what you have learned today to write out multiple expressions of a^6

Fig. 2 Problems used during the third segment

answers with explanations. Moving on to the third activity, Mr. Zhang showed four computation problems as written on the blackboard and asked four students to work on the blackboard and the rest of the class to do it on their own worksheets. The teacher then led the class to solve the rocket traveling problem presented at the beginning of the lesson. With some practice and discussion of power computation, the class finished the computation quite quickly. The teacher then provided two more open-ended problems (see Fig. 2), and students' trials and discussions helped push them to think beyond the case of positive integers for power computations. Finally, Mr. Zhang finished the lesson by reviewing the power computation formulas (as shown on PowerPoint) with students and asked students to complete their worksheet.

The Lesson's Main Features

On the surface, it seems that the lesson itself is straightforward. It shows a young and energetic teacher who made good uses of information technology to teach an otherwise purely mathematical content topic. Much of the class time was spent either on the teacher's explanation or students' solving problems. However, if we look further beyond the surface, our analyses of its three aspects (content, student, and instruction) indicate that the lesson contains several features that contributed to this lesson's success (see Li and Li 2009 for detailed analyses).

First, this is a goal-oriented lesson with its outcomes positively demonstrated throughout the lesson, especially at the end. The students were able not only to respond actively and correctly to most questions posted along the instruction process but also to differentiate these two computation rules and use them with possible extensions at the end. The lesson shows a clear and focused dealing of the mathematics content that emphasizes knowledge connections and differentiations, as well as its applications in solving real-world problems. Students' positive learning suggests that content requirements and its treatment were suitable to students' situation.

Second, students in the lesson were motivated to explore, deduct, compare, and use the rules for two power computations. Students' interest and engagement were cultivated through the teacher's careful design and use of different tasks and exercise problems, as well as his questioning and timely praises, for example, the design and use of the rocket launching video clip at the beginning and the sets of sequenced exercise problems solved by students in small groups. Students were kept on tasks through solving and discussing these exercise problems with adequate difficulty level to them. Multiple solutions to the same problem were greatly encouraged and shared in the class. Students were assumed responsibilities to come up as well as justify their solutions. They enjoyed these activities even more when experiencing success with their own efforts along the way.

Finally, the lesson's success also relied on the teacher's design and capability to carry out the lesson. The teacher did not simply tell students the power computation rules. Rather, he provided students opportunities to explore, share, and discuss different solutions to generate knowledge. He also employed multiple methods to facilitate frequent and various interactions with students that helped keep them on task and obtain feedback for adjusting the instruction progress. The teacher not only used the common methods of questioning, discussions, and having individual students come to share their solutions on the blackboard but also adopted small group collaborations, group competitions, and the adequate use of information technology. Although the teacher used multiple methods in teaching, overall the lesson is coherent and focused in content. The teacher tried to bring the lesson full circle at the end by solving the problem posed at the beginning. The class presented a harmonious atmosphere which shows that the teacher did well in piecing together different aspects to reach good instructional effects.

This exemplary lesson embodies the many features that were revealed by others in previous studies about Chinese mathematics classroom instruction (e.g., Li and Huang 2013). Even more, the lesson also shows the importance of instructional content dealing. While the design and use of challenging tasks and exercise problems are important as also pointed out by others (e.g., Fan et al. 2004; Stigler and Stevenson 1991), our analyses of this lesson suggest that the task design and use need to be based on the teacher's in-depth understanding of the content topic in relation to students. The tasks and exercise problems were not randomly chosen, nor were they chosen simply because they are fun or interesting. In fact, Mr. Zhang mentioned that he received other teachers' help in selecting and revising tasks and exercise problems. Task design and selection as shown in this lesson were deliberated to serve the needs of achieving the lesson's objectives.

The Teacher's Lesson Explaining and Reflection

Mr. Zhang's lesson explaining covers eight main sections: textbook analyses, instructional design ideas, analyses of students' situation, methods for dealing the important and difficult points of teaching, instructional methods and learning methods, instructional segments, after-lesson reflections, and an appendix of excerpts from students' great work. His lesson explaining fittingly presents what Mr. Zhang thought about the lesson in its multiple aspects. In particular, Mr. Zhang paid great attention to the content and textbook treatment. For example, the teacher went to great details in explaining what he perceived as the important and difficult content points as well as his proposed methods of teaching.

Mr. Zhang stated two important content points of teaching for this lesson: (1) knowing the process of deriving the computational formulas of "the multiplication of powers with the same base" and "the power of powers" and (2) the applications of these two computation formulas. In order to teach these important content points well, Mr. Zhang proposed the use of two instructional methods. The first is to use problem comparison, let students solve new problems, and then derive the computation formulas under the teacher's guidance. This approach aims to address the first important content point of teaching. The second approach is to design and use three

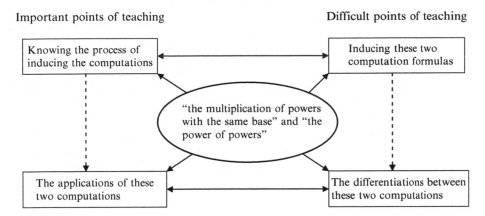

Important points of teaching   Difficult points of teaching

Fig. 3 Relationships between the important and difficult content points of teaching

sets of exercise problems with gradually increasing difficulty and let students solve these exercise problems as to stress the second important point of teaching.

Mr. Zhang also indicated two difficult content points of teaching for this lesson: (1) the induction of the computational formulas of "the multiplication of powers with the same base" and "the power of powers" and (2) the differentiations between these two computations. Correspondingly, Mr. Zhang put forward two methods for addressing these two difficult points. The first method is to take the induction of these two computation formulas one by one. He proposed to guide students to derive the computation formula of "the multiplication of powers with the same base" first and then let students have group explorations and model the process to derive the formula for computing "the power of powers." This method also tends to foster students' participation and collaboration and let them experience success through explorations. The second method is to design and use three sets of exercise problems, with the first set on simple applications of these two different computation formulas, the second on differentiating and judging the correctness of given computations, and the third on the mixed use of these computation formulas.

The two important content points and two difficult points of teaching refer to two different aspects of the same mathematical knowledge. The following figure shows their connections and differences.

Figure 3 shows that Mr. Zhang was able to identify and articulate the important and difficult points of teaching with the same content as placed in the center oval. The teacher put a great deal of thought in differentiating the closely related aspects of the mathematics content from the curriculum perspective (i.e., the two important points of teaching at the left side), as well as from the students' perspective (i.e., the two difficult points of teaching at the right side). The two important points of teaching are also related along the process of lesson instruction (shown as a dotted arrow line); the same goes for the case of the two difficult points of teaching. Moreover, Mr. Zhang came up with specific methods to address these important and difficult points of teaching. As described above, the methods he proposed for addressing the first important and difficult points of teaching do not refer to the same thing. Whereas the methods proposed for addressing the second important and difficult points of teaching refer to the design and use of the same three sets of exercise problems, they differ on the aspects being focused. For addressing the second important point of teaching, the design and use of these three sets of exercise problems as a whole are proposed as a method. In contrast, it is the nature of these three different sets of exercise problems that are specifically designed to help address the second difficult point of teaching. Here, students' four common mistakes in power computations were all addressed: $a \cdot a^3 = a^3, a + a^2 = a^3, a^3 \cdot a^3 = a^9$, and $(a^3)^5 = a^8$. The teacher's content treatment and proposed instructional methods show his in-depth thinking about the content, students, and what he can do through classroom teaching.

Mr. Zhang also wrote an after-lesson reflection. He thought by himself that this was a successful lesson in many ways. Specifically, he elaborated on his reflections of what he did while introducing the content topic at the beginning of the lesson, his lesson preparation, and his rationale behind the use of specific teaching methods in the classroom. At the same time, Mr. Zhang pointed out that he needed to further improve his capability to lead the class. For instance, he thought that he did not manage well when he mistakenly wrote $(m^2)^3 \cdot (m^3)^2$ instead of $(m^2)^3 \cdot (m^2)^2$. During the lesson, he confessed that he had written it incorrectly, but he reflected that this could be turned into an opportunity to teach the students to read the problem carefully or to use them as two different problems and let students explore the possibility of using two different solution methods. Given his less than 2 years' teaching experiences at that time, Mr. Zhang's reflections suggest that he knew his weakness and tended to improve his own teaching skills.

The Lesson's Quality as Evaluated Through Teaching Contests

Main Components of Evaluation Used in the Teaching Contests

Based on the specific requirements of a contest, different components of teaching evaluation were developed and used to judge the quality of the contested aspects. It should be noted here that the evaluation criteria, reflecting new and updated instruction ideology, evolve over time. The contestants knew what aspects were commonly evaluated in teaching contests during that period, although they might not have the exact criteria used in the contest evaluation. The contest announcement specified the purpose, scope, and the timeline of the contest and what the contestants needed to prepare and/or submit for joining the contest.

At the district level, the contest was organized to focus on the teaching skills. The contest consisted of three parts: lesson instruction design, lesson explaining, and classroom lesson instruction. For each part, a specific evaluation chart was used for rating. These three parts bore different weights, in this case 20, 20, and 40 points, respectively. The contest results were then based on the contestants' summary points earned from these three parts plus the contestants' self-reflections (20 points) on the lesson that was submitted.

The evaluation form for rating classroom lesson instruction places great emphases on the design of instructional content and students' learning. It is expected that the teacher needs to have an accurate analyses and understanding of the textbook, identify and handle the important and difficult content points of teaching well, and set up adequate instructional objectives. At the same time, the evaluation form highlights the importance of considering students' reality and motivating them to learn. It also contains specific aspects related to the teacher's use of instructional methods, classroom environment, and instructional effects.

The contest that Mr. Zhang joined at the city level was a contest of videotaped classroom instruction under the new curriculum. An independent evaluation chart was also developed and used for judging the quality of the submitted videotaped lessons. The evaluation sheet shows an equally distributed emphasis on six aspects (i.e., instructional objectives, lesson-type characteristics and content design, instructional methods, students' activity, interactions and feedback, and classroom organization), plus one aspect with a slightly less weight (i.e., instructional effects). These seven aspects together present a broad coverage of classroom instruction components that can contribute to the lesson quality.

Committee's Evaluation

For the final contest at the district level, the evaluation committee provided a written evaluation of Mr. Zhang's videotaped lesson, his written lesson instruction design, and his performance in lesson explaining. The following is the committee's evaluation of Mr. Zhang's lesson instruction:

> *For the classroom lesson instruction*: Can develop a problem situation based on a novel task that is of interest to students; have natural and effective teacher-students interactions, reflect well the student-centered instructional concept in every instructional segment, can follow the eighth graders' development characteristics to satisfy their psychological needs of expressing themselves actively to demonstrate their capability of pattern discovery as well as to be acknowledged, have a harmonious classroom atmosphere, the teacher has a relatively strong capability in leading the class learning and structuring the textbook content for teaching; the teacher's language use is concise and encouraging, and the teacher can effectively use modern instructional technology; the teacher uses an analogical approach in handling the textbook content, which helps students to better understand the connections and differences between the two computations and thus overcome the difficult content point of teaching fairly well; the instruction stresses the important content points of teaching, and has good instructional effects.

The committee's evaluations basically follow the aspects provided in the evaluation form. In particular, the evaluation committee was happy with the way that Mr. Zhang introduced the content topic with a novel problem and approach, motivated students to learn through continuous interactions, and generated and followed the class's group dynamics. The committee also praised Mr. Zhang's understanding and treatment of the textbook content and his handling of the important as well as difficult content points in teaching.

For the contests at the city level, the evaluation committee did not generate a written evaluation, but formed oral evaluative comments. Because the evaluation was done more than a year ago, the contest organizer was only able to recall some of the evaluative comments made at that time. In general, the city-level evaluation committee's comments were consistent with the evaluation that Mr. Zhang received at the district level, except for the lesson-explaining competition. The consistent evaluative comments suggest an emphasis on the teacher's understanding and handling of the instructional content as related to the specific group of students' learning, as well as the teacher's capability in employing different methods to make students' learning of such content effective.

Other Experts' Evaluation of the Exemplary Lesson: Views and Comments

In October 2007, seven mathematics educators and teachers were asked to watch the prize-winning videotaped lesson and provide their comments via a prede-signed mail survey. Although some of these educators and teachers knew each other professionally, they were invited separately for this survey. Table 2 summarizes the general background information about these seven educators and teachers.

All of these interviewees are either experienced mathematics educators or mathematics teachers. Because China practices a professional ranking and promotion system, the senior rank is the highest professional rank for teachers and "exceptional teacher" is an honorary title awarded to some senior-rank teachers who are exceptionally good (e.g., Li et al. 2011). "Teaching researcher" (*jiaoyanyuan*) is a special position similar to the instructional coordinator or supervisor

Table 2 Background information of the seven mathematics educators and teachers

Code	Professional rank	Highest degree	Years of teaching	Job nature
T1	Professor	Bachelor	40	University professor in math education, also in charge of editing the textbook
T2	Senior-rank teacher	Bachelor	27	High school teacher
T3	Exceptional teacher	Bachelor	30	Teaching researcher for middle school
T4	Exceptional teacher	Bachelor	25	Teaching researcher for middle school
T5	Professor and exceptional teacher	Bachelor	32	Professor at a teacher training school, also the writer of the chapter taught by Mr. Zhang
T6	Senior-rank teacher	Bachelor	20	Middle school teacher
T7	Senior-rank teacher	Bachelor	26	Middle (and high) school teacher

in the United States. Every school district, county, and city in China establishes such a teaching research office for every school subject, including mathematics. Teaching researchers are normally recruited and selected from teachers who have exceptional teaching performance and/or leadership. All teaching researchers interviewed in this study had a designated focus on middle school mathematics in different cities.

Among the seven experts, four gave 4 out of 5 points, one 4.6 points, and two 5 points. These present an average evaluation score of 4.4 out of 5 points. If taking the full credit of 5 points as excellent, the numerical evaluation results suggest that all these interviewees rated this lesson as very good or excellent. The result is consistent with the teaching contest committee's evaluation in general.

While the numerical result presents an overall picture of these experts' evaluations, their comments show their thinking and the rationale behind their ratings. In particular, we found that the teachers who gave the highest ratings focused more on the instruction. They especially like Mr. Zhang's use of the novel problem and information technology for introducing the content topic, his approach of gradually unpacking the knowledge for students' learning, and his fostering of students' interest in exploration and their thinking. For example, the following are part of two expert teachers' comments:

> I like this lesson. This lesson adapted an entertainment format that is attractive to modern middle school students. It focused on the knowledge exploration, understanding, summarization, and reinforcement. The lesson made its progress gradually from one level to next and it was embedded in students' competitions among small groups. The lesson resulted in very good effects, and brought the teacher and students as well as students themselves closer. [T6]

> In dealing the exercise problem of $(m^2)^3(m^2)^2$, the teacher paid attention to different methods. He kept leading and encouraging students to go on blackboard to show these two different methods. [T4]

In contrast, the more critical mathematics educators and teachers seemed to focus on the content and somewhat on the student. In fact, the two experts who also developed the textbook gave their evaluation point of 4 and questioned the teacher's treatment of the textbook content. For example, the following is part of the textbook editor's comments about the teacher's restructuring of the textbook content:

> Of course, the content treatment needs further considerations. The problem is that although these two computation rules have a close and logical connection, they stay at different levels. The first rule (the multiplication of powers with the same base) should be the base for the second rule (the power of exponents), and the second rule is the application and further development of the first rule. If taking a methodological view, the first rule is the base for all the computations of powers. It is also the starting point for learning power computations, thus it is important to emphasize its learning and should not share its emphasis with the learning of other rules. ... Finally, putting these two rules together for students to learn, the teacher paid special attention to relevant exercises on comparisons, diagnoses and analyses, correcting errors, and syntheses. Thus, it seems that not enough practices and reinforcement was given to each individual rule. [T1]

In fact, T1's comments were in sharp contrast to Mr. Zhang's design idea in restructuring the textbook content for teaching. While Mr. Zhang wanted to emphasize these knowledge connections, the textbook editor believed that these knowledge points deserve different instructional attentions. Interestingly, the textbook chapter writer (T5) also voiced his concerns about Mr. Zhang's content treatment, albeit in a different way:

> This lesson used the rocket traveling distance as the initial problem context, then reviewed basic concepts of power. This content arrangement may not be adequate, and lack clear requirements. For this lesson's content, it is not necessary to find and use a real-world problem as the initial context. [T5]

In addition to the concerns about the content treatment, there were some other suggestions related to students. For example, T2, T5, and T7 suggested that the teacher could encourage and engage students more. Those experts provided not only detailed comments about the lesson strengths and weakness but also specific suggestions for making alternative changes to the lesson (e.g., T1 and T7). Their comments and suggestions reflect their thinking about the content and different ways of designing and arranging the content to benefit students' learning.

Discussion and Conclusion

What Can We Learn from This Exemplary Lesson About Mathematics Classroom Instruction Excellence Valued in China?

This study examined the features of an exemplary mathematics lesson that was identified and awarded through teaching contests. In particular, we took the case study approach. Our analysis of a prize-winning lesson suggests that the lesson contained many features that were also praised and identified by other researchers in previous studies about Chinese mathematics classroom instruction. The lesson progressed smoothly with the use of well-designed and structured computation problems. One key feature related to the lesson's content treatment is the teacher's clear identification and handling of both important and difficult points of teaching the content topic, which reflects the teacher's careful and intensive study of the textbook. By comparing with the textbook, we found that the teacher selected and used only three computation problems from the textbook. Basically, the teacher either re-designed or added most of the lesson's computation problems to address these important and difficult points of teaching.

Moreover, the teacher also made a good use of multiple methods to engage students, such as solving several sets of problems with variations, discussions, multiple solutions to one problem, individual seatwork in conjunction with small group collaborations, and group competition. The teacher tried to transfer the knowledge development and justification responsibilities to students. In particular, the students were given opportunities to explore, discuss, share, and justify solutions. Students' knowledge development process were guided by the teacher and his use of problem sets. The lesson shows frequent and various interactions between the teacher and students, in addition to students' own efforts individually and in groups. Overall, the lesson is coherent, polished, and focused.

Importantly, the lesson's features as summarized above are consistent with what was commonly valued in the two teaching contests in China. The emphases of these features in teaching contests support the perception that these features are not unique to the particular lesson focused on in this study. In fact, our survey of seven other mathematics educators and teachers also suggests that the lesson's quality is commonly acknowledged in China. Although there were some variations across these seven experts in terms of the lesson's design and strengths, their comments are all about some of these features. The variations presented mainly focus on alternative ways of content treatment. The diversity in Chinese teachers' thinking about the lesson's content treatment actually suggests that a lesson's content focus and organization deserve great attention and thought.

Although the study focused on a specific lesson, what we aimed to learn from the case is not just about this particular lesson. Rather, what we wanted to learn is what features made this particular lesson gain high evaluations. We also tried to verify whether these features are commonly recognized by different entities and individuals in China. The consistency in recognizing and valuing the features, as presented in this specific lesson, supports our assumption of what we can learn from the case study about excellent mathematics classroom instruction identified through teaching contests in China.

Teaching Contest as a Platform to Promote Mathematics Classroom Instruction Excellence and Teacher Professional Development

It was indicated at the beginning of this chapter that China has a different cultural view of teaching as a professional practice than the West. This study provided detailed information about one particular aspect of the Chinese teaching culture: teaching contests. In a way, the study helped reveal how mathematics teaching can be competed and compared and what features Chinese teachers may focus on, a seemingly unrealistic undertaking in the West. In fact, the prize-winning lesson made it possible for us to learn beyond what can possibly be learned from experts' teaching in the West (e.g., Borko and Livingston 1989; Leinhardt 1989). While experts' teaching is commonly analyzed in terms of aspects specified by a researcher, the nature of the prize-winning lesson identified through teaching contests in China allowed us to learn, not only about the lesson itself, but also about the cultural values embodied through the identification process. At the same time, it should also be noted that ranking is not the only purpose, and sometimes not even the main purpose, for teaching contests – especially at the national level. The event organizers also aim to provide a platform for teachers to display exemplary lesson instruction, to exchange their experiences in solving teaching problems, or to identify excellent young teachers. In fact, the national teaching contests are now termed the national exemplary lesson demonstration contests (Li and Li 2013).

The teaching contest, as a platform valued in China, also helps promote mathematics teachers' professional development. Surveys with Mr. Zhang and the contest organizers revealed that teaching contests promote mathematics instruction excellence mainly in two ways:

1. One way is to promote discussions about the quality of classroom instruction and to identify high-quality classroom instruction for possible broad sharing and dissemination. For example, the nationwide teaching contests' organizers published and distributed selected prize-winning lesson videos after the contests. Some of the prize-winning instructional designs were also posted on the Internet. According to the contest organizers, however, more efforts would be needed to promote mathematics classroom instruction excellence identified through teaching contests at both the district and the city levels.
2. Another way is to motivate teachers' participations and to further their professional development, especially for junior teachers. According to Mr. Zhang, the process of joining a teaching contest was a great learning experience. Participating teachers usually tried their best to make efforts in understanding mathematics, teaching, and students as learners. They spent a lot of time before the lesson instruction to identifying important content points and difficult points through studying the textbook and looking for effective teaching methods to stress the important points and help the learners overcome possible difficulties. They often consulted with their colleagues for possible improvement and tried to use new technology innovatively to help the lesson instruction. The process of preparing and improving demonstration lesson itself provides a great learning opportunity for participating teachers. Certainly, participating teachers also need to be psychologically prepared to accept possible failures in a teaching contest.

In addition to these two ways, teaching contests have also been used implicitly or explicitly to identify and promote innovative classroom instruction, such as those valued in current school mathematics reform (Liu and Li 2010).

Our recent study of the exemplary lesson demonstrations at the national level in China also identified multiple merits of this professional activity (Li and Li 2013). They include (1) promoting curriculum development and teachers' professional development, (2) helping "produce" a large number of young exemplary teachers, (3) helping propel teaching research activity to go further in the entire country, and (4) providing a great opportunity for young excellent teachers to develop and showcase their teaching skills. These merits are consistent with what are identified in this study, but are larger in terms of their scopes and effects. Although some of these merits may also be available in many top-down training models often provided in the West, teaching contests in China present a unique type of professional activity that stems from teachers' daily instructional activity and promotes teachers' innovation, discussion, sharing, and improvement of classroom teaching.

Acknowledgements Special thanks go to the teacher who taught the exemplary lesson to share with us about himself, his lesson preparation, and thinking in great details. The authors are grateful to the teaching contest organizers as well as participating Chinese mathematics educators and teachers for their time and contributions.

References

Berends, M. (2006). Survey methods in educational research. In J. L. Green, G. Camilli, & P. B. Elmore (Eds.), *Handbook of complementary methods in education research* (pp. 623–640). Mahwah: Lawrence Erlbaum Associates.

Borko, H., & Livingston, C. (1989). Cognition and improvisation: Differences in mathematics instruction by expert and novice teachers. *American Educational Research Journal, 26*, 473–489.

Fan, L.-H., Wong, N.-Y., Cai, J., & Li, S. (Eds.). (2004). *How Chinese learn mathematics – Perspectives from insiders*. Singapore: World Scientific.

Gu, L.-Y., Huang, R., & Marton, F. (2004). Teaching with variation: A Chinese way of promoting effective mathematics learning. In L.-H. Fan, N.-Y. Wong, J. Cai, & S. Li (Eds.), *How Chinese learn mathematics – Perspectives from insiders* (pp. 309–347). Singapore: World Scientific.

Hiebert, J., Gallimore, R., Garnier, H., Givvin, K. B., Hollingsworth, H., Jacobs, J., et al. (2003). *Teaching mathematics in seven countries: Results from the TIMSS 1999 video study* (NCES 2003-013). Washington, DC: Department of Education, US National Center for Education Statistics.

Leinhardt, G. (1989). Math lessons: A contrast of novice and expert competence. *Journal for Research in Mathematics Education, 20*, 52–75.

Li, Y., & Even, R. (2011). Approaches and practices in developing teachers' expertise in mathematics instruction: an introduction. *ZDM – The International Journal on Mathematics Education, 43*, 759–762.

Li, J., & Li, Y. (2013). The teaching contest as a professional development activity to promote classroom instruction excellence in China. In Y. Li & R. Huang (Eds.), *How Chinese teach mathematics and improve teaching* (pp. 204–220). New York: Routledge.

Li, Y., & Huang, R. (Eds.). (2013). *How Chinese teach mathematics and improve teaching*. New York: Routledge.

Li, Y., Huang, R., Bao, J., & Fan, Y. (2011). Facilitating mathematics teachers' professional development through ranking and promotion in Mainland China. In N. Bednarz, D. Fiorentini, & R. Huang (Eds.), *International approaches to professional development of mathematics teachers* (pp. 72–85). Ottawa: University of Ottawa Press.

Li, Y., & Li, J. (2009). Mathematics classroom instruction excellence through the platform of teaching contests. *ZDM – The International Journal on Mathematics Education, 41*, 263–277.

Liu, J., & Li, Y. (2010). Mathematics curriculum reform in the Chinese mainland: Changes and challenges. In F. K. S. Leung & Y. Li (Eds.), *Reforms and issues in school mathematics in East Asia* (pp. 9–31). Rotterdam: Sense.

Ma, L. (1999). *Knowing and teaching elementary mathematics: Teachers' understanding of fundamental mathematics in China and the United States*. Mahwah: Lawrence Erlbaum.

Peng, A. (2007). Knowledge growth of mathematics teachers during professional activity based on the task of lesson explaining. *Journal of Mathematics Teacher Education, 10*, 289–299.

Stigler, J. W., & Stevenson, H. W. (1991). How Asian teachers polish each lesson to perfection. *American Educator, 15*(1), 12–20, 43–47.

Stigler, J. W., Fernandez, C., & Yoshida, M. (1996). Traditions of school mathematics in Japan and American elementary classrooms. In L. P. Steffe, P. Nesher, P. Cobb, G. A. Goldin, & B. Greer (Eds.), *Theories of mathematical learning* (pp. 149–175). Mahwah: Lawrence Erlbaum Associates.

Wang, J., & Paine, L. (2003). Learning to teach with mandated curriculum and public examination of teaching as contexts. *Teaching and Teacher Education, 19*, 75–94.

Yang, Y., & Ricks, T. E. (2013). Chinese lesson study: Developing classroom instruction through collaborations in school-based teaching research group activities. In Y. Li & R. Huang (Eds.), *How Chinese teach mathematics and improve teaching* (pp. 51–65). New York: Routledge.

Part IV
Advances in Theory and Methods for Assessing and Studying Mathematics Classroom Instruction

Preface to Part IV

Norma Presmeg

In comparison with the millennia in which mathematics has existed as a distinct branch of knowledge, *mathematics education* as a field of study in its own right is young indeed (Sierpinska and Kilpatrick 1998). Based at first on a psychological model of teaching and learning, this field started having its own dedicated associations, conferences, and journals (as opposed to being an offshoot of psychology or mathematics) in the 1970s, as reflected in names such as *International Group for the Psychology of Mathematics Education* (PME), which had its origins at a meeting of mathematicians and mathematics educators in 1976. At that stage in its evolution, mathematics education research emulated the scientific disciplines involving psychometric research. The drive for *rigor* resulted in controlled experiments, hypothesis testing using statistical methods, aptitude-treatment interaction studies, and time sampling, as the acme of scientific research, even in venues as complex, and as human, as classrooms in which mathematics was being taught and learned. There were some exceptions to this trend, which was particularly strong in the USA. For instance, in the USSR, Krutetskii (1976) deplored the waste of the "riches"—in much Western research—of the information that became available for analysis in clinical interview methodologies such as those he used in his studies of "capable" mathematics students: studies that were no less stringent in quality criteria than those involving statistical methods of analysis.

During the 1980s and 1990s, a much-needed swing of the pendulum brought qualitative methodologies to the fore in mathematics education research, accompanied by a recognition that much learning of mathematics takes place in social settings within institutions and therefore that theories based on sociology were perhaps just as relevant, if not more so, than psychological theories of learning by individuals. It was during this period that the International Committee of PME contemplated

N. Presmeg (✉)
5160 Candlewood Court, Maryville, TN 37804-4680, USA
e-mail: npresmeg@msn.com

Y. Li et al. (eds.), *Transforming Mathematics Instruction: Multiple Approaches and Practices*, Advances in Mathematics Education, DOI 10.1007/978-3-319-04993-9_22, © Springer International Publishing Switzerland 2014

	Theoretical issues	Methodological issues
Design that aims to assess classroom instruction	A	B
Design that aims to study classroom instruction	C	D

Fig. 1 Grid for analysis of foci of chapters in Part V

changing the name of this association from the *Psychology* of Mathematics Education to something more amenable to the changed nature of the questions being investigated in the field. (The membership voted to retain the name of PME, largely for historical reasons.) The 2000s saw a swing away again from the predominant qualitative research methodologies to a more balanced perception that qualitative and quantitative designs may be complementary, having different strengths and omissions. They may be suited to different research questions, and one of the various *mixed methods* designs may provide a richer view of a phenomenon of teaching and learning than either type independently.

Against this introductory backdrop, the following six chapters in this part of the book provide an interesting medley of questions investigated, theoretical perspectives adopted or implied, and methodologies designed to study these questions. It is useful to consider a grid, in comparing and contrasting these chapters, in which theory and methods are juxtaposed against designs that aim to assess, and designs that aim to study, various issues of teaching and learning mathematics in classroom situations (Fig. 1).

Various chapters in this part place different emphases on the elements of the four cells in Fig. 1. In each case, the research question being investigated determines this emphasis, at least in part. All of these chapters address questions that concern aspects of the teaching and learning mathematics in group settings, and all place an emphasis on particular methodologies that are suited to the various topics of investigation. Thus, all would have a check mark in cell D of the grid in Fig. 1. However, with regard to cells A, B, and C, the similarities end, and each of these chapters has thus a unique contribution to make in this part of the book.

The chapter by Harel, Fuller, and Soto has a strong theoretical orientation. The question of focus is as follows: "What does an implementation of DNR look like in a classroom?" The investigation concerns the potential effect of teaching actions on student learning, where the acronym DNR stands for the three principles involved, namely, the duality principle, the necessity principle, and the repeated-reasoning principle. The investigation is less about *assessing* the effect of such teaching than on *studying* it: the "teacher researcher" is characterized as an expert in implementation of DNR from the outset, and this expertise is taken for granted throughout the chapter. For this chapter, I would place check marks in cells C and D of the grid. As in all of the chapters, the authors emphasize the results of the investigation of their particular question: within the complex endeavor of such teaching, these authors conclude that DNR provides one theoretical framework with the potential to transform instruction.

The chapter by Jaworski is also designed to address the complexity of mathematics classroom processes, in particular the teaching of first year engineering students at university level. Because studying and assessing such processes are aims of the investigation, the chapter addresses all four of the cells of the grid in Fig. 1. The emphasis is on theoretical formulations of *inquiry*, *community*, and *critical alignment*, based on developmental processes including *documentational genesis* and *instrumentation theory*. The overarching framework is taken from Vygotskian activity theory. The assessment component of the research is guaranteed by the presence of an external researcher, the "research officer (RO)," in addition to the researchers studying the topic in the internal research team. Thus, the analysis was carried out at two levels that were interrelated, each addressing aspects of the inherent "overwhelming complexity" in studying and promoting development of mathematics teaching and learning in such a setting.

In contrast to the strong theoretical orientation of the chapter by Jaworski, the chapter by Even concentrates on the methodological aspects of investigating key factors involved in shaping students' opportunities to learn mathematics in classroom settings. Thus, for this chapter, check marks are in cells B and D in Fig. 1. Theoretical aspects are implicit in the "carefully designed conceptual frameworks" of the two studies reported, but the emphasis is on the novel methodology, in which the same teacher is observed teaching different classes, or teachers in different schools are observed teaching the same algebra curriculum, with some unexpected results.

Community college trigonometry is the setting for the research by Mesa and Land, in which they study and assess different elements of teaching where a lecture mode is the primary means of instruction. One could place checkmarks in all the cells of the grid in Fig. 1, but the emphasis is on B and D, the methodology. The "Novelty of Mathematical Questions" posed by the lecturers gives an indication of levels of difficulty, whereas the analysis of "Teacher Moves" addresses the ways that the teachers manage the dialogue that occurs. The complexity of the data analysis that results from the methodology causes the researchers to use color coding as a means of managing this complexity; the flexibility of the methods and decisions "in the moment" rather than planned beforehand is reminiscent of some aspects of grounded theory research. The effectiveness of the methodology is illustrated in the results that emerge, which would not have been apparent in less fine-grained research.

The chapter by Boston is again primarily concerned with methods of assessing and studying instructional quality (cells B and D in the grid), in this case by means of collections of student work. The methodology involves both parametric and nonparametric statistical analysis. The emphasis on assessment is stronger than in the other chapters of this part of the book: in fact, *evaluation* (in which numerical scores are assigned to assess quality) is a focus. The usefulness of rubrics in studying collections of student work to assess instructional quality is illustrated in classroom teaching in schools, as well as in professional development initiatives.

Examples are the focus of the chapter by Zaslavsky and Zodik, both in the context of example generation by teachers and in the investigation of example-based reasoning in classrooms. A convincing case is made for the importance of research on generation and use of examples in mathematics classrooms, from the perspectives of both teaching and learning. Although theoretical elements are implicit in the conceptual formulation, the emphasis is on studying these topics through the methodology described (cell D in the grid in Fig. 1). The richness of the research is illustrated in two carefully chosen generic tasks addressing two different mathematical concepts, namely, irrational numbers and periodic functions.

From this brief synopsis, it may be seen that the chapters in this part are diverse and unique in the ways that they address the investigation of issues in classroom mathematics instruction. The complexity of this endeavor comes through in most of the chapters. The endeavor to "transform mathematics instruction" (the focus of the title of this book) is matched by the advances that have taken place in theoretical formulations and in research methodologies in the last few decades. The journey is by no means complete, but these chapters give glimpses of ways that may be taken in research that seeks to address the complexity of issues in the classroom teaching and learning of mathematics.

References

Krutetskii, V. A. (1976). *The psychology of mathematical abilities in schoolchildren*. Chicago: University of Chicago Press.
Sierpinska, A., & Kilpatrick, J. (Eds.). (1998). *Mathematics education as a research domain: A search for identity*. Dordrecht: Kluwer Academic Publishers.

DNR-Based Instruction in Mathematics: Determinants of a *DNR* Expert's Teaching

Guershon Harel, Evan Fuller, and Osvaldo D. Soto

Abstract This chapter examines the classroom implementation of a theoretical framework for the teaching and learning of mathematics—called *DNR-based instruction in mathematics*—focusing on characteristics of the implementation of DNR to help learners transition between *proof schemes*. Three episodes from a professional development program for middle and high school teachers are analyzed to reveal the teaching behaviors of an expert *DNR* instructor. Complexities highlighted include (1) how the instructor balanced the intended mathematical content with the learners' current understandings, (2) the interplay of the questions *whether* a result holds and *why* it holds, and (3) how the instructor created *intellectual need* for new ideas. As a by-product, learning outcomes of this effort are also examined.

Keywords DNR-based instruction • Proof • Proof schemes • Theoretical framework • Professional development

G. Harel (✉)
Department of Mathematics, University of California, San Diego,
9500 Gilman Drive, La Jolla, CA 92093-0112, USA
e-mail: harel@math.ucsd.edu

E. Fuller
Department of Mathematics, Montclair State University,
9910 Fragrant Lilies Way, Laurel, MD 20723, USA
e-mail: fuller.evan@gmail.com

O.D. Soto
Department of Mathematics, Patrick Henry High School, University of California,
San Diego, via Dr. Guershon Harel, 9500 Gilman Drive, La Jolla, CA 92093-0112, USA
e-mail: osoto@sandi.net

Y. Li et al. (eds.), *Transforming Mathematics Instruction: Multiple Approaches and Practices*, Advances in Mathematics Education, DOI 10.1007/978-3-319-04993-9_23, © Springer International Publishing Switzerland 2014

Introduction

This chapter examines the classroom implementation of *DNR-based instruction in mathematics* (DNR). DNR is a theoretical framework for the teaching and learning of mathematics, whose objective is to provide language and tools to formulate and address critical curricular and instructional concerns. The question of focus in this paper is: what does an implementation of DNR look like in the classroom? The structure of DNR makes the mathematical setting important, so we look at an especially relevant setting: helping learners transition between *proof schemes*. In examining DNR, we will analyze the instructional aspects of the transition between *proof schemes*: from the *external conviction* and *empirical proof schemes* to the *transformational proof schemes*, focusing, in particular, on the transition from *result pattern generalization* (RPG, a form of empirical reasoning) to *process pattern generalization* (PPG, a form of deductive reasoning). These italicized terms are discussed at length elsewhere (see, e.g., Harel 2001). We briefly outline the DNR framework, along with these terms, in the next section.

Selected DNR Constructs

DNR can be thought of as a system consisting of three categories of constructs: premises, concepts, and claims. These claims include instructional principles—assertions about the potential effect of teaching actions on student learning, which are subsumed under three foundational principles: the *duality principle*, the *necessity principle*, and the *repeated-reasoning principle,* hence, the acronym DNR. For a fuller discussion of DNR, see Harel (2008a, b). Of relevance to this chapter is the *necessity principle: for students to learn what we intend to teach them, they must see a need for it, where "need" refers to intellectual need.*

The *Knowing-Knowledge Linkage Premise,* one of the DNR's eight premises, asserts that problem solving is the means—the only means—to learn. When one encounters a problematic situation, one necessarily experiences phases of disequilibrium, often intermediated by phases of equilibrium. Disequilibrium, or perturbation, is a state that results when one encounters an obstacle. Its cognitive effect is that it "forces the subject to go beyond his current state and strike out in new directions" (Piaget 1985, p. 10). Equilibrium is a state when one perceives success in removing such an obstacle. In Piaget's terms, it is a state when one modifies her or his viewpoint (accommodation) and is able, as a result, to integrate new ideas toward the solution of the problem (assimilation).

DNR defines perturbation in terms of two types of human needs: *intellectual need* and *affective need. Intellectual need* is different from *affective need.* Intellectual need has to do with disciplinary knowledge being born out of people's current knowledge through problematic situations. Affective need, on the other hand, has to do with people's desire, volition, interest, self-determination, and the like. Before one immerses oneself in a problem, one must desire, or at least be willing, to engage in the problem, and once one has engaged in a problem, often persistence and perseverance are needed to continue the engagement. These characteristics are manifestations of affective needs: motivational drives to initially engage in a problem and to pursue its solution. The existence of these needs is implied from another DNR premise, the *Epistemophilia Premise*, which asserts that people desire to solve problems and look for problems to solve—they do not passively wait for disequilibrium!

This brings us to DNR's definition of *learning:* learning is a continuum of disequilibrium-equilibrium phases manifested by (a) intellectual and affective needs that instigate or result from these phases and (b) *ways of understanding* or *ways of thinking* that are utilized and newly constructed during these phases.

The terms *way of understanding* and *way of thinking* have a special, technical meaning in DNR. For this paper's purposes, it is sufficient to think of ways of understanding (WoU) as one's particular conceptualizations of definitions, theorems, proofs, problems and their solutions, and so on. Ways of thinking (WoT), on the other hand, are the conceptual tools that are necessary for an individual to construct these conceptualizations. WoT are classified into three categories: problem-solving approaches, proof schemes, and beliefs about mathematics. Of particular interest in this chapter are proof schemes.

Harel and Sowder (1998) offered a taxonomy of proof schemes consisting of three classes: *external conviction, empirical,* and *deductive.* Proving within the *external conviction* class depends on (a) an authority such as a teacher or a book (the *authoritative proof scheme*), (b) strictly the appearance of the argument (the *ritual proof scheme,* e.g., proofs in geometry must have a two-column format), or (c) symbol manipulations, with the symbols or the manipulations having no coherent system of referents in the eyes of the student (the *non-referential symbolic proof scheme*).

The *empirical* class is marked by reliance on either (a) evidence from examples of direct measurements of quantities, substitutions of specific numbers in algebraic expressions, and so forth (the *inductive proof scheme*) or (b) visual perceptions (the *perceptual proof scheme*).

The *deductive* class consists of two categories. Relevant to this paper is the *transformational proof scheme* category. Its essential characteristics are generality, operational thought, and logical inference. The generality characteristic has to do with an individual's understanding that the goal is to justify a "for all" argument, not isolated cases, and that no exception is allowed. The operational thought characteristic manifests itself when an individual forms goals and subgoals and attempts to anticipate their outcomes during the proving process. Finally, when an individual understands that justifying in mathematics must ultimately be based on logical inference rules, the logical inference characteristic is being employed.

Empirical reasoning is a common and robust WoT among many students and even among teachers (Healy and Hoyles 2000; Blanton et al. 2009). A special case of this WoT is *result pattern generalization (RPG)*. Its counterpart, *process pattern generalization (PPG)*, belongs to the deductive proof schemes category. Observing that the sum of the first n consecutive odd natural numbers is n^2 because the value checks for $n = 1, 2, 3, 4$ is RPG. Proving this fact by looking at the effect of adding the next odd number (e.g., informal mathematical induction) is PPG. Thus, process pattern generalization is a WoT in which one's proving is based on regularity in the process (though it might be initiated by regularity in the result), whereas result pattern generalization is a WoT in which one's proving is based solely on regularity in the result—obtained by substitution of numbers, for instance. The question of how to help learners transition from RPG to PPG has been the focus of our research for some time.

Teaching Behaviors and Related Literature

Our characterizations of DNR-based instruction consider both *teaching actions* (what the teacher actually does in particular instances) and *teaching behaviors* (conceptual patterns that these many actions provide evidence for). One immediate implication of DNR for instruction is that teachers must seek out and make use of students' ideas as the basis for class discussion while simultaneously considering institutionally desirable mathematics. Given DNR's definition of learning, it is incumbent upon the teacher to create models of students' mathematics and select suitable problematic situations for the purposes of advancing students' WoU and WoT toward particular goals. The teacher formulates these goals and problematic situations in advance and reformulates them on the fly as he gathers more evidence from students.

Several studies have analyzed pedagogical practices using similar lenses to our pairing of teaching action and behavior. Sherin (2002) used a case study of middle school teachers to examine pedagogical tensions involved in trying to use students' ideas as the basis for class discussion while also ensuring that the discussion is mathematically productive. Sherin's idea of filtering, "used to emphasize that any new content raised by the teacher is based on a narrowing of ideas raised already by the students" (p. 200), raises a concern similar to our question (below) about how TR chose what aspects of participant contributions to focus on.

Reid and Zack (2009) examined the teaching of proof by looking for commonalities between Zack's 5th grade teaching and two teaching experiments in grades 5 and 8 conducted by Lampert and Boero, respectively. They found that encouraging students to state their conjectures and prove them is an important teaching action common to the three experiments. This teaching action also plays a role in our analysis below.

Lehrer et al. (2013) constructed models for the evolving state of students' ways of thinking by carefully examining the kinds of questions students asked during the course of instruction. They analyzed the extent to which a question by a student created opportunities for exploring new "mathematical terrain" and used the results of these analyses to create new problems that would potentially intellectually necessitate higher levels of questions oriented toward more advanced ways of thinking.

Mehan's (1979) *reproducible patterns of initiation, reply,* and *evaluation* point to the crucial role the use of authority plays in a teacher's practice. The use of authority is an important aspect of DNR as well.

Methods

To illustrate aspects of DNR-based instruction in mathematics, we analyze data that was collected in a sequence of teaching experiments (in the sense of Steffe and Thompson 2000), where the lead researcher was the teacher (hereafter, referred to as TR for teacher-researcher). These experiments took place during two intensive month-long summer professional development institutes for middle and high school algebra teachers (referred to as participants).

Three teaching episodes—each related to a single problem, the discussion of which spanned multiple days—were chosen based on (1) instances where TR attempted to promote the transition between RPG and PPG WoT, (2) our desire to include a wide spectrum of time across both summer institutes, and (3) space limitations. Each problem involved substantial time spent on group work to solve the problem, as well as public presentation and discussion of solutions. The mathematical context and purposes of the problem being worked on were taken into account at all times. The analysis of the participants' behaviors led to models for the mathematics of the learners at different times.

During the data analysis, video and transcripts of the institutes were reviewed by each team member. Research team members continually generated questions about TR's teaching practices and attempted to find evidence that could help answer them. Each teaching episode begins with a set of main questions that will be addressed by the data, and our analysis of each episode focuses on these questions. From this process, a large number of teaching actions emerged and were classified into several themes, some of which match existing literature (e.g., Mehan's (1979) reproducible patterns of initiation, reply, and evaluation and Sherin's (2002) idea generation, comparison and evaluation, filtering, and seeding the discussion with new ideas). Our themes concern Whether, When, and How issues are treated. *Whether* concerns teaching decisions in which TR chooses whether to focus on something that comes up, such as an aspect of a participant solution (e.g., an error). *When* concerns sequencing of classroom activities, such as when TR raises questions or shifts the direction of the discussion. *How* concerns details of the implementation of decisions on Whether and When, such as the way in which TR requests evaluation of presented solutions. In the analysis below, each question is labeled with its theme (Whether, When, or How). The themes are not disjoint, but they do emphasize different aspects of teaching behaviors.

We emphasize that this chapter does not intend to show evidence that the participants held particular proof schemes at points in time. First, there is not enough space here to do so. Second, this would detract from the primary goal of our analysis—to examine an expert implementation of DNR. This implementation begins with the premise—based on prior experiences with participants—that learners held primarily external convictions and empirical proof schemes. Although we build models for students' mathematics, these models are incomplete and used to contextualize the teaching actions, rather than to test TR's assumptions. We ask that the reader keep this important point in mind throughout the remainder of this chapter.

Episode 1: Investment Problem

The following problem was the first problem given to participants (on the first day of the first summer institute):

Jill and Jack invested money in a mutual fund for 1 year. Jill invested $23,000 and Jack $22,950. Their broker deducted a 5.5 % commission before turning the rest of the money over to the mutual fund. During the year, the value of each share of the mutual fund increased by 11.85 %. What percentage return on their investment did Jill and Jack realize?

Main Questions

- How does TR choose what aspects of participant contributions to focus on? (Whether)
- When does TR present his own solutions? (When)
- What governs TR's treatment of errors? (Whether)

Purpose of the Problem

The context was chosen to be concrete and about a concept—percentage—that the participants, as teachers, deem important. The following are a priori objectives stated by TR (to the research team):

1. Intellectually necessitate the question of whether the rate of return would be dependent or independent of the initial investment. The difference between the investment quantities was only $50.
2. Generate surprise that the rate of return is independent of the initial investment. The problem does not ask participants to explain the fact that the percent return is independent of the investment. Had the problem included such a question, it would have weakened the element of surprise. More important, the aim was that participants develop the WoT of raising questions about relationships between different quantities on their own.

3. Begin to develop the WoT of utilizing the power of algebra to ascertain, persuade, and explain. This WoT, dubbed *referential symbolic*,[1] is one by which a solver sets the problem in algebraic terms and applies algebraic rules to determine a solution.

4. Use participants' responses as objects of debate, whereby they become cognizant of their own justifications—a necessary step toward comparing RPG justifications with PPG justifications. Based on prior experience, TR anticipated heavy use of RPG by the participants for this problem.

The computation of the percentage return quantity is a process that starts with the initial investment quantity and, through a sequence of arithmetic operations, leads to the percentage return quantity. It was assumed by TR—based on his prior knowledge of a similar population of participants—that this computational process, in and of itself, constitutes evidence for the participants that the percentage return is *dependent* on the investment, since the value of the percentage return was determined by operations on the value of the investment. Hence, the realization that the percentage return does not change when the investment is different is likely to lead to a surprise—an intellectual perturbation. The teacher could have chosen a large difference between the values of the investments, which might have made the perturbation more pronounced. The choice of the small difference was intentional, to create a debate within the small working groups as to whether the equal values for the percentage return are due to the closeness between the investment values—a debate that might create a sequence of perturbation-equilibration stages such as this:

A. Equal percentage returns (perturbation).
B. Attributed to a "small" difference between the investment values (equilibration).
C. Checking other values with "large" differences (perturbation).
D. Conjecture: the return will always be the same (equilibration).
E. Checking a few other cases (further equilibration, since the empirical proof scheme is common).
F. What makes the return always be the same? (perturbation).

Question Analysis and Teaching Actions

How Does TR Choose What Aspects of Participant Contributions to Focus On? (Whether)

We correctly expected TR to focus on aspects of conviction and causality.[2] There is evidence to indicate that the problem was successful in creating disequilibrium about whether the percentages being the same was due to the small difference in

---

[1] This is the counterpart to the aforementioned non-referential symbolic proof scheme.

[2] A detailed discussion of causality is beyond the scope of this chapter. Here, it suffices to think of causality as a strong understanding of why a result holds.

Jack's and Jill's investments. Carly[3] said, "But just to double check we went back and did a really easy number that, *cause we were so close*, we went back and did 1,000." After Carly's group and one other had presented their solutions, in which the returns were the same, TR asked something to the effect[4]:

Is getting the same percentage a surprising fact? … How are we so sure that the percentage return is independent of the initial investment?

Participants displayed RPG (e.g., trying other numbers) and PPG reasoning (one participant observed that the calculations involve multiplying then later dividing by the principal, so this amount cancels out). TR continued by probing causality (addressed to a particular group, but during a public discussion):

… in all of these cases the percentage return came out the same. That gives us conviction. But what makes the result to be the way it is?

Overall, TR did *not* focus on particular calculations, but rather on general (PPG) reasoning that makes the return be independent of the initial investment.

When Does TR Present His Own Solutions? (When)

In response to TR's question above (what makes the result to be the way it is), Randy presented the only PPG solution. There is evidence that TR wished to postpone this solution until late in the discussion, and we believe the reason for this was to have participants consider his question for a significant amount of time before resolving it. TR only called on Randy when another participant pointed out that TR cannot see Randy's hand raised, and TR responds that he had already seen it.

After Randy's presentation, TR presented his own version of Randy's solution, in which the initial investment is denoted by *A*—rather than a number. He also spent a fair amount of time discussing how algebra showed why the percentage increase was independent of the initial investment. This seemed to be a first step in having students appreciate PPG reasoning and the power of algebra, and it fits with his stated goal of beginning to develop the referential symbolic WoT.

What Governs TR's Treatment of Errors? (Whether)

Carly's group calculated the yield by looking only at the gain on the investment, not subtracting the commission. This could be argued to be an error in modeling the problem situation. Indeed, Donna challenged their step. In this case, TR did not treat what was done as an error. He explicitly chose to focus on the fact that the found percentages are the same, not the actual values found. TR thus put attention on the

---

[3] All names are pseudonyms.

[4] Here and elsewhere, quotes from TR are modified slightly for clarity and brevity.

conjecturing and proving acts, at the expense of the modeling act. We would expect this decision based on the problem goals.

There is an additional computational error that was not mentioned by anyone. When Randy presented his calculations, he obtained an incorrect amount for the increase in value of Jack and Jill's combined investments. We have no evidence for whether TR noticed this error and let it pass or did not realize there was an error, but TR focused on generic features of Randy's argument rather than the particular values.

Episode 2: Quilt Problem

On the 13th day of the first summer institute, the following problem was posed:

A company makes square quilts. Each quilt is made out of small congruent squares, where the squares on the main diagonals of the quilt are black and the rest of the squares are white. The cost of a quilt is calculated as follows:

Materials: $1 for each black square, $0.50 for each white square
Labor: $0.25 for each square

April, Bonnie, and Chad ordered three identical quilts. Each of the three filled out a different order form. April entered the number of black squares in the black cell. The other two entered the same number as April's, but accidentally Bonnie entered her number in the whites cell, and Chad entered his number in the total cell. April was charged $139.25. How much money were Bonnie and Chad charged?[5]

Number of black squares	Number of white squares	Total of squares

Main Questions

- How does TR's request for evaluation of solutions delineate empirical and deductive approaches? (How)
- When and why does TR use his authority to shift attention? (When)
- When does TR raise issues of certainty and causality? (When)
- How does TR model desirable behaviors? (How)

---

[5] Although this problem has some depth, the reader can understand the discussion merely by considering how many squares are white versus black on an $n \times n$ quilt.

Purpose of the Problem

The problem had many purposes, but the one most central to this analysis was to delineate empirical and deductive approaches. TR's model[6] of participant WoU and WoT had changed as follows. Initially, participants had strong empirical proof schemes. At this point, the class as a whole saw empirical reasoning as manifested in tables. They were at a preliminary disequilibrium in that they began to realize a need to step away from empirical reasoning, because deductive proofs give more: an understanding of why. TR believed that presenters now felt intrinsic pressure to go beyond empirical solutions. Thus, a major purpose of this problem was to further encourage the transition away from empirical solutions, by inducing participants to compare solutions in the hope they will prefer deductive ones.

In addition, TR's experience in past summer institutes was that participants confused empirical proofs with iterative searches: a sequential examination of mathematical objects to find one satisfying certain properties (here, a quilt was the object, and the property was a total cost of $139.25). Previous participants rejected iterative searches and exhaustive proofs[7] at a certain stage, perhaps because exhaustive proofs do not appear sufficiently causal or because they confused empirical proofs and iterative searches. This year, TR hoped to use the quilt problem to explicitly bring up the difference between empirical proofs and exhaustive proofs or iterative searches, in particular leading participants to understand that the latter are mathematically acceptable.

Question Analysis and Teaching Actions

How Does TR's Request for Evaluations of Solutions Delineate Empirical and Deductive Approaches? (When)

TR asked Julie to present first, because her solution could help address the difference between empirical proofs and solutions that use a table but are essentially deductive. Julie's presented solution seemed to have been influenced by other participant's comments (rather than being a faithful reproduction of what she had done). Julie drew the 1×1, 2×2, 3×3, 4×4, and 5×5 cases, indicating how many more black squares than the previous case were present. She decided to also look at costs, and TR asked her to show her original table, which she drew as in Fig. 1.

Although these did not all appear on the board, she claimed that her original table had been filled in for all sizes up to a 13×13 quilt, where she found that the

---

[6] Recall that we do not make and substantiate claims about the actual transition between proof schemes; rather, we report TR's model (as reported or inferred).

[7] Proving a statement by showing that it holds in different cases, whose union is the whole set under consideration.

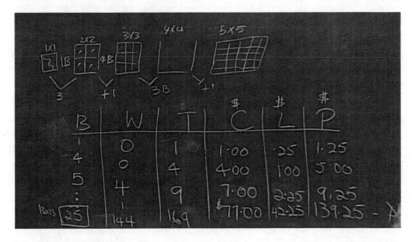

Fig. 1 Julie's work for quilt problem

purchase price was equal to $139.25, fulfilling the constraints of the first quilt in the problem. Julie claimed to have used a geometric pattern to determine the cost of the second quilt in the problem, but she was not able to do anything for the third quilt.

After Julie finished her presentation, without any prompting from TR, Carly asked "…did you draw pictures up to the 13 to get those numbers for the chart?" Julie's response was rather vague: she claimed to have observed a pattern for the increase in the number of black squares from quilt to quilt when she generated her table: adding 3, 1, 3, 1 and so on. When pushed, she acquiesced to Carly's suggestion that she figured out whites and total from the pattern.

After this exchange, TR asked "What do you think of this solution? Is it an acceptable solution? [participants say yes] Is this [an] empirical solution? … Did she generalize from several examples?" This teaching action of asking for evaluation is expected and plays an important role in delineating empirical and deductive solutions. It appears that TR intended Julie's solution to be viewed as elementary but mathematically legitimate (i.e., not empirical). In particular, there is evidence (beyond his self-report) that TR expected to convince participants that Julie's solution was not empirical. When the class responded that she did empirically generalize, he asked what she generalized, and numerous participants responded simultaneously, mostly citing the 3-1-3-1 pattern (see Fig. 1). TR countered, "but she didn't use that pattern," while participants insisted she did. This prompted TR to shift from his plan of evaluating the solution back to understanding what was done in the solution.

When and Why Does TR Use His Authority to Shift Attention? (When)

In this instance, TR had observed Julie working and was confident that he knew what she had done, expecting to make a point about her WoT. However, several vocal participants argued that she had empirically generalized her 3-1-3-1 pattern to fill in her table. Presumably, these participants were convinced of this by Julie's response to Carly and the structure of her presentation: presenting the pattern early and drawing only the first five cases—with only the first two shaded. After some back and forth, TR used his authority to focus on the case-by-case process of counting the number of blacks in a quilt rather than the issue of whether the pattern was used: he presented long monologues without seeking feedback and talked over a couple quiet comments by Julie and another participant. Such use of authority would be condemned by constructivism but was necessary in order to shift toward the intended issue: distinguishing empirical proofs from general use of a table. We note that participants were vocal in talking about the pattern but quiet on other issues. Thus, it might be argued that they only partly accepted the shift in attention. At the end of the monologue, TR returned to the 3-1-3-1 pattern and proceeded to prove it.[8] Based on TR's observation of participant reactions, he felt that they would continue to dwell on the pattern, and he thus chose to address it explicitly and provide a clear example of deductive reasoning.

How Does TR's Request for Evaluation of Solutions Delineate Empirical and Deductive Approaches? (Continued)

After completing his proof, TR asked Melody, "what have we done here? … From a teaching point of view." Sometimes, TR summarized. Other times, such as this case, TR asked participants to summarize. There are several reasons that having a participant summarize can be helpful:

(a) It helps TR determine the extent to which participants are following.
(b) It gives participants a chance to participate in the community and to solidify their understanding.
(c) It allows TR time to construct and reflect on participants' current WoU and WoT.

We conjecture that (a) and (b) are the primary reasons for this teaching action, based partly on some participant questions about the proof shortly before. TR built on Melody's summary to provide his own. In particular, Melody mentioned that they were testing whether the pattern works, and TR said that they utilized the power of algebra to show that the pattern works all the time. TR also said, "we learned that this solution is an exhaustive one." This relates back to the teaching action of asking for evaluation, which was interrupted by disagreement over what Julie did.

---

[8] The proof involved directly counting the number of black squares in a generic even or odd quilt and then taking the difference for successive quilts.

When Does TR Raise Issues of Certainty and Causality? (When)

The next presenter, Donna, drew a table with the side dimension and the number of black squares in a quilt. Donna claimed that, due to the 25 cent ending in the price of the quilt, it could not have even dimensions, so she didn't derive the equation for even quilts. TR then asked the class "Do you buy this?" and they provided guttural confirmation.

As a teaching action, questioning the validity of a claim seems to serve the purpose of destabilizing a participant by raising doubt. Donna had only vaguely justified her claim, so TR asked for further justification. Although the class was willing to accept the claim, TR said, "I am not convinced. I don't know why." TR (retrospectively reported) was acting and knew why he was not convinced but thought it was within the grasp of some participants to both find what is lacking in the explanation and provide further justification. One participant asked whether Donna charted the cost in each case like Julie, to which Donna responded that she calculated a few costs. TR latched onto this and suggested that she derived her claim from a few examinations, to which she agreed. He asked, "How do we know that the even [quilt] will not work beyond the several examinations?" Donna said she knows there isn't going to be, and TR responded, "...that's not the point I'm focusing on... I'm dying to know why," thus shifting the focus to causality.

Questioning the validity of Donna's claim and shifting the focus to causality are quite important to the goal of moving participants toward deductive proof schemes. Previous teaching experiments had suggested that questioning the validity of participants' claims is generally ineffective at creating intellectual need to advance proof schemes, raising the question of why TR tried it.

TR's experience is that formulas are self-supporting and it is more difficult to destabilize participants' certainty in a (correct) formula. Although Donna's literal wording that labor cost on an even quilt always "comes out to be an even number" is mathematically incorrect (we believe she intended "even" to be "whole"), the issue addressed by the class is why "You never have 25 cents leftover," which is a true assertion but one for which no formula has been produced—leaving a chance for destabilization. He thus attempted to perturb Donna with regard to both the validity and the cause of her assertion. Part of the reason for this dual focus is that he wanted participants to eventually recognize that assertions for which only a few examples have been checked not only lack explanatory power but also can be incorrect.

We saw no evidence that participants felt intellectual need to justify Donna's claim that an even quilt cannot provide a solution. However, the classroom was set up so that TR was a participant in the mathematical community. As such, he had the right to check claims or ask for more explanation. All participants respected his right to question the assertion, although Donna seemed to think that her initial explanation was sufficient until pushed further by TR. She then attempted a symbolic proof that built on her initial reasoning, but she was unable to complete it, even with the help of other participants. Nevertheless, TR's attention to causality led Donna to attempt a deductive argument.

Fig. 2 Donna's initial
quilt table

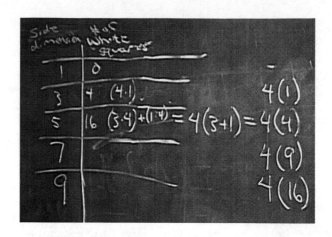

How Does TR Model Desirable Behaviors? (How)

Through an exchange with other participants, Donna attempted to formalize her reasoning to support the claim "you never have 25 cents leftover with an even quilt." After several minutes, TR put the discussion on hold. He said that it is common to encounter a problem but leave it for the moment and come back to it later, and that's what is being done. Part of the reason for this teaching action was to preserve the flow of Donna's solution, which was being interrupted by this issue. However, it also served to clarify and model a deductive WoT that every claim in an argument must be justifiable, but it does not need to be proven at that moment. TR could have quickly presented his own deductive argument for the claim. In our retrospective discussion with TR, he indicated that he did not do so because he felt creating such an argument was within the grasp of most participants. Indeed, later that day (not analyzed in this chapter), a participant provided a correct deductive proof that the side length must be odd to result in 25 cents leftover.

Donna continued her solution by writing an expression for the price of an odd quilt in terms of its side dimension x. A participant asked her to explain where she got $(x-1)^2$ for the number of whites, which she agreed to do. She presented a table, whose entries she obtained by counting white squares on drawn quilts (Fig. 2).

She explained that she found a relationship: for a given odd side dimension, the number of whites could be found by subtracting 1 from the side dimension, dividing the result by 2, squaring this, and then multiplying it by 4. She illustrated this for the 5×5 quilt and, at the request of TR, also the 7×7 (Fig. 3).

This was how she found that the number of white squares could be represented as $4\left(\dfrac{x-1}{2}\right)^2$ or $(x-1)^2$.

This work is clear evidence of RPG reasoning: Donna found the pattern by examining a few cases in her table. Nevertheless, she also showed a sophisticated ability to deal with numerical expressions that are not in a closed form. Overall,

Fig. 3 Donna's further quilt calculations

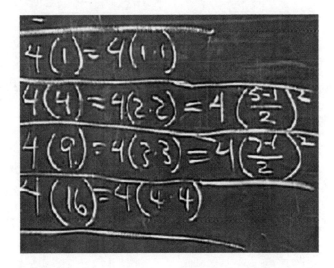

Donna displayed evidence of a referential symbolic proof scheme: she used her own symbol system and variables, exhibiting comfort with fractions.

Donna attempted to relate her expression $4\left(\dfrac{x-1}{2}\right)^2$ back to the geometry of the problem, possibly with the goal (conscious or unconscious) of making the solution more deductive: "…the 4 stands for those 4 sides." However, Donna did not explain the meaning of subtracting 1 or dividing by 2. TR stopped her with the following exchange.

TR: …as teachers, what do you think about this process? [11 second pause] You don't think about it? Is everything ok? You accept that. Beautiful reasoning, right? She made tremendous intellectual effort to bring this into a general form. We all agree upon that? Are we 100 % happy? Mathematically speaking. Yes or no? There are 2 possibilities: either you are happy or not.

Participant: Are you?

Class: [Laughs].

TR: Who cares about me?

Participant: We do.

This is another example of TR asking for evaluation of a solution. The request for evaluation was open-ended. Participants' slow response and question "are you [happy]?" suggest that participants wanted to know what TR thought rather than judging based on their own criteria. We also note that the way TR asked for evaluation praised the solution. This is important because TR did not want participants to throw out empirical reasoning as a conjecturing tool. Instead, they should ask each time: how do I know it always works and what makes it work? In this case, the few participant responses were positive (e.g., "we asked for her to explain that and that explains it so yes, in that sense I'm happy") and no participant raised issues of

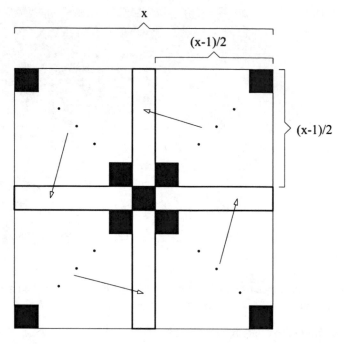

Fig. 4 TR's quilt diagram

certainty or causality. TR asked how we know that the formula will work for a very large odd number and then had the class take a break.

When Does TR Raise Issues of Certainty and Causality? (Continued)

After the break, TR made an explicit shift from certainty to causality: "you are so certain that this is always going to happen … We are also interested in what makes it happen all the time." Without giving participants further time to respond, he shared his own insight regarding a (PPG) proof of the pattern.

TR began by considering a generic $x \times x$ quilt, where x is odd. His proof involved finding a geometric interpretation for Donna's formula. He explained that, if we remove the center row and column of squares (containing the black square shared by both diagonals), the quilt would have four square corners with $\left(\dfrac{x-1}{2}\right)^2$ cells each. So, excluding the removed row and column, there would be $4\left(\dfrac{x-1}{2}\right)^2$ squares in the four square corners (see Fig. 4). He went on to explain that each black square along the diagonal corresponded to a square that had been removed by eliminating the row and column containing the center black square (arrows in figure indicate the correspondence). Finally, he claimed that his explanation constituted a reason for Donna's expression to hold in all cases.

How Does TR Model Desirable Behaviors? (Continued)

We note that providing his own deductive solution contrasts with what TR did for Donna's claim about the dimension needing to be odd. We suspect that the difference is that TR believed participants were capable of appreciating a deductive explanation for Donna's formula but not of finding such an explanation themselves. TR thus modeled the kind of deductive explanation he hoped participants would start producing. At least one participant clapped when TR finished the proof, and the whole class seemed to take pleasure in it. This response suggests that at least some participants were ready for a PPG solution and appreciated it. In DNR, the teacher can present a proof from beginning to end when students are ready to appreciate it.

When presenting his proof, TR emphasized that his solution depended on Donna's work and that he could not have created it without her insights. He shared his struggle: while she explained her solution, he was wondering why it would work all the time and how it related to the structure of the quilt—searching for a reason for the pattern to hold and eventually finding it. Sharing his own struggle demonstrated that TR is also reasoning and promotes the WoT that doing mathematics takes time and struggle. Building upon students' current WoU and WoT is critical in DNR, and one obvious way to do this is to present a solution that builds on student ideas. Thus, TR modeled DNR principles and tried to catalyze the empirical/deductive transition by showing participants how they could build on their own or each other's reasoning. He emphasized the pleasure derived from the fact that they are now both certain and understand a source of the pattern, with the implication that they should seek this kind of pleasure in the future.

Episode 3: Stair-Like Structure Problem

On the first day of the second summer institute,[9] the following problem was posed:

A figure such as the one below is called a stair-like structure. You have 1,176 identical square pieces. Can you use all the pieces to construct a stair-like structure?

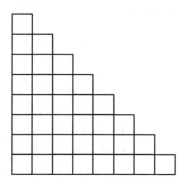

---

[9] One year after the first, with a few follow-up sessions in between.

Fig. 5 Donna's stair table

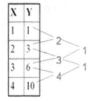

Main Questions

- How does TR model desirable behaviors? (How)
- When does TR raise issues of certainty and causality? (When)
- How does TR reinforce desirable reasoning? (How)

Purpose of the Problem

We see the major goal of the problem to be distinguishing between RPG and PPG approaches by attending to the difference between certainty and causality. Thus, it had similar purposes to the Quilt Problem, with an expectation that participants' WoT would have advanced.

Question Analysis and Teaching Actions

How Does TR Model Desirable Behaviors? (How)

Donna presented the first solution to this problem. She drew a table of x, "level" or "number of flights of stairs," versus y, "number of blocks needed in order to build that staircase." She filled in the first 4 rows of this table and said she saw a pattern. She looked at changes between successive y values, then changes between those changes (see Fig. 5), which she found to be constant. This told her that she had a quadratic pattern.

TR paused to see if anyone had questions, and Jenny said she did not see how Donna's observation "tells her" that the pattern is quadratic. TR fleshed out this question as two conjectures that he wrote on the board:

1. If the difference between any two consecutive elements in a pattern is constant, then that pattern is linear. Why?
2. If the second difference between any two consecutive elements in a pattern is constant, then that pattern is quadratic. Why?

We conjecture that TR had Donna pause at this point both because he perceived some confusion from other participants and because she used a fact that was not

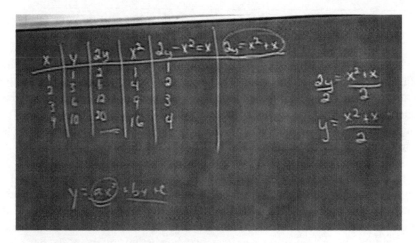

Fig. 6 Donnas extended stair table

known to the class. The pause communicated that participants should raise a question, thus reinforcing or modifying the didactical contract.

Jenny's question to Donna seemed to be about how to know that the pattern is quadratic, rather than a justification of this fact. However, TR used this opportunity to address a WoT that is part of his agenda: the problem-solving approach of recognizing conjectures as not truly known, but using them for now. He is explicit about this WoT: "…we'll put it aside. We'll raise a question and in this way, we'll enrich our knowledge about the mathematics that we know." Thus, we see the teaching behavior of purposely interpreting student statements and questions in a broader context. That is, when a participant raises a question that provides an indirect avenue for addressing some important issue, TR will reinterpret the question in a way he suspects was not intended by the participant in order to get at the issue he wants.

It was intentional for TR to raise the two conjectures written on the board but not resolve them. TR chose to accept this mathematical "error" partly because he wanted to maintain the flow of the mathematics. Moreover, TR believed that participants were capable of appreciating the conjectures but not yet proving them.

Donna continued her solution by drawing an extended table (Fig. 6).

From this table, she found the pattern $2y=x^2+x$, so $y=\dfrac{x^2+x}{2}$.

She then wrote $1{,}176=\dfrac{x^2+x}{2}$ and got $x=48$, which meant the answer to the problem is "yes."

When Does TR Raise Issues of Certainty and Causality? (When)

After Donna's solution, TR asked "So, are there questions here or comments?… If this were in your class and Donna produced this solution, what would be your reaction?" After some responses, he asked "what will be your response to Donna as a teacher?" and finally "within this problem, are we happy? Is this complete mathematically?"

We expect TR to advance his goal of distinguishing RPG and PPG approaches by asking for evaluation. In this case, TR began with more neutral and open-ended questions. When TR asked if the solution was mathematically complete, participants seemed happy and no participant objected to the RPG nature of the solution. Next, a lengthy exchange occurred. First, at TR's prompting, Donna shared that she based her solution "on just these four cases." TR raised the question, "does this relationship hold for every x?" and then asked if it would be artificial for students. Donna responded "you're going to get a lot of blank stares" and Reginald mentioned that recognizing and accepting patterns is encouraged. After repeatedly asking whether the pattern will continue, TR shifted to asking why it works, e.g., "Fine. This is going always to happen, but what causes this to be so?" TR asked if participants appreciate the latter question. It is not clear how many of them do, but no one attempts an answer.

It is important that TR questioned the validity of a claim and shifted the focus to causality in the same exchange. We wondered why so much time was spent on the former, when it was previously noted that formulas can be self-supporting, so that TR is unlikely to destabilize participants' certainty regarding Donna's formula. The question of whether the pattern will continue to hold did not come up naturally. It appears that participants did not appreciate it, and TR himself recognized that it "is artificial" and "you do not seem to be very impressed by that question."

TR explicitly said to participants that the question of whether the pattern will continue is meaningful to him, and we believe that he is trying to make it meaningful to them by connecting it to the question of why the pattern holds. DNR states that the goals are to lead participants toward institutionalized WoU and WoT, which require that they understand the difference between deductive and empirical justifications. At the same time, TR could not (according to DNR principles) simply tell them the difference between RPG and PPG. Thus, TR persisted in asking questions. There is a tension between wanting participants to think you share their understanding and wanting them to appreciate issues you consider important. Despite TR labeling the question as artificial for the participants, his repetition of it might indicate to participants that they should be asking such a question. The nature of TR's interaction with Donna shows that the institute is an environment in which participants can disagree with the instructor but still be persuaded of the value in his approach. One of TR's goals in persisting with this question was to show participants that it may be necessary at times to help students address questions that seem artificial to them; ideally, this would be done by asking other questions or problems to provide intellectual necessity for the original question.

Stepping back from this particular case, part of our goal in this research was to look at subtle teaching actions that were used to help participants transition from RPG to PPG. The espoused approach of TR is to emphasize causality for a long time and then try to help participants start to ask the question of whether a result holds. However, we see that the actual implementation involves a more

Fig. 7 TR's doulbed staircase

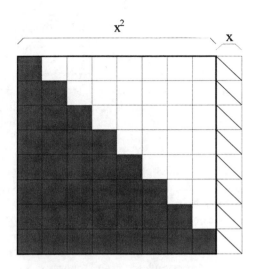

consistent relationship between whether and why a pattern holds. We saw TR raise the question of whether a pattern continues to hold during the Quilt Problem, and here he persisted with this question longer because he thought participants were closer to appreciating it. The relationship between certainty and causality has not been definitively established yet, and TR was proceeding without complete information. He felt a tension between wanting to be persuasive and not wanting to preach. In general, he tried to encourage independent reasoning by controlling overall goals of the institute but not forcing participants to follow a particular path toward them.

How Does TR Reinforce Desirable Reasoning? (How)

After raising the question of why Donna's pattern holds, TR presented his own proof of this fact in a similar manner as he did for the Quilt Problem—one of many similarities. In his extension of Donna's solution, TR asked what it means to double y and then added a rotated version of the stair-like structure to the existing diagram of an 8-step stair-like structure on the overhead, forming a rectangle (see Fig. 7). He emphasized that it can be any number of steps and this will still work. Then, he asked what it means to take away x^2 and drew a square of side 8 in red. TR noted that what is left is a single column with x squares, so "we explained the cause of that conjecture to happen."

During and after his proof, TR repeatedly emphasized the importance of Donna's work: "she very beautifully identified and established a very nice conjecture…her work there was indispensable" and "[his proof] doesn't count [for] anything if you don't have the conjecture." The teaching behavior of emphasizing empirical work as a starting point is a consistent feature of ATI, and we saw a similar emphasis for the Quilt Problem. TR's message is not that empirical reasoning should be avoided, but that it represents only a starting point and not a complete solution.

After finishing his proof, TR asked students to compare the conjecture with the proof. In this case, the comparison is between Donna's preliminary work and his completion of her solution. A few participants said it is powerful to have the diagram explain the symbols. TR emphasized that his proof did not come easily, but that he had to think about how to put meaning into the symbols (echoing what he said for the Quilt Problem). One WoT being reinforced here is that finding solutions often requires time and thought, not just quick answers. Another is the referential symbolic WoT, which he demonstrated by showing how useful it was for him: "…what is the meaning of $2y$? Remember, we attend to the meaning of the symbols all the time."

We conjecture that TR hoped to elicit some comment that his solution was more complete. Although participants express positive regard, no one suggests that TR's solution was more mathematically appropriate, correct, or complete. They appeared to see it as complementing Donna's solution because it explains more, but they do not yet appreciate that Donna's solution was not a valid proof.

Conclusion

Themes from the Three Episodes

Whether

A central aspect of DNR (though not unique to DNR) is attention to each learners' current state of mathematics understanding. TR had preconceived expectations regarding participants' mathematics knowledge going into the institute (e.g., he expected most to exhibit RPG reasoning), but he continually refined his models of participants' mathematics based on what he observed. These models guide all aspects of instruction, such as what questions are asked (problems or discussion questions), which participants are called on, and what TR presents to the class.

We noted an instance in the investment problem where TR did not address a modeling error because he wanted to keep attention focused on the conjecturing and proving acts. Also, when a computational error occurred, TR continued discussing the form of the argument instead of dealing with the error—although it is not clear if he noticed the computational error or not, this still indicates a focus away from the computations and result. During the stair-like structure problem, TR chose to leave a mathematical "error" unattended in order to maintain the flow of an argument and to model a problem-solving approach. Overall, TR focused on issues concerning the primary WoT that he wanted to address at the time, and other aspects were often set aside. He refrained from pointing out some errors that he might have considered important, in order to maintain the flow of a solution or keep participants' attention.

When

All three episodes involved TR raising questions about first certainty and then cause. However, the time spent pushing these issues increased from each episode to the next, in keeping with the presumed increased comfort participants had with these questions—although we note that they did not display an appreciation for certainty questions by the third episode.

TR chose to sequence his own deductive arguments in the flow of class discussions about the solutions to problems, and he did so when participants seemed to feel an intellectual need for understanding why a solution worked. We noted in the analysis that implementation of DNR necessarily entails building onto participants' WoU and WoT. In one case, a participant's generic argument was used to model how algebraic symbolism—with meaning—could be used to show a general result. In other cases, TR took advantages of situations when he had evidence to believe the participants cared a lot about a particular question (e.g., the 3-1-3-1 pattern), so that the discussion could not move on without a resolution. In a different case, TR noted retrospectively that when he felt creating a deductive argument was within the grasp of most participants, he chose not to present one.

DNR strikes a balance between considerations of the mathematical content (as is primary in traditional college instruction) and the mind of the learner (as is primary in constructivism). Thus, TR was willing to make small compromises in either direction to further his goals. We might characterize his style as opportunistic: he had clear goals and took advantage of any opportunity to create intellectual need that would help advance these goals.

How

Requesting an evaluation of solutions is an important teaching action in TR's practice. By requesting evaluations TR sought to determine how participants felt about the solution and what (if anything) they felt was lacking. His goal was to help participants delineate empirical and deductive solutions and determine what each provides: only certainty in the former but causality also in the latter. However, this had to be carefully implemented, as he did not wish to characterize participant solutions as incorrect or not useful. Thus, the nature of the evaluation involved mainly greater positive attention on PPG solutions, rather than negative attention on RPG solutions.

Two of the episodes involved TR demonstrating the power of algebra to help address questions, thus promoting referential symbolic reasoning, an important goal of the institute and part of deductive reasoning. Two episodes involved geometric patterns that were very amenable to RPG/PPG, and both times TR built upon an RPG solution to provide his own PPG proof, thus attempting to promote this action as desirable reasoning. It is important that TR did not simply present a PPG solution (e.g., his favorite one) after eliciting a participant's RPG one. Instead, he expended effort to create a new PPG solution that would use the same structure as the participant solution.

General Conclusions

As mentioned earlier, TR is a DNR expert. Moreover, the setting for this instruction is unusual: a full-time professional development institute, with few of the constraints that are a part of school or university instruction. Nevertheless, since our goal is not to find generalizable results, but rather to characterize DNR, this ideal setting is appropriate.

Teachers often have a great deal of uncertainty about what to do, and TR is no exception. His goal was to destabilize participants and create intellectual need whenever possible. We contend that, by examining a few situations where TR was uncertain about what to do or deviated from his plan, this chapter illuminates aspects of DNR that remain hidden when reading a theoretical description of its constructs.

Despite understanding the key determinants of teacher behavior within DNR, other members of the research team had trouble predicting what TR would do next at various points. Thus, learning to teach according to DNR is a complex endeavor that cannot be reduced to a set of guidelines. Our analysis in this chapter has demonstrated some of these complexities and how they can be negotiated. We do not expect this to provide a practical guide to implementing DNR, nor do we expect many readers to implement DNR. Rather, we believe that math educators can gain general insights by examining issues that arise when teaching by means of one theoretical framework with the potential to transform instruction. We hope that instructors of all types have benefited from the elucidation of these issues.

References

Blanton, M., Stylianou, D., & Knuth, E. J. (2009). *Teaching and learning proof across the grades: A K-16 perspective*. New York: Routledge.

Harel, G. (2001). The development of mathematical induction as a proof scheme: A model for DNR based instruction. In S. Campbell & R. Zazkis (Eds.), *The learning and teaching of number theory* (pp. 185–212). Dordrecht: Kluwer.

Harel, G. (2008a). DNR perspective on mathematics curriculum and instruction: Focus on proving, Part I. *Zentralblatt fuer Didaktik der Mathematik, 40,* 487–500.

Harel, G. (2008b). DNR perspective on mathematics curriculum and instruction, Part II. *Zentralblatt fuer Didaktik der Mathematik, 40,* 893–907.

Harel, G., & Sowder, L. (1998). Students' proof schemes: Results from exploratory studies. In A. Schoenfeld, J. Kaput, & E. Dubinsky (Eds.), *Research in collegiate mathematics education III* (pp. 234–283). Providence: American Mathematical Society.

Healy, L., & Hoyles, C. (2000). A study of proof conceptions in algebra. *Journal for Research in Mathematics Education, 31*(4), 396–428.

Lehrer, R., Kobiela, M., & Weinberg, P. J. (2013). Cultivating inquiry about space in a middle school mathematics classroom. *ZDM—The International Journal on Mathematics Education, 45*(3), 365–376.

Mehan, H. (1979). *Learning lessons: The social organization of classroom instruction*. Cambridge, MA: Harvard University Press.

Piaget, J. (1985). *The equilibration of cognitive structures: The central problem of intellectual development*. Chicago: University of Chicago Press.

Reid, D., & Zack, V. (2009). Aspects of teaching proving in upper elementary school. In M. Blanton, D. Stylianou, & E. Knuth (Eds.), *Teaching and learning proof across the grades: A K-16 perspective* (pp. 133–146). New York: Routledge.

Sherin, M. G. (2002). A balancing act: Developing a discourse community in a mathematics classroom. *Journal of Mathematics Teacher Education, 5*, 205–233.

Steffe, L. P., & Thompson, P. W. (2000). *Teaching experiment methodology: Underlying principles and essential elements*. Hillsdale: Lawrence Erlbaum Associates.

Unifying Complexity in Mathematics Teaching-Learning Development: A Theory-Practice Dialectic

Barbara Jaworski

Abstract This chapter addresses theory in relation to mathematics teaching and learning development, drawing on a research study to exemplify theoretical perspectives. In particular it addresses difficulties and issues which arise in a developmental process, from both theoretical and practice-based points of view. The areas of theory are those of *inquiry, community and critical alignment*, which address developmental processes in mathematics learning and teaching; *documentational genesis and instrumentation theory*, which address the development of knowledge in teaching; and finally the use of a framework from *activity theory*, which addresses issues and tensions that emerge from observation and analysis in the research. The illustrative research study addresses perceptions of learning and its outcomes between a teaching team and a cohort of engineering students learning mathematics in a university system. Overall the chapter seeks to address complexity in the developmental process and important synergies between theory, practice and research.

Keywords Mathematics teaching development • Inquiry communities in learning and teaching mathematics • Documentational genesis • Activity theory • University mathematics teaching

Introduction

In the teaching and learning of mathematics, it has been observed frequently that students' mathematical learning does not accord with what society and the educational establishment would like to see (e.g. Artigue et al. 2007; Hawkes and Savage

B. Jaworski (✉)
Mathematics Education Centre, Loughborough University,
Loughborough LE11 3TU, UK
e-mail: b.jaworski@lboro.ac.uk

Y. Li et al. (eds.), *Transforming Mathematics Instruction: Multiple Approaches and Practices*, Advances in Mathematics Education, DOI 10.1007/978-3-319-04993-9_24, © Springer International Publishing Switzerland 2014

2000; Romberg and Carpenter 1986). Perceived reasons for this differ according to those making the judgement. One area of theory suggests that students (at school or university) engage with mathematics at instrumental, operational or procedural levels in which concepts are touched on only superficially and learning is by rote memorisation rather than in-depth engagement (Brown 1979; Hiebert 1986; Skemp 1976). Research has shown that the nature of teaching rooted in social practice within schools and classrooms can promote comfortable ways of being rather than the struggle to deal with concepts more rigorously (Brown and McIntyre 1993; Doyle 1988). Further, research into students' transition from school to university reveals difficulties for students in dealing with the expectations of formality and abstraction at the higher levels without adequate preparation at the school level (Hawkes and Savage 2000; Hernandez-Martinez et al. 2011; Nardi 2008).

The teaching-learning process in mathematics is complex. Although mathematics can be argued to be central to many other disciplines and to aspects of everyday life, mathematics is nevertheless an abstract subject whose very abstraction challenges the teaching-learning process. In order for students to develop mathematical understandings, teachers have to create opportunities for students to engage mathematically; to learn to express mathematical ideas; to make, justify and prove mathematical conjectures; and to use mathematics to solve problems. The developmental research process inquires into the design of mathematical tasks and their impact on students, as well as exploring approaches to engaging students and evaluating their outcomes.

This chapter addresses theoretical perspectives relating to the use of developmental research both in studying the development of teaching and learning in mathematics and in promoting such development. Teachers seek to develop their teaching in order to provide better learning opportunities in mathematics for their students. Research documents this process and the issues it raises. In addition, the nature of developmental research is such that the research process provides stimulation and feedback to teachers seeking to improve their practice, so that the research itself becomes a tool for teaching development (Jaworski 2003). In this work, theory and practice are dialectically integrated: theory informs the design of teaching and its approaches to learning, and reflections of and analyses from practice enable theoretical development. This integration results in the growth of knowledge *in* practice and *about* practice: we learn, as practitioners (teachers), within our practice (teaching) and, as researchers, we are able to synthesise from local findings for more general applicability. I provide examples below.

In this developmental activity, we (the teams of researchers with whom I have worked) take a sociocultural position rooted in the work of Vygotsky and his followers in order to try to make sense of the complex issues involved. This position suggests that learning and teaching cannot be separated from the total social context of which they are a part. Any mathematics classroom, lecture theatre or seminar room forms a social setting in which learners engage with each other, with the teacher and with mathematics.[1] Learning is regarded as participation in social practice within cultural

---

[1] Relevant here is a special issue of the journal ZDM (*ZDM*, Vol. 4, Issue 5) which focuses on the didactical triangle of teacher, student and mathematics and important relations between mathematics teaching and learning.

worlds with the mediation of elements of community, systems, tools and actions. Vygotsky's central claim that learning takes place on two planes in which the social plane is pre-eminent is interpreted through Wertsch's (1991) perspective of 'goal-directed action' such that 'human action typically employs 'mediational means' such as tools and language' and 'the relationship between action and mediational means is so fundamental that it is more appropriate, when referring to the agent involved, to speak of 'individual(s)-acting-with-mediational-means' than to speak simply of 'individual(s)'' (p. 12). From these theoretical starting points, the chapter focuses on theory as follows:

(a) Theory of *community of inquiry*, which is central to a developmental research approach, and the important construct of *critical alignment* (e.g. Jaworski 2008a): these areas of theory are central to promoting the learning of mathematics and the learning of mathematics teaching.
(b) Theory of documentational genesis (e.g. Gueudet and Trouche 2011a, b), linked to instrumentation theory: these areas of theory address the development of teaching and of knowledge in teaching, with particular focus on a teacher's use of tools and resources including technological tools, and the corresponding growth of knowledge in teaching.
(c) Activity theory (e.g. Leont'ev 1979; Engeström 1999) as an analytical tool: this develops directly from our sociocultural basis set out briefly above and seeks to make sense of complexity in the process of analysis in relating teaching to learning, particularly where findings/results/outcomes appear to be in tension.

Although theoretically focused, the chapter draws on recent research to exemplify and illuminate theoretical ideas and their use. This research focused on an innovation in the teaching to first year engineering students at university level[2] and involved teachers as researchers in collaboration between research and practice. The project (Engineering Students Understanding Mathematics – ESUM) was funded by the Royal Academy of Engineering in the UK National HE STEM[3] programme. Here a teaching team designed an innovation (involving a new teaching approach) to an established, introductory mathematics module for engineering students in order to promote students' more conceptual understandings of mathematics. The innovation was researched through practitioner inquiry and outsider researcher observation and analysis; research revealed issues and tensions between teaching goals and students' perspectives and approaches to learning.

---

[2] Space here has not allowed a *dual* focus on the development of teaching at both school and university levels. Developmental research *at school level* focusing on inquiry approaches to developing teaching, used by teachers and didacticians, with activity theory analyses can be found in Jaworski and Goodchild (2006) and Jaworski (2008a).

[3] HE STEM has been a major government-sponsored programme in higher education focusing on the subjects science, technology, engineering and mathematics. Funding has been available for projects promoting teaching and learning development within this programme.

Overall, the chapter expands on the elements mentioned briefly above and seeks to provide a rationale to demonstrate how this combination of theory and methodology allows us to address the complexity of developing teaching and learning in mathematics and mathematics teaching. In order to do this, the chapter begins in the section "Developmental research and introduction of the research study" with an exposition of developmental research and some relevant details of the ESUM study. In the section "Theories of inquiry community and critical alignment", I go on to introduce the key theories of inquiry community and critical alignment, illuminating these in the section "Exemplifying theory through the research study" with references to ESUM. The section "Tools, tasks and resources: instrumentation theory and documentational genesis" discusses the use of the theory of documentational genesis through a need to analyse teaching development and its relations to the use of tools, tasks and resources in the ESUM study. The section "Tackling complexity: activity theory as an analytical tool" shows how activity theory has been used to provide a framework for analyses in order to address the overall complexity in the research studies. Finally, the section "Discussion" draws together these elements.

Developmental Research and Introduction of the Research Study

Developmental research is research which has the intention not only to chart, monitor or evaluate the developmental process but also to contribute to that development (Jaworski 2003). It is

> research which both studies the developmental process and, simultaneously, promotes development through engagement and questioning. ... Not only are research questions defined and explored ... but the whole research process is subject to question and exploration. We look critically at our research activity while engaging in and with it. (Jaworski and Goodchild 2006, p. 353)

The goals of such research are:

- To promote the development of teaching in mathematics, and teachers' better understandings of teaching for students' mathematical development;
- To document any issues and tensions in the developmental process and its outcomes, particularly in relation to the situations and cultures in which teaching and learning take place;
- To develop knowledge both in local practice and for more generalised understandings of teaching for learning in mathematics.

In the ESUM study, a team of three mathematics educators in a UK university designed and implemented an innovation in teaching a mathematics module for first year engineering students (e.g. Jaworski and Matthews 2011). The entire process was researched, aided by an external researcher (research officer, RO) employed for the purpose. The innovation was designed to improve mathematical learning outcomes for the students and, specifically, to promote more *conceptual* learning of mathematics, based on observations that teaching and learning had, in the past, taken rather instrumental forms (Hiebert 1986; Jaworski 2008b; Skemp 1976). The developmental nature of this research was interpreted through our use of *inquiry*. We sought ways of bringing inquiry into our practices at differing levels in order to promote developments in practice and associated growth of knowledge in practice – *insider research* – and we also collected data from activity in order to perform rigorous analyses related to clearly defined research questions – *outsider research* (Bassey 1995; Jaworski 2004a). In the ESUM project, the teaching team (insider researchers) designed and taught the module (one was the *lecturer*); the research officer (outsider researcher) collected data from events and joined members of the teaching team in analysing this data. Thus, some members of the teaching team acted as both insider and outsider researchers.

We collected data from our activity through observations of lectures and tutorials (with audio recording), lecturer reflections, student surveys and audio-recorded interviews and focus groups, together with documentation from the design and planning. The innovation included the use of inquiry-based tasks in a setting involving small group activities, use of a GeoGebra environment (http://www.geogebra.org/cms/en/) and assessment through a small group project. Teachers reflected on teaching design and implementation as these progressed and made modifications to their practice in response to findings from the observations and reflection.

The 'lecturer' offered lectures and tutorials to the cohort of students and worked closely with the RO who attended and observed all these events. The reflections of the lecturer, either in written form or in oral form through 'conversations' with the RO and a graduate tutorial assistant, formed important data. The lecturer thus acted as a practitioner-researcher at the teaching-learning interface in close collaboration with the RO who was able, through her comments and questions, to help objectify the lecturer's more subjective observations. Meetings with other members of the team allowed such observations to be considered at an even more critical level. For example, when it seemed to the lecturer that questioning in lectures was having a positive effect in student engagement, the researcher pointed out certain students who rarely responded and who seemed less engaged. The lecturer was then challenged to find ways of engaging these students while avoiding confrontation. When this was discussed with the team, the suggestion to offer a task for discussion in pairs and, over time, to develop an expectation that the lecturer might ask any pair for their response was made. This new suggestion could then be tested in practice. Thus, the team formed a small 'inquiry community'. Development can be seen in growth of knowledge in practice deriving from these stages of critical reflection. The whole developmental process was documented through analysis of collected data against research questions.

The focus of analysis was the teaching and its development. Thus the unit of analysis was the teaching event and student responses to that event. No fine-grained study was made of student learning. It can be seen that analysis took place at two levels, roughly the insider and outsider levels, although there was close synergy between the levels. At the insider level it was less formal and more immediate, feeding back into practice and promoting ongoing development.

Theories of Inquiry Community and Critical Alignment

Established 'ways of being' in schools or university might be characterised as *communities of practice* in the terms of Lave and Wenger (1991) or of Wenger (1998) in which the *practice* is the interaction of teachers and students, with its own norms and expectations related to learning mathematics. These communities operate with elements of *mutual engagement, joint enterprise* and *shared repertoire* (Wenger 1998). For example, teachers and students *work together* in classrooms or lecture theatres (mutual engagement); they have required goals and outcomes such as completion of tasks, success in assessment and appropriate behaviour (joint enterprise), and they follow established routines such as use of textbooks, classroom groupings, homework or coursework (shared repertoire). Wenger suggests that to *belong* to a community of practice, or to have *identity* within a community of practice, requires *engagement, imagination* and *alignment*. One has to take part in the practice, be overtly a member of the community and 'join in' (engagement); developing a personal trajectory within the practice requires participants to visualise their role (imagination); it is necessary to participate according to the norms and expectations the community has developed within the practice, to *align* with them (alignment). Being a student in a classroom or a university or being a teacher or lecturer involves having identity in the community of practice and hence engaging with the practice, using imagination to have a role in the practice and aligning with its norms and expectations. However, alignment with existing norms and expectations of ongoing practice can result in perpetuation of undesirable outcomes from that practice. This is particularly relevant to established practices in schools and higher education in which instrumental forms of teaching and learning (e.g. Hiebert 1986; Skemp 1976) result in 'impoverished' mathematical environments (Pring 2004, p. 18) in which students practice mathematical techniques but rarely gain deeper insights to mathematical concepts.

An inquiry approach is designed explicitly to address these issues. Inquiry involves asking questions and seeking answers, addressing problems and seeking solutions, exploring, investigating and looking critically at what we are doing and achieving (Cochran Smith and Lytle 1999; Mason et al. 1982; Schoenfeld 1985). The theory is that, through such engagement, through a critical questioning approach to what we do, we can gain knowledge that enables us to do it better and more knowledgeably. The 'better' here implies a way of being (Jaworski 2004b) or seeing rather than an objectively better form of practice (since the latter depends on the nature of judgement). Wells (1999) refers to this as 'metaknowing', knowing about knowing: we become more aware, more knowledgeable, about what we do as we do it. Mason (2002) calls it the 'discipline of noticing': by overtly noticing what we are doing, we have the possibility to do it differently, to inquire into new possibilities. With inquiry, the community of practice is transformed into a *community of inquiry,* belonging to which requires engagement and imagination and, of course, alignment. However, with inquiry we do not engage uncritically; we notice and question what we do, so that alignment becomes *critical*. Therefore, identity within a community of inquiry requires engagement, imagination and *critical alignment*; it involves working within established norms and expectations while questioning their provenance and exploring alternatives (Jaworski 2006). It is the concept of critical alignment which distinguishes a community of inquiry from a community of practice.

Exemplifying Theory Through the Research Study

In the research study, inquiry was operational at three levels:

1. *Inquiry in mathematics*: First we introduced inquiry in mathematics, seeking to promote students' conceptual engagement with mathematics through an inquiry-based approach. This involved our design of inquiry-based tasks, for use in lectures or tutorials, in which students' exploratory activity would promote engagement with mathematics and in which questioning between teachers and students would reveal relationships and alternative ways of expressing mathematical ideas. An aim was to link formality and abstraction with conceptual insight.

2. *Inquiry in mathematics teaching*: Second, it was a fundamental goal to promote development in teaching. Therefore we undertook inquiry into teaching: the 'innovation' was predesigned by the teaching team and put into practice by the lecturer with ongoing inquiry into the teaching process as described above. We demonstrated our use of inquiry cycles as shown in the figure below.

Plan/design for teaching
Teach: act and observe (collect data)   The developmental
Reflect and analyse   process
Feedback to future planning

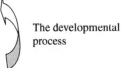

With the inclusion of elements of 'observe' and 'analyse', the inquiry cycle extends beyond a normal teaching cycle (of plan → teach → reflect → feedback). Such cycles reflect a *systematic* approach to development and have elements in common with iterative cycles in action research and design research (Elliott 1991; Kelly 2003). As in action research, the cycles are intended to have action outcomes in terms of development of practice and learning through development; as in design research, there is often some design of tasks, or process, and this is evaluated and developed through successive cycles. Through such cycles, teachers learn about approaches to teaching and their outcomes. However, the developmental process here is fluid and adaptable to context, experience and circumstance; rather than describing it as systematic in an objective sense, it might be seen more as *evolutionary* over time (Jaworski 1998). Participants grow into inquiry ways of being: they start by using inquiry as a tool: for example, by using an inquiry-based task or by introducing some form of questioning approach and developing this over time, often lengthy periods of time.

3. *Inquiry in the research process*: If we see research as 'systematic inquiry made public' (Stenhouse 1984, p. 77), then it is clear that inquiry is central to research. So the third level at which inquiry was operational was in developmental research itself. The roles of insider and outsider were very important here, both involving inquiry into the developmental process, the first promoting development in practice and the second analysing that development and contributing to theory. It was important to communicate and disseminate findings. In the ESUM project, our funders, the Royal Academy of Engineering, organised dissemination meetings, and we were asked to publish case studies on their website (http://www.hestem.ac.uk/resources/case-studies) and in a dedicated book (The Royal Academy of Engineering 2012). We have also made presentations at international conferences and published in refereed journals.

I continue this section with a short vignette to illustrate our development of inquiry processes at these three levels.

Impact of Inquiry-Based Tasks on Students

The principal aim of the ESUM project was to promote students' more conceptually based (less instrumental) learning of mathematics. In discussion with colleagues in the Department of Materials Engineering, we agreed that developing students' engagement with mathematical concepts in exploratory ways would be consistent with their development as engineers. We worked from the premise that (suitably designed) inquiry-based tasks would engage students in deeper levels of thinking about mathematical concepts than might be the case with more traditional tasks. We designed an innovation with four key elements and put this into practice within the normal constraints of the university system. These constraints included the size of the student cohort, a programme of lectures and tutorials in line with other modules, a module specification (curriculum) to which we were obliged to work and the usual forms of university accommodation for teaching sessions. The four elements of our innovation were:

1. Use of inquiry-based questions and tasks
2. Use of an electronic medium juxtaposing algebraic and graphical representations (GeoGebra)
3. Small group activity in tutorials
4. An assessed small group project including a peer assessment process

We were given two lectures (in regular lecture theatres) and one tutorial (in a computer laboratory environment) per week for 14 weeks. In lectures, material was presented and GeoGebra used, in dynamic mode, as a demonstration tool.

The lecturer asked many questions, in order to involve students, some of which were explicitly open ended or inquiry based. For example, in the topic area of real-valued functions of one variable, we posed the task:

Consider the function $f(x) = x^2 + 2x$ (x is real).
(a) Give an equation of a line that intersects the graph of this function:
    (i) Twice   (ii) Once   (iii) Never   (Adapted from Pilzer et al. 2003, p. 7)
(b) If we have the function $f(x) = ax^2 + bx + c$.
    What can you say about lines which intersect this function twice?
(c) Write down equations for three straight lines and draw them in GeoGebra.
(d) Find a (quadratic) function such that the graph of the function cuts one of your lines *twice*, one of them *only once* and the third *not at all* and show the result in GeoGebra.
(e) Repeat for three *different* lines (what does it mean to be different?).

Part (a) was used in a lecture, where it was judged that students could engage quickly with the task and provide feedback to the lecturer. Students were expected to be familiar with this function and able to imagine or sketch a graph readily. Thus, imagining lines which would intersect the graph was seen not to be a difficult task for these students. Thus they could talk to each other about possible lines. Their initial responses expressed equations of horizontal lines (e.g. (i) $y = 2$ (ii) $y = -1$ (iii) $y = -3$). They found it harder to think about non-horizontal lines. When the lecturer asked for non-horizontal lines, examples were forthcoming from just a few students. The lecturer used GeoGebra to show these lines and to encourage students' visualisation. This allowed for some quick discussion across the lecture theatre to involve students, help them to see that different answers are possible and discuss the quality of the answers and what we can learn from them.

This activity and discussion should not delay the progress of the lecture extensively – it was always a balance between promoting students' engagement and dealing with a suitable range of topics to cover the syllabus. The lecturer experimented with tasks such as this to gain insight into students' perspectives and to encourage their active participation. Lecturer reflection raised issues such as the value of outcomes versus the time factors involved. An issue that became visible was that of students' perceptions of mathematical representation and formality. In their A level studies,[4] students had used notation in procedural ways to specific ends. For example, they could quickly invert a simple function (such as $f(x) = (5x - 3)/2$) to find the 'inverse' function ($f^{-1}(x) = (2x + 3)/5$), usually by writing $y = f(x)$ (e.g. $y = (5x - 3)/2$) and rearranging an equation involving y and x to get $x = f^{-1}(y)$ (e.g. $x = (2y - 3)/5$). They extended this liberally to non-linear and many-one functions without consideration of the *meanings* of function and inverse. However, when given definitions of function and inverse, some were unable to see the

---

[4]A level GCE (Advanced Level General Certificate of Education) is a national examination (at 16+) with high stakes outcomes for higher-level study. Many UK universities require the highest grade in A level to qualify for university study in mathematics.

distinctions being made and therefore did not see the importance of the definitions and associated notations. Their perceptions of graphical representations were similarly instrumental: where tasks sought to develop connections between the algebraic and the graphical, students' focus on 'plotting' a graph detracted from seeing the generality of a function in its graph and the value of being able to vary parameters quickly to generate families of graphs and provide insight into the represented functions. The lecturer had to balance time factors, with quality time in lectures spent on tasks to shift these perceptions; inquiry-based tutorial tasks were designed and used with such aims in mind.

Thus, parts (b) to (e) of the above task were designed for use in a tutorial where students could work flexibly in their small groups with access to GeoGebra on their computers; the lecturer and a graduate assistant would circulate, engaging groups in discussion and trying to discern the quality of students' engagement and understanding. For example, in part (b) GeoGebra 'sliders' would allow students to vary a, b and c for a quadratic function and explore a variety of lines crossing the functions in order to visualise a line and relate to its algebraic equation, thus enabling them to make some (algebraic) form of general statement about such lines. GeoGebra supports quick experimentation. Parts (d) and (e) offered a more serious challenge, which was designed to be especially valuable for students who thought they knew all about quadratic functions. Thus, students should be drawn into mathematical inquiry and enabled to gain more familiarity with functions, graphs, functional notation and relationships between all of these. Further analysis of such inquiry-based tasks, relating to mathematical competencies, is presented in Jaworski (in press).

The lectures were intended to introduce mathematical material and start an inquiry process demonstrated in the use of GeoGebra. Small group work in tutorials allowed more flexibility of engagement with an emphasis on conceptual understanding. It was here that an inquiry community was envisaged and sought. Observations showed a range of differences across groups, with some groups engaging well with inquiry-based tasks and demonstrating in-depth mathematical understanding, particularly in discussion with the lecturer or graduate assistant. Others seemed to engage only when the lecturer was within earshot, and networking media proved to be a distraction. Some students filled their screen with graphs so that it was hard to see differences or discern features. Some used the sliders without stopping to question what they saw to be happening. Perceived commitment on the part of students was very variable with certain students seeming to believe they had not much to learn beyond their A level studies, seeing the graphical work as boring because they did not engage with deeper questions. For the teaching team, this was an important recognition which had to be fed into design and planning and was thus a practical instantiation of critical alignment in insider research. As a result of such critical recognition, the lecturer has been able to modify the approach to (try to) interact more effectively with such students.

After completion of the module, the RO and one of the teaching team conducted one-one and focus group interviews with the students. It was expected that, though students were no longer immersed in module tasks, they were still reasonably close enough to the events to reflect on their experiences. Analyses showed that despite inquiry approaches, some students maintained highly instrumental views on what it means to learn mathematics and ways in which the module supported this (or not!). For example, in one focus group, a student made the following remark:

> I found GeoGebra almost detrimental because it is akin to getting the question and then looking at the answer in the back of the book. I find I can understand the graph better if I take some values for x and some values for y, plot it, work it out then I understand it … if you just type in some numbers and get a graph then you don't really see where it came from. (Focus group 1)

For the lecturer who had tried hard to help students see values in GeoGebra use, such a comment was salutary! Such findings fed back into subsequent deliveries of this module (e.g. see Jaworski and Matthews 2011). We used activity theory to draw attention to differences in perspective between students and the teaching team, as discussed further below (Jaworski et al. 2012).

Tools, Tasks and Resources: Instrumentation Theory and Documentational Genesis

The inherent complexity here of inquiry community within inquiry community (e.g. inquiry in mathematics in tutorials within teaching team inquiry into suitable approaches to working with students) leads to research questions about the mediating roles of the tasks, tools and other resources that are central to innovation in developing teaching, as well as to the ways in which teachers develop their use. The use of inquiry-based tasks is essential to the inquiry approach; the use of GeoGebra as a medium for representation and experimentation was important for promoting students in-depth engagement with mathematics in coordination with inquiry-based tasks. We see the tasks and GeoGebra as *mediational tools* central to creating an inquiry community and to fostering critical alignment. The developmental of teaching depended on our use and knowledge of such tools.

The theory of documentational genesis focuses on resources and their 'schemes of utilisation' in tracing teachers' knowledge of teaching (Gueudet and Trouche 2011a, b). It is based on theory of instrumentation which is concerned with the relationship between an instrument and a person's use of that instrument. The theory of instrumentation (e.g. Trouche and Drijvers 2010) is concerned with learning that takes place as the user of the tool, the learner, interacts with the tool: it links a user with the tools he or she uses in a two-directional appropriation. From user to tools is a process of *instrumentalisation* in which the user appropriates the tool (instrument) to his or her use of it. In the opposite direction, a process of *instrumentation* involves the user in learning the idiosyncrasies of the tool in order to use it effectively. So, for example, with GeoGebra, instrumentation can be seen in the user learning what GeoGebra has to offer (such as the facility of using sliders to vary parameters) and its modes of use, becoming fluent with use in order to be able to achieve a desired purpose. Instrumentalisation involves the user in utilising the tool according to his or her explicit aims and requirements, that is, turning the tool to the user's desired purpose. It seems clear that both are needed for effective use of the tool. We learned that instrumentalisation took very different forms for the student (taking a strategic approach) and the teaching team (taking a conceptual approach).

Documentational genesis is a process through which teaching develops, and the teacher becomes a more knowledgeable practitioner. The teacher, as user of resources, tasks and tools (instruments in the teaching process), develops a repertoire through this use and associated 'schemes of utilisation' (Gueudet and Trouche 2011a, b) seen to develop through the instrumentation process. The teacher has a reason for using any tool related to her didactical purposes. Thus, she needs to know the tool and how to use it effectively (instrumentation). Didactical purpose will be interpreted through an instrumentalisation process, bending the tool to her own use of it. Through a repertoire of resource use, the teacher develops knowledge in teaching, related to the use of tools to promote students' learning. Thus, in her use of resources, the teacher becomes a more knowledgeable practitioner, this knowledge being the developing *document* in documentational genesis.

As an example, consider the use of inquiry-based questions and tasks in the ESUM project. We see these tasks as tools mediating students' engagement and mathematical understanding. Effective use of the tool means that we see the kinds of engagement and understanding that we seek as teachers. Our process of instrumentation involves seeking out inquiry-based questions, exploring their nature and becoming skilled in their design. Instrumentalisation involves our use of lectures and tutorials, fitting the questions or tasks to the constraints of university context and adapting them to achieve our goals for students' learning. Where we are dissatisfied with the outcomes of use, our inquiry into their use develops a feedback cycle through which we learn and which enables us to adapt the instrument for future use. The document that emerges from such a process reflects the knowledge we have gained through our use and adaptation of the tool (i.e. in the tasks we have (re)designed).

Alternatively, we might consider the contribution of GeoGebra as a tool. Feedback from students at the end of the module suggested that many had found the use of GeoGebra in dynamic mode to demonstrate functional relationships in a lecture as too slow, delaying the progress of the lecture. They suggested that static mode would be better because it would be quicker. This made clear that their focus was on the (procedural) outcomes of GeoGebra use, rather than on the relationships revealed through graphs drawn in dynamic mode. The challenge for the teaching team here was to design approaches which would make clearer the relational focus and draw students' attention away from the delays within the electronic system. This required teacher attention to the affordances and demands of GeoGebra, the mathematics in focus at a crucial time and the encompassing orchestration of the teacher. Through critical alignment, such considerations led to teachers making changes locally, to gaining new awarenesses in practice and more knowledge in teaching generally. These are essential ingredients of the documentational process.

The theory of documentational genesis is valuable because it focuses our attention specifically on the processes of teaching in relation to the resources we use, our specific uses of them and our learning through this use. For example, it was a significant recognition that instrumentalisation with GeoGebra was fundamentally different for students and teachers that allowed us to reconceptualise its use.

Tackling Complexity: Activity Theory as an Analytical Tool

The theories outlined above enable us to consider learning at a range of levels within developmental practice (e.g. engineering students learning mathematics, teachers learning about the use of resources in teaching, teachers learning to promote students' more conceptual understandings of mathematics). Within a sociocultural frame, learning is seen as participation within social and cultural worlds, conceptualised, as indicated, in terms of communities of practice and inquiry. Here, practice is seen as mathematical practice and as practice in the teaching and learning of mathematics, and an inquiry community involves a fundamental inquiry basis for engagement in practice. However, it is impossible to consider such practices without regard for the broader frames in which they are situated: the institutional and the societal. Teachers work within schools and classrooms or in university environments; they are people with social and political influences and perspectives; the same is true of students who are motivated by a range of factors and influenced by student culture. A. N. Leont'ev makes the following point, 'in a society, humans do not simply find external conditions to which they must adapt their activity. Rather these social conditions bear with them the motives and goals of their activity, its means and modes. In a word, society produces the activity of the individuals it forms' (1979, pp. 47–48). According to Wertsch (1991, p. 27), rather than 'the idea that mental functioning in the individual derives from participation in social life', 'the specific structures and processes of intramental processing can be traced to their genetic precursors on the intermental plane'. The key idea here is that human activity is motivated within the sociocultural and historical processes of human life and comprises (mediated) goal-directed action. We might see this as relating strongly to the formation of students of mathematics within the cultures and systems in which mathematics learning and teaching take place. For example, students learn mathematics within school culture; this includes working towards and being successful in A level examinations as a prerequisite for university study. School cultures are very different from university cultures. The expectations of students learning mathematics in the university include higher degrees of abstraction and formalism than they have encountered in schools (Hernandez-Martinez et al. 2011; Nardi 2008).

Activity theory offers perspectives of activity in a holistic sense – according to Leont'ev, 'Activity is the non-additive, molar unit of life … it is not a reaction, or aggregate of reactions, but a system with its own structure, its own internal transformations, and its own development' (1979, p. 46). We cannot divorce mathematics learning from the totality of its situation and the context in which it is rooted. The theories set out above help us to conceptualise inquiry communities, to define critical alignment and to make sense of teaching development. However, in our analyses of/during the project, we have been faced with issues, tensions or contradictions which these theories have not been helpful in addressing. These include tensions between teachers' ways of conceptualising teaching and learning in a university environment and the more strategic goals of students in learning mathematics. For this purpose we have used activity theory as a tool in the analytical process, thus including such complexity of factors in a unifying whole in which tensions and issues can be both accommodated and addressed. In the following, I draw on what Simon Goodchild and I wrote in our PME paper in 2006 in which we referred to tensions and contradictions in our activity with teachers in developmental research relating to school classrooms (Jaworski and Goodchild 2006, pp. 3–355). The ESUM project has used activity theory in a similar way.

> Leont'ev (1979) proposed a three-tiered explanation of activity. First, human activity is always energised by a motive. Second, the basic components of human activity are the actions that translate activity motive into reality, where each action is subordinated to a conscious goal. Activity can be seen as comprising actions relating to associated goals. Thirdly, operations are the means by which an action is carried out, and are associated with the conditions under which actions take place. Leont'ev's three tiers or levels can be summarised as:
>
> activity <--> motive;   actions <--> goals;   operations <--> conditions.
>
> Leont'ev writes emphatically about the movement of the elements between the 'levels' within an activity system: activity can become actions and actions develop into activity, goals become motives and vice-versa, similarly with operations and conditions. The crucial differences seem to be: first, goals are conscious, if the motive of activity becomes conscious it becomes a motive-goal; second, motive is about an energizing force for the activity and the actions, it is not something that is attained but rather drives the activity forward; on the other hand goals are results that can be achieved. Leont'ev writes "The basic 'components' of various human activities are the actions that translate them into reality, We call a process an action when it is subordinated to the idea of achieving a result, i.e. a process that is subordinated to a conscious goal". (Leont'ev 1979, pp. 59–60; Jaworski and Goodchild 2006)

This conceptualisation of activity is useful in providing a framework for analysis. We have done this in the ESUM project, and it has allowed us to deal with issues and tensions revealed in analyses – first of all through *recognition* and then through *juxtapositioning*, allowing us to see ways through the apparent contradictions. Here we juxtapose teaching perspectives with student perspectives, as revealed through our analyses, at each of the three levels.

Table 1 illustrates *recognition* and *juxtapositioning*, summarised as follows: first, aspects of activity revealed (recognised) in analysis and, second, through the two-column structure, positioning them so that apparent contradictions stand out. These allow us, forcefully, to be aware of the issues that we have to address in working towards more desirable outcomes in our project.

Juxtapositioning here shows two activity systems, two cultures acting side by side. The teaching position and the student position are as different *worlds* (Holland et al. 1998). For example, for teachers, the use of resources, inquiry-based tasks and a GeoGebra environment exists to create opportunities for students to conceptualise mathematics; teachers operate from within this world. For students, use of these

Table 1 Juxtaposing activity in teaching and for students in the ESUM project according to Leont'ev's three levels

Level	Teaching	Students
1	*Activity* is mathematics teaching-learning. For the teacher(s) it is *motivated* by the desire for students to gain a deep conceptual-relational understanding of mathematics. We might in this case call it 'teaching for learning'	For students the *activity* is learning within the teaching environment and with respect to many external factors (youth culture, school-based expectations of university, etc.) and is (probably) *motivated* by the desire to get a degree in the most student-effective way possible
2	Here, *actions* are design of tasks and inquiry-based questions – with *goals* of student engagement, exploration and getting beyond a superficial and/or instrumental view of mathematics. *Actions* include use of GeoGebra with the *goal* of providing an alternative environment for representation of functions offering ways of visualising functions and gaining insights into function properties and relationships. *Actions* include forming students into small groups and setting group tasks with the *goals* to provide opportunity for sharing of ideas, learning from each other and articulating mathematical ideas	For students, *actions* involve taking part in the module: attending lectures and tutorials, using the LEARN page, using the HELM books, etc. with *goals* related to student epistemology. So *goals* might include attending lectures and tutorials because this is where you are offered what you need to pass the module; clear views on what ought to be on offer and what you expect from your participation; wanting to know what to do and how to do it; wanting to do the minimum amount of work to succeed; wanting to understand; wanting to pass the year's work
3	Here we see operations such as the kinds of interactions used in lectures to get students to engage and respond, the ways in which questions are used, the operation of group work in tutorials and the interactions between teachers and students. The conditions include all the factors of the university environment that condition and constrain what is possible – for example, if some tutorials need to be in a computer lab, then they all have to be; lectures in tiered lecture theatres constrain conversations between lecturer and students when tasks are set	*Operations* include degrees of participation – listening in a lecture, talking with other students about mathematics, reading a HELM book to understand some bit of mathematics, using the LEARN page to access a lecture, PowerPoint, etc. The conditions in which this takes place include timetable pressure, fitting in pieces of coursework from different modules around given deadlines, balancing the academic and the social, getting up late and missing a lecture. They also include the organisation of lectures and tutorials and participating within modes of activity which do not fit with your own images of what should be on offer

Adapted from Jaworski et al. (2012, p. 151)

resources is what is required of them to reach their own 'strategic' goals: their world involves doing what is required to be successful in their academic programme and get high grades. Their vision of what this does or can involve is different from the teachers' vision.

I have suggested above that the use of resources – tasks and tools – has an important mediating function in the learning of students of mathematics or of teachers in developmental activity. However, the complexity in activity systems is such that we cannot isolate particular mediational influences. Tensions and contradictions can arise due to parts of the activity system as a whole working against each other in influencing learning outcomes.

Discussion

Here, I reflect on the three areas of theory and their contribution to teaching development and end with some thoughts on their value for future practice.

Rooted in significant documented developmental research, the inquiry approach sets out overtly to introduce new ways of teaching according to explicit goals for students' learning and to inquire into the practices that result. The designed innovation uses inquiry-based approaches to learning, seeking to engage students in working with mathematics at deeper, more conceptual levels than the instrumental approaches which are common. Those who teach have to do so within the affordances and constraints of the university system. An inquiry approach affords possibilities to work within the existing system while looking critically at ways of being and doing. New approaches sit alongside traditional ones, and teacher inquiry focuses on the extent to which goals seem to be achieved in relation to approaches used. This is critical alignment. For example, in the traditional lecture, inquiry-based tasks for students seek to engage students more overtly. We see that some students are not engaged, and this raises further questions for the lecturer with regard to interpretation of the theory of inquiry within the traditional lecture mode. The curriculum has to be 'covered': so the lecturer has to decide how much time can be spent on small group activity within a lecture. A compromise is to maintain the more traditional lecture and make small group activities more effective within the tutorials. Here, we see choices for the lecturer and the teaching team. The research activity of the RO, collecting data, acting as a sounding board, feeding back to the teaching and, ultimately, synthesising from analyses, provides a more global perspective.

The use of resources is crucial to the teaching approach. We have seen above the teaching goals surrounding the use of inquiry-based tasks and GeoGebra. Research has shown also the very different perspectives of students towards these resources. The resources are only effective to the extent that they are used in alignment with their intentions. One important outcome of this research has been the recognition of ways in which students have used and perceived their use of the resources. The teacher has to work with students' perspectives, which are embedded within students' own cultures, deriving from school, friends, family and social life, and succeed in developing an academic culture conducive to achieving teaching goals. If we take GeoGebra as an example, the teacher has first to learn to use GeoGebra herself in order to see how it can *afford* (Gibson 1977) what she wants for student activity: this is her own instrumentation and instrumentalisation. She introduces the resources to students in ways intended to enable them to become fluent with the resource and use it in the ways the teaching team has designed. Students then undertake their own instrumentation and instrumentalisation. They are quick to appreciate the technical affordances of the resource (instrumentation). It is in their instrumentalisation that issues arise. For example, they see the resource as giving them the answer to how the graph of a given function (algebraic representation) should look, rather than as a means of varying parameters to enable inquiry into the nature of given functions. Perceiving this, the teacher has to use her skills in questioning (in a tutorial) to engage students in using the resource in inquiry mode. The interview feedback at the end of the module showed the extent to which this had been (un)successful for some students. Thus, for the teacher, inquiry into utilisation of the resource leads to a deeper knowledge of the teaching-learning interface surrounding the contribution of the resource to teaching goals. This growth of knowledge for the teaching team is their documentational genesis: it is essentially valuable for the local (in the moment) and more global (planning for the future) design of teaching. Thus, we see that innovation and inquiry, in relation to the development of resource utilisation, are central to a growth of knowledge in teaching.

I come finally to the complexity of the system as a whole and the use of activity theory. Analysis of data had involved in-depth study of end-of-project interviews with the findings linked to data from lectures, tutorials, student surveys and project writing, and teacher reflections. It was clear that we were being shown distinct differences between how we had perceived students' involvement with tasks and their actual involvement. This led us to various levels of thinking: ways in which interactions with students in tutorials might have achieved a deeper engagement with mathematical concepts, how the lecture mode afforded (or not) the possibility to frame a deeper conceptual focus and how we might use resources differently.

These are local instantiations of an inquiry approach and our (local) growth of knowledge, encompassing new awarenesses at a number of levels as exampled above. More significantly, we recognise deeper levels of awareness and understanding. Teachers engage from teacher perspectives and students from student perspectives – it seems trite to write this. However, the weight of influence of these different perspectives underpins the difficulties we perceive within the mathematical learning outcomes for our students. The seminal report from Hawkes and Savage and colleagues (2000) pointed to 'The Mathematics Problem'. Artigue et al. (2007) drew attention to a range of problems highlighted in their extensive literature review. I am not pretending that the insights presented above provide '*the* answers' to these problems. However, I do believe that, through developmental research within an inquiry approach, activity theory enables us to gain insight to the deeper nature of the problems, which then affords the awarenesses (knowledge) that allow us to make changes. Such changes require new ways of being, new ways of seeing the educational environment in which we work in relation to who our students are and how we can work with them to achieve the mathematical outcomes we seek.

In conclusion, I point to the overwhelming complexity in studying the development of teaching and learning in mathematics while promoting such development, with important emphasis on relations between those participating. The several areas of theory all make a contribution to the overall approaches to, conceptualisations of and outcomes from these complex processes or activity systems. There is, of course, much more that could be said.

Acknowledgement I would like to acknowledge the contributions of Janette Matthews, Carol Robinson and Tony Croft, without whom the examples from research would not have been possible. I also thank two anonymous reviewers for their insights which helped me address important issues in an earlier draft.

References

Artigue, M., Batanero, C., & Kent, P. (2007). Mathematics thinking and learning at post secondary level. In F. Lester (Ed.), *Second handbook of research on mathematics teaching and learning*. Charlotte: Information Age Publishing.

Bassey, M. (1995). *Creating education through research*. Edinburgh: British Educational Research Association.

Brown, M. (1979). Cognitive development in the learning of mathematics. In A. Floyd (Ed.), *Cognitive development in the school years*. London: Croom Helm.

Brown, S., & McIntyre, D. (1993). *Making sense of teaching*. Buckingham: Open University Press.

Cochran Smith, M., & Lytle, S. L. (1999). Relationships of knowledge and practice: Teacher learning in communities'. In A. Iran-Nejad & P. D. Pearson (Eds.), *Review of research in education* (pp. 249–305). Washington, DC: American Educational Research Association.

Doyle, W. (1988). Work in mathematics classes: The context of students' thinking during instruction. *Educational Psychologist, 23*(2), 167–180.

Elliott, J. (1991). *Action research for educational change*. Milton Keynes: Open University Press.

Engeström, Y. (1999). Activity theory and individual and social transformation. In Y. Engeström, R. Miettinen, & R.-L. Punamäki (Eds.), *Perspectives on activity theory* (pp. 19–38). Cambridge: Cambridge University Press.

Gibson, J. J. (1977). The theory of affordances. In R. E. Shaw & J. Bransford (Eds.), *Perceiving, acting and knowing* (pp. 67–82). Hillsdale: Lawrence Erlbaum Associates.

Gueudet, G., & Trouche, L. (2011a). Mathematics teacher education advanced methods: An example in dynamic geometry. *ZDM Mathematics Education, 43*, 399–411.

Gueudet, G., & Trouche, L. (2011b). Communities, documents and professional geneses: Interrelated stories. In G. Gueudet, B. Pepin, & L. Trouche (Eds.), *Mathematics curriculum material and teacher development*. New York: Springer.

Hawkes, T., & Savage, M. (Eds.). (2000). *Measuring the mathematics problem*. London: The Engineering Council.

Hernandez-Martinez, P., Williams, J., Black, L., Pampala, M., & Wake, G. (2011). Students' views on their transition from school to college mathematics: Rethinking 'transition' as an issue of identity. *Research in Mathematics Education, 13*, 119–130.

Hiebert, J. (1986). *Conceptual and procedural knowledge: The case of mathematics*. Hillsdale: Erlbaum.

Holland, D., Lachicotte, W., Skinner, D., & Cain, C. (1998). *Identity and agency in cultural worlds*. Cambridge: Harvard University Press.

Jaworski, B. (1998). Mathematics teacher research: Process, practice and the development of teaching. *Journal of Mathematics Teacher Education, 1*(1), 3–31.

Jaworski, B. (2003). Research practice into/influencing mathematics teaching and learning development: Towards a theoretical framework based on co-learning partnerships. *Educational Studies in Mathematics, 54*(2–3), 249–282.

Jaworski, B. (2004a). Insiders and outsiders in mathematics teaching development: The design and study of classroom activity. *Research in Mathematics Education, 6*, 3–22.

Jaworski, B. (2004b). Grappling with complexity: Co-learning in inquiry communities in mathematics teaching development. In M. J. Høines & A. B. Fuglestad (Eds.), *Proceedings of the 28th conference of the International Group for the Psychology of Mathematics Education* (Vol. 1, pp. 17–32). Bergen: Bergen University College.

Jaworski, B. (2006). Theory and practice in mathematics teaching development: Critical inquiry as a mode of learning in teaching. *Journal of Mathematics Teacher Education, 9*(2), 187–211.

Jaworski, B. (2008a). Building and sustaining inquiry communities in mathematics teaching development: Teachers and didacticians in collaboration. In K. Krainer & T. Wood (Eds.), *Volume 3 of the International handbook of mathematics teacher education: Participants in mathematics teacher education: Individuals, teams, communities and networks* (pp. 309–330). Rotterdam: Sense Publishers.

Jaworski, B. (2008b). Helping engineers learn mathematics: A developmental research approach. *Teaching Mathematics and Its Applications, 27*(3), 160–166.

Jaworski, B. (in press). Mathematical meaning-making and its relation to design of teaching. In *Proceedings of the 8th Congress of the European Society for Research in Mathematics Education*.

Jaworski, B., & Goodchild, S. (2006). Inquiry community in an activity theory frame. In J. Novotná, H. Morová, M. Krátká, & N. Stehlíková (Eds.), *Proceedings of the 30th conference of the International Group for the Psychology of Mathematics Education* (pp. 3353–3360). Prague: Charles University Prague.

Jaworski, B., & Matthews, J. (2011). Developing teaching of mathematics to first year engineering students. *Teaching Mathematics and Its Applications, 30*(4), 178–185.

Jaworski, B., Robinson, C., Matthews, J., & Croft, A. C. (2012). Issues in teaching mathematics to engineering students to promote conceptual understanding: A study of the use of GeoGebra and inquiry-based tasks. *The International Journal for Technology in Mathematics Education, 19*(4), 147–152.

Kelly, A. E. (2003). Research as design. *Educational Researcher, 32*(1), 3–4.

Lave, J., & Wenger, E. (1991). *Situated learning: Legitimate peripheral participation*. Cambridge, MA: Cambridge University Press.

Leont'ev, A. N. (1979). The problem of activity in psychology. In J. V. Wertsch (Ed.), *The concept of activity in Soviet psychology* (pp. 37–71). New York: M. E. Sharpe.

Mason, J. (2002). *Researching your own practice: The discipline of noticing*. London: Routledge/Falmer.

Mason, J., Burton, L., & Stacey, K. (1982). *Thinking mathematically*. London: Addison Wesley.

Nardi, E. (2008). *Amongst mathematicians: Teaching and learning mathematics at university level*. London: Springer.

Pilzer, S., Robinson, M., Lomen, D., Flath, D., Hughes Hallet, D., Lahme, B., Morris, J., Mccallum, W., & Thrash, J. (2003). *Conceptests to accompany calculus* (3rd ed.). Hoboken: Wiley.

Pring, R. (2004). *Philosophy of education*. London: Continuum.

Romberg, T. A., & Carpenter, T. A. (1986). Research on teaching and learning mathematics: Two disciplines of scientific inquiry. In M. C. Wittrock (Ed.), *Handbook of research on teaching* (3rd ed., pp. 850–873). New York: Macmillan.

Schoenfeld, A. (1985). *Mathematical problem solving*. New York: Academic.

Skemp, R. (1976). Relational understanding and instrumental understanding. *Mathematics Teaching, 77*, 20–26.

Stenhouse, L. (1984). Evaluating curriculum evaluation. In C. Adelman (Ed.), *The politics and ethics of evaluation*. London: Croom Helm.

The Royal Academy of Engineering. (2012). *Enhancing engineering in higher education: Outputs of the National HE STEM Programme*. London: Author.

Trouche, L., & Drijvers, P. (2010). Handheld technology for mathematics education: Flashback into the future. *ZDM Mathematics Education, 42*, 667–681.

Wells, G. (1999). *Dialogic inquiry*. Cambridge: Cambridge University Press.

Wenger, E. (1998). *Communities of practice*. Cambridge: Cambridge University Press.

Wertsch, J. V. (1991). *Voices of the mind*. Cambridge, MA: Harvard University Press.

The Interplay of Factors Involved in Shaping Students' Opportunities to Learn Mathematics

Ruhama Even

Abstract This chapter examines the interplay of several key factors involved in shaping students' opportunities to learn mathematics. It draws on studies conducted as part of the research program *Same Teacher—Different Classes*, all of which use the same novel research methodology: multiple case studies, where each case includes a teacher who teaches mathematics using the same curriculum program or syllabus in two classes. The first three sections examine ways by which the interplay between class characteristics and the characteristics of its teacher shapes students' opportunities to learn mathematics, revealing different kinds of interactions between these two factors. The fourth section brings another factor into play by examining the interplay among class characteristics, characteristics of the teacher, and characteristics of the mathematics topic (a central component of the curriculum) and how they shape students' opportunities to learn mathematics. The interplay of factors involved in shaping students' opportunities to learn mathematics is examined in two different settings: (1) teaching the same probability syllabus in high-school classes having different matriculation levels and (2) teaching the same algebra curriculum program in 7th grade classes in different schools.

Keywords Interplay of factors shaping mathematics teaching and learning • Curriculum enactment • Teaching approaches • Teaching styles • Mathematics addressed in class • Students' opportunities to learn mathematics

R. Even (✉)
Department of Science Teaching, Weizmann Institute of Science, Rehovot 76100, Israel
e-mail: ruhama.even@weizmann.ac.il

Y. Li et al. (eds.), *Transforming Mathematics Instruction: Multiple Approaches and Practices*, Advances in Mathematics Education, DOI 10.1007/978-3-319-04993-9_25,
© Springer International Publishing Switzerland 2014

Introduction

In many countries, a common response to calls to improve mathematics teaching and learning is developing new curricula (e.g., the massive waves of "new math" curricula in the 1960s and various curriculum development projects of the 1990s). This includes adapting principles and standards for school mathematics, revising the mathematical content to be studied, and developing new curriculum programs (e.g., textbooks, teacher guides, and other learning and teaching materials).

However, the curriculum is only one factor that influences students' opportunities to learn mathematics. Accumulating research suggests that students' opportunities to learn mathematics vary across different classes, even when they use the same textbook (e.g., Manouchehri and Goodman 2000; Remillard and Bryans 2004; Tirosh et al. 1998). The differences found are often attributed to teacher-related factors, such as teacher knowledge and beliefs. These studies highlight the prominent and indispensable role that teachers play in influencing how the curriculum is enacted in the classroom, and they underscore teachers' central role in determining the nature of the learning experiences provided to students—a role that no curriculum program by itself can fulfill.

Nevertheless, research reveals that aspects not directly or solely related to the curriculum or the teacher are also involved in shaping students' opportunities to learn mathematics. Some are class-related aspects (i.e., aspects related to the group of students), such as students and parents' expectations and demands, students' profiles, classroom norms, and learning environments (e.g., Chazan 2000; Herbel-Eisenmann et al. 2006; Lloyd 2008; Tarr et al. 2008).

The curriculum, the teacher, and the class are therefore key factors in shaping students' opportunities to learn mathematics. Yet, not much is known about how these factors interact. To date, the interplay of these factors has received little research attention and is often considered "noise" by researchers. This chapter centers on the interplay of those factors. It draws on the research program *Same Teacher—Different Classes* (Even 2008), which focuses purposely on studying the interactions among curricula, teachers, and classes in different situations. To study these interactions, we compare teaching and learning mathematics in different classes of the same teacher as well as of different teachers and examine the enacted curricula (e.g., the mathematical ideas addressed in class), the teaching practices (e.g., teachers' response to, and use of, students' talk and actions), the classroom culture (e.g., the nature of argumentation), etc. All studies that belong to the *Same Teacher—Different Classes* research program use the same novel research methodology: multiple case studies in which each case includes a teacher who teaches mathematics using the same curriculum program or syllabus in two classes. In this way, some aspects are kept relatively constant; this enables careful examination of the interactions among curricula, teachers, and classes, which are not easily otherwise detectable.

The main part of this chapter includes four sections that illustrate what might be gained and what the challenges might be when using this methodology for assessing or studying mathematics classroom instruction. The first three sections examine the ways by which the interplay between characteristics of the class and characteristics of the teacher shape students' opportunities to learn mathematics, revealing different kinds of interactions between these two factors. The fourth section brings another factor into play: It examines the ways by which the interplay among characteristics of the class, characteristics of the teacher, and the mathematics topic shapes students' opportunities to learn mathematics. The interplay of these factors is examined in different settings. The first two sections are based on case studies of teaching the same probability syllabus in high-school classes having different matriculation levels (conducted in collaboration with Tova Kvatinsky—for more information about this set of studies, see Even and Kvatinsky (2009, 2010)). The last two sections are based on case studies of teaching the same algebra curriculum program in 7th grade classes in different schools (conducted in collaboration with Tammy Eisenmann and Michal Ayalon—for more information about this set of studies, see Eisenmann and Even (2009, 2011) and Ayalon and Even (2010, in press)).

Teaching Approaches and Classes Having Different Achievement Levels

In what ways does the achievement level of the class shape students' opportunities to learn mathematics? The prevalent view, as well as the research literature, suggests a rather straightforward answer to this question: In low-achieving classes mathematics teachers tend to focus less on developing understanding, thinking, and problem solving and more on mechanistic answer finding, memorizing, and rule-following (e.g., Raudenbush et al. 1993; Zohar et al. 2001). These findings imply that the achievement level of the class directly determines the degree of emphasis on students' understanding in class.

However, the differences reported in the literature between mathematics teaching in high- and in low-achieving classes are based mainly on teachers' self-reports (questionnaires and interviews), that is, teachers' views and conceptions, and not on detailed analyses of teaching practices and classroom interactions in high- and low-achieving classes. Research also shows that, usually, the more competent teachers teach classes of high-achieving students, whereas the less competent ones teach the low-achieving students (Yair 1997). Thus, it is not clear whether the differences reported in the literature between emphasis on students' understanding during mathematics teaching in high- and in low-achieving classes are related to differences between the teachers teaching in the respective classes and are not necessarily directly associated with the achievement level of the class.

In addressing this shortcoming of current research, we investigated whether teachers tend to adopt the teaching for the mechanistic answer-finding approach more when teaching classes of low-achieving students by analyzing actual practices of teaching mathematics and classroom interactions in classes having different levels taught by the same teacher (Even and Kvatinsky 2009). We focused on two aspects that are associated in the literature with the development of understanding (e.g., Cobb et al. 2001; Even and Lappan 1994; Wood et al. 2006): (1) students' opportunities to play a significant and influential role in the class discourse and (2) students' opportunities to make decisions about ways of solving mathematics problems in class.

The participants were Betty and Gloria (pseudonyms), two high-school teachers teaching in the same school. Both teachers had many years of experience in teaching mathematics and in preparing students for the matriculation examination[1] in mathematics, and both had a reputation of being competent and responsible teachers. Each teacher taught the topic of probability in two classes—one class of lower-achieving students and another class of higher-achieving students. No differences were noted between the compositions of the two same-level classes (each taught by a different teacher), which was in line with the school policy. All four classes were preparing for the matriculation examination in mathematics at the time of the study, and they followed the same syllabus. The same-level classes used the same textbooks. Moreover, the two teachers often collaborated in planning which tasks—all taken from the textbooks they were using—they would use in their teaching, and as a result, about half of the tasks worked on in class were identical in the two same-level classes. The teachers also jointly prepared identical exams for their same-level classes throughout the school year.

The main data source was derived from observing all probability lessons in each class for one school year (except for one topic taught only at the higher level)—a total of 46 lessons. An individual semi-structured interview was also conducted with each teacher, focusing on the teachers' views of teaching probability in different-level classes and whether they thought there were differences in how they taught the two classes.

A detailed data analysis included the whole-class work, using two units of analysis: (1) utterances, for examining students' opportunities to play a significant and influential role in the class discourse, and (2) activity (i.e., the whole-class works on one probability problem), for examining students' opportunities to make decisions about ways of solving mathematics problems in class. Using utterances, we employed the coding system developed in the TIMSS-Video Study (Hiebert et al. 2003; Stigler et al. 1999; Stigler and Hiebert 1999) for class talk, with some modifications. The coding included six categories for teachers' talk (e.g., elicitation, answering one's own questions) and five categories for students' talk (e.g., student response, student elicitation). Teacher elicitation was then coded in more detail using five categories; among them is content elicitation, again coded in detail, depending on whether the focus was on elicitation of factual information or on students' ideas. Six whole-class activities and two full lessons were analyzed using utterances as the unit of analysis in each class. The activities analyzed in the two same-level classes (different teachers) consisted of classwork on identical probability problems, chosen randomly from the common problems on which both same-level classes worked.

---

[1] High-school graduation national exams, a prerequisite for higher education in Israel.

The sampled activities were validated by randomly selecting two full lessons from each class and analyzing all activities included in each lesson. Statistical analyses of utterances were performed on (a) quantitative measurements (e.g., the number of teacher utterances and the number of elicitation utterances) and (b) percentages of some totals (e.g., the percentage of elicitation utterances out of the total number of teacher's utterances and the percentage of response utterances out of the total number of students' utterances). Using an activity as the unit of analysis, we analyzed the whole-class work on all the problems solved during the observed lessons—a total of 193 activities. We focused on decisions related to choosing methods of solving problems and solutions to present and share with the whole class. (More details can be found in Even and Kvatinsky (2009).)

Analysis revealed that the teachers did not always behave similarly in the two classes they taught. Although rather small, these differences were consistently of the same nature for each teacher. Betty's teaching was generally characterized by greater use of a teaching for mechanistic answer-finding approach in her lower-achieving class than in her higher-achieving class (e.g., asking students to memorize and follow rules in order to get correct final answers; rarely allowing students to present their work to the whole class, and then, only if it was correct and done in the way she desired). However, in contrast, Gloria's teaching was generally characterized by greater use of a teaching for understanding approach, emphasizing thinking, understanding, and problem solving in her lower-achieving class than in her higher-achieving class (e.g., encouraging students to propose and justify alternative solutions and to present and discuss their work with the whole class).

Yet, the analysis also revealed that Betty and Gloria's teaching approaches were fundamentally different from each other. Betty's teaching was not only characterized by a greater use of various characteristics of the mechanistic answer-finding approach in her lower-achieving class than in her higher-achieving class—in both of her classes, Betty emphasized mechanistic answer finding. In contrast, Gloria's teaching was characterized by a greater use of various features of a teaching for understanding approach in her lower-achieving class than in her higher-achieving class—and in both of her classes, she emphasized thinking, understanding, and problem solving. Thus, apparently both Betty and Gloria's teaching approaches were amplified to some degree in their lower-level class.

Betty's amplified teaching approach in the lower-achieving class is in agreement with the literature, which suggests that teachers tend to adopt a teaching for mechanistic answer-finding approach more when teaching in classes of lower-achieving students. However, Gloria's amplified teaching approach in the lower-achieving class, namely, of adopting more extremely a teaching for understanding approach, is contrary to this prevalent view.

One way to resolve this irregularity in findings from other studies is to argue that Gloria is the exception; that is, like Betty, teachers tend to adopt characteristics of a teaching for a mechanistic answer-finding approach more when they teach in lower-achieving classes. However, based on the detailed analysis conducted and supported by the views about desired mathematics teaching explicitly expressed by the teachers in their respective interviews, we proposed another way to resolve this inconsistency: As caring teachers, although very different from each other, both Betty and Gloria used the resources available to them and drew on their preferred instructional strategies—their teaching approach—in attempting to meet the demands of the students, which they perceived to be more challenging. Hence, it may not be surprising that each teaching approach was amplified to some degree in the lower-level class. In their own way, each teacher tried to help more those students who had encountered more difficulties—the low-achieving students—and they did so by using the resources available to them: enhancement of their teaching approaches.

These findings suggest that in contrast to the prevalent view, teachers like Gloria, whose teaching approach is characterized mainly by emphasis on understanding, may not emphasize understanding less in low-achieving classes. Thus, to a large extent, it is the fundamental teaching approach of the classroom teacher that may determine students' opportunity to learn mathematics with a focus on understanding, and not solely or directly the achievement level of the class.

Teaching Approaches and the Mathematics Addressed in Classes Having Different Achievement Levels

In a follow-up study, we continued to explore ways by which the teaching approach of the classroom teacher shapes students' opportunities to learn mathematics, by comparing the mathematical content that Betty and Gloria addressed in class (Even and Kvatinsky 2010). One way to examine this is to compare the coverage of chapters, units, or topics (e.g., Cueto et al. 2006; Porter 2002; Tarr et al. 2006). The use of this measure showed that Betty and Gloria followed the same national syllabus and covered the same mathematical topics. Moreover, the same-level classes (taught by different teachers) used the same textbooks and worked on many identical textbook problems. However, such measures are not suitable for examining more complex aspects of the mathematics taught in class.

For this study we developed a framework especially for analyzing the mathematics addressed in probability lessons. The framework is comprised of five interconnected aspects: (1) essential features and the strength of probability theory, (2) approaches to probability, (3) probability representations and models, (4) basic repertoire, and (5) the nature of probability theory. We examined references related to each of the 193 probability problems worked on in class. When noteworthy, we also counted the number of problems where specific references were made and performed a statistical analysis in order to compare the respective percentages of problems between the two classes of each teacher and between the two teachers. (More details can be found in Even and Kvatinsky (2010).)

Our analysis revealed that differences in the mathematics that was addressed in the probability lessons were considerably more substantial between the two teachers than between the two classes of each teacher and that, basically, mathematical ideas associated with probability theory were addressed similarly in the two classes of each teacher but somewhat differently in the classes of different teachers. For example, although both teachers referred to uncertainty—a fundamental characteristic of probability theory—Gloria did so much more often than Betty did. Similarly, Gloria's classes were exposed to additional representations of formal notation, such as graphs, pictures, tree diagrams, and tables, significantly more than Betty's classes were. Moreover, only Gloria introduced the experimental approach, extending the narrow view of probability commonly presented in text-books using only the classical approach. Furthermore, Betty made available to learn a basic repertoire of examples of different rules, and probability was presented in her classes as a domain that deals with final results where every problem has only one correct solution, reached by memorizing and following rules developed by experts. In contrast, Gloria made available to learn a basic repertoire of examples of important ideas and concepts, and probability was presented in her classes as a domain that deals with the construction and examination of various ways of solving problems.

The finding that differences in the mathematics that was addressed in the proba-bility lessons were considerably more substantial between the two teachers than between the classes of each teacher is somewhat surprising at first, because the two classes of each teacher were at different achievement levels. Consequently, even though all classes followed the same syllabus, the two classes of each teacher used different textbooks and worked on different textbook problems, whereas the same-level classes (taught by different teachers) used the same textbooks and worked on many identical textbook problems. Likewise, the teachers jointly prepared identical exams for their same-level classes throughout the school year, which were different for different-level classes of each teacher, taking into consideration the different nature of the matriculation exam for each level.

Hence, the differences in the mathematics that was addressed in the probability lessons appeared to be mainly related to differences between teachers, which prevailed over the difference between the achievement levels of their two classes. A major difference between Betty and Gloria lies in their teaching approaches. And, indeed, the differences in the mathematics that was addressed in the proba-bility lessons seem to be linked to the teachers' different teaching approaches. The mathematics that Betty addressed in class fit her mechanistic answer-finding teaching approach and the different mathematics that Gloria addressed in class fit her emphasis on thinking, understanding, and problem solving. Consequently, students of the two teachers did not only study the topic of probability differently— they also studied different mathematical ideas associated with probability theory. These findings suggest that teachers who adopt different teaching approaches, to some extent, make available to learn different mathematics even when they use the same textbooks. Thus, again, apparently it is the main teaching approach that the classroom teacher adopts that largely shapes students' opportunity to learn particu-lar mathematical ideas, rather than solely or directly the achievement level of the class or the textbook chosen.

Teaching Approaches and the Mathematics Addressed in Classes That Use the Same Textbook

Are students that have the same teacher and use the same textbook but are in different classes offered the same opportunities to learn mathematics? The previous section suggests that this might be the case. The findings of the probability research studies presented previously indicated that students' opportunities to learn mathematics were similar in both of Betty's classes, even though the students studied at different achievement levels, using different textbooks (although they followed the same syllabus). Similarly, in both of Gloria's classes, students' opportunities to learn mathematics were similar, yet different from those of Betty's students. Unfortunately, the literature provides little information about the enacted curriculum in different classes of the same teacher using the same textbook. To study this matter more thoroughly, we examined students' opportunities to learn mathematics when the same algebra textbook was used in four beginning algebra classes, where two classes were taught by one teacher, Sarah, and the other two by another teacher, Rebecca (pseudonyms) (Ayalon and Even 2010; Eisenmann and Even 2009, 2011).

Both teachers followed rather closely the lesson plans suggested in the textbook, characterized by work on investigation tasks for much of the class time, recommended for small-group work, followed by whole-class work aimed at advancing students' mathematical understanding and conceptual knowledge. Yet Sarah and Rebecca exhibited different teaching approaches during the whole-class work component of the lessons. Sarah incorporated aspects of direct teaching and provided explicit explanations of central mathematical ideas and solutions of key tasks. She was responsive to students' contributions only when they fit her lesson plan. In contrast, Rebecca adopted aspects of inquiry-based teaching. She rarely provided explicit explanations of central ideas or solutions of tasks. Moreover, she seldom explicitly appraised students' work. Instead, Rebecca encouraged students to propose their own ideas during whole-class work. This was followed up by additional questions. She was responsive in her teaching to students' mathematical class behavior and performance.

Analysis of classroom students' participation indicated that each of the respective teachers' two classes exhibited distinctive characteristics. One of Sarah's classes was characterized by active participation of most students. In contrast, Sarah's other class was characterized by a lack of student participation and frequent disciplinary problems. One of Rebecca's classes was cooperative, with highly motivated students. In Rebecca's other class, most students actively participated, although at times they experienced difficulties in learning the mathematics.

Examination of the mathematical content offered to students, by measuring the extent of coverage of chapters, units, or topics, indicated that both Sarah and Rebecca followed the teaching sequence suggested by the textbook, and generally covered the same textbook units, and based classwork almost entirely on textbook tasks. Thus, the teaching sequence in each of the four classes was basically identical, and all classes largely covered the same mathematics subtopics.

However, in-depth analyses of the mathematics addressed in class portrayed a somewhat different picture. For the in-depth analysis, we used a framework developed by Kieran (2004) that distinguishes among three types of school algebra activities, classified by Kieran as the core of school algebra. These include (1) generational activities, which involve the forming of expressions and equations that are the objects of algebra (e.g., writing a rule for a geometric pattern); (2) transformational activities, which are "rule-based" activities (e.g., collecting like terms, simplifying expressions, factoring, and substituting); and (3) global/meta-level activities, which include general mathematical processes that are not exclusive to algebra (e.g., problem solving, modeling, generalizing, predicting, justifying, and proving).

The main data source for this study was derived from observing the teaching of two beginning algebra topics—*forming and investigating algebraic expressions* and *equivalence of algebraic expressions*—in each of the four classes (15–19 lessons in each class; a total of 67 lessons). An individual semi-structured interview was also conducted with each teacher, focusing on the ways the teachers perceived the curriculum program and the differences in teaching it in the two classes. Using an activity (i.e., classwork on one algebra task) as the unit of analysis, we coded all class activities into one or more of the following categories: generational, transformational, and global/meta-level algebraic activity. We also recorded the time spent on each activity. The number of activities in each category and the time devoted to them, in each of the classes, were then compared. (More details can be found in Eisenmann and Even (2009, 2011).)

A comparison of the distributions of these three types of algebraic activity revealed similarities as well as differences between the two teachers and between the two classes of each teacher. In Sarah's case, the distributions of each type of algebraic activity were nearly similar in the two classes, although the class with disciplinary problems had fewer opportunities than did the class with active students' participation to engage during whole-class work in global/meta-level algebraic activities, such as hypothesizing, justifying, and proving. Examination of Sarah's use of the textbook revealed that some of the global/meta-level textbook tasks were enacted only in the class with active students' participation. Moreover, there were also several cases in which the same textbook task was enacted in the class with active students' participation as a global/meta-level activity but not so in the class with disciplinary problems. This was done by transforming global/meta-level textbook tasks into non-global/meta-level tasks.

In Rebecca's case, the differences between her two classes were more profound. Rebecca's highly motivated class had more opportunities to engage in global/meta-level algebraic activities than the class that had experienced difficulties, whereas the class that had experienced difficulties had more opportunities to engage in transformational activities, such as collecting like terms, simplifying expressions, factoring, and substituting numerical values into expressions. Examination of Rebecca's use of the textbook revealed that, like in Sarah's case, some of the global/meta-level textbook tasks were enacted only in the highly motivated class. Also, there were times when the same textbook task was enacted in the highly motivated class as a global/meta-level activity by transforming non-global/meta-level textbook tasks into global/meta-level tasks, but not so in the class that had experienced difficulties.

These findings suggest that the two classes of each teacher were offered a somewhat different type of mathematics. In both teachers' cases, the decline of global/meta-level activities in one class appeared to be related to the interplay between the teaching approach of the teacher and the students' classroom participation and contribution to the mathematics discourse in class. In Sarah's case, the decline of global/meta-level activities in one of her classes seemed to be largely related to the lack of students' cooperation and to the many discipline problems that caused interruptions in the class mathematics activity. Furthermore, students in this class, in contrast to the other class, often did not complete the assigned small-group work, which was planned as a basis for the more advanced whole-class activities. This situation made it difficult to enact global/meta-level activities during the whole-class work, and consequently, Sarah implemented fewer thinking-related activities and more basic and practice activities during this component of the lesson. However, Sarah's strict adherence to the lesson plans recommended in the textbook, coupled with her use of direct teaching during whole-class work, contributed to a small gap between her two classes regarding students' opportunities to engage in global/meta-level algebraic activities.

In Rebecca's case, the decline of global/meta-level activities in the class that had experienced difficulties seemed to be mainly related to the nature of students' contribution to the mathematical discourse in class, coupled with Rebecca's ongoing responsiveness to students' contribution and participation in class. With the students in the class that readily cooperated with her in global/meta-level activities and even initiated them, Rebecca emphasized this type of algebraic activities, even beyond what was available in the textbook. However, in the class that had experienced difficulties, students seldom cooperated with her when she tried to work on global/meta-level activities. Instead, they often wanted to make sure that they knew how to reach the correct result and encouraged her to emphasize transformational (rule-based) activities.

Mathematical Topics, Teaching Approaches, and the Mathematics Addressed in Classes That Use the Same Textbook

In a follow-up study, we examined how students' opportunities to learn mathematics are shaped by the interplay of the class, the teacher, and the mathematical topic—an important component of the curriculum (Ayalon and Even 2010, in press). The finding that, of Rebecca's two classes, the class that had experienced difficulties had more opportunities to engage in transformational activities than did the highly motivated class, whereas no such difference occurred in Sarah's two classes, intrigued us. Thus, we conducted our investigation in the context of transformational algebraic activity in Sarah and Rebecca's classes.

For this purpose, we categorized transformational activities into different roles, uses, and characteristics, as revealed during work in the four classes—some of which represent invalid mathematical ideas that were suggested by students (e.g., substituting numerical values into expressions as a means of developing a sense about the behavior of expressions, substituting numerical values into expressions as a means of proving non-equivalence, substituting numerical values into expressions as a means of proving equivalence (mathematically invalid), expanding and simplifying expressions as a means of maintaining/proving equivalence, and technical practice in simplifying expressions). We then compared the percentage of time and the distribution of each kind of transformation-related work in the teaching sequence between two classes taught by the same teacher and also across two topics: *forming and investigating algebraic expressions* and *equivalence of algebraic expression*. These topics were chosen because transformational algebraic activity plays different roles in each topic. With *equivalence of algebraic expressions*, transformational algebraic activity (i.e., manipulating expressions using properties of real numbers and substituting numerical values into expressions) is central to proving the equivalence or non-equivalence of expressions. With *forming and investigating algebraic expressions*, transformational algebraic activity (i.e., substituting numerical values into expressions) is a useful means for developing a sense of the behavior of expressions (Even 1998). Each of those different roles of transformational algebraic activity requires a different kind of reasoning—deductive with *equivalence of algebraic expressions* and inductive with *forming and investigating algebraic expressions*. Deductive reasoning is known to be difficult for students (Harel and Sowder 2007), whereas inductive reasoning is considered to be the simplest and most pervasive form of everyday problem-solving activities (Nisbett et al. 1983) and, as research suggests, is often students' preferred way to form and test mathematical conjectures (e.g., Harel and Sowder 2007). (For more details, see Ayalon and Even (2010, in press).)

Analysis of the whole-class work that was associated with transformational algebraic activity during the teaching of the two topics revealed that the opportunities to engage in transformational activity related to the topic *forming and investigating algebraic expressions* were similar in Sarah's two classes as well as in Rebecca's two classes. In fact, they were similar in all four classes. However, substantial differences were found between Rebecca's classes—but not between Sarah's classes—with regard to the opportunities to engage in transformational activities related to the topic *equivalence of algebraic expressions*. In this regard, Rebecca's highly motivated class was similar to Sarah's two classes. Conversely, the class that had experienced difficulties, unlike Rebecca's other class, repeatedly engaged in substituting numerical values into expressions as a means of proving equivalence—a method that is often used by students to (invalidly) prove equivalence (e.g., Smith and Phillips 2000). Moreover, this class had considerably fewer opportunities than did the other class to engage in simplifying and expanding expressions as a means of maintaining or proving equivalence. Instead, this class extensively engaged in the technical practice of simplifying expressions. Based on the detailed analysis of the classroom discourse in each class, we proposed that these findings (the similarities as well as the differences) are related to the interplay among the nature of the specific mathematical topic, the specific teacher, and the specific class.

As mentioned earlier, work associated with the topic *equivalence of algebraic expressions* involves extensive deductive reasoning, which is known to be difficult for students, and counteracts students' tendency to use inductive reasoning (e.g., Harel and Sowder 2007). And indeed, our analysis revealed that both of Rebecca's classes, who, in line with her teaching approach, were encouraged to propose their own ideas about how to prove equivalence, indeed suggested ideas that resembled inductive reasoning, involving substituting numerical values into expressions. Yet the two classes proposed different ways of using substitution of numerical values into expressions as a means of proving equivalence. In the highly motivated class, the ideas that resembled inductive reasoning had a valid mathematical flavor. For example, students proposed substituting all numbers—then added that this could not be realized—and therefore suggested substituting "representative" numbers. Although adhering to the idea of substituting numbers, students in this class understood that substituting numerical values into expressions is a useful means of examining the potential of equivalence but is not appropriate in proving equivalence. In contrast, in the class that had experienced difficulties, the prevailing idea was that substituting a few numbers per se is an appropriate means of proving the equivalence of given expressions. The different mathematical discourses that developed in her classes led Rebecca, who was attentive to her students' mathematical performance, to provide each of her classes with different experiences related to simplifying and expanding expressions. The class that had appeared to understand the concept of equivalence was given more opportunities to simplify and expand expressions as a means of maintaining or proving equivalence, an idea known to be difficult for students (Kieran 2007). However, to address the recurring usage of substitution as a means of proving equivalence by the other class, while avoiding overloading the students with additional challenging ideas, and in line with her teaching approach of not providing explicit explanations of central ideas or explicit appraisal of students' work, Rebecca chose to devote a considerable amount of time in this class to the technical practice of simplifying expressions.

Unlike Rebecca, and in accordance with her direct teaching approach, when teaching the topic *equivalence of algebraic expressions*, Sarah simply explicated in both classes that substitution could not be used to prove that two given expressions are equivalent because there might be a number that has not yet been substituted, but its substitution in the two given expressions would result in different values. In both classes Sarah presented this idea to motivate students to look for a different method to show equivalence. She then directly introduced the use of properties of real numbers to manipulate expressions as a means of proving equivalence. When, later, a student once suggested substituting numerical values into expressions as a means of proving equivalence, Sarah immediately rejected it and repeated the above explanation. By providing explicit explanations of how to prove equivalence, and by not allowing students to alter her lesson plans, there was little opportunity for students to suggest their own (valid or invalid) ideas during whole-class work about ways of proving equivalence (e.g., the use of substitution). Consequently, students' opportunities to engage in transformational activities related to the topic *equivalence of algebraic expressions* were similar in Sarah's two classes.

In contrast to the nature of the transformation-related work associated with the topic *equivalence of algebraic expressions*, transformation-related work associated with the topic *forming and investigating algebraic expressions* basically involves inductive reasoning. Consequently, the transformation-related work associated with developing meaning for expressions, such as substituting numerical values into expressions to learn about the behavior of expressions, was well suited to the students' preferences. Therefore, both Sarah and Rebecca could follow rather closely the lesson plans suggested in the textbook, as they often did, without dealing with students' major difficulties. Consequently, Sarah and Rebecca's contrasting teaching approaches did not appreciably influence students' opportunities to engage in transformational activity related to the topic *forming and investigating algebraic expressions*, and thus these opportunities were generally similar in all four classes.

Conclusion

The fact that when using the same curriculum materials, different teachers teach mathematics differently, as was shown in our studies, is not entirely surprising and has been documented by empirical research (e.g., Manouchehri and Goodman 2000; Remillard and Bryans 2004; Tirosh et al. 1998). However, by using carefully designed conceptual frameworks that enabled us to examine fundamental aspects of the mathematics taught in class, beyond textbook or topic coverage, our studies revealed that students of different teachers did not only study mathematics differently but there were also differences in the mathematics addressed in those classes. The differences found appeared to be linked to the teacher's teaching approach. These findings suggest that teachers who adopt different teaching approaches, to some extent, tend to teach different mathematics even when they use the same curriculum materials.

Noteworthy information was revealed when, instead of focusing solely on the comparison between teachers, different classes taught by the same teacher were also compared. For example, the detailed information about actual teaching practices and classroom interactions in different classes with the same teacher allowed us to detect a rather surprising finding, which is contrary to the prevalent view portrayed in modern literature about teachers' tendency to focus less on developing understanding and more on mechanistic answer finding when teaching low-achieving classes. Furthermore, our studies showed that differences in the mathematics addressed occurred not only between classes of different teachers but also between different classes of the same teacher who used the same curriculum materials. For example, careful examination of the types of the algebraic activities enacted in different classes of the same teacher allowed us to detect differences in the classes' opportunities to engage in global/meta-level algebraic activities. These findings highlight the indispensable role that the class (i.e., the group of students), and not only the teacher, plays in determining students' opportunities to learn mathematics.

However, the findings from the research program *Same Teacher—Different Classes* suggest additional important implications. Our findings clearly exemplify how the interplay among the teacher, the class, and the curriculum shapes students' opportunities to learn mathematics. For example, it was the interplay among the following factors: Rebecca's fundamental teaching approach, the specific characteristics of each of her classes, and the unique characteristics of the topic *equivalence of algebraic expressions* that greatly contributed to differences between her two classes, regarding students' opportunities to engage in a transformational activity related to this topic. Likewise, it was the interplay among the following factors: her fundamental teaching approach, the specific class characteristics, and the unique characteristics of the topic *forming and investigating algebraic expressions* that contributed to the similarity between her two classes and in students' opportunities to engage in a transformational activity related to this topic.

Although research revealed important, though limited information about factors involved in shaping students' opportunities to engage in argumentative activity, the interplay of these factors has received little research attention, and not much is known about how these factors interact with each other. The unique methodology of the research program *Same Teacher—Different Classes*, which examines teaching and learning mathematics in different classes with the same teacher and with different teachers, enabled us to carefully examine interactions among curricula, teachers, and classes that are not easily detectable, and it revealed the complex ways in which they shape students' opportunities to learn mathematics. As this chapter suggests, attending to the interplay among teachers, the curriculum, and classes has great potential to contribute to sophisticated understanding of teaching and learning in the classroom in general and to curriculum enactment in particular. Our findings help explain discrepancies between the written and the enacted curriculum, among the ways different teachers enact the same curriculum materials, and among the ways the same teacher enacts the same curriculum materials in different classes.

We previously described what might be gained when using the unique methodology of the research program *Same Teacher—Different Classes*, which is based on multiple case studies, where each case includes a teacher who teaches mathematics using the same curriculum program or syllabus in two classes. The findings obtained from using this methodology laid the groundwork for follow-up studies by revealing new research questions that are important to pursue. For example, what roles does the achievement level of the class or disciplinary problems play in curriculum enactment and in students' opportunities to learn mathematics? Is there a teaching approach that is suitable for all classes and for all mathematical topics? However, one of the challenges we now face lies in moving from small-scale to large-scale research studies. Similarly, our initial work on designing and adopting conceptual frameworks that can be used to examine the mathematics addressed in class is a promising tool for analyzing complex aspects of the mathematics addressed in different classes. However, suitable conceptual frameworks that can be used to examine the mathematics taught in class are sparse, and therefore this is another area that could benefit from stronger and more systematic work in the future.

References

Ayalon, M., & Even, R. (2010). The nature of transformational algebraic activities addressed in different classes of the same teacher. In P. Brosnan, D. B. Erchick, & L. Flevares (Eds.), *Proceedings of the 32nd conference of the North American chapter of the International Group for the Psychology of Mathematics Education* (Vol. VI, pp. 178–185). Columbus: PME-NA.

Ayalon, M., & Even, R. (in press). Students' opportunities to engage in transformational algebraic activity in different beginning algebra topics and classes. *International Journal of Science and Mathematics Education.*

Chazan, D. (2000). *Beyond formulas in mathematics and teaching: Dynamics of the high school algebra classroom.* New York: Teachers College Press.

Cobb, P., Stephan, M., McClain, K., & Gravemeijer, K. (2001). Participating in classroom mathematical practices. *The Journal of the Learning Sciences, 10*(1&2), 113–163.

Cueto, S., Ramirez, C., & Leon, J. (2006). Opportunities to learn and achievement in mathematics in a sample of sixth grade student in Lima, Peru. *Educational Studies in Mathematics, 62,* 25–55.

Eisenmann, T., & Even, R. (2009). Similarities and differences in the types of algebraic activities in two classes taught by the same teacher. In J. T. Remillard, B. A. Herbel-Eisenmann, & G. M. Lloyd (Eds.), *Mathematics teachers at work: Connecting curriculum materials and classroom instruction* (pp. 152–170). New York: Routledge.

Eisenmann, T., & Even, R. (2011). Enacted types of algebraic activity in different classes taught by the same teacher. *International Journal of Science and Mathematics Education, 9,* 867–891.

Even, R. (1998). Factors involved in linking representations of function. *Journal of Mathematical Behavior, 17,* 105–121.

Even, R. (2008). Offering mathematics to learners in different classes of the same teacher. In O. Figueras & A. Sepúlveda (Eds.), *Proceedings of the joint meeting of the 32nd conference of the International Group for the Psychology of Mathematics Education, and the XX North American chapter* (Vol. 1, pp. 51–66). Morelia: PME.

Even, R., & Kvatinsky, T. (2009). Approaches to teaching mathematics in lower-achieving classes. *International Journal of Science and Mathematics Education, 7*(5), 957–985.

Even, R., & Kvatinsky, T. (2010). What mathematics do teachers with contrasting teaching approaches address in probability lessons? *Educational Studies in Mathematics, 74,* 207–222.

Even, R., & Lappan, G. (1994). Constructing meaningful understanding of mathematics content. In D. B. Aichele & A. F. Coxford (Eds.), *Professional development for teachers of mathematics, 1994 yearbook* (pp. 128–143). Reston: NCTM.

Harel, G., & Sowder, L. (2007). Toward a comprehensive perspective on proof. In F. K. Lester (Ed.), *Second handbook of research on mathematics teaching and learning: A project of the National Council of Teachers of Mathematics* (pp. 805–842). Charlotte: Information Age.

Herbel-Eisenmann, B. A., Lubienski, S. T., & Id-Deen, L. (2006). Reconsidering the study of mathematics instructional practices: The importance of curricular context in understanding local and global teacher change. *Journal of Mathematics Teacher Education, 9,* 313–345.

Hiebert, J., Gallimore, R., Garnier, H., Givvin, K. B., Hollingsworth, H., Jacobs, J., et al. (2003). *Teaching mathematics in seven countries: Results from the TIMSS 1999 Video Study* (CDRom). Philadelphia: NCES.

Kieran, C. (2004). The core of algebra: Reflections on its main activities. In K. Stacey, H. Chick, & M. Kendal (Eds.), *The future of the teaching and learning of algebra: The 12th ICME Study* (pp. 21–33). Dordrecht: Kluwer.

Kieran, C. (2007). Learning and teaching algebra at the middle school through college levels. In F. K. Lester (Ed.), *Second handbook of research on mathematics teaching and learning: A project of the National Council of Teachers of Mathematics* (pp. 707–762). Charlotte: Information Age.

Lloyd, G. M. (2008). Teaching high school mathematics with a new curriculum: Changes to classroom organization and interactions. *Mathematical Thinking and Learning, 10*, 163–195.

Manouchehri, A., & Goodman, T. (2000). Implementing mathematics reform: The challenge within. *Educational Studies in Mathematics, 42*, 1–34.

Nisbett, R., Krantz, D., Jepson, C., & Kunda, Z. (1983). The use of statistical heuristics in everyday inductive reasoning. *Psychological Review, 90*, 339–363.

Porter, A. C. (2002). Measuring the content of instruction: Uses in research and practice. *Educational Researcher, 31*(7), 3–14.

Raudenbush, S. W., Rowan, B., & Cheong, Y. F. (1993). Higher order instructional goals in secondary schools: Class, teacher and school influences. *American Educational Research Journal, 30*, 523–555.

Remillard, J. T., & Bryans, M. (2004). Teacher's orientations toward mathematics curriculum materials: Implications for teacher learning. *Journal for Research in Mathematics Education, 35*, 352–388.

Smith, J. P., & Phillips, E. A. (2000). Listening to middle school students' algebraic thinking. *Mathematics Teaching in the Middle School, 6*(3), 156.

Stigler, J. W., & Hiebert, J. (1999). *The teaching gap: Best ideas from the world's teachers for improving education in the classroom.* New York: Free Press.

Stigler, J. W., Gonzales, P. A., Kawanka, T., Knoll, S., & Serrano, A. (1999, February). *The TIMSS videotape classroom study: Methods and findings from an exploratory research project on eighth-grade mathematics instruction in Germany, Japan, and the United States.* http://nces. ed.gov/pubsearch/pubsinfo.asp?pubid=1999074

Tarr, J. E., Chávez, Ó., Reys, R. E., & Reys, B. J. (2006). From the written to enacted curricula: Intermediary role of middle school mathematics in shaping students' opportunity to learn. *School Science and Mathematics, 106*(4), 191–201.

Tarr, J. E., Reys, R., Reys, B., Chávez, O., Shih, J., & Osterlind, S. J. (2008). The impact of middle-grades mathematics curricula and the classroom learning environment on student achievement. *Journal for Research in Mathematics Education, 39*(2), 247–280.

Tirosh, D., Even, R., & Robinson, N. (1998). Simplifying algebraic expressions: Teacher awareness and teaching approaches. *Educational Studies in Mathematics, 35*, 51–64.

Wood, T., Williams, G., & McNeal, B. (2006). Children's mathematical thinking in different classroom cultures. *Journal for Research in Mathematics Education, 37*(3), 222–255.

Yair, G. (1997). Teachers' polarization in heterogeneous classrooms and the social distribution of achievements: An Israeli case study. *Teaching and Teacher Education, 13*, 279–293.

Zohar, A., Degani, A., & Vaaknin, E. (2001). Teachers' beliefs about low achieving students and higher order thinking. *Teaching and Teacher Education, 17*, 469–485.

Methodological Considerations in the Analysis of Classroom Interaction in Community College Trigonometry

Vilma Mesa and Elaine Lande

Abstract We report analyses of classroom interaction in trigonometry classes taught at an American community college focusing on two dimensions: the mathematical novelty of questions that instructors and students ask and the interactional moves that the instructors use to encourage student involvement in the lesson. The analyzed lessons were particularly challenging because existing frameworks for analyzing classroom behavior did not account for the cases in which the delivery mode was lecture. We discuss the analytical strategies we used and show data to illustrate how they help us in capturing the complexity of classroom interaction and differences between instructors when lecture is the primary mode of instructional delivery. We conclude with suggestions for further work.

Keywords Classroom interaction • Lecture • Trigonometry • Teacher Moves • Questions

Since the publication of the *Professional Standards for Teaching Mathematics* (National Council of Teachers of Mathematics 1991), research in mathematics education has focused on how instructors and students manage interactions in the classroom. Attention to classroom interaction has long been of paramount importance in education, but the NCTM publication brought to light the need for creating different interaction dynamics in mathematics classes. Increased student participation

V. Mesa (✉)
School of Education, University of Michigan,
4041 SEB 610 East University, Ann Arbor, MI 48109-1259, USA
e-mail: vmesa@umich.edu

E. Lande
Mathematics Education, School of Education, University of Michigan,
4002 SEB 610 East University, Ann Arbor, MI 48109-1259, USA
e-mail: elande@umich.edu

Y. Li et al. (eds.), *Transforming Mathematics Instruction: Multiple Approaches and Practices*, Advances in Mathematics Education, DOI 10.1007/978-3-319-04993-9_26,
© Springer International Publishing Switzerland 2014

in math classes has been heralded as an important element of good teaching practice at the postsecondary level (Blair 2006), but the extent to which these practices are common in tertiary education is unknown.

Community colleges in the United States offer an important setting to investigate postsecondary teaching practice. Community colleges are a type of postsecondary institution that provides the first 2 years of baccalaureate degrees and vocational, technical, and enrichment education. These institutions are typically open access and nonresidential, and they serve the communities in which they are located. In addition, they are less expensive relative to other postsecondary institutions. Community colleges are an attractive option to students for all these reasons. Courses are offered at many hours during the day and on weekends, allowing students to keep full-time jobs while they take classes. Community college classes are usually small (under 40 students), thereby allowing more opportunities for instructor-student interaction. Community colleges enroll a significant number of undergraduate students each year: in 2006, 50 % of the total undergraduate population and nearly 49 % of all undergraduate students taking a mathematics course were enrolled at the community college (Dowd et al. 2006; Rodi 2007). An important feature of these mathematics classes is the prominence of lecture as a preferred mode of instructional delivery. In 2-year colleges, for example, 74 % of class sections in college algebra, 81 % in trigonometry, and 93 % in differential equations used predominantly lecture (Lutzer et al. 2007, p. 146).

The impetus of this chapter comes from dissatisfaction with existing frameworks that investigate classroom interaction, as such frameworks are mostly geared towards *standards-based* mathematics education. These frameworks leave large portions of interaction unexamined, because they are grouped under a single label (e.g., lecture, initiation-response-evaluation/feedback [IRE/F]). In lessons in which the teacher lectures most of the time, the frameworks generally do not provide enough detail about what happens in any given class and do not differentiate across instructors. And although using open-ended activities that students explore in small groups and discuss as a large group may lead to the development of important mathematical competencies, our sense is that most of the mathematics classes in postsecondary education do not use this type of teaching. Our own experience working with instructors considered outstanding by their institutions is that student participation is usually initiated by the teacher and is mostly centered around memorizing and practicing routine procedures (Mesa 2010, 2011; Mesa et al. 2014). If we want to change how students engage with mathematics, and increase their opportunities to learn authentic mathematics, a better characterization of the complexity of classroom interactions that are happening in this setting is fundamental.

In this chapter, we describe what we have learned from the analyses of 21 trigonometry lessons taught at a community college by five different instructors. In these analyses, we describe the novelty of the mathematical questions that were posed and how the instructors managed interactions in the classroom over time.

The chapter is organized into three sections. We start by briefly stating the theoretical grounding for this work and relevant prior research on classroom interaction. We then describe the methodology and the two analyses we conducted with the trigonometry lessons. In the final section, we discuss the affordances and challenges of the analyses, the ways in which they complement each other, and the areas for further investigation.

Theoretical Background

We define instruction as the shared work on mathematical content between teachers and students within environments (the classroom, the school, and the community); this work changes over time (Cohen et al. 2003). This definition gives us a point of entry into the complexity of any given classroom and also the ability to shift attention from the teacher, the student, or the content to the interactions between them, through which teaching, learning, and knowledge are manifested. By *content*, we specifically refer to knowledge, skills, and dispositions that instructors, institutions, or society deem appropriate for students to learn. This definition acknowledges that learning happens all the time, even in cases in which an observer judges the teaching as leading to "impoverished" learning.

Many scholars have established, both theoretically and empirically, that classroom interactions matter for student learning. Social constructivist theories of learning acknowledge that learning does not happen in a vacuum, it is mediated by the interactions and the tools (e.g., language) available to learners at any given time (Bakhtin 1981; Vygotsky 1986). Seminal work in elementary mathematics classrooms in the late 1980s and early 1990s based on this theory highlighted that the ways in which teachers and students interact with mathematical content in their classrooms shape what children believe mathematics is about (Yackel and Cobb 1996; Yackel et al. 1990). In response to this change in thinking, the community shifted its attention from teachers and students and their beliefs, attitudes, or knowledge (e.g., Fennema and Sherman 1986; Secada 1995; Thompson 1992) to classroom processes (e.g., Moschkovich 1996) and to the way in which those processes evolved and developed in real classrooms (Cobb et al. 2001). Driven also by a desire to improve instruction, this work promoted a vision of classroom mathematical activity centered on complex mathematical tasks and questions, which would allow students to struggle with mathematics in the same way as mathematicians would (Schoenfeld 1992).

A comparable interest exists in postsecondary education. Observational studies in college classrooms have characterized student learning as a "spectator sport": "little participation occurs, few students are involved, and teacher questions focus on recall rather than critical thinking" (Nunn 1996, p. 245). Scholars have advocated shifting from a "teaching" to a "learning" paradigm (Bass 1999), in which student participation and engagement with the content during classrooms becomes central. Although there is an important body of work promoting the use of "active learning" strategies in higher-education classrooms (e.g., Frederick 1987; Johnson et al. 1998; Prince 2004), very few faculty actually use them in their lectures (e.g., Dancy and Henderson 2009). Likewise, teaching approaches such as inquiry-based learning in mathematics (Coppin et al. 2009) have been confined to a few faculty members within math departments.

In reviewing the literature, we found two areas that were important in analyzing the interaction between the teacher, the students, and the content. One was the nature of the questions asked by the teachers and students, and the other was the extent to which instructors used strategies that opened the dialogue and invited students into the mathematical conversation.

The Nature of Questions Matters

There is a substantial agreement among scholars about the importance of questions and tasks for promoting students' learning. Scholars in cognitive psychology (e.g., Anderson et al. 2001) highlight the importance of organizing instruction using questions that address different types of knowledge (factual, procedural, conceptual, and metacognitive) and that engage different levels of cognitive processes (remembering, understanding, applying, analyzing, creating, and evaluating). Ideally, instruction is such that all types of knowledge and all different processes are addressed, yet some studies report that recall questions are the most common type used in college classrooms (Barnes 1983; Nunn 1996; Pollio 1989).

A meta-analysis of the parameters of discourse present in nine well-known strategies for text discussion in small groups revealed that the quality of teacher and student questions (specifically novel questions), uptakes, the presence of elaborated explanations, and the density of reasoning words were features of discussions that were deemed productive (i.e., they developed high-level thinking and comprehension) "despite the highly situated nature of small group discussions" (Soter et al. 2008, p. 373). Interestingly, Soter and colleagues' analysis of who spoke the most (either students or teachers, using number of words as a metric) did not support the idea that approaches dominated by teacher talk were less productive than approaches dominated by student talk, but rather that the nature of the questions was more important.

Research on tasks used in mathematics classrooms also indicates that tasks addressing novel mathematical questions are preferred over tasks focusing on routine or repetitive activities (Doyle 1984, 1988). In addition, the way in which the tasks are enacted in the classroom matters. Students of teachers who tend to reduce the cognitive complexity of tasks by asking simpler, more routine questions perform worse on standardized tests than students of teachers who tend to maintain or increase the cognitive complexity of the tasks they work on (e.g., Silver and Stein 1996; Stein et al. 1996).

How Teachers Invite Students into the Conversation Matters

Work in linguistics, specifically with the engagement system (Martin and White 2005), has highlighted that speakers use language to engage others by way of the interplay between two major discursive voices, *monogloss* and *heterogloss*.

A monogloss voice seeks to give facts that ostensibly concede no room for the negotiation of meaning. For example, to attempt to persuade an audience to the speaker's side, he or she can skillfully use assertive discourse devices to elicit confidence in the statement he or she is making. On the other hand, a heterogloss voice seeks to engage the audience using a variety of linguistic resources and to open up or close down options for dialogue, each of these conveying a varied strength of engagement (Martin and White 2005).

It would be erroneous to classify any lecture as strictly monoglossic. Instructors can use language to open up the conversation, via heteroglossic moves. Some of these devices have been identified as having the potential for increasing students' involvement in the classroom and for changing their own positioning towards doers of mathematics (Males et al. 2010; Mesa and Chang 2010). Smith and Higgins (2006) have proposed that more than the types of questions that teachers ask, the manner in which they react to students' responses can make a difference in the classroom, specifically in creating more interactive learning environments. In college classrooms, Nunn (1996) found that behaviors that create a supportive atmosphere (i.e., praising students, indicating that an answer is right, and using students' names) were significantly correlated to the amount of time a student participated (p. 258). Thus, both the type of questions asked and the teacher's responses to the questions can signal that student participation is welcome, and facilitate student engagement with the content.

Given the predominant role of lecture as a preferred delivery method in post-secondary mathematics, and the scarcity of existing frameworks to capture what happens in lectures, we sought to use these two criteria, the Novelty of Mathematical Questions posed during class and the Teacher (linguistic) Moves observed during lecture, to characterize mathematics lectures. One of our main purposes was to see whether we could use these two attributes to characterize instruction (i.e., the interaction between students, teachers, and the content, over time, and within a particular environment) when the primary delivery mode is lecture. Also, we sought to determine whether this process allowed us to differentiate across instructors who lecture.

Method

The setting for this study is a large suburban community college in Michigan with an approximate enrollment of 12,000 students and an average yearly retention rate of 50 %. At the time of data collection (2008–2009), the mathematics department had 16 full-time and 75 part-time instructors and offered an average of 22 different courses per term, including remedial math courses (e.g., fundamental math, beginning and intermediate algebra), college courses for professional and liberal arts degrees (e.g., business, health, and education), STEM preparatory courses (college algebra, college trigonometry, and precalculus), and college courses for STEM degrees (e.g., calculus, linear algebra, and differential equations). Like other community colleges across the United States, students may also obtain their general

Table 1 Instructor characteristics

Instructor	Academic background	Years of college teaching experience	Status
Ed	Mathematics, BS, MS	3	Part-time
Elizabeth	Mathematics, BS, MA	7	Full-time
Elliot	Economics, BS	6	Part-time
Emmett[a]	Physics, PhD	16	Full-time
Evan	Physics, BS; Mathematics, BS; Mathematics, MA	8	Part-time

[a]Emmett taught three sections of the course

education diploma (GED) at this college. This particular college was chosen because students' evaluation of teaching in the mathematics department was high (above 4.2 on a scale from 1 to 5), which suggests high student satisfaction with instruction in the department. In addition, the department had recently appointed a very dynamic department chair, committed to investing time in improving teaching. Moreover, like other colleges in the state, the faculty felt pressure to increase passing rates in their courses. The department received substantial support from the administration to engage in activities that would address the low passing rate problem (e.g., support for a faculty development group, time off for periodic evaluation of curriculum and syllabi, incentives for managing the coordination of the large number of part-time instructors, a college-wide program to address students' orientations towards learning).

As part of a larger study, we had been interviewing and observing 12 instructors teaching college algebra, trigonometry, and precalculus (over 80 lessons). For this particular paper, we analyzed 21 lessons that were on the same subject, trigonometry, which gave us the most variation in terms of teachers' characteristics and therefore gave us interesting differences to capture when teaching the same content. During the 2008–2009 school year, we observed seven trigonometry sections taught by five instructors (Table 1). After producing our initial descriptions, we met with each instructor to share our views of their interactions in the classroom (who participates, number of questions, use of IRE/F patterns, cognitive demand of tasks). In these meetings, we sought to identify whether what we have captured was reflective of instructors' standard practices and their rationale for organizing the interaction in the way they did. All teachers confirmed that our descriptions were accurate and provided further insights about their practices.

Each section met 2 days a week for 85 min per class. Each section was observed three times on consecutive days; we avoided exams in order to maximize the time that students and instructors interacted with each other and with the content. One instructor, Emmett was observed in three different sections, for a total of nine times. The lessons were audiotaped, and extensive field notes were taken that included the work on the board and other observations not captured by the audiotape (e.g., students leaving or entering the room, overall class mood, teacher movement in the room, where the students sat, and who asked or answered questions). After each class, instructors commented on events that happened during the lesson, or that departed from other lessons observed (e.g., calling students by name to answer questions, sending students to the board, assigning seatwork), and about how representative of other lessons in the semester the observed class was. The purpose was to determine what counted as "common" or "standard" practice and what was considered extraordinary. The audio recordings of the lessons were transcribed, with the length of pauses 3 s or more in speech noted; the transcripts were augmented with the work done on the board.

Analyses

The analyses of the classroom transcripts attended to two dimensions of the interaction: the Novelty of Mathematical Questions posed during class and the Teacher Moves we observed during the lecture. These afforded us several units of analysis: the questions posed, the turns in which teachers initiated an interaction, and the time that was allotted to certain Teacher Moves. We also contextualized these by the different types of activities (introducing New Material, doing Review, and Other— e.g., test-taking, discussing class logistics) that were evident in the lessons. Whereas the Novelty of Mathematical Questions analysis seeks to give an indication of the difficulty of the questions asked by both students and teachers, the Teacher Moves analysis attends solely to the way in which the teachers manage the dialogue that occurs in the classroom.

Novelty of Mathematical Questions

We see mathematical questions as opportunities that instructors create to engage students in mathematical activities. With this framework, we sought to characterize the opportunities that are created by describing how novel the questions are. We developed this scheme by drawing from frameworks that analyze questions in classrooms (Nystrand et al. 2003; Wells and Arauz 2006), specifically in mathematics (Nathan and Kim 2009; Truxaw and DeFranco 2008), and augmenting the frameworks based on our data. We started by synthesizing features of these various frameworks (e.g., cognitive demand, authenticity, uptake, teacher evaluation) and then created a categorization of questions that we applied to several of our transcripts, attending to content, intention, execution, and novelty. First, we identified all questions that both instructors and students asked. Next, we took each teacher question and determined whether the question was mathematically oriented or not (content) and whether the instructor expected to obtain an answer from the students (intention). Those questions that were mathematically oriented and for which the instructor expected to obtain an answer became the focus of the analysis. We refer to these questions as the mathematical questions asked by the teacher. We further categorized these questions, indicating if the students answered the question or if the teacher paused and gave the students an opportunity to answer the question (execution) and if students were expected to know the answer or how to procedurally figure out the answer given what had been covered in the class (novelty).

The questions that were not mathematically oriented were questions about classroom procedures (e.g., "So how's it going? Questions on the trig?"), discourse management (e.g., "Could you repeat that?"), and rhetorical questions, including a type of question that we called statement-right (e.g., "Let's see, from 0 to 180°, that's the window we're looking for, right?"). We did not include statement-right questions because they were not usually open to discussion—the teachers were only looking for the listener's agreement.

In terms of execution, mathematical questions asked by the teachers could be aborted. This occurred when the question was not followed by a student response, either because the teacher did not provide enough pause time for the students (3 s or more) or because he or she reworded or answered the question himself or herself (e.g., "And what's cosine of $-x$? That's just cosine of x itself"). In terms of novelty, mathematical questions asked by teachers or students were *Routine* when students were expected to know the answer or to know how to procedurally figure out the answer using information given in the class, or in previous classes or courses (e.g., "If I'm talking about negative pi over 2, which direction am I going first of all?" "What's the result?"). They were *Novel* when students were not expected to already know the answer or the procedure to figure out the answer. Novel questions included those that required students to explain new connections between mathematical notions or connections to real-world scenarios (e.g., "Why is it sometimes that if the light is getting old that you're able to see it flicker?"), to figure out something new using information that had not been discussed in the class (e.g., "And what's cosine of $-x$?"), or that encouraged students to think about a new mathematical notion (e.g., "b approaches 1, and a approaches 0. What do you think is going to happen to the ratio?"). Student questions that inquired about the how or why of the mathematics (e.g., "Doesn't shifting affect whether it would be sine or cosine?") were considered Novel, whereas student questions seeking for a specific, direct answer (e.g., "It needs to be in radians right, not in degree mode?") were considered Routine. We made the classification taking into account the talk and content that preceded and followed the question. A team of five researchers using NVivo coded the mathematical questions. Cohen's κ, used to determine pair-wise agreement of the coding of teacher questions, ranged from .62 to .80.

Teacher Moves

For the second analysis, we used a framework for describing teacher moves in primary and secondary English and mathematics lessons developed by Mary Kay Stein and colleagues (Scherrer and Stein 2012). This framework attends specifically to the ways in which teachers initiate interaction and how they sustain it.

Although developed for helping teachers enact standards-based practice, this framework contained moves that could account for actions that are seen in lecture-based lessons in ways that other frameworks did not. An earlier version of this framework had two categories of moves, those that initiate the discussion (initiating moves) and those that invite more participation from students (rejoinder moves). We added three codes to this framework: Statement of Problem, an initiating move, to indicate when a new problem started; Response Right; and Response Wrong—rejoinder moves—to mark moves in which the instructor explicitly states that a student response is correct or incorrect. The Statement of Problem code was important for us because, unlike the context in which Stein and colleagues were working, we did not have many open-ended tasks that were posed to the students; instead, the instructors brought many examples and solved many problems on the board that were an important feature of the lessons. Likewise, Response Right and Response Wrong appeared frequently in the data, and we agreed that it was an important feature to capture (see also Nunn 1996).

We also made two modifications to this framework as we applied it to our data. First, rather than coding at the turn level as Scherrer and Stein did, we coded by groups of clauses that conveyed the meaning proposed by the codes in the framework. We called these clauses or groups of clauses, moves. This allowed the initiating moves to be mutually exclusive, and the rejoinder moves to be "added on" to an initiating move, thus allowing us to tease out the type of invitations that teachers used to engage students in the dialogue. Second, and because we wanted to have a group of codes that were mutually exclusive and would allow us to code all possibilities of dialogue in the classroom (reform oriented or not), we reclassified the code *Collect* as an initiating move (see Table 2).

To facilitate discussion of the moves, we further categorized them into the two main voices, monogloss and heterogloss. Heterogloss moves were further classified depending on whether the move sought to expand or contract the conversation or whether it was possible, in context, for the move to be used either way. We classified one code, *Provide Information*, as Monogloss; eight codes, *Think Aloud, Literal, Lot, Repeat, Response Right, Response Wrong, Terminal,* and *Uptake-Literal,* as Heterogloss-Contract; three codes, *Launch, Collect,* and *Pushback,* as Heterogloss-Expand; and four codes, *Re-Direct, Re-Initiate, Connect,* and *Uptake,* as Heterogloss moves that could be either contracting or expanding the conversation depending on the context. The Statement of Problem code was not included in this classification because it was not considered germane to the analysis (see Fig. 1). In Table 3, we provide examples of this classification. In some of these examples, we include additional text that was used in making the classification; the underlined text was coded as the specific move.

A two-person team, including one who participated in the Novelty of Mathematical Question analysis team, coded the Teacher Moves. They coded 30 min of a lesson independently using the code descriptions. Agreement on the initiating codes was 78 and 76 % on the rejoinder moves. The discrepant cases were discussed, allowing us to make our definitions clearer. With the revised system, one person coded the rest of the lessons.

Table 2 Framework for analyzing Teacher Moves

Initiating Moves (mutually exclusive assignment)

1. Collect: Teacher seeks to gather more responses to a question from more students[a]
2. Launch: Teacher asks an open-ended question meant to invite student thinking
3. Literal: Teacher asks a question seeking retrieval of factual information. The teacher often is looking for a specific answer
4. Provide Information: Teacher gives information (answer or method) related to the instructional task at hand. Teacher reviews or reveals relevant information from prior work.
5. Re-direct: Teacher asks a question that invites student thinking in a different direction from a preceding question. The initial question was never fully answered.
6. Re-initiate: Teacher asks a question that repeats the same or slightly reworded question.
7. *Statement of Problem: Teacher poses the problem to be worked on.*
8. Think Aloud: Teacher talks about how she or he is thinking about a passage or a problem.

Rejoinder Moves (assigned individually or in addition to initiating moves)

9. Connect: Teacher asks a question or makes a statement so the students make an explicit connection.
10. (parking-)Lot: Teacher acknowledges student responses and states that the class will deal with them later.
11. Pushback: The teacher challenges a student response in order to encourage students to rethink or defend their responses.
12. Repeat: Teacher echoes a student response.
13. *Response Right: Teacher tells the student that his or her response or contribution is correct.*
14. *Response Wrong: Teacher tells the student that his or her response or contribution is incorrect.*
15. Terminal: An utterance that discontinues a student's response and often implicitly or explicitly evaluates students' responses.
16. Uptake-Literal: Teacher asks a question for retrieving factual information building on a student response.
17. Uptake: Teacher uses a student response to extend, deepen, clarify, or elaborate the discussion.

Other

18. No Code: A move cannot be categorized using one of the codes above. These included classroom management comments, administrative announcements, references to the textbook, and personal stories unrelated to the content.

Adapted from Scherrer and Stein (2012)

Notes: Italicized text corresponds to codes added to the original framework proposed by Scherrer and Stein. a. This category was a Rejoinder move in the Scherrer and Stein paper

Episode Parsing

We contextualized these two analyses by parsing the transcripts into three mutually exclusive episodes that occurred in the classroom, namely, *New Material*, *Review*, and *Other*. In *New Material* episodes, teacher and students discussed material that had not been presented previously in the course. In *Review* episodes, teachers and students discuss material covered in a previous class, solutions to past assignments (e.g., homework, quizzes, or examinations), or topics or examples that would be covered on a future examination. Episodes classified as *Other* included discussions that were independent of mathematical content (e.g., providing dates for upcoming

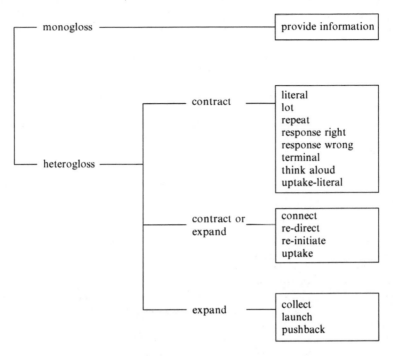

Fig. 1 Classification of Teacher Moves according to monogloss-heterogloss voices

Table 3 Examples of Teacher Moves from the corpus

Monogloss	
Provide Information	T: Today we're gonna wrap up section 3.1 on graphing [six basic] trig functions, remember we got through sine, cosine and tangent [on Tuesday] and we're going wrap up doing the other three which actually follow uh, pretty easily from the graphs of sine, cosine, and tangent.
Heterogloss Contract	
Literal	T: so in this example, $y = x^2$, what's the range?
Lot	T: Well that's, yeah, and that actually will not give rise to 'cannot define,' let's hold off on that for a second. Where are the places where we would be dividing by zero, for cotangent?
Repeat	M: Arbitrarily small.
	T: Arbitrarily small. Does everyone see that?
Response Right	M: And you kind of do this for anything with a negative because if you add a full period it shouldn't change anything, right?
	T: Correct. So anytime you get a negative radian answer you know that it's supposed to be positive, you start adding periods, however many periods you need.
Response Wrong	T: But where would the 120 be? What letter would be 120?
	M: [B]
	T: Not B. Sorry?

(continued)

Table 3 (continued)

Terminal	T: Then can I write the function now?
	M: Um, no.
	T: Heck yeah, we got it, right? So we can now say y is 30 sin pi over seven
	T. Ok. Cool
Think Aloud	T: Ok, I want to draw the graph for this function, so x is between 0 and 2π. The way I'm going to do it, so let's see. Just base this of off what I know about this regular sine. Let's draw the graph of, say, sine x. (Pause 10 seconds) This is, well, $y = \sin x$
Uptake-Literal	T: What effect, what would this pi over two affect?
	M: Period.
	T: Period, right? It would affect period. And, we know something about period, don't we?
	M: It's fourteen seconds.
Heterogloss Expand	
Collect	T: I'll get what?
	M: Sine squared.
	T: (writes on board) What else?
	M: Minus 2 sine cosine.
Launch	T: We found the A and B and we wrote this. So now let's talk about well what's that mean. What's does that mean? This thirty. Well what are we answering first?
Pushback	T: What's our y-axis?
	M: Uhh.
	M2: [it is] feet.
	T: Oh, really? Hmm, why is this feet? Does that help or no? Ok.
	M: Why would it be the y-axis if x can measure the amplitude?
Heterogloss Contract or Expand	
Connect	**Contract:**
	T: .0125. So it's 1/100 of a second roughly. That's the time it takes for one wave, that's the time it takes to complete one wave. This is the lowest frequency of a male speech. Now the highest for a male is 240 and the lowest for a female is 140. The range they're giving you from 80 to 240, that's the range of male speech. 140 to 500 is the range of female speech. Compact disc is from 0 to 22,050. It makes sense because it has all kinds of sounds coming from a compact disc. Piano is from 28 to 4,186. And human hearing is from 20 to 20,000 hertz. Ok. Any questions? There are more applications that have to do with electricity, we're running out of time so we'll get to these applications next time. I do have your quizzes.
	Expand:
	T: So, I'm going to back up over here, I just want to try and draw some parallels. What do we know about this?
Re-Direct	**Contract:**
	T: And how do we find C from that number? What do we do to it? If sine C equals this number here, what would C be? (pause 6 sec) Let me calculate that number. We need 5 divided by 7.6. 5 divided by 7.6 is .65789.
	Expand:
	T: What's the unit of the phase shift? (pause 5 sec) First of all what is a phase?

(continued)

Table 3 (continued)

Re-Initiate	**Contract:**
	T: But where would the 120 be? What letter would be 120?
	Expand:
	T: For this particular frequency, how do we find the time? What do we do to frequency to find the time?
Uptake	**Contract:**
	M: It's going to shrink
	T: It shrinks by a factor of
	M: One-third.
	T: Yeah.
	Expand:
	T: Ok. Any suggestions on that?
	M2: (laughs) The rate.
	T: We could look at a rate! That's a good idea!

Note: Underlined text was used to make the classification

tests, taking an in-class examination, returning graded work). Each transcript was parsed into these three mutually exclusive episodes. The parsing was done prior to the coding of questions and moves. A team of three researchers, the two authors and a graduate student, parsed the lesson transcripts, with weekly discussions to determine final episodes.

Results

We present the results of the two main analyses performed, the Novelty of Mathematical Questions and the Teacher Moves. We present these results as they unfold over time and relative to the type of episodes.

Novelty of Mathematical Questions

Table 4 shows the frequency of mathematical questions and the proportion of Novel questions asked by the teachers over the three lessons observed including the proportion of those questions that were aborted.

In Table 4 we see that instructors asked a large number of mathematical questions in each 85-min class period (average=55, min=38, max=85). Most of these questions were Routine (70 %), which suggests that students were more frequently expected to give answers they already knew rather than answers they did not. In other words, students were not asked to struggle with the content that was being presented very often, a key characteristic of these lectures. This percentage is lower than what Nunn (1996), citing Barnes (1983), reported: 80 % of questions that faculty ask in mathematics classes are of the lowest cognitive level (recall of

Table 4 Average frequency per 85-min class period of mathematical questions: frequency and percent of teacher and student Novel questions, Novel and Routine teacher questions aborted, and Novel teacher questions not aborted

| | Teacher mathematical questions | | | | | | | Student mathematical questions | | |
| | Novel questions | | Aborted questions | | Novel questions not aborted | | | Novel questions | | |
Instructor	N	n	%[a]	%[b] Novel	%[c] Routine	n	%[a]	N	n	%[d]
Ed	85	24	29	18	17	20	23	14	7	54
Elizabeth	73	25	35	30	24	18	24	8	2	25
Elliot	52	10	19	24	7	7	14	41	8	20
Emmett 1	55	14	25	37	38	9	16	5	3	57
Emmett 4	39	11	29	38	40	7	18	12	6	49
Emmett 5	38	19	50	34	23	13	33	9	2	27
Evan	46	12	26	66	43	4	9	4	2	45
Average	55	16	30	33	26	11	20	13	4	32

[a]Percent calculated out of all mathematical questions asked in the lessons
[b]Percent calculated out of all Novel questions asked in the lessons
[c]Percent calculated out of all Routine questions asked in the lessons
[d]The percentage of Novel student questions is calculated before rounding the average number of student mathematical and Novel questions

facts, p. 245). In addition, on average, 33 % of Novel questions were aborted compared to 26 % of Routine questions aborted ($\chi^2(1) = 5.94$, $p < .05$). Thus, these instructors were more likely to abort Novel questions than Routine questions, and the number of Novel questions that students were engaged in was small (average = 11, min = 4, max = 20).

Table 4 also presents the frequencies and proportions of questions students asked by type over the three lessons observed. Overall, about one third of the questions students asked were coded as Novel, but there is substantial variation in the amount of questions students asked (mean = 13, min = 4, max = 41) and in the number and proportion of Novel questions asked (mean = 4, min = 2, max = 8). It is also notable that there is variation for the instructor who taught three sections of the same course.

Teacher Moves

We coded in total 5,094 Teacher Moves across all the lessons. Among the initiating moves, *Provide Information*, *Literal*, and *No Code* accounted for the majority of these moves (46 %, 33 %, and 13 %, respectively; see Table 5). Thus, consistent with images of lectures, the teachers in these classes delivered the content at hand and asked the students very specific, pointed questions. The 658 moves that were categorized as *No Code* corresponded to classroom management comments (238, 34 %), references

Table 5 Frequency of initiating Teacher Moves by instructor across all observed lessons

	Initiating moves								
	COL	LAU	LIT	NC	PIn	ReD	ReI	SoP	ThA
Ed (n=913)	1	3	278	137	415	5	25	12	37
Elizabeth (n=958)	0	0	318	155	384	4	33	11	53
Elliot (n=1,158)	0	0	340	155	612	1	10	18	22
Emmett 1 (n=528)	0	0	202	50	232	2	20	19	3
Emmett 4 (n=523)	0	0	190	48	252	0	14	19	0
Emmett 5 (n=526)	0	0	200	42	239	5	29	8	3
Evan (n=488)	0	0	168	71	213	2	16	6	12
Total (N=5,094)	1	3	1,696	658	2,347	19	147	93	130
Percent (%)	0	0	33	13	46	0	3	2	3

COL Collect, LAU Launch, LIT Literal, NC No Code, PIn Provide Information, ReD Re-Direct, ReI Re-Initiate, SoP Statement of Problem, ThA Think Aloud

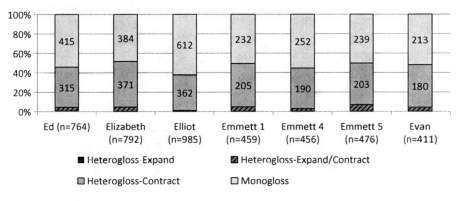

Fig. 2 Average distribution of heterogloss versus monogloss initiating moves by instructor (N=4,436, excludes No Code, n=658 and Statement of Problem moves, n=93)

to the textbook (202, 28 %), administrative announcements (201, 28 %), personal stories unrelated to the content (59, 7 %), and inaudible text (32, 3 %).

Figure 2 shows the distribution of these moves in terms of the Heterogloss-Monogloss classifications. The figure excludes the *No Code* moves (n=658) and the *Statement of Problem* moves (n=93).

In general, the figure shows remarkable similarities across teachers in the absence of Heterogloss-Expand initiating moves (only 4 moves in all by Ed) and limited use of moves that may be considered Heterogloss-Expand (Heterogloss-Expand/Contract moves). We see differences across the teachers, however, in terms of the *number* of moves they used. Three teachers—Ed, Elizabeth, and Elliot—used over 750 moves, whereas Emmett and Evan used less than 500 moves. It is also remarkable that Elliot had almost three times as many Monogloss moves (*Provide Information*) as Emmett or Evan and almost 1.5 times as many as Ed or Elizabeth, indicating that the length of each Monogloss move is shorter in Elliot's class. Proportionally, there is

Table 6 Frequency of rejoinder Teacher Moves by instructor across all observed lessons

	Rejoinder moves								
	CON	Lot	PBK	REP	RR	RW	TRM	U	UL
Ed ($n=165$)	19	2	2	64	44	5	6	20	3
Elizabeth ($n=184$)	15	3	5	74	27	3	18	34	5
Elliot ($n=220$)	5	1	4	85	47	0	26	49	3
Emmett 1 ($n=75$)	3	0	0	40	6	0	7	18	1
Emmett 4 ($n=64$)	10	0	0	29	2	0	4	18	1
Emmett 5 ($n=82$)	11	0	2	32	10	2	4	20	1
Evan ($n=67$)	12	1	1	22	12	3	5	11	0
Total ($N=857$)	75	7	14	346	148	13	70	170	14
%[a]	9	1	2	40	17	2	8	20	2
%[b]	2	0	0	8	3	0	2	4	0

CON Connections, *PBK* Pushback, *REP* Repeat, *RR* Response Right, *RW* Response Wrong, *TRM* Terminal, *U* Uptake, *UL* Uptake-Literal
[a]Percent taken out of the rejoinder moves only
[b]Percent taken out of all moves, excluding No Code

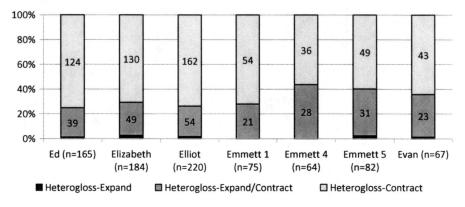

Fig. 3 Distribution of heterogloss versus monogloss rejoinder moves by instructor ($N=857$)

consistency across teachers in their use of Heterogloss-Contract moves (around 40 %). In general, this classification suggests that about half of the Teacher Moves are Monogloss; while teachers do use Heterogloss moves, these tend to be contracting, thus closing the conversation rather than expanding it.

The rejoinder moves were assigned concurrently with initiating moves, but could be assigned independently or concurrently with other rejoinder moves. Rejoinder moves were used less frequently than initiating moves—they only accounted for 17 % of all the moves the teachers used. Among the rejoinder moves, *Repeat*, *Uptake*, and *Response Right* were the most frequently assigned (respectively, 40 %, 20 %, and 17 % of the total; see Table 6).

Figure 3 represents the distribution of these moves in terms of the Heterogloss-Monogloss classification (see Fig. 1) over the three lessons observed per instructor.

We see some variation across teachers in their use of rejoinder moves. Proportionally, Emmett 4, Emmett 5, and Evan use Heterogloss-Contract moves about 60 % of the time, whereas for the other instructors, this proportion is nearly 70 %. Again, there is variation in the number of rejoinder moves: three teachers—Ed, Elizabeth, and Elliot—used these moves over 150 times across the three lessons observed, whereas Emmett and Evan used these types of moves less than 100 times. Again, this analysis corroborates that, in general, even with Heterogloss moves, which seek students' engagement in the conversation, these instructors tended to use contracting rather than expanding moves.

Episodes

Regarding the episodes, on average, 70 % of the class time was devoted to presenting *New Material* (min = 40 %, max = 88 %), 24 % was devoted to *Review* (min = 2 %, max = 53 %), and 6 % (min = 0 %, max = 17 %) was devoted to *Other* activities (assessment, discussions before or after class).

Representing the Novelty of Mathematical Questions and Teacher Moves Analyses Simultaneously

The previous analyses portray similar enactments of lessons, with some variation across teachers regarding the ways in which the teachers used questions and moves in their lessons, but do not provide an idea of how these questions and moves are deployed over time. To get a view of this process, we mapped the two codings over the duration of the lesson and accounted for the different class episodes. These maps show a very detailed, yet complicated view of these lessons.

For representation purposes, we used different shadings to differentiate the Novelty of Mathematical Questions and the types of Teacher Moves: black represents Novel questions, moves that are Heterogloss-Expand (*Collect, Launch,* and *Pushback*), and those moves that could be either Heterogloss-Expand or Contract (*Connect, Re-Direct, Re-Initiate,* and *Uptake*); dark gray represents Heterogloss-Contract moves (*Think Aloud, Literal, Lot, Repeat, Response Right, Response Wrong, Terminal,* and *Uptake-Literal*); and light gray represents Routine questions and Monogloss moves (*Provide Information*). We used the same shading scheme for student questions and dark-gray dots to represent when students otherwise interacted—either in responding to a teacher question or providing other utterances, such as volunteering information. To better represent the Teacher Moves, we divided them into two categories: (a) those best represented as an instance in time (*Collect, Launch, Pushback, Connect, Re-Direct, Re-Initiate, Uptake, Literal, Lot, Repeat, Response Right, Response Wrong, Terminal,* and *Uptake-Literal*) and (b) those best represented as an interval of time (*Provide Information* and *Think Aloud*). We used dots and Xs to make it easier to visualize the data. The representations also include the type of activities that were done in the lesson, mainly presenting *New Material* (black) and doing homework or exam *Review* (light gray). Elliot's 2nd lesson is an example of what this representation looks like (Fig. 4).

To make evident the affordances, specifically the differences that can be captured with these representations, we present 20 min of a lesson from Elizabeth, Elliott, Emmett, and Evan (Fig. 5). These four segments were taken from episodes in which *New Material* was being discussed. Each segment was chosen because it illustrates possible differences between classrooms, as well as the complexity of interaction within a classroom. The representation shows that the relationship between the types of questions asked, teacher moves, and student participation is not a simple one. In addition, adding the time component within and across lessons provides a richer picture of the dynamics of the classroom interaction.

In the 20-min segment of Elizabeth's lesson, we can see that she uses both Novel and Routine questions at about the same frequency, the Teacher Moves are mostly Heterogloss-Contract, and the intervals of providing information are frequent, but relatively short. The students are quite engaged in this class both in asking and responding to questions or volunteering information. In the 20-min segment of Elliot's lesson, students are also quite engaged and frequently ask questions, even though he asks questions much less frequently and uses less Heterogloss moves than Elizabeth. The 20-min segments from Emmett's and Evan's lessons show cases in which the students are not very active. In both of these segments, the total amount of time *providing information* and the length of each occurrence is greater than in Elizabeth's and Elliot's, and the use of Heterogloss moves is infrequent and mostly contracting. The segment of Emmett's class has no teacher questions, whereas Evan's segment includes quite a few Novel questions but very few Routine questions. Evan's representation illustrates a phenomenon that we observed frequently—instructors asking Novel questions that were not answered, either because the teacher rephrased the question to make it simpler for the student or because the teacher answered it.

A representation[1] of the full lessons from our seven sections illustrates the different ways in which instructors interacted with the students. The representations are similar in that they show an infrequent use of Novel questions and of Heterogloss-Expand moves. The full-lesson representation reveals other interesting features, such as the differences in student participation and the Novel questions teachers asked between Monogloss moves. When the three diagrams of the three consecutive lessons are put side by side, we notice an interesting consistency, suggesting, perhaps unsurprisingly, that the individual teachers follow a similar pattern as they teach their lessons day in and day out. This consistency is useful in characterizing what teachers do with their lessons, and it suggests that teachers have *signatures*, or particular ways of organizing instruction that are recognizable and predictable.

---

[1] Available from the authors.

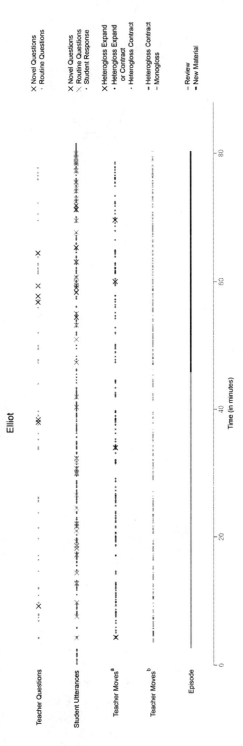

Fig. 4 Representations of the novelty of teacher questions, student utterances, and Teacher Moves, as they unfolded in Elliot's second lesson. *Notes*: a. Includes the following moves: Collect, Launch, Pushback, Connect, Re-direct, Re-initiate, Uptake, Literal, Lot, Repeat, Response Right, Response Wrong, Terminal, and Uptake-Literal. b. Includes the following moves: Provide Information and Think Aloud

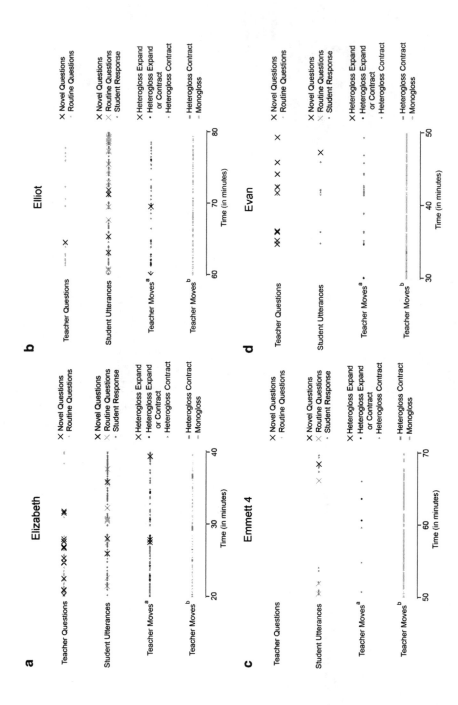

Fig. 5 Representations of the novelty of teacher questions, student utterances, and Teacher Moves, as they unfolded over a 20-min segment of New Material, for four instructors: (**a**) Elizabeth's first lesson, (**b**) Elliot's second lesson, (**c**) Emmett 4's first lesson, and (**d**) Evan's first lesson. *Notes*: a. Includes the following moves: Collect, Launch, Pushback, Connect, Re-direct, Re-initiate, Uptake, Literal, Lot, Repeat, Response Right, Response Wrong, Terminal, and Uptake-Literal. b. Includes the following moves: Provide Information and Think Aloud

Discussion

While the two analyses emphasize the complexity of teaching mathematics and the importance of both mathematical questions and teaching moves, combining them gives a richer picture of classroom interactions. These two analyses separately show regular patterns in the classroom interaction of these trigonometry lessons. The analysis of the mathematical questions shows a consistent pattern; the level of mathematics students are expected to engage with is low—the questions are mostly Routine and teachers interrupt the thinking process by aborting a sizable proportion of questions posed. The analysis of the Teacher Moves reveals how instructors use various additional ways to engage students beyond asking questions, although this is also limited. For the most part, teachers use *Provide Information* and rarely use Heterogloss-Expand moves, such as *Collect* or *Pushback*.

By representing the two analyses together, we see that even with the commonalities of interaction seen in the tables and figures, there are visible differences in how the questions and moves unfold over time. While some instructors use moves that limit the amount of student participation, others use moves that seek it. We see with these combined representations, however, that in these lessons which would have been rated "traditional" or "lecture" instructors provide many opportunities for student engagement with the material and that the way in which these instructors use these devices varies.

Before discussing the affordances and challenges of using this methodology to understand the classroom interaction, we give some interpretations of why we see these behaviors.

Interpreting the Findings

Part of the reason for instructors offering mostly Routine questions at the same time that they provide opportunities for student engagement might be rooted in their belief that students who attend community college have experienced failure in previous mathematics courses, which has left them with low confidence in their ability to do mathematics. Thus, instructors, in an effort to help them gain confidence, will ask questions that they think students can answer without risking failure. As a result, the questions they ask tend to be of a routine nature, thus creating a situation in which students are rarely exposed, or expected to answer difficult questions, therefore constraining opportunities for the students (Mesa 2010, 2012). Another possibility is that teachers fear that students might not be able to take on Novel questions on their own or without the appropriate scaffolding. This was partially confirmed in a later study with Elliot (not reported here), in which we suggested that he engage students in a group activity that involved solving a problem that they had not seen before (graphing inverse tangent, after seeing how inverse sine was graphed using values from the unit circle). During the planning sessions, Elliot disagreed with the idea of asking students to do something he had not modeled for them before (doing at least a few of the key values for tangent), and although he agreed to give the task to the students, during the lesson, he stepped into the solution process, providing the information he felt was necessary for a successful completion of the task and effectively reducing the complexity of the activity for the students. His concerns for the well-being of the students and his doubts that they would be able to generate the graph greatly impacted how the task unfolded.

Part of the reason teachers do not use Novel questions and Heterogloss-Expand moves (*Uptake, Pushback, Collect*) more frequently might be that teachers do not know how to use them in the classroom or may not be aware of their benefits for student learning. In general, community college instructors have little time or opportunity to participate in faculty development programs, and when available, these programs may not be geared specifically towards mathematics or towards managing classroom discourse (Sowder 2007). While some colleges have programs for faculty, their teaching load (five courses per term) may impede their participation (Grubb and Associates 1999). We can argue that teachers' lack of knowledge about the role of language in opening or closing mathematical discussions may explain some of these results; it is also possible that the instructors' perception of the nature of trigonometry may suggest that Monogloss and Heterogloss-Contract moves are more appropriate. Trigonometry is perceived as a course with an extensive amount of information that students need to be exposed to and achieve competency in using. Instructors indicate that the most efficient way to make this content available to students is by providing that information directly, illustrating how to solve the problems, and providing a template for students to repeat the process. Given the limited amount of time in a semester to accomplish this task, instructors may see engaging in explorations (e.g., *Launches* and *Uptakes* with Novel questions) as working against their responsibility to make sure that students have seen all the content of the course.

Affordances and Challenges in Using This Methodology

The analyses of the Novelty of Mathematical Questions and Teacher Moves, both individually and together, show the importance of attending to these two aspects when describing classroom interaction. While this is not necessarily new, representing both the Novelty of Mathematical Questions and Teacher Moves over time reveals various patterns across teachers that otherwise would go unnoticed. Only after we represented the results of these analyses together could we corroborate the differences that we experienced while observing these classes. Thus, these representations allow for a better description of the nature of the classroom interaction that occurred in these classes.

As we indicated earlier, one advantage of combining these two ways of looking at classroom data is that it provides richer descriptions for how teaching actions unfold in the classroom, particularly in cases which other analyses would simply classify the teachers' work as "traditional." Our methodology seeks to understand from the perspective of the local system how instruction happens and the value that teachers give to this form of interaction. Assuming that lecturing or providing information is uniformly "bad" is problematic because we fail to see what exists in this context that promotes student confidence and learning of the material. We argue that there is a role for researchers in making visible how instructors manage instruction and in finding ways to represent and describe their work that captures the complexity of what they do. This analysis allows us to observe important differences in how interaction in the classroom is organized, differences that would not have been possible to describe with one of the analyses alone. Another important benefit of our analyses is that they allow us to see how lessons unfold over time and to understand the back and forth interactions between teachers and students in ways that might not be apparent by using transcripts or one of the analyses alone.

A major challenge of this methodology lies in managing the level of detail that it seeks to achieve. What is the appropriate unit of analysis that one needs to attend to? In our case, we have several units of analysis: the questions, the utterances, and time. Coordinating these into a single representation was a challenge. Whereas seeing these images side by side shows different patterns or signatures in these teachers' lessons (especially when their three lessons are put together), the amount of information presented can be overwhelming. We have spent a great deal of energy in looking for ways to convey the richness of the analyses and at the same time seeking to synthesize the patterns that we observe. No representation can be good enough to approach reality, but the ones that we proposed give us a good idea of how lessons evolved over time and how teachers managed interaction in the classroom.

Future Research

Whereas these analyses and representations are revealing, they are also limited in several ways. Attempting to characterize what teachers do from these three lessons alone could be misleading. However, we believe that the analyses capture important characteristics of lectures that current frameworks don't examine. These analyses can be easily replicated and can produce reliable information about the activities in the classroom.

One major task that lies ahead is developing a system that would allow a comparison, numerical or qualitative, that can account for the differences observed in these lessons. The representations we use provide an account for these differences by contrasting how questions and moves unfold over time. Another task that lies ahead is proposing ways to measure the differences that are observed in these representations that better capture the differences over the five teachers and seven sections and take into account all the lessons observed.

We could then use such measures to answer questions such as follows: Are Heterogloss-Expand moves more likely to be used in tandem with Novel or with

Routine questions? Are there particular patterns in the use of Heterogloss-Expand, Heterogloss-Contract, or Monogloss moves and questions? Are there differences between the use of these moves and use of Novel questions when teachers conduct a Review or when they present New Material? Making these representations highlights that time is an important aspect of the analysis; how these activities unfold over time can shed light on the complexity of teachers' work.

An important feature of lectures is the preponderance of providing information, which is the core of such a teaching methodology. Further research is needed in order to determine the conditions under which this mode of instruction, augmented with the Heterogloss moves that we see and with the Novel questions posed, is beneficial to students. Does this mode of instruction combined with students' practice and individual work produce sustained learning and good outcomes in the course? This seems to be a strongly held belief of community college mathematics instructors, yet we have not been able to establish whether this is the case or not.

Repeating these analyses with other courses (e.g., basic algebra, calculus) would allow us to see the extent to which these findings depend on the course content and to explore the role of teachers' perceptions of their students' abilities on these findings. It would be important, for example, to determine whether instructors teaching courses beyond trigonometry would ask more Novel questions and use more engaging moves with their students, under the assumption that the content is more interesting or that their students are more capable. Contrasting these results with courses for honor students would also be useful in testing the hypothesis that teachers' perceptions of their students determine the extent to which they ask more Novel questions or use more engaging moves with the students. Such information can be used to design programs for faculty development that increases instructors' knowledge of ways to use Novel questions and interactional moves that engage students with mathematics in ways that preserve its depth and complexity.

References

Anderson, L. W., Krathwohl, D. R., Airasian, P. W., Cruikshank, K. A., Mayer, R. E., Pintrich, P. R., & Wittrock, M. C. (Eds.). (2001). *A taxonomy for learning, teaching, and assessing*. New York: Longman.

Bakhtin, M. M. (1981). *The dialogic imagination*. Austin: University of Texas Press.

Barnes, C. P. (1983). Questioning in the college classroom. In C. L. Ellner & C. P. Barnes (Eds.), *Studies of college teaching* (pp. 61–81). Lexington: D.C. Heath.

Bass, R. (1999). The scholarship of teaching: What's the problem? *Inventio: Creative thinking about learning and teaching, 1*. Available at: http://www.doiiit.gmu.edu/archives/feb98/rbass.htm

Blair, R. (Ed.). (2006). *Beyond crossroads: Implementing mathematics standards in the first two years of college*. Memphis: American Mathematical Association of Two Year Colleges.

Cobb, P., Stephan, M., McClain, K., & Gravemeijer, K. (2001). Participating in classroom mathematical practices. *The Journal of the Learning Sciences, 10*(1/2), 113–163.

Cohen, D. K., Raudenbush, S. W., & Ball, D. L. (2003). Resources, instruction, and research. *Educational Evaluation and Policy Analysis, 25*, 119–142.

Coppin, C. A., Mahavier, W. T., May, E. L., & Parker, G. E. (2009). *The Moore method: A pathway to learner-centered instruction*. Washington, DC: The Mathematical Association of America.

Dancy, M. H., & Henderson, C. (2009). Pedagogical practices of physics faculty. *AIP Conference Proceedings, 1179*(1), 121–124.

Dowd, A., Bensimon, E. M., Gabbard, G., Singleton, S., Macias, E., Dee, J. R., Giles, D. (2006). *Transfer access to elite colleges and universities in the United States: Threading the needle of the American dream*. Jack Kent Cooke Foundation, Lumina Foundation, Nellie Mae Education Foundation. Retrieved from http://www.jkcf.org/assets/1/7/Threading_the_Needle-Executive_ Summary.pdf.

Doyle, W. (1984). Academic tasks in classrooms. *Curriculum Inquiry, 14*, 129–149.

Doyle, W. (1988). Work in mathematics classes: The context of students' thinking during instruction. *Educational Psychologist, 23*, 167–180.

Fennema, E., & Sherman, J. (1986). *Fennema-Sherman mathematics attitudes scales: Instruments designed to measure attitudes towards the learning of mathematics by females and males*. Madison: Wisconsin Center for Education Research.

Frederick, P. J. (1987). Student involvement: Active learning in large classes. In M. Weimer (Ed.), *Teaching large classes well* (pp. 45–56). San Francisco: Jossey-Bass.

Grubb, N. W., & Associates. (1999). *Honored but invisible: An inside look at teaching in community colleges*. New York: Routledge.

Johnson, D. W., Johnson, R. T., & Smith, K. A. (1998). Cooperative learning returns to college: What evidence is there that it works? *Change, 30*(4), 27–35.

Lutzer, D. J., Rodi, S. B., Kirkman, E. E., & Maxwell, J. W. (2007). *Statistical abstract of undergraduate programs in the mathematical sciences in the United States: Fall 2005 CBMS survey*. Washington, DC: American Mathematical Society.

Males, L. M., Otten, S., & Herbel-Eisenmann, B. (2010). Challenges of critical colleagueship: Examining and reflecting on study group interactions. *Journal of Mathematics Teacher Education, 13*, 459–471. doi:10.1007/s10857-010-9156-6.

Martin, J. R., & White, P. R. R. (2005). *The language of evaluation: Appraisal in English*. New York: Palgrave-Macmillan.

Mesa, V. (2010). Student participation in mathematics lessons taught by seven successful community college instructors. *Adults Learning Mathematics, 5*, 64–88.

Mesa, V. (2011). Similarities and differences in classroom interaction between remedial and college mathematics classrooms in a community college. *Journal of Excellence in College Teaching, 22*(4), 21–56.

Mesa, V. (2012). Achievement goal orientation of community college mathematics students and the misalignment of instructors' perceptions. *Community College Review, 40*(1), 46–74. doi:10.1177/0091552111435663.

Mesa, V., & Chang, P. (2010). The language of engagement in two highly interactive undergraduate mathematics classrooms. *Linguistics and Education, 21*(2), 83–100.

Mesa, V., Celis, S., & Lande, E. (2014). Teaching approaches of community college mathematics faculty: Do they relate to classroom practices? *American Educational Research Journal, 51*, 117–151. doi:10.3102/0002831213505759.

Moschkovich, J. (1996). Learning math in two languages. In L. Puig & A. Gutiérrez (Eds.), *Proceedings of the 20th conference of the International Group of the Psychology of Mathematics Education* (Vol. 4, pp. 27–34). Valencia: Universidad de Valencia.

Nathan, M. J., & Kim, S. (2009). Regulation of teacher elicitations in the mathematics classroom. *Cognition and Instruction, 27*(2), 91–120.

National Council of Teachers of Mathematics. (1991). *Professional standards for teaching mathematics*. Reston: Author.

Nunn, C. (1996). Discussion in the college classroom: Triangulating observational and survey results. *The Journal of Higher Education, 67*(3), 243–266.

Nystrand, M., Wu, L. L., Gamoran, A., Zeiser, S., & Long, D. A. (2003). Questions in time: Investigating the structure and dynamics of unfolding classroom discourse. *Discourse Processes, 35*(2), 135–198.

Pollio, H. R. (1989). *Any questions now?* Knoxville: University of Tennessee.

Prince, M. (2004). Does active learning work? A review of the research. *Journal of Engineering Education, 93*(3), 223–231.

Rodi, S. B. (2007). *Snapshot of mathematics programs at two-year colleges in the U.S.* Austin: Austin Community College. Available at: http://www.amatyc.org.

Scherrer, J., & Stein, M. K. (2012). Effects of a coding intervention on what teachers learn to notice during whole-group discussion. *Journal of Mathematics Teacher Education*. doi:10.1007/s10857-012-9207-2.

Schoenfeld, A. H. (1992). Learning to think mathematically: Problem solving, metacognition, and sense making in mathematics. In D. A. Grouws (Ed.), *Handbook of research on mathematics teaching and learning* (pp. 334–370). New York: Macmillan.

Secada, W. G. (1995). Social and critical dimensions for equity in mathematics. In W. G. Secada, E. Fennema, & L. B. Adajian (Eds.), *New directions for equity in mathematics education* (pp. 146–164). New York: Cambridge University Press.

Silver, E. A., & Stein, M. K. (1996). The QUASAR project: The "revolution of the possible" in mathematics instructional reform in urban middle schools. *Urban Education, 30*, 476–521.

Smith, H., & Higgins, S. (2006). Opening classroom interaction: The importance of feedback. *Cambridge Journal of Education, 34*, 485–502.

Soter, A. O., Wilkinson, I. A., Murphy, P. K., Rudge, L., Reninger, K., & Edwards, M. (2008). What the discourse tells us: Talk and indicators of high-level comprehension. *International Journal of Educational Research, 47*, 372–391.

Sowder, J. (2007). The mathematical education and development of teachers. In F. Lester (Ed.), *Second handbook of research on mathematics teaching and learning* (pp. 157–224). Charlotte, NC: Information Age.

Stein, M. K., Grover, B. W., & Henningsen, M. (1996). Building capacity for mathematical thinking and reasoning: An analysis of mathematical tasks used in reform classrooms. *American Educational Research Journal, 33*, 455–488.

Thompson, A. (1992). Teachers' beliefs and conceptions: A synthesis of the research. In D. Grouws (Ed.), *Handbook of research on mathematics teaching and learning* (pp. 127–146). New York: Macmillan.

Truxaw, M. P., & DeFranco, T. C. (2008). Mapping mathematics classroom discourse and its implications for models of teaching. *Journal for Research in Mathematics Education, 39*(5), 489–525.

Vygotsky, L. S. (1986). *Thought and language* (A. Kozulin, Trans.). Cambridge, MA: MIT Press.

Wells, G., & Arauz, R. M. (2006). Dialogue in the classroom. *The Journal of the Learning Sciences, 15*(3), 379–428.

Yackel, E., & Cobb, P. (1996). Sociomathematical norms, argumentation, and autonomy in mathematics. *Journal for Research in Mathematics Education, 27*, 458–477.

Yackel, E., Cobb, P., Wood, T., Wheatley, G., & Merkel, G. (1990). The importance of social interaction in children's construction of mathematical knowledge. In T. Cooney (Ed.), *Teaching and learning mathematics in the 1990s*. Reston: National Council of Teachers of Mathematics.

Assessing Instructional Quality in Mathematics Classrooms Through Collections of Students' Work

Melissa D. Boston

Abstract This chapter explores the use of collections of students' work as a reflection of instructional quality. Sets of students' written work can provide indicators of the *conditions* of learning, representing the norms and instructional practices impacting students' mathematical thinking as they produced the work. I present a methodology for analyzing sets of students' written work using the Instructional Quality Assessment (IQA) Mathematics Assignment rubrics. I will summarize research validating the use of students' work as an indicator of instructional quality, provide examples to illustrate how to use the IQA rubrics to evaluate collections of students' work, describe ways of analyzing IQA data, and share research projects in which student-work collections and the IQA rubrics were used to (1) assess instructional quality in mathematics at the district level and (2) evaluate the effectiveness of professional development initiatives. The chapter will close with a discussion of the strengths and limitations of the IQA specifically and the use of students' work as a data source more broadly.

Keywords Students' work • Instructional quality • Professional development research • Task implementation • Cognitive demand

As schools across the country begin to implement the Common Core State Standards in Mathematics (Common Core State Standards Initiative [CCSSI] 2011), school leaders will need methods of assessing the progress of mathematics teaching and learning in their schools, particularly in the direction of the Standards for Mathematical Practice. While students' achievement on standardized tests or the analysis of value-added measures provide indirect representations of teaching quality, direct assessments of instructional quality based on classroom observations and collections of

M.D. Boston (✉)
School of Education, Duquesne University, Pittsburgh, PA, USA
e-mail: bostonm@duq.edu

Y. Li et al. (eds.), *Transforming Mathematics Instruction: Multiple Approaches and Practices*, Advances in Mathematics Education, DOI 10.1007/978-3-319-04993-9_27,
© Springer International Publishing Switzerland 2014

instructional artifacts (e.g., tasks and students' work) can supplement and explain student achievement data and indicate pathways for instructional improvement (Pianta and Hamre 2009; Stein and Matsumura 2008). Lesson observations, instructional tasks, and samples of students' work provide windows into the practices in which teachers and students engage in the process of teaching and learning mathematics. In addition to providing data on students' learning, sets of students' written work can also provide an indicator of the *conditions* of learning, representing the norms and instructional practices impacting students' mathematical thinking as they produced the work (Matsumura et al. 2002). Through collections of student work, researchers and school administrators can analyze the quality of mathematics instruction at the scale of an entire school or district, between different districts, or between schools within the same district. Collections of students' work can aid researchers in analyzing the effectiveness of professional development initiatives or curriculum implementations and can provide school leadership with internal assessments of teaching quality to serve both diagnostic and evaluative purposes.

This chapter explores the use of collections of students' work in research on instructional quality. I present a methodology for analyzing sets of students' written work using the Instructional Quality Assessment (IQA) Mathematics Assignment rubrics. This set of rubrics is part of the larger IQA toolkit, a validated measure developed to assess instruction in mathematics and reading/language arts through lesson observations and collections of students' work (Boston 2012; Matsumura et al. 2008). I will summarize research validating the use of students' work as an indicator of instructional quality and describe research projects using the rubrics to (1) assess instructional quality in mathematics at the district level and (2) evaluate the effectiveness of a professional development initiative. The chapter will close with a discussion of the strengths and limitations of the IQA specifically and the use of students' work as a data source more broadly.

Using Student Work as a Reflection on Instruction

Sets of students' written work on mathematical tasks have been used successfully in professional development settings to provide windows into students' thinking, enabling teachers to consider the variety of strategies and reasoning students may use to solve a given task, identify the range of understanding across a set of students, and plan ways to provide support or ask questions that build and develop students' mathematical thinking (Cobb et al. 2009; Kazemi and Franke 2004; Smith 2001). Analyzing sets of students' work can also provide data and initiate conversations about the *nature of instruction* that supported students to produce the mathematical work and thinking. For example, consider the reflection on instruction when (a) students solved the task in more than one way even though the directions did not specifically request multiple strategies, (b) all or most students did not complete the cognitively challenging parts of the task, or (c) many student-work samples look "template" (Boston 2008; Matsumura and Boston 2006; Steele and Boston 2012).

Sets of students' written work can provide insight into the teacher's expectations for what "counts" as a written explanation or whether the teacher's instructional practices maintained or diminished opportunities for cognitively challenging work (Boston and Steele in press).

Matsumura and colleagues' research (e.g., Matsumura 2003; Matsumura et al. 2002) validated the collection and analysis of students' work as a reflection of teachers' instructional practice. In comparison to classroom observations, collections of students' work are harder to manipulate in ways that please researchers and encapsulate longer periods of instructional time and more activities in a classroom (Clare and Aschbacher 2001). As an alternative or supplement to classroom observations, collecting student work is less invasive to the instructional process and requires fewer resources than conducting observations (live, audiotaped, or videotaped). Collections of students' work also provide artifacts of the instructional episode that can be shared and discussed amongst researchers, school leaders, professional development providers, and/or mathematics teachers. In this way, collections of students' work (and the tools or rubrics used to analyze students' work) can serve as *boundary objects*, tools used together by different stakeholders in the educational system to improve instruction at scale (Stein and Coburn 2007). While the actual collections of students' work serve as resources to promote discussion and reflection on instruction, the tools used to analyze students' work identify what is important and valued in students' outcomes *and* the type of instruction that supported students to reach those outcomes. Ideally, these tools also indicate pathways for instructional improvement and provide a means of assessing improvement, thereby communicating a vision of quality mathematics instruction and setting benchmarks for effective instructional practice. The following section describes the vision of and benchmarks for high-quality mathematics instructional set forth by the IQA Mathematics Assignment rubrics.

Vision of Instructional Quality in Mathematics

The vision of high-quality mathematics instruction at the foundation of the IQA Mathematics Assignment rubrics is consistent with the recommendations by the National Council of Teachers of Mathematics (2000) and the Common Core State Standards Initiative's Standards for Mathematical Practice (CCSSI 2011). Specifically, components of quality mathematics instruction identified by the IQA include the following: (1) the teacher presents students with a cognitively challenging mathematical task (e.g., as defined by Stein et al. (2009)); (2) in completing the task, students engage in high-level thinking (e.g., problem-solving, justifying or proving claims or conjectures, identifying and generalizing patterns, or making sense of or connecting mathematical ideas, procedures, or representations), with the teacher providing enough support to maintain students' engagement in high-level processes without taking away students' opportunities for thinking and reasoning (e.g., see Henningsen and Stein's (1997) factors for maintenance of high-level cognitive demands); (3) students' written work (in the student-work collection)

| **Potential of the Task** |
| The highest level of thinking required to successfully complete the instructional task(s) in the samples of students' work and identified by the teacher on the cover sheet. For assignments with multiple tasks, the score received by the largest number of tasks is used; average score is used in a tie. |
| **Implementation** |
| The highest level of engagement evidenced in the majority of student work samples. |
| **Rigor of Teacher's Expectations** |
| The highest level of cognitive demand expected of students, as indicated on the cover sheet, including copies of any rubrics or criteria sheets used to assess students' work. |
| **Clarity and Detail of Teacher's Expectations** |
| The clarity and detail of teachers' expectations for high-quality work, as indicated on the cover sheet, including copies of any rubrics or criteria sheets given to students for their work on the task. |
| **Students' Access to Teacher's Expectations** |
| Ways in which expectations for students' work are communicated to all students, as described on the cover sheet. |

Fig. 1 IQA Mathematics Assignment rubrics

or discussion following the task (in lesson observations) includes complete and thorough explanations, justifications, or representations of mathematical ideas; and (4) teachers maintain and publically express expectations for high-level thinking, specific to the mathematical and cognitive demands of the task. Research has consistently confirmed that these four aspects of classroom instruction impact student achievement (Boaler and Staples 2008; Cobb et al. 1997; Hufferd-Ackles et al. 2004; Stein and Lane 1996; Stigler and Hiebert 2004; Tarr et al. 2008).[1] Hence, the IQA Mathematics Assignment rubrics assess the quality of a mathematics lesson using a small number of indicators empirically associated with students' learning. Figure 1 describes the five dimensions[2] of the IQA Mathematics Assignment rubrics: *Potential of the Task, Implementation, Rigor of Teacher's Expectations, Clarity and Detail of Teacher's Expectations*, and *Students' Access to Teacher's Expectations*. Through these rubrics, the IQA provides data to address the following research questions:

1. What is the rigor of the mathematical tasks in the collection of students' work?
2. What is the rigor of task implementation, as evidenced in the students' work? Were high-level task demands maintained or reduced?
3. What is the rigor of teachers' expectations for students' work? Did teachers' expectations align with the cognitive demands of the task(s)? To what extent did the rigor of task implementation align with the rigor of teachers' expectations?
4. To what extent were the teachers' expectations clear and accessible?

---

[1] Thorough descriptions of the conceptual underpinnings of the IQA rubrics are provided in Boston (2012).

[2] A sixth rubric, *Rigor of Students' Written Responses*, was developed but is no longer used due to high correlation with the *Implementation* rubric.

The next section describes how to use the IQA Mathematics Assignment rubrics to analyze collections of students' work.

The IQA Mathematics Assignment Rubrics

The collection and analysis of students' work in the IQA Mathematics Assignment rubrics is grounded in a body of research indicating that collections of students' work provide stable indicators of classroom practice highly correlated with observed instruction (Borko et al. 2003; Clare and Aschbacher 2001; Matsumura et al. 2002). Specific to the IQA rubrics, scores on lesson observation and student-work collections exhibit significant correlations ($r = .68$, $p < .01$) (Matsumura et al. 2008). Design and generalizability studies conducted on the IQA Mathematics Assignment rubrics indicate that four sets of student-work per teacher, with 4–6 samples in each set, can serve as a valid indicator of classroom practice (Matsumura et al. 2008). This research also indicated that the IQA Mathematics Assignment scores were significantly correlated with students' scores on all subscales (i.e., total mathematics, procedures, problem-solving) of the Stanford Achievement Test, 10th Edition (SAT-10).

The protocol for the IQA student-work collection was also informed by the aforementioned design studies (e.g., Matsumura et al. 2008). Each teacher was asked to provide four assignments with six samples of students' work per assignment. To minimize sampling variability, teachers were explicitly asked to submit students' work on instructional tasks that require students to "show written mathematical work and explanations." Teachers completed a cover sheet for each assignment, identifying the task(s) students were asked to solve, directions given to students, and the expectations for students' work. Teachers were also asked to submit copies of the instructional task(s) and any rubrics, criteria sheets, or scoring guides used with the task(s). Raters utilize these artifacts to score the Mathematics Assignment rubrics listed in Fig. 1. Each rubric is rated on a scale of 0–4 (0 indicates the construct was absent), with score levels representing a continuum of quality *and* discrete categories of performance. This allows for quantitative analysis and for descriptive interpretations of the results (i.e., what each score level "looks like" for a given construct). Stein and colleagues' levels of cognitive demand (Stein et al. 1996, 2009) informed the development of the score levels for *Potential of the Task, Implementation,* and *Rigor of Teacher's Expectations.*

Each set of student work was scored by two raters. For the IQA Mathematics Assignment rubrics, raters participate in a 2-day training session and are provided with a scoring manual containing samples of tasks, sets of students' work, and cover sheets (with teacher's expectations) illustrating the score levels for each rubric. Rater pairs must achieve at least 80 % exact-point agreement on sample packets of student work prior to rating student-work collections for research. Similarly, rater pairs should achieve at least 80 % exact-point agreement on a subset of at least 20 % of the sets of students' work in a data collection before rating sets of student work individually. In rater-training experiences, newly trained raters without mathematics education backgrounds (e.g., graduate students in initial certification elementary education programs) achieved poor levels of reliability (63.5 % exact-point agreement), IQA project members in mathematics and reading comprehension exhibited acceptable levels of reliability (76.3 % exact-point agreement), and "expert raters" (mathematics education researchers and doctoral students) exhibited excellent levels of reliability (exact-point agreements of 85 % and higher).

Scoring the Potential of the Task and Implementation Rubrics

As indicated in Fig. 1, the *Potential of the Task* rubric is rated based on the instructional task identified by the teacher on the "Student Work Collection Cover Sheet." An instructional task is defined as "a mathematical problem, exercise, or set of problems/exercises with the purpose of focusing students' attention on a particular mathematical idea" (Stein et al. 2009). Excerpts from the *Potential of the Task* and *Implementation* rubric are provided in Fig. 2. When scoring *Potential of the Task*, raters reference a set of sample criteria and characteristics to supplement the rubric description. Once they have identified the elements of the task that contribute to the *Potential of the Task* score, scoring *Implementation* merely requires raters to determine whether or not those elements materialized in students' work. Three examples are provided to illustrate the scoring of these rubrics.

Example 1: Place Value Fractions and Decimals

Figure 3 provides two samples of student work from a 6th grade classroom. The task "Re-write the decimals as fractions... Re-write the fractions as decimals..." scores a 1 for *Potential of the Task*. All of the given fractions (except the Bonus) have denominators that are powers of 10, and rewriting them as decimals requires students' knowledge of place value (i.e., no computation is necessary to successfully change 6/100 into a decimal, as might be required for 3/14, for instance). Students are asked to "rewrite" decimals as fractions and vice versa, which does not imply the use of a procedure (i.e., there is no indication that students are to divide the numerator by denominator). The task does not score a 2 because no computation is necessary to successfully complete the task. *Implementation* also receives a score of 1, since (as demonstrated in the sample) the majority of students "provide answers only."

Example 2: Shading Squares

Figure 4 provides two student-work samples from a 6th grade classroom working on the Shading Squares task. In the part of the task featured in Fig. 4, students are asked to shade in 6 of 40 grid squares and to use the diagram to explain the percent of the

Potential of the Task rubric		*Implementation* rubric
4	The task has the potential to engage students in exploring and understanding the nature of mathematical concepts, procedures, and/or relationships, such as (from Stein, etal., 2009): • Doing mathematics: using complex and non-algorithmic thinking (i.e., there is not a predictable, well-rehearsed approach or pathway explicitly suggested by the task, task instructions, or a worked-out example); or • Procedures with connections: applying a broad general procedure that remains closely connected to mathematical concepts. The task must explicitly prompt for evidence of students' reasoning and understanding. For example, the task MAY require students to: • solve a genuine, challenging problem for which students' reasoning is evident in their work on the task; • develop an explanation for why formulas or procedures work; • identify patterns;...justify generalizations based on these patterns;...	Student-work indicates the use of complex and non-algorithmic thinking, problem solving, or exploring and understanding the nature of mathematical concepts, procedures, and/or relationships (i.e., there is evidence of at least one of the descriptors of a "4" in the *Potential of the Task* rubric.)
3	The task has the potential to engage students in complex thinking or in creating meaning for mathematical concepts, procedures, and/or relationships. However, the task does not warrant a "4" because: • the task does not explicitly prompt for evidence of students' reasoning and understanding. • students may need to identify patterns but are not pressed to form or justify generalizations; students may be asked to use multiple strategies or representations but the task does not explicitly prompt students to develop connections between them;...	Student work indicates that students engaged in problem-solving or in creating meaning for mathematical procedures and concepts BUT student work lacks explicit evidence of complex thinking required for "4" (i.e., the *Potential of the Task* was rated as 3 or 4, ...and there is a lack of evidence of the appropriate descriptors for a 4, but there is evidence of at least one descriptor of a 3.)
2	The potential of the task is limited to engaging students in using a procedure that is either specifically called for or its use is evident based on prior instruction, experience, or placement of the task.... The task does not require students to make connections to the concepts or meaning underlying the procedure being used... (e.g., practicing a computational algorithm).	Students engage with the task at a procedural level. Students apply a demonstrated or prescribed procedure. Students show or state the steps of their procedure, but do not explain or support their ideas. ..
1	The potential of the task is limited to engaging students in memorizing or reproducing facts, rules, formulae, or definitions...	Students engage with the task at a memorization level... (e.g., provide answers only), OR even though a procedure is required or implied by the task, only answers are provided in students' work; there is no evidence of the procedure used by students.

Fig. 2 Excerpts of the IQA Mathematics Assignment rubrics for *Potential of the Task* and *Implementation*

area that is shaded. The task scores a 4 for *Potential of the Task*, since "the task has the potential to engage students in exploring and understanding the nature of mathematical concepts, procedures, and/or relationships" (e.g., percent as "per 100," a visual representation of percent using an area model and the relationship between fractions and percents), and the task explicitly prompts for evidence of students' thinking and reasoning. The majority of student-work samples include explicit evidence of students' thinking and reasoning, in a way that explains the meaning of percent as "per 100"; hence, the *Implementation* also scores a 4. Across the set of student work, students use a variety of strategies and provide unique explanations. If the majority of students had provided inadequate explanations, the *Implementation* score would have fallen to a 3. If the majority of student-work samples used the same strategy or computation, looked "template," or provided similarly worded explanations, the *Implementation* score would have fallen to a 2 (as an indication that a set procedure was provided at some point during students' work on the task).

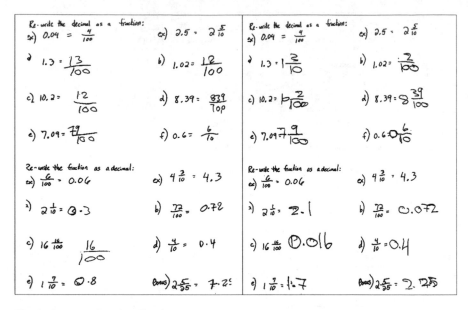

Fig. 3 Two samples of students' work from the Place Value Fractions and Decimals task

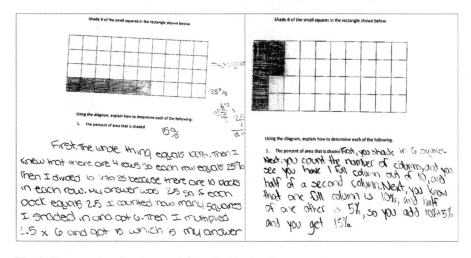

Fig. 4 Two samples of student work from the Shading Squares task

Example 3: Grouping Flowers

Figure 5 provides two samples of students' work from a 4th grade classroom. The "Grouping Flowers" task provides students with a situation involving equal groups of flowers, as a context for multiplication (part a) and division (part b). The task explicitly asks students to "show all of your work," "explain your thinking" (part a), and "explain why you did each step" (part b). For these reasons, the *Potential of the Task* score is a 4. However, most samples of student work do not

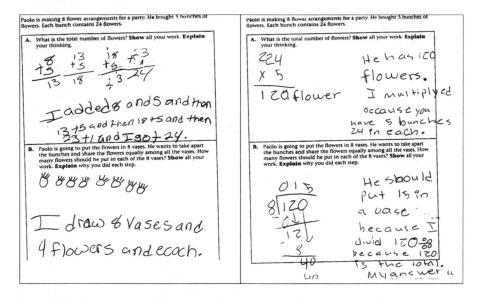

Fig. 5 Two samples of student work from the Grouping Flowers task

provide evidence of students' understanding of the connection between equal groupings and multiplication/division. In the majority of students' work, students applied a random procedure that does not reflect the action in the problem. Because "students show or state the steps of their procedure, but do not explain or support their ideas," and the majority of students' work does not indicate "that students engaged in … creating meaning for mathematical procedures and concepts," *Implementation* scores a 2. If the majority of student-work samples provided implicit evidence of students' connections between equal groups and multiplication or division, even with inadequate explanations, *Implementation* would score a 3. If the majority of student-work samples featured explanations that explicitly described the connection between equal groups and multiplication or division (i.e., "I multiplied because you have 5 bunches 24 in each"), *Implementation* would score 4.

In summary, a set of students' work receives one score for *Potential of the Task* and one score for *Implementation*. In the analysis, comparing *Potential of the Task* scores with *Implementation* scores (as paired values) helps determine whether students' opportunities to engage in thinking and reasoning were maintained during the instructional episode. *Implementation* scores can be higher than *Potential of the Task* scores. For example, student-work collections with a *Potential of the Task* score of 3 sometimes receive an *Implementation* score of 4 when students provide explanations in their work even though not explicitly prompted by the task. However, we rarely see a student-work collection with a *Potential of the Task* score of 1 or 2 (tasks with low-level cognitive demand) receive an *Implementation* score of 3 or 4 (evidence of high-level thinking and reasoning). More frequently, *Implementation* scores fall lower than *Potential of the Task* scores, as tasks that begin with high-level demands (*Potential of the Task* scores of 3 or 4) frequently receive a 2 for

	Rigor of Teacher's Expectations	Clarity and Detail of Teacher's Expectations	Students' Access to Teacher's Expectations
4	The majority of the teacher's expectations are for students to engage with the high-level demands of the task, such as using complex thinking and/or exploring and understanding mathematical concepts, procedures, and/or relationships.	The expectations are very clear and explicit regarding the quality of work expected. The criteria for quality work are appropriately detailed. The expectations and levels of quality are task-specific.	Teacher provides and discusses the expectations or criteria for student work (e.g., scoring guide, rubric, etc.) with students in advance of their completing the assignment and includes a model of high-quality work.
3	At least some of the teacher's expectations are for students to engage in complex thinking or in understanding important mathematics... • the expectations are appropriate for a task that lacks the complexity to be a "4"; • the expectations do not reflect the potential of the task to elicit complex thinking... • the teacher expects complex thinking, but the expectations do not reflect the mathematical potential of the task.	The expectations are clear regarding the quality of work expected. Expectations are task-specific. However, there is no elaboration of what level of quality is expected for each criterion.	Teacher provides and discusses the expectations or criteria for student work (e.g., scoring guide, rubric, etc.) with students in advance of their completing the assignment.
2	The teacher's expectations focus on skills that are germane to student learning, but these are not complex thinking skills (e.g., expecting use of a specific problem solving strategy, expecting short answers based on memorized facts, rules or formulas; expecting accuracy or correct application of procedures rather than on understanding mathematical concepts).	The expectations for the quality of student's work are broadly stated and unelaborated (i.e., a standard rubric).	Teacher provides a copy of the expectations or criteria for assessing student work (e.g., scoring guide, rubric, etc.) to students in advance of their completing the assignment, but does not publicly discuss the expectations or criteria with the entire class.
1	The teacher's expectations do not focus on substantive mathematical content (e.g., activities or classroom procedures such as following directions, effort, producing neat work, or following rules for cooperative learning).	The teacher's expectations for the quality of student's work are unclear OR the expectations for quality work are not shared with students.	Teacher does not share the criteria for assessing students' work with the students in advance of their completing the assignment...

Fig. 6 Excerpts from IQA Mathematics Assignment rubrics for *Rigor of Teacher's Expectations*, *Clarity and Detail of Teacher's Expectations*, and *Students' Access to Teacher's Expectations*

Implementation when the student-work indicates the use of a common, prescribed procedure. Tasks that receive a 4 for *Potential of the Task* can also fall to an *Implementation* of 3 when the student-work lacks high-quality explanations.

Scoring the Teachers' Expectations Rubrics

The IQA Mathematics Assignment rubrics assessing teachers' expectations are provided in Fig. 6. Teachers submit "Student Work Collection Cover Sheets" (informed by Clare 2000), identifying the instructional tasks, explaining their expectations, and providing any rubrics or grading criteria for each set of students' work. When scoring the teacher's expectations rubrics, raters use information provided by the teacher on the cover sheet, particularly question 4. For the *Rigor of Teacher's Expectations*, raters look for expectations or criteria that align with high-level cognitive demands and reflect the main mathematical ideas in the task. For *Clarity and Detail of Teacher's Expectations*, raters identify whether the expectations are task specific and provide enough information to discern high-, medium-, and low-quality work. In scoring *Students' Access to Teacher's Expectations*, raters consider the extent to which the grading criteria, levels of quality, and examples of high-quality work are shared with the class. Any reference to students' prior engagement in high-level thinking and reasoning (e.g., the use of multiple representations or strategies) or to examples of high-quality explanations in students' prior work can count as models. The examples of completed cover sheets in Fig. 7a, b will be used to describe the scoring of the teachers' expectations rubrics.

Hexagon Pattern Cover Sheet

Figure 7a provides the cover sheet for the Hexagon Pattern student-work collection (grade 6). The teacher expected students to generalize a pattern, to describe the "general rule of finding the perimeter" in "sentence form" and by using "a variable formula," and to relate their descriptions to the diagram of the train. The teacher indicates that high-quality work requires "a good explanation of how they came up with the variable expression. Especially relating it to the diagrams they draw." These descriptors for students' work align with score level 4 on the *Potential of the Task* rubrics and capture the thinking skills and mathematical purpose of the patterning task. Hence, the *Rigor of Teacher's Expectations* scores a 4. Without the push for an explanation or for the connection between the descriptions, variable expressions, and diagram of the pattern, the *Rigor of Teacher's Expectations* would score a 3. The expectations are also task specific and delineate different levels of quality, so the *Clarity and Detail of Teacher's Expectations* also receives a 4. If the teacher did not provide specific indicators of the different levels of quality (e.g., instead indicated "all criteria are met" for high quality), or indicated that a general rubric was used to guide and assess students' work on the task (e.g., "students used their problem-solving rubric") without connection to the specific mathematical ideas in the task, the *Clarity and Detail* would receive a score of 3 or 2, respectively. Note that the rubric provided by the teacher (not provided here) was specific to patterning tasks and contained the criteria identified by the teacher. Because the teacher indicates that "Expectations were discussed in class and related to the rubric criteria which were developed by combined classes" and "We went over the previous problem we had done before doing this one," *Students' Access to Teacher's Expectations* also receives a 4, as the previous problem was also a pattern-generalizing problem. Without reference to the class discussion of a previous [patterning] problem or connection to the rubric criteria (i.e., a model and criteria for high-quality work), *Students' Access* would score a 3. Without reference to a class discussion of the teacher's expectations (e.g., "directions were printed on the handout" or "students have a rubric that they can use for reference"), *Students' Access* would score a 2.

Instructional Quality Assessment
Collection of Assignments and Student Work
Cover Sheet for Participants[*]

Please answer all questions as specifically as possible. We're especially interested in question #4 to help us understand the assignment and student work.

Please check: This assignment is **typical** ☐ or **especially challenging** ☒.

1. Attach the assignment and any instructions that were given to students. If this is not possible, use the space below to state the task and describe the instructions.
   Students were to determine the perimeter for the hexagon train and create a formula to find the perimeter.

2. If this task was drawn from a published source, please provide the following information:
   a. title: *None*
   b. volume :
   c. publisher

3. What kinds of activities did your students engage in while working on this assignment?
   Students used pattern blocks to draw their trains. We went over the previous problem we had done before doing this one. We worked with a partner instead of a group to discuss the problem.

4. What expectations were <u>given to students</u> for quality work? (Please include as many details as possible and attach grading criteria, if any, or describe your grading criteria. If your students used a criteria chart or rubric that was posted in the classroom, please sketch or describe it here.)

   Expectations: *Students were expected to write the description of their procedure in sentence form and relate their description to their diagram of the train. Students were also expected to use a variable formula to express a general rule of finding the perimeter. They are always expected to label all their answers and do their work neatly.*

   Grading-High: *Giving the perimeters, a variable expression, and a good explanation of how they came up with the variable expression. Especially relating it to the diagrams they draw.*

   Medium: *Giving the perimeters and a variable expression but not giving a clear explanation of how they arrived at the solution.*

   Low: *Giving the perimeters and possibly a variable expression but not explaining how they arrived at the solution.*

5. How did you share your grading criteria with students before the assignment was due? (e.g.: develop criteria with students, discuss expectations/scoring guides with students in class) *Expectations were discussed in class and related to the rubric criteria which were developed by combined classes. The criteria are posted in class and referred to often.*

---

[*] *This cover sheet was adapted from Clare, L. (2000). Using Teachers' Assignments as an Indicator of Classroom Practice. Los Angeles: UCLA Center for the Study of Evaluation.*

Fig. 7a Hexagon pattern cover sheet

Instructional Quality Assessment
Collection of Assignments and Student Work
Cover Sheet for Participants[*]

Please answer all questions as specifically as possible. We're especially interested in question #4 to help us understand the assignment and student work.

Please check: This assignment is **typical** ☒ or **especially challenging** ☐.

1. Attach the assignment and any instructions that were given to students. If this is not possible, use the space below to state the task and describe the instructions.
    The assignment was to solve and graph inequalities using multiplication and division properties.

2. If this task was drawn from a published source, please provide the following information:
    a. title: *N/A- Handout*
    b. volume :
    c. publisher

3. What kinds of activities did your students engage in while working on this assignment?

    As an introduction we discussed, how, why, and when situations involving inequalities arise.

4. What expectations were <u>given to students</u> for quality work? (Please include as many details as possible and attach grading criteria, if any, or describe your grading criteria. If your students used a criteria chart or rubric that was posted in the classroom, please sketch or describe it here.)

    Expectations: *My students always understand that quality work involves neatness, accuracy, and checks for accuracy.*

    Grading-High: *All problems attempted with a minimum (1 or 2) missed.*

    Medium: *All problems attempted with 3 or 4 mistakes.*

    Low: *Incomplete work with multiple mistakes.*

5. How did you share your grading criteria with students before the assignment was due? (e.g.: develop criteria with students, discuss expectations/scoring guides with students in class)
    Grading criteria is an ongoing process in my class. I constantly encourage and praise completeness, neatness, and accuracy.

---

[*] *This cover sheet was adapted from Clare, L. (2000).* Using Teachers' Assignments as an Indicator of Classroom Practice. *Los Angeles: UCLA Center for the Study of Evaluation.*

Fig. 7b Graphing inequalities cover sheet

Graphing Inequalities Cover Sheet

Figure 7b provides a cover sheet from the Graphing Inequalities student-work collection (grade 7). The *Rigor of Teacher's Expectations* scores a 2, since students were expected to neatly and accurately "solve and graph inequalities using multiplication and division properties," skills germane to students' learning of mathematics but not complex thinking skills. The teacher's response to item 5, "Grading criteria is an ongoing process in my class. I constantly encourage and praise completeness, neatness, and accuracy," provides no indication that any criteria, levels of quality, or models of high-level work were shared or discussed with students prior to students' work on the task. Thus, both *Clarity and Detail of Teacher's Expectations* and *Students' Access to Teacher's Expectations* score a 1. If the teacher had indicated that he/she had posted the criteria on the board, both scores would increase to a 2. In this example, the teacher's expectations as written cannot advance beyond a 2 for *Clarity and Detail*, but different actions by the teacher could result in a 3 (e.g., reviewing the grading scale with the class) or 4 (e.g., reviewing the grading scale and providing a model of an accurate response) for *Students' Access*.

In summary, in addition to the scores for *Potential of the Task* and *Implementation*, a collection of students' work also receives scores for each of the three teacher's expectations rubrics.

Analyzing IQA Scores

As described in the previous sections, each collection of students' work receives 5 scores, one for each of the rubrics identified in Fig. 1. The scores can be interpreted as a continuous scale of increasing quality from 0 to 4, or they can be considered discrete categories of performance. If perceived as a continuous scale, mean scores and t-tests can be used to describe and analyze the data. Sets of student work can be analyzed individually (where n is the number of sets of students' work), or they can be grouped by teacher (where n is the number of teachers). When grouped by teacher, each teacher's score from their four individual collections of student work was averaged for each rubric (i.e., the four scores for the *Potential of the Task* are averaged into one *Potential of the Task* mean score for each teacher). Then, across teachers, an overall mean score is obtained for each rubric. Since scores of 1 and 2 represent low levels of quality and scores of 3 and 4 represent high levels of quality for each rubric, a mean of 2.5 is considered to be the demarcation line between consistently high-quality and consistently low-quality constructs for each teacher and overall. A composite or "overall" student-work score is useful for correlating student-work performance to student achievement data, but not recommended for formative assessments of instructional quality as combining the rubric scores diminishes their interpretive value.

If scores are considered to be discrete categories of performance, medians and modes are used for descriptive purposes, and nonparametric tests and tests for frequency and proportions are used for the analyses. Frequencies of high (3 or 4) vs. low (1 or 2) scores in each construct are important to report and analyze when comparing data over time, because a variety of changes in scores can affect the mean in ways that would not necessarily indicate an increase in teachers' selection or implementation of cognitively challenging tasks or in teachers' expectations. For example, a 1-point increase from a mean score close to 1 to a mean score close to 2 could be statistically significant but would not indicate a shift in instructional practices from low-level to high-level tasks, implementation, or expectations.

Frequencies of high vs. low scores are also particularly helpful in identifying pathways for improvement. Frequencies with important interpretive value between *Potential of the Task* and *Implementation* include (1) the percent of student-work collections with high scores for *Potential of the Task* that were maintained as high-level *Implementation* vs. fell to low-level *Implementation*; (2) the percent of student-work collections with *Potential of the Task* scores of 4 that received a 3 for *Implementation*, often indicating low-quality explanations; and (3) the percent of student-work collections with high scores for *Potential of the Task* that received a 2 for *Implementation*, indicating that the tasks became proceduralized. For the set of rubrics assessing teachers' expectations, insightful frequencies to analyze and report include (1) the percent of high-level tasks (*Potential of the Task* at a 3 or 4) with high scores vs. low scores for *Rigor of Teachers' Expectations*, indicating the extent to which teachers' expectations reflected the cognitive demands of the task), and (2) similarly, the percentages of high-level *Implementation* with high vs. low scores for the *Rigor of Teachers' Expectations*, indicating the level of consistency in the rigor of mathematical work and thinking that a teacher expected vs. the level of rigor actually evident in the students' work. Note that high scores for the *Clarity and Detail of Teacher's Expectations* and *Students' Access to Teacher's Expectations* can be deceiving, as sets of student work can receive high scores on these rubrics with tasks having low-level cognitive demands and task implementation that reduce the cognitive demands of the task (e.g., providing modeling that is too explicit). Hence, as a supplement to interpreting only overall rubric means, separately analyzing descriptive statistics for student-work collections containing high-level tasks (e.g., the *Potential of the Task* scores of 3 or 4) from student-work collections containing low-level tasks (e.g., the *Potential of the Task* scores of 1 or 2) may provide greater insight into instructional quality and highlight areas for instructional improvement. For example, if sets of scores for a teacher or school indicate a consistent decline from high-level tasks (e.g., the *Potential of the Task* scores of 3 or 4) to low-level implementation (e.g., *Implementation* scores of 1 or 2), high scores for the *Clarity and Detail of Teacher's Expectations* and *Students' Access to Teacher's Expectations* may signal a need for teachers to consider how to communicate clear expectations without over-structuring students' mathematical work and thinking.

Statistical tests (parametric or nonparametric) provide additional insights into instructional quality. For example, comparing scores for the *Potential of the Task* and *Implementation* as paired values for each set of student work can indicate whether high-level task demands were maintained during implementation (no significant differences) or declined during implementation (if *Implementation* is significantly lower than the *Potential of the Task*). The *Potential of the Task* and the *Rigor of Teacher's Expectations* should not to be significantly different and, beyond that, should be highly correlated. This would indicate that teachers recognized the main mathematical ideas in the task and the potential of the task to elicit students' thinking. Similarly, *Implementation* and the *Rigor of Teacher's Expectations* should be correlated and not significantly different, indicating that student work provides evidence of the level of rigor expected by the teacher. Whether using discrete or continuous analyses, descriptive statistics on the overall collection of students' work can indicate the success of teachers as a group in selecting and implementing cognitively challenging tasks, holding expectations for students to engage in high-level mathematical work and thinking, and communicating these expectations clearly and publicly to students.

Ethics of Using the IQA for Evaluative and Diagnostic Purposes

In school systems where the use of cognitively challenging instructional tasks is a clear criterion for high-quality instruction, the analysis of student-work collections using the IQA Mathematics Assignment rubrics can provide an assessment of teachers' best efforts to select and implement cognitively challenging instructional tasks, for evaluative or diagnostic purposes. Recall that teachers are explicitly asked to provide samples of students' work that illustrate students' mathematical work and explanations. Hence, across a school or district, teachers' opportunities to have formed an understanding of what "counts" as high-quality work and explanations, of the type of instructional tasks and instructional practices identified by the IQA as supporting students' learning in mathematics, are necessary in order for IQA results to have value. Evaluating teachers on components of instruction of which they are unaware or have not been given an opportunity to develop would be unethical. The IQA, and any tool or rubric, should only be used in an evaluative capacity when (1) teachers are aware of and understand the criteria on which their instructional practices are being assessed (e.g., through district statements of expectations for instructional quality, goals for district- or school-wide reform, professional development opportunities, etc.), (2) teachers are supported to develop the instructional practices identified in the assessment (e.g., through professional development or curricular resources), and (3) only school- or district-level data are reported (not teacher-level data). In this way, the IQA (or other tool) would provide an evaluation of teaching, not an evaluation of teachers, describing key elements of the instructional practices in mathematics in a school or district.

As a diagnostic tool, teacher- or school-level data from the IQA can provide insight into the success of professional development initiatives or curriculum implementations, particularly those designed specifically to facilitate teachers' selection and implementation of cognitively challenging instructional tasks. However, depending on the research design and the number of student-work collections, generalizations to teachers' everyday practice may not be appropriate, and the use of teacher-level data is appropriate for diagnostic purposes or formative assessments only. In the next sections, I describe specific studies in which subsets of the research questions were explored through collections of students' work to assess district-wide reform efforts and to evaluate the effectiveness of a university-based professional development initiative.

Using the IQA Mathematics Assignment Rubrics in Research

The IQA Mathematics Assignment rubrics are useful in a variety of research settings, such as (1) assessing instructional quality at the scale of a school or district, (2) evaluating the effectiveness of professional development initiatives, or (3) monitoring the implementation of *Standards*-based curricula. Herein, I will discuss studies of the first two types; see Boston and Steele (in press) for use of the IQA in a curriculum implementation study.

School- or District-Level Assessment

The IQA Mathematics Assignment rubrics were used to compare elementary students' opportunities to learn mathematics in two mid-sized urban school districts (Districts A and B), similar demographically but different in their use of a *Standards*-based vs. traditional curriculum and in the nature and extent of professional development opportunities provided to mathematics teachers. District A had implemented a long-standing professional development (PD) program specific to the teaching of mathematics with *Standards*-based curricula at the elementary and middle school level and very closely aligned with the constructs measured by the IQA. For District A, the IQA served to assess teachers' instructional practices following the PD and curriculum implementation efforts to identify successes and areas of improvement. District B was just beginning to implement reform-based initiatives in PD and curriculum; hence, in District B, the IQA provided a baseline assessment of teachers' instructional practices to inform the direction of the PD and curriculum reform efforts. The districts consisted of a diverse population of students (16 % African American, 8 % Asian, 63 % Latino, 11 % white, 2 % others), 19 % of whom were English language learners. Two procedures were used to minimize sampling variability. First, data collection was limited to 2nd and 4th grade classrooms only, with seven teachers from each district providing students' work. Second, in each district, teachers were asked to submit four sets of student work where "students demonstrate their mathematical work and thinking." One teacher in District A provided only three student-work sets, resulting in an overall data set of 55 sets of student work from 14 teachers.

Table 1 provides the descriptive data for both districts. Statistically significant differences, favoring the district utilizing the *Standards*-based curriculum and providing content-specific professional development (District A), existed in each dimension of the IQA Mathematics Assignment rubrics (Boston and Wolf 2006). This finding provided the IQA team with construct validity; the IQA Mathematics Assignment rubrics were capable of differentiating mathematics instruction between districts and hence were measuring what was intended. Most importantly, the IQA rubrics provided data to inform instructional improvements in both districts. The district with lower scores

Table 1 Descriptive data on elementary mathematics assignments in Districts A and B

		Number (%) of student-work sets at each score level[a]			
		Low-level demands		High-level demands	
	Mean (SD)	1	2	3	4
District A ($n=27$ assignments; 7 teachers)					
Potential of the Task	*3.15 (.53)	0 (0 %)	2 (8 %)	19 (70 %)	6 (22 %)
Implementation	*2.63 (.79)	4 (15 %)	3 (11 %)	19 (70 %)	1 (4 %)
Rigor of Teachers' Expectations	*3.07 (.39)	0 (0 %)	1 (4 %)	23 (85 %)	3 (11 %)
District B ($n=28$ assignments; 7 teachers)					
Potential of the Task	1.93 (.72)	8 (29 %)	14 (50 %)	6 (21 %)	0 (0 %)
Implementation	1.61 (.69)	14 (50 %)	11 (39 %)	3 (11 %)	0 (0 %)
Rigor of Teachers' Expectations	1.96 (.58)	5 (18 %)	19 (68 %)	4 (14 %)	0 (0 %)

*Significantly higher than District B at $p<.05$
[a]No scores of 0 were received for any rubric dimension

(District B) realized the value of a *Standards*-based curriculum, as the *Potential of the Task* mean score of 1.93 indicated that the sample of instructional tasks provided students opportunities to engage primarily in procedural and memorization tasks. Lack of high-quality tasks effectively limited *Implementation* to a mean of 1.61 and the *Rigor of Teacher's Expectations* to a mean of 1.96, as teachers' expectations for students' work and the student-work samples provided evidence of low-level cognitive demands consistent with the level of the tasks. Means from the collection of student work from District A were above the demarcation line of 2.5 in each construct (with a *Potential of the Task* mean of 3.15, *Implementation* mean of 2.63, and *Rigor of Teachers' Expectations* mean of 3.07), indicating that students in the sample were consistently presented with cognitively challenging tasks and rigorous expectations and produced high-quality mathematical work. The student-work collection from District A was significantly higher than District B, with differences in means greater than one point in each dimension. However, low percentages of tasks, task implementations, and teachers' expectations at a level 4 indicate that the sample of students' work from District A did not indicate that students were prompted to explain their thinking by the instructional tasks or by teachers' expectations, nor did the student work provide evidence of high-quality written mathematical explanations. This finding might suggest a pathway for professional development efforts, both with this sample of teachers and perhaps across the district more broadly.

Evaluating Professional Development Initiatives

The analysis of collections of students' work provides a methodology for evaluating the effectiveness of professional development (PD) initiatives, if the instructional practices advocated by the PD are aligned with the constructs assessed by the IQA. Collections of students' work can be analyzed before and after teachers' participation in a professional development workshop, to identify instructional change consistent with the workshop's goals and purposes. Alternatively, when the logistics of a PD initiative inhibit the collection of pre-workshop data (i.e., summer workshops or other circumstances where researchers do not have access to teachers' classroom prior to the start of the workshop), post-workshop collections of students' work can indicate whether teachers are able to enact instruction consistent with the intent of the PD. Collections of students' work can also be utilized as data on teachers' instructional practices when participants or school districts are not amenable to classroom observations or when a project lacks the resources to conduct classroom observations.

With their focus on tasks and task implementation, the IQA Mathematics Assignment rubrics were ideally suited to assess instructional change in secondary mathematics teachers participating in the Enhancing Secondary Mathematics Teacher Preparation (ESP) project (Boston 2006; Boston and Smith 2009, 2011). The ESP project selected 19 teachers from different school districts (within the same urban-suburban region) to participate in a 2-year initiative focused on the selection and implementation of cognitively challenging tasks in their own classrooms (Year 1) and as the teachers served as mentors to preservice teachers (Year 2). The Year 1 workshop consisted of six full-day sessions, held monthly on Saturdays throughout the 2004–2005 school year. The primary workshop activities included solving cognitively challenging tasks, reflecting on task demands and task implementation, analyzing episodes of instruction (video and written cases) and sets of students' work, and sharing personal successes and challenges in implementing cognitively challenging tasks in their own classrooms.

ESP teachers submitted data collections consisting of five consecutive days of instructional tasks and three sets of students' work (from within the 5-day period) at three points throughout the school year, coinciding with the beginning, middle, and end of their participation in the Year 1 workshop. Teachers were also observed once within each 5-day period. Instructional tasks, lesson observations, and collections of students' work were analyzed using the IQA Mathematics Assignment rubrics for *Potential of the Task* and *Implementation*, consistent with the focus of the ESP professional development initiative. The teachers' expectations rubrics were not utilized in the assessment, since those constructs were not prominent aspects of teachers' professional learning experiences in the ESP workshop. Sixteen ESP teachers submitted complete student-work collections in the fall (resulting in 48 sets of students' work), and 13 teachers submitted complete student-work collections in the spring (39 sets of students' work). Two raters individually scored a subset of 20 % of the student-work sets, reaching exact-point agreement of 85 %; the remaining student-work sets were then scored by an individual rater.

Analysis of students' work indicated significant improvement in teachers' selection and implementation of cognitively demanding mathematical tasks over the course of the workshop. Mann-Whitney tests for nonparametric data indicated that the *Potential of the Task* means increased significantly from 2.63 at the beginning (fall) to 3.03 at the end (spring) of the Year 1 workshop ($z = 2.35$; $p < .01$[one tailed]), and *Implementation* means increased significantly ($z = 2.94$; $p = .002$ [one tailed]) from 2.27 to 2.86. More critically, student-work data also indicated a significant improvement in the teachers' ability to maintain the cognitive demands of high-level tasks. In fall, low-level tasks (i.e., *Potential of the Task* scores of 1 or 2) present 52 % vs. 48 % of the time over high-level tasks (i.e., *Potential of the Task* scores of 3 or 4), but by spring, this ratio had shifted to 77 % vs. 23 % in favor of high-level tasks. Similarly, *Implementation* increased from 25 % (12 out of 48) high-level in fall to 67 % (26 out of 39) high-level in spring. Chi-squared tests indicated that the increases in the number of high-level instructional tasks ($\chi2(2) = 16.18$; $p < .01$) and the number of high-level implementations ($\chi2(2) = 16.11$; $p < .001$) in students' work were significant from fall to spring. These statistics also suggest that fewer high-level tasks in the student-work collection declined during implementation in the spring data collection than in the fall, and a chi-squared test indicated that the change was significant ($\chi2(2) = 7.96$; $p = .02$). In other words, significantly more tasks at a score of 3 or 4 for the *Potential of the Task* were maintained at a score level of 3 or 4 for *Implementation*. This is a valuable finding regarding change in teachers' instructional practices following their participation in the ESP professional development workshop, as students' engagement with cognitively challenging tasks significantly impacts their mathematical learning, and US teachers' inability to maintain high-level cognitive demands was a significant factor differentiating instruction in US classrooms from higher-performing countries on the Third International Mathematics and Science Study (TIMSS) (Stigler and Hiebert 2004). Of course, not all teachers participating in the same PD initiative exhibit the same level of change in instructional practices. The student-work analysis also provided teacher-level data for diagnostic purposes and enabled the ESP researchers to consider "cases" of teachers who did or did not exhibit change in their selection and implementation of cognitively challenging instructional tasks. Interestingly, we were able to identify three distinct groups of teachers according to their level of instructional change across the set of 18 ESP teachers: (1) no change (two teachers) or improving tasks only (three teachers); (2) improving tasks and task implementation (eight teachers); and (3) enhancing preexisting practices in implementing high-level tasks (five teachers). The cases are reported in Boston and Smith (2009, 2011).

Conclusion: Affordances and Constraints of Using the IQA

Using collections of students' work as data on instructional quality is important to mathematics education research for several reasons. Assessing the quality of mathematics instruction continues to increase as an area of public concern. Currently, student achievement tests, value-added measures, and classroom observations serve as the primary sources of data on instructional quality. The use of student achievement data and value-added data as indicators of teacher quality can be misleading, as students' performance on standardized tests can be impacted by numerous factors beyond teachers and teaching (McCaffrey et al. 2003). While classroom observations are ideal for assessing instructional quality, and a number of validated classroom observation instruments exist (in general and specific to mathematics), classroom observations require resources in time, money, and personnel (Borko et al. 2003; Matsumura et al. 2008).

Collections of student work provide an accessible source of data on instructional quality for researchers from small projects to projects working at the scale of large school systems. Collections of student work can supplement classroom observations by providing additional windows into teachers' instructional practices and students' opportunities for learning. Alternatively, they can also serve as data on instructional practices when classroom observations are not feasible due to constraints in time, resources, or district permission. Collections of student work may be considered preferable to classroom observations in that they are less intrusive and less resource intensive. Sampling variability can be minimized by specifying mathematical topics or types of tasks. While this is also true of lesson observations, collections of student work do not require instruction to be altered so that a particular task or mathematical topic is presented on a specific day and time, as would be required for a lesson observation. Finally, collections of students' work filter out distractions that occur throughout a lesson that do not pertain to the constructs being assessed on the rubrics (i.e., warm-up activities, checking homework, classroom discipline).

Certain constraints exist in using collections of students' work to assess instructional quality. Student work does not portray teacher questioning, whole group discussions, or the nature of teacher-student and student-student interactions within the classroom, all of which are important elements of classroom instruction that impact students' opportunities for learning mathematics. The IQA Mathematics Assignment rubrics are designed to assess instructional quality through a specific lens, which may limit their broad application. For example, samples of students' work from a series of tasks designed to improve students facility with specific procedures would not score highly on the IQA, though the instructional activities may be appropriate for the given context and goals (i.e., preparing students to take AP tests). When the IQA is not aligned with the goals of instructional practice in a school or district, professional development initiative, or curriculum implementation, researchers or school administrators may need to find or develop rubrics to assess collections of students' work consistent with their specific goals and outcomes.

In closing, the analysis of collections of students' work can serve as a valuable methodology for mathematics education research. Specific to the use of the IQA Mathematics Assignment rubrics, collections of student work can bridge research and practice by informing instructional improvements or enhancements to professional development workshops by providing descriptive, diagnostic data at the teacher, school, and district level. In current work with colleagues (e.g., Boston et al. 2011; Boston and Steele in press), collections of students' work and the IQA Mathematics Assignment rubrics are being used to enhance school leaders' ability to support ambitious mathematics instruction, aligned to the CCSS-M, in their schools.

References

Boaler, J., & Staples, M. (2008). Creating mathematical futures through an equitable teaching approach: The case of Railside School. *Teachers College Record, 110*, 8–9.

Borko, H., Stecher, B., Alonzo, A., Moncure, S., & McClam, S. (2003). *Artifact packages for measuring instructional practice: A pilot study* (CSE Technical Report No. 615). Los Angeles: University of California, National Center for Research on Evaluation, Standards, and Student Testing (CRESST).

Boston, M. D. (2006). Developing secondary mathematics teachers' knowledge of and capacity of implement instructional tasks with high-level cognitive demands (Doctoral dissertation, University of Pittsburgh). *Dissertation Abstracts International* (Publication No. AAT 3223943).

Boston, M. D. (2008). *Using student work to identify meaningful differences in students' opportunities to learn mathematics*. Paper presented at the annual meeting of the American Association of Colleges for Teacher Education, New Orleans, LA.

Boston, M. D. (2012). Assessing the quality mathematics instruction. *Elementary School Journal, 113*, 76–104.

Boston, M. D., & Smith, M. S. (2009). Transforming secondary mathematics teaching: Increasing the cognitive demands of instructional tasks used in teachers' classrooms. *Journal for Research in Mathematics Education, 40*, 119–156.

Boston, M. D., & Smith, M. S. (2011). A 'task-centric approach' to professional development: Enhancing and sustaining mathematics teachers' ability to implement cognitively challenging mathematical tasks. *ZDM: International Journal of Mathematics Teacher Education, 43*, 965–977. doi:10.1007/s11858-011-0353-2.

Boston, M. D., & Steele, M. S. (in press). Analyzing students' work to reflect on instruction: The Instructional Quality Assessment as a tool for instructional leaders. Accepted by *National Council of Supervisors of Mathematics Journal of Mathematics Education Leadership*, December 2012.

Boston, M., & Wolf, M. K. (2006). *Assessing academic rigor in mathematics instruction: The development of Instructional Quality Assessment toolkit* (CSE Report #672). Los Angeles: University of California, National Center for Research on Evaluation, Standards, and Student Testing (CRESST).

Boston, M. D., Gibbons, L., & Henrick, E. (2011). *Using classroom observation instruments to improve principal's capacity as instructional leaders in mathematics*. Paper presentation at the annual meeting of the American Education Research Association, New Orleans, LA.

Clare, L. (2000). *Using teachers' assignments as an indicator of classroom practice* (CSE Report #532). Los Angeles: University of California, National Center for Research on Evaluation, Standards, and Student Testing (CRESST).

Clare, L., & Aschbacher, P. (2001). Exploring the technical quality of using assignments and student work as indicators of classroom practice. *Educational Assessment, 7*, 39–59.

Cobb, P., Boufi, A., McClain, K., & Whitenack, J. (1997). Reflective discourse and collective reflection. *Journal for Research in Mathematics Education, 28*, 258–277.

Cobb, P., Zhao, Q., & Dean, C. (2009). Conducting design experiments to support teachers' learning: A reflection from the field. *Journal of the Learning Sciences, 18*, 165–199.

Common Core State Standards Initiative. (2011). *Common Core State Standards in Mathematics*. Retrieved February 15, 2013, from http://www.corestandards.org/Math

Henningsen, M., & Stein, M. K. (1997). Mathematical tasks and student cognition: Classroom-based factors that support and inhibit high-level mathematical thinking and reasoning. *Journal for Research in Mathematics Education, 28*, 524–549.

Hufford-Ackles, K., Fuson, K., & Sherin, M. G. (2004). Describing levels and components of a math-talk learning community. *Journal for Research in Mathematics Education, 35*(2), 81–116.

Kazemi, E., & Franke, M. L. (2004). Teacher learning in mathematics: Using student work to promote collective inquiry. *Journal of Mathematics Teacher Education, 7*, 203–235.

Matsumura, L. C. (2003). *Teachers' assignments and student work: Opening a window on classroom practice* (CSE Technical Report No. 602). Los Angeles: University of California, National Center for Research on Evaluation, Standards, and Student Testing (CRESST).

Matsumura, L. C., & Boston, M. (2006). *Measuring the quality of mathematics instruction in urban elementary and middle schools*. Paper presented at the annual meeting of the American Education Research Association, San Francisco, CA.

Matsumura, L. C., Garnier, H., Pascal, J., & Valdés, R. (2002). Measuring instructional quality in accountability systems: Classroom assignments and student achievement. *Educational Assessment, 8*, 207–229.

Matsumura, L. C., Garnier, H., Slater, S. C., & Boston, M. D. (2008). Toward measuring instructional interactions "at-scale". *Educational Assessment, 13*, 267–300.

McCaffrey, D. F., Lockwood, J. R., Koretz, D. M., & Hamilton, L. S. (2003). *Evaluating value-added models for teacher accountability* (MG-158-EDU). Santa Monica: RAND.

National Council of Teachers of Mathematics. (2000). *Principles and standards for school mathematics*. Reston: Author.

Pianta, R. C., & Hamre, B. K. (2009). Conceptualization, measurement, and improvement of classroom processes: Standardized observations can leverage capacity. *Educational Researcher, 38*, 109–119.

Smith, M. S. (2001). *Practice-based professional development for teachers of mathematics*. Reston: NCTM.

Steele, M. S., & Boston, M. D. (2012). *Using student work as a reflection on instruction*. Paper presentation at the research pre-session of the National Council of Teachers of Mathematics Annual Meeting, Philadelphia, PA.

Stein, M. K., & Coburn, C. (2007). *Architectures for learning: A comparative analysis of two urban school districts*. Seattle: University of Washington, Center for the Study of Teaching and Policy.

Stein, M. K., & Lane, S. (1996). Instructional tasks and the development of student capacity to think and reason: An analysis of the relationship between teaching and learning in a reform mathematics project. *Educational Research and Evaluation, 2*, 50–80.

Stein, M. K., & Matsumura, L. C. (2008). Measuring instruction for teacher learning. In D. Gitomer (Ed.), *Measurement issues and the assessment of teacher quality* (pp. 179–205). Thousand Oaks: Sage Publications.

Stein, M. K., Grover, B., & Henningsen, M. (1996). Building student capacity for mathematical thinking and reasoning: An analysis of mathematical tasks used in reform classrooms. *American Educational Research Journal, 33*, 455–488.

Stein, M. K., Smith, M. S., Henningsen, M., & Silver, E. A. (2009). *Implementing standards-based mathematics instruction: A casebook for professional development* (2nd ed.). New York: Teachers College Press.

Stigler, J. W., & Hiebert, J. (2004). Improving mathematics teaching. *Educational Leadership, 61*, 12–16.

Tarr, J. E., Reys, R. E., Reys, B. J., Chavez, O., Shih, J., & Osterlind, S. (2008). The impact of middle grades mathematics curricula on student achievement and the classroom learning environment. *Journal for Research in Mathematics Education, 39*, 247–280.

Example-Generation as Indicator and Catalyst of Mathematical and Pedagogical Understandings

Orit Zaslavsky and Iris Zodik

Abstract This chapter examines the activities of example-generation and example-verification from both the teaching and learning perspectives. We closely examine how engaging learners in generating and verifying examples of a particular mathematical concept as a group activity serves both as an indicator of learners' understandings and a catalyst for enhancing their understanding and expanding their example space that is associated with the particular concept. We present two cases that illustrate how the mathematics instruction may look when classroom activities and discussions build on example-generation and example-verification – the first case focuses on the concept of an irrational number and the second on the notion of a periodic function. The learners in these cases are in-service secondary mathematics teachers (MTLs), and the teacher is a mathematics teacher educator (MTE). We show how this kind of learning environment lends itself naturally to genuine opportunities for learners to engage in meaningful mathematics, to share and challenge their thinking, and to sense the need for unpacking mathematical subtleties regarding definitions and ideas. For practicing and prospective mathematics teachers, engaging in such activity and experiencing the potential learning opportunity that it offers is also likely to convince them to implement this approach in their classrooms.

Keywords Example-generation • Example-verification • Example space • Concept image • Concept definition • Professional development • Irrational numbers • Periodic functions

O. Zaslavsky (✉)
New York University, 2 Washington Square Village, Apt. 9B,
New York, NY 10012, USA

Technion – Israel Institute of Technology, Technion City, Haifa 32000, Israel
e-mail: oritrath@gmail.com

I. Zodik
Technion – Israel Institute of Technology, 11 HaEshel Street,
P.O.B. 12864 Nesher 36860, Israel
e-mail: iris.zodik@gmail.com

Y. Li et al. (eds.), *Transforming Mathematics Instruction: Multiple Approaches and Practices*, Advances in Mathematics Education, DOI 10.1007/978-3-319-04993-9_28,
© Springer International Publishing Switzerland 2014

The significant role of examples in learning and teaching mathematics stems from the central role that examples play in mathematics and mathematical thinking. Examples are an integral part of mathematics and a critical element of expert knowledge (Rissland 1978). In particular, examples are essential for generalization, abstraction, analogical reasoning, and proof. In addition to the central role examples play in mathematics, examples constitute a fundamental part of a good explanation, which is considered a building block for good teaching (Leinhardt 2001). According to Leinhardt (2001, p. 347), "For learning to occur, several examples are needed, not just one; the examples need to encapsulate a range of critical features; and examples need to be unpacked, with the features that make them an example clearly identified."

The task of choosing an example to illustrate a mathematical idea is a nontrivial one (Zaslavsky 2008, 2010). The choice of an example for teaching is often a trade-off between one limitation and another. Choosing examples for teaching mathematics entails many complex and even competing considerations, some of which can be made in advance and others only come up during the actual teaching (Zodik and Zaslavsky 2008, 2009).

The choice of examples presents the teacher with a challenging responsibility, especially since the specific choice and treatment of examples may facilitate or hinder learning (Zaslavsky and Zodik 2007). The knowledge teachers need for meeting this challenge by judiciously constructing and selecting mathematical examples is a special kind of knowledge. It can be seen as core knowledge needed for teaching mathematics. In addition, engaging in generating or choosing instructional examples can be a driving force for enhancing teachers' knowledge (Zodik and Zaslavsky 2009). This process builds on and facilitates teachers' knowledge of pedagogy, mathematics, and student epistemology. In Ball et al.'s (2008) terms, it encompasses knowledge of content and students and knowledge of content and teaching, as well as "pure" content knowledge unique to the work of teaching.

As mentioned above, teachers' specific choices of examples shape students' learning. Thus, by examining the quality of the instructional examples that a teacher uses, we may learn much about the quality of the mathematics classroom instruction. Moreover, teachers' use of examples often leads to learning opportunities for themselves through which they gain pedagogical and/or mathematical insights (Zodik and Zaslavsky 2009).

In examining the quality of instructional examples, there are two main attributes that make an example pedagogically useful according to Bills et al. (2006). First, an example should be "transparent" to the learner, that is, it should be relatively easy to direct the learner's attention to the features that make it exemplary. It should also foster generalization, that is, it should highlight the critical features of an example of the illustrated case and at the same time point to its arbitrary and changeable features.

This notion of transparency is consistent with Mason and Pimm's (1984) notion of generic examples that are transparent to the general case, allowing one to see the general through the particular, and with Peled and Zaslavsky's (1997) discussion of the explanatory nature of examples. Examples with some or all of these qualities have the potential to serve as a reference or model example (Rissland 1978), with which one can reason in other related situations and can be helpful in clarifying and resolving mathematical subtleties. Generally, an example should be examined in context. Any example carries some attributes that are intended to be exemplified and others that are irrelevant. Skemp (1987) refers to the irrelevant features of an example as its "noise," while Rissland (1991) suggests that "one can view an example as a set of facts or features viewed through a certain lens" (p. 190).

We hereby examine the activity of example-generation and example-verification from both teaching and learning perspectives (which are tightly related). By example-verification we refer to the act of examining whether and justifying why a certain example satisfies its intended requirements (e.g., the definition of the exemplified concept). In this process it is possible that the learners articulate certain criteria that are useful in the verification stage. From a teaching perspective, we look at a mathematics teacher educator's (MTE, mathematics teacher educator) example use in professional development workshops for in-service secondary mathematics teachers. In this context, the participants of these workshops are mathematics teachers who are learners of both mathematics and pedagogy (MTL, mathematics teacher as learner). The MTE's example use includes the following (interconnected) instructional moves: (1) the opportunities that the MTE offers the learners to engage in example-generation and example-based reasoning; (2) specific examples that the MTE brings in order to illustrate or expand a mathematical concept or idea; and (3) ways in which the MTE responds to the participants' utterances and actions during the workshop, in order to help them better understand some mathematical subtleties (in particular utterances and actions that reflect a misconception or limited concept image or example space). From a learning perspective, we examine example-generation and example-verification by MTLs, the participants of these workshops, and how these shape their mathematical and pedagogical understandings.

According to Bills et al. (2006), the collection of examples to which an individual has access at any moment and the richness of interconnection between those examples constitute his or her accessible example space. A personal example space is defined as what is accessible in response to a particular situation and to particular prompts and propensities. Example spaces are not just lists, but have internal idiosyncratic structure in terms of how the members and classes in the space are interrelated. Example spaces can be explored or extended by searching for peculiar examples as doorways to new classes or by being given further constraints in order to focus on particular characteristics of examples. In our work, we consider an example space as the collection of examples one associates with a particular concept at a particular time or context. According to Mason and Goldenberg (2008), what determines the use of a concept is the example space one associates with it. This notion is closely related to Vinner and Tall's idea of concept image (Vinner 1983; Tall and Vinner 1981). Vinner and Tall use the term concept image to describe the total cognitive structure that is associated with a particular concept, which includes all the mental pictures and associated properties and processes. "It is built up over the years through experiences of all kinds, changing as the individual meets new stimuli and matures... Different stimuli can activate different parts of the concept image, developing them in a way which need not make a coherent whole" (Tall and Vinner 1981, p. 152). Example spaces also are dynamic and evolving. Thus, in orchestrating learning it is important that the teacher identifies (limited) concept images and prototypical views of certain concepts, which the learners hold, and facilitates the expansion beyond "more of the same" examples. According to Mason and Goldenberg (2008), some parts of an example space may be more accessible at a given time than others. The less accessible parts await an appropriate trigger to be used (Watson and Mason 2005). Sometimes one has a general sense of examples without the specifics of an example, while at other times some specific examples come to mind readily. In a group activity or discussion, an example suggested by one member may trigger access to a further class of examples for other members. When learners compare their examples, they often extend and enrich their example space. Moreover, once a connection is made, it is strengthened and more likely to come to mind in the future (Mason and Goldenberg 2008).

Learners' example spaces play a major role in what sense they can make of the tasks they are offered, the activities they engage in, and how they interpret what the teacher says and does. Zaslavsky and Peled (1996) point to the possible effects of limited example spaces that teachers hold with respect to a binary operation on their ability to generate examples of binary operations that are commutative but not associative or vice versa. Watson and Mason (2005) regard the notion of a personal example space as a tool for helping learners and teachers become more aware of the potential and limitations of experience with examples. Experiencing extensions of one's example space (if sensitively guided) contributes to flexibility of thinking and empowers the appreciation and adoption of new concepts.

In our work, we closely examine how engaging learners in generating and verifying examples of a particular mathematical concept during a group activity serves both as an indicator of learners' understandings as well as a catalyst for enhancing their understanding and expanding their example space associated with the particular concept. This type of activity can be seen as a rich open-ended task (Hazzan and Zazkis 1999; Zaslavsky 1995), for which a teacher needs to be able to act in the moment (Mason and Spence 1999). This implies that it is likely to create a learning opportunity not only for the learners but also for the teacher. Moreover, on the one hand the demands on the teacher require a special kind of knowledge, and on the other hand these demands may lead to the expansion of this knowledge.

It follows that examples serve both as *indicators* of and *catalysts* for teaching and learning. These interconnected roles that can be triggered by learners' generated examples are presented in Fig. 1. Note that in this framework we include example-verification as part of the act of example-generation, although the verification part can be addressed separately and applied also for examples that are given without engaging in the generation stage. The act of example-verification is closely connected to Vinner and Tall's notion of concept definition. Mostly, the verification requires checking whether the example satisfies the concept definition – whether it is the mathematical agreed upon definition or the definition the individual holds and operates with.

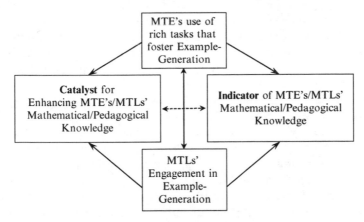

Fig. 1 A framework for examining the potential of rich tasks that foster example-generation as indicators and catalysts

The above framework suggests that mathematical and pedagogical knowledge can both be reflected and enhanced by (well designed) processes of example-generation and example-verification (e.g., Zaslavsky and Peled 1996); these processes may reveal (mis)conceptions, limitations/strengths in accessing appropriate examples, the scope of examples associated with a particular concept, the degree of fluency in giving an appropriate example, and the ability to reason with examples and verify that an example satisfies the conditions it should. At the same time, these processes may enhance the mathematical and pedagogical example spaces teachers and learners hold.

In this chapter, we focus on two rich cases that illustrate how mathematics instruction may look, when classroom activities and discussions include example-generation and example-based reasoning. We illustrate how this kind of learning environment lends itself naturally to genuine opportunities for learners to engage in meaningful mathematics, to share and challenge their thinking, and to sense the need for unpacking mathematical subtleties regarding definitions and ideas. This approach satisfies the necessity principle and raises an intellectual need to delve deeper into and beyond existing knowledge (Harel 2013). For practicing and prospective mathematics teachers, engaging in such activity and experiencing the potential learning opportunity that it offers is also likely to convince them to implement this approach in their classrooms.

Design Considerations for Eliciting Learners' Example-Generation and Example-Verification Reasoning

As described earlier, the teacher in our study was an MTE (the first author of this chapter) who worked with in-service secondary mathematics teachers (MTLs). Thus, the learners in this group were practicing secondary mathematics teachers.

The goals for the workshops were twofold: from a pedagogical viewpoint, the goal was to facilitate the participants' appreciation of the act of generating and verifying examples in the course of learning mathematics; from a mathematical viewpoint, the goal was to challenge the participants' existing example spaces (or concept images) with respect to some mathematical concepts; the intention was to enhance their understandings and expand their example spaces beyond prototypical and familiar/common instances to include more sophisticated examples. These two goals are interrelated, as by experiencing in person how one expands his or her example space through this activity, it is likely that one will attribute this growth to the activity and the learning environment and gain appreciation of this type of activity.

We used the generic task of "Give an example of ..., and another one ..., and now another one, different from the previous ones ..." Note that a version of this type of task appears in several publications (e.g., Hazzan and Zazkis 1999; Mason and Goldenberg 2008; Watson and Shipman 2008). In this type of task, the learner is required to give an appropriate example of a given mathematical concept spontaneously, one by one, while making notable variations from one example to the other. By asking for "notable variations," we expect the learner to move beyond repetition of similar and closely related examples. The task calls for mathematical fluency and for moving from common and familiar (often prototypical) examples to more sophisticated ones. It also requires constant comparisons between similarities and differences that facilitate mathematical connections between objects, which are considered an indication of understanding (NCTM 2000). For (in-service) teachers this kind of task may be seen as a simulation of real classroom situations that call for teachers' example-generation. It also provides the teachers with a less familiar type of learning experience that may encourage them to implement with their own students.

The choice of the above generic task was just the first stage. The second stage was to choose mathematical concepts for this task. We considered concepts like an irrational number, a trapezoid, a periodic function, an odd function, and a pair of congruent triangles. For each concept we anticipated some mathematical and pedagogical insights that the MTLs might gain through this activity. For example, with respect to an irrational number, we hoped to expand beyond the common view that an irrational number is either a root of a prime number (e.g., $\sqrt{5}$) or a transcendental number (e.g., π). For a periodic function, we hoped to expand beyond the common view that periodic functions are solely or mostly trigonometric functions (Van Dormolen and Zaslavsky 2003). We were aware that this kind of task may provoke additional mathematical subtleties and unforeseen claims and ideas raised by the learners.

In this chapter, we focus on two (rich) cases that convey the learning opportunities that this type of task may provide. We argue that this task may equally be implemented with practicing/prospective mathematics teachers (MTLs) as well as with K-12 students.

Each session began by asking for a teacher (MTL) to volunteer to take a leading role in this activity. The volunteer was asked to give an example of a certain concept, and then another one different than the previous, and so on. Case 1 focused on the notion of an irrational number, while Case 2 on a periodic function. The rest of the group were asked to verify each example that was proposed by the volunteering teacher, that is, to check whether it was indeed an example of the concept in question (i.e., satisfies its definition), or to take part in proposing different examples in the event that the volunteer ran out of examples.

Overview of Two Cases

Below, we provide accounts of the two cases that illustrate how the activity of generating examples can be both an indicator of the learners' understandings of irrational numbers and periodic functions and a catalyst for refining and crystallizing some understandings. We include excerpts that convey the thought processes involved in the example-generation and example-verification activities and discussions that accompanied these activities.

For each case, we examined the actual examples that were suggested by the MTLs, the order in which they were generated, and the time that elapsed between one generated example and the next. The time intervals indicate the level of fluency in generating new examples, which reflects the learner's example space and concept image. (We use the notions of concept image and example space interchangeably). We also looked at the discussions that were orchestrated by the MTE in response to MTLs' examples and tried to capture the kinds of understandings that were enhanced. Similar to Zaslavsky and Shir (2005) and Zodik and Zaslavsky (2007), we traced MTLs' shifts in acceptance or rejection of examples, as indication of their learning. These discussions, triggered by MTLs' example-generation, were regarded as learning events.

For Case 1, there were two main events that we call *learning events* (LE) that were evoked by certain examples. Both were triggered by two different incorrect examples. These two LEs (LE-1.1 and LE-1.2) addressed disagreements and uncertainty in the group, helped move beyond prototypical examples, and led to unpacking some mathematical subtleties related to differences between an acceptable example and an unacceptable one. For Case 2 there were three main learning events (LE-2.1, LE-2.2, and LE-2.3) that were triggered by shifts from a set of familiar/accessible examples to less familiar and more sophisticated ones.

Case 1: Generating Examples of an Irrational Number

As mentioned above, we chose the concept of an irrational number, in order to examine the concept images teachers held and to push them to expand their example spaces of irrational numbers. We relied on our own personal experiences as well as the experiences of colleagues. More specifically, as Mason and Goldenberg (2008) claim, "most learners think first of $\sqrt{2}$ or π. If there is no further discussion, these may constitute their accessed example space (accessed at that time, even though

Table 1 The sequence of examples generated by teachers for an irrational number

Part 1

Example no.	1	2	3	4	5	6	LE-1.1
The example	$\sqrt{2}$	$\sqrt[3]{5}$	π	$\sqrt[3]{3}$	e	$0.\dot{3}$	Addressing a misconception
							Moving beyond prototypical examples
Time (in seconds)	2	2	1	1	14	8	900 (15 min.)

Part 2

Example no.	7	8	LE-1.2
The example	sin 64°	$\log(x)$	Back to infinite decimals and beyond repeating decimals
Time (in seconds)	16	39	180 (3 min.)

Note: LE stands for a learning event. Time was measured between each two consecutive examples, except for examples 1 and 7. For example 1, the time was measured from the moment they were asked to give an example of an irrational number until they came up with the first one; for example 7, the time was measured from the moment they were asked again, after LE-1.1, to give another example of an irrational number till they came up with one

other examples may be accessible at other times)" (p. 186, ibid.). As shown in Table 1, indeed, these two examples were included in the initial set of examples that were offered.

The task called not only for example-generation but also for example-verification, i.e., checking that a suggested number is indeed irrational. The process of verification calls for an examination of the definition of an irrational number. As indicated in the flow and utterances of Case 1, relying on the definition of an irrational number in order to verify that a number is irrational was particular challenging, as it requires showing that a number *cannot* be represented as a quotient of two integers (the denominator of which is nonzero). Thus, logically, it is much easier to show that a number is rational than that it is irrational. Even so, showing that $0.3\dot{3}$ is a rational number was a nontrivial task for the MTLs.

Table 1 presents the examples in the order that they were given.

As shown in the above Table 1, after giving the most accessible examples rather quickly/automatically, generating a less familiar example was more difficult and required more time. In terms of indication of the understanding of the learner, there were two instances in which the examples that were given did not satisfy the necessary conditions (for a number to be an irrational number): $0.3\dot{3}$ and $\log(x)$. These incorrect examples led to two learning events, LE-1.1 and LE-1.2.

LE-1.1

Prior to LE-1.1 the examples that were suggested were closely related to those anticipated by Mason and Goldenberg (2008). As shown in Table 1, these examples were suggested rather fluently (by one of the MTLs), taking from 1 to 14 s. For each example, the rest of the group members had to verify that it is indeed an irrational number. For the first five examples, this was not an issue, as there appeared to be a shared knowledge that roots of a prime number and transcendental numbers are always irrational numbers. Thus, there was no need to rely on a formal definition. However, $0.33\dot{3}$, the sixth example suggested by Hassan, the MTL, reflected a misconception of his. In response, Noa, another MTL, said that $0.33\dot{3}$ is not irrational because $0.33\dot{3} = \frac{1}{3}$. This caused disagreement between the group members: some (incorrectly) agreed with Hassan that it was irrational, some thought like Noa that it was rational, and some were indecisive. In terms of Zaslavsky (2005), this was an authentic conflict that created uncertainty and evoked discussion that constituted a meaningful learning event; the uncertainty called for example-verification. It appeared that the participants knew the definition of an irrational number, but weren't sure how to apply it to $0.33\dot{3}$, namely, whether or not $0.33\dot{3} = \frac{1}{3}$. Note that this was a spontaneous event that the MTE did not anticipate; it set the grounds for addressing the question of whether repeating decimals are always rational numbers. The following is an excerpt of the discussion.

Hassan: $0.33\dot{3}$ cannot be precisely $\frac{1}{3}$ because $\frac{1}{3}$ is something else; it is one over three but not $0.33\dot{3}$.

MTE: Does anyone think differently?

Ella: I recall teaching this topic to my 9th grade students several years ago. I taught them a procedure that appeared in the textbook, which transformed $0.33\dot{3}$ back to a proper fraction, $\frac{1}{3}$.

MTE: Did you actually write the equal sign?

Ella: Yes. We also showed that $0.499\dot{9} = \frac{1}{2}$ and that $0.99\dot{9} = 1$.

Noa: $0.99\dot{9}$ is not 1 because it does not come from a fraction, but $0.33\dot{3}$ is equal to $\frac{1}{3}$.

Without specifying the procedure, Ella knew it was possible to transform $0.33\dot{3}$ into a proper fraction $\left(\frac{1}{3}\right)$. Thus, she was convinced that the two numbers, $0.33\dot{3}$ and $\frac{1}{3}$, were equal. Note that the procedure that Ella referred to is probably the common procedure of multiplying the number $0.33\dot{3}$ by 10 and then subtracting $0.33\dot{3}$ from the product $3.33\dot{3}$. This procedure applies to $0.499\dot{9}$ as well as to $0.99\dot{9}$.

Noa made the distinction between the two cases; she agreed that $0.33\dot{3} = \frac{1}{3}$, but pointed out that the related case of $0.99\dot{9}$ differed from the previous one, as in her mind $0.99\dot{9} \neq 1$. To justify this contradicting statement, she explained that the criterion for determining whether a repeating decimal is rational or not is by checking whether it could be obtained as a result of the long division algorithm. Thus, according to Noa, $0.33\dot{3} = \frac{1}{3}$ because $0.33\dot{3}$ is a result of dividing 1 into 3, while $0.99\dot{9} \neq 1$ because $0.99\dot{9}$ cannot be obtained by dividing two integers.

Rachel articulated a different conflict stemming from Noa's assertion, by showing that if we agree that $0.33\dot{3} = \frac{1}{3}$, then it follows that $0.66\dot{6} = \frac{2}{3}$; then on the one hand, $\frac{1}{3} + \frac{2}{3} = 1$; yet on the other hand, $0.33\dot{3} + 0.66\dot{6} = 0.99\dot{9}$; so if $0.99\dot{9} \neq 1$, then we get a contradiction. Rachel concluded by saying that this means that $0.33\dot{3} \neq \frac{1}{3}$ (see Fig. 2).

Fig. 2 Case 1, Rachel's
conflict

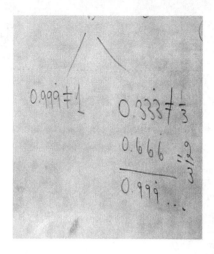

At this point Benny felt he needed to remind the group what the formal definition of a rational number is. In response, Ilan questioned the definition, by arguing that on the one hand we know that π is irrational; however, $\pi = \dfrac{22}{7}$. This appeared to him as a contradiction. To resolve this conflict, Hanna made the distinction between an approximation and an equality: "π is not exactly $\dfrac{22}{7}$ although we use this fraction to calculate (an approximation of) π, while $\dfrac{1}{3}$ is exactly $0.33\dot{3}$."

In response to the MTE's probe for more views on these issues, Hassan suggested looking at $0.33\dot{3}$ as the sum of a converging geometric sequence $\left(\dfrac{3}{10} + \dfrac{3}{10^2} + \dfrac{3}{10^3} + \cdots \right)$. Yet, looking at it this way did not seem to help him decide whether or not $0.33\dot{3} = \dfrac{1}{3}$. He was missing the idea that this infinite sum is defined as the limit of the geometric series, and it can be shown that this limit is exactly $\dfrac{1}{3}$.

This event ended with the MTE inviting them to continue contemplating the issues that were raised in this session over the next week and to try resolving some of the conflicts they had encountered. As an additional tool to compare two numbers, she suggested considering the difference between the two numbers; that is, in order to compare the numbers a and b, we can look at the difference a-b. In the meeting on the following week, time was devoted to resolve the issue of whether any repeating decimal is a rational number and why $0.99\dot{9} = 1$.

At the end of this part, the MTE returned to the main task and asked for additional examples of irrational numbers. The first reaction by Reli was "let's take *sinus*." It appeared that she was trying to search in a totally different domain for an example that would be different than the previous ones. Following a long silence, the MTE asked whether she thought sin 30° would be an appropriate example. This was immediately rejected by several participants, who acknowledged that it is a rational number, $\dfrac{1}{2}$.

Thus, Reli suggested the next example (Example 7, sin 64°). Everyone seemed to agree that this was an irrational number, as they recalled that with the formulae for the sine of the sum and difference of angle measures, they could calculate the values of the sine function, where there are only very few integer angle measures for which the sine value is rational, e.g., $\sin 0°, \sin 30°, \sin 90°, \sin 150°$. Inspired by Reli's shift to trigonometric functions, Noa suggested looking at the logarithm function $\log(x)$. Here too they recalled that only specific values are rational (e.g., for values of x that are rational powers of 10) and realized that without specifying the value of x in $\log(x)$, it is not an example at all. Noa's example triggered the next learning event.

LE-1.2

The formal definition of an irrational number does not convey the full scope of the irrational number concept. One of the MTE's goals was to facilitate a concept image that includes any infinite non-repeating decimal number as an irrational number (while accepting any repeating decimal as a rational number). Even when it was established that an infinite non-repeating decimal number is irratio-nal, the question of how to construct an example of such a number remained open. None of the MTLs was able to suggest one (we did get such an example in a similar workshop where leading secondary mathematics teachers participated). Thus, at this stage the MTE put forth the following example for discussion: 0.10110111011110... (the MTE explained that this pattern of increasing the number of 1 s between two 0 s continues indefinitely). Clearly, this (type of) example was not part of the MTLs' example spaces. This too created a learning opportunity facilitated by the MTE, through which the example spaces of the learners gradually expanded.

One issue that came up was the limitation of representing a non-repeating infinite decimal. Another one was the connection between knowing that any rational number can be represented as either a repeating decimal or a finite one and knowing that any non-repeating decimal must be irrational. The big question MTLs raised was "how can we be sure whether a number is an irrational number?" These were questions that they admitted that they had not been thinking of before. The issues discussed were new to them. Some felt that having examined the previous example (0.10110111011110...) opened to them a whole collection of non-repeating decimals that they could construct. This was a manifestation of the expansion of their example spaces.

Case 2: Generating Examples of a Periodic Function

Similar to our considerations for irrational numbers, we chose the concept of a periodic function in order to examine the current concept images teachers held and push them to expand their example spaces associated with periodicity (Shama 1998). Van Dormolen and Zaslavsky (2003) discuss the meta-concept of a mathematical definition and illustrate it with the notion of a periodic function. They suggest the following pseudo-definition (p. 92, ibid. see Fig. 3).

A periodic function is a function that can be constructed in the following way: divide the x-axis into equal-length segments, such as, for example, ... , [−39,−26], [−26,−13], [−13, 0], [0, 13], [13, 26], [26, 39], ... Take any of these segments, no matter which one, and define a function on it, no matter how (e.g., as in Fig. 1).

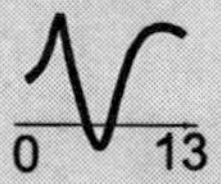

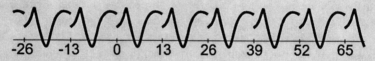

Fig. 1

Then define another function on the whole x-axis, such that on each segment it behaves in the same way as the first function (as in Fig. 2).

Fig. 2

Then the new function is a periodic function. Its values are repeated regularly.

Fig. 3 A constructive "definition" of a periodic function, taken from Van Dormolen and Zaslavsky (2003)

Although the above definition is not a valid mathematical definition, it is a useful "definition" from a pedagogical standpoint. This type of (often overlooked) example construction conveys the essence of the notion of a periodic function. Inspired by this work, it appeared that the notion of a periodic function would lend itself well to generating and verifying examples; it was anticipated that the MTLs would mainly think of trigonometric functions as examples of periodic functions; thus, there would be many learning opportunities to expand their example spaces.

Table 2 presents the examples of periodic functions in the order that they were given.

Table 2 conveys the turning points in how the participants viewed a periodic function. For this task, Benny was the MTL who volunteered to give a range of examples of a periodic function. After giving 3 familiar, rather prototypical, and highly accessible examples (examples 1, 2, and 3 in Table 2), all drawn from the domain of trigonometric functions, Benny ran out of examples. This led to LE-2.1, in which Reli took a leading role by suggesting moving from the domain of trigonometric functions to special kinds of sequences. Based on Reli's idea, the group members helped her construct a specific example. This learning event triggered the first shift from regarding periodic functions as mostly (or even solely) combinations of trigonometric functions to

Table 2 The sequence of examples generated by teachers for a periodic function

Part 1

Example no.	1	2	3	LE-2.1
The example	$f(x) = \sin(x)$	$f(x) = \cos(x)$	$f(x) = \sin(x) \cdot \cos(x)$	Moving beyond Trig, to *Example 4* $1, -1, 1, -1, \ldots$
Time (in seconds)	1	1		360 (6 min.)

Part 2

Example no.	5	6	LE-2.2
The example	$-1, 1, -1, 1, \ldots$	$f(x) = \begin{cases} 2, & \text{when } x \text{ is even} \\ 3, & \text{when } x \text{ is odd} \end{cases}$	What does it mean to be "different"? Entering graphs into the discussion
Time (in seconds)	10	13	188 (appx. 3 min.)

Part 3

Example no.	7	8 and 9	LE-2.3
The example	$f(x) = x - [x]$	$f(x) = \dfrac{[x]}{x}$ $f(x) = \dfrac{x}{[x]}$	How can we be sure the examples satisfy the definition? Using alternative representations to answer this question
Time (in seconds)	23	3	720 (12 min.)

Note: LE stands for a learning event. Example 4 was jointly constructed in the course of LE-2.1. Time was measured between each two consecutive examples, except for examples 1, 5, 7, and 8. For example 1, the time was measured from the moment they were asked to give an example of a periodic function until they came up with the first one; for example 5, the time was measured from the moment they were asked again, after LE-2.1, to give another example of a periodic function till they came up with one; for example 7, the time was measured from the moment they were asked again, after LE-2.2, to give another example of a periodic function till they came up with one. For example 8, the time was measured from the moment they were asked again, after LE-2.3, to give another example of a periodic function till they came up with one including as periodic functions also certain non-trigonometric functions. Example 4 (which was constructed at this stage) (LE-2.1) can be seen as a breakthrough in participants' views on periodic functions. It led to the construction of examples 5 and 6, by Hassan and Mary, respectively. These examples triggered the next learning event (LE-2.2), as several participants, including Hanna, questioned the extent to which examples 4, 5, and 6 are essentially different. Following the discussions in LE-2.2, a more sophisticated example emerged (example 7), involving a floor function (by Hassan). This example led to a long discussion including group work surrounding ways to verify that example 7 is indeed a periodic function. Some verified this based on the symbolic representation of the function and some used its graphical representation. These different approaches evoked a comparison between these representations and set the grounds for the originally intended approach described in Van Dormolen and Zaslavsky (2003), as cited earlier. Interestingly, while periodicity lends itself naturally to visual representations, this idea did not occur spontaneously. However, at a certain point, the MTE suggested approaching the examples of a periodic function graphically (in the spirit of Van Dormolen and Zaslavsky 2003).

We now turn to the three learning events, LE-2.1, LE-2.2, and LE-2.3.

LE-2.1

After establishing that the familiar trigonometric functions, as well as certain combinations of them (in this case, a product of two trigonometric functions), are also periodic functions, Reli volunteered to continue Benny's role and shared her considerations with the entire group. It took some iterations until she was able to come up with a specific example that followed her reasoning. This discussion helped the group to shift to a less familiar type of periodic function – Example 4 (see Fig. 5).

Reli: I am thinking of a geometric sequence, something discrete. not continuous.
MTE: Why not continuous?
Reli: I'm looking for a collection of points.
MTE: Why?
Reli: Because a sequence is not continuous.
MTE: OK. So indeed a geometric sequence is a discrete function. But where is the period? Can anyone help Reli find a geometric sequence that is periodic?
Hassan: $1, -1, 1, -1, \ldots$
Dave: Oh, this reminds me of a sine.
Noa: How can we express this symbolically? That is, with a formula?
Hanna: $a = 1, q = -1$.
MTE: So what is the power of -1?
Hassan: $2n - 1$
MTE: Does everyone agree?
Galit: $2n + 1$
MTE: Does everyone agree?
Ella: $n + 1$

Fig. 4 Case 2, Example 4 on
the white board at the end of
LE-2.1

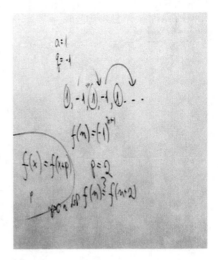

MTE: Does everyone agree?

[Several MTLs say yes; no one expresses disagreement]

MTE: OK, so we have $f(n)=a_n=(-1)^{n+1}$, for any natural number n. Now, what is the period?

Hanna: What do you mean by the period?

MTE: A number p that satisfies $f(x)=f(x+p)$, for any value of x in the domain of f. The main idea is that if we add the period to x we will reach "the same place," that is, the function will have the same value.

Hassan: So the period is 2 (see Fig. 4).

MTE: Look how long it took us to jointly construct and verify an example that was not part of your "toolbox," according to Reli's guidelines. The only examples that were readily accessible to all of you were the trigonometric ones.

LE-2.2

Following Example 4 (i.e., $f(n)=(-1)^{n+1}$), Hassan suggested Example 5, and Mary suggested Example 6. As a consequence, Hanna questioned the difference between examples 4, 5, and 6. She actually argued that all three examples are very similar to the example discussed in LE-2.1. She did not articulate why she thought so. To support her claim, the MTE sketched the graphs of Examples 4 and 6 (see Fig. 5).

Hanna: Now, with these graphs, I see why these examples are basically the same; for $f(n)=(-1)^{n+1}$ [Example 4], there are two "rows," one above the x-axis and one below; and for $f(x)=\begin{cases} 2, & \text{when } x \text{ is even} \\ 3, & \text{when } x \text{ is odd} \end{cases}$, [Example 6], there are similar "rows," both above the x-axis.

Fig. 5 Case 2, the graphs of
Examples 4 and 6

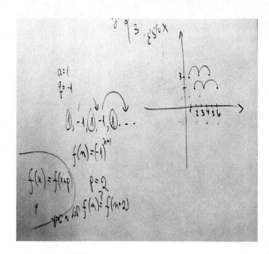

MTE: Note the connection between representations and the fact that one
         representation highlighted certain features that the other one did not.

Hanna: Noa said before that instead of writing the example as $f(n)=(-1)^{n+1}$, we
         could have written it as $f(n)=\begin{cases} -1, & \text{when } n \text{ is even} \\ 1, & \text{when } n \text{ is odd} \end{cases}$. This would
         convey how similar these two examples are, even without the graphs.

These observations led naturally to considering the case of a constant function
and then to the next example, Example 7, which was dramatically different than the
previous ones.

LE-2.3

In response to the MTE's invitation to give another example of a periodic function,
distinct from the ones suggested up to this stage, Hassan suggested example 7. This
came as a surprise to the other members of the group (except for Benny, who had contemplated the idea of examining floor functions but wasn't sure how to verify them).

The MTE asked everyone to concentrate on verifying that $f(x)=x-[x]$ is a valid
example of a periodic function. Some chose an analytic approach and others moved
to a graphical representation.

Edna volunteered to come to the board and sketch the graph of example 7.
At first she sketched the graph only for positive numbers. Edna shared her
reluctance to graph the part for negative numbers, as she was not certain about the
way the function behaves for negative numbers. To help her, the MTE asked what
the value of the function is for (−1.3). This helped Edna see the behavior of the

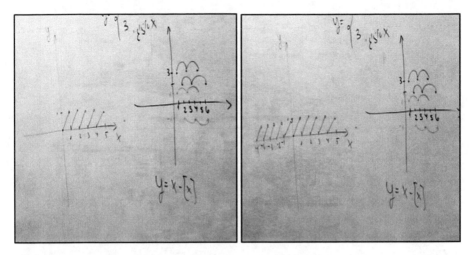

Fig. 6 Case 2, the graph of Example 7 before (on the *left*) and after the discussion (on the *right*)

graph for this domain, and thus she was able to complete it and observe its properties (see Fig. 6).

The participants who approached the question by a graphical representation at the end of the discussion (as on the right part of Fig. 6), as well as those who analyzed the analytic representation of the function, in order to verify that this was indeed an example of a periodic function, all reached an agreement that it satisfied the definition of a periodic function. Some noticed that this periodic function is the difference between two nonperiodic functions. Moreover, they were able to see and justify that the period of this function is 1.

Following this discussion (LE-2.3), and in response to the MTE's invitation to give another example of a periodic function, two MTLs suggested simultaneously very similar examples (8 and 9). The MTE probed for verification of these examples. It was previously established for Example 7 that if f is the floor function $f(x)=[x]$ and g is the identity function $g(x)=x$, then $h=g-f$ is a periodic function, even though g and f are not periodic.

It appears that following a similar line of thought, the MTLs anticipated that the two quotient functions $h = \dfrac{g}{f}$ and $h = \dfrac{f}{g}$ would also be periodic. However, Examples 8 and 9 do not satisfy the necessary conditions for a periodic function. Figure 7 illustrates this graphically.

To conclude the activities related to a periodic function, after the participants came up with the rest of the examples (Examples 8 and 9), the MTE introduced the idea of constructing an example of a periodic function without knowing, or even being able to know, its analytic representation. Basically, it was similar to the "copying" approach of Van Dormolen and Zaslavsky (2003) presented earlier.

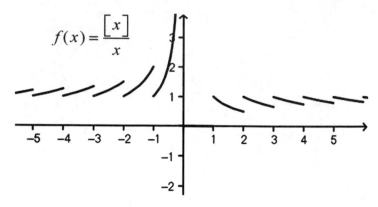

$$f(x) = \frac{[x]}{x}$$

Fig. 7 Case 2, the graph of Example 8

Discussion and Conclusion

In this chapter we presented an example-generation/example-verification eliciting learning environment. The two cases described above share the rich, open-ended, generic task on which they are built, yet address two different mathematical concepts. By reflecting on these cases, we hope to shed light on the affordances and limitations of this kind of learning environment and characterize the kind of teaching it requires.

This learner-centered environment is characterized by generating examples of a given concept followed by the naturally evolving need to verify that the proposed examples satisfy the definition of the given concept or other sufficient conditions of the concept. The teacher's main roles are choosing the focal mathematics concept and orchestrating the discussions; it is critical that the teacher persists and pushes the learners to continue generating more and more examples that are different than the previous ones. As we see in Fig. 8, the learning occurs once we go beyond the familiar and the accessible. It is also important that the teacher encourages genuine discussions and debates with minimal interference and at the same time offers useful prompts when learners face an impasse or when there is an opportunity to draw learners' attention to a mathematical subtlety that may otherwise be overlooked. When learners seem to have run out of examples, the teacher may offer ideas for generating additional examples that could serve to push learners beyond their existing/current concept images and example spaces, as appears in the teacher-generated example in Fig. 8. This kind of teaching requires constant in-the-moment decision-making, which is a serious challenge for teachers (Mason and Spence 1999).

Figure 8 captures the essence of this form of instruction. The first five examples that were generated by the learners serve as indicators of how they think about irrational numbers, that is, what comes first to their mind. This serves as important information for the teacher – a way to assess and get at the learners' current thinking or more specifically – the learners' current example spaces.

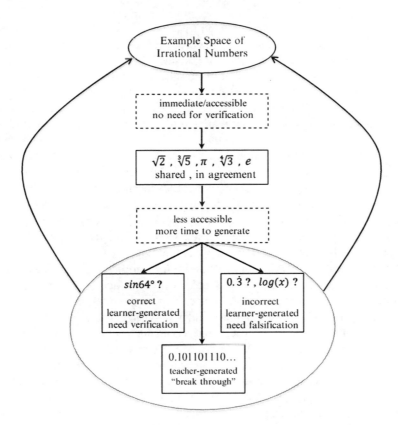

Fig. 8 The learning cycle fostered by engaging in a group activity of example-generation of irrational numbers

It appears from these examples that the MTLs' example spaces of irrational numbers included any root of a prime number as well as transcendental numbers or at least the "famous" ones – π and e. These examples are straightforward, taken as shared, and do not raise the need for verification. The teacher's role at this stage is to encourage the learners to continue generating more, yet different, examples. As indicated in Fig. 8, this led to less accessible examples, or examples that have not yet been considered – some correct and some incorrect. All of the examples that were given at this stage raised some degree of uncertainty (see the question marks in the diagram), in particular $0.33\dot{3}$ (followed by $0.99\dot{9}$). This example was an indicator that some MTLs (wrongly) included repeating decimals in their example space of irrational numbers. The teacher's role at this stage is to facilitate discussion that addresses this perplexity and fosters the learners' need to justify and convince each other, as well as themselves.

Note that the teacher offered several prompts along the way. For example, when Reli suggested to take the *sinus* function as an example of an irrational number, the teacher responded with an example to consider – sin 30°. With no further interference by the teacher, Reli realized that she needed to think more carefully about an appropriate example and generated sin 64°. Verifying that this is indeed an irrational number is not a trivial task that remained open.

As mentioned above, another role of the teacher is to put forth more sophisticated and unfamiliar examples for discussion. In the case of the irrational numbers, the example the teacher offered for discussion, 0.101101101111..., came as a surprise to the entire group, which not only realized that this was another (very different) example of an irrational number but at the same time provided a tool for constructing a whole new family of non-repeating decimals. In Case 2, the teacher also ended the meeting with an example that created a "breakthrough" in the group's current thinking by constructing a function similar to the one cited from Van Dormolen and Zaslavsky (2003), which uses the copying approach. The idea that one can construct a periodic function graphically without knowing its analytic representation was new to the group and allowed the expansion of the ways in which they think of a periodic function and tools to construct other periodic functions.

In terms of example-generation as a catalyst for learning, Fig. 8 indicates that all the examples that were offered at the less accessible stage led to expansion and refinement of the group's example space. Some examples helped expand the example space by adding new examples and new verification tools, and some led to its refinement by eliminating examples that should not be part of the example space. In terms of the work on concept image, we can say that $0.33\dot{3}$ was now regarded a non-example rather than an example of an irrational number. Similarly, after more extensive discussions and debates, $0.99\dot{9}$ too was accepted as a rational number, that is, a non-example of an irrational number. Note that understanding that $0.99\dot{9} = 1$ is a deep and cognitively demanding task (Conner 2013; Tall 1977). Dubinsky et al. (2005) discuss the difficulty with this equality compared to a similar one: $0.33\dot{3} = \dfrac{1}{3}$. In our work, this phenomenon was manifested in a spontaneous way, as a result of engaging in example-generation.

Interestingly, we can easily substitute the examples in Fig. 8 that were drawn from Case 1 with the examples of Case 2. This supports the generality of the process described in Fig. 8. In Case 2 there were also immediate examples (the first three) followed by attempts to construct less familiar examples – some correct and some incorrect. In both cases, there were attempts to search for examples in domains that were not initially associated with the focal concept (in the case of irrational numbers, there was an attempt to look for examples that relate to trigonometric and logarithmic functions, while in the case of the periodic function, there was an attempt to look for sequences and floor functions).

It should be noted that different examples are available at different times according to what triggers them, and what comes to mind in the moment is situated and dependent on many factors. "In a group, one person's example can trigger access to a further class of examples for someone else. Furthermore, each time a connection is made it is strengthened and more likely to come to mind in the future" (Mason and Goldenberg 2008, p. 188). "We acknowledge, that absence of evidence is not evidence of absence and that, when asking learners to reveal their grasp of a concept, the fact that they don't display an example does not necessarily imply that it is not within their accessible space; it could be that they have not yet perceived a reason to express it" (ibid., p. 189).

Although our learners were in-service secondary mathematics teachers, and the teacher was a mathematics teacher educator (MTE), depending on the mathematical concept, this kind of learning environment may equally be suitable for various learners, including preservice mathematics teachers and secondary school students. In fact, several teachers who encountered (as learners) the affordances of this learning environment expressed the appreciation they gained and their intention to implement a similar approach with their students.

References

Ball, D. L., Thames, M. H., & Phelps, G. (2008). Content knowledge for teaching: What makes it special? *Journal of Teacher Education, 59*(5), 389–407.

Bills, L., Dreyfus, T., Mason, J., Tsamir, P., Watson, A., & Zaslavsky, O. (2006). Exemplification in mathematics education. In J. Novotná, H. Moraová, M. Krátká, & N. Stehliková (Eds.), *Proceedings of the 30th conference of the International Group for the Psychology of Mathematics Education* (Vol. 1, pp. 126–154). Prague: PME.

Conner, A. (2013). Authentic argumentation with prospective secondary teachers: The case of 0.999.... *Mathematics Teachers Educator, 1*(2), 69–77.

Dubinsky, E., Weller, K., McDonald, M., & Brown, A. (2005). Some historical issues and paradoxes regarding the concept of infinity: An APOS analysis: Part 2. *Educational Studies in Mathematics, 60*, 253–266.

Harel, G. (2013). Intellectual need. In K. R. Leatham (Ed.), *Vital directions for mathematics education research* (pp. 119–151). New York: Springer.

Hazzan, O., & Zazkis, R. (1999). A perspective on "give and example" tasks as opportunities to construct links among mathematical concepts. *Focus on Learning Problems in Mathematics, 21*(4), 1–14.

Leinhardt, G. (2001). Instructional explanations: A commonplace for teaching and location for contrast. In V. Richardson (Ed.), *Handbook of research on teaching* (4th ed., pp. 333–357). Washington, DC: American Educational Research Association.

Mason, J., & Goldenberg, P. (2008). Shedding light on and with example spaces. *Educational Studies in Mathematics, 69*, 183–194.

Mason, J., & Pimm, D. (1984). Generic examples: Seeing the general in the particular. *Educational Studies in Mathematics, 15*(3), 277–290.

Mason, J., & Spence, M. (1999). Beyond mere knowledge of mathematics: The importance of knowing-to act in the moment. *Educational Studies in Mathematics, 38*, 135–161.

National Council of Mathematics (NCTM). (2000). *Principles and standards for school mathematics*. Reston: Author.

Peled, I., & Zaslavsky, O. (1997). Counter-examples that (only) prove and counter-examples that (also) explain. *FOCUS on Learning Problems in Mathematics, 19*(3), 49–61.

Rissland, E. L. (1978). Understanding understanding mathematics. *Cognitive Science, 2*(4), 361–383.

Rissland, E. L. (1991). Example-based reasoning. In J. F. Voss, D. N. Parkins, & J. W. Segal (Eds.), *Informal reasoning in education* (pp. 187–208). Hillsdale: Lawrence Erlbaum Associates.

Shama, G. (1998). Understanding periodicity as a concept with a Gestalt structure. *Educational Studies in Mathematics, 35*(3), 255–281.

Skemp, R. R. (1987). *The psychology of learning mathematics: Expanded American edition.* Hillsdale: Lawrence Erlbaum Associates.

Tall, D. O. (1977). *Cognitive conflict and the learning of mathematics.* Paper presented to the International Group for the Psychology of Mathematics Education, Utrecht, Holland.

Tall, D. O., & Vinner, S. (1981). Concept image and concept definition in mathematics, with particular reference to limits and continuity. *Educational Studies in Mathematics, 12,* 151–169.

Van Dormolen, J., & Zaslavsky, O. (2003). The many facets of a definition: The case of periodicity. *Journal of Mathematical Behavior, 22*(1), 91–106.

Vinner, S. (1983). Concept definition, concept image and the notion of function. *International Journal of Mathematical Education in Science and Technology, 14,* 293–305.

Vinner, S. (1991). The role of definitions in the teaching and learning of mathematics. In D. O. Tall (Ed.), *Advanced mathematical thinking* (pp. 65–81). London: Kluwer Academic.

Watson, A., & Mason, J. (2005). *Mathematics as a constructive activity: Learners generating examples.* Mahwah: Erlbaum.

Watson, A., & Shipman, S. (2008). Using learner generated examples to introduce new concepts. *Educational Studies in Mathematics, 69,* 97–109.

Zaslavsky, O. (1995). Open-ended tasks as a trigger for mathematics teachers' professional development. *For the Learning of Mathematics, 15*(3), 15–20.

Zaslavsky, O. (2005). Seizing the opportunity to create uncertainty in learning mathematics. *Educational Studies in Mathematics, 60,* 297–321.

Zaslavsky, O. (2008). Meeting the challenges of mathematics teacher education through design and use of tasks that facilitate teacher learning. In B. Jaworski, & T. Wood (Eds.), *The mathematics teacher educator as a developing professional,* Vol. 4 of T. Wood (Series Ed.), *The international handbook of mathematics teacher education* (pp. 93–114). Rotterdam: Sense Publishers.

Zaslavsky, O. (2010). The explanatory power of examples in mathematics: Challenges for teaching. In M. K. Stein & L. Kucan (Eds.), *Instructional explanations in the disciplines* (pp. 107–128). New York: Springer.

Zaslavsky, O., & Peled, I. (1996). Inhibiting factors in generating examples by mathematics teachers and student teachers: The case of binary operation. *Journal for Research in Mathematics Education, 27*(1), 67–78.

Zaslavsky, O., & Shir, K. (2005). Students' conceptions of a mathematical definition. *Journal for Research in Mathematics Education, 36*(4), 317–346.

Zaslavsky, O., & Zodik, I. (2007). Mathematics teachers' choices of examples that potentially support or impede learning. *Research in Mathematics Education, 9,* 143–155.

Zodik, I., & Zaslavsky, O. (2007). Exemplification in the mathematics classroom: What is it like and what does it imply? In D. Pitta-Pantazi & G. Philippou (Eds.), *Proceedings of the fifth congress of the European Society for Research in Mathematics Education* (pp. 2024–2033). Larnaca: University of Cyprus.

Zodik, I., & Zaslavsky, O. (2008). Characteristics of teachers' choice of examples in and for the mathematics classroom. *Educational Studies in Mathematics, 69,* 165–182.

Zodik, I., & Zaslavsky, O. (2009). Teachers' treatment of examples as learning opportunities. In M. Tzekaki, M. Kaldrimidou, & C. Sakonidis (Eds.), *Proceedings of the 33rd conference of the International Group for the Psychology of Mathematics Education* (Vol. 5, pp. 425–432). Thessaloniki: PME.

Part V
Commentary

Transforming Research to Transform Mathematics Instruction

Deborah Loewenberg Ball and Mark Hoover

Abstract Transforming mathematics instruction is an ambitious aim and requires careful attention to the interactions among teachers, students, and content in classrooms. The authors of this volume have, in a variety of ways, attended to this crucial dynamic, whether through a focus on professional learning, curricular innovation, or other levers to change the quality and outcomes of mathematics instruction. They have also sought to focus on ways in which the work of teaching contributes to these interactions and, in doing so, have innovated with approaches for studying and understanding teaching practice. In reflecting on their work, we highlight challenges to the development of research on teaching and ways in which the projects and studies discussed in the volume contribute to the advancement of the field and suggest next steps for its development.

Keywords Research on teaching • Instructional improvement • Instructional interactions • Theory of teaching • Methods for studying teaching

This book comprises a collection of projects and studies aimed at transforming mathematics instruction, using curriculum and teacher professional development to leverage change. With an eye on improved student learning of mathematics, the chapters' authors navigate the complex environments of teaching and learning. Doing this requires influencing the primary interactions that shape students' learning opportunities—namely, the interactions among teachers and students around content in classrooms. The relationship between levers for change—such as curriculum

D.L. Ball (✉) • M. Hoover
School of Education, University of Michigan,
610 E. University Ave., Ann Arbor, MI 48109-1259, USA
e-mail: dball@umich.edu; mhoover@umich.edu

Y. Li et al. (eds.), *Transforming Mathematics Instruction: Multiple Approaches and Practices*, Advances in Mathematics Education, DOI 10.1007/978-3-319-04993-9_29,
© Springer International Publishing Switzerland 2014

materials and professional development—and instructional interactions is complex. In order for such efforts to succeed, understanding these dynamics is vital.

In describing the relationship between curriculum and instruction in his chapter in Part II, Silver writes about the importance of understanding instructional interactions:

> The effects of curriculum changes are mediated by a number of factors and actors, among which are teachers and students. The implemented curriculum is largely a function of the actions and reactions of teachers and students in classrooms, and it is constrained by a complex array of cultural, historical, political, and social factors.

The projects and research reported in this volume focus on these "actions and reactions of teachers and students." From this perspective, the choice of the term "instruction" in the title of this volume stands out. Although, in common usage, "instruction" is often taken to refer to what teachers do, the knowledge they impart when they teach, or the giving of directions, education researchers have increasingly used the term to refer to the deliberate interactions of instruction (see, e.g., Cohen et al. 2003). The chapters in this volume are in varying ways centering mathematics education improvement research on the nexus through which transformation must happen—*instructional interactions in classrooms*.

The centrality of these interactions for improving teaching and learning has been written about elsewhere. In brief, improvement in educational outcomes depends on changes in what teachers and students do with content in classrooms, and teaching is the deliberate activity responsible for those interactions. We frame our comments on the contributions of the research reported in this volume by considering three challenges of attending to instructional interactions in sufficiently nuanced ways:

- Difficulties in gaining analytic traction on instruction and teaching
- Still nascent methods available for studying instruction and teaching
- Confounding of the notion of a theory of teaching with specific approaches to teaching

We use these challenges to highlight the progress this volume represents and key issues for ongoing progress in our field.

One persistent challenge is that instructional interactions and the work of teaching that shapes them tend to remain relatively invisible. There are several explanations for this. First, instructional interactions tend to be under-conceptualized. Descriptions of classroom learning often focus more on student contributions or behaviors than on those of the teacher. This is particularly true in classrooms in which students are actively engaged in ideas and discourse. Accounts of such "student-centered" classrooms often refer admiringly to the teacher as merely "facilitating" or "standing off to the side"; classroom activity is often attributed to the task or the environment more than to the active structuring and work of the teaching. The pervasive dichotomization of "teacher-centered" and "student-centered" classrooms pulls analytic attention away from the instructional interactions of teachers and students around content and tasks which are inherent in all classrooms (Cohen et al. 2003).

A second explanation for the tendency to under-notice teaching is rooted in the aptly named "apprenticeship of observation" (Lortie 1975). This refers to the idea that we have all been exposed to extensive hours of teaching, yet the perspective gained on teaching is from the "student's side of the desk." Although active agents in instruction, students are not usually attuned to the work of teaching that shapes classroom life. Even when invested in learning, students are not responsible for the learning of others in the ways that teachers are. They are not in a position to be reflective or analytic about what they see. Indeed, students often resist engagement and seek to minimize effort and work actively against the efforts of teaching and learning as commonly construed. As former students, both teachers and researchers come to the practice and study of teaching with taken-for-granted views as well as strong convictions born of familiarity. For example, we think we know whether students are interested or engaged based on visual cues, which are often quite far off. We think we know what students understand and often fall prey to both excessive generosity and over-criticism. We infer teachers' motives and miss significant actions and talk. Researchers, like others, are susceptible to overconfident judgments about teaching that follow from student-based impressions. We have experienced this in our own work and see it as complicating research efforts in the field.

Disciplined study of instruction can open new perspectives on the work of teaching and its relation to the work of learning. What makes this far from straightforward, however, is the relatively under-theorized state of research on instruction and teaching. Learning is well theorized—indeed, many are inclined to assume that a theory of learning is a theory of teaching (e.g., consider how often one hears of "constructivist teaching"). This fails to attend to the difference between a focus on individuals when considering learning—sociocultural theories acknowledged—and the need to focus on interactions among groups of individuals when considering instruction. Research on learning has a comfortable theoretical home within the discipline of psychology. In contrast, research on teaching lacks a similar theoretical base (Ball and Forzani 2007). It has no clear disciplinary home and little established professional knowledge and language on which to draw (Jackson 1968; Lortie 1975). Thus, analytic tools for research on teaching, including language, concepts, and categories, are limited. This limitation extends to representations of teaching (Lampert 2001), to the parsing of teaching (Grossman et al. 2009), and to technical knowledge and language for talking about teaching or its improvement (Hiebert et al. 2002).

A new field of research often must bootstrap itself into existence; conceptual tools may need to be posited just to provide a foothold for initial research. Early-stage research of an under-theorized phenomenon may require extensive investment in developing, testing, and synthesizing analytic tools essential for disciplined study. A new field is also susceptible to a tendency to identify features, without adequately addressing the need to ensure that the features being identified contribute to an understanding of how the phenomenon works and what is involved in improving it. Research on teaching has been slow to develop and still requires significant conceptual work as it frames its core questions, methods, and theoretical foundations. As we argue below, this volume reflects important progress being made in the field to address this challenge.

A related part of the challenge is the underdevelopment of methods for studying instruction and teaching. As Ball and Forzani (2007) argue, research that focuses on instructional dynamics probes not only activities and features of teachers, students, and content but also the "mutual adjustment that shapes student learning, instructional practice, or policy implementation" (p. 531). Instruction is a form of human interaction, but it is a very distinctive form and may call for distinctive methods. In addition, methods for probing these interactions might be drawn from psychology, sociology, anthropology, or elsewhere, but such research may require the development of methods specifically suited for documenting and investigating the distinctive nature of instructional interaction, with its distinctive distribution of responsibility, object of focus for social interaction (viz., a subject area), and goal of effecting student learning. Methods drawn from other disciplines may be better suited for addressing the driving questions of those disciplines, rather than the core problems of instructional practice, and may bring with them native orientations to theory inherent in those disciplines. These concerns arise for us from our impression that research studies concerned with improving teaching and learning have a tendency to veer away from the direct study of instructional dynamics and their role in the improvement of teaching and learning. This happens in the formulation of research questions, the design of methods that strategically address instructional dynamics, and the formulation of results so that they actually contribute to understanding instructional dynamics (Thames and Van Zoest 2013). In the end, methods for analyzing interactions often flounder or become indirect. The chapters of this volume explore a variety of novel methods that address this underlying challenge.

Not all of the chapters involve the study of instruction or teaching, yet those that do include a wide range of novel approaches for studying it. For example, Boston uses the examination of student work as a basis for making (actionable) inferences about teaching practice; Zaslavsky and Zodik trace backward from specific learning events to infer what teachers did to facilitate that learning; Ni, Li, Zhou, and Li use questions from teachers, responses from students, and teachers' reactions to students' responses to analyze the quality of instructional interaction; and Liljedahl perturbs instruction (with random group assignments) and then observes interactions as a way to conceptualize what might be important for shaping those interactions.

In addition, several chapters discuss methods that might be used, and several propose novel methods for making practice study-able in the context of professional education. For instance, in thinking about the study of instruction in the context of professional education, Jacobs, Koellner, John, and King describe a *problem-solving cycle* design that embeds the learning of teaching in facilitated analysis of instruction. As do others, they use a rotating analytic attention to content, students, and teaching to bring discipline to the examination of instruction. Huang and Li describe the use of exemplary lesson development, critically reviewed using publically available standards, as one component of a coherent national in-service professional system that includes exemplary lesson development, teaching research activities, and skill competitions, all of which involve forms of public teaching and professional commentary. In this case, methods for analyzing practice have been institutionalized and are part of professional practice. We are struck by the extent to which approaches to the professional education of teachers are investing in layered designs that directly include teaching, artifacts of teaching, and the study of teaching as components of the teaching and learning of teaching. In doing so, these efforts are contributing to research on teaching and to the development of suitable methods. Our impression is that the wide variety of methods for analyzing mathematics instruction visible in this volume reflects the need in the field to develop useful methods for the study of instructional practice.

The current lack of established methods and exploration of novel methods for analyzing instruction is also visible in the prominence of what might be considered indirect approaches to the study of instruction and the absence of direct studies of teaching or instructional interactions. For instance, most of the chapters in Part I, which focuses on instructional practice, are structured in relation to the nature and substance of the curriculum. For example, Vorhölter, Kaiser, and Ferri advance a modeling curriculum in tandem with their discussion of instructional practice, and da Ponte, Branco, and Quaresma argue that exploration tasks provide an important setting for changing instructional interactions in classrooms. In addition, while focusing on professional education, many of the chapters in Part III invest significantly in articulating the instructional practice or the curriculum targeted by the professional education discussed, and several use professional education as a vehicle for engaging in the study of instruction.

In part, this reflects the interrelationships among instruction, curriculum, and the learning of teaching. Artifacts, data, and methods overlap and overrun one another across the parts. In Part III on professional education, Smith et al. argue for "reasoning-and-proving" as important curricular content for transforming instruction, and they use their cases as much to articulate an understanding of the instructional practice that they have been developing as to serve as materials for professional education. A more unusual instance of this crossover dynamic is Watanabe's historical account of Japanese curricular changes, where in several places he suggests that an analysis of curriculum materials may provide information about common teaching practices and where learning about practice over time in a professional community may have led to changes in textbooks, rather than the more common reverse relationship where curricula are used to effect changes in practice, which he also discusses.

Several factors might contribute to this crossover dynamic among the parts of this volume. One is the complex interrelationships among curriculum, teaching, teacher learning, and instructional improvement. Another is the lack of established analytic tools that would allow researchers to treat factors in a modular way. Third, an exploration of method is needed to get at the instructional dynamics and use of factors such as curriculum or teacher learning to create identifiable and study-able change in instructional interactions.

A final challenge for research that accounts for dynamics of instruction is the need to disentangle two distinct aims of scholarship on teaching. Research on teaching might contribute to a *theory* of teaching—that is, an explanatory conceptualization or model of the work of teaching. Alternatively, researchers might seek to specify an *approach* to teaching—that is, describe a specific way of teaching, not to conceptualize tasks inherent to instruction. Research of the first type might aim to create a general model of teachers' actions across the board, such as Schoenfeld's (2010) theory of goal-oriented decision making. Or it might aim to identify core practices that are defensible in a broad professional community and can be effectively taught and learned in professional education, such as Grossman et al.'s (2009) characterization of decompositions of teaching into learnable, re-composable practices. Such research attempts to be ecumenical with regard to preferred methods of teaching. It approaches the problem of how to teach from the standpoint of understanding inherent demands and core components. In contrast, research of the second type might aim to identify a particular approach, without suggesting that the approach is the only defensible alternative, such as Cohen and Lotan's research on complex instruction and its use of product evaluation criteria and equal-status role assignments in small-group problem solving (see, e.g., Cohen and Lotan 2003; Cohen et al. 2002). Research of this type approaches the problem of how to teach from the standpoint of positing a particular strategy and arguing for its effectiveness.

We acknowledge that these different aims are interrelated and are often combined within a single program of work. In Lampert's (2001) analysis of teaching practice, she identifies endemic "problems of teaching," such as "covering the curriculum" and achieving "closure." As she writes,

> The problems in teaching are many. Teachers face some students who do not want to learn what they want to teach, some who already know it, or think they do, and some who are poorly prepared to study what is taught. They must figure out how to teach each student while working with a class of students who are all different from one another. (p. 1)

She goes on to name other problems—dealing with multiple policy signals about what to teach, managing time and interruptions, and solving these many different problems at the same time. Here Lampert is articulating a theory of the work of instruction. But she also focuses her work on what she calls "teaching with problems"—that is, "a particular kind of teaching" (p. 3) advocated by reformers who seek more intellectually challenging and complex learning opportunities and outcomes.

As Lampert's careful analysis demonstrates, the design of any high-quality specific approach is based on general principles and implies a set of foundational demands and core components of teaching. In her work, over time she has developed a theory of instruction; what was at first a specific approach can thus be used to explain fundamental aspects of the work of teaching. Cohen and Lotan's "complex instruction" also began by developing a specific approach to teaching, with particular aims. Although complex instruction has not yet become a theoretical lens for understanding the work of teaching in general, it may develop into one. The interconnections of general theory and definition of specific approaches can be seen in the need to illustrate the theory with concrete images of enactment, which then involve particular choices in approach. For instance, the core tasks of teaching proposed by Grossman and others, as they are more and more fully specified, can easily be interpreted as representing preferred approaches to teaching. At some point in its rendering in practice, a theory becomes an approach, or a collection of approaches, however universal its conception or widespread its application. A theory's use to guide practice ends up being shaped by preferred forms of implementation. Furthermore, any theory is, after all, only one alternative theory among many. We acknowledge that the distinction we make here between a theory of teaching and an approach is a matter of describing two sides of the same coin.

However, we suggest that inadequate attention to this distinction weakens research on teaching and that increased attention would improve the overall quality of research in two important ways. It would improve quality and it would coordinate different work in the field. One issue that has plagued education research for over a century has been a tendency to slip into ideological advocacy by using research to argue (whether overtly or not) for approaches to teaching that embed specific political and social values. We recognize that our view on this is not universally shared—that many researchers see education research as an important form of social and political action. Although sympathetic to this view, and struggling with it in our own work, we see this as creating a significant challenge for making actual, cumulative progress on core problems of education. Research reports that are couched as being research on general principles when they actually (or also) advocate for a particular approach with embedded, unexamined commitments complicate the research process. We suggest that having clearer language for describing the focus of a piece of research with regard to where it falls on the spectrum from specific approach to theoretical principle would reduce the chances of slipping unnoticed into advocacy being passed off as disciplined research.

A second issue that has plagued education research, in particular research on teaching, is the challenge of orchestrating research studies that together, across researchers and over time, accumulate knowledge and understanding of teaching. Research on learning has built robust theories of learning in the past century. Research on teaching has not. To do so, as with any theory-building effort, requires orchestration between research on general theories and the development of well-understood techniques. Analogous to the ways that funding agencies might use a cycle of discovery, innovation, and application to consider the portfolio of research they fund, mathematics education researchers might benefit from clearer articulation of a cycle between approach development and theory building as it designs and communicates research on teaching.

This volume takes up these different challenges and suggests potential for future progress. Many of the chapters put forward a vision of teaching seen as "good," where judgment about what counts as good is drawn from a range of sources—reform calls and policy documents (e.g., Goos, Geiger, and Dole; Ni, Li, Zhou, and Li; or Oliveira and Mestre), past programs of research or syntheses of such programs (e.g., Stephan, Underwood-Gregg, and Yackel; Gravemeijer; or Jaworski), existing large-scale efforts deemed relatively successful (e.g., Watanabe; Huang and Li; Borko, Jacobs, Seago, and Mangram; Yang; or Li and Li), or novel approaches informed by extensive background and experience (e.g., Leikin; Liljedahl; or Zaslavsky and Zodik). Each paints its own picture, using overlapping yet unique language and categories. Even ones that share significant historical roots, such as Stephan, Underwood-Gregg, and Yackel's chapter on guided reinvention and Gravemeijer's synthesis of inquiry-oriented practices, both of which draw from *Realistic Mathematics Education* as developed in the Netherlands, weave in and out of using the same and different terms. The relationship between them is often intriguing, yet not easy to discern clearly. Jaworski's chapter on communities of inquiry and the use of activity theory to make sense of the teacher's unique role is situated in sociocultural theory, but the characterization of critical alignment in a community of inquiry has a certain resonance with the characterizations of instruction provided by Gravemeijer and by Stephan, Underwood-Gregg, and Yackel. It is not clear to us what to make of these similarities and differences, but we are struck and intrigued by them. Similarly, several chapters identify the cognitive demand of tasks and support for mathematical talk as key. Yet, trying to make sense of the intersections in language, meaning, and principles across different scholars is not easy.

Reading across all of the chapters, we are impressed by an intriguing sense of convergence in the many different visions put forward. The three chapters we just mentioned (each appearing in a different part of the volume) have great resonance and connection, but the convergence is not limited to these. Many of the chapters that advance particular kinds of tasks or curricula include many of the same themes, identifying similar features of certain tasks and talk. While trying to neatly capture these themes is certainly beyond our intellectual dexterity, we wonder if the rather striking similarity in visions of "good" mathematics teaching across such disparate chapters—analyzing Japanese textbooks, case-based professional education focused on reasoning-and-proving, state curriculum mandates in Portugal, and teaching contests in China—attests to a bridging between the approaches and converging principles in research on mathematics instruction. In light of our comments above, we propose that being more explicit about theory, investing in building common language and framing, and eschewing the tendency to advocate for preferred approaches might facilitate even greater convergence, and greater clarity in emerging principles, and might support the production of useful theory in research on teaching.

Although we note significant common ground in the research reflected in this volume, we would be remiss not to mention several chapters that point clearly at how much further we have to go in our efforts to understand teaching and the interactions of instruction. For instance, Liljedahl explores a somewhat paradoxically naive, intriguing, practical, and self-aware proposal for using visibly random daily group assignments in secondary mathematics classes as a way to manage the important different threads in the dynamics of instruction, such as different agendas of students and teachers and the goal of focusing on academic work. Among other things, his analysis draws attention to how much we do not yet understand regarding even how to think about the most basic factors influencing the dynamics in mathematics instruction. Likewise, Even's report on the *Same Teacher—Different Classes* research program, which uses a comparative method across cases that hold some of the key factors in the dynamics of instruction constant while others vary, exposes in a different way the extensive work ahead in developing theoretical work on teaching that provides leverage for understanding the role and interplay of different factors in the dynamics of instruction. Different yet, Zaslavsky and Zodik's exploration of example generation and example-based reasoning exposes a small but important aspect of mathematical practice that in all likelihood matters for the work of teaching. Understanding how and where it arises in the work of teaching is an important topic that will contribute much to conceptualizing and theorizing about instructional interactions and the work of teaching. This valuable research additionally helps to point out that there are other similar important pieces of the puzzle waiting to be addressed.

We thank all of the scholars contributing to this volume for the opportunity to reflect on the many important programs of work being conducted in the field today and on the progress being made and needing to be made to reach the shared goal of transforming mathematics instruction into the dynamic and effective professional practice that we know it can be.

References

Ball, D. L., & Forzani, F. M. (2007). What makes education research "educational"? *Educational Researcher, 36*(9), 529–540.

Cohen, E. G., & Lotan, R. A. (2003). Equity in heterogeneous classrooms. In J. Banks & C. Banks (Eds.), *Handbook of multicultural education* (2nd ed.). New York: Teachers College Press.

Cohen, E. G., Lotan, R. A., Abram, P. L., Scarloss, B. A., & Schultz, S. E. (2002). Can groups learn? *Teachers College Record, 104*, 1045–1068.

Cohen, D., Raudenbush, S., & Ball, D. (2003). Resources, instruction, and research. *Educational Evaluation and Policy Analysis, 25*(2), 1–24.

Grossman, P., Compton, C., Igra, D., Ronfeldt, M., Shahan, E., & Williamson, P. (2009). Teaching practice: A cross-professional perspective. *Teachers College Record, 111*(9), 2055–2100.

Hiebert, J., Gallimore, R., & Stigler, J. W. (2002). A knowledge base for the teaching profession: What would it look like and how can we get one? *Educational Researcher, 31*(5), 3–15.

Jackson, P. (1968). *Life in classrooms.* New York: Holt, Rinehart, & Winston.

Lampert, M. (2001). *Teaching problems and the problems of teaching.* New Haven: Yale University Press.

Lortie, D. C. (1975). *Schoolteacher: A sociological study.* Chicago: University of Chicago Press.

Schoenfeld, A. H. (2010). *How we think: A theory of goal-oriented decision making and its educational applications.* New York: Routledge.

Thames, M. H., & Van Zoest, L. (2013). Building coherence in research on mathematics teacher identity, knowledge and beliefs by developing practice-based approaches. *ZDM—The International Journal on Mathematics Education, 43*(3), 583–594.

Author Biographies

Fran Arbaugh is an associate professor in the Department of Curriculum and Instruction in the College of Education at Pennsylvania State University. Her research interests include the design and implementation of teacher development programs (both preservice and in-service) and how and what teachers learn from these programs. Her work in mathematics teacher education is widely published for both research and practitioner audiences. She is currently the coprincipal investigator of the NSF-funded CORP (Cases of Reasoning and Proving in Secondary Mathematics) Project that is creating materials intended to develop teachers' knowledge related to reasoning and proof and their ability to support students' engagement in these mathematical practices.

Dr. Arbaugh has been acknowledged for her work in mathematics teacher education through the receipt of a number of awards over the past decade, including being named a *William T. Kemper Fellow for Teaching Excellence* at the University of Missouri and being the *Missouri Council of Teachers of Mathematics Post-Secondary Mathematics Teacher of the Year*, both in 2007. She is currently an active member of the Pennsylvania Association of Teachers of Mathematics (PAMTE) and serves as the president of the Association of Mathematics Teacher Educators (AMTE).

Deborah Loewenberg Ball is the William H. Payne Collegiate Professor in education at the University of Michigan and an Arthur F. Thurnau Professor. She currently serves as dean of the School of Education and as director of TeachingWorks. She is a fellow of the American Mathematical Society and of the American Educational Research Association and an elected member of the National Academy of Education. Ball also serves on the National Science Board, the Mathematical Sciences Research Institute, and is the chair of the Spencer Foundation board. Ball's research focuses on the practice of mathematics instruction, the nature, role, and effects of mathematical knowledge for teaching, and on the improvement of teacher training and development. Ball taught elementary school for over 15 years and continues to teach mathematics to fifth grade students every summer in the Elementary Mathematics Laboratory. Ball earned her bachelor's, master's, and doctoral degrees at Michigan State University.

Y. Li et al. (eds.), *Transforming Mathematics Instruction: Multiple Approaches and Practices*, Advances in Mathematics Education, DOI 10.1007/978-3-319-04993-9,
© Springer International Publishing Switzerland 2014

Hilda Borko is a professor of education at Stanford University. She received her BA in psychology, MA in philosophy education, and PhD in educational psychology, all from the University of California, Los Angeles. Dr. Borko's research explores teacher cognition, the process of learning to teach, and the impact of teacher professional development programs on teachers and students. Her current research program includes a field test of the Problem-Solving Cycle professional development program for mathematics teachers (with Jennifer Jacobs and Karen Koellner) and a study of the effectiveness of a PD program to improve discourse and inquiry in science classrooms (with Jonathan Osborne). She recently completed a project to develop a portfolio-based measure of assessment practices in science classrooms (with Brian Stecher and Felipe Martinez). Dr. Borko is a member of numerous professional organizations in education and psychology. She served as president of the American Educational Research Association (2003–2004) and is a member of the US National Academy of Education. She was chair of the National Academy of Education/Spencer Postdoctoral Fellowship Selection Committee and a member and chair of various committees for the American Educational Research Association, Association of Mathematics Teacher Educators, American Psychological Association, and National Academy of Education.

Rita Borromeo Ferri got her master's degree in primary education in 1999 from the University of Siegen and received both her PhD in Mathematics Education and her master's degree in Secondary Mathematics from the University of Hamburg in 2004, where she also acquired her Habilitation in Mathematics Education in 2010. She worked as a teacher at primary and secondary schools in Germany and was a visiting professor of Mathematics Education at the University of Siegen in 2007 and at the University of Hamburg from 2007 to 2011. Since 2011 she is a professor of Mathematics Education (for secondary level) at the University of Kassel. She was vice-chair of ICTMA-14 (International Conference on the Teaching of Mathematical Modelling and Applications) in 2009 at the University of Hamburg. Her current research areas include applications and modeling in mathematics education, mathematical thinking styles, and higher mathematics education.

Melissa D. Boston is an associate professor in the School of Education at Duquesne University (Pittsburgh, PA), where she teaches mathematics content and pedagogy courses for preservice secondary mathematics and elementary teachers. Melissa is the lead developer of the Instructional Quality Assessment (IQA) Mathematics Toolkit, which is a set of rubrics for analyzing mathematics teachers' instructional practices via classroom observations and collections of students' work. Melissa was awarded the Association of Teacher Educators' 2008 Distinguished Dissertation Award for her dissertation research on teachers' learning and instructional change following their participation in a professional development workshop. Melissa has published articles in *Elementary School Journal, Journal for Research in Mathematics Education, Journal of Mathematics Teacher Education, ZDM: The International Journal on Mathematics Education, Educational Assessment, Mathematics Teaching in the Middle School,* and NCTM Yearbooks, and she assisted in the publication of materials to be used in professional development settings, entitled *Improving Instruction in Mathematics: Using Cases to Transform Mathematics Teaching and Learning*. Melissa has served on the NTCM "Student Explorations in Mathematics" committee (member, 2007–2008; cochair, 2009) and currently serves as the associate editor of the AMTE/NCTM online journal *Mathematics Teacher Education*.

Justin Boyle is an assistant professor at the University of New Mexico in the College of Education within the Teacher Education Department specializing in mathematics teacher (prospective and in-service) learning and practice. He teaches instructional methods to preservice secondary mathematics teachers and follows their learning into the classroom during their student teaching. He is interested in how teacher learning experiences and knowledge impact their classroom practice and their students' understanding of mathematics.

His experience and interest in mathematics education began as an undergraduate teaching assistant almost 20 years ago. He served as a secondary mathematics teacher in Northern California for 6 years. While a graduate student, he worked on the NSF-funded Cases of Reasoning and Proving in Secondary Classrooms (CORP) Project, which aims to develop curriculum materials for teachers to learn, enact, and integrate reasoning-and-proving tasks throughout the secondary courses they teach. He was awarded a STaR (Service, Teaching, and Research) fellowship, which is designed to support promising new mathematics education faculty across the country.

Neusa Branco has a bachelor's degree in teaching of mathematics (2002) and master's degree in mathematics education (2008) by the Faculty of Sciences of the University of Lisbon and a doctoral degree in mathematics education by the Institute of Education of the University of Lisbon (2013). She began her professional activity as a school mathematics teacher (during 5 years) and is currently Professor of the Higher School of Education of Santarém (Portugal). In the last years, she has been member of several research projects in mathematics education and directed master students in preservice teacher education. She co-coordinates an educational program of preservice elementary and kindergarten teachers. Her current main research interests are the teaching and learning of algebra and teacher education for the elementary years.

David Clarke is professor in the Melbourne Graduate School of Education at the University of Melbourne and director of the International Center for Classroom Research (ICCR). Over the last 20 years, his research activity has centered on capturing the complexity of classroom practice through a program of international video-based classroom research. The ICCR provides the focus for collaborative activities among researchers from more than 20 countries. Professor Clarke has worked with school systems and teachers throughout Australia and in the USA, Canada, Sweden, Germany, the Netherlands, Italy, Korea, Singapore, China, Japan, Malaysia, and the Federated States of Micronesia. Research collaborations also include the Czech Republic, Finland, Israel, New Zealand, Norway, Portugal, South Africa, and the UK. Other significant research by Professor Clarke has addressed teacher professional learning, metacognition, problem-based learning, and assessment (particularly the use of open-ended tasks for assessment and instruction in mathematics). His current research activities involve multi-theoretic research designs, cross-cultural analyses, discourse in and about classrooms internationally, curricular alignment, and the challenge of research synthesis in education.

João Pedro da Ponte has a bachelor's degree in mathematics from the Faculty of Sciences of the University of Lisbon (1979), a doctoral degree in mathematics education by the University of Georgia (USA) (1984), and aggregation in education by the University of Lisbon (1995). He began his professional activity as a school mathematics teacher and is currently professor and director of the Institute of Education of the University of Lisbon. He has been a visiting professor in universities at Brazil, Spain, and the USA. He has coordinated several research projects in the areas of mathematics education, teacher education, and information and communication technologies (ICT) and directed a high number of master and doctoral students. He is (co)author of several books and articles in national and international journals and associate editor of the *Journal of Mathematics Teacher Education*. He coordinated a government report about preservice teacher education (2006) and a new mathematics curriculum for basic education (2007). Currently, his main research interests are the teaching and learning of algebra and statistics and the development of mathematics reasoning.

Shelley Dole is an associate professor in the School of Education at the University of Queensland, where she coordinates Mathematics Curriculum Studies for prospective primary and middle school teachers in the preservice Bachelor of Education program. Over the 20 years she has been involved with education, she has taught in primary, secondary, and tertiary teaching institutions throughout Australia. Her research interests include mathematics curriculum change and innovation; learning difficulties, misconceptions, and conceptual change associated with learning mathematics; and particularly rational number topics of ratio and percent and the development of proportional reasoning and multiplicative structures. She has lead two major Australian Research Council projects focusing on numeracy across the curriculum and the development of proportional reasoning, with teachers and schools in Queensland and South Australia. In 2009, she won a University of Queensland Award for Teaching Excellence and in 2010 was the recipient of an Australian Award for University Teaching.

Ruhama Even is full professor at the Weizmann Institute of Science, the Rudy Bruner Chair of Science Teaching, and head of the Mathematics Group in the Department of Science Teaching. Her main research interests include education and professional development for math teachers and teacher educators, comparative analysis of textbooks, and the interactions among math curriculum, teachers, and classrooms. She is section editor of the *Encyclopedia of Mathematics Education*, has been member of the International Committee of PME, and cochair of ICMI Study 15 on the professional education and development of teachers of mathematics. Ruhama Even earned her PhD in Mathematics Education from Michigan State University in 1989.

Evan Fuller is an assistant professor at Montclair State University. He has a doctorate in Combinatorics from the University of California, San Diego, with a focus in mathematics education. He studies the strategies used by undergraduate mathematics majors to read and produce proofs, different dimensions of understanding gained by reading a proof, and conditions that aid these dimensions of understanding. He also investigates the effectiveness of professional development programs for mathematics teachers.

Vince Geiger is an associate professor of education at Australian Catholic University in Queensland, Australia. He is the deputy director of Australian Catholic University's Mathematics Teaching and Learning Research Centre and the deputy head of School for Research in the Faculty of Education, Queensland campus. Vince is a past president of the Australian Association of Mathematics Teachers and is an associate editor of the *Mathematics Education Research Journal*. He is actively involved in programs related to the professional learning of teachers. His research interests include teachers' pedagogy associated with effective numeracy practice, the use of digital tools in enhancing mathematics teaching and learning, mathematical modeling as a vehicle for the effective teaching and learning of mathematics, the professional learning of primary and secondary teachers, and the development of tertiary mathematics educators as researchers.

Merrilyn Goos is a professor of education at the University of Queensland, Australia, where she has worked for 20 years as a mathematics teacher educator and mathematics education researcher. For the last 5 years, she served as director of the university's Teaching and Educational Development Institute, working with all faculties and disciplines to improve the quality of teaching and learning in the university. Her work as a university teacher has been recognized through a national teaching excellence award and a national teaching fellowship aimed at building capacity for assessment leadership in university course coordinators. Her research interests include mathematics teacher education, the professional formation of mathematics teacher educators, numeracy education in school and nonschool contexts, school reform, and teaching and learning in higher education. She is currently president of the Mathematics Education Research Group of Australia and an associate editor of *Educational Studies in Mathematics*.

Koeno P.E. Gravemeijer is professor emeritus in science and technology education at the Eindhoven University of Technology in the Netherlands. Earlier he was professor in mathematics education at Utrecht University (Utrecht, the Netherlands) and Vanderbilt University (Nashville, USA). His research interests concern curriculum development, instructional design, domain-specific instruction theories (in particular the theory for realistic mathematics education, RME), teacher professional development, the use of computer tools, and students' use of symbols and modeling. In relation to the latter, he developed the so-called "emergent modeling" design heuristic. Next to his research activities, he also has been involved in instructional design. He has been the leading author of an RME textbook series for Dutch primary schools, and he was involved in the development of the textbook series for the American Middle School, "Mathematics in Contexts"—a collaborative project of the Dutch Freudenthal Institute and the University of Wisconsin-Madison.

Guershon Harel research interest is cognition and epistemology of mathematics and their application in mathematics curricula and the education of mathematics teachers. His research focus has been on the conceptualization of proof, the learning and teaching and linear algebra, and the development of quantitative reasoning. His DNR-based instruction framework has evolved from these lines of research. He is the author/coauthor of over 100 research papers and has edited two books. He has been funded by NSF, US Department of Education, and California Department of Education to conduct research and teacher professional development projects on these subjects.

Mark Hoover is a research scientist in the School of Education at the University of Michigan. His research investigates the practice of teaching mathematics and the improvement of practice, focusing on the work entailed in teaching, the mathematical demands of that work, and ways in which these contribute to learning to teach. He is interested specifically in equitable teaching practice, measures of teacher knowledge and practice, and designs for collective work on teaching. He developed and directs the Secondary Mathematics Laboratory with Bob Moses and the Algebra Project and coleads research projects on mathematical knowledge for teaching with Deborah Ball and Hyman Bass. Hoover earned a BS in mathematics at Alfred University, master's degrees at the University of North Carolina in statistics and sociocultural anthropology, and two PhDs, one in computer science at the University of New Mexico and the second in education at the University of Michigan.

Rongjin Huang is an associate professor of mathematics education at the Middle Tennessee State University. He is one of the Chinese team leaders for the Learner's Perspective Study. His research interests include mathematics classroom research, mathematics teacher education, and comparative mathematics education. He has conducted several research projects and published scholarly works extensively. He is a coeditor of three Chinese books and three English books, including *How Chinese Teach Mathematics and Improve Teaching* (2013, Routledge). He is a guest editor of *ZDM: The International Journal on Mathematics Education*. He has been actively involved in organization of activities at various national and international conferences such as AERA, NCTM, and ICME.

Jennifer Jacobs is a research faculty associate in the Institute of Cognitive Science at the University of Colorado at Boulder. Her areas of specialization are teaching practices and beliefs and mathematics professional development. She received her PhD from UCLA in 1999.

Barbara Jaworski is professor of mathematics education in the Mathematics Education Centre at Loughborough University and Doctor Honoris Causa at the University of Agder, Norway. She was formerly professor of mathematics education at the University of Agder and before that a reader at the University of Oxford.

She has a career that spans mathematics teaching at secondary level and first year university level, teacher education at secondary level, and teaching and supervision of doctoral students. Her research has been mainly into the development of mathematics teaching through research and through partnerships between teachers and teacher educators or didacticians. She was for 6 years editor in chief of the *Journal of Mathematics Teacher Education* and for 4 years president of ERME, the European Society for Research in Mathematics Education. Her research currently is into the development of mathematics teaching at the university level.

Tyrone John who obtained his MSE from Fordham University in 2008, is a doctoral student in Urban Education at the City University of New York. He is also a high school mathematics teacher at Queens Gateway to Health Sciences Secondary School. His research focuses on mathematics professional development, teacher learning, and students' mathematical thinking. He received his MSE from Fordham University in 2008.

Gabriele Kaiser holds a master's degree as a teacher of mathematics and humanities for lower and upper secondary level, completed at the University of Kassel in 1978 with the first state degree. After having worked at school and completing the second state degree, she worked as a scientific assistant at the Department of Mathematics at the University of Kassel, where she received her doctorate in mathematics education in 1986 with a study on applications and modeling. Based on a grant for postdoctoral research by the German Research Society (DFG), she undertook her postdoctoral study in pedagogy on international comparative studies at the University of Kassel, which she completed in 1997. Since 1998, she is full professor for mathematics education at the University of Hamburg. In 2010 she took up the position as vice dean of the Faculty of Education, Psychology, and Human Movement. Since 2005 she serves as editor in chief of *ZDM: The International Journal on Mathematics Education* published by Springer. She is convenor of the 13th International Congress on Mathematics Education (ICME-13), which will take place in 2016 at the University of Hamburg.

Her areas of research include modeling and applications in school, international comparative studies, gender and lingual-cultural aspects in mathematics education, and empirical research on teacher education.

Carolyn D. King is an assistant professor of mathematics at Queensborough Community College, City University of New York. Her research focuses on mathematics education and the underrepresentation of minorities in STEM. She received her PhD from City University of New York in 2013.

Karen Koellner is an associate professor of mathematics education at the Hunter College, City University of New York. Her research focuses on mathematics teacher learning, teacher leader learning, and students' mathematical thinking. She received her PhD from Arizona State University in 1998.

Elaine Lande is a doctoral candidate in mathematics education at the School of Education of the University of Michigan. She uses systemic functional linguistics to investigate instructional decisions and their relation to professional obligations in community college mathematics. Ms. Lande has been an instructor at Henry Ford Community College, Washtenaw Community College, Madonna University, and Wayne State University. She holds an MS in mathematics from Wayne State University, a BS in mathematics from Madonna University, and an AS in liberal arts from Henry Ford Community College.

Roza Leikin is a professor of the Department of Mathematics Education, the head of the Graduate Program in the Education of Gifted at the Faculty of Education, and the head of the Interdisciplinary RANGE Center (Research and Advancement of Giftedness and Excellence) in the University of Haifa. She is the president of the International Group for Mathematical Creativity and Giftedness (http://igmcg.org). Dr. Leikin is the head of the National Advisory Committee in Mathematics Education of the Israel Ministry of Education. Her areas of expertise include mathematics teacher knowledge and education, mathematics challenges in education, mathematical creativity, giftedness, and the relationships between them. Lately her research is focusing on multidimensional examination of mathematical giftedness including neurocognitive examination of mathematical abilities. Multiple Solution Tasks in mathematics are one of the central issues in her research and design activities. Dr. Leikin published more than 100 research papers in edited journals, books, and conference proceedings. She coedited several books and special journal issues in the fields of mathematics teacher educations and mathematical creativity and giftedness.

Jun Li is an associate professor in the Department of Mathematics of the East China Normal University. She has special interest in studying students' understanding of mathematics, especially in the field of statistics and probability. She is also interested in some other topics, such as curriculum study, teacher training, using technology in classrooms, and culture's influence on mathematics education. She is a member of the writing group of the Standards of Mathematics Curriculum for Senior High Schools issued by the Ministry of Education of China in 2003. She is also one of the authors of a mathematics textbook being used in junior high schools in China.

Qiong Li is an associate professor in the Teacher Education Research Center, Beijing Normal University in China. Her research focuses on teacher cognition and development. In recent years, her research projects have focused on curriculum reform in mathematics and its impact on classroom teaching and learning and how to promote teacher professional development. She received her PhD from the Chinese University of Hong Kong in educational psychology.

Shiqi Li is a professor of mathematics education at the East China Normal University. He is also the deputy director of Institute of Mathematics Education at ECNU. His main research interests include mathematics learning, instruction, and teacher education, and he has published many papers and books in these areas. Professor Li plays active roles in national and international academic communities, such as being the former president of Mathematics Education Research Association of China; IPC member of ICME 12, ICMI Study 15, and EARCOME 2, 3, 4, and 5; and member of the editorial board of several national and international mathematics education journals. He was invited as a speaker at many local and international academic exchanges, including ICME regular lecture, plenary panel, EARCOMEs, symposiums, and seminars in many countries including Japan, Korea, the UK, Australia, the USA, Spain, Singapore, and Germany.

Xiaoqing Li obtained her PhD degree from the Chinese University of Hong Kong, specializing in educational psychology. Her thesis title is "Quality of instructional explanation and its relation to student learning in primary mathematics." She is currently working as an assistant professor in the Psychology Department of Shenzhen University in China. Her research interests include classroom processes, curriculum and instruction, mathematics education, educational assessment, and teacher education.

Yeping Li is a professor of mathematics education, holder of the Claude H. Everett, Jr. Endowed Chair in Education, and head of the Department of Teaching, Learning and Culture at Texas A&M University. His research interests focus on issues related to mathematics curriculum and teacher education in various education systems and understanding how factors related to mathematics curriculum and teachers may come together to shape effective classroom instruction. He is the founding editor-in-chief of the *International Journal of STEM Education* published by Springer and also the editor of a monograph series *Mathematics Teaching and Learning* published by Sense Publishers. In addition to coediting over 10 books and special journal issues, he has published more than 100 articles that focus on three related topic areas of study (i.e., mathematics curriculum and textbook studies, teachers and teacher education, and classroom instruction). He has also organized and chaired many group sessions at various national and international professional conferences, such as ICME-10 in 2004, ICME-11 in 2008, and ICME-12 in 2012. He received his PhD in Cognitive Studies in Education from the University of Pittsburgh, USA.

Peter Liljedahl is an associate professor of mathematics education in the Faculty of Education at Simon Fraser University in Vancouver, Canada. Peter is a former high school mathematics teacher who has kept his research interest and activities close to the classroom. He consults regularly with teachers, schools, school districts, and ministries of education on issues of pertaining to the improvement of teaching and learning.

Charmaine Mangram is a doctoral candidate in the Curriculum and Teacher Education program at Stanford's Graduate School of Education. She studies mathematics teacher professional development for in-service secondary mathematics teachers and parental practices involving mathematics. Her doctoral work explores how parents understand school mathematics curricular changes and how their understanding impacts their parental practices around homework. Charmaine works with Dr. Hilda Borko as a research assistant on the research project, Toward a Scalable Model of Mathematics Professional Development: A Field Study of Preparing Facilitators to Implement the Problem-Solving Cycle (iPSC). Prior to enrolling in Stanford, she served as a mathematics instructional coach for Los Angeles Unified School District with the goal of helping teachers incorporate conceptually focused mathematics lessons into their daily practice. Before becoming a coach, Charmaine taught high school mathematics in public schools in Los Angeles, CA, and Mercedes, TX. She left the classroom to pursue her passion to empower parents to be partners in their children's mathematics education by founding the nonprofit Parents' Academic Support Network with several college friends and teaching colleagues.

Vilma Mesa is an assistant professor of education at the University of Michigan. She investigates the role that resources play in developing teaching expertise in undergraduate mathematics, specifically at community colleges and in inquiry-based learning classrooms. She has conducted several analyses of textbooks and evaluation projects on the impact of innovative mathematics teaching practices for students in science, technology, engineering, and mathematics. She has a BS in computer sciences and a BS in mathematics from the University of Los Andes in Bogotá, Colombia, and a master's degree and a PhD in mathematics education from the University of Georgia.

Célia Mestre is a PhD candidate in mathematics education at the University of Lisbon, Portugal, and has a master's degree from the same university. She has 15 years of experience as an elementary school teacher and taught one of the primary classes where the new Portuguese mathematics curriculum was first experimented. She has experience as teacher educator in in-service courses in mathematics education for elementary teachers. Her research interests center on students' algebraic thinking, particularly on the developing of generalization and symbolization processes by elementary school students.

Yu-Jing Ni is a professor of educational psychology at the Chinese University of Hong Kong. Her research areas include cognitive development, numerical cognition, mathematics education, classroom processes, educational assessment, and evaluation. She served as an editor for the volume "Educational Evaluation" of *International Encyclopedia of Education, 3rd edition* (2010, Elsevier, UK), and a guest editor for the special issue "Curricular effect on the teaching and learning of mathematics: Findings from two longitudinal studies from the USA and China" for *International Journal of Educational Research* (Vol. 50(2), 2011). She obtained her PhD degree from University of California at Los Angeles.

Hélia Oliveira is an assistant professor of mathematics education at the Institute of Education of the University of Lisbon, Portugal. She received her PhD from the same university in 2004, with a study on beginning mathematics teachers' identity. She teaches a range of courses in mathematics education both for preservice and in-service mathematics teachers. Her research interests have centered in recent years on student's learning of algebra and numbers as well as on the development of mathematics teacher's knowledge and practices. Presently, she is coordinating a national research project in statistical literacy and producing multimedia resources for teacher education and doing research associated with their use.

Norma Presmeg is professor emerita in Mathematics Department at Illinois State University. She has done research on visualization in the teaching and learning of mathematics since she completed her PhD research on this topic at Cambridge University in 1985. Other research interests include the role of culture in mathematics education, the use of metaphor and metonymy in mathematical thinking, and semiotic theoretical frameworks for research on mathematics teaching and learning at all levels, but particularly in high schools and at college. She is the editor in chief of *Educational Studies in Mathematics.*

Marisa Quaresma has a bachelor's degree in the teaching of mathematics and natural sciences (2005) by the Higher School of Education of Setúbal (Portugal) and master's degree in mathematics education (2010) by the Institute of Education of the University of Lisbon. Currently, she is a doctoral candidate in mathematics education at this institute and a mathematics and science teacher at 5th and 6th grades. In the last years, she has been member of several research projects in mathematics education and also a teacher educator for in-service elementary school teachers. She is (co)author of several book chapters and articles in national and international journals and congress research reports. Her current main research interests are the teaching and learning of rational numbers and the development of mathematics reasoning.

Nanette Seago project director at WestEd, conducts research and designs professional development materials that prepare middle and high school mathematics teachers to more effectively teach challenging mathematical concepts. Currently, as project director for WestEd's Science, Technology, Engineering, and Mathematics Program, she serves as principal investigator for a National Science Foundation project focused on the research and design of videocase materials for middle school teachers—*Learning and Teaching Geometry*—to be published by WestEd. She is co-PI of an Institute of Education Sciences project focused on researching the efficacy of videocase-based mathematics professional development materials, *Linear Functions for Teaching—An Efficacy Study of Learning and Teaching Linear Functions.* Since 2003, she has published two books, two manuals, six peer-reviewed scientific journal articles, and four peer-reviewed chapters in international educational research books. She is primary author of *Learning and Teaching Linear Functions*, video-based resources designed to better equip teachers to prepare and implement lessons that will help students develop conceptual understanding of linear functions. Additionally, she is coauthor of *Examining Mathematics Practice through Classroom Artifacts*, a book that helps teachers learn how to use classroom artifacts to assess students' thinking and understanding of mathematical content.

Edward A. Silver is the William A. Brownell Collegiate Professor of Education and professor of mathematics at the University of Michigan. His main teaching and advising responsibilities involve doctoral students in mathematics education. His scholarly interests include the study of mathematical thinking, especially mathematical problem solving and problem posing; the design and analysis of intellectually engaging and equitable mathematics instruction for students; innovative methods of assessing and reporting mathematics achievement; and effective models for enhancing the knowledge of teachers of mathematics. He has directed or codirected a number of projects in mathematics education, including the NSF-supported UPDATE project that had a pivotal role in the work reported in this book chapter. He has served as editor of the *Journal for Research in Mathematics Education* and as coeditor of *The Elementary School Journal*.

Margaret S. Smith is a professor in the Department of Instruction and Learning in the School of Education and a senior scientist at the Learning Research and Development Center, both at the University of Pittsburgh. She works with preservice secondary mathematics teachers at the University of Pittsburgh, with doctoral students in mathematics education and with practicing teachers and teacher leaders locally and nationally.

Over the past 20+years, she has been developing research-based materials for use in the professional development of mathematics teachers and studying what teachers learn from the professional development in which they engage. She is currently the coprincipal investigator of the NSF-funded CORP (Cases of Reasoning and Proving in Secondary Mathematics) Project that is creating materials intended to develop teachers' knowledge related to reasoning and proof and their ability to support students' engagement in these mathematical practices. She was a member of the Board of Directors of the National Council of Teachers of Mathematics (2006–2009). In 2009 she received the award for Excellence in Teaching in Mathematics Teacher Education from the Association of Mathematics Teacher Educators (AMTE). She is currently the editor of *Mathematics Teacher Educator*, a new journal copublished by NCTM and AMTE.

Osvaldo D. Soto is both a practicing high school teacher and a senior program associate for the math for America San Diego's (MfA SD's) Master Teaching Fellowship program. Along with Dr. Guershon Harel, Dr. Soto is responsible for overseeing the professional development of the teaching fellows on-site. Dr. Soto is currently a mathematics teacher at Patrick Henry High School where his classroom serves as a setting for fellows to see Dr. Harel's DNR-based instruction in practice. He recently completed his PhD in Mathematics and Science Education with Dr. Harel from a joint program between the University of California, San Diego, and San Diego State University. He also earned an MA degree in mathematics in 2004 from San Diego State.

While actively teaching in a high school setting and mentoring teachers in multiple school districts, Dr. Soto continues to conduct research and present findings in mathematics education, including the development of curricular materials and sharing of pedagogical methods for interns, new MfA SD fellows, and master teaching fellows. Dr. Soto's research interests include teacher change in the context of proof-centered professional development. His specific interest lies in investigating the connection between teachers' mathematical content knowledge and its influence on their teaching practice.

Michael D. Steele is an associate professor in the Department of Curriculum and Instruction in the School of Education at the University of Wisconsin-Milwaukee. He has worked with preservice secondary mathematics teachers at University of Wisconsin-Milwaukee and Michigan State University, with mathematics education doctoral students at Michigan State University and with practicing teachers and administrators across the Midwest. He is a member of the Professional Development Committee of the Association of Mathematics Teacher Educators and a regular presenter at the National Council of Teachers of Mathematics Research Conference and served on the editorial board of Review of Educational Research.

Dr. Steele's work focuses on supporting secondary mathematics teachers in developing mathematical knowledge for teaching, integrating content and pedagogy, through teacher preparation and professional development. He is the coprincipal investigator of the NSF-funded Mathematics Discourse in Secondary Classrooms (MDISC) project that is creating practice-based professional development materials to support teachers in learning productive and powerful discourse practices to support students' engagement in rich thinking and reasoning. He also studies the influence of curriculum as co-PI of the Mathematical Practices Implementation (MPI) study and Algebra I policy as co-PI of the Learning About New Demands in Schools: Considering Algebra Policy Environments (LANDSCAPE) project.

Michelle Stephan earned her EdD in Mathematics Education from the Peabody College of Vanderbilt University in 1998. She currently is an assistant professor at the University of North Carolina at Charlotte. Since earning her doctorate, Dr. Stephan has been interested in teaching and learning mathematics in inquiry environments. Her research focuses on analyzing students' learning in social context as the teacher enacted instructional sequences created with the realistic mathematics education (RME) design program. She worked with Paul Cobb, Erna Yackel, and Koeno Gravemeijer to create and enact instruction in the first-, third-, and middle-grade mathematics classrooms. During her time at Purdue University Calumet, she worked with colleagues to create and implement RME sequences in geometry, algebra, and differential equations at the undergraduate level.

More recently, she worked full time as a middle school teacher for 7 years. During that time, she worked with fellow teachers to design RME sequences for 7th and 8th grades. As a consequence of her intimate work with teachers, Dr. Stephan has become interested in creating professional learning environments in which teachers can work collaboratively to form a guided reinvention approach to teaching.

Gabriel Stylianides is a University of Oxford lecturer of mathematics education and a fellow of Worcester College. His research focuses on issues related to students' meaningful engagement in fundamental mathematical activities—notably reasoning and proving and algebraic thinking—at all levels of education including teacher education. In pursuing these research interests, he also addressed issues of curriculum, task design, instructional intervention, and technology. He has over 60 publications in refereed journals or refereed conference proceedings, and he received the 2011 AERA SIG/RME Early Career Publication Award. His research projects have been supported by the US National Science Foundation, the US Institute of Education Sciences, and the Spencer Foundation. He was recently a guest coeditor of a special issue on classroom-based interventions published in *ZDM: The International Journal on Mathematics Education*, and he is currently a guest editor of a special issue on reasoning and proving to appear in the *International Journal of Educational Research*. He is an editorial board member of the *International Journal of Educational Research* and the *Elementary School Journal*. He co-organized topic study groups at the 11th International Congress on Mathematical Education, the 2nd International GeoGebra Conference, and the 8th Congress of the European Society for Research in Mathematics Education.

Heejoo Suh is a graduate student in the Curriculum, Instruction, and Teacher Education program in the College of Education at Michigan State University. Her interests include teacher education and professional development, epistemologies of mathematics, empowering all students in a mathematics classroom, and roles of (multiple) language and discourse in teaching and learning mathematics. She has been teaching Korean language, culture, and history to Korean-American students at Sunday Korean language schools. She received her bachelor's degree in mathematics with 7–12 teacher certificate from Ewha Womans University in South Korea and a master's degree in mathematics education from the University of Michigan. While at the University of Michigan, she was a research assistant on the UPDATE project, and she has continued to remain involved in the project.

Peter Sullivan is a professor of science, mathematics, and technology at Monash University, Australia. His main professional achievements are in the field of research. His recent research includes four ARC-funded projects. He is an author of the popular teacher resource *Good questions for math teaching*. He was chief editor of the *Journal of Mathematics Teacher Education*, is immediate past president of the Australian Association of Mathematics Teachers, was the author of the shape paper that outlined the principles for the development of the Australian Curriculum in Mathematics, and was the author of the 2011 Australian Education Review on research informed strategies for teaching mathematics.

Diana Underwood-Gregg earned her PhD in Mathematics Education from Purdue University in 1994. She is currently an associate professor of mathematics education at Purdue University Calumet, Indiana.

She was strongly influenced by the early work on social and socio-mathematical norms by Paul Cobb and Erna Yackel. As a graduate student, she was introduced the instructional design theory of realistic mathematics education. This provided her with a framework for designing several instructional sequences for addressing beginning algebra concepts. She is currently working on developing a minor program in elementary school mathematics that would acculturate undergraduates in elementary education into the practices of a guided reinvention teacher. She also works closely with K-4th grade teachers in their classrooms as they begin to rethink their current practices for teaching mathematics.

Katrin Vorhölter got her master's degree as a teacher of mathematics and German language for lower and upper secondary level in 2005 from the University of Hamburg. She did her PhD in 2009 as a scholarship holder of the Graduate Research Group on Educational Experience and Learner Development, funded by the German Research Society, with a study about the influence of modeling tasks on students' individual sensemaking. Afterward she worked as a teacher at a Hamburger secondary school. Since 2011 she teaches at the University of Hamburg in the working group of didactics of mathematics future mathematics teachers. Her current research areas include applications and modeling in mathematics education, students' individual sensemaking, and metacognition.

Tad Watanabe is a professor of mathematics education at Kennesaw State University, Kennesaw, Georgia, USA. His research interests include prospective elementary school teachers' development of mathematical knowledge for teaching elementary school mathematics and mathematics education practices in Japan. He has examined and published articles on Japanese elementary school mathematics textbooks' treatment of multiplication, fractions, and percent, as well as their use of visual representations. He was a member of the project that translated a recent edition of Japanese elementary (Gr. 1–6) and lower secondary (Gr. 7–9) mathematics textbooks. Tad received his MS degree in mathematics from Purdue University and PhD in mathematics education from Florida State University.

Erna Yackel earned her PhD in mathematics education from Purdue University in 1984. She is professor emerita of mathematics education at Purdue University Calumet. Her work has been strongly influenced by her early involvement in classroom-based research with Paul Cobb and Terry Wood and later with Koeno Gravemeijer. Her understanding of the need to account for sociological as well as psychological aspects of students' learning in the classroom emerged in her early work with Cobb and Wood and in their collaboration with Heinrich Bauersfeld and colleagues. This work resulted in the development of the emergent perspective on mathematical learning. Later, their work with Koeno Gravemeijer introduced her to realistic mathematics education (RME) as providing a sound, theoretical basis for instructional design.

Since retiring several years ago, Yackel has devoted her efforts to providing professional support to elementary school teachers, primarily in urban settings in Northwest Indiana that serve highly diverse student populations, as they develop an inquiry form of instructional practice in mathematics. This work reflects and remains grounded in her interests in social and sociomathematical norms, classroom discourse, mathematical argumentation, and RME instructional design theory.

Yudong Yang is currently associate professor and deputy director of the Center for Teachers' Development in Shanghai Academy of Educational Sciences and has been deputy secretariat of Shanghai Committee of School Mathematics Teaching since 2008. His major research interests include mathematical teacher education, especially in-service teacher's professional learning in school-based teaching environment, and he is also a founded member of the WALS (World Association of Lesson Study). In recent research project sponsored by the Ministry of Education of China, he focused on the effectiveness of mathematical problem contexts. As an IPC member of ICMI Study 22, he is doing a study on task design with some international scholars led by Anne Watson from Oxford University.

Orit Zaslavsky received her BSc in mathematics and statistics from the Hebrew University of Jerusalem (1972) and her MSc (1980) and PhD (1987) in mathematics education from the Technion, Haifa (Israel Institute of Technology), to where she returned as a faculty member after a 2-year postdoctorate fellowship at LRDC, within the University of Pittsburgh. Since 2009 she is a professor of mathematics education at New York University (NYU). Zaslavsky's research focuses on mathematics teacher education. She was among the first scholars to study the development of mathematics teacher educators, from both theoretical and practical perspectives. She has investigated the nature of productive mathematics-related tasks and instructional examples in promoting mathematical thinking. Another focus of Zaslavsky's work is on mathematical proof and proving and on ways to facilitate the need for proof and to make proof more accessible to students. An overarching theme in her research is the role of examples – in proving, learning, and teaching.

Zaslavsky's contributions include a special coedited triple issue of *JMTE* "The Role and Nature of Mathematics-Related Tasks for Teacher Education" and a coedited book *Constructing Knowledge for Teaching Secondary Mathematics: Tasks to Enhance Prospective and Practicing Teacher Learning* (Springer). She also served as an associate editor of *JMTE* (2009–2011).

Dehui Zhou attained her PhD degree with honors in cognitive psychology from the University of Duisburg-Essen, Germany. After graduation, she worked as postdoctoral fellow first at the Educational Psychology Department of the Chinese University of Hong Kong and then at the Social Work Department of Hong Kong Baptist University. This demanding research work has broadened her research horizon in mathematics education, metaphoric conceptualization of marriage, and mental health. Currently, she is working at the Counseling and Psychology Department of Hong Kong Shue Yan University as assistant professor. Her academic interests include metaphor cognition, metaphor application in counseling practice, and individualized educational plan for preschool children with special educational needs (SEN).

Iris Zodik received her BSc (1992) in mathematics and computer science education and her MSc (cum laude, 2004) and PhD (2008) in mathematics education from the Technion, Haifa (Israel Institute of Technology). Her doctoral study yielded a conceptual framework that accounts for teachers' choice and the use of mathematical examples as part of their craft knowledge. Her research and development interests include facilitating school-based educational changes and implementation of innovative programs in educational systems, design principles of technology-enhanced learning environments, exemplification in mathematics education from both teachers' and students' perspectives, and teaching and learning in informal settings.

Iris has served as codirector and coinvestigator (with Orit Zaslavsky) on two large-scale research and development projects in mathematics education at the

Technion: (1) an outreach program for promoting excellence and fostering the mathematical potential of high-achieving students and (2) curriculum design, development, and experimentation of learning and teaching material in secondary mathematics that include mathematics textbooks, teacher guides, and a book for secondary mathematics teachers on mathematical and pedagogical aspects of teaching calculus. In addition, Iris holds the position of lecturer at the Technion, where she teaches undergraduate courses for prospective teachers.

Author Index

Subject Index

A
Activity theory, 411, 441, 442, 449, 451–455, 556
Advances, 150, 251, 261, 263, 271, 305, 328, 412, 416, 425, 430, 435, 447, 468, 510, 514, 526, 553
Algebraic thinking, 6, 114–122, 150, 173–195, 295, 299, 568, 571
Assessing, 4, 5, 22, 53, 235, 323, 410, 413, 501–521, 570
Australia, 3, 82, 561–563, 572

B
Beliefs, 28, 29, 60, 91, 128, 168, 248, 290, 329, 415, 460, 477, 495, 498, 564

C
Case study, 17, 83, 89, 92–96, 234–247, 339–341, 344–351, 355–380, 387, 388, 402, 403, 416
Change, 3, 15–19, 22, 23, 27, 47–48, 77, 90, 97, 119–121, 131, 133, 143, 148–151, 154–156, 161, 164, 166, 168, 169, 175, 179, 211, 212, 214, 218, 273, 292, 335–352, 356, 375–377, 393, 394, 419, 476, 485, 506, 519, 520, 549, 553, 562, 570
China, 3, 7, 8, 131, 148, 176, 218, 220, 222, 227, 232–235, 247, 248, 250, 255, 256, 355, 356, 359, 380, 384–389, 392, 400, 402–404, 556, 561, 566, 567, 574
Chinese mathematics classrooms, 150, 217–228, 233, 238, 355, 384, 402

Chinese mathematics teaching and learning, 150, 221, 222, 228
Classroom communication, 225
Classroom discourse, 106, 131, 217–228, 469, 573
Classroom instruction, 2–5, 7, 9, 21–33, 100, 147–150, 174, 193, 217–219, 221, 224, 226–228, 231–250, 273, 314, 330, 337, 339, 345, 355–380, 383–404, 461, 504, 526, 567
Classroom instruction analysis, 387, 391, 402
Classroom interaction, 42, 106, 260, 286, 461, 471, 475–498
Classroom practice, 33, 38, 48, 50–51, 53, 55, 85, 220, 227, 256, 286, 314, 322, 338, 505, 561
Classroom teaching of mathematics, 233, 357, 384, 387, 388
Cognitive coaching, 46, 51
Cognitive demand, 219, 221–226, 288, 358, 360–363, 366, 377, 480, 503–505, 509, 511, 515, 518, 520, 556
Collaboration, 8, 47, 48, 83, 85, 138, 140, 156, 194, 388, 396, 402, 441, 461, 561, 573
Concept definition, 528
Concept image, 527, 528, 530, 531, 535, 542
Contexts, 3, 5–9, 15, 17, 22, 24, 27, 28, 39, 40, 51, 82–85, 89–93, 95, 96, 99, 100, 104, 105, 108, 120, 121, 123, 147, 161, 173–195, 202, 222, 234, 237, 245, 247, 250, 256, 265, 270, 276, 279, 288, 295, 304, 314, 316, 317, 326, 329, 351, 352, 384, 388–392, 402, 411, 418, 431, 445, 450, 468, 481, 483, 484, 497, 508, 521, 527, 552, 563, 564, 571, 574

Y. Li et al. (eds.), *Transforming Mathematics Instruction: Multiple Approaches and Practices*, Advances in Mathematics Education, DOI 10.1007/978-3-319-04993-9, © Springer International Publishing Switzerland 2014